WORLD WAR II

MAP BY MAP

SMITHSONIAN
WORLD WAR II
MAP BY MAP

FOREWORD BY
PETER SNOW

THE SLIDE TO WAR 1918–1939

GERMANY TRIUMPHANT 1939–1941

CONTENTS

Penguin Random House

DK LONDON

Senior Editor Hugo Wilkinson
Project Editors Shashwati Tia Sarkar, Miezan van Zyl
Editor Polly Boyd
US Editors Megan Douglass, Lori Hand
Editorial Assistant Michael Clark
Project Assistant Briony Corbett
Managing Editor Angeles Gavira Guerrero
Associate Publishing Director Liz Wheeler
Publishing Director Jonathan Metcalf

Lead Senior Art Editor Duncan Turner
Senior Art Editor Sharon Spencer
Project Art Editor Steve Woosnam-Savage
Cartographer Ed Merritt
Jacket Design Development Manager Sophia MTT
Jacket Designer Surabhi Wadhwa
Jacket Editor Emma Dawson
Producer (Pre-production) Rob Dunn
Senior Producer Meskerem Berhane
Managing Art Editor Michael Duffy
Art Director Karen Self
Design Director Phil Ormerod

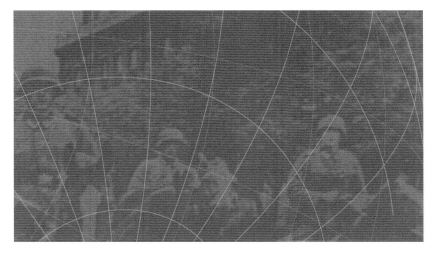

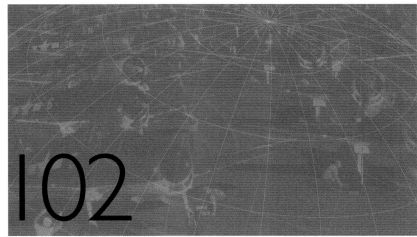

102

THE WIDENING WAR 1942

DK INDIA

Senior Editor Rupa Rao
Assistant Editors Aashirwad Jain, Sonali Jindal
Picture Researchers Akash Jain, Surya Sankash Sarangi
Picture Research Manager Taiyaba Khatoon
Jackets Editorial Coordinator Priyanka Sharma
Managing Editor Rohan Sinha
Managing Jackets Editor Saloni Singh
Pre-production Manager Balwant Singh
Cartographers Ashutosh Ranjan Bharti, Swati Handoo, Animesh Kumar Pathak
Cartography Manager Suresh Kumar

Lead Senior Art Editor Vaibhav Rastogi
Senior Art Editor Mahua Mandal
Project Art Editors Sanjay Chauhan, Anjali Sachar
Art Editors Rabia Ahmad, Mridushmita Bose, Debjyoti Mukherjee, Sonali Rawat Sharma
Managing Art Editor Sudakshina Basu
Senior Jackets Designer Suhita Dharamjit
Senior DTP Designers Harish Aggarwal, Vishal Bhatia, Jagtar Singh
Production Manager Pankaj Sharma

COBALT ID

Designer Darren Bland
Art Director Paul Reid
Editorial Director Marek Walisiewicz

CONTRIBUTORS

FOREWORD
Peter Snow CBE

CONSULTANT
Richard Overy, Professor of History, Exeter University

WRITERS
Simon Adams, Tony Allan, Kay Celtel, R.G. Grant, Jeremy Harwood, Philip Parker, Christopher Westhorp

156

TURNING THE TIDE   1943–1944

First American Edition, 2019
Published in the United States by DK Publishing, 1745 Broadway, 20th Floor, New York, NY 10019

Copyright © 2019 Dorling Kindersley Limited
DK, a Division of Penguin Random House LLC
23 24 10 9 8 7
020-311581-Sep/2019
Foreword copyright © 2019 Peter Snow

DK books are available at special discounts when purchased in bulk for sales promotions, premiums, fund-raising, or educational use. For details, contact: DK Publishing Special Markets, 1745 Broadway, 20th Floor, New York, NY 10019 SpecialSales@dk.com

A catalog record for this book is available from the Library of Congress.
ISBN: 978-1-4654-8179-5

Printed and bound in UAE
A WORLD OF IDEAS:
SEE ALL THERE IS TO KNOW
www.dk.com

Smithsonian Institution

CURATOR
Dr. F. Robert van der Linden, Chairman, Aeronautics Department, National Air and Space Museum

SMITHSONIAN ENTERPRISES
Product Development Manager Kealy Gordon

Editorial Director Ellen Nanney

Vice President, Consumer Brigid Ferraro **and Education Products**

Senior Vice President, Consumer Carol LeBlanc **and Education Products**

224

ENDGAME AND AFTERMATH 1944–1955

SMITHSONIAN

Established in 1846, the Smithsonian—the world's largest museum and research complex—includes 19 museums and galleries and the National Zoological Park. The total number of artifacts, works of art, and specimens in the Smithsonian's collections is estimated at 154 million, the bulk of which is contained in the National Museum of Natural History, which holds more than 126 million specimens and objects. The Smithsonian is a renowned research center, dedicated to public education, national service, and scholarship in the arts, sciences, and natural history.

FOREWORD

This is the most compelling work of military geography I've ever seen. It's a testament to the titanic scale of the conflict of 1939–1945, which dwarfs all others in world history. The ferocity of World War II— the level of its violence and the cost in human life—almost defies description: up to 80 million deaths; some 20 million on the battlefield; and around three times more than that among civilians caught up in the firestorm of bombing and all-embracing warfare on land, sea, and air. What these maps explain in intricate detail is the mobility and speed with which mechanized armies could sweep across vast areas, and with which warships and aircraft could inflict destruction at ranges never before dreamed of.

No earlier conflict has demanded such comprehensive mapping. No other conflict has been as challenging to the cartographer. Each of the pivotal moments of the war is marked by more movement and the exercise of more industrial might than in any previous war. It is maps such as these that can help us to envisage the scope, the size, and the sheer pace of Hitler's blitzkrieg, which crushed the Low Countries and France in the spring of 1940. Other instances of mass mobility are illuminated for us—the see-sawing of the rival armies in North Africa in 1940–1943, the great leap across the Mediterranean by Montgomery's and Patton's armies from North Africa to Sicily and Italy, the lightning Nazi assault on Stalin's Soviet Union, and

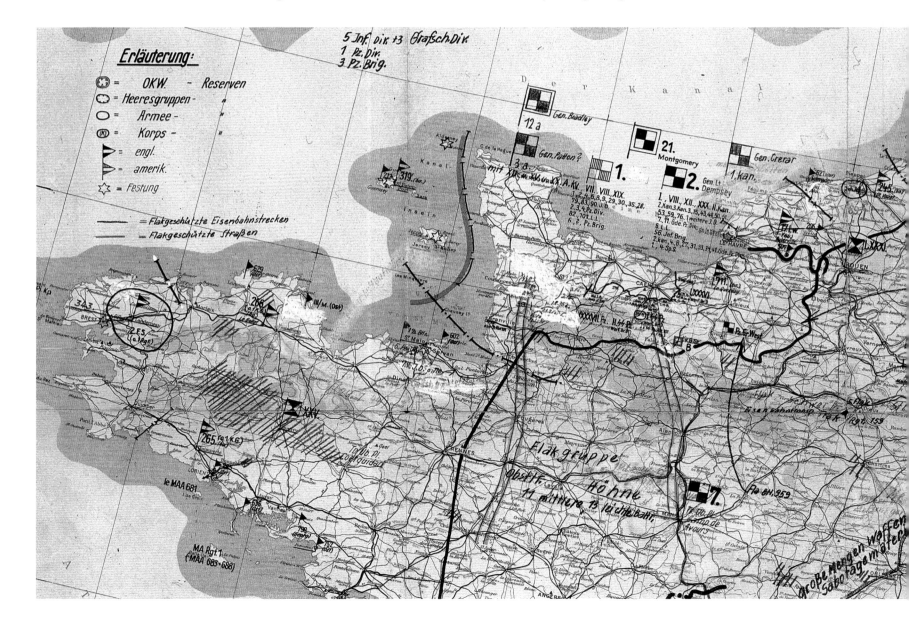

▽ **Contemporary map of action in Normandy**
This German situation map shows Axis and Allied troop movements
in 1944. Following the Allied counterinvasion of France on D-Day, the
two sides battled fiercely for control of territory in northern France,
Belgium, and the Netherlands in what was to be one of the pivotal
episodes of the war in Europe (see pp.190–191).

the astonishing turnaround after Stalingrad in 1942–1943. Perhaps most dramatically of all, we can see the greatest seaborne invasion of all time on D-Day in June 1944.

This book also reminds us that the war enveloped Asia. It describes the great naval battles of the Pacific that followed Japan's attack on Pearl Harbor on December 7, 1941. This was, in President Roosevelt's words, the "date which will live in infamy," propelling the US into the war. More than anything, it was the commitment of America's industrial might on the side of the Allies that spelled the end for Germany, Italy, and Japan. The set of maps describing the desperately hard-fought and costly series of battles that finally consumed Japan's short-lived

Pacific empire is an essential guide to the understanding of the massive task that confronted the US forces. This comprehensive picture of World War II is enhanced by further maps and features that illustrate the state of the world before and after the fighting, and the wider social, political, and economic aspects of the conflict. We also get a glimpse of the kind of mapping that was available to military commanders at the time. I've long been fascinated by the way good maps have helped me and other commentators explain the ups and downs of warfare. This book is right at the forefront of that great enterprise.

PETER SNOW, 2019

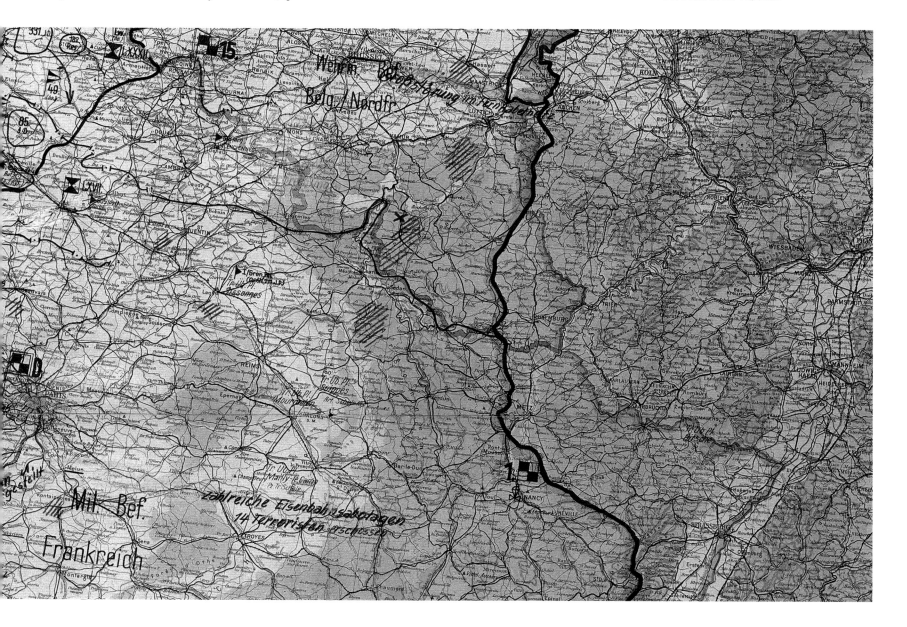

THE SLIDE TO WAR 1918–1939

MOUNTING TENSIONS AFTER WORLD WAR I LED TO INSTABILITY AND THE RISE OF EXTREMIST NATIONALISM IN EUROPE, WHILE CLASHES IN ASIA GATHERED MOMENTUM. A NEW GLOBAL WAR DREW NEAR.

△ **Nationalist propaganda**
This Spanish Civil War poster promotes the Nationalist cause. Fought between Republicans and Nationalists, the war epitomized the right–left divide that polarized Europe in the 1930s.

THE SEEDS OF WAR

The world of the 1920s and 1930s was scarred by ideological divisions, social conflicts, and economic collapse. Aggressive militarists intent on conquest rose to power in major states, notably Germany and Japan, and the clumsy efforts of liberal democracies to preserve the peace only precipitated a headlong rush to war.

It is a sad irony that the origins of World War II can be directly traced back to World War I, which was known as "the war to end war." This immensely destructive conflict bred a widespread popular longing for peace, but also left a heritage of grievance, insecurity, and instability. Germany in particular found it hard to come to terms with defeat, and the Versailles peace treaty, devised by the victorious powers in 1919, was bitterly resented by most Germans, who felt it was too punitive. The German Weimar Republic, the government founded in 1919, was weak, facing hyperinflation and armed revolts from both the right and the left.

From peace to rearmament

During the 1920s, there was encouraging evidence of recovery, with a marked improvement in international affairs. The League of Nations, set up in 1920

▷ **Japanese firepower**
The Type 92 heavy machine gun was one of the weapons adopted by Japan as it pursued military expansion in the 1930s.

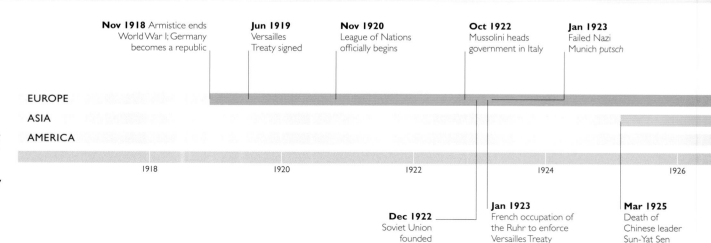

under the terms of the peace treaty, pursued ambitious plans for collective security and disarmament, although its authority was lessened by the refusal of the US to take part. After a crisis over enforcement of the Treaty of Versailles in 1923, Germany and France started making moves toward normalizing relations, but true stability proved elusive. The transformation of the former Russian Empire into the Soviet Union—a Communist state theoretically committed to world revolution—constituted a new unsettling factor in international politics. In Italy, also fatally destabilized by World War I, Fascist dictator Benito Mussolini took power. In China, Nationalists struggled to uphold a central government against Communists and warlords.

Hopes for a return to "normalcy" disappeared definitively with the onset of the Great Depression in 1929, after the Wall Street Crash. This crushing blow to the global economy had a devastating impact on a world riven by domestic and international tensions. As trade collapsed, major powers were tempted to seek economic security through political control of territory and resources. Faced with mass unemployment and falling living standards, many countries abandoned liberalism for authoritarian government. In Germany, the impact of the Depression turned Adolf Hitler's Nazi Party from a marginal extremist movement into a major

BETWEEN THE WARS

In Europe, a period of turmoil after the end of World War I was followed by relative stability in the mid-1920s. Then the onset of the Great Depression in 1929 propelled Hitler's rise to power in Germany. After that, German aggression led to crisis after crisis, until the fateful invasion of Poland that started World War II in Europe in September 1939. The Japanese invasion of China in 1937 had already led to war in Asia.

EUROPE

ASIA

AMERICA

Nov 1918 Armistice ends World War I; Germany becomes a republic

Jun 1919 Versailles Treaty signed

Nov 1920 League of Nations officially begins

Oct 1922 Mussolini heads government in Italy

Jan 1923 Failed Nazi Munich *putsch*

1918   1920   1922   1924   1926

Dec 1922 Soviet Union founded

Jan 1923 French occupation of the Ruhr to enforce Versailles Treaty

Mar 1925 Death of Chinese leader Sun-Yat Sen

◁ **Unopposed conquest**
Occupying Czechoslovakia without a fight, the German army parades through the streets of Prague before a sullen crowd in spring 1939.

political force. Marshaling German resentment against the Treaty of Versailles, Hitler linked solving Germany's economic problems to a reassertion of German military power. Within two years of Hitler becoming Chancellor of Germany in 1933, the country had embarked on open, full-scale rearmament. Meanwhile, in East Asia, an increasingly militarist Japan was tempted by Chinese weakness into encroachments that culminated in a full-scale invasion in 1937. Mussolini's Italy committed its own smaller-scale act of aggression with an invasion of Ethiopia in 1935. Revealed as impotent to prevent such breaches of world peace, the League of Nations faded into insignificance.

The lead-up to war

Britain and France, both liberal democracies, struggled to find an adequate response to the rise of naked aggression. They failed to take action when Hitler rearmed in defiance of the Treaty of Versailles. When civil war broke out in Spain in 1936, and Germany and Italy intervened on the side of right-wing rebels, the British and French stayed neutral, refusing to align with the ideologically opposed Soviet Union, which supported the Spanish government.

Belatedly, the democracies began to rearm, but they were desperate to avoid war with Germany, fearful of the possibly immediate effect of aerial bombardment. British prime minister Neville Chamberlain decided on a policy of appeasement, seeking to satisfy German grievances. In 1938, Hitler was allowed to absorb Austria and take the Sudetenland from Czechoslovakia. However, this was not enough for the Nazi leader. Instead, he actively desired war and conquest, making plans to reverse the verdict of World War I and establish German domination in Europe.

After Germany occupied Prague in March 1939, the British government decided to oppose any further Nazi expansionism. When Britain and France promised to assist Poland, Hitler's next target, a countdown to war began. Britain and France were still reluctant to ally with the Soviet Union. As they dallied, the Soviet dictator Joseph Stalin opted for a deal with Hitler, clearing the way for a German attack on Poland and the start of World War II.

"War is to man what motherhood is to woman …
I do not believe in perpetual peace."

BENITO MUSSOLINI, ITALIAN DICTATOR, 1939

▷ **The face of Fascism**
Italian Fascist leader Benito Mussolini set the model for the uniformed dictators who dominated Europe between the wars.

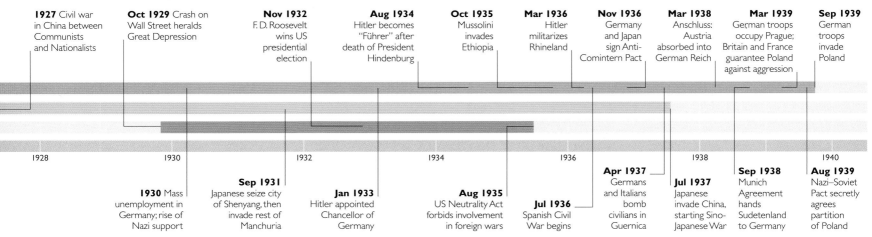

1927 Civil war in China between Communists and Nationalists

Oct 1929 Crash on Wall Street heralds Great Depression

Nov 1932 F. D. Roosevelt wins US presidential election

Aug 1934 Hitler becomes "Führer" after death of President Hindenburg

Oct 1935 Mussolini invades Ethiopia

Mar 1936 Hitler militarizes Rhineland

Nov 1936 Germany and Japan sign Anti-Comintern Pact

Mar 1938 Anschluss: Austria absorbed into German Reich

Mar 1939 German troops occupy Prague; Britain and France guarantee Poland against aggression

Sep 1939 German troops invade Poland

1928   1930   1932   1934   1936   1938   1940

1930 Mass unemployment in Germany; rise of Nazi support

Sep 1931 Japanese seize city of Shenyang, then invade rest of Manchuria

Jan 1933 Hitler appointed Chancellor of Germany

Aug 1935 US Neutrality Act forbids involvement in foreign wars

Jul 1936 Spanish Civil War begins

Apr 1937 Germans and Italians bomb civilians in Guernica

Jul 1937 Japanese invade China, starting Sino-Japanese War

Sep 1938 Munich Agreement hands Sudetenland to Germany

Aug 1939 Nazi–Soviet Pact secretly agrees partition of Poland

AVEZ VOUS PLACE DANS VOTRE COEUR POUR NOUS ?

◁ **War children**
This poster from 1917 asks "Have you room in your hearts for us?," appealing on behalf of the many thousands of French children left fatherless by World War I. The scale of the casualties had far-reaching implications in the combatants' home countries.

1920 Russia recognizes Finnish independence in the Treaty of Tartu.

1920 Estonia is liberated from Russia following a short war of independence.

1921 After a Russian defeat outside Warsaw, Poland and Russia reach agreement on their common border.

1921 Russia recognizes Latvian independence under the Treaty of Riga.

1920 Poland annexes Wilno from Lithuania, which it gains by plebiscite in 1922.

1922 Ireland is divided between a mainly Catholic Free State and a mainly Protestant six-county entity in the north.

1916 Irish Republicans launch the Easter Rising in Dublin against British rule.

1919 Saarland is placed under League of Nations mandate until reunited with Germany by plebiscite in 1935.

1923–1925 French and Belgian troops occupy the Ruhr after Germany fails to pay reparations.

1919 Rhineland is demilitarized until 1936.

1919 Alsace-Lorraine returns to France after 48 years of German rule.

1919 The former German city of Danzig becomes a Free City under the League of Nations.

1920 Teschen is partitioned between Poland and Czechoslovakia.

1920 A peace treaty is signed between Russia and Lithuania.

1919 The Treaty of St.-Germain sets new borders for Austria.

6 EUROPE IN DISPUTE 1919–1925

The treaties that ended the war in Europe attempted to resolve many outstanding territorial disputes. Most involved returning lands lost in previous wars or addressing the issues of ethnic groups living on the "wrong" side of a new border. Plebiscites—public referendums— were called to allow local people the final say on their future government.

○ Areas of dispute   ⚖ Plebiscites held

1920 The Treaty of Trianon settles new borders for Hungary.

1918 The Kingdom of the Serbs, Croats, and Slovenes is created from the Austro-Hungarian empire and Serbia; it is renamed Yugoslavia in 1929.

1918 Bessarabia is added to Romania.

1920–1922 Greeks occupy Eastern Thrace.

5 THE NEW TURKEY 1919–1923

Following an armistice with Ottoman Turkey in October 1918, the victorious Allies sought to partition the country in the 1920 Treaty of Sèvres. Turkish Nationalists under Mustafa Kemal rejected the treaty and gradually expelled the occupying Greek, Armenian, and French armies by 1922. The Ottoman sultanate was abolished and the new republic recognized by the 1923 Treaty of Lausanne, which approved Turkey's new borders.

☐ Turkey after Treaty of Sèvres
☐ Land restored to Turkey after Treaty of Lausanne, 1923
⧅ Annexed by Turkey, 1921

4 THE BREAKUP OF THE GERMAN EMPIRE 1918–1923

At the end of the war, Kaiser Wilhelm II fled to the Netherlands, and Germany became a republic. The Treaty of Versailles in 1919 imposed punitive terms on Germany. Land was lost to Denmark, Belgium, France, and Poland; its empire was removed, its armed forces reduced, and its fleet confiscated. Germany was also made to pay war reparations.

— German border, 1918
☐ Areas under League of Nations High Commissioners
👤 Ruhr under armed occupation
⧅ Demilitarized Rhineland

1925 Greece and Bulgaria are in conflict over Macedonia.

1919 Greece occupies Smyrna, leading to war with Turkey until 1922.

Map labels: SWEDEN, NORWAY, FINLAND, Petrograd, Åland Is., ESTONIA, Pskov, LATVIA, LITHUANIA, Wilno, WHITE RUSSIA, MEMEL TERRITORY, Danzig, EAST PRUSSIA, Allenstein, Marienwerder, POLISH CORRIDOR, Brest-Litovsk, POLAND, UKRAINE, DENMARK, SCHLESWIG-HOLSTEIN, North Sea, Baltic Sea, NORTHERN IRELAND, IRISH FREE STATE, Dublin, UNITED KINGDOM, NETHERLANDS, RUHR, Eupen, BELGIUM, LUXEMBOURG, GERMANY, UPPER SILESIA, RHINELAND, ALSACE-LORRAINE, FRANCE, SWITZERLAND, BOHEMIA, CZECHOSLOVAKIA, Teschen, RUTHENIA, AUSTRIA, SLOVAKIA, HUNGARY, TRANSYLVANIA, ROMANIA, BESSARABIA, Sopron, CARINTHIA, SLOVENIA, CROATIA, DALMATIA, KINGDOM OF SERBS, CROATS, AND SLOVENES, BOSNIA-HERZEGOVINA, SERBIA, MONTENEGRO, MACEDONIA, ITALY, Corsica, Adriatic Sea, ALBANIA, NORTHERN EPIRUS, WESTERN THRACE, EASTERN THRACE, Smyrna, GREECE, BULGARIA, SPAIN, Dodecanese Is., Crete

AFTER THE WAR

The borders of many European countries were redrawn after World War I, as empires collapsed and new countries were born. This new settlement was often violent, and left its own damaging legacy.

KEY

— National borders, 1923

TIMELINE

```
1
2
3
4
5
6
1915        1920        1925        1930
```

1 END OF THE RUSSIAN EMPIRE   1917–1921

The February Revolution of 1917 that overthrew the Romanov Czar and the October Revolution that ended the provisional government led to a Communist takeover of Russia. The Bolshevik regime arranged a cease-fire with Germany in December 1917, and in March 1918 signed the Treaty of Brest-Litovsk, renouncing its claims on Finland, the Baltic provinces, Poland, and Ukraine.

1918 Russia signs the Treaty of Brest-Litovsk, giving up its claims on lands west of the Brest-Litovsk line.

— Russian border, December 1917

- - - Brest-Litovsk treaty line

Areas temporarily autonomous or independent

2 THE BREAKUP OF THE AUSTRO-HUNGARIAN EMPIRE   1918–1920

The Hapsburg Empire's collapse led to three new states: Austria, Hungary, and Czechoslovakia. Former Austrian territory was added to Poland, Romania, and what later became Yugoslavia. Austria had to pay reparations, was forbidden to unite with Germany, and saw its army restricted. The old Kingdom of Hungary lost two-thirds of its land and many ethnic Hungarians to Romania and elsewhere.

— Austria-Hungary border, 1914

Rostov

Caucasus

AZERBAIJAN

GEORGIA

1915–1922 Around 1.5 million Turkish Armenians are killed by Turkish Nationalists.

ARMENIA

Black Sea

TURKISH ARMENIA

Lake Van

PERSIA

TURKEY

Anatolia

Ankara

1923 Ankara becomes new capital of Republican Turkey.

TURKISH KURDISTAN

3 EMERGING STATES   1918–1922

The collapse of the Ottoman, German, Russian, and Austro-Hungarian empires at the end of the war led to the formation of new states in central Europe: Estonia; Finland; Austria; Czechoslovakia; Poland; Hungary; Lithuania; Latvia; and the Kingdom of Serbs, Croats, and Slovenes. They were joined by the Irish Free State, which broke free from Britain in 1922 after a brutal civil war.

■ New states created

Cyprus

RUSSIA

THE LEGACY OF WORLD WAR I

The end of war in Europe in 1918 saw the collapse of four major empires. The map of the continent needed to be redrawn, and the future home of millions of people decided. As new states emerged and old conflicts were slowly resolved, the legacy of the war continued to be felt across Europe for many years.

The peace treaties that settled the future of Europe after 1919 were the result of numerous compromises between the "Big Four": the victorious Allied powers of the US, UK, France, and Italy. American president Woodrow Wilson wanted to forge a liberal peace settlement based on national self-determination, while French prime minister Georges Clemenceau wanted above all to ensure the future security of his country and make Germany pay for the war—a view that was shared by David Lloyd George, prime minister of Britain. The resulting treaties had the overall effect of pleasing no one, and left the people and governments of many countries profoundly dissatisfied with the outcome.

Territorial disputes continued to divide nations, notably in Eastern Europe, while actual fighting continued in Turkey until 1922. Many of the new states were crudely carved out of Austro-Hungary and the other old empires, while defeated Germany emerged as a shrunken republic and imperial Russia, excluded from the peace talks, became the world's first Communist state.

While some problems were addressed by the peace treaties, the legacy of the war had profound social, economic, and political consequences across Europe and Asia, and would become one of the defining causes of a new world war within 20 years.

"My home policy: I wage war. My foreign policy: I wage war. All the time I wage war."

GEORGES CLEMENCEAU, 1918

WRITING THE PEACE

The victorious Allied politicians and diplomats met in Paris in 1919 to draw up a series of treaties with the defeated Central Powers, each one named after the palaces, chateaux, and towns to the west of Paris where they were signed. The main treaty was signed with Germany at Versailles in June 1919, followed by St.-Germain-en-Laye with Austria in September 1919, Neuilly-sur-Seine with Bulgaria in November 1919, Trianon with Hungary in June 1920, and finally the abortive Sèvres treaty with Turkey in August 1920.

Signing the Treaty of Versailles

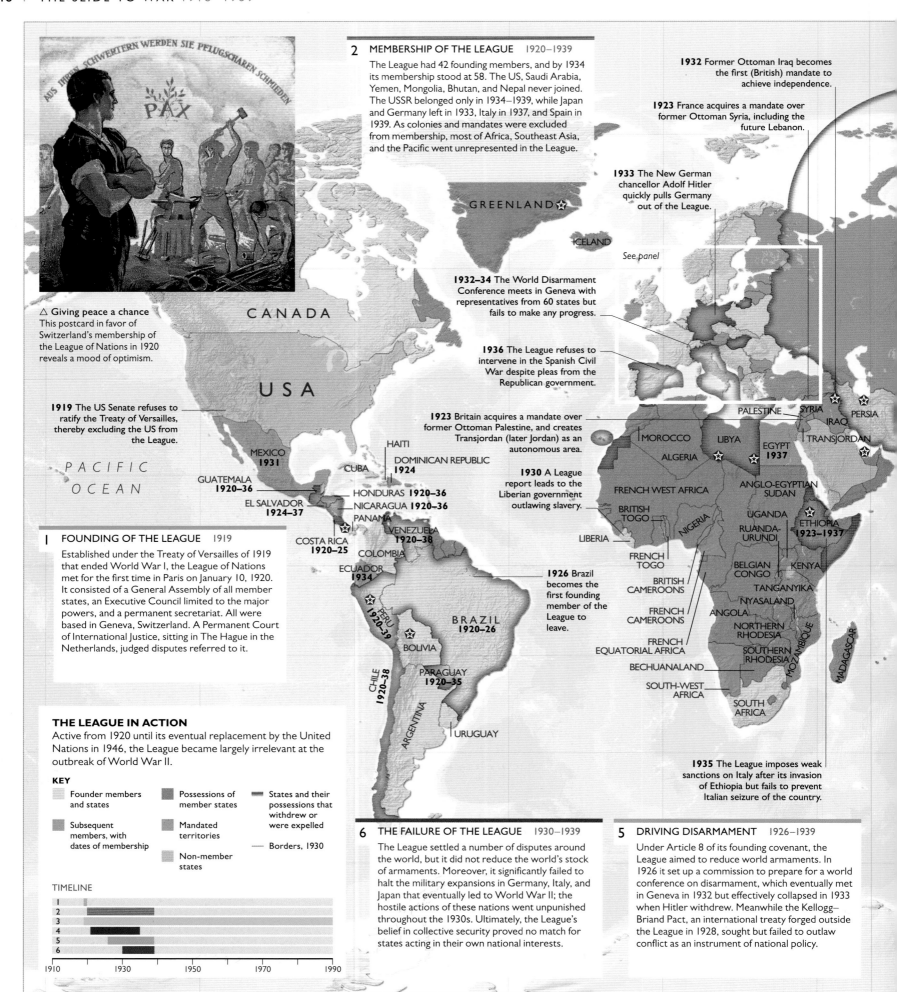

PAX
AUS IHREN SCHWERTERN WERDEN SIE PFLUGSCHAREN SCHMIEDEN

△ **Giving peace a chance**
This postcard in favor of
Switzerland's membership of
the League of Nations in 1920
reveals a mood of optimism.

2 MEMBERSHIP OF THE LEAGUE 1920–1939

The League had 42 founding members, and by 1934
its membership stood at 58. The US, Saudi Arabia,
Yemen, Mongolia, Bhutan, and Nepal never joined.
The USSR belonged only in 1934–1939, while Japan
and Germany left in 1933, Italy in 1937, and Spain in
1939. As colonies and mandates were excluded
from membership, most of Africa, Southeast Asia,
and the Pacific went unrepresented in the League.

1932 Former Ottoman Iraq becomes
the first (British) mandate to
achieve independence.

1923 France acquires a mandate over
former Ottoman Syria, including the
future Lebanon.

1933 The New German
chancellor Adolf Hitler
quickly pulls Germany
out of the League.

GREENLAND ☆

ICELAND

See panel

CANADA

1932–34 The World Disarmament
Conference meets in Geneva with
representatives from 60 states but
fails to make any progress.

USA

1919 The US Senate refuses to
ratify the Treaty of Versailles,
thereby excluding the US from
the League.

1936 The League refuses to
intervene in the Spanish Civil
War despite pleas from the
Republican government.

PACIFIC
OCEAN

1923 Britain acquires a mandate over
former Ottoman Palestine, and creates
Transjordan (later Jordan) as an
autonomous area.

PALESTINE ☆ SYRIA ☆ PERSIA ☆
IRAQ ☆
TRANSJORDAN ☆

MOROCCO LIBYA EGYPT ☆
1937
ALGERIA

ANGLO-EGYPTIAN
SUDAN

MEXICO
1931

HAITI

CUBA

DOMINICAN REPUBLIC
1924

1930 A League
report leads to the
Liberian government
outlawing slavery.

FRENCH WEST AFRICA

BRITISH
TOGO

UGANDA

RUANDA-
URUNDI

ETHIOPIA
1923–1937 ☆

GUATEMALA
1920–36

HONDURAS 1920–36
NICARAGUA 1920–36
PANAMA

EL SALVADOR
1924–37

NIGERIA
LIBERIA

KENYA

COSTA RICA
1920–25 ☆

VENEZUELA
1920–38

FRENCH
TOGO

BELGIAN
CONGO

TANGANYIKA

COLOMBIA

1926 Brazil
becomes the
first founding
member of the
League to
leave.

BRITISH
CAMEROONS

NYASALAND

ECUADOR
1934 ☆

FRENCH
CAMEROONS

ANGOLA

NORTHERN
RHODESIA

1 FOUNDING OF THE LEAGUE 1919

Established under the Treaty of Versailles of 1919
that ended World War I, the League of Nations
met for the first time in Paris on January 10, 1920.
It consisted of a General Assembly of all member
states, an Executive Council limited to the major
powers, and a permanent secretariat. All were
based in Geneva, Switzerland. A Permanent Court
of International Justice, sitting in The Hague in the
Netherlands, judged disputes referred to it.

PERU
1920–39 ☆

BRAZIL
1920–26

FRENCH
EQUATORIAL AFRICA

SOUTHERN
RHODESIA

BECHUANALAND

BOLIVIA ☆

CHILE
1920–38

PARAGUAY
1920–35

SOUTH-WEST
AFRICA

SOUTH
AFRICA

MOZAMBIQUE
MADAGASCAR

THE LEAGUE IN ACTION

Active from 1920 until its eventual replacement by the United
Nations in 1946, the League became largely irrelevant at the
outbreak of World War II.

ARGENTINA

URUGUAY

1935 The League imposes weak
sanctions on Italy after its invasion
of Ethiopia but fails to prevent
Italian seizure of the country.

KEY

▨ Founder members and states	▨ Possessions of member states	▬ States and their possessions that withdrew or were expelled
▨ Subsequent members, with dates of membership	▨ Mandated territories	— Borders, 1930
	▨ Non-member states	

TIMELINE

1
2
3
4
5
6

1910   1930   1950   1970   1990

6 THE FAILURE OF THE LEAGUE 1930–1939

The League settled a number of disputes around
the world, but it did not reduce the world's stock
of armaments. Moreover, it significantly failed to
halt the military expansions in Germany, Italy, and
Japan that eventually led to World War II; the
hostile actions of these nations went unpunished
throughout the 1930s. Ultimately, the League's
belief in collective security proved no match for
states acting in their own national interests.

5 DRIVING DISARMAMENT 1926–1939

Under Article 8 of its founding covenant, the
League aimed to reduce world armaments. In
1926 it set up a commission to prepare for a world
conference on disarmament, which eventually met
in Geneva in 1932 but effectively collapsed in 1933
when Hitler withdrew. Meanwhile the Kellogg–
Briand Pact, an international treaty forged outside
the League in 1928, sought but failed to outlaw
conflict as an instrument of national policy.

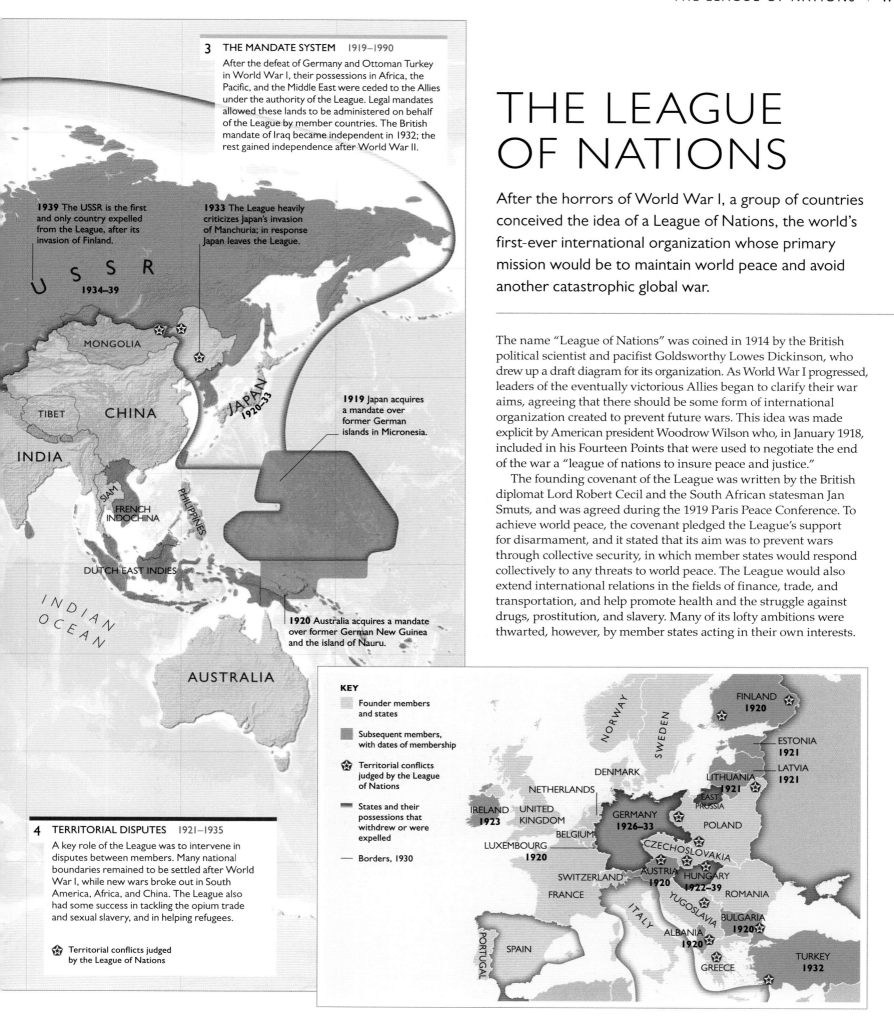

3 THE MANDATE SYSTEM 1919–1990

After the defeat of Germany and Ottoman Turkey in World War I, their possessions in Africa, the Pacific, and the Middle East were ceded to the Allies under the authority of the League. Legal mandates allowed these lands to be administered on behalf of the League by member countries. The British mandate of Iraq became independent in 1932; the rest gained independence after World War II.

1939 The USSR is the first and only country expelled from the League, after its invasion of Finland.

1933 The League heavily criticizes Japan's invasion of Manchuria; in response Japan leaves the League.

USSR
1934–39

MONGOLIA

TIBET   CHINA

INDIA

SIAM

FRENCH INDOCHINA

PHILIPPINES

JAPAN 1920–33

1919 Japan acquires a mandate over former German islands in Micronesia.

DUTCH EAST INDIES

INDIAN OCEAN

1920 Australia acquires a mandate over former German New Guinea and the island of Nauru.

AUSTRALIA

THE LEAGUE OF NATIONS

After the horrors of World War I, a group of countries conceived the idea of a League of Nations, the world's first-ever international organization whose primary mission would be to maintain world peace and avoid another catastrophic global war.

The name "League of Nations" was coined in 1914 by the British political scientist and pacifist Goldsworthy Lowes Dickinson, who drew up a draft diagram for its organization. As World War I progressed, leaders of the eventually victorious Allies began to clarify their war aims, agreeing that there should be some form of international organization created to prevent future wars. This idea was made explicit by American president Woodrow Wilson who, in January 1918, included in his Fourteen Points that were used to negotiate the end of the war a "league of nations to insure peace and justice."

The founding covenant of the League was written by the British diplomat Lord Robert Cecil and the South African statesman Jan Smuts, and was agreed during the 1919 Paris Peace Conference. To achieve world peace, the covenant pledged the League's support for disarmament, and it stated that its aim was to prevent wars through collective security, in which member states would respond collectively to any threats to world peace. The League would also extend international relations in the fields of finance, trade, and transportation, and help promote health and the struggle against drugs, prostitution, and slavery. Many of its lofty ambitions were thwarted, however, by member states acting in their own interests.

KEY

Founder members and states

Subsequent members, with dates of membership

⭐ Territorial conflicts judged by the League of Nations

States and their possessions that withdrew or were expelled

— Borders, 1930

4 TERRITORIAL DISPUTES 1921–1935

A key role of the League was to intervene in disputes between members. Many national boundaries remained to be settled after World War I, while new wars broke out in South America, Africa, and China. The League also had some success in tackling the opium trade and sexual slavery, and in helping refugees.

⭐ Territorial conflicts judged by the League of Nations

NORWAY   SWEDEN

FINLAND 1920

DENMARK

ESTONIA 1921

LATVIA 1921

LITHUANIA 1921

NETHERLANDS

IRELAND 1923   UNITED KINGDOM

EAST PRUSSIA

GERMANY 1926–33   POLAND

BELGIUM

LUXEMBOURG 1920

CZECHOSLOVAKIA

SWITZERLAND   AUSTRIA 1920   HUNGARY 1922–39

FRANCE

ITALY   YUGOSLAVIA   ROMANIA

BULGARIA 1920

ALBANIA 1920

PORTUGAL   SPAIN

GREECE   TURKEY 1932

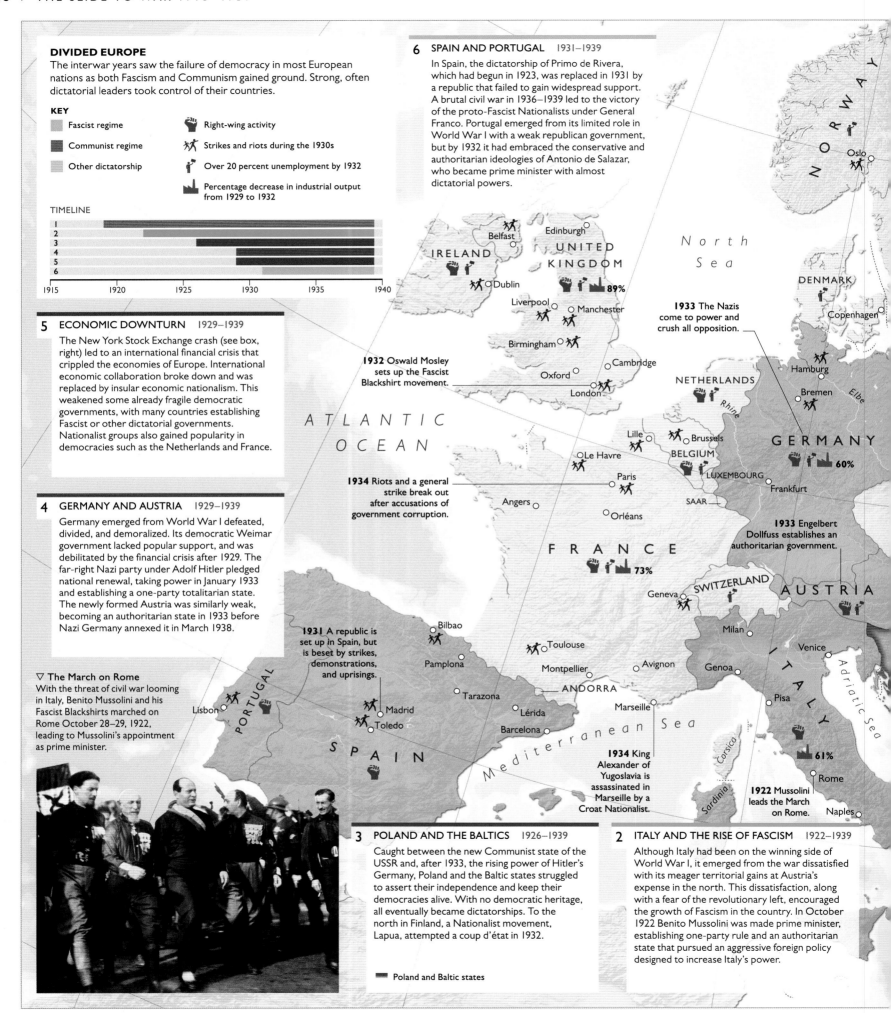

DIVIDED EUROPE

The interwar years saw the failure of democracy in most European nations as both Fascism and Communism gained ground. Strong, often dictatorial leaders took control of their countries.

KEY

- Fascist regime
- Communist regime
- Other dictatorship
- Right-wing activity
- Strikes and riots during the 1930s
- Over 20 percent unemployment by 1932
- Percentage decrease in industrial output from 1929 to 1932

TIMELINE

1915 1920 1925 1930 1935 1940

1
2
3
4
5
6

6 SPAIN AND PORTUGAL 1931–1939

In Spain, the dictatorship of Primo de Rivera, which had begun in 1923, was replaced in 1931 by a republic that failed to gain widespread support. A brutal civil war in 1936–1939 led to the victory of the proto-Fascist Nationalists under General Franco. Portugal emerged from its limited role in World War I with a weak republican government, but by 1932 it had embraced the conservative and authoritarian ideologies of Antonio de Salazar, who became prime minister with almost dictatorial powers.

5 ECONOMIC DOWNTURN 1929–1939

The New York Stock Exchange crash (see box, right) led to an international financial crisis that crippled the economies of Europe. International economic collaboration broke down and was replaced by insular economic nationalism. This weakened some already fragile democratic governments, with many countries establishing Fascist or other dictatorial governments. Nationalist groups also gained popularity in democracies such as the Netherlands and France.

4 GERMANY AND AUSTRIA 1929–1939

Germany emerged from World War I defeated, divided, and demoralized. Its democratic Weimar government lacked popular support, and was debilitated by the financial crisis after 1929. The far-right Nazi party under Adolf Hitler pledged national renewal, taking power in January 1933 and establishing a one-party totalitarian state. The newly formed Austria was similarly weak, becoming an authoritarian state in 1933 before Nazi Germany annexed it in March 1938.

▽ **The March on Rome**
With the threat of civil war looming in Italy, Benito Mussolini and his Fascist Blackshirts marched on Rome October 28–29, 1922, leading to Mussolini's appointment as prime minister.

1933 The Nazis come to power and crush all opposition.

1932 Oswald Mosley sets up the Fascist Blackshirt movement.

1934 Riots and a general strike break out after accusations of government corruption.

1933 Engelbert Dollfuss establishes an authoritarian government.

1931 A republic is set up in Spain, but is beset by strikes, demonstrations, and uprisings.

1934 King Alexander of Yugoslavia is assassinated in Marseille by a Croat Nationalist.

1922 Mussolini leads the March on Rome.

NORWAY

Oslo

North Sea

DENMARK

Copenhagen

Hamburg

Bremen Elbe

GERMANY 60%

NETHERLANDS

Rhine

Brussels

BELGIUM

LUXEMBOURG

Frankfurt

SAAR

FRANCE 73%

Paris

Le Havre

Angers

Orléans

Geneva SWITZERLAND AUSTRIA

Milan

Venice

Genoa

ITALY

Pisa

Adriatic Sea

Rome

Naples

Corsica

Sardinia

Mediterranean Sea 61%

SPAIN

Bilbao

Pamplona

Tarazona

Madrid

Toledo

Lérida

Barcelona

Toulouse

Montpellier

Avignon

Marseille

ANDORRA

PORTUGAL

Lisbon

IRELAND

Belfast

Dublin

Edinburgh

UNITED KINGDOM

Liverpool Manchester

Birmingham

Cambridge

Oxford

London 89%

ATLANTIC OCEAN

Lille

3 POLAND AND THE BALTICS 1926–1939

Caught between the new Communist state of the USSR and, after 1933, the rising power of Hitler's Germany, Poland and the Baltic states struggled to assert their independence and keep their democracies alive. With no democratic heritage, all eventually became dictatorships. To the north in Finland, a Nationalist movement, Lapua, attempted a coup d'état in 1932.

■ Poland and Baltic states

2 ITALY AND THE RISE OF FASCISM 1922–1939

Although Italy had been on the winning side of World War I, it emerged from the war dissatisfied with its meager territorial gains at Austria's expense in the north. This dissatisfaction, along with a fear of the revolutionary left, encouraged the growth of Fascism in the country. In October 1922 Benito Mussolini was made prime minister, establishing one-party rule and an authoritarian state that pursued an aggressive foreign policy designed to increase Italy's power.

1934 Acting head of state Konstantin Päts declares a state of emergency, claiming that the right-wing Vaps movement is planning a coup.

1934 Three-time prime minister Karlis Ulmanis establishes an authoritarian dictatorship.

1926 A coup d'état sets up an authoritarian government under Antanas Smetona.

1926 Dissatisfied with Poland's unstable democratic governments, former military commander Josef Pilsudski comes out of retirement to stage a coup.

63%

1919 Admiral Horthy forms an authoritarian regency in the new kingdom.

1929 King Alexander appoints a royal dictatorship to end the fighting between Serbs and Croats.

1938 King Carol II takes dictatorial powers.

1936 King Boris III establishes a royal dictatorship.

1936 A right-wing dictatorship under General Metaxas takes power.

HUNGARY AND THE BALKANS 1919–1939

Following the collapse of the Austro-Hungarian and Ottoman empires at the end of World War I, new states emerged in the Balkans. Their governments were typically weak and were replaced by royal or military dictatorships; the growing influence of Nazi Germany led to the formation of far-right groups in the region. In Hungary, resentment over the loss of territory under the 1920 Treaty of Trianon led to closer ties with Nazi Germany.

■ Balkan countries

EUROPE OF THE DICTATORS

The victors of World War I had been a coalition of democracies, but in the uncertain decades that followed, many European countries underwent major political upheaval. Economic problems only served to add to the instability of inter-war Europe.

After the end of the war in 1918 and the subsequent signing of various peace treaties, most European states—excepting the newly formed Communist state in Russia—were democracies. However, one by one these democratic regimes gave way to dictatorships. Italy was the first of these, when Mussolini took power in 1922, followed by Spain in 1923 and Poland in 1926. Democracy collapsed in the Baltic states between 1926 and 1934, while the Balkan states become dictatorships after 1929. The rise of Nazi rule after 1933 in Germany, and later in Austria, completed the picture.

"The Spanish national will was never freely expressed through the ballot box."

FRANCISCO FRANCO, 1938

This transformation was exacerbated by the economic crisis that swept across Europe after 1929. Rising unemployment and economic collapse undermined democratic governments and gave rise to right-wing and Fascist groups. These were often militaristic in structure and populist in appeal, providing their members with power that had not been available to them under democracy. By 1939, democratic rule existed only in Scandinavia, Britain and Ireland, France, the Benelux nations, and Switzerland. The rest of Europe was under dictatorial rule.

THE GREAT DEPRESSION

In October 1929, the long boom on the New York Stock Exchange came to a sudden end. American creditors began to call in foreign loans and the supply of international credit dried up. In response, the US government introduced tariffs in 1930 that restricted imports. Competitive protection by other countries followed, causing world trade to fall by almost two-thirds between 1929 and 1932. Prices and profits collapsed, output plummeted, and millions were left unemployed (right) and impoverished.

HITLER AND NAZI GERMANY

Although Hitler's attempted *putsch* (or coup) in 1923 failed, by 1930 the Nazi party had become a force to be reckoned with in Germany. The economic depression that followed the Wall Street crash of 1929 was crucial in winning them nationwide support.

△ **The Führer**
Adolf Hitler, in his uniform, poses for the camera. A picture of the *Führer* (leader) was a must in every German home.

Defeat in World War I had left Germany poor, resentful, and polarized between the political extremes of left and right. Many Germans were looking for strong, decisive leadership, which mainstream parties had failed to provide. Adolf Hitler emerged as leader of the National Socialist German Workers Party (NSDAP, known as the Nazi party) in the early 1920s, with great determination. As one commentator said, Hitler was "the living incarnation of the nation's yearning."

The Nazi program

Hitler's oratory was direct, aggressive, and uncompromising, as was his program. He pledged a national revolution that would restore German strength and dignity. His promises included an end to mass unemployment, abrogating the Treaty of Versailles, stopping the crippling war reparations Germany was forced to pay, and rebuilding the armed forces. Germany was listening. In the 1932 federal elections, the Nazis won 230 seats in the German *Reichstag* (parliament), making them the most powerful party in the country. After months of back room negotiations, in January 1933 a reluctant President Hindenburg was finally cajoled into appointing Hitler Chancellor. In March, the so-called Enabling Act gave Hitler emergency dictatorial powers. Its passage effectively marked the end of German democracy. The Nazis dubbed their new regime the Third Reich, or Third Empire, reflecting their ambitions.

JOSEPH GOEBBELS
1897–1945

Joseph Goebbels, a masterful orator, was one of Hitler's closest colleagues. In 1926, Hitler appointed Goebbels *Gauleiter* (district leader) of Berlin, and in 1933 promoted him to Propaganda Minister, with control over German radio, press, and cultural institutions. His propaganda sold the Nazi vision of German superiority and territorial expansion to the public.

Addressing the rally
The rally at Nuremberg, which was held annually from 1933 to 1938 and masterminded by the Propaganda Minister Joseph Goebbels, was a highlight of the Nazi year. Here, at the 1936 rally, massed troops at the Zeppelinfeld stadium listen attentively to Hitler's keynote speech.

CHINA IN TURMOIL

China between the two world wars was a country embroiled in internal conflict: its disunited provinces were ruled over by rival warlords and threatened by a growing Communist insurgency, while its national territory later came under attack from imperialist army forces from Japan.

The Chinese Revolution of 1911 began with a mutiny among troops in Wuchang in Hubei province, in central China. It rapidly led to the overthrow of the Manchu or Qing dynasty, whose autocratic rulers had controlled the country since 1644, and the formation of a republic in 1912. The first president of the republic, Yuan Shih-k'ai, tried to turn his office into a virtual dictatorship based on military force. However, on his death in 1916 China fragmented into a number of provincial military dictatorships run by local warlords who fought among themselves. Civil war raged throughout China until, under Chiang Kai-shek, China's

Nationalist Party, the Guomindang (GMD), was able to unite the east of the country by 1928. The GMD then slowly extended their control over the rest of the country by 1937.

Two forces emerged to oppose the Nationalists: the Chinese Communist Party (CCP), fighting for a social and economic revolution, and the Japanese army, intent on establishing an empire in China. The Communists were largely crushed in the cities in 1927, but the Japanese were a more formidable foe, absorbing the region of Manchuria in 1931 and the northern province of Jehol in 1932, and setting up a puppet state across northern China in 1935.

> "We shall not lightly talk about sacrifice until we are driven to the last extreme which makes sacrifice inevitable."
>
> CHIANG KAI-SHEK, 1935

CHIANG KAI-SHEK 1887–1975

Nationalist leader Chiang Kai-shek was born in Fenghua, a district of the city of Ningbo, in Zhejiang province. The son of a merchant, and a supporter of the new Chinese republic, he built up the Republican army and became commandant of the military school at Whampoa in 1924. His connections enabled him to take over the leadership of the Nationalist Guomindang (GMD) party and become commander-in-chief of the army in 1926. Despite successes against the warlords, Chiang's rule over China was never secure, as it was threatened by Communist insurgents and Japanese invasions. In 1949 he was defeated in the Chinese Civil War by the Chinese Communist Party (CCP) under Mao Zedong and retreated to Taiwan.

△ Director of the masses
Mao Zedong, leader of China's Communists, addresses followers during the Sino-Japanese war. In 1945, at the conflict's end, Mao commanded an army of over 1.2 million Chinese Communists.

1 THE NATIONALIST REVIVAL 1919–1937

Student demonstrations in Beijing in May 1919 initiated a wave of nationalist feeling across the country, which gave birth to the Chinese Communist Party (CCP) in 1921 and a revived Guomindang (GMD) in 1924. The GMD cooperated with the CCP and began a campaign of unification against warlord forces that culminated in the Northern Expedition of 1926–1928, which was led by Chiang Kai-shek. After its successful conclusion, the Communists were purged from power.

	Under direct control of the Nationalist government, 1928		Route of Northern Expedition
	Nationalist territory, 1929–1934		Pro-Nationalist forces
	Nationalist territory, 1935–1937		

Juyan

Qinghai

Wuwei

Lanzho

2 JAPANESE INVASION OF MANCHURIA 1931

Responding to an act of provocation (which was staged by the Japanese army), Japanese forces invaded Manchuria on September 19, 1931, seizing the key city of Shenyang. They went on to take the whole of Manchuria, establishing the state of Manchukuo in 1932 with the former Chinese boy emperor Pu Yi Hsuan-t'ung as puppet emperor. The invasion and occupation of Manchuria marked the start of Japanese imperial expansion into northern and eastern China.

	Invaded by Japan, 1931		Japanese invasion

Luding

DISUNITED CHINA

Republican China was initially ruled by a number of local warlords and was only united under Nationalist control in 1937. By then China faced Japanese armed incursions in the north and east of the country.

TIMELINE

1910　　　1920　　　1930　　　1940

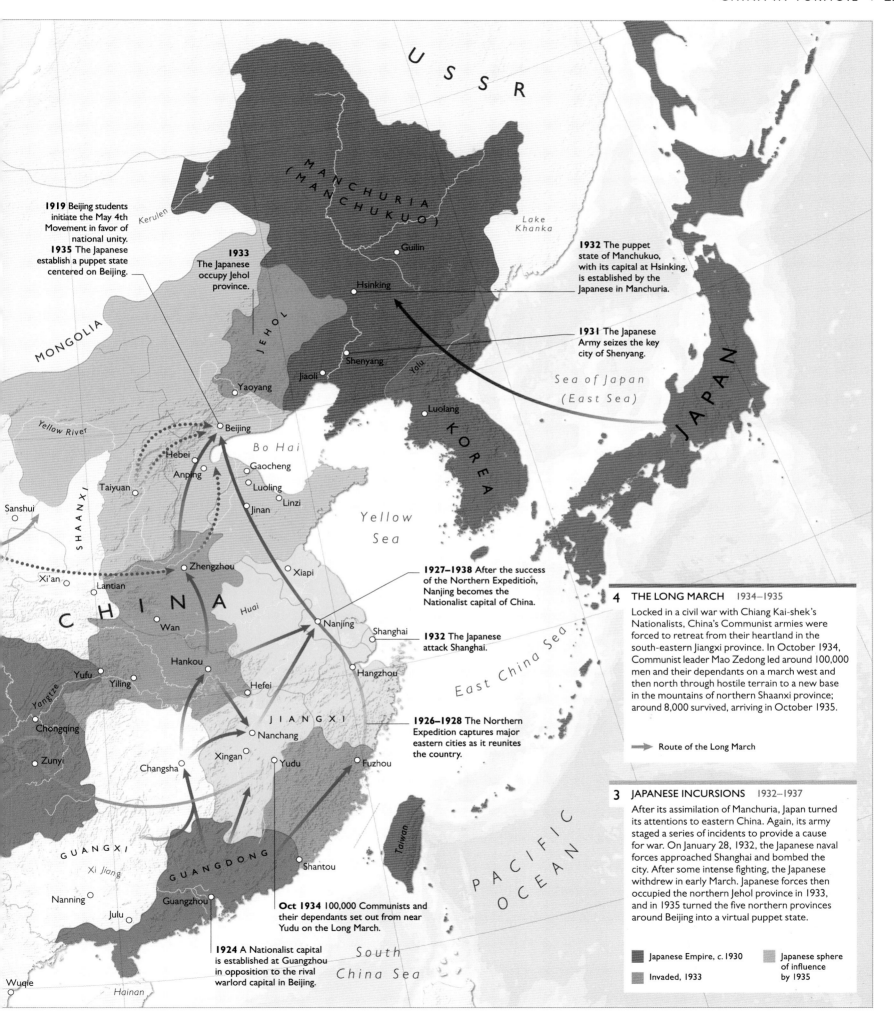

1919 Beijing students initiate the May 4th Movement in favor of national unity.

1935 The Japanese establish a puppet state centered on Beijing.

1933 The Japanese occupy Jehol province.

1932 The puppet state of Manchukuo, with its capital at Hsinking, is established by the Japanese in Manchuria.

1931 The Japanese Army seizes the key city of Shenyang.

1927–1938 After the success of the Northern Expedition, Nanjing becomes the Nationalist capital of China.

1932 The Japanese attack Shanghai.

1926–1928 The Northern Expedition captures major eastern cities as it reunites the country.

Oct 1934 100,000 Communists and their dependants set out from near Yudu on the Long March.

1924 A Nationalist capital is established at Guangzhou in opposition to the rival warlord capital in Beijing.

4 THE LONG MARCH 1934–1935

Locked in a civil war with Chiang Kai-shek's Nationalists, China's Communist armies were forced to retreat from their heartland in the south-eastern Jiangxi province. In October 1934, Communist leader Mao Zedong led around 100,000 men and their dependants on a march west and then north through hostile terrain to a new base in the mountains of northern Shaanxi province; around 8,000 survived, arriving in October 1935.

➤ Route of the Long March

3 JAPANESE INCURSIONS 1932–1937

After its assimilation of Manchuria, Japan turned its attentions to eastern China. Again, its army staged a series of incidents to provide a cause for war. On January 28, 1932, the Japanese naval forces approached Shanghai and bombed the city. After some intense fighting, the Japanese withdrew in early March. Japanese forces then occupied the northern Jehol province in 1933, and in 1935 turned the five northern provinces around Beijing into a virtual puppet state.

■ Japanese Empire, c. 1930
■ Invaded, 1933
■ Japanese sphere of influence by 1935

THE SPANISH CIVIL WAR

A prelude to World War II, the Spanish Civil War (1936–1939) was a bitter struggle between supporters of the democratically elected government and an emerging military dictatorship. Several other countries lent their support to each side.

During the 1930s, Spain was highly polarized, with major divisions between the church and state, urban and rural communities, liberal and conservative values, and the rich and poor. At one end of the political spectrum was the right-wing National Front (Nationalists), supported by the Falange (a Spanish Fascist party), monarchists, and some Catholics. At the other end was the left-wing Popular Front (Republicans), consisting of Communists, socialists, liberals, and anarchists.

The Republicans won the general election on February 16, 1936. Fearing a Communist revolution, the army officer and Nationalist leader General Francisco Franco launched a military uprising in Spanish Morocco and across south-western Spain. Pro-government groups fought against the Nationalist rebels, but Franco received significant help from Nazi Germany and Fascist Italy, both of which wanted to stop the spread of Communism in Europe. By November 1936, Franco's troops had reached the outskirts of Madrid—a Republican stronghold. Unable to capture the capital, the Nationalists besieged the city for over two years.

Although the Republicans continued to control eastern Spain and much of the south-east, Franco's forces were more organized and gradually took over areas previously under Republican control. The Nationalist victory at the Battle of Teruel (December 1937–February 1938) was a turning point in the war, and at the Battle of the Ebro (July–November 1938) the Republican troops were almost entirely eliminated. By spring 1939 the conflict was over, and Franco's government was accepted by most of Europe.

> *"… wherever I am there will be no Communism."*
>
> FRANCISCO FRANCO, QUOTED IN 1938

SPAIN IN WORLD WAR II

While Spain was a non-belligerent in World War II, it was not entirely neutral. Although Franco did not officially join the Axis alliance, he did support Germany by providing essential supplies and allowing thousands of Spaniards to volunteer in the Axis forces, albeit on condition that they did not fight the Western Allies. Spain and Germany came close to an alliance after the fall of France in June 1940, but Hitler considered Franco's demands too high and the two could not broker a deal. As the war progressed, Hitler considered an invasion of Spain, prompting Franco to move his forces to the border with France.

General Francisco Franco

---

1 THE WAR BEGINS JULY 1936

On July 17, 1936, Nationalist forces based in Spanish Morocco launched a coup against the newly elected Republican government. Franco took command of the Army of Africa—a Moroccan-based group of professional soldiers—on July 19. From July 27, Franco's army was flown from Morocco to Spain by German and Italian forces, and fighting soon spread through south-western Spain.

ATLANTIC OCEAN

2 INTERNATIONAL INTERVENTION 1936

Although 27 countries signed a non-intervention pact in September 1936, the ideological nature of the war gave it an international dimension. The Nationalists were aided by soldiers and equipment supplied by Fascist Italy and Nazi Germany. The Republicans were supported by the Communist government of Russia, and the government of Mexico, as well as by volunteers from International Brigades—left-wing fighters who came from all over the world to fight Fascism.

🚢 German support   🚢 Soviet support

🚢 Italian support

Aug 22, 1936 Portugal allows German ships to dock at Lisbon and from there dispatch war supplies into Nationalist territory.

Porto

Lisbon

PORTUGAL

3 ATROCITIES AGAINST CIVILIANS 1936–1939

Both sides committed atrocities against civilians during the war. The Republicans targeted anyone believed to be right wing, including teachers, lawyers, mayors, and landowners, and they ransacked many churches. Meanwhile, the Nationalists persuaded the Nazis and Italians to carry out attacks from the air, including raids on Guernica and Barcelona, which was bombed by Italian aircraft that flew from the Balearic Islands.

✊ Republican violence   ✊ Nationalist violence

▽ **Resisting the Nationalists**
The women's militia of the left-wing Popular Front march in Madrid in July 1936. A number of women fought in the Republican forces.

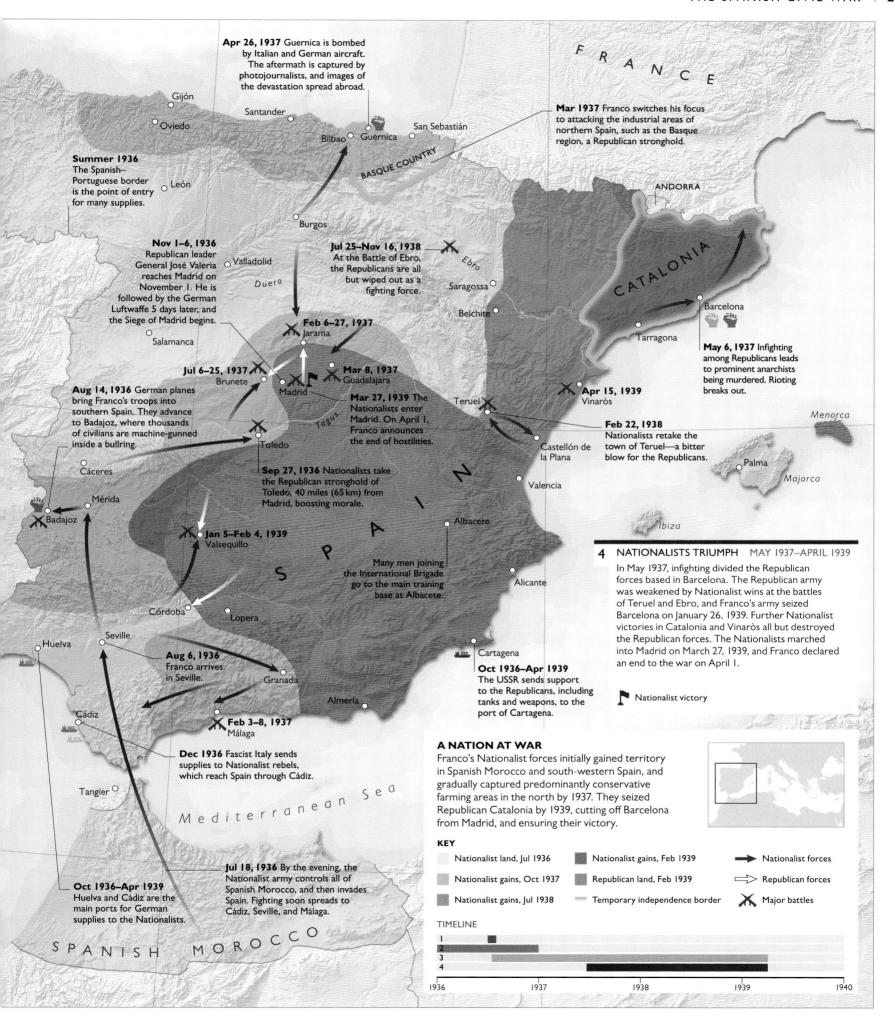

Apr 26, 1937 Guernica is bombed by Italian and German aircraft. The aftermath is captured by photojournalists, and images of the devastation spread abroad.

Mar 1937 Franco switches his focus to attacking the industrial areas of northern Spain, such as the Basque region, a Republican stronghold.

Summer 1936 The Spanish–Portuguese border is the point of entry for many supplies.

Nov 1–6, 1936 Republican leader General José Valeria reaches Madrid on November 1. He is followed by the German Luftwaffe 5 days later, and the Siege of Madrid begins.

Jul 25–Nov 16, 1938 At the Battle of Ebro, the Republicans are all but wiped out as a fighting force.

Feb 6–27, 1937 Jarama

Jul 6–25, 1937 Brunete

Aug 14, 1936 German planes bring Franco's troops into southern Spain. They advance to Badajoz, where thousands of civilians are machine-gunned inside a bullring.

Mar 8, 1937 Guadalajara

Mar 27, 1939 The Nationalists enter Madrid. On April 1, Franco announces the end of hostilities.

Apr 15, 1939 Vinaròs

May 6, 1937 Infighting among Republicans leads to prominent anarchists being murdered. Rioting breaks out.

Feb 22, 1938 Nationalists retake the town of Teruel—a bitter blow for the Republicans.

Sep 27, 1936 Nationalists take the Republican stronghold of Toledo, 40 miles (65 km) from Madrid, boosting morale.

Jan 5–Feb 4, 1939 Valsequillo

4 NATIONALISTS TRIUMPH MAY 1937–APRIL 1939

In May 1937, infighting divided the Republican forces based in Barcelona. The Republican army was weakened by Nationalist wins at the battles of Teruel and Ebro, and Franco's army seized Barcelona on January 26, 1939. Further Nationalist victories in Catalonia and Vinaròs all but destroyed the Republican forces. The Nationalists marched into Madrid on March 27, 1939, and Franco declared an end to the war on April 1.

⚑ Nationalist victory

Many men joining the International Brigade go to the main training base at Albacete.

Oct 1936–Apr 1939 The USSR sends support to the Republicans, including tanks and weapons, to the port of Cartagena.

Aug 6, 1936 Franco arrives in Seville.

Feb 3–8, 1937 Málaga

Dec 1936 Fascist Italy sends supplies to Nationalist rebels, which reach Spain through Cádiz.

A NATION AT WAR

Franco's Nationalist forces initially gained territory in Spanish Morocco and south-western Spain, and gradually captured predominantly conservative farming areas in the north by 1937. They seized Republican Catalonia by 1939, cutting off Barcelona from Madrid, and ensuring their victory.

Oct 1936–Apr 1939 Huelva and Cádiz are the main ports for German supplies to the Nationalists.

Jul 18, 1936 By the evening, the Nationalist army controls all of Spanish Morocco, and then invades Spain. Fighting soon spreads to Cádiz, Seville, and Málaga.

KEY

Nationalist land, Jul 1936	Nationalist gains, Feb 1939
Nationalist gains, Oct 1937	Republican land, Feb 1939
Nationalist gains, Jul 1938	Temporary independence border

➡ Nationalist forces
⇨ Republican forces
✗ Major battles

TIMELINE

1
2
3
4

1936   1937   1938   1939   1940

Map labels: Gijón, Oviedo, Santander, Bilbao, Guernica, San Sebastián, FRANCE, León, BASQUE COUNTRY, ANDORRA, Valladolid, Burgos, Duero, Ebro, Saragossa, CATALONIA, Belchite, Barcelona, Tarragona, Salamanca, Jarama, Madrid, Brunete, Tagus, Toledo, Teruel, Castellón de la Plana, Menorca, Cáceres, Mérida, Badajoz, Valencia, Palma, Majorca, Albacete, Ibiza, Córdoba, Lopera, Alicante, Huelva, Seville, Cartagena, Granada, Cádiz, Almería, SPAIN, Tangier, Mediterranean Sea, SPANISH MOROCCO

THE SINO-JAPANESE WAR

The Japanese attacked China in July 1937, marking the start of an eight-year war. The fighting was brutal; there were more than seven million military casualties on both sides and 17–22 million Chinese civilians lost their lives.

The hostilities that broke out in July 1937 were the culmination of a long-term Japanese aspiration to dominate China in order to gain access to raw materials, food, and labor. Having already captured Taiwan in 1895 (seen here in dark red), Manchuria in 1931, and Jehol province in 1933 (both seen in the right-hand pink area), Japan turned its attention to the rest of China. On July 7–9, 1937, the Japanese and Chinese exchanged fire over an incident involving a missing Japanese soldier at Wanping, 10 miles (16 km) south-west of Beijing. The Japanese opened fire on Marco Polo (Lugou) Bridge, a key access route to Beijing, and attacked Wanping. This skirmish developed into a major battle. Although a cease-fire was soon agreed, Japanese and Chinese forces continued to clash, leading to full-scale hostilities as the Japanese began to conquer northern China. Neither side officially declared war.

Invasion and expansion

Some Japanese forces then headed south; others landed on the east coast. In November they captured Shanghai after a three-month battle, and in December took Nanjing (both in the pink-tinted area on this map), where they perpetrated a major massacre. In 1938, they won a victory at Hankou against Chinese forces and Soviet volunteers led by Chiang Kai-shek. The four-month battle claimed around 1.2 million lives. These offensives were accompanied by the bombing of civilian targets, intended to destroy morale; Chongqing, for example, was bombed more than 200 times and had its center burned out. By 1941, Japan controlled much of eastern China and almost the entire coastline.

Chinese resistance

Despite these victories, the war turned into a stalemate. Chinese lines of communication stretched far into local territory, and Japan lacked the manpower to dominate the countryside. It was unable to defeat a major Communist guerrilla campaign in Shaanxi, nor could it repel two massive Nationalist and Communist counter-offensives, losing two major battles at Hankou and South Guangxi.

◁ **Massacre at Nanjing**
The Imperial Japanese Army entered Nanjing in January 1938. Up to 300,000 civilians are estimated to have been killed.

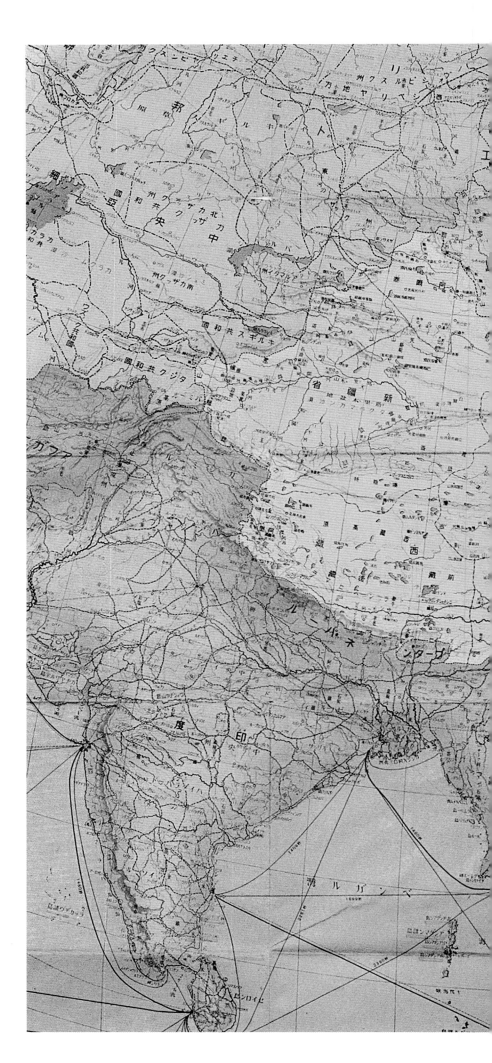

Japanese empire map, c. 1939
The red areas of this map show Japan's empire in 1930 including Korea and Taiwan; the right-hand pink area shows conquests of 1931–1933, including Manchuria. The pink tint shows gains in China by 1937, and the orange tint shows gains made in 1938–1939.

GERMANY AND ITALY EXPAND

In the years following World War I, the governments of Fascist Italy and Nazi Germany both pursued expansionist policies aimed at enlarging their territories and overcoming the terms of the 1919 Versailles Treaty. At the time, they met with little opposition from other European nations.

Although Italy was on the winning Allied side in World War I, it emerged from the conflict with high casualties, a crippled, indebted economy, and few territorial gains. This fueled great resentment at home, which was among the many factors that propelled Benito Mussolini's National Fascist Party to power in 1922.

Mussolini sought to bolster the nation's standing by expanding Italy's territories in the Mediterranean and in Africa in an attempt to build a second Roman Empire. The conquests of Ethiopia (1935) and Albania (1939) were successful parts of this process.

Hitler also had imperial ambitions, believing that Germany required *Lebensraum* (living space) to survive.

When he came to power in 1933, he intended to avenge the Treaty of Versailles and create a remilitarized, pan-German state in central Europe. As Germany began to rearm in defiance of Versailles, the Saarland and Rhineland returned to full German control in 1935–1936, Austria was united with Germany in 1938, and Czechoslovakia was occupied and divided in 1938–1939.

In response to these expansionist policies, the European powers of Britain and France did little to defend Versailles, instead choosing to appease the dictators in the hope that this would keep the peace. However, the failure of appeasement by the spring of 1939 forced both countries to prepare for the inevitability of renewed war in Europe.

> "It is not programs that are wanting for the salvation of Italy but men and will power."
>
> BENITO MUSSOLINI, SPEECH MADE IN UDINE, 1920

ALLIED REARMAMENT

After World War I, Britain and France reduced their military capacities, but the rise of the Nazi Party in Germany in 1933 forced a rethink. After 1936 Britain began to produce a new generation of tanks and artillery pieces, new aircraft carriers and battleships, and to develop the Spitfire and Hawker Hurricane fighter aircraft. France built the defensive Maginot Line along its eastern border with Germany and modernized its air force, the biggest in the world at the time.

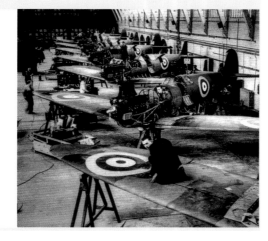

A British Spitfire production line

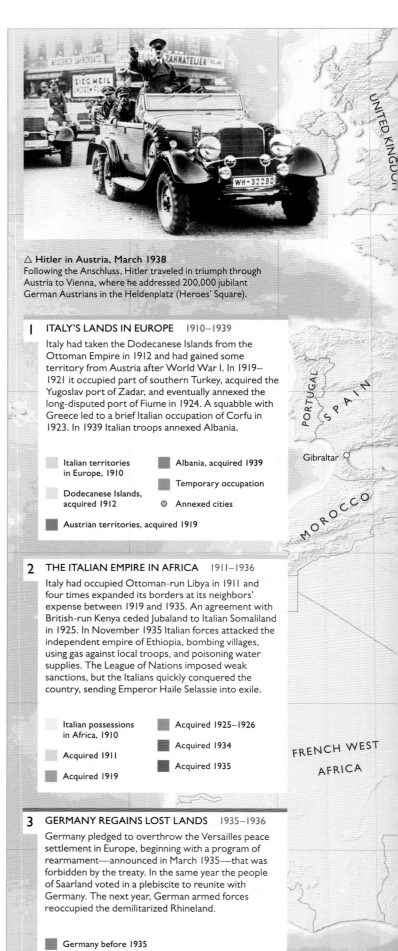

△ Hitler in Austria, March 1938
Following the Anschluss, Hitler traveled in triumph through Austria to Vienna, where he addressed 200,000 jubilant German Austrians in the Heldenplatz (Heroes' Square).

1 ITALY'S LANDS IN EUROPE 1910–1939

Italy had taken the Dodecanese Islands from the Ottoman Empire in 1912 and had gained some territory from Austria after World War I. In 1919–1921 it occupied part of southern Turkey, acquired the Yugoslav port of Zadar, and eventually annexed the long-disputed port of Fiume in 1924. A squabble with Greece led to a brief Italian occupation of Corfu in 1923. In 1939 Italian troops annexed Albania.

- ▢ Italian territories in Europe, 1910
- ▢ Dodecanese Islands, acquired 1912
- ▢ Austrian territories, acquired 1919
- ▢ Albania, acquired 1939
- ▢ Temporary occupation
- ⊚ Annexed cities

2 THE ITALIAN EMPIRE IN AFRICA 1911–1936

Italy had occupied Ottoman-run Libya in 1911 and four times expanded its borders at its neighbors' expense between 1919 and 1935. An agreement with British-run Kenya ceded Jubaland to Italian Somaliland in 1925. In November 1935 Italian forces attacked the independent empire of Ethiopia, bombing villages, using gas against local troops, and poisoning water supplies. The League of Nations imposed weak sanctions, but the Italians quickly conquered the country, sending Emperor Haile Selassie into exile.

- ▢ Italian possessions in Africa, 1910
- ▢ Acquired 1911
- ▢ Acquired 1919
- ▢ Acquired 1925–1926
- ▢ Acquired 1934
- ▢ Acquired 1935

3 GERMANY REGAINS LOST LANDS 1935–1936

Germany pledged to overthrow the Versailles peace settlement in Europe, beginning with a program of rearmament—announced in March 1935—that was forbidden by the treaty. In the same year the people of Saarland voted in a plebiscite to reunite with Germany. The next year, German armed forces reoccupied the demilitarized Rhineland.

- ▢ Germany before 1935
- ▢ Saarland, acquired 1935
- ▢ Rhineland, acquired 1936

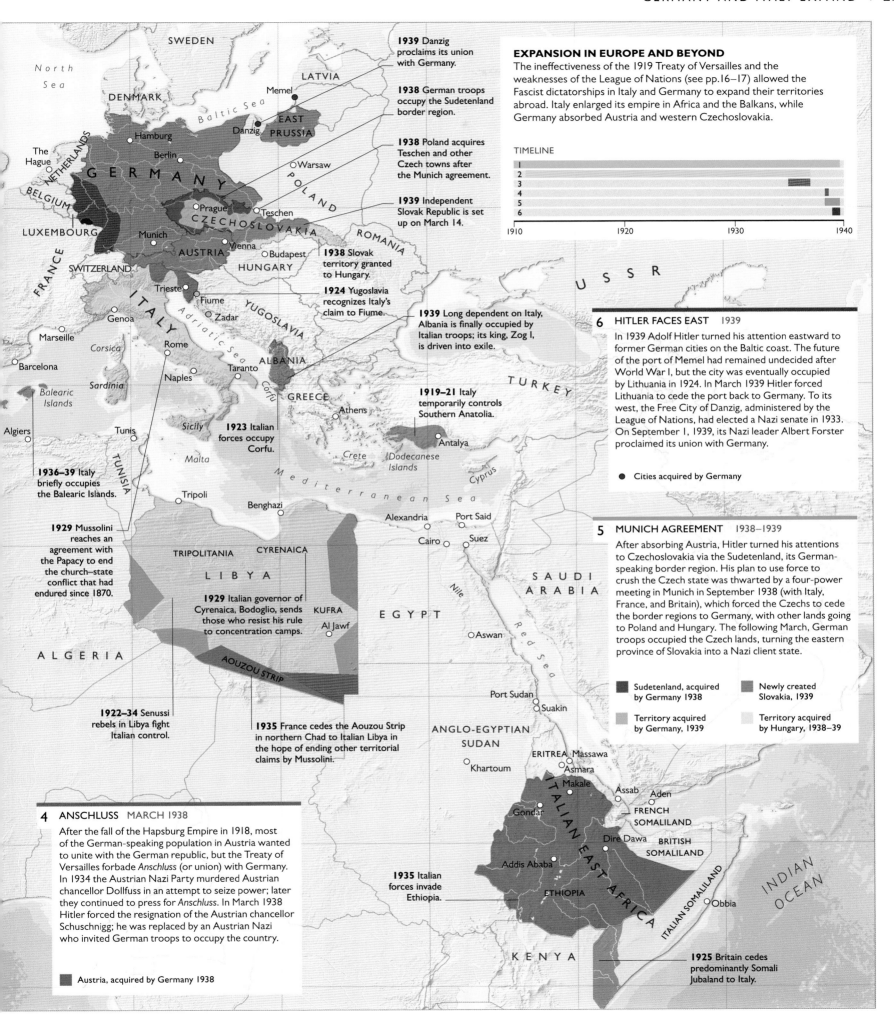

1939 Danzig proclaims its union with Germany.

1938 German troops occupy the Sudetenland border region.

1938 Poland acquires Teschen and other Czech towns after the Munich agreement.

1939 Independent Slovak Republic is set up on March 14.

1938 Slovak territory granted to Hungary.

1924 Yugoslavia recognizes Italy's claim to Fiume.

1939 Long dependent on Italy, Albania is finally occupied by Italian troops; its king, Zog I, is driven into exile.

1919–21 Italy temporarily controls Southern Anatolia.

1923 Italian forces occupy Corfu.

1936–39 Italy briefly occupies the Balearic Islands.

1929 Mussolini reaches an agreement with the Papacy to end the church–state conflict that had endured since 1870.

1929 Italian governor of Cyrenaica, Bodoglio, sends those who resist his rule to concentration camps.

1922–34 Senussi rebels in Libya fight Italian control.

1935 France cedes the Aouzou Strip in northern Chad to Italian Libya in the hope of ending other territorial claims by Mussolini.

1935 Italian forces invade Ethiopia.

1925 Britain cedes predominantly Somali Jubaland to Italy.

EXPANSION IN EUROPE AND BEYOND

The ineffectiveness of the 1919 Treaty of Versailles and the weaknesses of the League of Nations (see pp.16–17) allowed the Fascist dictatorships in Italy and Germany to expand their territories abroad. Italy enlarged its empire in Africa and the Balkans, while Germany absorbed Austria and western Czechoslovakia.

TIMELINE

6 HITLER FACES EAST 1939

In 1939 Adolf Hitler turned his attention eastward to former German cities on the Baltic coast. The future of the port of Memel had remained undecided after World War I, but the city was eventually occupied by Lithuania in 1924. In March 1939 Hitler forced Lithuania to cede the port back to Germany. To its west, the Free City of Danzig, administered by the League of Nations, had elected a Nazi senate in 1933. On September 1, 1939, its Nazi leader Albert Forster proclaimed its union with Germany.

● Cities acquired by Germany

5 MUNICH AGREEMENT 1938–1939

After absorbing Austria, Hitler turned his attentions to Czechoslovakia via the Sudetenland, its German-speaking border region. His plan to use force to crush the Czech state was thwarted by a four-power meeting in Munich in September 1938 (with Italy, France, and Britain), which forced the Czechs to cede the border regions to Germany, with other lands going to Poland and Hungary. The following March, German troops occupied the Czech lands, turning the eastern province of Slovakia into a Nazi client state.

■ Sudetenland, acquired by Germany 1938

■ Newly created Slovakia, 1939

■ Territory acquired by Germany, 1939

□ Territory acquired by Hungary, 1938–39

4 ANSCHLUSS MARCH 1938

After the fall of the Hapsburg Empire in 1918, most of the German-speaking population in Austria wanted to unite with the German republic, but the Treaty of Versailles forbade *Anschluss* (or union) with Germany. In 1934 the Austrian Nazi Party murdered Austrian chancellor Dollfuss in an attempt to seize power; later they continued to press for *Anschluss*. In March 1938 Hitler forced the resignation of the Austrian chancellor Schuschnigg; he was replaced by an Austrian Nazi who invited German troops to occupy the country.

■ Austria, acquired by Germany 1938

Synagogue ablaze
The main synagogue in Hanover, in northern Germany, was burned to the ground by Nazis on November 9, 1938. Jewish shops and dwellings in the city were also looted, and the furniture from homes was dragged into a square and burned.

KRISTALLNACHT

In November 1938, a 17-year-old Polish Jew, Herschel Grynszpan, assassinated Ernst vom Rath, a diplomat working at the German Embassy in Paris. This triggered a Nazi pogrom that would have disastrous consequences for Jews throughout the Third Reich.

In a matter of hours after vom Rath's death on November 9, Nazis throughout Germany went on a violent rampage, attacking synagogues and Jewish businesses and homes. The event came to be called *Kristallnacht* ("Crystal Night") for the shattered window glass that littered the streets. By the time the pogrom came to an end a day later, around 100 synagogues had been demolished and several hundred more severely damaged by fire. Many Jewish cemeteries had been desecrated, and at least 7,500 Jewish-owned shops had been sacked and looted.

△ **Mark of a Jew**
The pogrom had a lasting impact. By 1941, all Jews in Germany had to wear a yellow Star of David with the word *Jude* (Jew).

Cause and aftermath

Whether Hitler ever gave a specific order to launch the pogrom is uncertain. Goebbels, the Propaganda Minister, was quick to claim that the pogrom was an outburst of national anger in response to a cowardly attack. As well as inciting racial hatred through propaganda, the Nazis had institutionalized anti-semitism by teaching it in schools and introducing the Nuremberg Laws in 1935, which stripped Jews of German citizenship. Following the death of vom Rath, the Jews were fined one billion Reichsmarks and told to repair all the damage the pogrom had caused. About 30,000 Jewish men were arrested, most of whom were transported to concentration camps.

△ **Anti-Jewish boycott**
A Berlin shop window is vandalized during *Kristallnacht* with a poster warning shoppers not to buy from Jews. A correspondent in Berlin for the *Daily Telegraph* reported, "racial hatred and hysteria seemed to have taken complete hold of otherwise decent people."

COUNTDOWN IN EUROPE

In a frenzy of diplomatic activity before the war, nations formed alliances, offered guarantees, and—if not wishing to fight—proclaimed neutrality. The final piece of the jigsaw—the Nazi–Soviet Nonaggression Pact—was the most surprising diplomatic coup of the century.

The threat to world peace intensified through the 1930s as Germany and Italy expanded their imperial possessions in Europe, while to the east Japan entered into conflict with China (see pp.26–27). In response, the two major democracies in Europe—Britain and France—abandoned their policy of appeasing Hitler and Mussolini and moved to deterrence instead. On March 31, 1939, they made a guarantee to Poland that the western powers would come to its aid if the country was attacked, and extended similar assurances to Romania, Greece, and Turkey after the Italian annexation of Albania.

With the emergence of the two rival power blocs, several European nations grouped together to proclaim their neutrality, but such diplomatic alliances were nothing next to the announcement in August 1939 that the two ideological foes of Europe—Nazi Germany and the Communist USSR—had agreed a mutual nonaggression pact. Its secret clauses redrew the map of central and Eastern Europe and absorbed previously independent states into their two spheres of influence. With the safeguard of nonaggression, Hitler's Germany had now cleared the way for a successful invasion of Poland.

"In war, whichever side may call itself the victor, there are no winners, but all are losers."

NEVILLE CHAMBERLAIN, BRITISH PRIME MINISTER, 1938

JOSEPH STALIN 1879–1953

Born in Gori, Georgia, Josef Djugashvili was educated in a seminary but expelled for holding revolutionary views. Twice exiled by the Czarist government to Siberia, and from 1912 known as Stalin, or "Man of Steel," he helped Lenin during the October Revolution of 1917, becoming Commissar for Nationalities in the Bolshevik government. In 1922 he became General Secretary of the Party and used this to build his own power base. By the late 1920s he had established a dictatorship that lasted until his death in 1953.

A DIVIDED EUROPE
The rise of Nazi Germany and its alliance with Italy divided Europe into two camps. One group of nations attempted to remain neutral, while the USSR reached a surprising understanding with Nazi Germany.

TIMELINE

1936   1937   1938   1939   1940   1941

1   THE AXIS POWERS 1936–1940
On November 1, 1936, after the signing of a new set of protocols with Germany, the Italian dictator Benito Mussolini proclaimed the establishment of a Rome–Berlin "Axis." Italy and Germany formalized their alliance in the Pact of Steel on May 22, 1939. Meanwhile, Germany and Japan had signed the Anti-Comintern Pact against the USSR on November 25, 1936, which Italy joined in 1937. The ties between Japan, Germany, and Italy, who came to be called the "Axis powers," were strengthened by the Tripartite Pact of September 27, 1940.

■ European Axis powers, May 1939

Nov 1938 Strikes take place in France amid tension between Communists and the far right.

ATLANTIC OCEAN

2   COPENHAGEN DECLARATION JULY 1938
In July 1938 Norway, Sweden, Denmark, the Netherlands, Belgium, Finland, and the three Baltic states of Estonia, Latvia, and Lithuania signed a declaration in the Danish capital, Copenhagen, stating that they would remain neutral in any forthcoming European war. Most of these states, except Belgium, had been neutral or not yet independent in World War I, and wished to avoid being drawn into a future conflict.

■ Signatories of Copenhagen Declaration

Jan 26, 1939 General Franco's Nationalist troops capture Barcelona.

3   THE END OF APPEASEMENT 1939
After Germany broke the Munich Agreement of September 1938 (see pp.28–29) and occupied western Czechoslovakia, Britain and France offered guarantees to Poland (March 1939), Romania and Greece (April 1939), and Turkey (May 1939) that they would defend them from attack. With these guarantees in place, the German invasion of Poland in September 1939 triggered a declaration of war against Germany.

Apr 1, 1939 Franco declares victory in Madrid, ending the Spanish Civil War.

■ Allies and countries promised Allied assistance

GLASGOW   BELFAST   IRELAND   DUBLIN   UNITED KINGDOM   LONDON   FRANCE   PARIS   PORTUGAL   SPAIN   MADRID   BARCELONA

1939 Denmark signs a ten-year nonaggression pact with Germany.

Jul 1938 A declaration of neutrality is signed by nine states in Copenhagen.

Mar 22, 1939 Germany annexes the Baltic port of Memel from Lithuania.

1939 Originally assigned to Germany in the Nazi–Soviet Pact, Lithuania is later transferred to the Soviet sphere of influence.

Aug 1939 Hitler issues ultimatum claiming sovereignty over Free City of Danzig.

May 22, 1939 The Pact of Steel is signed in Berlin.

1939 Under the Nazi–Soviet Pact, Poland is to be split between Germany and the USSR and wiped off the map.

Mar 1938 *Anschluss:* Hitler annexes Austria.

Nov 1, 1936 In a speech in Milan, Mussolini uses the term "Axis" to denote his alliance with Nazi Germany.

Apr 7, 1939 Italian forces invade Albania.

△ **Hitler and the bear**
In a critique of the pact between the USSR and Germany, this French satirical cartoon from 1939 depicts Hitler and the USSR—the "bear"—wrestling over a map of Europe. The pact was negotiated in secret and was met with shock across Europe when it was announced.

5   THE EFFECTS OF THE PACT   1939–1940

Secret clauses in the pact were to affect the fate of neighboring countries. Germany gained a free hand in western Poland and Lithuania, while the influence of the USSR was to prevail over eastern Poland, Finland, Estonia, Latvia, and the Romanian province of Bessarabia. A later secret agreement on September 28, 1939, extended German control further into eastern Poland while giving the USSR a free hand in Lithuania. All the secret clauses were implemented by summer 1940.

🤝 Victims of the Pact

4   THE NAZI–SOVIET NONAGGRESSION PACT   AUGUST 23, 1939

On August 23, 1939, the German and Russian foreign secretaries Joachim von Ribbentrop and Vyacheslav Molotov signed a nonaggression pact. The published terms included pledges to maintain neutrality if either country was at war. This marked a major change in policy: the USSR, let down by the Munich Agreement, was now willing to precipitate war between "the two imperialist camps"; and Germany wanted to avoid possible Soviet interference in its invasion of Poland.

🤝 Signatories to the Nonaggression Pact

GERMANY TRIUMPHANT
1939–1941

AS THE AXIS ARMIES SWEPT ACROSS EUROPE AND PUSHED INTO THE
USSR, THE BALKANS, AND AFRICA, THE ALLIES FOUND THEMSELVES
BATTLING FOR SURVIVAL ON ALL FRONTS.

WAR IN EUROPE

The triumph of German armies in the first phase of World War II made Adolf Hitler the master of continental Europe. Under the leadership of Winston Churchill, Britain successfully resisted a German aerial onslaught, but with no immediate prospect of more than mere survival.

△ **Fleeing civilians**
A Parisian family sets out in search of a safe haven as German forces approach the French capital in 1940. Two-thirds of the city's population fled in panic to the countryside.

When World War II broke out in September 1939, there were no cheering crowds as there had been in World War I. The British and French governments reluctantly entered a conflict that they had not wanted, and took no action to aid the Poles, on whose behalf they had declared war on Germany. Quickly defeated and divided between Nazi Germany and the Soviet Union, Poland was subjected to the mass killing of its educated elite, and its Jews were driven into ghettos. Britain and France rejected a peace offer from Hitler after his victory in Poland, but had no desire for military action. The French army based itself on the Maginot Line, the fortifications that were supposed to block a German invasion, while a British Expeditionary Force headed to northern France. However, little actually happened, except at sea. The lack of military action led to this period being dubbed the "phony war."

In Britain, preparations for conflict had been under way long before war was officially declared. Civil defense programs set up to cope with air raids were implemented immediately, and blackouts were introduced in cities, although expectations that Germany would undertake a swift aerial attack proved

△ **Third Reich medal**
The Knight's Cross, introduced by Hitler in 1939, was awarded to German soldiers for acts of exceptional valor or skill in command.

mistaken. In British cities, children were evacuated days before the declaration of war, likewise the residents in France's frontier zone. By the time war broke out, Germany's economy had already been geared to war for over a year, and Britain and France had begun to rearm. Indeed, armaments programs and military conscription ended the mass unemployment of the interwar period.

Germany storms Europe

Some politicians, especially in France, would have preferred to fight the Soviet Union rather than Nazi Germany. They toyed with plans for intervention in support of Finland after it was attacked by the Soviets in the winter of 1939–1940. However, in spring 1940 this idea was abandoned as Germany took decisive and widespread military action. First, Hitler sent his armies northward into Denmark and Norway. He then followed this by launching a lightning offensive in France, Belgium, the Netherlands, and Luxembourg. Combining tanks and aircraft in fast-moving "Blitzkrieg" tactics, the Germans scored a series of astonishing victories. On the Western front, the French and British armies were routed in six weeks, although many soldiers escaped capture through the evacuation of Dunkirk in May–June 1940.

HITLER TRIUMPHANT

Nazi Germany conquered most of northern Europe in three short campaigns: the first against Poland in September 1939, the second in Scandinavia beginning in April 1940, and the third in Western Europe in May–June 1940. However, after France surrendered, Hitler failed to pursue an invasion of Britain with equal energy and willpower. The Luftwaffe's air attacks caused extensive damage but were inconclusive. Meanwhile the US was increasingly drawn into supporting the British war effort.

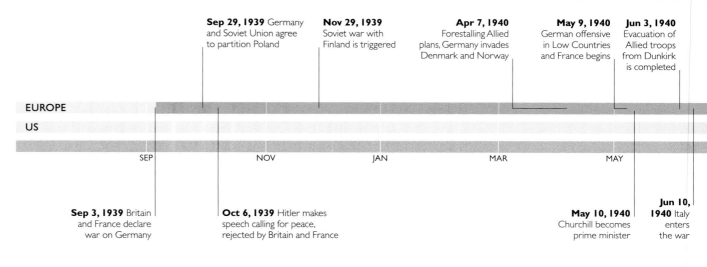

Sep 29, 1939 Germany and Soviet Union agree to partition Poland

Nov 29, 1939 Soviet war with Finland is triggered

Apr 7, 1940 Forestalling Allied plans, Germany invades Denmark and Norway

May 9, 1940 German offensive in Low Countries and France begins

Jun 3, 1940 Evacuation of Allied troops from Dunkirk is completed

EUROPE

US

SEP   NOV   JAN   MAR   MAY

Sep 3, 1939 Britain and France declare war on Germany

Oct 6, 1939 Hitler makes speech calling for peace, rejected by Britain and France

May 10, 1940 Churchill becomes prime minister

Jun 10, 1940 Italy enters the war

◁ **Rallying support**
Issued soon after Winston Churchill became prime minister in May 1940, this British poster was intended to encourage national unity.

▽ **Victory in Europe**
Seen here at a parade on his 50th birthday a few months before the war, Hitler seemed to be fulfilling his promises in the war's early stages, as Poland and then France fell to the Nazis.

France's surrender a few weeks later was followed by the creation of the Vichy French government—a regime dedicated to collaboration with the Nazis. Hitler and his allies had control of almost all continental Europe.

In Britain, the recently appointed prime minister, Winston Churchill, resolved to fight on. In summer 1940, Germany fought for control of the air over southern England while preparing for a seaborne invasion. Known as the Battle of Britain, the aerial conflict ended in stalemate, and Hitler's invasion plans were abandoned. However, throughout the following fall and winter, Britain's cities were battered by German bombers attacking at night in the "Blitz." At sea, German U-boats took a heavy toll on merchant shipping.

There was little that Britain could do at this stage to take the war to its enemy. Instead, Churchill opted for "economic warfare," consisting of ineffectual attempts to bomb German cities from the air and stir up resistance in occupied Europe.

"What the world did not deem possible, the German people have achieved …"

ADOLF HITLER, SPEECH, APRIL 6, 1941

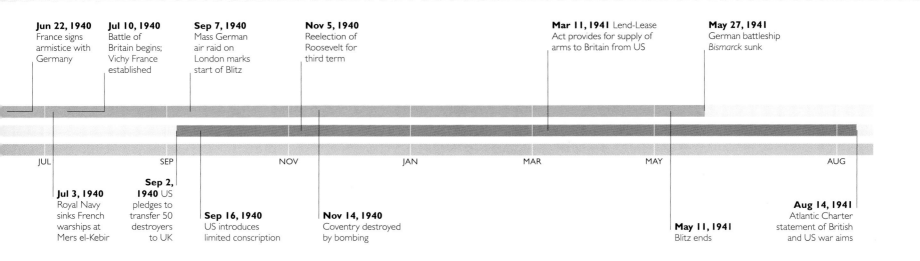

Jun 22, 1940
France signs armistice with Germany

Jul 10, 1940
Battle of Britain begins; Vichy France established

Sep 7, 1940
Mass German air raid on London marks start of Blitz

Nov 5, 1940
Reelection of Roosevelt for third term

Mar 11, 1941 Lend-Lease Act provides for supply of arms to Britain from US

May 27, 1941
German battleship *Bismarck* sunk

JUL   SEP   NOV   JAN   MAR   MAY   AUG

Jul 3, 1940
Royal Navy sinks French warships at Mers el-Kebir

Sep 2, 1940 US pledges to transfer 50 destroyers to UK

Sep 16, 1940
US introduces limited conscription

Nov 14, 1940
Coventry destroyed by bombing

May 11, 1941
Blitz ends

Aug 14, 1941
Atlantic Charter statement of British and US war aims

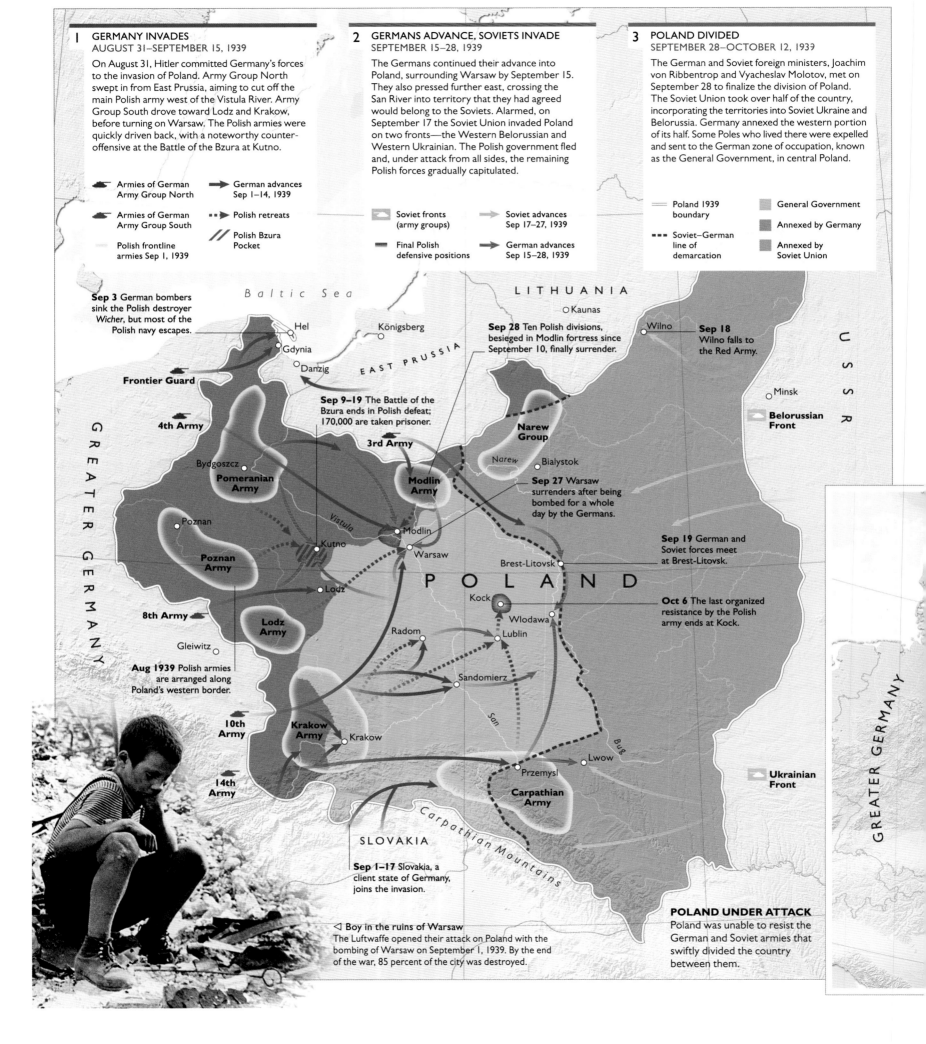

1 GERMANY INVADES
AUGUST 31–SEPTEMBER 15, 1939

On August 31, Hitler committed Germany's forces to the invasion of Poland. Army Group North swept in from East Prussia, aiming to cut off the main Polish army west of the Vistula River. Army Group South drove toward Lodz and Krakow, before turning on Warsaw. The Polish armies were quickly driven back, with a noteworthy counter-offensive at the Battle of the Bzura at Kutno.

- ◀ Armies of German Army Group North
- ◀ Armies of German Army Group South
- —— Polish frontline armies Sep 1, 1939
- → German advances Sep 1–14, 1939
- ▪▪▶ Polish retreats
- // Polish Bzura Pocket

2 GERMANS ADVANCE, SOVIETS INVADE
SEPTEMBER 15–28, 1939

The Germans continued their advance into Poland, surrounding Warsaw by September 15. They also pressed further east, crossing the San River into territory that they had agreed would belong to the Soviets. Alarmed, on September 17 the Soviet Union invaded Poland on two fronts—the Western Belorussian and Western Ukrainian. The Polish government fled and, under attack from all sides, the remaining Polish forces gradually capitulated.

- ◢ Soviet fronts (army groups)
- ▬ Final Polish defensive positions
- ⇨ Soviet advances Sep 17–27, 1939
- → German advances Sep 15–28, 1939

3 POLAND DIVIDED
SEPTEMBER 28–OCTOBER 12, 1939

The German and Soviet foreign ministers, Joachim von Ribbentrop and Vyacheslav Molotov, met on September 28 to finalize the division of Poland. The Soviet Union took over half of the country, incorporating the territories into Soviet Ukraine and Belorussia. Germany annexed the western portion of its half. Some Poles who lived there were expelled and sent to the German zone of occupation, known as the General Government, in central Poland.

- —— Poland 1939 boundary
- ▪▪▪ Soviet–German line of demarcation
- ▪ General Government
- ▪ Annexed by Germany
- ▪ Annexed by Soviet Union

Sep 3 German bombers sink the Polish destroyer *Wicher*, but most of the Polish navy escapes.

Sep 28 Ten Polish divisions, besieged in Modlin fortress since September 10, finally surrender.

Sep 18 Wilno falls to the Red Army.

Frontier Guard

Sep 9–19 The Battle of the Bzura ends in Polish defeat; 170,000 are taken prisoner.

Sep 27 Warsaw surrenders after being bombed for a whole day by the Germans.

Sep 19 German and Soviet forces meet at Brest-Litovsk.

Oct 6 The last organized resistance by the Polish army ends at Kock.

Aug 1939 Polish armies are arranged along Poland's western border.

Sep 1–17 Slovakia, a client state of Germany, joins the invasion.

Baltic Sea
LITHUANIA
USSR

Hel, Königsberg, Kaunas, Wilno, Gdynia, Danzig, EAST PRUSSIA, Minsk, Belorussian Front, 4th Army, Bydgoszcz, Pomeranian Army, Narew, Bialystok, Narew Group, 3rd Army, Modlin Army, Modlin, Poznan, Poznan Army, Vistula, Kutno, Warsaw, Brest-Litovsk, POLAND, Lodz, Lodz Army, Kock, Wlodawa, 8th Army, Gleiwitz, Radom, Lublin, Sandomierz, San, 10th Army, Krakow Army, Krakow, Carpathian Army, Lwow, Bug, Przemysl, 14th Army, Carpathian Mountains, Lwow, SLOVAKIA, GREATER GERMANY

◁ **Boy in the ruins of Warsaw**
The Luftwaffe opened their attack on Poland with the bombing of Warsaw on September 1, 1939. By the end of the war, 85 percent of the city was destroyed.

POLAND UNDER ATTACK
Poland was unable to resist the German and Soviet armies that swiftly divided the country between them.

POLAND DESTROYED

Poland emerged from World War I as an independent state after more than 200 years of subjugation. However, it took just a few weeks in 1939 for Germany and the Soviet Union to crush Polish resistance, divide the country, and begin brutalizing its population.

After Germany's expansion into Austria and Czechoslovakia, Hitler determined to attack Poland to regain lost territory and create *Lebensraum* ("living space") for his people, turning Poland into a German satellite state. Under the terms of the cynical pact that he had negotiated with the Soviet Union in 1939 (see pp.32–33), Poland was to be partitioned between the two powers; this enabled Germany to attack Poland without the fear of Soviet intervention.

On September 1, German troops moved into the country. Although France and Britain declared war on Germany on September 3, they reneged on their promise to provide military aid to Poland, giving Hitler a free hand.

Within a week, German "Blitzkrieg" tactics had squeezed Polish forces into the heart of Poland. When the Soviet army invaded from the east on September 17, Poland's fate was sealed. With its forces trapped between two enemies, Poland capitulated on September 28. The country was split into three: one zone was annexed by Germany, one by Soviet Russia, and the third—the General Government—was occupied by the Germans.

INVASION AND OPPRESSION

Poland was destroyed in a matter of weeks from August 31 to October 12, 1939. The Poles were seen by their occupiers as an inferior people and suffered deeply under the oppressive regimes imposed upon them.

TIMELINE

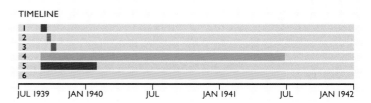

| | JUL 1939 | JAN 1940 | JUL | JAN 1941 | JUL | JAN 1942 |

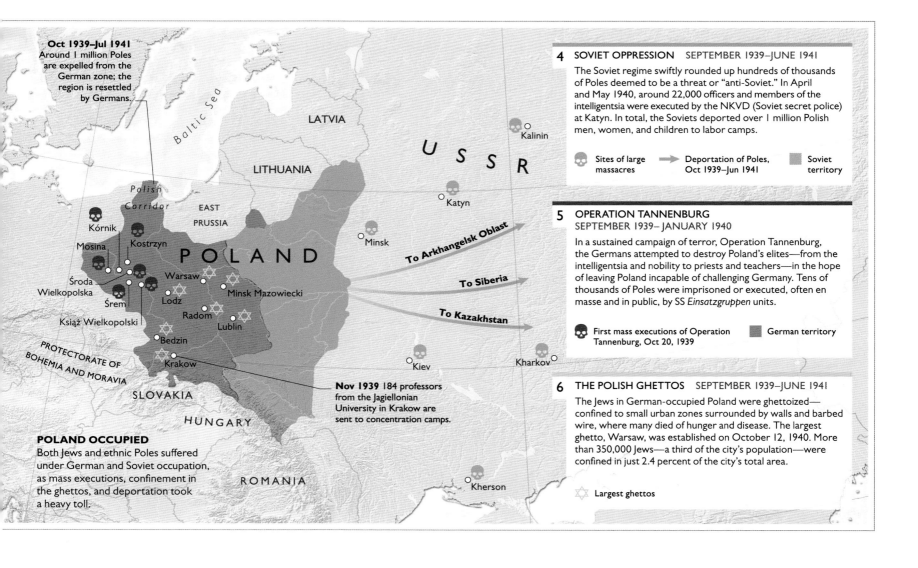

Oct 1939–Jul 1941
Around 1 million Poles are expelled from the German zone; the region is resettled by Germans.

Nov 1939 184 professors from the Jagiellonian University in Krakow are sent to concentration camps.

POLAND OCCUPIED
Both Jews and ethnic Poles suffered under German and Soviet occupation, as mass executions, confinement in the ghettos, and deportation took a heavy toll.

4 SOVIET OPPRESSION SEPTEMBER 1939–JUNE 1941

The Soviet regime swiftly rounded up hundreds of thousands of Poles deemed to be a threat or "anti-Soviet." In April and May 1940, around 22,000 officers and members of the intelligentsia were executed by the NKVD (Soviet secret police) at Katyn. In total, the Soviets deported over 1 million Polish men, women, and children to labor camps.

- Sites of large massacres
- → Deportation of Poles, Oct 1939–Jun 1941
- Soviet territory

5 OPERATION TANNENBURG
SEPTEMBER 1939– JANUARY 1940

In a sustained campaign of terror, Operation Tannenburg, the Germans attempted to destroy Poland's elites—from the intelligentsia and nobility to priests and teachers—in the hope of leaving Poland incapable of challenging Germany. Tens of thousands of Poles were imprisoned or executed, often en masse and in public, by SS *Einsatzgruppen* units.

- First mass executions of Operation Tannenburg, Oct 20, 1939
- German territory

6 THE POLISH GHETTOS SEPTEMBER 1939–JUNE 1941

The Jews in German-occupied Poland were ghettoized—confined to small urban zones surrounded by walls and barbed wire, where many died of hunger and disease. The largest ghetto, Warsaw, was established on October 12, 1940. More than 350,000 Jews—a third of the city's population—were confined in just 2.4 percent of the city's total area.

- ✡ Largest ghettos

Emergency measures
Fearing mass air attacks, including the use of poison gas, once war had been declared, governments took measures to ensure that civil defense could be carried out in major cities. Here fire-fighters in gas masks carry out an exercise in Paris in 1939.

THE PHONY WAR

Although the Allies declared war against Germany on September 3, 1939, there was little fighting on land until spring 1940. This lull in hostilities became known as the "phony war."

△ **Safety precautions**
In this British government propaganda poster, an air raid warden warns a schoolboy that he should leave London. In total, 1.5 million schoolchildren and mothers with babies were evacuated from the city.

The lack of fighting in western Europe during this time suited both sides: the Germans feared an Allied attack while they were engaged against Poland, and the French and British needed time to build up their forces. While preparations were underway and wartime emergency powers were imposed at home, military action was very limited. The British Expeditionary Force (BEF) was deployed to France on September 4, 1939, but took up defensive positions, and a French offensive against the Germans in the Saar on September 7 lasted only five days. British bombers flew over Germany, but merely dropped propaganda leaflets aimed at undermining German morale.

Hitler made a peace offer to Britain on October 6, 1939, but after Britain rejected it he ordered his generals to prepare for an invasion of France and Belgium. Initial plans were unsatisfactory, and a harsh winter meant that the attack was postponed 29 times. Instead, in April 1940, the Germans invaded Denmark and Norway, ending the phony war.

△ **Army in waiting**
The British Expeditionary Force was ordered into France on September 4, and within three weeks there were around 150,000 troops stationed there. Sent to the Franco-Belgian border, they had little to do for eight months but dig trenches and wait.

BATTLE OF THE RIVER PLATE

On the night of October 13–14, 1939, a German U-boat sank HMS *Royal Oak* at her berth in Scapa Flow, Britain's main naval base. The audacious attack was a blow to British morale, but just two months later the Royal Navy had claimed a victory against the odds in the first major naval battle of the war.

At the outbreak of war, Germany's naval strategy was to avoid direct combat between fleet units and instead use surface raiders and U-boats to sink Allied shipping wherever possible, severing Britain's maritime lifelines. Weeks before hostilities began, German warships and supply vessels went into the North and South Atlantic, and most of the U-boat fleet took up station in the North Sea and Atlantic approaches. There they awaited authorization to attack.

The flagship of the German navy (*Kriegsmarine*) was the *Admiral Graf Spee*, a fast, modern, heavily armed pocket battleship commanded by Hans Langsdorff. From late September to early December, *Graf*

Spee eluded detection and raided successfully, sinking nine Allied merchantmen totaling 55,000 tons (50,000 metric tons). The British and French navies organized hunting groups in areas throughout the North and South Atlantic, and in the early hours of December 13, *Graf Spee* was spotted. In the ensuing Battle of the River Plate, the smaller Royal Navy cruisers were able to harry *Graf Spee* and inflict damage that forced her to take refuge in a neutral port for repairs. The subsequent scuttling of *Graf Spee* was a major setback for the German navy, greatly undermining the original strategy of using its surface fleet to blockade British trade.

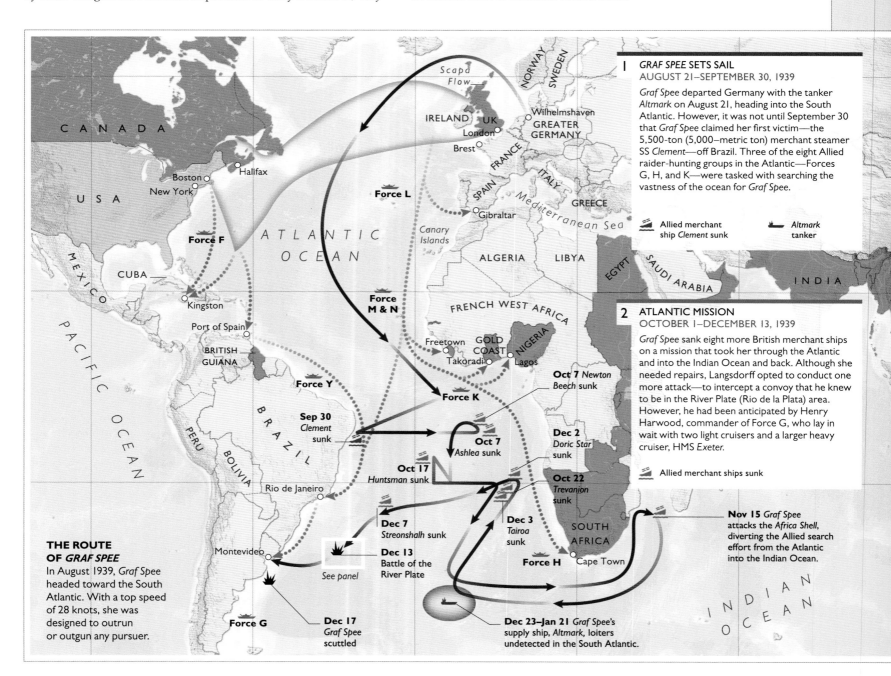

1 GRAF SPEE SETS SAIL
AUGUST 21–SEPTEMBER 30, 1939

Graf Spee departed Germany with the tanker *Altmark* on August 21, heading into the South Atlantic. However, it was not until September 30 that *Graf Spee* claimed her first victim—the 5,500-ton (5,000–metric ton) merchant steamer SS *Clement*—off Brazil. Three of the eight Allied raider-hunting groups in the Atlantic—Forces G, H, and K—were tasked with searching the vastness of the ocean for *Graf Spee*.

- Allied merchant ship *Clement* sunk
- *Altmark* tanker

2 ATLANTIC MISSION
OCTOBER 1–DECEMBER 13, 1939

Graf Spee sank eight more British merchant ships on a mission that took her through the Atlantic and into the Indian Ocean and back. Although she needed repairs, Langsdorff opted to conduct one more attack—to intercept a convoy that he knew to be in the River Plate (Rio de la Plata) area. However, he had been anticipated by Henry Harwood, commander of Force G, who lay in wait with two light cruisers and a larger heavy cruiser, HMS *Exeter*.

- Allied merchant ships sunk

THE ROUTE OF GRAF SPEE
In August 1939, *Graf Spee* headed toward the South Atlantic. With a top speed of 28 knots, she was designed to outrun or outgun any pursuer.

Nov 15 *Graf Spee* attacks the *Africa Shell*, diverting the Allied search effort from the Atlantic into the Indian Ocean.

Dec 23–Jan 21 *Graf Spee's* supply ship, *Altmark*, loiters undetected in the South Atlantic.

Dec 17 *Graf Spee* scuttled

Dec 13 Battle of the River Plate

See panel

Dec 7 *Streonshalh* sunk

Dec 3 *Tairoa* sunk

Dec 2 *Doric Star* sunk

Oct 22 *Trevanion* sunk

Oct 17 *Huntsman* sunk

Oct 7 *Ashlea* sunk

Oct 7 *Newton Beech* sunk

Sep 30 *Clement* sunk

Force G
Force H
Force Y
Force K
Force M & N
Force F
Force L

6 GRAF SPEE SCUTTLED
DECEMBER 13/14–19, 1939

Graf Spee sheltered in the neutral port Montevideo and was permitted to stay until December 17 to make repairs and off-load her wounded. On December 15, a German officer thought he spotted British ships approaching, and Langsdorff became convinced that superior forces lay in wait. Unwilling to lose Graf Spee, he took her into the estuary, and at around 8pm on December 17 she was scuttled. On December 19, Captain Langsdorff shot himself dead in a hotel room.

5 GRAF SPEE WITHDRAWS
6:30 AM–7:30 AM DECEMBER 13, 1939

Torpedoes fired by the British forced Graf Spee to lay down a smokescreen and turn away. Ajax launched her spotter plane at 6:37am. She and Achilles were closing range, firing heavily, drawing Graf Spee's main guns away from Exeter. Ajax was hit at 7:25am and had to turn east. Graf Spee was hit several dozen times and withdrew west into the River Plate Estuary.

 Ajax reconnaissance aircraft

4 EXETER DAMAGED
6 AM–6:30 AM DECEMBER 13, 1939

The British force spotted Graf Spee shortly after 6am. The British doctrine on the engagement of a superior ship had been developed by Harwood himself a few years earlier: he duly divided his force into two—Exeter turning north-west and Ajax and Achilles north-east—to split the fire from the heavily armed ship. Graf Spee opened fire and concentrated her 11-in guns on Exeter, which, by 6:30am, had been hit three times, losing a turret and her Walrus spotter aircraft.

TORPEDO FIRE

Exeter   Ajax

Ajax and Achilles combined

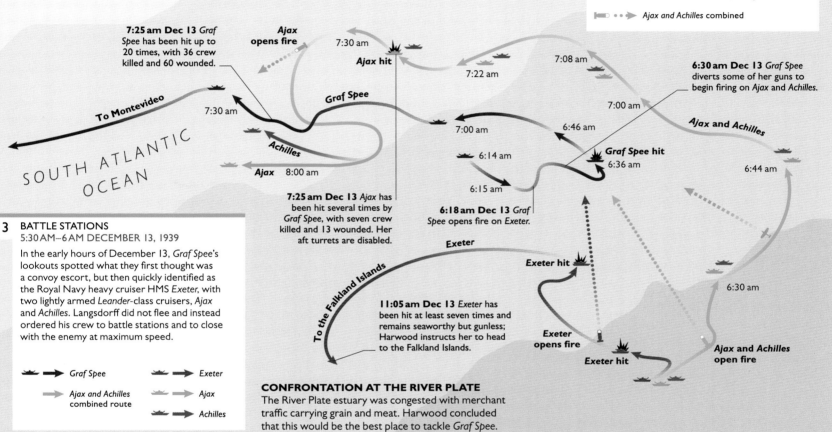

7:25am Dec 13 Graf Spee has been hit up to 20 times, with 36 crew killed and 60 wounded.

Ajax opens fire

Ajax hit

7:30 am

7:22 am

7:08 am

6:30am Dec 13 Graf Spee diverts some of her guns to begin firing on Ajax and Achilles.

7:00 am

Graf Spee

7:30 am

To Montevideo

7:30 am

7:00 am

6:46 am

Ajax and Achilles

Achilles

Graf Spee hit 6:36 am

6:44 am

SOUTH ATLANTIC OCEAN

Ajax   8:00 am

6:14 am

6:15 am

7:25am Dec 13 Ajax has been hit several times by Graf Spee, with seven crew killed and 13 wounded. Her aft turrets are disabled.

6:18am Dec 13 Graf Spee opens fire on Exeter.

Exeter hit

6:30 am

3 BATTLE STATIONS
5:30 AM–6 AM DECEMBER 13, 1939

In the early hours of December 13, Graf Spee's lookouts spotted what they first thought was a convoy escort, but then quickly identified as the Royal Navy heavy cruiser HMS Exeter, with two lightly armed Leander-class cruisers, Ajax and Achilles. Langsdorff did not flee and instead ordered his crew to battle stations and to close with the enemy at maximum speed.

Exeter

To the Falkland Islands

11:05am Dec 13 Exeter has been hit at least seven times and remains seaworthy but gunless; Harwood instructs her to head to the Falkland Islands.

Exeter opens fire

Exeter hit

Ajax and Achilles open fire

Graf Spee

Exeter

Ajax and Achilles combined route

Ajax

Achilles

CONFRONTATION AT THE RIVER PLATE

The River Plate estuary was congested with merchant traffic carrying grain and meat. Harwood concluded that this would be the best place to tackle Graf Spee.

ATLANTIC HUNTING GROUNDS

Atlantic shipping routes were vital to Britain's global war effort. The German raiding campaign against this shipping required supply vessels and good luck to remain undetected for extended periods.

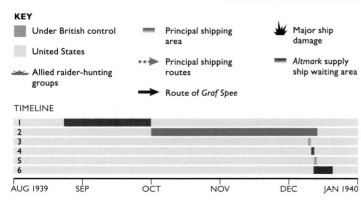

KEY

Under British control

United States

Allied raider-hunting groups

Principal shipping area

Principal shipping routes

Route of Graf Spee

Major ship damage

Altmark supply ship waiting area

TIMELINE

1						
2						
3						
4						
5						
6						

AUG 1939   SEP   OCT   NOV   DEC   JAN 1940

△ **Scuttling of Admiral Graf Spee**
Charges set on the pocket battleship Graf Spee were detonated on the evening of December 17, 1939, to scuttle the ship. Her sinking was witnessed by a crowd of more than 20,000 onlookers.

THE WINTER WAR IN FINLAND

The Soviet invasion of Finland in winter 1939 was met with ferocious resistance from a largely reservist Finnish army that was familiar with—and well trained for—the severe weather conditions. The damage inflicted by the Finns on their numerically superior enemy helped them negotiate a settlement that avoided their complete subjugation.

In the Molotov–Ribbentrop Pact of August 23, 1939, the Soviet Union and Germany secretly agreed to divide much of Europe between themselves in a way that anticipated the "territorial and political rearrangements" to come. According to this pact, the Baltic States and Finland fell into the Soviet sphere of influence, and it was not long before the Soviets demanded that Finland cede to them a number of strategically important territories on their shared border. Finland refused, and Stalin ordered an invasion, intending to install a compliant regime in Finland.

The Soviet attack began on November 30, 1939, and was undertaken initially by four armies of about 450,000 men. The plan was to reach Helsinki within three weeks. The main focus of the Soviet offensive was the Karelian Isthmus, where most of

the Finnish Army was deployed along the Mannerheim Line—a series of fortifications, anti-tank ditches, and obstacles built over two decades to deter Soviet aggression. The Soviet build-up gave the Finns time to assemble around 250,000 men, who had been trained in the use of *motti* tactics—encircling and breaking up enemy formations into isolated pockets, then destroying them.

Stout resistance and damaging counter-attacks from the Finns stalemated the Soviets in most of Finland by the end of December. The highly mobile Finnish ski patrol units wreaked havoc behind Soviet formations. However, by early February, a reorganized Red Army converted its superiority in manpower and equipment into success on the battlefield. Hostilities ended on March 13, 1940, with Finland ceding around ten percent of its territory to the USSR.

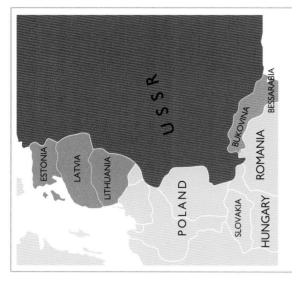

ESTONIA — LATVIA — LITHUANIA — POLAND — SLOVAKIA — HUNGARY — ROMANIA — BUKOVINA — BESSARABIA — U S S R

SOVIET ABSORPTION OF THE BALTIC AND BLACK SEA STATES

Following the Winter War, the Soviets annexed Estonia, Latvia, Lithuania, and parts of Romania—all areas recognized in the Molotov–Ribbentrop Pact as lying within the Soviet sphere of influence. These territories were incorporated into the Soviet Union as constituent republics in August 1940, and many of their residents, deemed "enemies of the people," were deported to Siberia or Kazakhstan.

KEY
- ⬛ Annexed from the Baltic States
- ⬛ Annexed from Romania

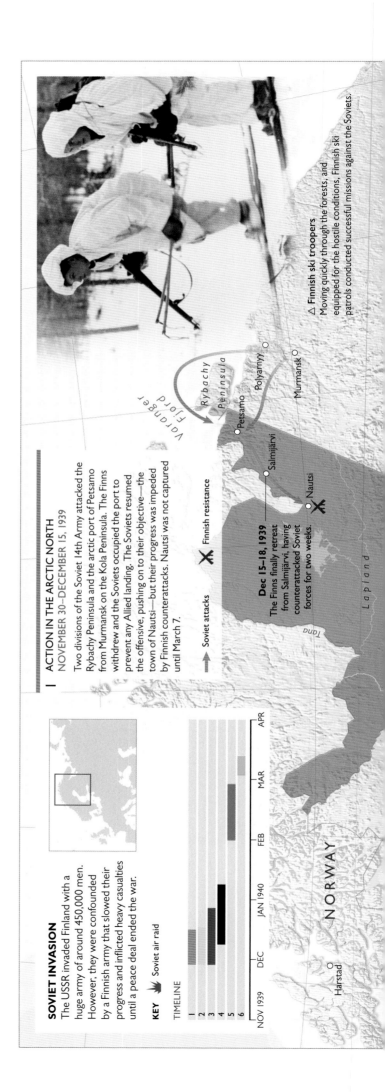

△ **Finnish ski troopers**
Moving quickly through the forests, and equipped for the hostile conditions, Finnish ski patrols conducted successful missions against the Soviets.

I **ACTION IN THE ARCTIC NORTH**
NOVEMBER 30–DECEMBER 15, 1939

Two divisions of the Soviet 14th Army attacked the Rybachy Peninsula and the arctic port of Petsamo from Murmansk on the Kola Peninsula. The Finns withdrew and the Soviets occupied the port to prevent any Allied landing. The Soviets resumed the offensive, pushing on to their objective—the town of Nautsi—but their progress was impeded by Finnish counterattacks. Nautsi was not captured until March 7.

Dec 15–18, 1939
The Finns finally retreat from Salmijärvi, having counterattacked Soviet forces for two weeks.

✕ Finnish resistance

⬆ Soviet attacks

Varanger Fjord — Rybachy Peninsula — Polyarnyy — Murmansk — Petsamo — Salmijärvi — Nautsi — Lapland — Tana — NORWAY — Harstad

SOVIET INVASION

The USSR invaded Finland with a huge army of around 450,000 men. However, they were confounded by a Finnish army that slowed their progress and inflicted heavy casualties until a peace deal ended the war.

KEY ✈ Soviet air raid

TIMELINE

NOV 1939 — DEC — JAN 1940 — FEB — MAR — APR

6 THE MOSCOW PEACE TREATY
MARCH 3–13, 1940

On March 3, the Soviets established a bridgehead to the west of Viipuri. A Finnish delegation in Moscow agreed to Soviet terms, and in the early hours of March 13 a peace treaty was signed. Around 10 percent of the territory that Finland had held since 1920 was ceded to the Soviets. However, the Red Army was seen to have been humiliated by the far weaker Finns; the USSR's international reputation was badly damaged, and on December 14, 1939, it was expelled from the League of Nations.

Territory ceded to the Soviets

Finland, March 1940

Dec 7–19, 1939 Heavily outnumbered, the Finns hold their line in the Kollaa River area north of Lake Ladoga.

Nov 26, 1939 The Mainila shots incident, a claim that the Finns had fired across the frontier, allows the USSR to depict Finland as an aggressor.

Dec 1, 1939 The Red Army installs a collaborationist "Finnish Democratic Republic" government in Terijoki.

Dec 16–19, 1939 Parts of a Soviet division are defeated at the Battle of Pelkosenniemi and have to retreat to Salla.

Dec 8–12, 1939 The first major Finnish victory of the war takes place at Tolvajärvi.

Dec 1939 Soviet aircraft attack Finnish ports and shipping. Shipborne antiaircraft batteries defend the Finnish coast.

Feb 11, 1940 A Soviet advance breaks the Mannerheim Line at Summa.

Nov 30, 1939 Soviet air raids on Helsinki kill almost 100 people.

Reinforcements

White Sea

U S S R

Lake Ladoga

Gulf of Bothnia

Gulf of Finland

Karelian Isthmus

F I N L A N D

S W E D E N

ESTONIA

Kandalaksha
Belomorsk
Kondopoga
Petrozavodsk
Salmi
Leningrad
Terijoki
Mainila
Summa
Viipuri
Svetogorsk
Kollaa
Kollaa River
Tolvajärvi
Äglajärvi
Ilomantsi
Repola
Savonlinna
Mikkeli
Kuopio
Kuhmo
Suomussalmi
Raate
Salla
Pelkosenniemi
Märkäjärvi
Kemijärvi
Kemi
Oulu
Kokkola
Vaasa
Pori
Turku
Porvoo
Helsinki

Torne
Ounas
Kemi

---

2 FINLAND BISECTED
NOVEMBER 30–DECEMBER 16, 1939

The Soviet 9th Army, positioned to the west of the White Sea, attempted a pincer-style offensive through central Finland. Its target was the capture of the rail junctions of Kemi and Oulu on the Gulf of Bothnia. Soviet divisions to the north became bogged down around Salla, while in the southern sector there was heavy Finnish resistance at Repola and Suomussalmi.

→ Soviet attacks
→ Finnish counterattacks
⋯→ Finnish reinforcements
✕ Finnish resistance

3 THE KARELIAN ISTHMUS
NOVEMBER 30–DECEMBER 24, 1939

The main Soviet attack, spearheaded by the 7th Army, was a thrust into the Karelian Isthmus—the wide stretch of land between the Gulf of Finland and Lake Ladoga. Their objective was Viipuri, a staging post on the route to Helsinki. However, the Finns held the Mannerheim Line, and their forces between Salmi and Ilomantsi blocked the Soviet 8th Army's attempts to flank the isthmus north of Lake Ladoga.

→ Soviet attacks
→ Finnish counterattacks
▭▭▭ Mannerheim Line

4 FINNISH VICTORIES
DECEMBER 7, 1939–JANUARY 7, 1940

A week after hostilities began, the Soviet 9th Army captured the village of Suomussalmi, but its progress was then checked by Finnish *motti* tactics. By the end of December the Finns had retaken the village and routed a Soviet division sent to provide relief. A large amount of Soviet equipment was seized, including tanks, artillery, and anti-tank guns. The Finns also overcame the Soviets at Tolvajärvi.

⌐ Finnish victory

5 A REINVIGORATED OFFENSIVE
FEBRUARY 1–27, 1940

Reinforced by the 13th Army, and now with new leadership, tactics, and close air support, the Soviets resumed their large-scale offensive in the Karelian Isthmus. The Mannerheim Line, which had held for two months, was finally breached, and by February 15 the Finnish General Headquarters at Mikkeli had ordered a withdrawal from the line as the Soviets poured forward.

→ Soviet attacks

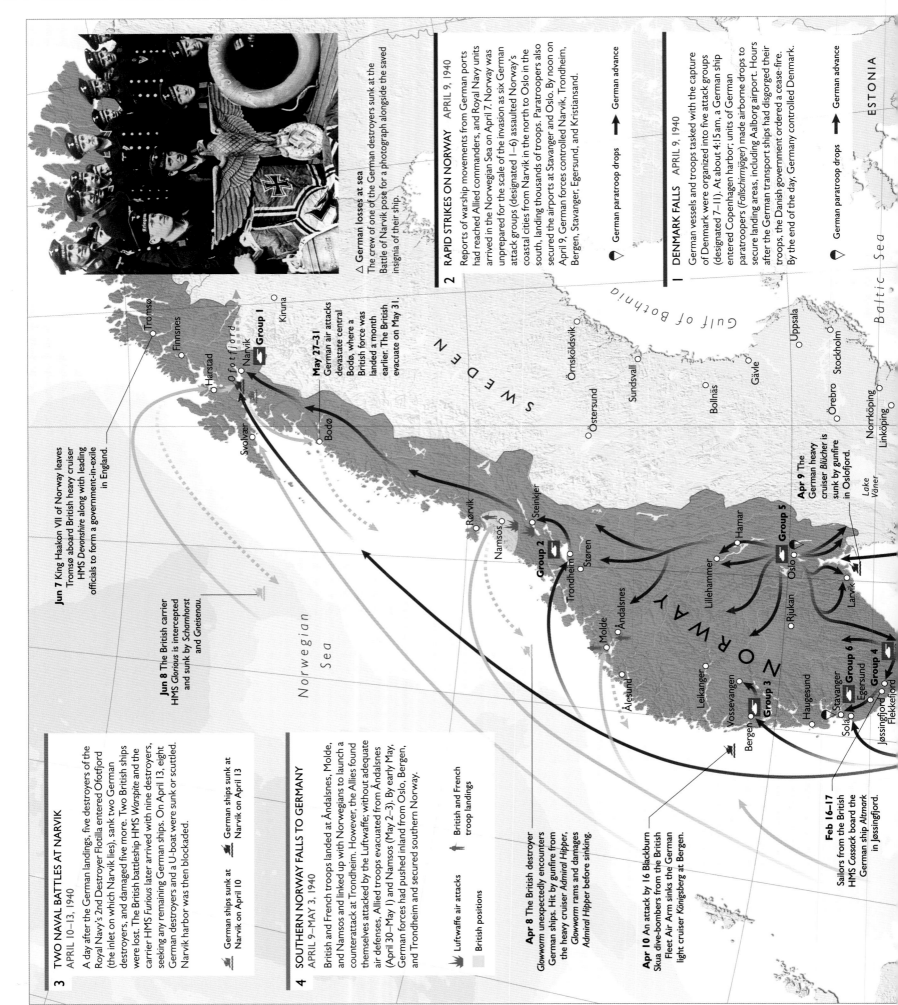

3 TWO NAVAL BATTLES AT NARVIK APRIL 10–13, 1940

A day after the German landings, five destroyers of the Royal Navy's 2nd Destroyer Flotilla entered Ofotfjord (the inlet on which Narvik lies), sank two German destroyers, and damaged five more. Two British ships were lost. The British battleship HMS Warspite and the carrier HMS Furious later arrived with nine destroyers, seeking any remaining German ships. On April 13, eight German destroyers and a U-boat were sunk or scuttled. Narvik harbor was then blockaded.

🚢 German ships sunk at Narvik on April 10   🚢 German ships sunk at Narvik on April 13

4 SOUTHERN NORWAY FALLS TO GERMANY APRIL 9–MAY 3, 1940

British and French troops landed at Åndalsnes, Molde, and Namsos and linked up with Norwegians to launch a counterattack at Trondheim. However, the Allies found themselves attacked by the Luftwaffe; without adequate air defenses, Allied troops evacuated from Åndalsnes (April 30–May 1) and Namsos (May 2–3). By early May, German forces had pushed inland from Oslo, Bergen, and Trondheim and secured southern Norway.

Apr 8 The British destroyer *Glowworm* unexpectedly encounters German ships. Hit by gunfire from the heavy cruiser *Admiral Hipper*, *Glowworm* rams and damages *Admiral Hipper* before sinking.

Apr 10 An attack by 16 Blackburn Skua dive-bombers from the British Fleet Air Arm sinks the German light cruiser *Königsberg* at Bergen.

↙ Luftwaffe air attacks
⬛ British positions
⬅ British and French troop landings

Jun 7 King Haakon VII of Norway leaves Tromsø aboard British heavy cruiser HMS Devonshire along with leading officials to form a government-in-exile in England.

Jun 8 The British carrier HMS *Glorious* is intercepted and sunk by *Scharnhorst* and *Gneisenau*.

May 27–31 German air attacks devastate central Bodø, where a British force was landed a month earlier. The British evacuate on May 31.

△ **German losses at sea**
The crew of one of the German destroyers sunk at the Battle of Narvik pose for a photograph alongside the saved insignia of their ship.

2 RAPID STRIKES ON NORWAY APRIL 9, 1940

Reports of warship movements from German ports had reached Allied commanders, and Royal Navy units arrived in the Norwegian Sea on April 7. Norway was unprepared for the scale of the invasion as six German attack groups (designated 1–6) assaulted Norway's coastal cities from Narvik in the north to Oslo in the south, landing thousands of troops. Paratroopers also secured the airports at Stavanger and Oslo. By noon on April 9, German forces controlled Narvik, Trondheim, Bergen, Stavanger, Egersund, and Kristiansand.

◐ German paratroop drops   ➔ German advance

1 DENMARK FALLS APRIL 9, 1940

German vessels and troops tasked with the capture of Denmark were organized into five attack groups (designated 7–11). At about 4:15am, a German ship entered Copenhagen harbor; units of German paratroopers (*Fallschirmjäger*) made airborne drops to secure landing areas, including Aalborg airport. Hours after the German transport ships had disgorged their troops, the Danish government ordered a cease-fire. By the end of the day, Germany controlled Denmark.

◐ German paratroop drops   ➔ German advance

Feb 16–17 Sailors from the British HMS *Cossack* board the German ship *Altmark* in Jøssingfjord.

Apr 9 The German heavy cruiser *Blücher* is sunk by gunfire in Oslofjord.

THE BATTLE FOR NORWAY

On March 1, 1940, Adolf Hitler signed the order for Operation Weserübung. The principal aim of this daring operation was to take control of Norway—a goal that also necessitated the occupation of Denmark. The invasion advanced Germany's aim of gaining greater access to the North Sea and provided a gateway to the Atlantic for its warships and submarines.

In July 1938, Norway and eight other countries declared their neutrality in any possible European conflict. Germany, in turn, agreed to respect Norway's integrity so long as its neutrality was not infringed by any other power. The peace was not to last.

Norway was of significant importance to Germany, not least because large quantities of iron ore from Sweden were shipped annually to Germany via the ice-free Norwegian port of Narvik. In addition, the German navy saw strategic advantages in establishing bases in Norway, because it would be far more difficult for an enemy to deny access to its long coastline than to blockade German ports.

The *Altmark* incident of February 1940 (see box, right) convinced Hitler that the British would not respect Norwegian neutrality. Fearing that the British would soon move to disrupt the vital trade in iron ore, the German high command planned an invasion of Norway, which began on April 9, 1940.

The focal point of the naval and land battles in Norway was the town of Narvik, which the Allies needed to occupy in order to retain a strategic foothold in Norway. The Allies decisively won the sea battles, with the German navy sustaining heavy losses. On land, however, the poorly equipped Allied troops were outnumbered and outgunned, and many were evacuated by the beginning of May. The Germans dominated the air through the Luftwaffe's 10th Air Corps (Fliegerkorps X), demonstrating the tactical importance of air superiority to achieving military aims on the modern battlefield.

The Allies abandoned their action in southern Norway after just three weeks, but fighting continued in the north, where the Norwegian and Allied forces eventually retook Narvik. However, German invasions in France and the Low Countries in May 1940 (see pp.48–49) dictated a withdrawal and evacuation because the remaining Allied soldiers were urgently needed elsewhere.

THE ALTMARK INCIDENT

From August to December 1939, the German supply ship *Altmark* (pictured below) refueled the warship *Admiral Graf Spee* during her raiding mission against Allied shipping in the South Atlantic (see pp.42–43). In January 1940, *Altmark* headed home, carrying prisoners from merchant ships sunk by *Admiral Graf Spee*. After neutral Norwegian destroyers prevented a Royal Navy interception, the British instructed the destroyer HMS *Cossack* to pursue *Altmark* into Jøssingfjord. On February 16, a boarding party armed with bayonets leaped onto *Altmark*, killing several guards but rescuing around 300 Allied POWs.

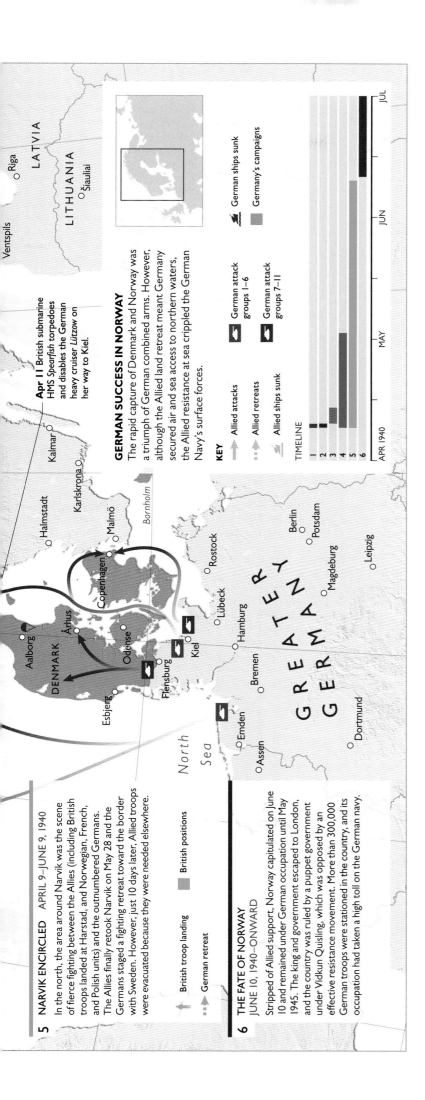

5 NARVIK ENCIRCLED APRIL 9–JUNE 9, 1940

In the north, the area around Narvik was the scene of fierce fighting between the Allies (including British troops landed at Harstad, and Norwegian, French, and Polish units) and the outnumbered Germans. The Allies finally retook Narvik on May 28 and the Germans staged a fighting retreat toward the border with Sweden. However, just 10 days later, Allied troops were evacuated because they were needed elsewhere.

Apr 11 British submarine HMS *Spearfish* torpedoes and disables the German heavy cruiser *Lützow* on her way to Kiel.

GERMAN SUCCESS IN NORWAY

The rapid capture of Denmark and Norway was a triumph of German combined arms. However, although the Allied land retreat meant Germany secured air and sea access to northern waters, the Allied resistance at sea crippled the German Navy's surface forces.

KEY

- Allied attacks
- Allied retreats
- Allied ships sunk
- German attack groups 1–6
- German attack groups 7–11
- German ships sunk
- Germany's campaigns

TIMELINE

1
2
3
4
5
6

APR 1940 | MAY | JUN | JUL

- British troop landing
- German retreat
- British positions

6 THE FATE OF NORWAY JUNE 10, 1940–ONWARD

Stripped of Allied support, Norway capitulated on June 10 and remained under German occupation until May 1945. The king and government escaped to London, and the country was ruled by a puppet government under Vidkun Quisling, which was opposed by an effective resistance movement. More than 300,000 German troops were stationed in the country, and its occupation had taken a high toll on the German navy.

LATVIA
Riga
Ventspils
LITHUANIA
Šiauliai
Kalmar
Karlskrona
Halmstadt
Karlskrona
Malmö
Copenhagen
Bornholm
Berlin
Potsdam
Rostock
Lübeck
Magdeburg
Leipzig
Aalborg
Århus
DENMARK
Odense
Esbjerg
Flensburg
Kiel
Hamburg
Bremen
Emden
Assen
Dortmund
GREATER GERMANY
North Sea

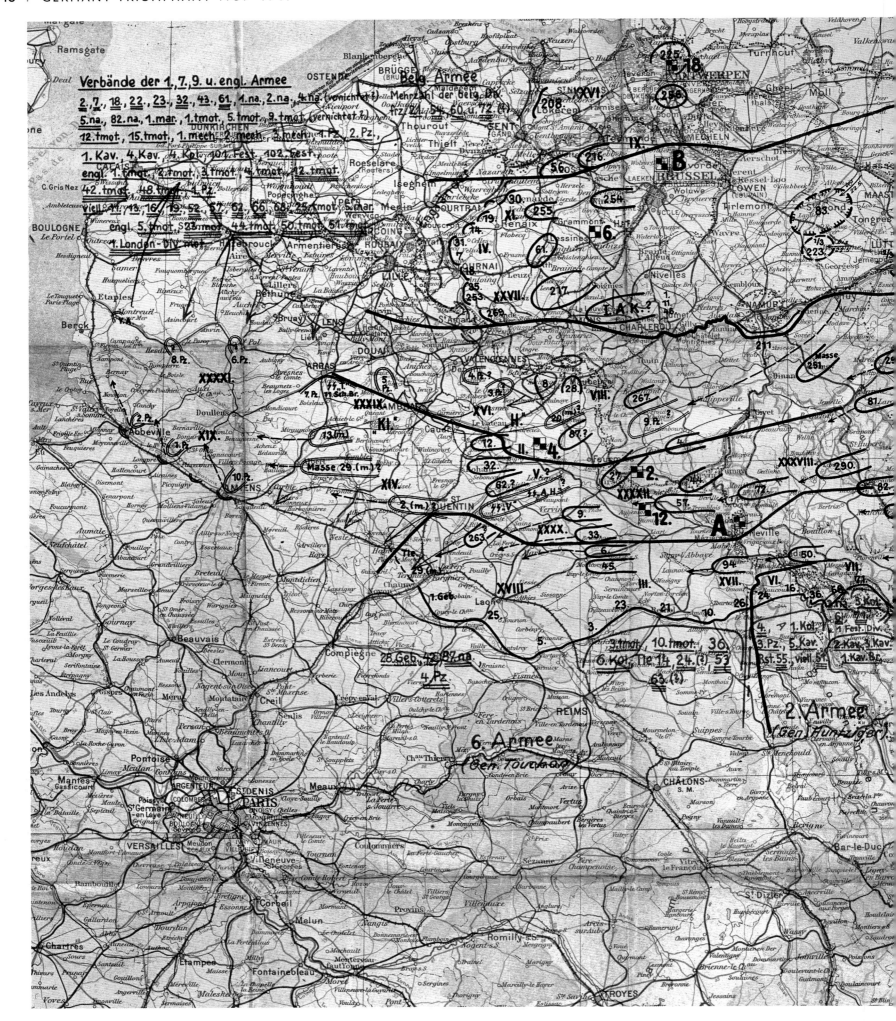

Wehrmacht map, May 21, 1940
With German (black) and Allied (red) units, this map shows the German advance by May 21. Both sides' headquarters are marked with flags. The French 2nd, 3rd, 4th, and 5th Armies are ranged along the French border east to west, while the British counterattack can be seen west of Lens.

THE GERMAN OFFENSIVE IN THE WEST

The Germans began their campaign in the west in May 1940. Within one day they had invaded the Low Countries, and within weeks they had swept across northern France to reach the Channel coast, trapping thousands of French and British soldiers around Dunkirk.

On May 10, Germany attacked the Netherlands, Belgium, and Luxembourg. Paratroopers were dropped in the Netherlands, taking key bridges and opening the way for ground forces. By May 12, German tanks had reached Rotterdam, which was heavily bombed by the Luftwaffe. The Dutch surrendered on May 14. In Belgium, German gliders dropped paratroopers onto the roof of Fort Eben-Emael, between Liège and Maastricht. They were joined by ground forces, which moved toward the British and French forces at the River Dyle in Belgium (see flag marked in Brussels). After 18 days of fighting, Belgium surrendered on May 28. Luxembourg surrendered in a matter of hours.

Breaching Allied defenses

British and French generals were sure that Germany could not penetrate France's fortified eastern border—the Maginot Line—or the densely forested Ardennes region. They were wrong. On May 12, panzer corps moved into the Ardennes and crossed the River Meuse at Sedan. This meant the Germans could advance to the Channel via the undefended countryside. To the south, the French fought to stop the Germans moving on Paris. However, Paris was not the goal, and on May 20 the Germans reached the Channel coast at Abbeville (center left) and trapped the Allies. The sole British tank division counterattacked Arras on May 21 (upper left), but to no avail. German forces pushed through Belgium, and panzers drew closer from the south and east. On May 20 Britain opted to evacuate its troops via Dunkirk.

▷ **German advance**
German infantry accompanied by a tank maneuver in the Ardennes in May 1940 during the Battle of France.

On land and in the air
Early in the German invasion of the USSR in June 1941, Heinkel 111 bombers fly over German motorized and infantry forces advancing in a column. It is likely this photo was manipulated for dramatic effect, possibly for propaganda.

BLITZKRIEG

The incredible speed at which Germany overran Poland, France, and other countries in the opening stages of the war exposed the inadequacy of the Allies' preparations. These campaigns became known as Blitzkrieg ("lightning war"), as they were sudden, intense, and devastating.

During World War I, the German high command developed a tactic of using *Sturmtruppen* ("stormtroopers") to punch through gaps in the enemy's line, followed by heavier infantry. By World War II, advances in technology—including superior tanks, aircraft capable of ground support roles, and enhanced radio communications—meant the German Wehrmacht could develop this tactic further, unleashing combined arms offensives to penetrate enemy lines, then fan out to their rear and envelop them in a *Kessel* ("cauldron").

The effects of Blitzkrieg were striking. Poland was overwhelmed in September 1939, as was France in May 1940. The panzer corps sliced through the French army, reaching the Channel coast and cutting off much of the Allied army. Variants of Blitzkrieg, including employing airborne troops to disorient the enemy by seizing objectives in the rear, also helped Germany win rapid victories in Belgium, the Netherlands, and Norway from April to June 1940.

Lessons learned
Blitzkrieg tactics became less effective as Germany's opponents learned counter-measures, such as attacking the flanks of an advance, and sacrificing territory to avoid becoming trapped. This was one of several reasons why Germany's attack on the USSR in 1941 (see pp.90–91) failed disastrously.

△ **German *Stahlhelm***
This steel helmet is typical of the protective gear issued to German infantry, who followed up the advances made by panzers.

△ **Operation Barbarossa**
When they invaded the USSR in June 1941, Germany made rapid advances against the Red Army, trapping huge pockets of troops. However, over-extended supply lines and bad weather meant the advance stalled around Moscow in December.

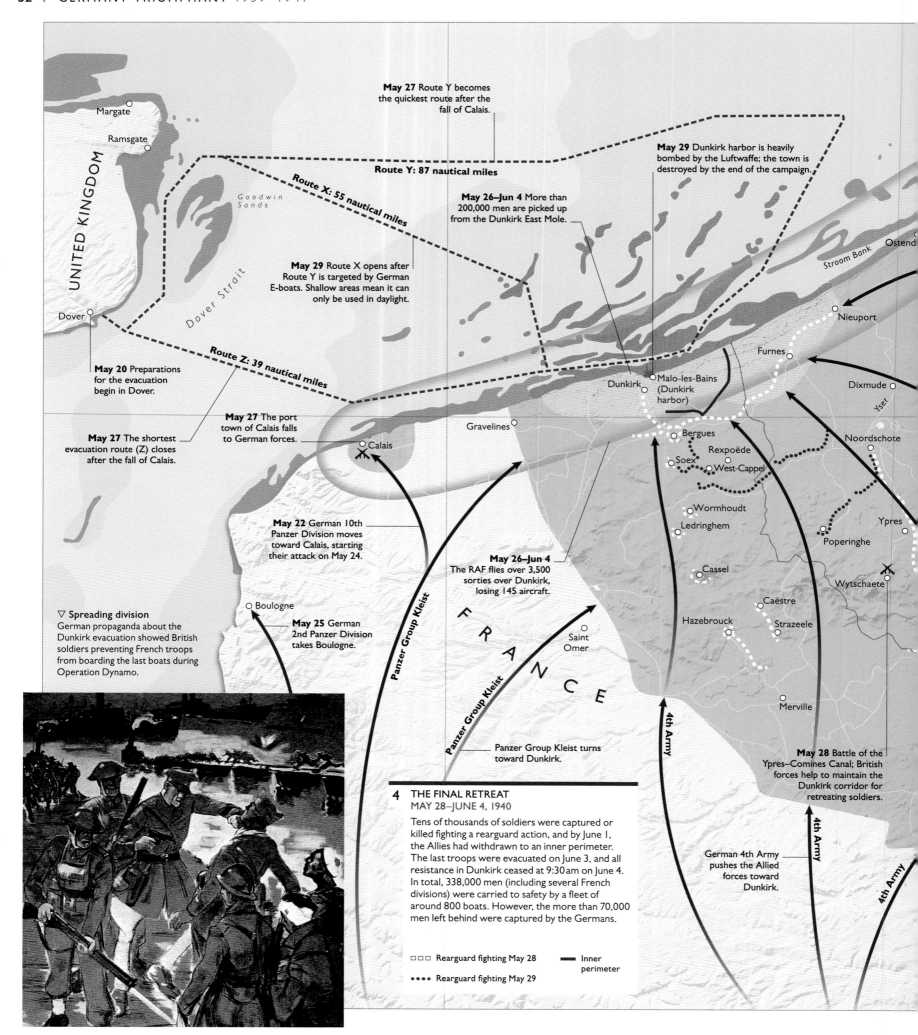

May 27 Route Y becomes the quickest route after the fall of Calais.

Route Y: 87 nautical miles

May 29 Dunkirk harbor is heavily bombed by the Luftwaffe; the town is destroyed by the end of the campaign.

Route X: 55 nautical miles

Goodwin Sands

May 26–Jun 4 More than 200,000 men are picked up from the Dunkirk East Mole.

May 29 Route X opens after Route Y is targeted by German E-boats. Shallow areas mean it can only be used in daylight.

Dover Strait

Route Z: 39 nautical miles

May 20 Preparations for the evacuation begin in Dover.

May 27 The port town of Calais falls to German forces.

May 27 The shortest evacuation route (Z) closes after the fall of Calais.

Dover

Margate

Ramsgate

UNITED KINGDOM

Stroom Bank

Ostend

Nieuport

Furnes

Dixmude

Gravelines

Dunkirk

Malo-les-Bains (Dunkirk harbor)

Yser

Bergues

Rexpoëde

Noordschote

Soex

West-Cappel

Wormhoudt

Ypres

Ledringhem

Poperinghe

Calais

May 22 German 10th Panzer Division moves toward Calais, starting their attack on May 24.

May 26–Jun 4 The RAF flies over 3,500 sorties over Dunkirk, losing 145 aircraft.

Cassel

Wytschaete

Caëstre

Strazeele

Hazebrouck

Boulogne

May 25 German 2nd Panzer Division takes Boulogne.

Panzer Group Kleist

Saint Omer

F R A N C E

Merville

▽ **Spreading division**
German propaganda about the Dunkirk evacuation showed British soldiers preventing French troops from boarding the last boats during Operation Dynamo.

Panzer Group Kleist

4th Army

4th Army

4th Army

4th Army

Panzer Group Kleist turns toward Dunkirk.

4   THE FINAL RETREAT
MAY 28–JUNE 4, 1940

Tens of thousands of soldiers were captured or killed fighting a rearguard action, and by June 1, the Allies had withdrawn to an inner perimeter. The last troops were evacuated on June 3, and all resistance in Dunkirk ceased at 9:30 am on June 4. In total, 338,000 men (including several French divisions) were carried to safety by a fleet of around 800 boats. However, the more than 70,000 men left behind were captured by the Germans.

□□□ Rearguard fighting May 28

•••• Rearguard fighting May 29

━━ Inner perimeter

German 4th Army pushes the Allied forces toward Dunkirk.

May 28 Battle of the Ypres–Comines Canal; British forces help to maintain the Dunkirk corridor for retreating soldiers.

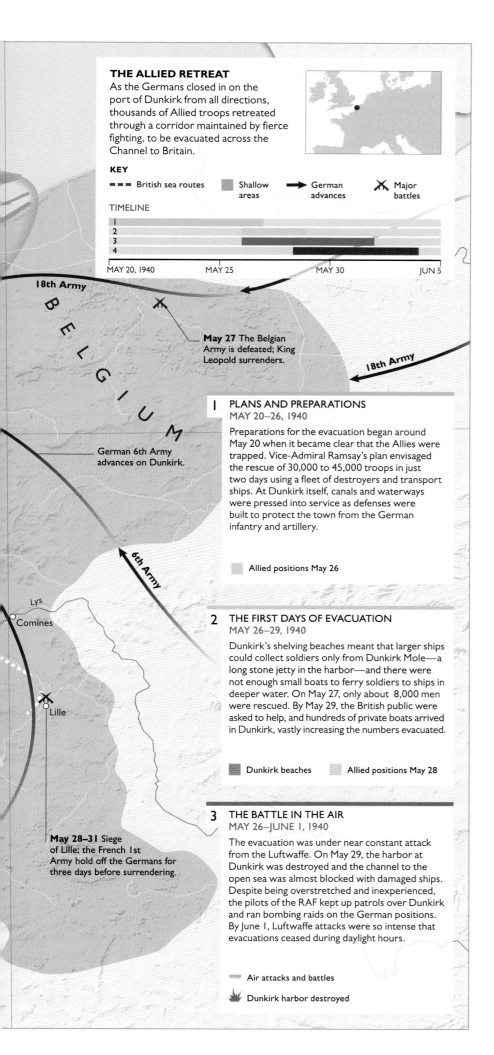

THE ALLIED RETREAT

As the Germans closed in on the port of Dunkirk from all directions, thousands of Allied troops retreated through a corridor maintained by fierce fighting, to be evacuated across the Channel to Britain.

KEY

- - - British sea routes

Shallow areas

→ German advances

✕ Major battles

TIMELINE

1
2
3
4

MAY 20, 1940　　MAY 25　　MAY 30　　JUN 5

18th Army

BELGIUM

May 27 The Belgian Army is defeated; King Leopold surrenders.

18th Army

German 6th Army advances on Dunkirk.

6th Army

Lys
Comines

1 PLANS AND PREPARATIONS
MAY 20–26, 1940

Preparations for the evacuation began around May 20 when it became clear that the Allies were trapped. Vice-Admiral Ramsay's plan envisaged the rescue of 30,000 to 45,000 troops in just two days using a fleet of destroyers and transport ships. At Dunkirk itself, canals and waterways were pressed into service as defenses were built to protect the town from the German infantry and artillery.

　■ Allied positions May 26

2 THE FIRST DAYS OF EVACUATION
MAY 26–29, 1940

Dunkirk's shelving beaches meant that larger ships could collect soldiers only from Dunkirk Mole—a long stone jetty in the harbor—and there were not enough small boats to ferry soldiers to ships in deeper water. On May 27, only about 8,000 men were rescued. By May 29, the British public were asked to help, and hundreds of private boats arrived in Dunkirk, vastly increasing the numbers evacuated.

　■ Dunkirk beaches　　■ Allied positions May 28

Lille

May 28–31 Siege of Lille; the French 1st Army hold off the Germans for three days before surrendering.

3 THE BATTLE IN THE AIR
MAY 26–JUNE 1, 1940

The evacuation was under near constant attack from the Luftwaffe. On May 29, the harbor at Dunkirk was destroyed and the channel to the open sea was almost blocked with damaged ships. Despite being overstretched and inexperienced, the pilots of the RAF kept up patrols over Dunkirk and ran bombing raids on the German positions. By June 1, Luftwaffe attacks were so intense that evacuations ceased during daylight hours.

　— Air attacks and battles
　✱ Dunkirk harbor destroyed

EVACUATING DUNKIRK

In just ten days from May 26 to June 4, 1940, 338,000 British and Allied troops were carried aboard a flotilla of boats and ships from Dunkirk to safety in Britain. Known as Operation Dynamo, it was the biggest military evacuation in history.

Barely one week after Hitler had ordered the invasion of France and the Low Countries, the German army had pushed the Allied forces into a corner of north-east France near the port of Dunkirk. Under attack from the Luftwaffe, the retreating soldiers of the British Expeditionary Force (BEF), together with their French, Canadian, and Belgian allies, faced roads blocked with vehicles and a flood of refugees. However, in one of the most pivotal decisions of the war, Hitler called a halt to the advance of his panzer divisions, giving the Allies sufficient breathing space to evacuate more than 330,000 men from the beaches of Dunkirk.

The evacuation was ordered by Winston Churchill and planned by logistics expert Vice-Admiral Bertram Ramsay from a room in the naval headquarters at Dover that once housed a dynamo (which gave the operation its name). It began on May 26. Even though the Germans did not launch a full-scale attack on the retreating Allies, the evacuation was accompanied by fierce fighting. Once on the beaches, soldiers often stood shoulder-deep in water, waiting for rescue, while the Germans bombed the sands from above.

Although the BEF left behind nearly all their equipment, the "miracle" of Dunkirk saved what Churchill called "the whole root and core and brain of the British Army" from a disastrous campaign. Without it, the Allied war effort would probably have collapsed.

THOSE LEFT BEHIND

Substantial Allied forces remained in France after the evacuation from Dunkirk; 35,000 French and as many British soldiers were forced to surrender. The majority were taken as POWs and forced to march for days before being transported to camps in Germany, where they remained for rest of the war. Several thousand French, British, and Canadian troops eluded capture, and by June 5 were ranged along the Somme, hoping to halt the German advance. Many were rescued in later evacuations.

Allied captives at Dunkirk

THE FALL OF FRANCE

After the evacuations at Dunkirk, the vastly outnumbered Allies fought fiercely but unsuccessfully to hold back Germany's advance into France. By June 22, 1940, France had signed an armistice and the country was split between the German-occupied north and Marshal Pétain's Vichy France.

On June 5, 1940, following the withdrawal of the British Expeditionary Forces, the Germans began the second stage of their invasion of France. Lacking significant British support (only one division, the 51st Highland, stayed in France), Maxime Weygand, chief of the Allied armies in France, was outgunned. With a depleted French army, he faced a near-impossible task—to defend a 560-mile (900-km) front from a German force of 10 panzer divisions and 130 infantry divisions.

Although their army fought fiercely, the French government was unwilling to commit to a long battle, abandoning Paris on June 10 and seeking an armistice on June 17. With the Allied

forces in the west evacuating, the armies in the east surrounded, and forces in the center fragmenting as the Germans swept on, France capitulated on June 22.

In the Franco–German Armistice, France was divided, with the north and west under German occupation, and the south (nominally) under French sovereignty. Charles de Gaulle, then the French under-secretary of national defense and war, refused to accept the surrender and led the Free French from London. By the end of June 1940, France had lost half her huge army as prisoners of war or casualties. The Western Front remained closed for four years until the D-Day landings of June 1944.

> "*Difficulty attracts the characterful man, for it is by grasping it that he fulfills himself.*"
>
> CHARLES DE GAULLE, *MEMOIRES DE GUERRE VOL 1, 1954*

DE GAULLE AND THE LONDON BROADCASTS

From a BBC studio in London, Charles de Gaulle broadcast a series of powerful speeches to the people of France in June 1940. He urged them to stand firm against the Germans: "Whatever happens, the flame of French resistance must not and shall not die." His words fanned the flames of resistance, but many of the French soldiers who had been evacuated from Dunkirk remained loyal to Vichy France and were unconvinced by De Gaulle's promises.

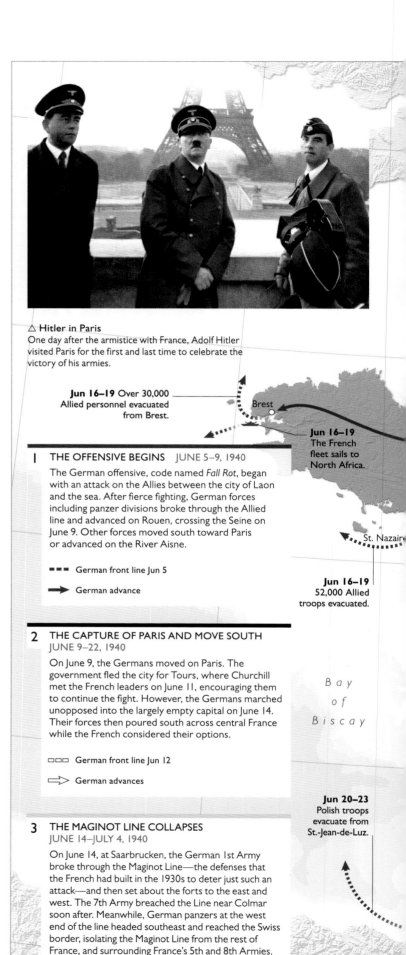

△ **Hitler in Paris**
One day after the armistice with France, Adolf Hitler visited Paris for the first and last time to celebrate the victory of his armies.

Jun 16–19 Over 30,000 Allied personnel evacuated from Brest.

Jun 16–19 The French fleet sails to North Africa.

1 THE OFFENSIVE BEGINS JUNE 5–9, 1940

The German offensive, code named *Fall Rot*, began with an attack on the Allies between the city of Laon and the sea. After fierce fighting, German forces including panzer divisions broke through the Allied line and advanced on Rouen, crossing the Seine on June 9. Other forces moved south toward Paris or advanced on the River Aisne.

- - - German front line Jun 5

→ German advance

Jun 16–19 52,000 Allied troops evacuated.

2 THE CAPTURE OF PARIS AND MOVE SOUTH JUNE 9–22, 1940

On June 9, the Germans moved on Paris. The government fled the city for Tours, where Churchill met the French leaders on June 11, encouraging them to continue the fight. However, the Germans marched unopposed into the largely empty capital on June 14. Their forces then poured south across central France while the French considered their options.

□□□ German front line Jun 12

⇒ German advances

Bay of Biscay

Jun 20–23 Polish troops evacuate from St.-Jean-de-Luz.

3 THE MAGINOT LINE COLLAPSES JUNE 14–JULY 4, 1940

On June 14, at Saarbrucken, the German 1st Army broke through the Maginot Line—the defenses that the French had built in the 1930s to deter just such an attack—and then set about the forts to the east and west. The 7th Army breached the Line near Colmar soon after. Meanwhile, German panzers at the west end of the line headed southeast and reached the Swiss border, isolating the Maginot Line from the rest of France, and surrounding France's 5th and 8th Armies.

■ Last French stronghold

□□□ German front line Jun 22

⇒ German advances

SPAIN

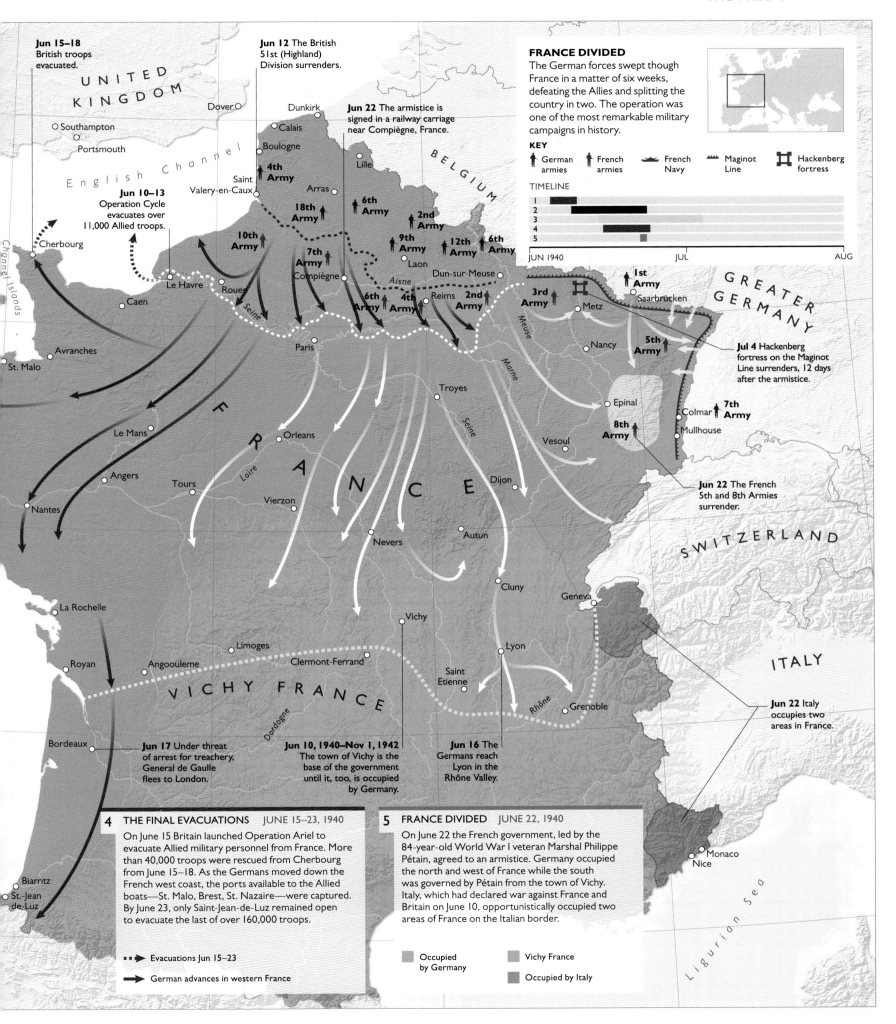

Jun 15–18
British troops evacuated.

Jun 12 The British 51st (Highland) Division surrenders.

Jun 22 The armistice is signed in a railway carriage near Compiègne, France.

UNITED KINGDOM

Dover

Southampton

Portsmouth

English Channel

Dunkirk

Calais

Boulogne

Lille

4th Army

Saint Valery-en-Caux

Arras

18th Army

6th Army

Jun 10–13 Operation Cycle evacuates over 11,000 Allied troops.

BELGIUM

2nd Army

Channel Islands

Cherbourg

10th Army

7th Army

Compiègne

Aisne

9th Army

Laon

12th Army

6th Army

Dun-sur-Meuse

1st Army

GREATER GERMANY

Le Havre

Rouen

Seine

6th Army

4th Army

Reims

2nd Army

3rd Army

Metz

Saarbrücken

Caen

Paris

Meuse

Nancy

5th Army

Jul 4 Hackenberg fortress on the Maginot Line surrenders, 12 days after the armistice.

Avranches

St. Malo

Marne

Epinal

Colmar

7th Army

Mullhouse

Le Mans

Seine

8th Army

F R A N C E

Orleans

Troyes

Vesoul

Jun 22 The French 5th and 8th Armies surrender.

Angers

Loire

Tours

Vierzon

Dijon

Nantes

SWITZERLAND

Nevers

Autun

Cluny

La Rochelle

Geneva

ITALY

Royan

Angouuleme

Limoges

Clermont-Ferrand

Vichy

Lyon

V I C H Y   F R A N C E

Saint Etienne

Dordogne

Grenoble

Rhône

Jun 22 Italy occupies two areas in France.

Bordeaux

Jun 17 Under threat of arrest for treachery, General de Gaulle flees to London.

Jun 10, 1940–Nov 1, 1942 The town of Vichy is the base of the government until it, too, is occupied by Germany.

Jun 16 The Germans reach Lyon in the Rhône Valley.

Biarritz

St.-Jean-de-Luz

Monaco

Nice

Ligurian Sea

FRANCE DIVIDED
The German forces swept though France in a matter of six weeks, defeating the Allies and splitting the country in two. The operation was one of the most remarkable military campaigns in history.

KEY

German armies | French armies | French Navy | Maginot Line | Hackenberg fortress

TIMELINE

1
2
3
4
5

JUN 1940   JUL   AUG

---

4   THE FINAL EVACUATIONS   JUNE 15–23, 1940

On June 15 Britain launched Operation Ariel to evacuate Allied military personnel from France. More than 40,000 troops were rescued from Cherbourg from June 15–18. As the Germans moved down the French west coast, the ports available to the Allied boats—St. Malo, Brest, St. Nazaire—were captured. By June 23, only Saint-Jean-de-Luz remained open to evacuate the last of over 160,000 troops.

5   FRANCE DIVIDED   JUNE 22, 1940

On June 22 the French government, led by the 84-year-old World War I veteran Marshal Philippe Pétain, agreed to an armistice. Germany occupied the north and west of France while the south was governed by Pétain from the town of Vichy. Italy, which had declared war against France and Britain on June 10, opportunistically occupied two areas of France on the Italian border.

- - -▶ Evacuations Jun 15–23

──▶ German advances in western France

Occupied by Germany

Vichy France

Occupied by Italy

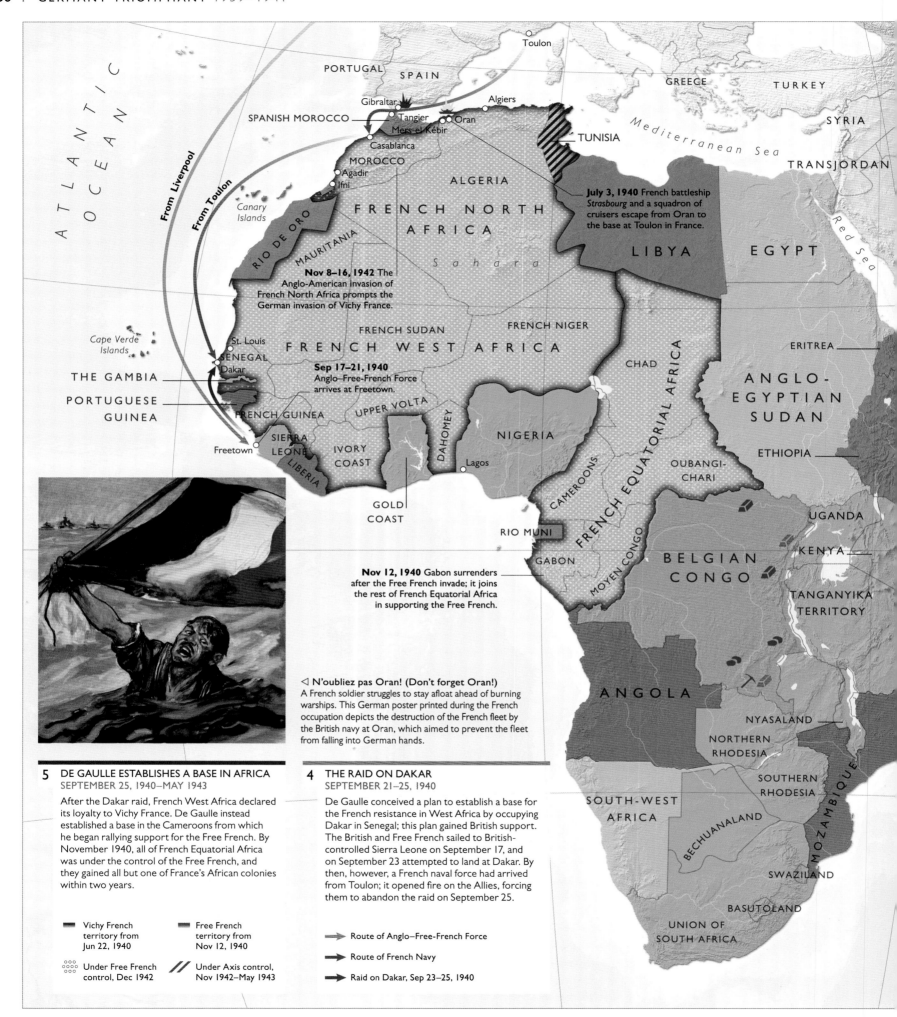

July 3, 1940 French battleship *Strasbourg* and a squadron of cruisers escape from Oran to the base at Toulon in France.

Nov 8–16, 1942 The Anglo-American invasion of French North Africa prompts the German invasion of Vichy France.

Sep 17–21, 1940 Anglo–Free-French Force arrives at Freetown.

Nov 12, 1940 Gabon surrenders after the Free French invade; it joins the rest of French Equatorial Africa in supporting the Free French.

◁ N'oubliez pas Oran! (Don't forget Oran!)
A French soldier struggles to stay afloat ahead of burning warships. This German poster printed during the French occupation depicts the destruction of the French fleet by the British navy at Oran, which aimed to prevent the fleet from falling into German hands.

5 DE GAULLE ESTABLISHES A BASE IN AFRICA
SEPTEMBER 25, 1940–MAY 1943

After the Dakar raid, French West Africa declared its loyalty to Vichy France. De Gaulle instead established a base in the Cameroons from which he began rallying support for the Free French. By November 1940, all of French Equatorial Africa was under the control of the Free French, and they gained all but one of France's African colonies within two years.

4 THE RAID ON DAKAR
SEPTEMBER 21–25, 1940

De Gaulle conceived a plan to establish a base for the French resistance in West Africa by occupying Dakar in Senegal; this plan gained British support. The British and Free French sailed to British-controlled Sierra Leone on September 17, and on September 23 attempted to land at Dakar. By then, however, a French naval force had arrived from Toulon; it opened fire on the Allies, forcing them to abandon the raid on September 25.

■ Vichy French territory from Jun 22, 1940

■ Free French territory from Nov 12, 1940

⁚⁚⁚ Under Free French control, Dec 1942

// Under Axis control, Nov 1942–May 1943

⟶ Route of Anglo–Free-French Force

➡ Route of French Navy

➡ Raid on Dakar, Sep 23–25, 1940

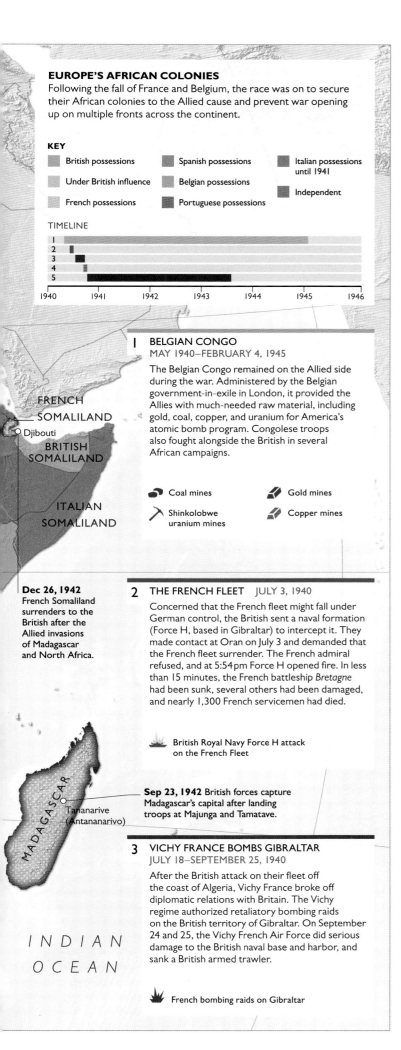

EUROPE'S AFRICAN COLONIES

Following the fall of France and Belgium, the race was on to secure their African colonies to the Allied cause and prevent war opening up on multiple fronts across the continent.

KEY

- British possessions
- Under British influence
- French possessions
- Spanish possessions
- Belgian possessions
- Portuguese possessions
- Italian possessions until 1941
- Independent

TIMELINE

1940 | 1941 | 1942 | 1943 | 1944 | 1945 | 1946

FRENCH SOMALILAND
Djibouti

BRITISH SOMALILAND

ITALIAN SOMALILAND

1 BELGIAN CONGO
MAY 1940–FEBRUARY 4, 1945

The Belgian Congo remained on the Allied side during the war. Administered by the Belgian government-in-exile in London, it provided the Allies with much-needed raw material, including gold, coal, copper, and uranium for America's atomic bomb program. Congolese troops also fought alongside the British in several African campaigns.

- Coal mines
- Shinkolobwe uranium mines
- Gold mines
- Copper mines

Dec 26, 1942 French Somaliland surrenders to the British after the Allied invasions of Madagascar and North Africa.

2 THE FRENCH FLEET JULY 3, 1940

Concerned that the French fleet might fall under German control, the British sent a naval formation (Force H, based in Gibraltar) to intercept it. They made contact at Oran on July 3 and demanded that the French fleet surrender. The French admiral refused, and at 5:54pm Force H opened fire. In less than 15 minutes, the French battleship *Bretagne* had been sunk, several others had been damaged, and nearly 1,300 French servicemen had died.

- British Royal Navy Force H attack on the French Fleet

Sep 23, 1942 British forces capture Madagascar's capital after landing troops at Majunga and Tamatave.

3 VICHY FRANCE BOMBS GIBRALTAR
JULY 18–SEPTEMBER 25, 1940

After the British attack on their fleet off the coast of Algeria, Vichy France broke off diplomatic relations with Britain. The Vichy regime authorized retaliatory bombing raids on the British territory of Gibraltar. On September 24 and 25, the Vichy French Air Force did serious damage to the British naval base and harbor, and sank a British armed trawler.

- French bombing raids on Gibraltar

MADAGASCAR

INDIAN OCEAN

Tananarive (Antananarivo)

POWER STRUGGLES IN AFRICA

The French and Belgian colonial possessions in Africa represented both a threat and an opportunity to the Allies in 1940. If they could be kept out of Axis control, these territories promised vast resources of material and people for the Allied struggle.

After the fall of Belgium and France in June 1940 (see pp.54–55), Belgium's African possessions joined the Allied war effort. However, the position of France's colonies in Africa was more complex. Just as France itself was divided—into occupied France and Vichy France—so were the loyalties of her colonial possessions. The French colonists in Algeria stuck firmly by the Vichy regime, but others—such as Feliz Éboué, the governor of Chad—were disgusted by the Vichy capitulation and supported Charles de Gaulle's Free French. For de Gaulle, the colonies offered a huge reserve of troops with which he could build an army to regain France; however, they would also pose a threat to the Allies if they fell into Axis hands. These concerns prompted Allied attacks on the French Fleet in Algeria, and later on Madagascar (as well as Syria in the Middle East), and generated Allied support for de Gaulle's attempt to land at Dakar in French West Africa. Yet suspicion abounded: the French were wary of British ambition in Africa and the Middle East, and the Allies—along with many of the French who supported them—were unsure of de Gaulle's capabilities. Still, by November 1942, all but one of France's colonies in Africa and the Middle East had been successfully tied to the Allied cause.

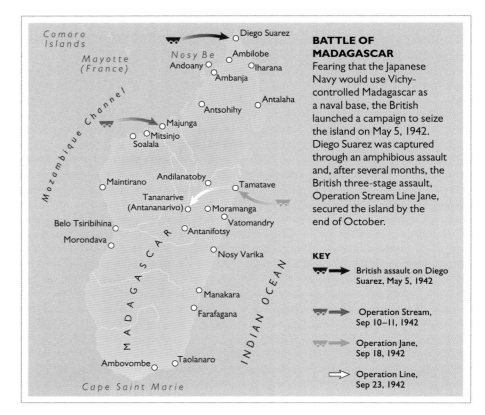

BATTLE OF MADAGASCAR

Fearing that the Japanese Navy would use Vichy-controlled Madagascar as a naval base, the British launched a campaign to seize the island on May 5, 1942. Diego Suarez was captured through an amphibious assault and, after several months, the British three-stage assault, Operation Stream Line Jane, secured the island by the end of October.

KEY

- British assault on Diego Suarez, May 5, 1942
- Operation Stream, Sep 10–11, 1942
- Operation Jane, Sep 18, 1942
- Operation Line, Sep 23, 1942

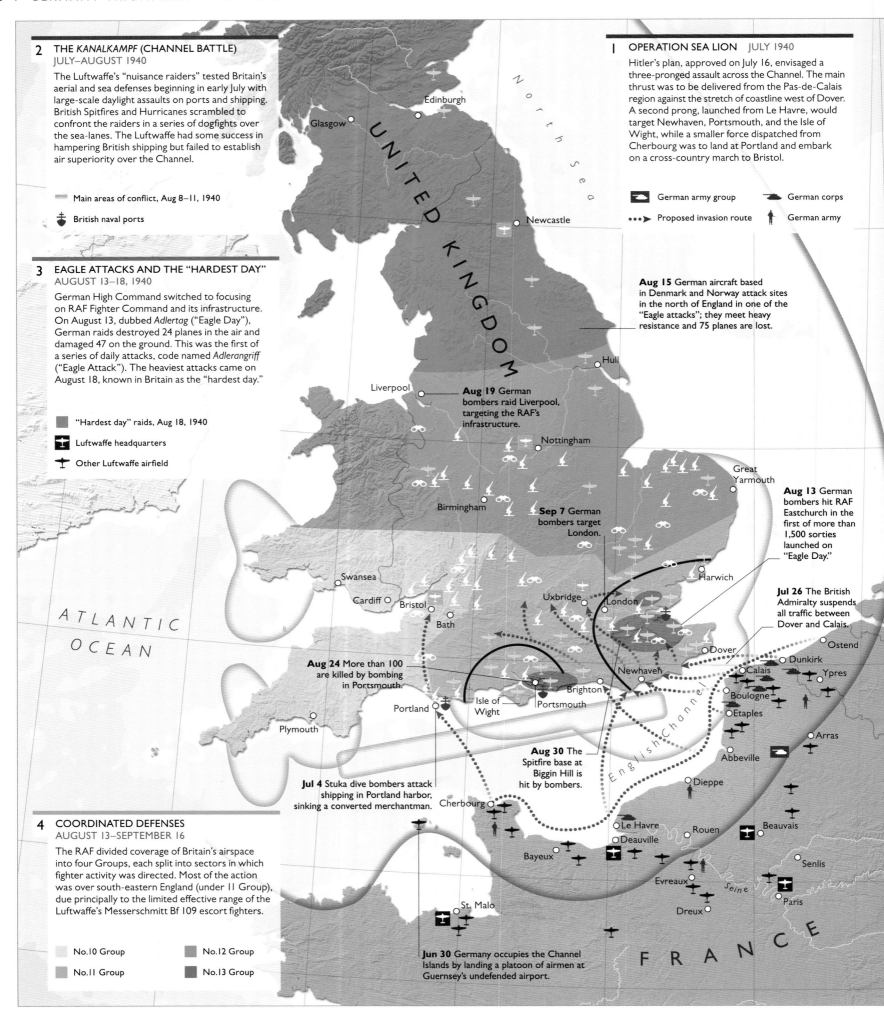

2 THE *KANALKAMPF* (CHANNEL BATTLE)
JULY–AUGUST 1940

The Luftwaffe's "nuisance raiders" tested Britain's aerial and sea defenses beginning in early July with large-scale daylight assaults on ports and shipping. British Spitfires and Hurricanes scrambled to confront the raiders in a series of dogfights over the sea-lanes. The Luftwaffe had some success in hampering British shipping but failed to establish air superiority over the Channel.

⬚ Main areas of conflict, Aug 8–11, 1940

⚓ British naval ports

3 EAGLE ATTACKS AND THE "HARDEST DAY"
AUGUST 13–18, 1940

German High Command switched to focusing on RAF Fighter Command and its infrastructure. On August 13, dubbed *Adlertag* ("Eagle Day"), German raids destroyed 24 planes in the air and damaged 47 on the ground. This was the first of a series of daily attacks, code named *Adlerangriff* ("Eagle Attack"). The heaviest attacks came on August 18, known in Britain as the "hardest day."

⬚ "Hardest day" raids, Aug 18, 1940

✠ Luftwaffe headquarters

✈ Other Luftwaffe airfield

4 COORDINATED DEFENSES
AUGUST 13–SEPTEMBER 16

The RAF divided coverage of Britain's airspace into four Groups, each split into sectors in which fighter activity was directed. Most of the action was over south-eastern England (under 11 Group), due principally to the limited effective range of the Luftwaffe's Messerschmitt Bf 109 escort fighters.

⬚ No.10 Group   ⬚ No.12 Group

⬚ No.11 Group   ⬚ No.13 Group

1 OPERATION SEA LION   JULY 1940

Hitler's plan, approved on July 16, envisaged a three-pronged assault across the Channel. The main thrust was to be delivered from the Pas-de-Calais region against the stretch of coastline west of Dover. A second prong, launched from Le Havre, would target Newhaven, Portsmouth, and the Isle of Wight, while a smaller force dispatched from Cherbourg was to land at Portland and embark on a cross-country march to Bristol.

⬛▶ German army group   ⬛ German corps

•••▶ Proposed invasion route   ⬚ German army

Aug 15 German aircraft based in Denmark and Norway attack sites in the north of England in one of the "Eagle attacks"; they meet heavy resistance and 75 planes are lost.

Aug 19 German bombers raid Liverpool, targeting the RAF's infrastructure.

Sep 7 German bombers target London.

Aug 13 German bombers hit RAF Eastchurch in the first of more than 1,500 sorties launched on "Eagle Day."

Jul 26 The British Admiralty suspends all traffic between Dover and Calais.

Aug 24 More than 100 are killed by bombing in Portsmouth.

Aug 30 The Spitfire base at Biggin Hill is hit by bombers.

Jul 4 Stuka dive bombers attack shipping in Portland harbor, sinking a converted merchantman.

Jun 30 Germany occupies the Channel Islands by landing a platoon of airmen at Guernsey's undefended airport.

North Sea

UNITED KINGDOM

ATLANTIC OCEAN

English Channel

FRANCE

Edinburgh
Glasgow
Newcastle
Hull
Liverpool
Nottingham
Great Yarmouth
Birmingham
Harwich
Swansea
Cardiff
Bristol
Bath
Uxbridge
London
Dover
Ostend
Dunkirk
Calais
Ypres
Newhaven
Boulogne
Brighton
Etaples
Portsmouth
Isle of Wight
Portland
Arras
Abbeville
Plymouth
Dieppe
Cherbourg
Le Havre
Rouen
Beauvais
Deauville
Bayeux
Senlis
Evreaux
Seine
Dreux
Paris
St. Malo
Guernsey

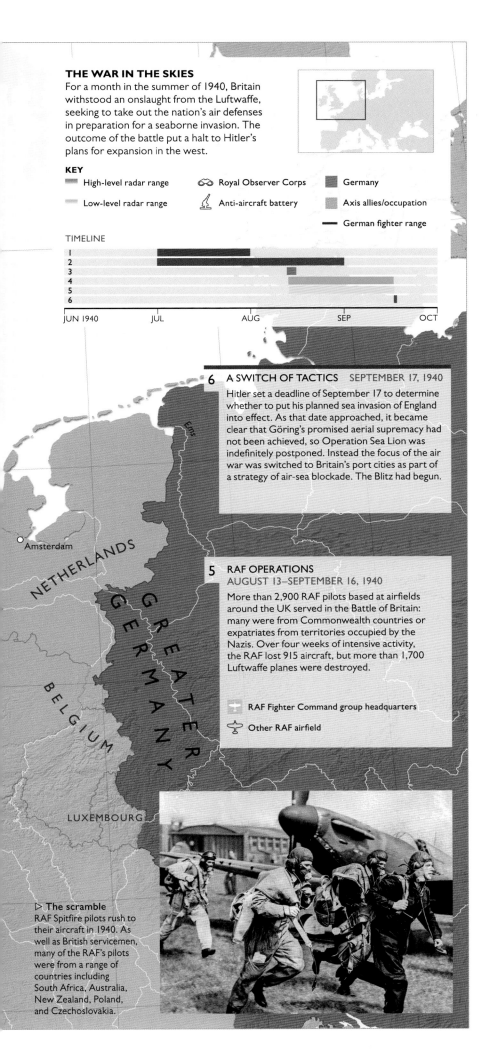

THE WAR IN THE SKIES

For a month in the summer of 1940, Britain withstood an onslaught from the Luftwaffe, seeking to take out the nation's air defenses in preparation for a seaborne invasion. The outcome of the battle put a halt to Hitler's plans for expansion in the west.

KEY

High-level radar range	Royal Observer Corps	Germany
Low-level radar range	Anti-aircraft battery	Axis allies/occupation
	German fighter range	

TIMELINE

1
2
3
4
5
6

JUN 1940   JUL   AUG   SEP   OCT

6 A SWITCH OF TACTICS   SEPTEMBER 17, 1940

Hitler set a deadline of September 17 to determine whether to put his planned sea invasion of England into effect. As that date approached, it became clear that Göring's promised aerial supremacy had not been achieved, so Operation Sea Lion was indefinitely postponed. Instead the focus of the air war was switched to Britain's port cities as part of a strategy of air-sea blockade. The Blitz had begun.

Amsterdam

NETHERLANDS

GREATER GERMANY

BELGIUM

5 RAF OPERATIONS
AUGUST 13–SEPTEMBER 16, 1940

More than 2,900 RAF pilots based at airfields around the UK served in the Battle of Britain: many were from Commonwealth countries or expatriates from territories occupied by the Nazis. Over four weeks of intensive activity, the RAF lost 915 aircraft, but more than 1,700 Luftwaffe planes were destroyed.

RAF Fighter Command group headquarters

Other RAF airfield

LUXEMBOURG

▷ **The scramble**
RAF Spitfire pilots rush to their aircraft in 1940. As well as British servicemen, many of the RAF's pilots were from a range of countries including South Africa, Australia, New Zealand, Poland, and Czechoslovakia.

THE BATTLE OF BRITAIN

After the fall of France, the British Empire stood alone against Nazi Germany. With his offer of peace rejected, Hitler planned an invasion of England. For this, he needed first to control the sea-lanes in the English Channel—and that meant commanding the skies above.

With Britain reeling after the fall of France (see pp.54–55), Hitler expected to impose a negotiated peace on his own terms. However, when Churchill made it clear that this was not an option, Hitler determined to force the nation to capitulate. Plans were drawn up for Operation Sea Lion—a coordinated shipborne assault on England's south coast. To make this happen, Hermann Göring, chief of the Luftwaffe, promised to eliminate Britain's Royal Air Force (RAF) within four weeks. The plan failed. In the years leading up to war, Britain had enhanced its air defenses with innovations such as radar and better coordination of aircraft from the ground. Meanwhile, signals intelligence including the top-secret Ultra decryptions (see pp.170–171) gave the RAF some advance knowledge of German plans—and, ultimately, Britain's Spitfire and Hurricane aircraft proved more than a match for German Messerschmitts in the dogfights over the Channel.

Thwarted in his attempt to subdue Britain's air defenses, Hitler turned instead to a strategy of bombing raids on British port cities, launching the nighttime Blitz on London and other industrial centers (see pp.60–61) as part of his air-sea blockade. However, Hitler's failure to defeat the RAF was perhaps his first major setback of the war, dealing a blow to his reputation for invincibility.

THE HAWKER HURRICANE

The Hurricane entered service in December 1937, and by August 1940 more than 2,300 had been delivered to the RAF. In the Battle of Britain they outnumbered Spitfires by almost two to one. Highly maneuverable, they brought down more enemy aircraft than any other British planes in the course of 1940. Over the following two years they were gradually replaced as dog-fighters by the more modern Spitfires.

Damage survey
A map of London shows the bomb damage caused to buildings in Bermondsey and Wapping. Black and purple indicate complete destruction or irreparable damage. Pink sites indicate severe damage that could be repaired, although repairs would be expensive.

THE BLITZ

In September 1940, Hitler made the fateful decision to switch the focus of Luftwaffe air attacks from RAF airfields to Britain's cities. His aim was to damage manufacturing centers and ports and to break civilian morale, forcing Churchill to sue for peace.

The Blitz (German for "lightning") was the word coined by the British press for the intense bombing campaign conducted by the Luftwaffe. The first attack over London on September 7, 1940, was followed by 57 consecutive nights of bombing raids on the capital, as well as raids on other major cities. The Blitz continued until May 1941.

Hitler still hoped to invade Britain, and bombing London was part of that plan, with the aim of softening up the British population. The fighting reached a climax on September 15, when waves of German planes launched an all-out attack on London but failed to achieve a decisive breakthrough. The devastating raid on Coventry on November 14–15 signaled that other industrial centers were also at risk. This single attack claimed the lives of 568 people and left around one-third of the city's houses uninhabitable. Over the next six months, the Luftwaffe carried out heavy raids on Belfast, Birmingham, Bristol, Cardiff, Clydebank, Hull, Manchester, Plymouth, Portsmouth, Sheffield, Southampton, and Swansea. Liverpool and Merseyside suffered the worst destruction of any area outside London, with 1,900 killed and 70,000 made homeless.

By May 1941, Hitler had turned his attention to the Soviet Union. The last major raid on London took place on May 10, when 1 sq mile (2.8 sq km) of the city center was set on fire and the Houses of Parliament took a dozen hits. Bombing continued to the end of the war, but not on the same scale.

The effects of the Blitz

During the campaign, there were 127 large-scale night raids (71 in London), during which some 50,700 tons (46,000 metric tons) of high explosives were dropped on Britain's cities, in addition to 110,000 incendiary bombs. The raids killed more than 43,000 civilians and destroyed or damaged two million homes. By February 1941, 1.37 million civilians had been evacuated from areas affected by the bombing.

Although the effects of the Blitz were devastating, Hitler's plan failed. British war production was reduced by no more than five percent during the Blitz, while popular morale, dented at times by the destruction, never collapsed.

▷ **Image of resistance**
This famous image shows St. Paul's Cathedral in London, lit up by fire and surrounded by smoke, during a night raid on December 29, 1940.

BRITAIN AT BAY

After France capitulated to Hitler in June 1940, the British Empire was the only major power fighting the Germans and Italians. While the Royal Air Force readied itself to battle the Luftwaffe for control of the skies, the British people prepared themselves for a German invasion.

△ **Digging for victory**
This poster was part of a campaign to encourage the British to grow their own food. Garden plots sprang up in open spaces everywhere.

Even before France's surrender, the British government was making plans for the possibility of an invasion by Germany. On May 14, 1940, Anthony Eden, Prime Minister Winston Churchill's new Secretary of State for War, broadcast an appeal for part-time volunteers to fight alongside the army in the event of such an incursion. The response was immediate. Within 24 hours, some 250,000 men had enlisted in the Local Defense Volunteers; by the end of June, numbers had increased to nearly 1,500,000. In July, on the orders of Churchill, they were given the more martial-sounding title of the Home Guard.

An all-out effort

The country was preparing itself for total war. British factories and shipyards churned day and night manufacturing guns, tanks, aircraft, and warships. Gasoline had been rationed since the beginning of the war, and food rationing, which had begun in January 1940, was tightened. Butter, sugar, bacon, and ham were the first foods to be rationed, followed by preserves, syrup, golden syrup, cheese, tea, margarine, and cooking fats. Clothes were also rationed, and the government issued a pamphlet popularizing the slogan "Make Do and Mend."

The most significant shortage was that of manpower. In December 1941, the call-up age limits for men were reduced to 18 and raised to 51. Most revolutionary of all, women were conscripted. By the end of 1942, 10 million British women aged between 19 and 50 were registered for war work, many taking the place of men in the armed forces.

THE HOME GUARD AT WAR

The Home Guard were trained in small arms and anti-tank weapons to be used against an invading force; German orders were to shoot them out of hand. Some saw action in the Battle of Britain (see pp.58–59) manning anti-aircraft guns. Secret "Auxiliary Units" were trained in guerrilla warfare and sabotage.

Entertainment in wartime, 1940
During the Blitz, thousands sought refuge from the bombing in London's underground stations. Aldwych station was the first to develop into an air-raid shelter, with sleeping bunks and occasional concerts, as seen here, to boost morale.

THE U-BOAT WAR BEGINS

The German High Command used every means at its disposal to cut Britain's vital maritime supply routes. Its most effective weapon was the German submarine fleet, the U-boats, which was increasingly successful in attacking Atlantic shipping lanes from 1939 to 1941.

Germany's U-boats had played a major role in World War I, sinking almost 5,000 ships. From the start of the hostilities in 1939, Hitler looked again to the submarine fleet, commanded by Admiral Karl Dönitz (see p.168), to starve Britain into submission.

For a time the campaign came close to success, particularly after the fall of France and Norway opened up new ports from which the U-boats could operate. Germany's early successes persuaded Hitler to divert resources to submarine production. At first Britain was desperately short of warships to escort merchant shipping and of planes to provide air cover, and the Royal Canadian Navy played a vital role in protecting Atlantic shipping. However, the tide began to turn against the U-boats as the Allies improved their protective measures, developed technology to detect the raiders, and gained better intelligence about U-boat deployment. In 1939, the US established the Pan-American Security Zone, an area extending 300–1,000 nautical miles from the coast of the Americas in which the US Navy escorted merchant ships. After the US formally entered the war in 1941, the US Navy actively engaged German naval vessels in the Atlantic.

> "The only thing that really frightened me during the war was the U-boat peril."
>
> WINSTON CHURCHILL, *THE SECOND WORLD WAR*, 1949

THE *UNTERSEEBOOT* (U-BOAT)

Prohibited after World War I, German submarine construction recommenced in the mid 1930s. By 1939, 57 boats served under the skillful command of Admiral Karl Dönitz. Most were small, 825-ton (750-metric ton) Type VII (Sea Wolf) vessels, featuring a new diesel-electric propulsion system. The Type VIIC model had a top speed of 17 knots on the surface and 7.5 knots submerged, and carried 14 torpedoes or tube-launched mines.

U-boats at the port of Kiel

BATTLE OF THE ATLANTIC

The Atlantic Ocean became a battleground as Hitler attempted to cut Britain's supply lines. The Allies' ability to protect shipping with naval and air escorts was crucial. The map shows borders up to May 1941, before the invasion of the USSR (see pp.90–91) caused frontiers to fluctuate.

KEY

Territory under Allied influence

Territory under Axis control

Territory under Vichy France

Extent of Pan-American Security Zone

Major convoy routes

TIMELINE

1 2 3 4 5

1939 1940 1941 1942

▽ **Sinking of HMS *Royal Oak*, 1939**
This painting depicts the attack on *Royal Oak*, anchored at Scapa Flow, Scotland, by German submarine U-47. The sinking, and the loss of 833 lives, was a huge blow to British morale.

Dec 11, 1941
The US plays a non-combatant role until Germany declares war on it, in support of Japan.

Oct 1939
Pan-American Security Zone established.

5 ALLIES GAIN A FORWARD BASE JULY 1941

The British had established a garrison on (neutral) Iceland in May 1940, fearing that the island would be used by Germany. Aircraft from Iceland helped plug the gap in Allied air cover that had turned the mid-Atlantic into a favorite hunting ground for U-boat commanders. In July 1941, American forces took over defense of the island, freeing up British troops for service in North Africa.

— Extent of British air cover by Jul 1941

CANADA

LABRADOR

NEWFOUNDLA

USA

Halifax

New York

Bermuda

Gulf of Mexico

Bahamas

CUBA

BRITISH HONDURAS

HONDURAS

Jamaica

HAITI

DOMINICAN REPUBLIC

NICARAGUA

Caribbean Sea

Puerto Rico

PAN-AMERICAN

Trinidad

VENEZUELA

BRITISH GUIANA

SURINAM

BRAZIL

FRENCH GUIANA

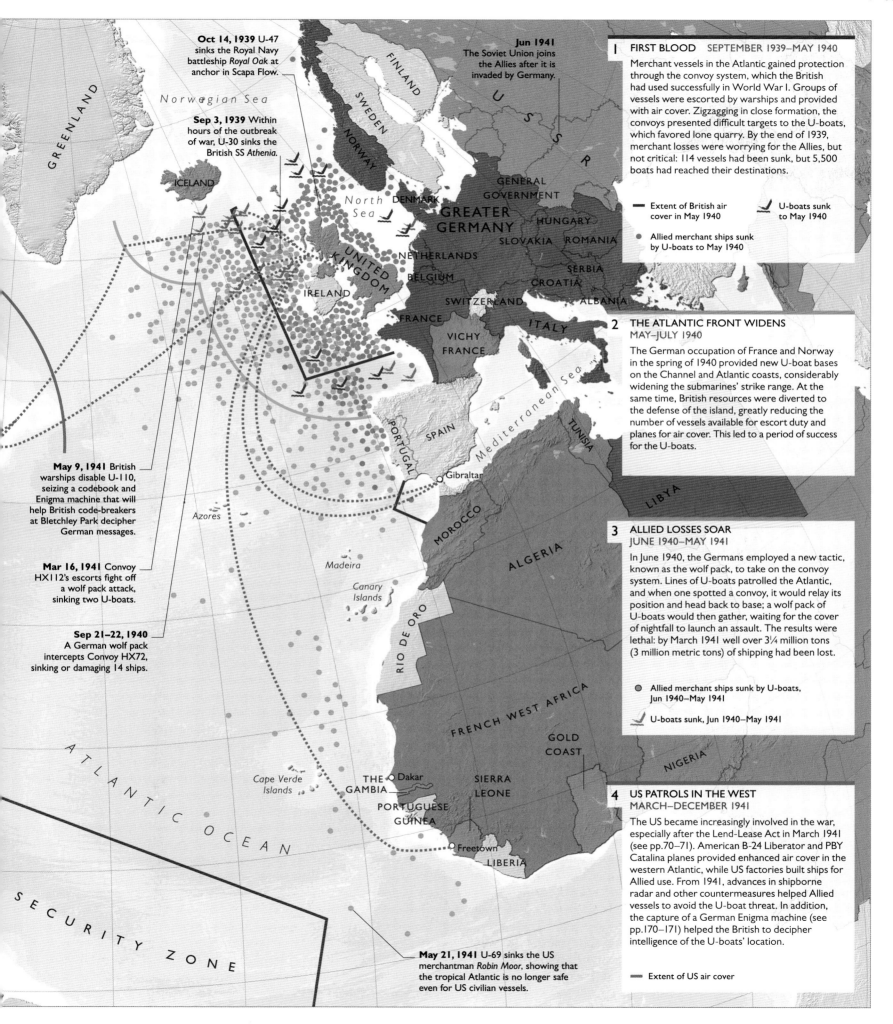

Oct 14, 1939 U-47 sinks the Royal Navy battleship *Royal Oak* at anchor in Scapa Flow.

Sep 3, 1939 Within hours of the outbreak of war, U-30 sinks the British SS *Athenia*.

Jun 1941 The Soviet Union joins the Allies after it is invaded by Germany.

May 9, 1941 British warships disable U-110, seizing a codebook and Enigma machine that will help British code-breakers at Bletchley Park decipher German messages.

Mar 16, 1941 Convoy HX112's escorts fight off a wolf pack attack, sinking two U-boats.

Sep 21–22, 1940 A German wolf pack intercepts Convoy HX72, sinking or damaging 14 ships.

May 21, 1941 U-69 sinks the US merchantman *Robin Moor*, showing that the tropical Atlantic is no longer safe even for US civilian vessels.

1 FIRST BLOOD SEPTEMBER 1939–MAY 1940

Merchant vessels in the Atlantic gained protection through the convoy system, which the British had used successfully in World War I. Groups of vessels were escorted by warships and provided with air cover. Zigzagging in close formation, the convoys presented difficult targets to the U-boats, which favored lone quarry. By the end of 1939, merchant losses were worrying for the Allies, but not critical: 114 vessels had been sunk, but 5,500 boats had reached their destinations.

— Extent of British air cover in May 1940

⌇ U-boats sunk to May 1940

● Allied merchant ships sunk by U-boats to May 1940

2 THE ATLANTIC FRONT WIDENS MAY–JULY 1940

The German occupation of France and Norway in the spring of 1940 provided new U-boat bases on the Channel and Atlantic coasts, considerably widening the submarines' strike range. At the same time, British resources were diverted to the defense of the island, greatly reducing the number of vessels available for escort duty and planes for air cover. This led to a period of success for the U-boats.

3 ALLIED LOSSES SOAR JUNE 1940–MAY 1941

In June 1940, the Germans employed a new tactic, known as the wolf pack, to take on the convoy system. Lines of U-boats patrolled the Atlantic, and when one spotted a convoy, it would relay its position and head back to base; a wolf pack of U-boats would then gather, waiting for the cover of nightfall to launch an assault. The results were lethal: by March 1941 well over 3¼ million tons (3 million metric tons) of shipping had been lost.

● Allied merchant ships sunk by U-boats, Jun 1940–May 1941

⌇ U-boats sunk, Jun 1940–May 1941

4 US PATROLS IN THE WEST MARCH–DECEMBER 1941

The US became increasingly involved in the war, especially after the Lend-Lease Act in March 1941 (see pp.70–71). American B-24 Liberator and PBY Catalina planes provided enhanced air cover in the western Atlantic, while US factories built ships for Allied use. From 1941, advances in shipborne radar and other countermeasures helped Allied vessels to avoid the U-boat threat. In addition, the capture of a German Enigma machine (see pp.170–171) helped the British to decipher intelligence of the U-boats' location.

— Extent of US air cover

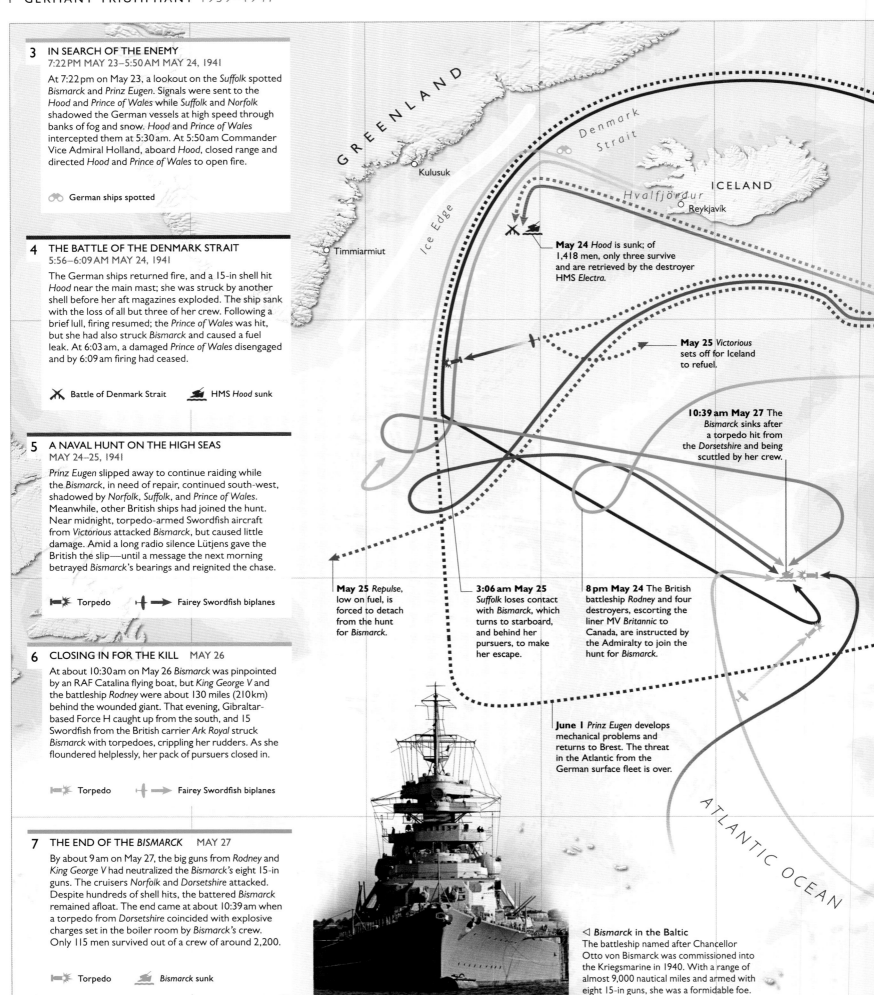

3 IN SEARCH OF THE ENEMY
7:22 PM MAY 23–5:50 AM MAY 24, 1941

At 7:22 pm on May 23, a lookout on the *Suffolk* spotted *Bismarck* and *Prinz Eugen*. Signals were sent to the *Hood* and *Prince of Wales* while *Suffolk* and *Norfolk* shadowed the German vessels at high speed through banks of fog and snow. *Hood* and *Prince of Wales* intercepted them at 5:30 am. At 5:50 am Commander Vice Admiral Holland, aboard *Hood*, closed range and directed *Hood* and *Prince of Wales* to open fire.

German ships spotted

4 THE BATTLE OF THE DENMARK STRAIT
5:56–6:09 AM MAY 24, 1941

The German ships returned fire, and a 15-in shell hit *Hood* near the main mast; she was struck by another shell before her aft magazines exploded. The ship sank with the loss of all but three of her crew. Following a brief lull, firing resumed; the *Prince of Wales* was hit, but she had also struck *Bismarck* and caused a fuel leak. At 6:03 am, a damaged *Prince of Wales* disengaged and by 6:09 am firing had ceased.

Battle of Denmark Strait   HMS *Hood* sunk

5 A NAVAL HUNT ON THE HIGH SEAS
MAY 24–25, 1941

Prinz Eugen slipped away to continue raiding while the *Bismarck*, in need of repair, continued south-west, shadowed by *Norfolk*, *Suffolk*, and *Prince of Wales*. Meanwhile, other British ships had joined the hunt. Near midnight, torpedo-armed Swordfish aircraft from *Victorious* attacked *Bismarck*, but caused little damage. Amid a long radio silence Lütjens gave the British the slip—until a message the next morning betrayed *Bismarck*'s bearings and reignited the chase.

Torpedo   Fairey Swordfish biplanes

6 CLOSING IN FOR THE KILL   MAY 26

At about 10:30 am on May 26 *Bismarck* was pinpointed by an RAF Catalina flying boat, but *King George V* and the battleship *Rodney* were about 130 miles (210 km) behind the wounded giant. That evening, Gibraltar-based Force H caught up from the south, and 15 Swordfish from the British carrier *Ark Royal* struck *Bismarck* with torpedoes, crippling her rudders. As she floundered helplessly, her pack of pursuers closed in.

Torpedo   Fairey Swordfish biplanes

7 THE END OF THE *BISMARCK*   MAY 27

By about 9 am on May 27, the big guns from *Rodney* and *King George V* had neutralized the *Bismarck*'s eight 15-in guns. The cruisers *Norfolk* and *Dorsetshire* attacked. Despite hundreds of shell hits, the battered *Bismarck* remained afloat. The end came at about 10:39 am when a torpedo from *Dorsetshire* coincided with explosive charges set in the boiler room by *Bismarck*'s crew. Only 115 men survived out of a crew of around 2,200.

Torpedo   *Bismarck* sunk

May 24 *Hood* is sunk; of 1,418 men, only three survive and are retrieved by the destroyer HMS *Electra*.

May 25 *Victorious* sets off for Iceland to refuel.

10:39 am May 27 The *Bismarck* sinks after a torpedo hit from the *Dorsetshire* and being scuttled by her crew.

May 25 *Repulse*, low on fuel, is forced to detach from the hunt for *Bismarck*.

3:06 am May 25 *Suffolk* loses contact with *Bismarck*, which turns to starboard, and behind her pursuers, to make her escape.

8 pm May 24 The British battleship *Rodney* and four destroyers, escorting the liner MV *Britannic* to Canada, are instructed by the Admiralty to join the hunt for *Bismarck*.

June 1 *Prinz Eugen* develops mechanical problems and returns to Brest. The threat in the Atlantic from the German surface fleet is over.

◁ *Bismarck* in the Baltic
The battleship named after Chancellor Otto von Bismarck was commissioned into the Kriegsmarine in 1940. With a range of almost 9,000 nautical miles and armed with eight 15-in guns, she was a formidable foe.

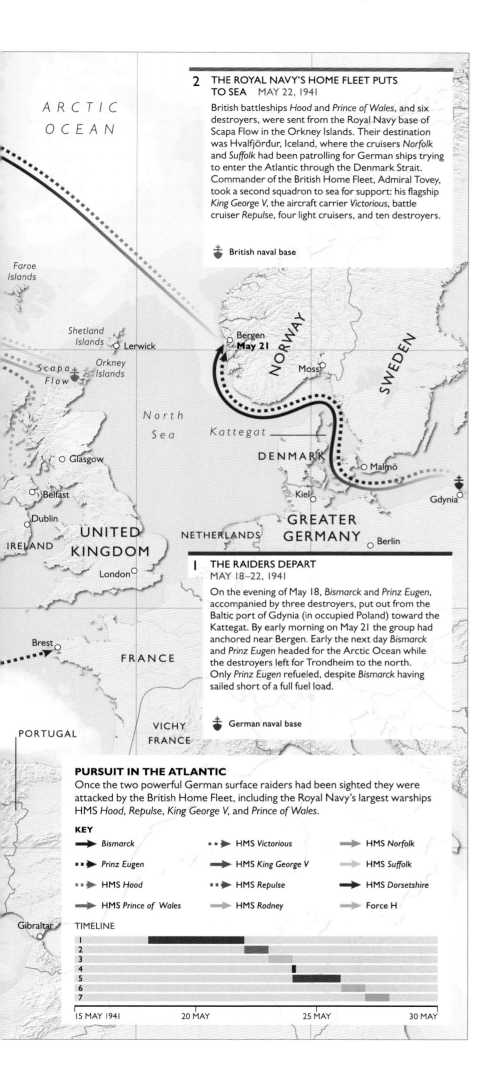

2 THE ROYAL NAVY'S HOME FLEET PUTS TO SEA MAY 22, 1941

British battleships *Hood* and *Prince of Wales*, and six destroyers, were sent from the Royal Navy base of Scapa Flow in the Orkney Islands. Their destination was Hvalfjörður, Iceland, where the cruisers *Norfolk* and *Suffolk* had been patrolling for German ships trying to enter the Atlantic through the Denmark Strait. Commander of the British Home Fleet, Admiral Tovey, took a second squadron to sea for support: his flagship *King George V*, the aircraft carrier *Victorious*, battle cruiser *Repulse*, four light cruisers, and ten destroyers.

⚓ British naval base

1 THE RAIDERS DEPART MAY 18–22, 1941

On the evening of May 18, *Bismarck* and *Prinz Eugen*, accompanied by three destroyers, put out from the Baltic port of Gdynia (in occupied Poland) toward the Kattegat. By early morning on May 21 the group had anchored near Bergen. Early the next day *Bismarck* and *Prinz Eugen* headed for the Arctic Ocean while the destroyers left for Trondheim to the north. Only *Prinz Eugen* refueled, despite *Bismarck* having sailed short of a full fuel load.

⚓ German naval base

PURSUIT IN THE ATLANTIC

Once the two powerful German surface raiders had been sighted they were attacked by the British Home Fleet, including the Royal Navy's largest warships HMS *Hood*, *Repulse*, *King George V*, and *Prince of Wales*.

KEY

➡ *Bismarck*
••➡ *Prinz Eugen*
••➡ HMS *Hood*
➡ HMS *Prince of Wales*

••➡ HMS *Victorious*
➡ HMS *King George V*
••➡ HMS *Repulse*
➡ HMS *Rodney*

➡ HMS *Norfolk*
➡ HMS *Suffolk*
➡ HMS *Dorsetshire*
➡ Force H

TIMELINE

15 MAY 1941 — 20 MAY — 25 MAY — 30 MAY

SINKING OF THE *BISMARCK*

On May 18, 1941, the German navy began Operation Rheinübung, part of the effort to isolate Britain by targeting merchant ships in the Atlantic. The vessels used in this operation were the heavy cruiser *Prinz Eugen* and the largest warship in the German fleet, *Bismarck*.

From January to March 1941, the German navy had deployed two battleships—*Scharnhorst* and *Gneisenau*—in the Atlantic under the command of Admiral Günther Lütjens. Maintained by supplies from support vessels and tankers, they destroyed or captured 22 Allied merchant ships. After the pair had to return to port for repairs, two new warships—*Prinz Eugen* and the formidable battleship *Bismarck*—were sent into the Atlantic under the same command with orders to continue the task.

On May 20, Allied intelligence sources in Scandinavia spotted the German ships as they made their way from the Baltic port of Gdynia. Four days later they were intercepted in the Denmark Strait, between Iceland and Greenland, by the British battle cruiser HMS *Hood* and the battleship HMS *Prince of Wales*. The ensuing battle was followed by an epic, three-day chase on the high seas, during which dozens of Allied warships converged on the *Bismarck*. Eventually, the *Bismarck* was sunk with the loss of around 2,100 men, including Günther Lütjens. In the aftermath, between June 3 and June 15 the Royal Navy sank or seized seven of the nine tankers and supply ships that had made raiding ventures into the Atlantic possible. Germany's hopes of conducting any similar operations in future had been gravely damaged.

AIRCRAFT CARRIERS IN WORLD WAR II

By the 1930s air power was eclipsing the battleship as the dominant weapon of naval warfare. At the time war broke out, aircraft carriers were a vital maritime offensive weapon, as combat aircraft could attack enemy ships at greater range than gun batteries and with a higher level of accuracy. However, once within range of the enemy, carriers were vulnerable to attacks themselves. Here a squadron of torpedo-armed Fairey Swordfish—also used in the attack on the *Bismarck*—prepares to launch from the British carrier HMS *Ark Royal* during the war.

THE END OF US NEUTRALITY

At the start of World War II, the US took a neutral position. However, President Franklin Roosevelt reversed this stance, rearming the US and increasing aid to Britain. By December 1941, the US was fully involved in the war.

△ **Anti-war lobby**
Formed in 1940, the America First Committee lobbied against US intervention in Europe. It attracted 800,000 members.

The US's involvement in World War I had not been universally popular, and after the war ended, the US reduced its navy and army to fewer than 135,000 men. In 1937, it passed a Neutrality Act, forbidding the sale of arms to countries at war. However, as Germany and Japan became more aggressive, President Roosevelt sought to counter the powerful political voices that counseled keeping out of foreign conflicts.

The US takes up arms

After war broke out in September 1939, Roosevelt persuaded Congress to repeal the arms embargo, but recipients could only acquire arms with cash payments. He also ordered a major rearmament, buying 270 warships and increasing the army to over 1.6 million by December 1941. Roosevelt increased aid to Britain by the Lend-Lease Act (see pp.70–71), which allowed raw materials and military aid to go to the Allies on credit. After the Japanese attacked the US naval base at Pearl Harbor, Hawaii, in December 1941 (see pp.110–111), the neutralist sentiment vanished and the US joined the war.

△ **The Atlantic Charter meeting**
British prime minister Winston Churchill heads to Newfoundland, Canada, in August 1941, for a meeting with Roosevelt. The two leaders drew up a joint declaration known as the Atlantic Charter, which set out their goals for the war and its aftermath.

Marines prepare for war
New recruits undergo basic training at the Parris Island Recruit Depot, South Carolina. As part of Roosevelt's rearmament effort, between 1939 and 1941 the Marines expanded nearly four-fold.

LEND-LEASE

The Lend-Lease Act, passed by the US Congress in March 1941, provided assistance to Britain's war effort while allowing the US to maintain its neutrality. The policy ensured a flow of food, fuel, and matériel to Allied forces that the Axis powers could not match.

Following neutrality legislation in 1937, US companies could not export military goods to warring nations. However, President Roosevelt was committed to helping the fight against Fascism by all means short of war, and this sentiment underpinned policies such as the 1940 Destroyers for Bases Agreement, in which the US transferred destroyers to the British in exchange for land for US military bases. Lend-Lease was another such policy, under which the US could loan war matériel to the Allies. Roosevelt justified its implementation with a simple analogy—if a neighbor's house was on fire it was simply common sense to lend him a garden hose. Lend-Lease unlocked a wealth of supplies for the Allies, ranging

> *"We defend and we build a way of life, not for America alone, but for all mankind."*
>
> FRANKLIN D. ROOSEVELT, MAY 1940

from ordnance, oil, aircraft, tanks, and ships to tooth powder and salt cellars. The policy helped to save Britain, which was running desperately short of food and fuel in 1941. At first, the recipients were Britain and the Commonwealth countries, but within a year, Lend-Lease was providing aid to the Soviet Union and China. From 1942, it became increasingly significant as the war extended to the Pacific following the events of Pearl Harbor (see pp.110–111). By the end of the war, over $49 billion of American aid had been transported around the world to 40 countries.

US ISOLATIONISM IN WORLD WAR II

The US was determined to stay neutral in 1939. The country had suffered significant casualties in World War I, and debts owed by the Allies had caused resentment. There was little desire to become embroiled in another "foreign affair." However, knowing that the war threatened America's security, President Roosevelt worked to weaken the Neutrality Acts of the 1930s. With Lend-Lease, he hoped America could arm the fight for democracy while avoiding direct conflict.

President Franklin D. Roosevelt signing the Lend-Lease Act

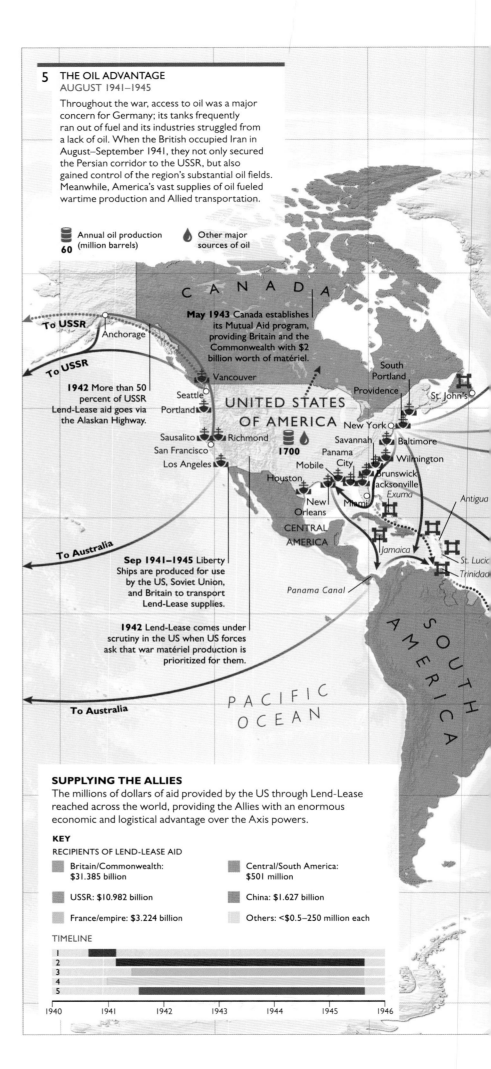

5 THE OIL ADVANTAGE
AUGUST 1941–1945

Throughout the war, access to oil was a major concern for Germany; its tanks frequently ran out of fuel and its industries struggled from a lack of oil. When the British occupied Iran in August–September 1941, they not only secured the Persian corridor to the USSR, but also gained control of the region's substantial oil fields. Meanwhile, America's vast supplies of oil fueled wartime production and Allied transportation.

60 Annual oil production (million barrels)

Other major sources of oil

To USSR

To USSR

May 1943 Canada establishes its Mutual Aid program, providing Britain and the Commonwealth with $2 billion worth of matériel.

1942 More than 50 percent of USSR Lend-Lease aid goes via the Alaskan Highway.

Anchorage

Vancouver

Seattle

Portland

UNITED STATES OF AMERICA

Sausalito
San Francisco
Los Angeles
Richmond
1700

New York
Savannah
Panama
Mobile   City
Houston
New Orleans
Miami

Baltimore
Wilmington
Brunswick
Jacksonville
Exuma

South Portland
Providence
St. John's

Antigua

CENTRAL AMERICA

Jamaica

St. Lucia
Trinidad

Panama Canal

To Australia

Sep 1941–1945 Liberty Ships are produced for use by the US, Soviet Union, and Britain to transport Lend-Lease supplies.

1942 Lend-Lease comes under scrutiny in the US when US forces ask that war matériel production is prioritized for them.

To Australia

S O U T H   A M E R I C A

PACIFIC OCEAN

SUPPLYING THE ALLIES

The millions of dollars of aid provided by the US through Lend-Lease reached across the world, providing the Allies with an enormous economic and logistical advantage over the Axis powers.

KEY
RECIPIENTS OF LEND-LEASE AID

- Britain/Commonwealth: $31.385 billion
- USSR: $10.982 billion
- France/empire: $3.224 billion
- Central/South America: $501 million
- China: $1.627 billion
- Others: <$0.5–250 million each

TIMELINE

	1940	1941	1942	1943	1944	1945	1946
1							
2							
3							
4							
5							

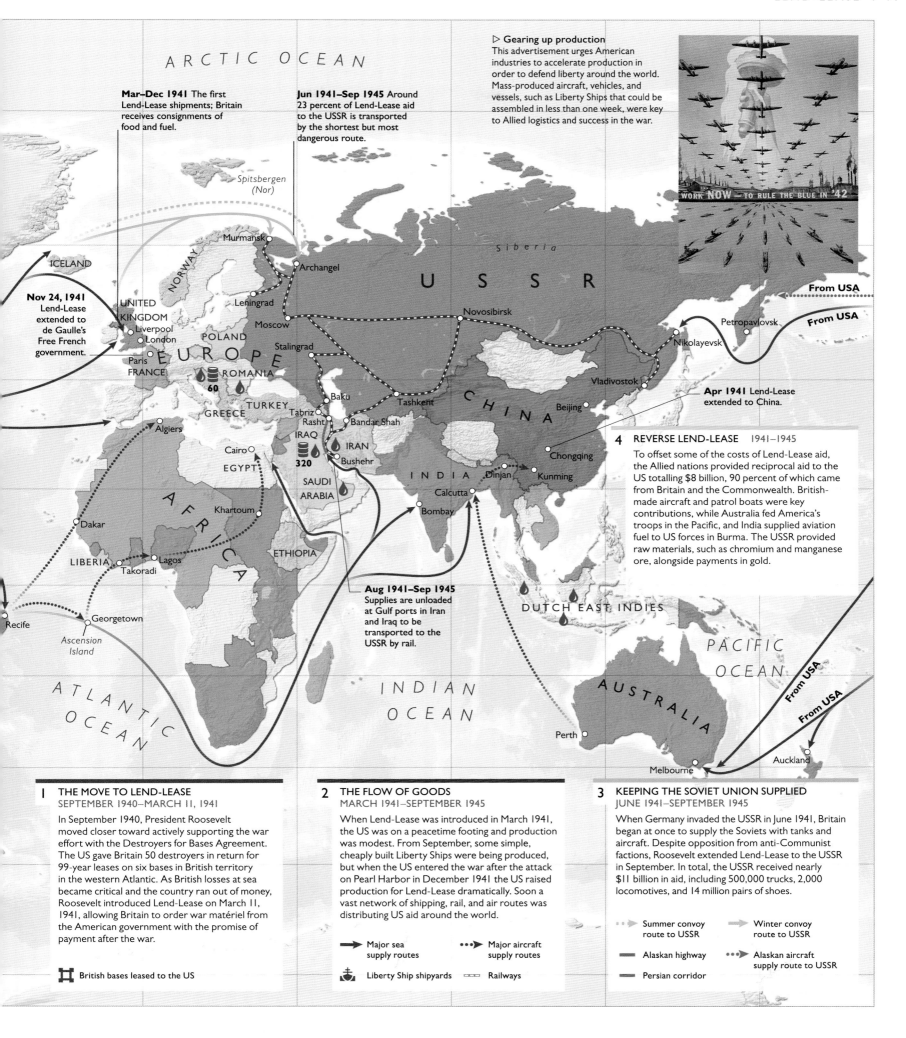

Mar–Dec 1941 The first Lend-Lease shipments; Britain receives consignments of food and fuel.

Jun 1941–Sep 1945 Around 23 percent of Lend-Lease aid to the USSR is transported by the shortest but most dangerous route.

▷ **Gearing up production**
This advertisement urges American industries to accelerate production in order to defend liberty around the world. Mass-produced aircraft, vehicles, and vessels, such as Liberty Ships that could be assembled in less than one week, were key to Allied logistics and success in the war.

WORK **NOW** – TO RULE THE BLUE IN '42

Nov 24, 1941 Lend-Lease extended to de Gaulle's Free French government.

Apr 1941 Lend-Lease extended to China.

4 REVERSE LEND-LEASE   1941–1945

To offset some of the costs of Lend-Lease aid, the Allied nations provided reciprocal aid to the US totalling $8 billion, 90 percent of which came from Britain and the Commonwealth. British-made aircraft and patrol boats were key contributions, while Australia fed America's troops in the Pacific, and India supplied aviation fuel to US forces in Burma. The USSR provided raw materials, such as chromium and manganese ore, alongside payments in gold.

Aug 1941–Sep 1945 Supplies are unloaded at Gulf ports in Iran and Iraq to be transported to the USSR by rail.

1 THE MOVE TO LEND-LEASE
SEPTEMBER 1940–MARCH 11, 1941

In September 1940, President Roosevelt moved closer toward actively supporting the war effort with the Destroyers for Bases Agreement. The US gave Britain 50 destroyers in return for 99-year leases on six bases in British territory in the western Atlantic. As British losses at sea became critical and the country ran out of money, Roosevelt introduced Lend-Lease on March 11, 1941, allowing Britain to order war matériel from the American government with the promise of payment after the war.

⊟ British bases leased to the US

2 THE FLOW OF GOODS
MARCH 1941–SEPTEMBER 1945

When Lend-Lease was introduced in March 1941, the US was on a peacetime footing and production was modest. From September, some simple, cheaply built Liberty Ships were being produced, but when the US entered the war after the attack on Pearl Harbor in December 1941 the US raised production for Lend-Lease dramatically. Soon a vast network of shipping, rail, and air routes was distributing US aid around the world.

→ Major sea supply routes
•••▶ Major aircraft supply routes
⚓ Liberty Ship shipyards
▭▭ Railways

3 KEEPING THE SOVIET UNION SUPPLIED
JUNE 1941–SEPTEMBER 1945

When Germany invaded the USSR in June 1941, Britain began at once to supply the Soviets with tanks and aircraft. Despite opposition from anti-Communist factions, Roosevelt extended Lend-Lease to the USSR in September. In total, the USSR received nearly $11 billion in aid, including 500,000 trucks, 2,000 locomotives, and 14 million pairs of shoes.

•••▶ Summer convoy route to USSR
▶ Winter convoy route to USSR
▬ Alaskan highway
•••▶ Alaskan aircraft supply route to USSR
▬ Persian corridor

THE MEDITERRANEAN AND MIDDLE EAST

Italy's entry into World War II extended the conflict south into the Mediterranean region. After multiple failures by the Italian forces, Germany went to the rescue, and the Axis powers fought major tank battles against the British in the North African desert.

△ **Operation Compass**
In December 1940, British forces advanced to attack the Italians in the Western Desert, Egypt. Around 133,000 Italians were taken prisoner by British troops.

When war broke out in September 1939, Italy remained neutral, despite its alliance with Nazi Germany—a union grandiosely dubbed the "Pact of Steel." Knowing his country's military weakness, the Fascist dictator Benito Mussolini waited until the French were clearly beaten before declaring war on the Allies in June 1940. With France out of the picture, and Britain focused on its life-or-death struggle against Germany, it seemed an ideal opportunity for Italy to pursue its imperial ambitions around the Mediterranean.

In autumn 1940, Italy launched offensives from its North African colony, Libya, into Egypt, and from Albania (which they had occupied since spring 1939) into Greece. Despite Britain's desperate circumstances at that time, Winston Churchill was prepared to devote valuable resources to defend Egypt. Technically an independent, neutral country, it was in reality under British influence, and the Suez Canal was seen as a vital link to the British Empire in Asia. Maintaining a supply of oil from the Middle East was also a priority.

Poorly equipped and badly led, the Italian forces suffered disastrous defeats on all fronts. Italy quickly lost its East African colonies and most of Libya to the British, and was equally defeated by the Greeks. Although Hitler saw the Mediterranean and North Africa as distractions from more important matters, he sent German forces into the region to save Italy from disaster.

The Germans head southward

In spring 1941, having conquered Yugoslavia, German troops continued south into Greece and Crete in the last of their Blitzkrieg offensives; Britain sent forces to intervene. In North Africa, the arrival of the tanks of the Afrika Korps, led by the German general Erwin Rommel, placed Egypt under threat. There was heavy fighting between Britain and the Axis powers in the Western Desert. Meanwhile, the naval war in the Mediterranean centered on British efforts to block supplies to Rommel and keep a convoy route open between their bases at Gibraltar and Alexandria via Malta. Although the Royal Navy's warships were relatively well equipped, land-based Luftwaffe aircraft caused the British a lot of damage.

Britain's position was rendered more vulnerable by the hostile attitude of Francoist Spain and Vichy France, both

◁ **Parachutist's badge**
German airborne troops, marked by their distinctive badge, played a significant role in the Blitzkrieg offensives early in the war.

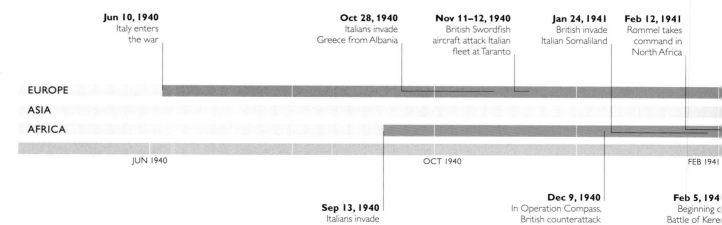

CHANGES IN FORTUNE

The war in the Mediterranean region had two distinct phases. From June 1940 to spring 1941, Italy suffered defeats on all fronts. Then the arrival of German air and land forces shifted the balance in favor of the Axis, although not decisively. Battered by British victories at Taranto, Italy, and Cape Matapan, Greece, the Italian navy could never control the Mediterranean. The British were frequently outfought by Rommel in North Africa, but mounted repeated counteroffensives.

Jun 10, 1940
Italy enters the war

Oct 28, 1940
Italians invade Greece from Albania

Nov 11–12, 1940
British Swordfish aircraft attack Italian fleet at Taranto

Jan 24, 1941
British invade Italian Somaliland

Feb 12, 1941
Rommel takes command in North Africa

EUROPE

ASIA

AFRICA

JUN 1940

OCT 1940

FEB 1941

Sep 13, 1940
Italians invade Egypt from Libya

Dec 9, 1940
In Operation Compass, British counterattack Italians in Egypt

Feb 5, 194[1]
Beginning o[f] Battle of Kere[n] in Eritre[a]

◁ **Greece conquered**
German troops raise the swastika on the Acropolis in Athens, having captured the Greek capital after a three-week campaign in April 1941.

officially neutral states, but leaning heavily toward collaboration with Nazi Germany. Colonies loyal to Vichy France controlled the western half of North Africa, but Britain succeeded in gaining Syria for the Free French (General De Gaulle's forces, which continued to fight with the Allies against the Axis powers after the fall of France). Generally, the British were successful in shoring up their position in the Middle East, securing the support of most Jewish settlers in Palestine, and bringing Iraq and Iran into line when their rulers leaned toward the Axis.

The Allies hold their own

Hitler never devoted sufficient resources to the Western Desert Campaign, or to the Mediterranean generally, to achieve decisive results. Malta was heavily bombed by German and Italian aircraft but was never invaded, despite being only 50 miles (80 km) from Italy. This failure to seize an obvious prize was typical of an Axis policy that lacked resolute focus. For Britain, on the other hand, North Africa became very important strategically, because it was the only place where the enemy could be engaged on land. By 1942–1943, operations in the Mediterranean and North Africa were central to Allied strategy.

▷ **The Battle of Crete**
German paratroopers land in a mass assault on Crete in May 1941. Despite fierce local and Allied defense, the German forces captured the Greek island after 13 days of fighting.

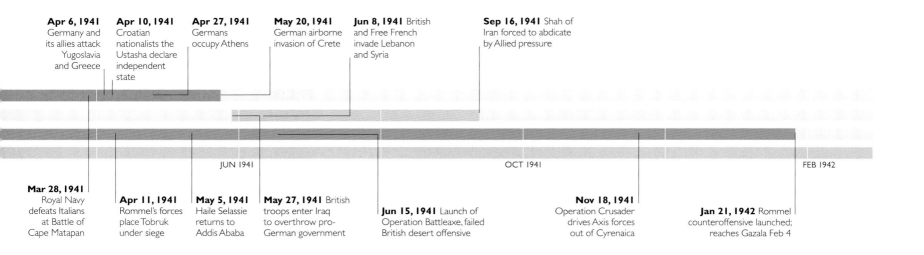

Apr 6, 1941 Germany and its allies attack Yugoslavia and Greece

Apr 10, 1941 Croatian nationalists the Ustasha declare independent state

Apr 27, 1941 Germans occupy Athens

May 20, 1941 German airborne invasion of Crete

Jun 8, 1941 British and Free French invade Lebanon and Syria

Sep 16, 1941 Shah of Iran forced to abdicate by Allied pressure

JUN 1941

OCT 1941

FEB 1942

Mar 28, 1941 Royal Navy defeats Italians at Battle of Cape Matapan

Apr 11, 1941 Rommel's forces place Tobruk under siege

May 5, 1941 Haile Selassie returns to Addis Ababa

May 27, 1941 British troops enter Iraq to overthrow pro-German government

Jun 15, 1941 Launch of Operation Battleaxe, failed British desert offensive

Nov 18, 1941 Operation Crusader drives Axis forces out of Cyrenaica

Jan 21, 1942 Rommel counteroffensive launched; reaches Gazala Feb 4

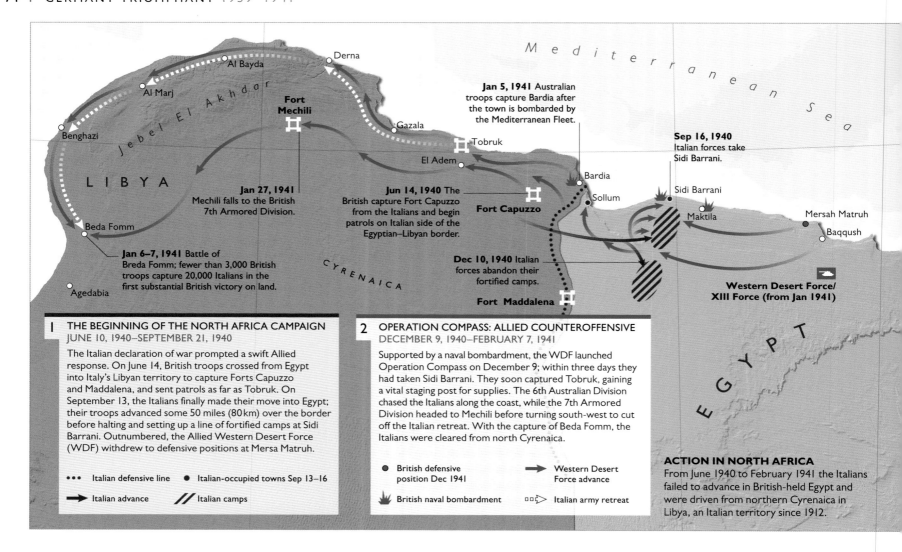

Jan 5, 1941 Australian troops capture Bardia after the town is bombarded by the Mediterranean Fleet.

Sep 16, 1940 Italian forces take Sidi Barrani.

Jan 27, 1941 Mechili falls to the British 7th Armored Division.

Jun 14, 1940 The British capture Fort Capuzzo from the Italians and begin patrols on Italian side of the Egyptian–Libyan border.

Jan 6–7, 1941 Battle of Breda Fomm; fewer than 3,000 British troops capture 20,000 Italians in the first substantial British victory on land.

Dec 10, 1940 Italian forces abandon their fortified camps.

Western Desert Force/ XIII Force (from Jan 1941)

1 THE BEGINNING OF THE NORTH AFRICA CAMPAIGN
JUNE 10, 1940–SEPTEMBER 21, 1940

The Italian declaration of war prompted a swift Allied response. On June 14, British troops crossed from Egypt into Italy's Libyan territory to capture Forts Capuzzo and Maddalena, and sent patrols as far as Tobruk. On September 13, the Italians finally made their move into Egypt; their troops advanced some 50 miles (80 km) over the border before halting and setting up a line of fortified camps at Sidi Barrani. Outnumbered, the Allied Western Desert Force (WDF) withdrew to defensive positions at Mersa Matruh.

- ••• Italian defensive line
- • Italian-occupied towns Sep 13–16
- → Italian advance
- // Italian camps

2 OPERATION COMPASS: ALLIED COUNTEROFFENSIVE
DECEMBER 9, 1940–FEBRUARY 7, 1941

Supported by a naval bombardment, the WDF launched Operation Compass on December 9; within three days they had taken Sidi Barrani. They soon captured Tobruk, gaining a vital staging post for supplies. The 6th Australian Division chased the Italians along the coast, while the 7th Armored Division headed to Mechili before turning south-west to cut off the Italian retreat. With the capture of Beda Fomm, the Italians were cleared from north Cyrenaica.

- • British defensive position Dec 1941
- → Western Desert Force advance
- ✲ British naval bombardment
- □□▷ Italian army retreat

ACTION IN NORTH AFRICA
From June 1940 to February 1941 the Italians failed to advance in British-held Egypt and were driven from northern Cyrenaica in Libya, an Italian territory since 1912.

ITALY'S CAMPAIGNS IN AFRICA

Italian dictator Benito Mussolini saw the outbreak of war as an opportunity to pursue his imperial ambitions in Africa. He embarked on two disastrous campaigns against the British in Egypt, Anglo-Egyptian Sudan, and British Somaliland, which backfired and resulted in Italy's expulsion from northern Libya and Ethiopia.

Italy did not follow its Axis partner Germany into war in September 1939, but entered the conflict later, in June 1940, when Mussolini judged that the Allies would soon be defeated. His initial aim was to expand Italy's colonies in Libya, Ethiopia, Eritrea, and Italian Somaliland by taking territory from the British. With superior numbers in the air and on the ground, Italy posed a threat to Britain's positions in Anglo-Egyptian Sudan, Kenya, and the Horn of Africa, as well as British bases in Egypt and the vital supply route of the Suez Canal.

Italian forces invaded Sudan in early July 1940, but did not push deep into British territory, switching to assault British Somaliland in August, and then the Egyptian border in September. By the end of October, however, Italy had opened up a new front in Greece (pp.78–79) and did not appear to be planning new moves in Africa.

In December, the British launched Operation Compass against the Italian invaders in Egypt and then swept on through northern Libya, clearing the Italians out of the region in early February 1941. By then, British forces—supported by Ethiopian chieftains rallied by Emperor Haile Selassie—had launched counterattacks in East Africa. By May, only few pockets of Italian resistance remained.

ITALY'S EMPIRE
Italy's imperial ambitions were dealt a blow when its soldiers failed to make inroads in Egypt against the British, instead losing control of vital territory in Libya. The Italians were also driven from their East African colonies of Italian Somaliland, Eritrea, and the Ethiopian Empire, held since 1936.

KEY

- Under British influence by Jun 1940
- Italian Empire Jun 1940
- French and French mandated territories Jun 1940
- Italian forts
- Allied army units
- Major battles

TIMELINE

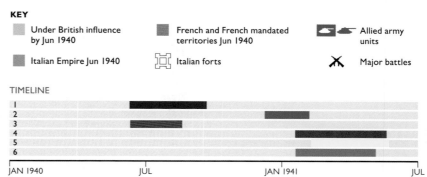

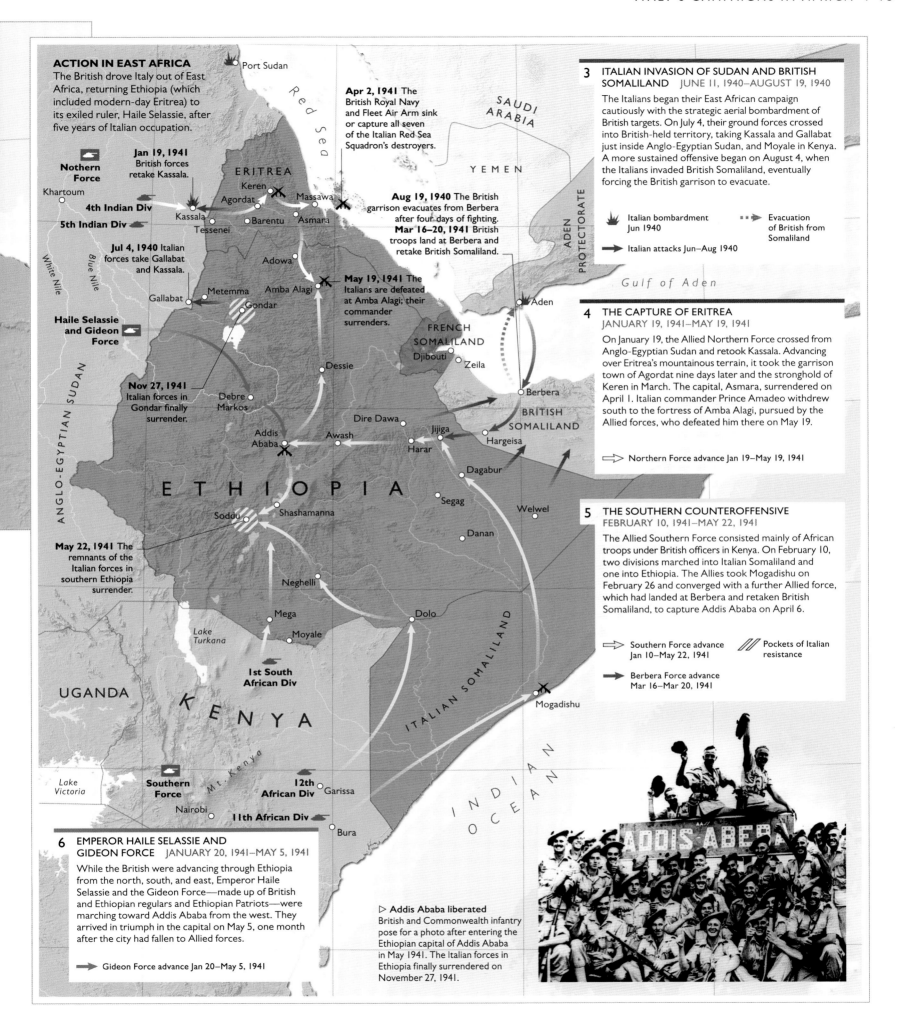

ACTION IN EAST AFRICA

The British drove Italy out of East Africa, returning Ethiopia (which included modern-day Eritrea) to its exiled ruler, Haile Selassie, after five years of Italian occupation.

Nothern Force

Jan 19, 1941 British forces retake Kassala.

4th Indian Div

5th Indian Div

Jul 4, 1940 Italian forces take Gallabat and Kassala.

Haile Selassie and Gideon Force

Nov 27, 1941 Italian forces in Gondar finally surrender.

May 22, 1941 The remnants of the Italian forces in southern Ethiopia surrender.

1st South African Div

Southern Force

12th African Div

11th African Div

Apr 2, 1941 The British Royal Navy and Fleet Air Arm sink or capture all seven of the Italian Red Sea Squadron's destroyers.

Aug 19, 1940 The British garrison evacuates from Berbera after four days of fighting.
Mar 16–20, 1941 British troops land at Berbera and retake British Somaliland.

May 19, 1941 The Italians are defeated at Amba Alagi; their commander surrenders.

3 ITALIAN INVASION OF SUDAN AND BRITISH SOMALILAND   JUNE 11, 1940–AUGUST 19, 1940

The Italians began their East African campaign cautiously with the strategic aerial bombardment of British targets. On July 4, their ground forces crossed into British-held territory, taking Kassala and Gallabat just inside Anglo-Egyptian Sudan, and Moyale in Kenya. A more sustained offensive began on August 4, when the Italians invaded British Somaliland, eventually forcing the British garrison to evacuate.

- Italian bombardment Jun 1940
- Italian attacks Jun–Aug 1940
- Evacuation of British from Somaliland

4 THE CAPTURE OF ERITREA
JANUARY 19, 1941–MAY 19, 1941

On January 19, the Allied Northern Force crossed from Anglo-Egyptian Sudan and retook Kassala. Advancing over Eritrea's mountainous terrain, it took the garrison town of Agordat nine days later and the stronghold of Keren in March. The capital, Asmara, surrendered on April 1. Italian commander Prince Amadeo withdrew south to the fortress of Amba Alagi, pursued by the Allied forces, who defeated him there on May 19.

- Northern Force advance Jan 19–May 19, 1941

5 THE SOUTHERN COUNTEROFFENSIVE
FEBRUARY 10, 1941–MAY 22, 1941

The Allied Southern Force consisted mainly of African troops under British officers in Kenya. On February 10, two divisions marched into Italian Somaliland and one into Ethiopia. The Allies took Mogadishu on February 26 and converged with a further Allied force, which had landed at Berbera and retaken British Somaliland, to capture Addis Ababa on April 6.

- Southern Force advance Jan 10–May 22, 1941
- Berbera Force advance Mar 16–Mar 20, 1941
- Pockets of Italian resistance

6 EMPEROR HAILE SELASSIE AND GIDEON FORCE   JANUARY 20, 1941–MAY 5, 1941

While the British were advancing through Ethiopia from the north, south, and east, Emperor Haile Selassie and the Gideon Force—made up of British and Ethiopian regulars and Ethiopian Patriots—were marching toward Addis Ababa from the west. They arrived in triumph in the capital on May 5, one month after the city had fallen to Allied forces.

- Gideon Force advance Jan 20–May 5, 1941

▷ **Addis Ababa liberated**
British and Commonwealth infantry pose for a photo after entering the Ethiopian capital of Addis Ababa in May 1941. The Italian forces in Ethiopia finally surrendered on November 27, 1941.

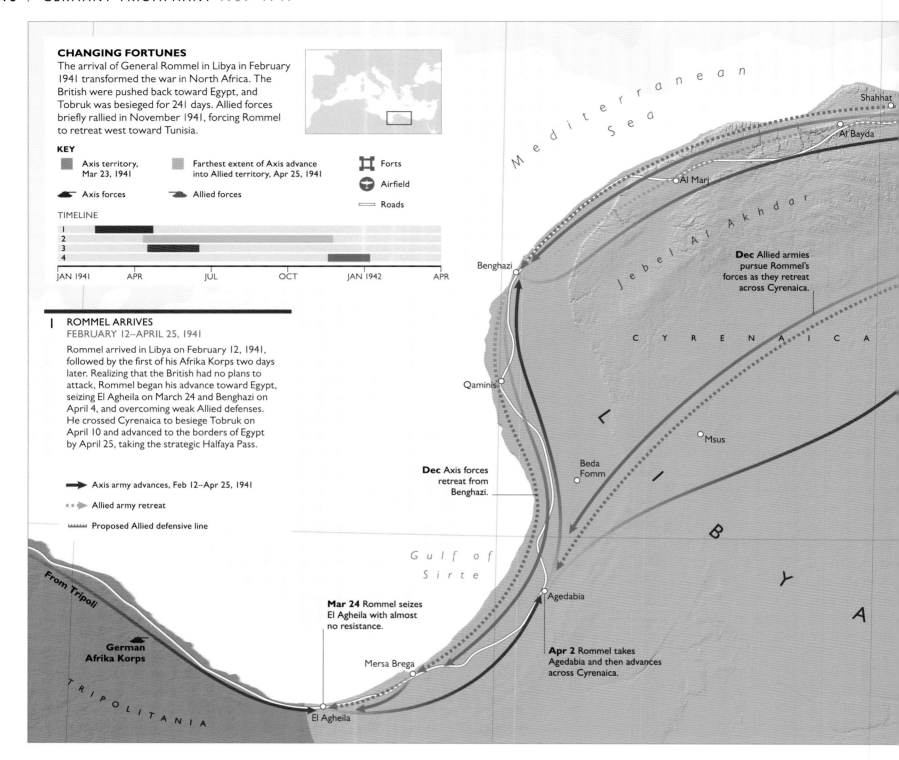

CHANGING FORTUNES

The arrival of General Rommel in Libya in February 1941 transformed the war in North Africa. The British were pushed back toward Egypt, and Tobruk was besieged for 241 days. Allied forces briefly rallied in November 1941, forcing Rommel to retreat west toward Tunisia.

KEY

- Axis territory, Mar 23, 1941
- Farthest extent of Axis advance into Allied territory, Apr 25, 1941
- Forts
- Axis forces
- Allied forces
- Airfield
- Roads

TIMELINE

1 2 3 4

JAN 1941 APR JUL OCT JAN 1942 APR

ROMMEL ARRIVES
FEBRUARY 12–APRIL 25, 1941

Rommel arrived in Libya on February 12, 1941, followed by the first of his Afrika Korps two days later. Realizing that the British had no plans to attack, Rommel began his advance toward Egypt, seizing El Agheila on March 24 and Benghazi on April 4, and overcoming weak Allied defenses. He crossed Cyrenaica to besiege Tobruk on April 10 and advanced to the borders of Egypt by April 25, taking the strategic Halfaya Pass.

→ Axis army advances, Feb 12–Apr 25, 1941

▪▪▸ Allied army retreat

Proposed Allied defensive line

Dec Allied armies pursue Rommel's forces as they retreat across Cyrenaica.

Dec Axis forces retreat from Benghazi.

Mar 24 Rommel seizes El Agheila with almost no resistance.

Apr 2 Rommel takes Agedabia and then advances across Cyrenaica.

From Tripoli

German Afrika Korps

TRIPOLITANIA

Mediterranean Sea

Shahhat

Al Bayda

Al Marj

Jebel Al Akhdar

Benghazi

Qaminis

CYRENAICA

Msus

Beda Fomm

LIBYA

Gulf of Sirte

Agedabia

Mersa Brega

El Agheila

ROMMEL ENTERS THE DESERT WAR

By February 1941, the Italians were struggling in their war against the Allies in North Africa. Their incursions into Egypt had failed, and they had been chased out of Cyrenaica in northern Libya. Hitler was anxious to save Italy from defeat and sent his favorite general, Erwin Rommel, with a German armored expeditionary force—the Afrika Korps—to rescue the situation.

Rommel's orders on arriving in Libya were to stand on the defensive and prevent any further Italian retreats, but the German general—who had proved his flair for tank warfare in France—had an instinct for attack. Knowing that the British forces facing him had been weakened by the diversion of troops to Greece (see pp.80–81), he launched a probing offensive in late March and found that his tanks could outmaneuver the British with ease.

Rommel soon began an eastward advance, forcing the Allies to retreat in disarray from Libya into Egypt. In early April, the 9th Australian Division found itself marooned in the port of Tobruk, surrounded by the enemy, and far behind the new front line. Rommel had orders to take Tobruk, but the Australian forces there, resupplied by sea, held a defensive perimeter against attack by superior German forces throughout the next six months. British counterattacks from Egypt in May and June failed to break the

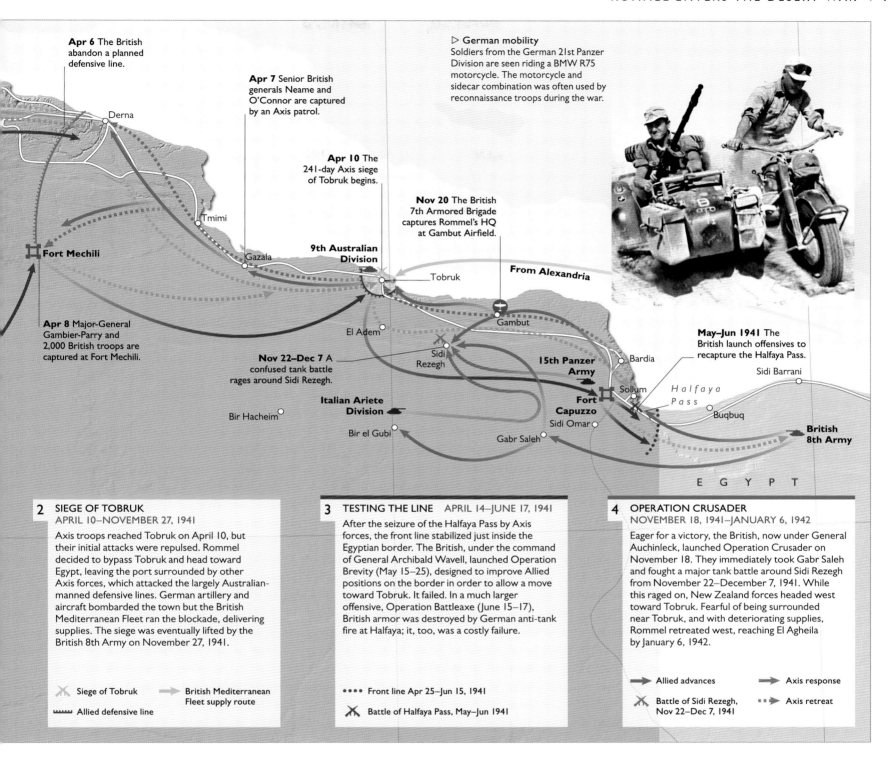

Apr 6 The British abandon a planned defensive line.

Apr 7 Senior British generals Neame and O'Connor are captured by an Axis patrol.

Apr 10 The 241-day Axis siege of Tobruk begins.

Nov 20 The British 7th Armored Brigade captures Rommel's HQ at Gambut Airfield.

▷ **German mobility**
Soldiers from the German 21st Panzer Division are seen riding a BMW R75 motorcycle. The motorcycle and sidecar combination was often used by reconnaissance troops during the war.

Derna

Tmimi

Fort Mechili

Gazala

9th Australian Division

Tobruk

From Alexandria

Gambut

Apr 8 Major-General Gambier-Parry and 2,000 British troops are captured at Fort Mechili.

Nov 22–Dec 7 A confused tank battle rages around Sidi Rezegh.

El Adem

Sidi Rezegh

15th Panzer Army

Bardia

May–Jun 1941 The British launch offensives to recapture the Halfaya Pass.

Sidi Barrani

Italian Ariete Division

Bir Hacheim

Bir el Gubi

Fort Capuzzo

Sidi Omar

Sollum

Halfaya Pass

Buqbuq

Gabr Saleh

British 8th Army

E G Y P T

---

2 SIEGE OF TOBRUK
APRIL 10–NOVEMBER 27, 1941

Axis troops reached Tobruk on April 10, but their initial attacks were repulsed. Rommel decided to bypass Tobruk and head toward Egypt, leaving the port surrounded by other Axis forces, which attacked the largely Australian-manned defensive lines. German artillery and aircraft bombarded the town but the British Mediterranean Fleet ran the blockade, delivering supplies. The siege was eventually lifted by the British 8th Army on November 27, 1941.

✕ Siege of Tobruk
⟶ British Mediterranean Fleet supply route
⌇⌇⌇ Allied defensive line

3 TESTING THE LINE APRIL 14–JUNE 17, 1941

After the seizure of the Halfaya Pass by Axis forces, the front line stabilized just inside the Egyptian border. The British, under the command of General Archibald Wavell, launched Operation Brevity (May 15–25), designed to improve Allied positions on the border in order to allow a move toward Tobruk. It failed. In a much larger offensive, Operation Battleaxe (June 15–17), British armor was destroyed by German anti-tank fire at Halfaya; it, too, was a costly failure.

•••• Front line Apr 25–Jun 15, 1941
✕ Battle of Halfaya Pass, May–Jun 1941

4 OPERATION CRUSADER
NOVEMBER 18, 1941–JANUARY 6, 1942

Eager for a victory, the British, now under General Auchinleck, launched Operation Crusader on November 18. They immediately took Gabr Saleh and fought a major tank battle around Sidi Rezegh from November 22–December 7, 1941. While this raged on, New Zealand forces headed west toward Tobruk. Fearful of being surrounded near Tobruk, and with deteriorating supplies, Rommel retreated west, reaching El Agheila by January 6, 1942.

⟶ Allied advances   ⟶ Axis response
✕ Battle of Sidi Rezegh, Nov 22–Dec 7, 1941   ⇢ Axis retreat

---

siege of Tobruk, and in July, a frustrated Churchill dismissed the area commander, General Archibald Wavell, replacing him with General Claude Auchinleck. The new commander was given substantial reinforcements, especially tanks, and the British desert forces—which included Australians, New Zealanders, Poles, South Africans, Indians, and Free French troops—were reorganized as the British 8th Army.

On November 18, Auchinleck took the offensive in Operation Crusader. Again the British armor was outfought by Rommel's more experienced tank commanders, but at a crucial moment Rommel lost contact with his enemy, advancing into empty desert while, further north, 8th Army infantry pressed towards Tobruk. The siege was lifted on November 27 and Rommel soon conducted a full-scale retreat, falling back as far as El Agheila—the first position he had captured from the British, the previous March.

FIELD MARSHAL ERWIN ROMMEL

Field Marshal Erwin Rommel (1891–1944) was one of the leading tank commanders of World War II, earning himself the nickname *der Wüstenfuchs*, "the Desert Fox," for his wily strategic command. His British adversaries admired his chivalry, and the war in North Africa has been called the "war without hate." Although a supporter of Adolf Hitler and the Nazi seizure of power in 1933, Rommel was a reluctant Nazi. In 1944 he was implicated in the July 20 plot to assassinate Hitler (see pp.196–197); he was allowed to take his own life rather than face trial.

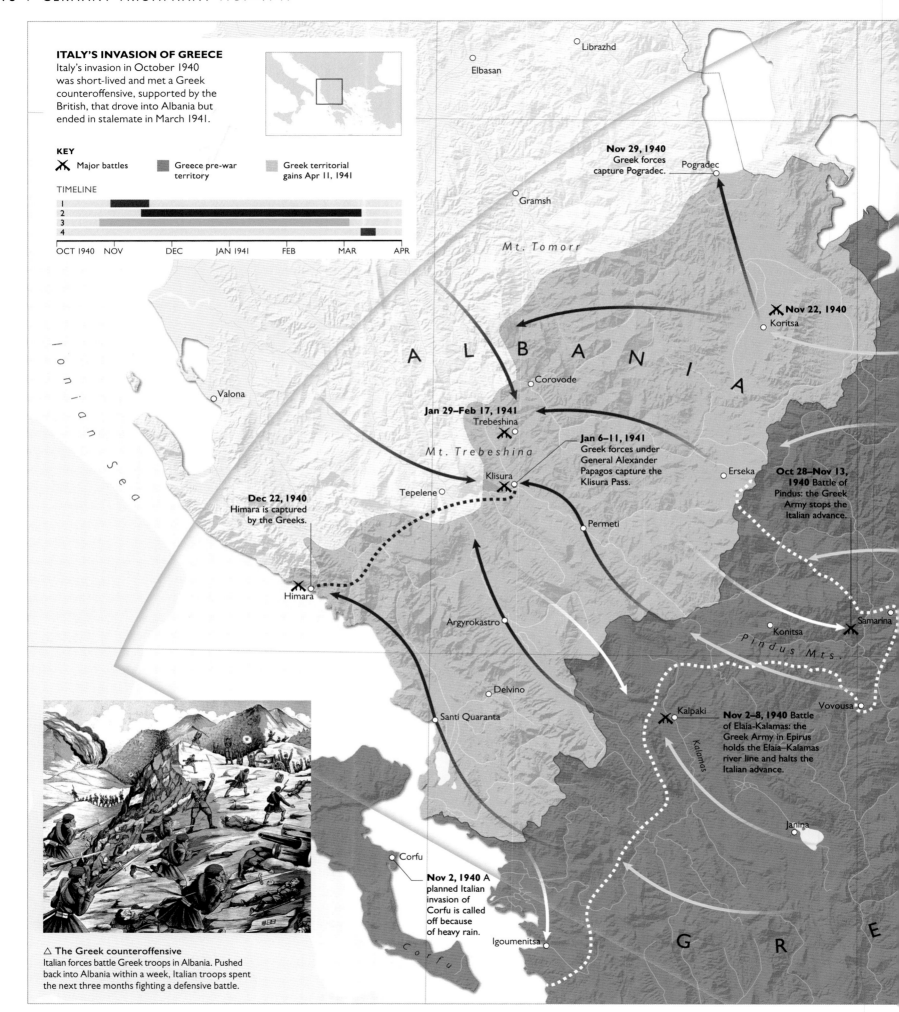

ITALY'S INVASION OF GREECE

Italy's invasion in October 1940 was short-lived and met a Greek counteroffensive, supported by the British, that drove into Albania but ended in stalemate in March 1941.

KEY

✗ Major battles

█ Greece pre-war territory

█ Greek territorial gains Apr 11, 1941

TIMELINE

1
2
3
4

OCT 1940 NOV DEC JAN 1941 FEB MAR APR

Nov 29, 1940 Greek forces capture Pogradec.

Nov 22, 1940 Koritsa

Jan 29–Feb 17, 1941 Trebeshina

Jan 6–11, 1941 Greek forces under General Alexander Papagos capture the Klisura Pass.

Oct 28–Nov 13, 1940 Battle of Pindus: the Greek Army stops the Italian advance.

Dec 22, 1940 Himara is captured by the Greeks.

Nov 2–8, 1940 Battle of Elaia-Kalamas: the Greek Army in Epirus holds the Elaia–Kalamas river line and halts the Italian advance.

Nov 2, 1940 A planned Italian invasion of Corfu is called off because of heavy rain.

Mt. Tomorr

Mt. Trebeshina

Pindus Mts.

Ionian Sea

Kalamas

Corfu

Librazhd

Elbasan

Gramsh

Pogradec

Valona

Corovode

Erseka

Klisura

Tepelene

Permeti

Himara

Argyrokastro

Samarina

Konitsa

Vovousa

Delvino

Kalpaki

Santi Quaranta

Janina

Corfu

Igoumenitsa

A L B A N I A

G R E[E]

△ **The Greek counteroffensive**
Italian forces battle Greek troops in Albania. Pushed back into Albania within a week, Italian troops spent the next three months fighting a defensive battle.

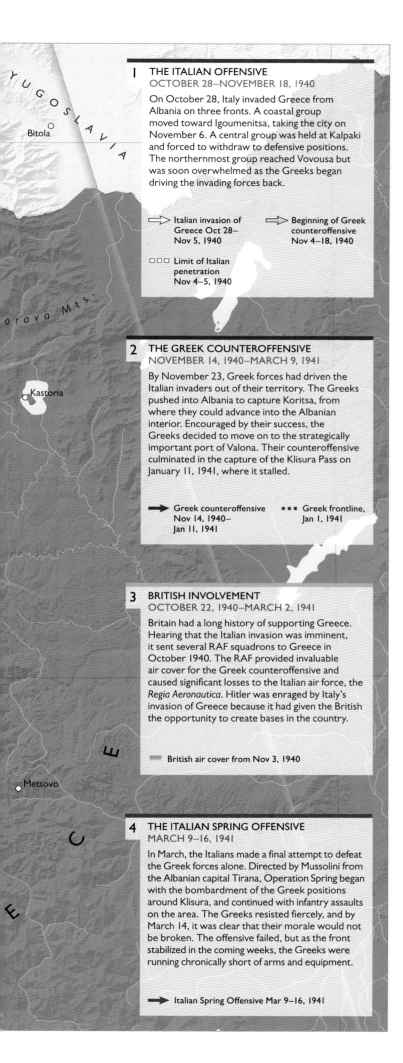

1 THE ITALIAN OFFENSIVE
OCTOBER 28–NOVEMBER 18, 1940

On October 28, Italy invaded Greece from Albania on three fronts. A coastal group moved toward Igoumenitsa, taking the city on November 6. A central group was held at Kalpaki and forced to withdraw to defensive positions. The northernmost group reached Vovousa but was soon overwhelmed as the Greeks began driving the invading forces back.

⇨ Italian invasion of Greece Oct 28–Nov 5, 1940

⇨ Beginning of Greek counteroffensive Nov 4–18, 1940

▢▢▢ Limit of Italian penetration Nov 4–5, 1940

2 THE GREEK COUNTEROFFENSIVE
NOVEMBER 14, 1940–MARCH 9, 1941

By November 23, Greek forces had driven the Italian invaders out of their territory. The Greeks pushed into Albania to capture Koritsa, from where they could advance into the Albanian interior. Encouraged by their success, the Greeks decided to move on to the strategically important port of Valona. Their counteroffensive culminated in the capture of the Klisura Pass on January 11, 1941, where it stalled.

➡ Greek counteroffensive Nov 14, 1940–Jan 11, 1941

∎∎∎ Greek frontline, Jan 1, 1941

3 BRITISH INVOLVEMENT
OCTOBER 22, 1940–MARCH 2, 1941

Britain had a long history of supporting Greece. Hearing that the Italian invasion was imminent, it sent several RAF squadrons to Greece in October 1940. The RAF provided invaluable air cover for the Greek counteroffensive and caused significant losses to the Italian air force, the *Regia Aeronautica*. Hitler was enraged by Italy's invasion of Greece because it had given the British the opportunity to create bases in the country.

▬ British air cover from Nov 3, 1940

4 THE ITALIAN SPRING OFFENSIVE
MARCH 9–16, 1941

In March, the Italians made a final attempt to defeat the Greek forces alone. Directed by Mussolini from the Albanian capital Tirana, Operation Spring began with the bombardment of the Greek positions around Klisura, and continued with infantry assaults on the area. The Greeks resisted fiercely, and by March 14, it was clear that their morale would not be broken. The offensive failed, but as the front stabilized in the coming weeks, the Greeks were running chronically short of arms and equipment.

➡ Italian Spring Offensive Mar 9–16, 1941

THE GRECO-ITALIAN WAR

At war with the Allies since June 10, 1940, Italy had begun to fulfill its imperial ambitions with invasions of France, British Somaliland, and Egypt. In October 1940, it launched the invasion of Greece— a disastrous offensive that achieved nothing other than to test the relationship between Italy and Germany.

In October 1940, the Balkans were broadly pro-German, and Greece's own right-wing dictator—General Metaxas— had confirmed Greece's neutrality. This suited Hitler, because it allowed him to pursue his plans for the invasion of the Soviet Union without distraction. However, Mussolini had designs on Greece and was impatient for conquests to match those of his German allies.

Mussolini accused the Greeks of aiding the British in the Mediterranean, and on October 28 issued an ultimatum demanding free passage for his troops to occupy strategic points in Greek territory. When Metaxas rejected the ultimatum, Italy invaded from Albania.

The Italian forces crossed the border at three points, but were soon caught in bitter fighting with a fiercely patriotic and tenacious Greek army in the unforgiving terrain of the mountains along the Albanian–Greek border.

By early November, a Greek counter-offensive had pushed the Italians back into Albania, and the Greek army was soon advancing through the country. The counteroffensive halted by early January 1941, leaving the Italians to attempt one last offensive in March. It achieved little, but it did highlight the vulnerability of the Greek army, influencing Hitler's later decision to send his own armies into the region.

"We do not argue with those who disagree with us, we destroy them."

BENITO MUSSOLINI, 1936

ITALY'S IMPERIAL AMBITIONS

After its unification in the mid-19th century, Italy built a small empire that included the Dodecanese Islands and territories in East and North Africa. From the 1920s, Mussolini— whose Fascist Party was named after the bundle of wooden rods (or *fasces*) that was a symbol of Roman authority—sought to reclaim the glory of Ancient Rome. He gradually strengthened Italy's power in Libya, and conquered Ethiopia in 1935. Four years later, Albania was incorporated into Italy, and the invasion of Greece in 1940 was the next logical step in his plan to dominate the Mediterranean.

Italian imperial propaganda shows Mussolini and Vittorio Emanuele III superimposed on a graphic of Italy's planned African empire.

GERMANY PUSHES SOUTH

Italy's unsuccessful invasion of Greece forced Hitler to postpone his planned invasion of the USSR and concentrate on securing the Balkans. With the support of its regional allies, Germany invaded Yugoslavia and Greece in April 1941, taking both in under a month.

While Italy was fighting its ineffectual war with Greece (see pp.78–79), Hitler had been persuading and pressurizing the states in the Balkan region to join the defensive alliance known as the Tripartite Pact. By March 1, 1941, all the states except Yugoslavia and Greece had joined. German troops had begun to arrive in Romania and Hungary in November 1940, and—as the Italians prepared their counteroffensive against Greece in Albania—the German 12th Army moved into Bulgaria on March 2, 1941.

Alarmed by the arrival of German forces on Greece's borders, the British responded by sending an expeditionary force (W Force, named after its commander, Lieutenant-General Henry Maitland Wilson) from Egypt to Greece. On March 25, Yugoslavia yielded to pressure to join the Tripartite Pact, but a coup on March 27 gave power to a group of anti-Pact air force officers. When they signed a nonaggression pact with the Soviet Union and began talks with Britain about a Balkan coalition, Hitler immediately began planning the simultaneous invasion of Yugoslavia and Greece. The Yugoslav people were forced to defend a 1,000-mile (1,600-km) frontier with ill-equipped divisions numbering barely half the 50 fielded by Germany. Most of the Greek forces were in Albania, leaving only the Greek 2nd Army and W Force to defend the eastern route into Greece. On April 6, the Germans unleashed their blitzkrieg. By April 28, Yugoslavia had surrendered, and the Allies been driven out of Greece.

THE EXPANSION OF THE TRIPARTITE PACT

On September 27, 1940, Germany, Italy (including Albania), and Japan had signed a defense alliance known as the Tripartite Pact. Unwilling to become embroiled in a war in the notoriously complex Balkan region, Hitler sought the support of the Balkan countries through diplomacy, and by the end of November 1940, Hungary, Romania, and Slovakia had all joined the Pact. Bulgaria joined on March 1, 1941. Threatened by the German, Hungarian, and Italian troops building up along its borders, Yugoslavia joined the pact on March 25. But on March 27, Yugoslavia revoked, forcing Germany to expand its invasion plans.

KEY

■ Initial signatories	■ Joined Nov 24, 1940
■ Joined Nov 20, 1940	■ Joined Mar 1, 1941
■ Joined Nov 23, 1940	■ Joined Mar 25, 1941

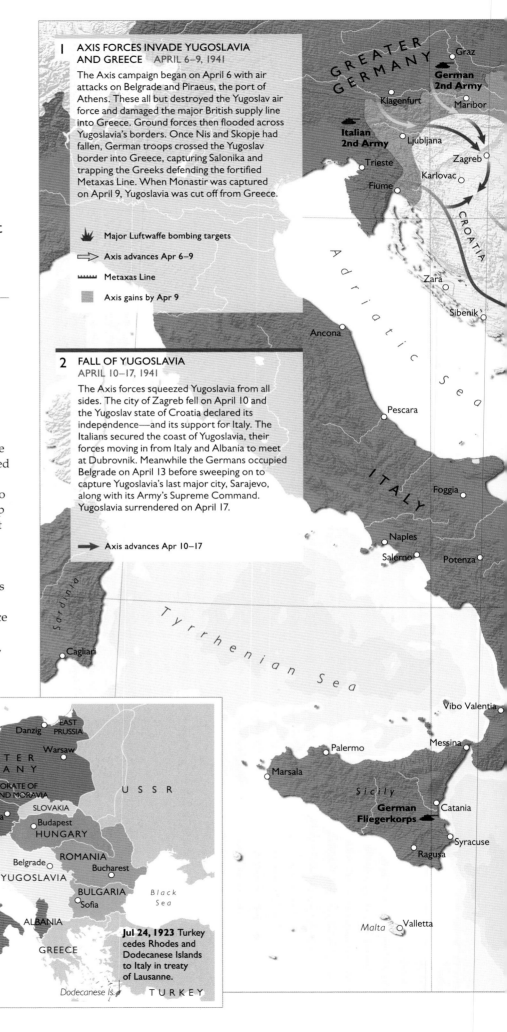

1 AXIS FORCES INVADE YUGOSLAVIA AND GREECE APRIL 6–9, 1941

The Axis campaign began on April 6 with air attacks on Belgrade and Piraeus, the port of Athens. These all but destroyed the Yugoslav air force and damaged the major British supply line into Greece. Ground forces then flooded across Yugoslavia's borders. Once Nis and Skopje had fallen, German troops crossed the Yugoslav border into Greece, capturing Salonika and trapping the Greeks defending the fortified Metaxas Line. When Monastir was captured on April 9, Yugoslavia was cut off from Greece.

- ✺ Major Luftwaffe bombing targets
- ⇨ Axis advances Apr 6–9
- ᴧᴧᴧᴧ Metaxas Line
- ■ Axis gains by Apr 9

2 FALL OF YUGOSLAVIA APRIL 10–17, 1941

The Axis forces squeezed Yugoslavia from all sides. The city of Zagreb fell on April 10 and the Yugoslav state of Croatia declared its independence—and its support for Italy. The Italians secured the coast of Yugoslavia, their forces moving in from Italy and Albania to meet at Dubrovnik. Meanwhile the Germans occupied Belgrade on April 13 before sweeping on to capture Yugoslavia's last major city, Sarajevo, along with its Army's Supreme Command. Yugoslavia surrendered on April 17.

- ➡ Axis advances Apr 10–17

Jul 24, 1923 Turkey cedes Rhodes and Dodecanese Islands to Italy in treaty of Lausanne.

Veszprem
Lake Balaton
HUNGARY
Bekescsaba
Tirgu Mures
Pecs
Apr 11–12 The Hungarian Army overruns part of northern Yugoslavia, which is then annexed by Hungary.
Hungarian 3rd Army
Arad
Subotica
Timisoara
Sibiu
Osijek
German XLI Panzer Corps
ROMANIA
Novi Sad
Deta
Drava
Banja Luka
Tuzla
Sava
Belgrade
Turnu-Severin
Pitesti
Valjevo
YUGOSLAVIA
Kragujevac
Apr 6 The German XIV Panzer Corps invades from Bulgaria; it reaches Belgrade on April 12.
Alexandria
Razgrad
Uzice
Danube
Sarajevo
Pleven
Mostar
Nis
BULGARIA
German XIV Panzer Corps
Pristina
Sofia
Stara Zagora
German 12th Army
Niksic
Pec
Urba
German XL Motorized Corps
Dubrovnik
Podgorica
Krainitzi
Plovdiv
Maritsa
Skopje
Adrianople
Apr 17 The Yugoslav government is evacuated to Athens, before moving to London.
Scutari
Veles
Belitza
Krumovo
Italian 9th Army
Peshkopi
Tirana
Durazzo
Italian 11th Army
Seres
Kavala
Greek 2nd Army
Monastir
Salonika
Thasos
Alexandroupoli
Brindisi
ALBANIA
Florina
Samothrace
Koritsa
Katerina
Polygyros
Taranto
Lecce
Valona
Mount Olympus
Lemnos
Greek 1st Army
British W Force
Aegean Sea
Gulf of Taranto
Janina
Larissa
Corfu
Volos
Ionian Sea
GREECE
Apr 9 Trapped by the fall of Salonika, the Greek 2nd Army surrenders.
Khios
Thermopylae
Apr 25 German paratroopers land in Corinth.
Agrinio
Chalcis
Patras
Thebes
Euboea
Megara
Athens
Piraeus
Corinth
Tinos
Pirgos
Nafplio
Ermoupoli
Peloponnesus
Paros
Kalamata
Monemvasia
Apr 6–7 Piraeus is virtually destroyed by Luftwaffe bombing raids and the explosion of the British ammunition ship *Clan Fraser*.
Cerigo
Maleme   Canea   *Crete*

THE AXIS CAMPAIGN IN THE BALKANS

Axis forces swiftly overwhelmed Yugoslavia and Greece in April 1941. The British were forced to retreat to Crete, leaving the entire Balkans in Axis hands.

KEY

Axis territories, Apr 6, 1941   Axis armies   Allied armies

TIMELINE

1
2
3
4
APR 1, 1941   APR 15   MAY 1

△ **Athens falls**
German soldiers ride a Stug III assault gun in Athens, with the ruins of the Acropolis visible in the background. The first German forces—motorcycle troops—entered the city on April 27, 1941, and were followed by armor and infantry.

TURKEY

3   GREECE OVERRUN
APRIL 10–27, 1941

With the Germans threatening their rear from Monastir, the British W Force began to withdraw from the defensive Aliakmon Line on April 10, and pulled back to Mount Olympus. Over the next two weeks, the German forces pushed farther south, driving a wedge between W Force and the Greek 1st Army in Albania; by this time, the Italians had also retaken their Albanian territories. The Greek 1st Army surrendered on April 20.

▬▬▬ Aliakmon Line   •••• W Force position Apr 16

→ Axis advances Apr 10–27

4   THE BRITISH EVACUATION
APRIL 20–28, 1941

Facing the advancing German forces alone, the British made plans to evacuate. W Force fell back to Thermopylae, where its commander, Lieutenant-General Henry Maitland Wilson, planned to fight a rearguard action to protect the withdrawing troops. Evacuations to Crete began on April 22. Three days later, German paratroopers landed at the Corinth Canal and crossed to Patras, driving the last Allied forces from the Peloponnesus.

••• British evacuation routes Apr 22–28   📍 German paratrooper assault May 25

⚓ Main evacuation ports

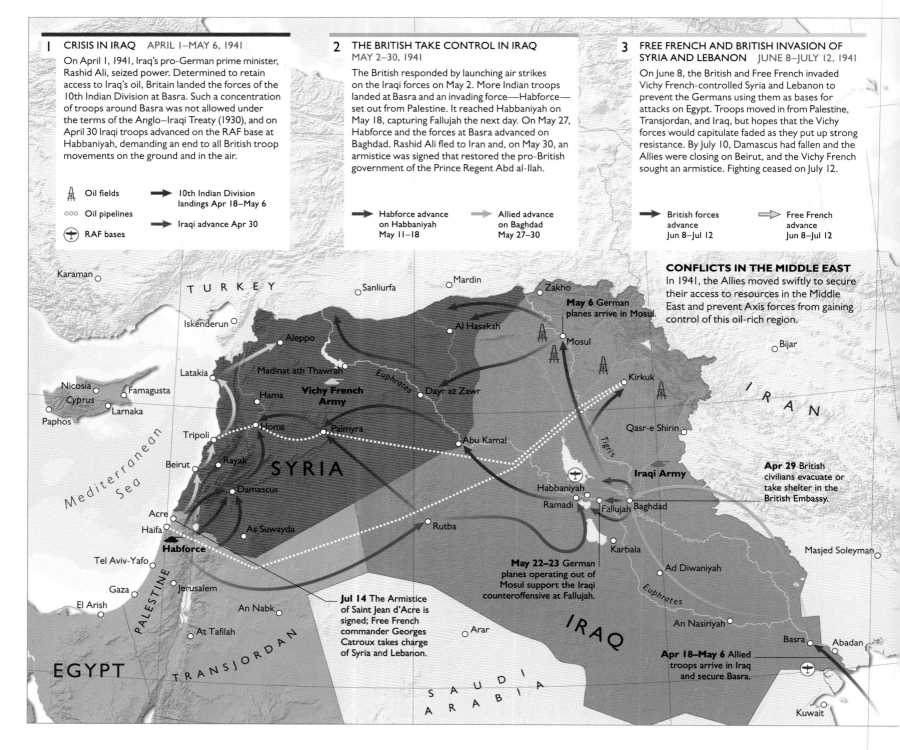

1 CRISIS IN IRAQ APRIL 1–MAY 6, 1941

On April 1, 1941, Iraq's pro-German prime minister, Rashid Ali, seized power. Determined to retain access to Iraq's oil, Britain landed the forces of the 10th Indian Division at Basra. Such a concentration of troops around Basra was not allowed under the terms of the Anglo–Iraqi Treaty (1930), and on April 30 Iraqi troops advanced on the RAF base at Habbaniyah, demanding an end to all British troop movements on the ground and in the air.

🛢 Oil fields
ooo Oil pipelines
⊕ RAF bases

➡ 10th Indian Division landings Apr 18–May 6
➡ Iraqi advance Apr 30

2 THE BRITISH TAKE CONTROL IN IRAQ MAY 2–30, 1941

The British responded by launching air strikes on the Iraqi forces on May 2. More Indian troops landed at Basra and an invading force—Habforce—set out from Palestine. It reached Habbaniyah on May 18, capturing Fallujah the next day. On May 27, Habforce and the forces at Basra advanced on Baghdad. Rashid Ali fled to Iran and, on May 30, an armistice was signed that restored the pro-British government of the Prince Regent Abd al-Ilah.

➡ Habforce advance on Habbaniyah May 11–18
➡ Allied advance on Baghdad May 27–30

3 FREE FRENCH AND BRITISH INVASION OF SYRIA AND LEBANON JUNE 8–JULY 12, 1941

On June 8, the British and Free French invaded Vichy French-controlled Syria and Lebanon to prevent the Germans using them as bases for attacks on Egypt. Troops moved in from Palestine, Transjordan, and Iraq, but hopes that the Vichy forces would capitulate faded as they put up strong resistance. By July 10, Damascus had fallen and the Allies were closing on Beirut, and the Vichy French sought an armistice. Fighting ceased on July 12.

➡ British forces advance Jun 8–Jul 12
➡ Free French advance Jun 8–Jul 12

CONFLICTS IN THE MIDDLE EAST

In 1941, the Allies moved swiftly to secure their access to resources in the Middle East and prevent Axis forces from gaining control of this oil-rich region.

May 6 German planes arrive in Mosul.

Apr 29 British civilians evacuate or take shelter in the British Embassy.

May 22–23 German planes operating out of Mosul support the Iraqi counteroffensive at Fallujah.

Apr 18–May 6 Allied troops arrive in Iraq and secure Basra.

Jul 14 The Armistice of Saint Jean d'Acre is signed; Free French commander Georges Catroux takes charge of Syria and Lebanon.

Map labels: Karaman, TURKEY, Sanliurfa, Mardin, Zakho, Iskenderun, Aleppo, Al Hasakah, Mosul, Bijar, Latakia, Madinat ath Thawrah, Euphrates, Dayr az Zawr, Kirkuk, Nicosia, Famagusta, Cyprus, Larnaka, Hama, Vichy French Army, Qasr-e Shirin, IRAN, Paphos, Tripoli, Homs, Palmyra, Abu Kamal, Tigris, Beirut, Rayak, SYRIA, Acre, Haifa, Damascus, Habbaniyah, Ramadi, Fallujah, Baghdad, Iraqi Army, Masjed Soleyman, Habforce, As Suwayda, Rutba, Karbala, Tel Aviv-Yafo, Ad Diwaniyah, Gaza, PALESTINE, Jerusalem, An Nabk, Arar, Euphrates, An Nasiriyah, Basra, Abadan, El Arish, At Tafilah, TRANSJORDAN, IRAQ, EGYPT, SAUDI ARABIA, Kuwait, Mediterranean Sea

THE ALLIES SECURE THE MIDDLE EAST

Between April and July 1941, Allied ground forces—supported by squadrons from the Royal Air Force and the Royal Australian Air Force—took control of Vichy Syria, Lebanon, and Iraq, creating a bloc that offered access to oil and protection for their other territories in the region.

KEY

▨ British-controlled territory
▨ Axis-controlled territory
▨ Pro-Axis territory
◺ Vichy French Army
◄ British and Commonwealth forces
◄ Iraqi Army

TIMELINE

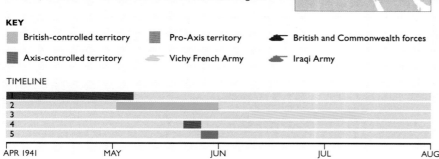

APR 1941   MAY   JUN   JUL   AUG

△ **British troops captured**
British troops surrender during the German invasion of Crete in May 1941. Code named Operation Mercury, the invasion involved the mass deployment of *Fallschirmjäger* (paratroopers).

THE MIDDLE EAST AND EASTERN MEDITERRANEAN

In 1941 the Allies faced a series of challenges that ended with Axis powers dominating the eastern Mediterranean. However, the Allies strengthened their position in the Middle East, securing oil and supply routes from Iraq to the USSR that would prove invaluable in the months to come.

The Allies experienced mixed fortunes in the Middle East and east Mediterranean in the first half of 1941. They were chased out of Greece by the German advance in April (see pp.80–81) and suffered a further humiliation in Crete in May. There, they were ousted by a surprise airborne assault, despite having known that the Germans had planned to invade since April. The loss of Crete deprived the Allied forces of around 16,000 men—either dead or captured—and cost the Royal Navy nine ships, with another 13 damaged. It was followed by more failure, when a British attempt to relieve Tobruk

in North Africa in June ended in disaster. Yet Hitler failed to capitalize on the dominance of the Mediterranean that the Axis powers had won through the conquest of the Balkans and Crete, and their success in North Africa. Instead, the Germans turned their attention to the Soviet Union.

The Allies were left to consolidate the gains they had begun to make in the Middle East. By mid-June, they had wrested control of Iraq from its pro-German leader, Rashid Ali, and had launched a successful invasion of Vichy-held Syria.

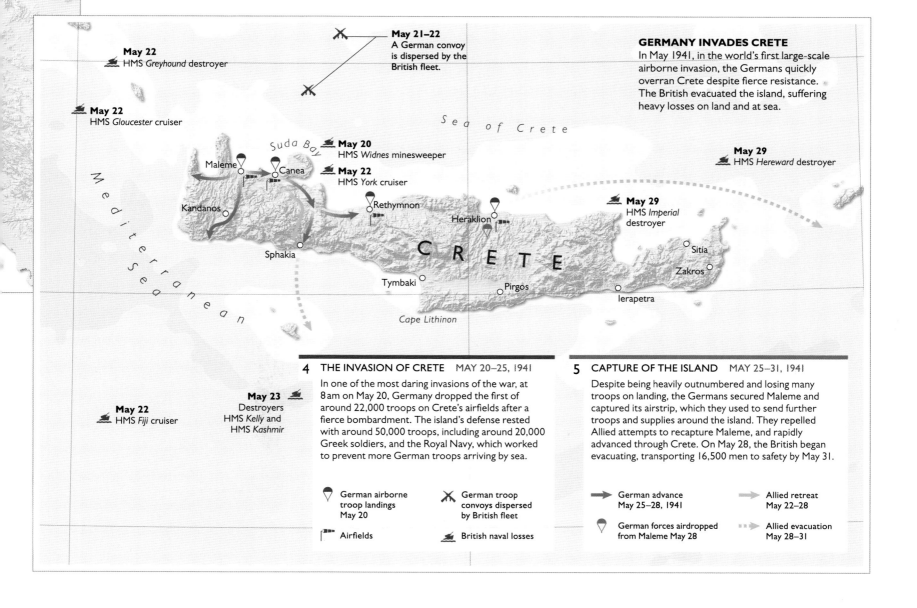

May 22
HMS *Greyhound* destroyer

May 21–22
A German convoy is dispersed by the British fleet.

May 22
HMS *Gloucester* cruiser

GERMANY INVADES CRETE
In May 1941, in the world's first large-scale airborne invasion, the Germans quickly overran Crete despite fierce resistance. The British evacuated the island, suffering heavy losses on land and at sea.

Sea of Crete

Suda Bay

May 20
HMS *Widnes* minesweeper

May 22
HMS *York* cruiser

May 29
HMS *Hereward* destroyer

Maleme
Canea

Kandanos

Rethymnon

May 29
HMS *Imperial* destroyer

Heraklion

Mediterranean Sea

Sphakia

C R E T E

Sitia

Zakros

Tymbaki

Pirgos

Ierapetra

Cape Lithinon

May 22
HMS *Fiji* cruiser

May 23
Destroyers
HMS *Kelly* and
HMS *Kashmir*

4 THE INVASION OF CRETE MAY 20–25, 1941
In one of the most daring invasions of the war, at 8 am on May 20, Germany dropped the first of around 22,000 troops on Crete's airfields after a fierce bombardment. The island's defense rested with around 50,000 troops, including around 20,000 Greek soldiers, and the Royal Navy, which worked to prevent more German troops arriving by sea.

5 CAPTURE OF THE ISLAND MAY 25–31, 1941
Despite being heavily outnumbered and losing many troops on landing, the Germans secured Maleme and captured its airstrip, which they used to send further troops and supplies around the island. They repelled Allied attempts to recapture Maleme, and rapidly advanced through Crete. On May 28, the British began evacuating, transporting 16,500 men to safety by May 31.

- German airborne troop landings May 20
- Airfields
- German troop convoys dispersed by British fleet
- British naval losses

- German advance May 25–28, 1941
- German forces airdropped from Maleme May 28
- Allied retreat May 22–28
- Allied evacuation May 28–31

Celeken

Caspian Sea

WAR IN THE MEDITERRANEAN

From Italy's entry into World War II until 1943, Allied and Axis forces were engaged in a naval battle for control of the Mediterranean. Each strove to destroy the other's supply lines while keeping their own open, and to inflict as much damage as possible on their enemy's ability to wage war at sea.

The Italians entered the war on June 10, 1940, with a totally modernized fleet, replete with fast new battleships, cruisers, and destroyers, which outmatched the British Royal Navy's capabilities in the Mediterranean. They harbored high ambitions in the region, wishing to oust Britain from Egypt—where British troops were stationed to protect the nation's financial and strategic interests—and extend Mussolini's "New Roman Empire" into Nice, Corsica, Tunisia, and the Balkans.

The British, meanwhile, sought to hold the three key points in the Mediterranean—Gibraltar, Malta, and the Suez Canal—that would allow them to keep open supply routes across the Mediterranean and support Greece and Turkey should they enter the war.

Malta, in particular, was crucial (see pp.86–87). Sitting at the gateway to the eastern Mediterranean, it provided a stopping point for Allied convoys and a base from which to attack the Axis supply routes to North Africa.

Air power was vital in keeping the convoys moving, and both sides were able to take advantage of the short distances from their bases in Europe and North Africa, and of the good visibility in the Mediterranean skies. The Italians, however, lacked a fleet air arm, while the British had several aircraft carriers operating in the area.

For much of the first year, the Allies had the upper hand in the Mediterranean, but in December 1941, they lost the advantage when the Italians destroyed several of their battleships.

> "This tiny island [Malta] is a vital feature in the defense of our Middle East position."
>
> HASTINGS ISMAY, BRITISH GENERAL, 1942

THE SUBMARINE WAR

British submarines played a vital role in disrupting the Axis supply lines across the Mediterranean, sinking over 440,000 tons (400,000 metric tons) of Axis shipping between January 1941 and December 1942. German U-boats joined Italian submarines in September 1941 and destroyed 12 merchant vessels, HMS *Ark Royal*, and HMS *Barham* before the end of the year. However, the U-boats were themselves in danger from the Allies' radar-equipped aircraft; none survived the war in the Mediterranean.

Destruction of HMS *Barham*

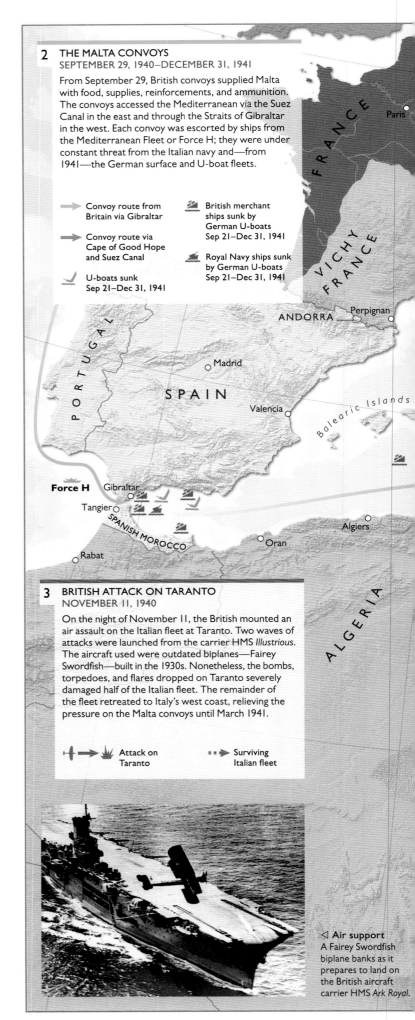

2 THE MALTA CONVOYS
SEPTEMBER 29, 1940–DECEMBER 31, 1941

From September 29, British convoys supplied Malta with food, supplies, reinforcements, and ammunition. The convoys accessed the Mediterranean via the Suez Canal in the east and through the Straits of Gibraltar in the west. Each convoy was escorted by ships from the Mediterranean Fleet or Force H; they were under constant threat from the Italian navy and—from 1941—the German surface and U-boat fleets.

→ Convoy route from Britain via Gibraltar

→ Convoy route via Cape of Good Hope and Suez Canal

⌄ U-boats sunk Sep 21–Dec 31, 1941

British merchant ships sunk by German U-boats Sep 21–Dec 31, 1941

Royal Navy ships sunk by German U-boats Sep 21–Dec 31, 1941

3 BRITISH ATTACK ON TARANTO
NOVEMBER 11, 1940

On the night of November 11, the British mounted an air assault on the Italian fleet at Taranto. Two waves of attacks were launched from the carrier HMS *Illustrious*. The aircraft used were outdated biplanes—Fairey Swordfish—built in the 1930s. Nonetheless, the bombs, torpedoes, and flares dropped on Taranto severely damaged half of the Italian fleet. The remainder of the fleet retreated to Italy's west coast, relieving the pressure on the Malta convoys until March 1941.

→ Attack on Taranto

⇢ Surviving Italian fleet

◁ **Air support**
A Fairey Swordfish biplane banks as it prepares to land on the British aircraft carrier HMS *Ark Royal*.

1 THE BATTLE OF THE MEDITERRANEAN BEGINS
JUNE 11–NOVEMBER 11, 1940

The Italians began the Battle of the Mediterranean with a bombing raid on Malta on June 11, and the British scored their first hit when they sank the Italian destroyer *Espero*, which was escorting a convoy to Benghazi on June 28. The first major clash between the Italian and British fleets occurred on July 9 at the Battle of Calabria. Neither side scored a decisive victory, and both avoided further large-scale action until November.

⟶ Italian bombing raid on Malta, Jun 11, 1940

🚢 British attack on Italian convoy

NAVAL BATTLES

The Mediterranean was the site of the largest conventional sea battles of the war outside the Pacific theater, as the British Royal Navy fought the Italian and German fleets for control of the convoy routes taking vital supplies and reinforcements to North Africa.

KEY

▨ Areas controlled by Vichy France, 1940

▨ Areas controlled by Italy, 1940

▨ Areas under British influence, 1940

▨ Areas controlled by Germany, 1940

☐ Neutral / not yet involved in the war

— Borders, Dec 1940

✕ Major battles

🚢 British fleets

🚢 Italian fleet

TIMELINE

1 2 3 4 5 6

JAN 1940   JUL   JAN 1941   JUL   JAN 1942

Nov 27, 1941 Battle of Cape Spartivento; the Italians attack a convoy en route to Malta.

9 Jul 1940 Calabria

Duisberg Convoy

28–29 Mar 1941 Cape Matapan

Nov 8–9, 1941 Battle of Duisburg Convoy; the Royal Navy sinks all seven merchant ships and a destroyer in a German convoy.

Dec 13, 1941 Battle of Cape Bon; two Italian cruisers carrying supplies to the Luftwaffe in North Africa are sunk.

Mediterranean Fleet

Nov 25, 1941 HMS *Barham* is hit and sunk by three torpedoes; 862 die and 449 survive.

Italian fleet

4 BATTLE OF CAPE MATAPAN
MARCH 28–29, 1941

On March 28, the Italians sent a small fleet to Crete to intercept British convoys that were carrying troops to Greece. However, the RAF spotted the Italian ships, and the British Mediterranean Fleet moved in from Alexandria and opened fire on their enemy. The battle lasted into the night, and the British sank three Italian cruisers, two destroyers, and damaged the battleship *Vittorio Veneto* in a significant victory, after which the Italian fleet avoided major battles.

⟶ Allied troop convoys to Greece

5 STRIKING THE AXIS CONVOYS
APRIL–DECEMBER 1941

The nine warships lost to the Luftwaffe during the defense and evacuation of Crete (see pp.82–83) in May 1941 highlighted just how vulnerable the British navy was in the eastern Mediterranean. However, the Allies continued to strengthen their position in the central Mediterranean, making several successful attacks on Axis convoys—particularly in the Battles of the Duisburg Convoy and Cape Bon—that left the Axis powers in North Africa short of fuel.

⟶ Axis convoy routes

6 THE AXIS POWERS IN THE ASCENDANT
DECEMBER 19–31, 1941

The Allies suffered a setback when ships returning to Alexandria ran into a minefield off the coast of Tripoli on December 19. Two ships were sunk and two were badly damaged, reducing the Allies' ability to threaten the Axis convoys. Later that day, the Italians disabled two battleships and damaged a destroyer in Alexandria harbor. While the Royal Navy recovered, the Italian fleet dominated the central and eastern Mediterranean.

✴ Italian minefield

🔥 Raid on Alexandria Dec 19, 1941

THE SIEGE OF MALTA

The British colony of Malta was strategically important to the Allies, who used the island as a base to attack the Axis forces' supply lines in the central Mediterranean. As a result, neutralizing the island became an Axis priority.

△ **Courage recognized**
Britain's King George VI awarded the George Cross to Malta in April 1942, in recognition of the population's remarkable bravery.

Following Mussolini's declaration of war on Britain on June 10, 1940, the Italian air force launched their first attacks on Malta. The capital city of Valletta, including its port (known as the Grand Harbor), and Hal Far (one of Malta's three airfields) were blitzed. The Luftwaffe soon joined the assault with further aerial bombing.

Starvation threat

The siege reached its climax in spring 1942, when the Germans decided to bomb and starve the island into submission. Food, fuel, and other essentials ran short as convoys trying to reach Valletta were decimated. Facing almost continual air raids, the islanders were housed in caves and tunnels that could withstand bombs, which helped them survive the repeated attacks. Eventually the Allies broke through Axis lines in August 1942 and delivered supplies to the besieged island. Operation Pedestal, as this convoy was known, suffered heavy casualties, but Malta was saved. By the time the siege ended in November 1942, the Axis air forces had attacked the island 3,343 times, winning Malta the unwanted distinction of being the most bombed place on Earth.

△ **Italian air attack on Malta**
An Italian Savoia-Marchetti SM.81 tri-motor bomber makes its bomb run over Malta's Grand Harbor naval base, in Valletta. The *Regia Aeronautica* (Italian air force) had 350 bombers ready for action only 20 minutes' flying time away from the island.

Under fire
Naval officers and ratings line the deck of
the light cruiser HMS *Penelope*, moored in the
Grand Harbor, Valletta. The ship's starboard
side was so severely cratered by bomb
splinters that the crew nicknamed the cruiser
HMS *Pepperpot*.

GERMANY'S WAR WITH THE USSR

Hitler's invasion of the Soviet Union in June 1941 transformed the scale of the war in Europe. Despite putting almost four million soldiers into battle, the Germans failed to achieve the rapid victory they had hoped for.

△ **Soviet armor**
First deployed in 1941, the Soviet T-34 tank proved possibly the most effective armored vehicle of World War II. Over 60,000 were manufactured during the war.

In August 1939, Stalin made a nonaggression pact with Hitler. This allowed the Soviets to extend their territory westward—through the partition of Poland with Nazi Germany, and the occupation of Estonia, Lithuania, Latvia, and Bukovina, taken from Germany's ally Romania. Although Stalin behaved as a friendly neutral to Germany, providing vital supplies that sustained the German war effort, the Soviet economy and the Red Army were meanwhile being mobilized for war.

Planning Operation Barbarossa

For Hitler, no agreement with the Soviet Union could ever be other than temporary. His enduring hostility to Marxism, his belief in the racial inferiority of Slavs, and his aspiration to find *Lebensraum* ("room to live") for German settlers in the East made the Soviet Union a target for aggression. In December 1940, despite still being at war with Britain, Hitler decided to invade the Soviet Union, in a campaign known as Operation Barbarossa. The planning made plain the Nazis' intention to carry out mass murder of civilians, through killing squads and deliberate starvation. Joining the German forces were the armies of its allies, such as Romania, Hungary, and Italy, as well as ideologically motivated anticommunist volunteers from other countries, including France, Spain, and Portugal.

◁ **Ruthless warfare**
German infantry employ a flamethrower to clear a bunker during the invasion of the USSR in 1941. German soldiers had orders to fight especially fiercely against the Red Army.

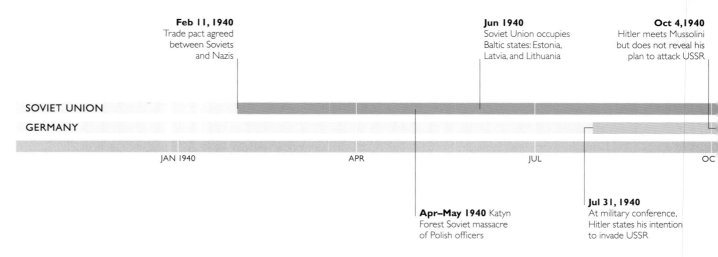

GERMANY INVADES THE EAST
Invading the Soviet Union, Hitler's armies sought to destroy Stalin's Red Army in a series of massive encirclements. But German victories at Smolensk and Kiev, in which hundreds of thousands of Soviet soldiers were taken prisoner, failed to end Soviet resistance. Stopped outside Moscow in December, the Germans were driven back by a Soviet counteroffensive, but they were still in control of a vast area of Soviet territory, from the gates of Leningrad to the Crimea.

Feb 11, 1940 Trade pact agreed between Soviets and Nazis

Jun 1940 Soviet Union occupies Baltic states: Estonia, Latvia, and Lithuania

Oct 4, 1940 Hitler meets Mussolini but does not reveal his plan to attack USSR

SOVIET UNION

GERMANY

JAN 1940   APR   JUL   OC

Apr–May 1940 Katyn Forest Soviet massacre of Polish officers

Jul 31, 1940 At military conference, Hitler states his intention to invade USSR

◁ **Russian winter**
The Wehrmacht experienced great difficulty in coping with the extreme winter conditions encountered in the Soviet Union. In December 1941, a German officer recorded temperatures of −36.5°F (−38°C) outside Moscow.

Early successes for Germany

In 1941, the Soviet Union was not in a very strong military position. The world's first Communist state had achieved rapid industrialization under its dictator Joseph Stalin, but in 1937–1938, during Stalin's "Great Purge" campaign, a substantial percentage of senior Soviet army officers had been denounced as traitors and were shot, imprisoned, or dismissed. The Red Army's mediocre performance in the Winter War against Finland in 1939–1940 had confirmed suspicions that, despite its large size, the army might suffer from poor morale and leadership. Stalin's brutal rule had certainly alienated many of the Soviet people, especially in Ukraine, where a famine killed millions in the 1930s.

Despite ample warnings of an imminent invasion, Stalin's forces were not well deployed when the blow struck in June 1941. The first few months after the launch of Operation Barbarossa brought a series of catastrophic defeats for the Red Army, and Leningrad was placed under siege. The Germans were initially welcomed as liberators in many areas, such as Lithuania and western Ukraine, but brutal mistreatment soon alienated local populations.

The tide turns

After its initial panic, the Soviet regime held together, shifting its heavy industry eastward out of the invaders' reach, and using ruthless measures to compel its soldiers to fight in desperate counterattacks. They also received military supplies from the Allied forces. The Red Army held out against Germany in Moscow, thwarting Hitler's plans

"Communism is a colossal danger for our future … This is a war of annihilation."

ADOLF HITLER, SPEECH TO HIS SENIOR OFFICERS, MARCH 30, 1941

to take the capital within four months. By the time winter had set in, the German army had been significantly weakened and were ill-equipped to stand the perishingly cold weather conditions. A spirit of determination set in among the Soviet people. Meanwhile, in Germany, as the army's casualty list lengthened, civilian morale for the first time showed signs of wavering.

▽ **Prisoners of war**
During Operation Barbarossa over two million Soviet soldiers were taken prisoner. Few survived captivity, most dying of starvation, maltreatment, exposure, and disease.

Apr 13, 1941 Soviet Union and Japan sign neutrality pact

Jul 12, 1941 Britain and Soviet Union agree to ally in fight against Germany

Sep 8, 1941 Siege of Leningrad begins

Sep 19, 1941 Fall of Kiev

Oct 10, 1941 Zhukov given command of defense of Moscow

Oct 11, 1941 First British Arctic convoy reaches Archangel

Dec 5, 1941 German advance halted 15 miles (24km) from central Moscow

Dec 6, 1941 Beginning of Zhukov counterattack that pushes Axis troops back from Moscow

JAN 1941   APR   JUL   OCT   DEC

Dec 18, 1940 Hitler orders planning for invasion of Soviet Union

Jun 22, 1941 Operation Barbarossa, invasion of Soviet Union, launched

May 2, 1941 German Hunger Plan envisages mass starvation of Slavs to free up food for Germans

Jul 16, 1941 Axis forces take Smolensk

Sep 29–30, 1941 About 34,000 Jews massacred by Germans and their allies at Babi Yar

Oct 11, 1941 American Lend-Lease to USSR passed by Congress

Oct 22–24, 1941 Some 30,000 Jews massacred in Odessa

Dec 17, 1941 Germans attack Sevastopol in Crimea

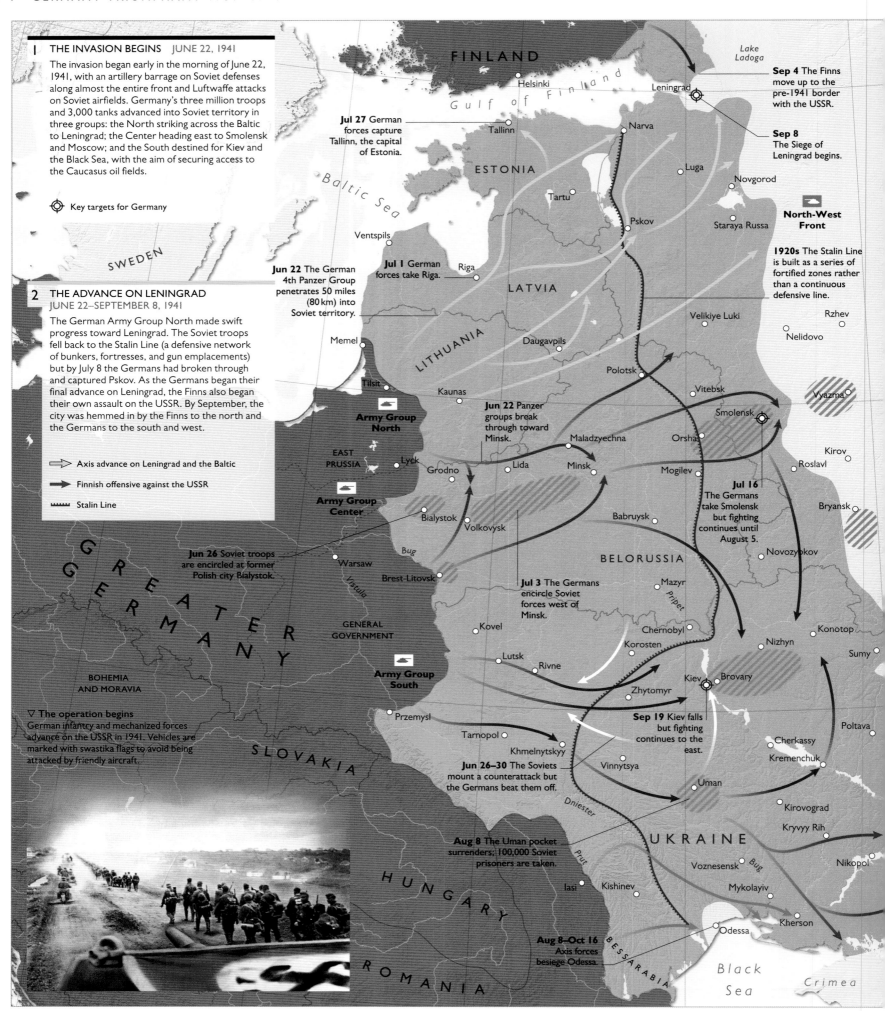

1 THE INVASION BEGINS JUNE 22, 1941

The invasion began early in the morning of June 22, 1941, with an artillery barrage on Soviet defenses along almost the entire front and Luftwaffe attacks on Soviet airfields. Germany's three million troops and 3,000 tanks advanced into Soviet territory in three groups: the North striking across the Baltic to Leningrad; the Center heading east to Smolensk and Moscow; and the South destined for Kiev and the Black Sea, with the aim of securing access to the Caucasus oil fields.

⊕ Key targets for Germany

2 THE ADVANCE ON LENINGRAD
JUNE 22–SEPTEMBER 8, 1941

The German Army Group North made swift progress toward Leningrad. The Soviet troops fell back to the Stalin Line (a defensive network of bunkers, fortresses, and gun emplacements) but by July 8 the Germans had broken through and captured Pskov. As the Germans began their final advance on Leningrad, the Finns also began their own assault on the USSR. By September, the city was hemmed in by the Finns to the north and the Germans to the south and west.

⇨ Axis advance on Leningrad and the Baltic

➤ Finnish offensive against the USSR

⋯⋯ Stalin Line

▽ The operation begins
German infantry and mechanized forces advance on the USSR in 1941. Vehicles are marked with swastika flags to avoid being attacked by friendly aircraft.

Sep 4 The Finns move up to the pre-1941 border with the USSR.

Sep 8 The Siege of Leningrad begins.

Jul 27 German forces capture Tallinn, the capital of Estonia.

North-West Front

1920s The Stalin Line is built as a series of fortified zones rather than a continuous defensive line.

Jun 22 The German 4th Panzer Group penetrates 50 miles (80 km) into Soviet territory.

Jul 1 German forces take Riga.

Jun 22 Panzer groups break through toward Minsk.

Jul 16 The Germans take Smolensk but fighting continues until August 5.

Jun 26 Soviet troops are encircled at former Polish city Bialystok.

Jul 3 The Germans encircle Soviet forces west of Minsk.

Sep 19 Kiev falls but fighting continues to the east.

Jun 26–30 The Soviets mount a counterattack but the Germans beat them off.

Aug 8 The Uman pocket surrenders; 100,000 Soviet prisoners are taken.

Aug 8–Oct 16 Axis forces besiege Odessa.

Army Group North

Army Group Center

Army Group South

EAST PRUSSIA

GENERAL GOVERNMENT

BOHEMIA AND MORAVIA

GREATER GERMANY

SLOVAKIA

HUNGARY

ROMANIA

FINLAND

ESTONIA

LATVIA

LITHUANIA

BELORUSSIA

UKRAINE

BESSARABIA

CRIMEA

Baltic Sea

Gulf of Finland

Lake Ladoga

Black Sea

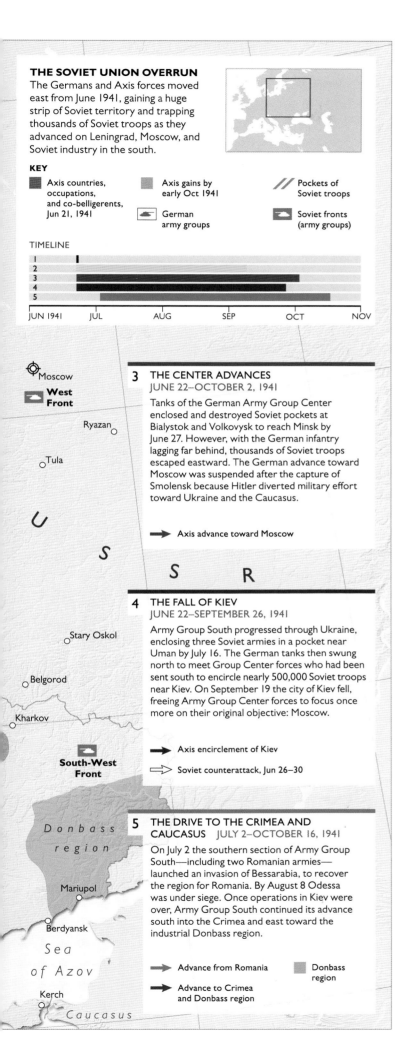

THE SOVIET UNION OVERRUN
The Germans and Axis forces moved east from June 1941, gaining a huge strip of Soviet territory and trapping thousands of Soviet troops as they advanced on Leningrad, Moscow, and Soviet industry in the south.

KEY

▮ Axis countries, occupations, and co-belligerents, Jun 21, 1941

▮ Axis gains by early Oct 1941

// Pockets of Soviet troops

◼ German army groups

◼ Soviet fronts (army groups)

TIMELINE

```
1
2
3
4
5
JUN 1941   JUL   AUG   SEP   OCT   NOV
```

3 THE CENTER ADVANCES
JUNE 22–OCTOBER 2, 1941

Tanks of the German Army Group Center enclosed and destroyed Soviet pockets at Bialystok and Volkovysk to reach Minsk by June 27. However, with the German infantry lagging far behind, thousands of Soviet troops escaped eastward. The German advance toward Moscow was suspended after the capture of Smolensk because Hitler diverted military effort toward Ukraine and the Caucasus.

→ Axis advance toward Moscow

4 THE FALL OF KIEV
JUNE 22–SEPTEMBER 26, 1941

Army Group South progressed through Ukraine, enclosing three Soviet armies in a pocket near Uman by July 16. The German tanks then swung north to meet Group Center forces who had been sent south to encircle nearly 500,000 Soviet troops near Kiev. On September 19 the city of Kiev fell, freeing Army Group Center forces to focus once more on their original objective: Moscow.

→ Axis encirclement of Kiev

⇨ Soviet counterattack, Jun 26–30

5 THE DRIVE TO THE CRIMEA AND CAUCASUS JULY 2–OCTOBER 16, 1941

On July 2 the southern section of Army Group South—including two Romanian armies—launched an invasion of Bessarabia, to recover the region for Romania. By August 8 Odessa was under siege. Once operations in Kiev were over, Army Group South continued its advance south into the Crimea and east toward the industrial Donbass region.

→ Advance from Romania

→ Advance to Crimea and Donbass region

▮ Donbass region

OPERATION BARBAROSSA

In June 1941, Hitler launched Operation Barbarossa, the invasion of Soviet territories. Ranged across a vast front that stretched 1,000 miles (1,600 km) from the Baltic to the Black Sea, Germany and its Axis allies advanced at an extraordinary pace, besieging Leningrad and reaching within striking distance of Moscow by early October.

The peace between Germany and the USSR that had been agreed in the Nazi–Soviet non-aggression pact of August 1939 (see pp.32–33) proved to be short-lived. Hitler believed the Slav people to be *Untermenschen* ("sub-humans") and wanted to take the USSR's vast territories for *Lebensraum* ("living space") for Germans. Operation Barbarossa, named after the Holy Roman Emperor who pursued German dominance in Europe, was Hitler's plan to invade the USSR with three million Germans and one million men from Axis Hungary, Romania, Slovakia, and Italy; Finland joined as a co-belligerent.

The German commanders were confident that Operation Barbarossa would be over quickly; they thought the Red Army was weak, and that German air power would provide a superior edge. The campaign did indeed start well: by July, the Germans had advanced 400 miles (640 km) and defeated large groups of Soviet forces around Minsk and Smolensk. The Red Army suffered enormous losses as Stalin refused to acknowledge the extent of the danger and willingly sacrificed men in defense of the cities.

By October, Kiev had fallen, Leningrad was surrounded with the help of the Finns (see pp.94–95), and Axis forces had reached the Crimea. However, the German troops were exhausted, their supply lines were stretched and, as they prepared to advance on Moscow, they were about to face the deadly cold of a Russian winter.

> *"The ideology that dominates us is in diametrical contradiction to that of Soviet Russia."*
>
> ADOLF HITLER, MAY 1935

STALIN'S PARANOIA AND PURGE OF THE ARMY

By the time of the German invasion in 1941, the Red Army was fatally short of experienced personnel; only a quarter of its officers had been in post for over a year. Paranoid about political opponents, Stalin had embarked on a Great Purge of the Communist party in 1936. By 1939, three of the five Marshals of the Soviet Union (right) were dead, along with hundreds of army officers.

GERMANY AND USSR AT HOME

Germany and the USSR both geared their economies to meet the demands of total war. The Soviets were more effective, manufacturing weapons that were cheaper and easier to make than those produced by the Germans.

△ **Fighting for the fatherland**
Armbands such as this were issued to members of the *Volkssturm* ("People's Militia"), a German militia formed of civilians conscripted into service.

The Soviet people suffered extreme deprivation as they fought what was christened the "Great Patriotic War." A ruthless focus on arms production meant that most civilians lived in near-starvation, working a 66-hour week while receiving half the rations of their German counterparts. At least 18 million civilians died, but a mixture of coercion, hatred for the "Fascist enemy," and Russian nationalism kept the people working.

In Germany, despite superior resources, production did not match the pace of the Soviets until the war industry was reorganized in 1942 (see pp.174–175). After this, German output rose steeply, with women playing an increasingly important role. Rationing was introduced from 1939, but privations increased from 1943 as Allied bombing raids intensified and disrupted food supplies. The civilian death toll rose, and millions were evacuated from German cities.

Dictatorships at war

The two totalitarian regimes both conducted forced population transfers. Germany imported more than 7 million civilians and prisoners of war from the occupied countries for forced labor, while the USSR transported hundreds of factories and their workers east beyond the Ural mountains to protect their war industry from the German advance in the west. Both regimes also exploited slave labor from concentration camps and gulags (Soviet prison camps).

▷ **Life goes on**
Young girls play with their dolls in a Munich street, undeterred by the shells stacked in front of their homes. As the Allied bombing raids increased in number and intensity, thousands of children were evacuated from German cities to keep them safe.

Komsomol workers' brigade
A forewoman of a Komsomol (All-Union Leninist Young Communist League) workers' brigade supervises rifle assembly at a Soviet military plant. Arms production in both the Soviet Union and Germany reached its peak in 1944.

THE SIEGE OF LENINGRAD

One of the most grueling blockades in history, the siege of Leningrad saw hundreds of thousands of civilians perish as the Germans and their Finnish allies encircled the city, bombarding and starving its people for 872 days.

The German army advanced on Leningrad in August 1941, two months after their invasion of the USSR. By September 8, the Germans in the south and the Finns in the north began closing in on the city. They severed all rail routes and land routes, cutting the city's supply lines.

In late September, Hitler changed tactics and issued orders to besiege Leningrad, to bombard and starve the people rather than accept surrender, and to raze the city to the ground. For over two years, heavy artillery fire and aerial bombing destroyed Leningrad's infrastructure, and an estimated 650,000 people died from artillery attacks, air raids, starvation, disease, and hypothermia.

Survival against the odds

Cut off from its major supply routes, Leningrad's survival depended entirely on Lake Ladoga to the northeast, the only means by which supplies could reach the city from elsewhere in the Soviet Union. Each summer, barges carried food, fuel, and munitions across the lake to the city. Each winter, when the lake froze over, provisions were driven across it on narrow and dangerous ice roads. Known as the "Road of Life," the route was also the main evacuation route for over one million civilians escaping the starving city. Soviet antiaircraft artillery and fighter planes protected the road against attack, but as the Germans regularly attacked convoys, travel was still dangerous.

Soviet forces made several attempts to break the blockade. An advance by the Leningrad and Volkhov Fronts in August–October 1942 ended in stalemate, but in Operation Iskra ("Spark") in January 1943 the Soviets broke through German lines to create a corridor to the city on the southern shore of Lake Ladoga. A railway was built in the corridor, providing faster transport than the Lake Lagoda routes. In January 1944, the Soviets finally broke the blockade. They drove out the Germans and recaptured the Moscow–Leningrad railway on January 27, ending the 872-day siege. In 1945, the city was awarded the Order of Lenin and in 1965 it was given the title the Hero City of the Soviet Union.

◁ **Attacking the city**
Soldiers of the Wehrmacht observe German attacks on Leningrad's defensive line in late 1941.

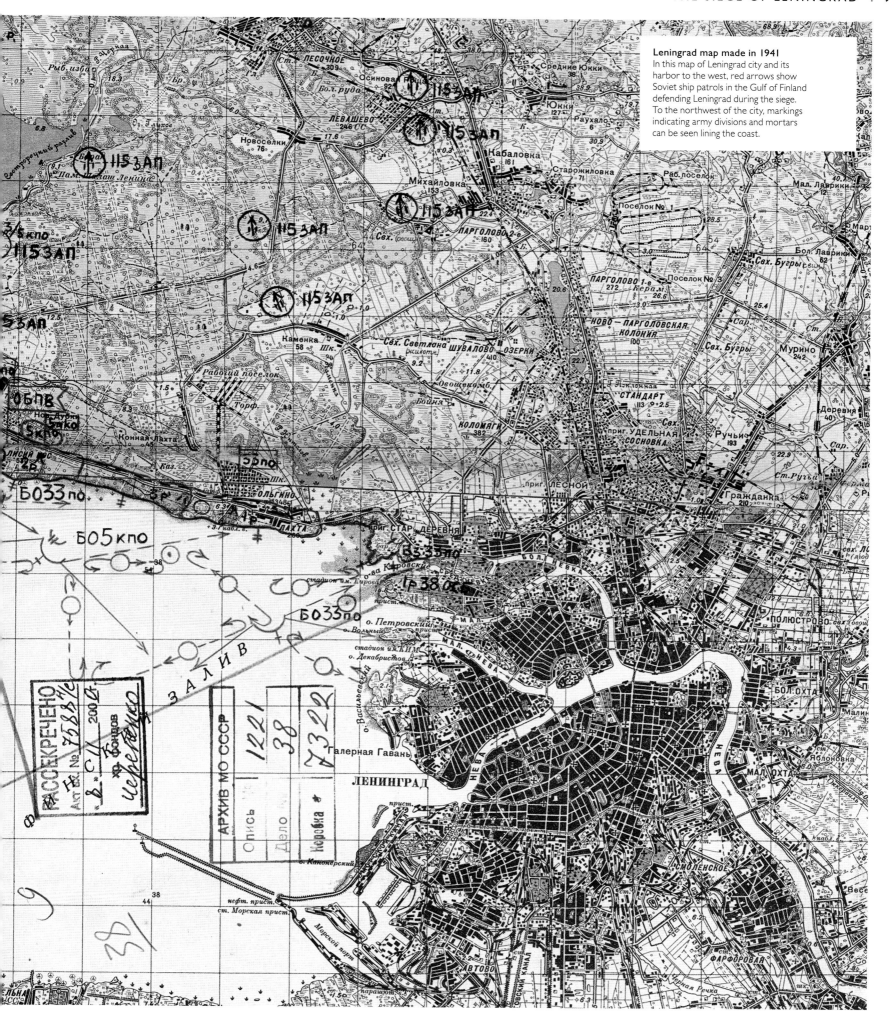

Leningrad map made in 1941
In this map of Leningrad city and its harbor to the west, red arrows show Soviet ship patrols in the Gulf of Finland defending Leningrad during the siege. To the northwest of the city, markings indicating army divisions and mortars can be seen lining the coast.

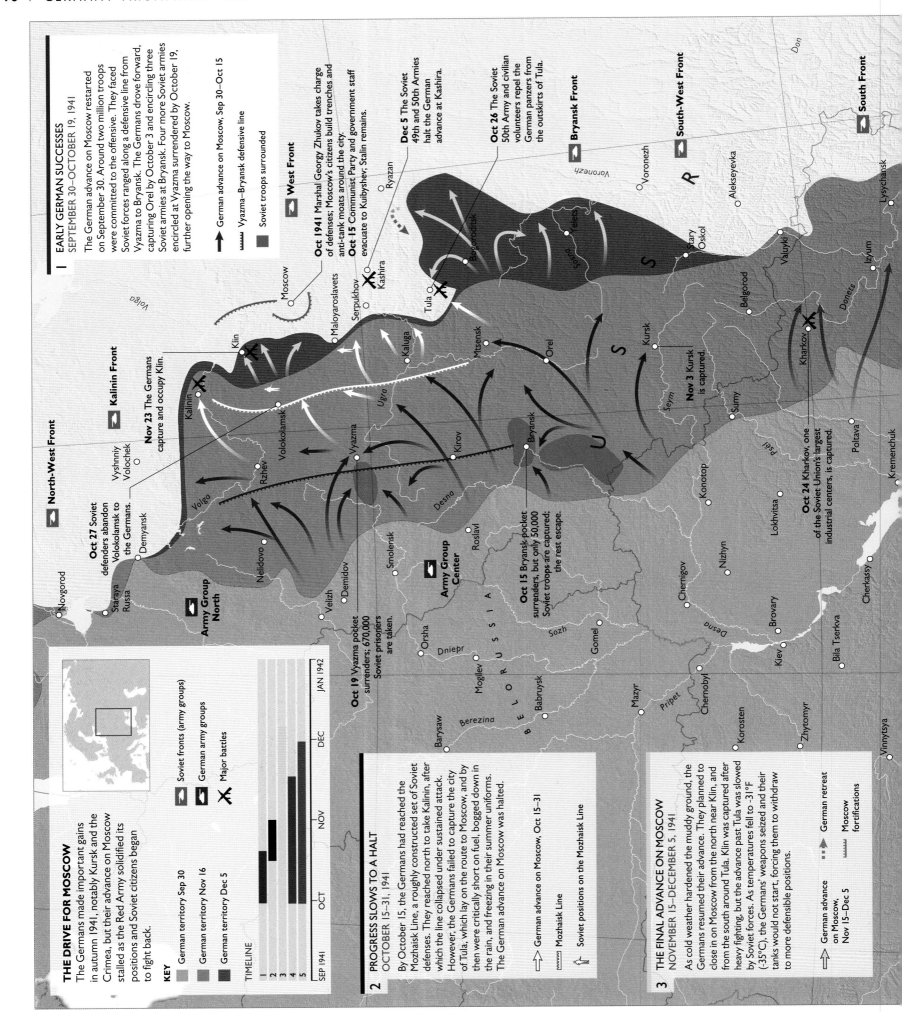

THE DRIVE FOR MOSCOW

The Germans made important gains in autumn 1941, notably Kursk and the Crimea, but their advance on Moscow stalled as the Red Army solidified its positions and Soviet citizens began to fight back.

KEY

- German territory Sep 30
- German territory Nov 16
- German territory Dec 5

- Soviet fronts (army groups)
- German army groups
- Major battles

TIMELINE

SEP 1941   OCT   NOV   DEC   JAN 1942

1 | EARLY GERMAN SUCCESSES
SEPTEMBER 30–OCTOBER 19, 1941

The German advance on Moscow restarted on September 30. Around two million troops were committed to the offensive. They faced Soviet forces ranged along a defensive line from Vyazma to Bryansk. The Germans drove forward, capturing Orel by October 3 and encircling three Soviet armies at Bryansk. Four more Soviet armies encircled at Vyazma surrendered by October 19, further opening the way to Moscow.

→ German advance on Moscow, Sep 30–Oct 15
⌐⌐⌐ Vyazma–Bryansk defensive line
■ Soviet troops surrounded

West Front

Oct 1941 Marshal Georgy Zhukov takes charge of defenses; Moscow's citizens build trenches and anti-tank moats around the city.

Oct 15 Communist Party and government staff evacuate to Kuibyshev; Stalin remains.

Dec 5 The Soviet 49th and 50th Armies halt the German advance at Kashira.

Oct 26 The Soviet 50th Army and civilian volunteers repel the German panzers from the outskirts of Tula.

Bryansk Front

South-West Front

North-West Front

Kalinin Front

Nov 23 The Germans capture and occupy Klin.

Oct 27 Soviet defenders abandon Volokolamsk to the Germans.

Army Group North

Oct 19 Vyazma pocket surrenders; 670,000 Soviet prisoners are taken.

Army Group Center

Oct 15 Bryansk pocket surrenders, but only 50,000 Soviet troops are captured; the rest escape.

Nov 3 Kursk is captured.

Oct 24 Kharkov, one of the Soviet Union's largest industrial centers, is captured.

South Front

2 | PROGRESS SLOWS TO A HALT
OCTOBER 15–31, 1941

By October 15, the Germans had reached the Mozhaisk Line, a roughly constructed set of Soviet defenses. They reached north to take Kalinin, after which the line collapsed under sustained attack. However, the Germans failed to capture the city of Tula, which lay on the route to Moscow, and by then were critically short on fuel, bogged down in the rain, and freezing in their summer uniforms. The German advance on Moscow was halted.

→ German advance on Moscow, Oct 15–31
⌐⌐⌐ Mozhaisk Line
✈ Soviet positions on the Mozhaisk Line

3 | THE FINAL ADVANCE ON MOSCOW
NOVEMBER 15–DECEMBER 5, 1941

As cold weather hardened the muddy ground, the Germans resumed their advance. They planned to close in on Moscow from the north near Klin, and from the south around Tula. Klin was captured after heavy fighting, but the advance past Tula was slowed by Soviet forces. As temperatures fell to -31°F (-35°C), the Germans' weapons seized and their tanks would not start, forcing them to withdraw to more defensible positions.

⇢ German advance on Moscow, Nov 15–Dec 5
➤ German retreat
⌐⌐⌐ Moscow fortifications
⇨ German advance on Moscow, Nov 15–Dec 5

THE GERMAN ADVANCE ON MOSCOW

After the success of Operation Barbarossa, Germany's invasion of the USSR, Hitler launched Operation Typhoon, a renewed push on Moscow. He believed it would be "the last, great, decisive battle of the war." The campaign, however, ended in a retreat that dealt a serious blow to Hitler's plan to destroy the Soviet Union.

During Operation Barbarossa (see pp.90–91), the Germans considered Moscow less important than other strategic targets. The push on the capital was delayed by the advance into the Ukraine for resources—a source of dispute between Hitler and his generals—and recommenced only in late September 1941, by which time the heavy rains were turning the roads into quagmires. This, along with fuel shortages and a failure to replace damaged tanks, slowed German progress and sapped morale. Moreover, it seemed that despite the capture of millions of Red Army troops, the USSR had millions more in reserve. The Red Army was regularly replenished, and even joined by civilian

volunteers. By December 5, 1941, the Germans had failed to capture Moscow, and winter was upon them. Unprepared for the bitter cold and fatally overstretched against a determined Red Army, their casualties mounted. By Christmas that year, over 100,000 German soldiers had frostbite and over 250,000 had died.

In the south, meanwhile, the Germans had succeeded in taking the Crimea, but their advance on the Caucasus was hampered, as in the north, by overstretched supply lines and exhausted troops. When Red Army soldiers recaptured Rostov at the end of November, they highlighted just how vulnerable the Germans really were.

EVACUATION OF SOVIET INDUSTRIAL AREAS

The German advance threatened Soviet industries producing vital ammunition (pictured above) and other war materiel. In 1941, the Soviets began to evacuate factories and their workforces to safety in Siberia and beyond the Ural mountains. Over 1,500 large plants were relocated.

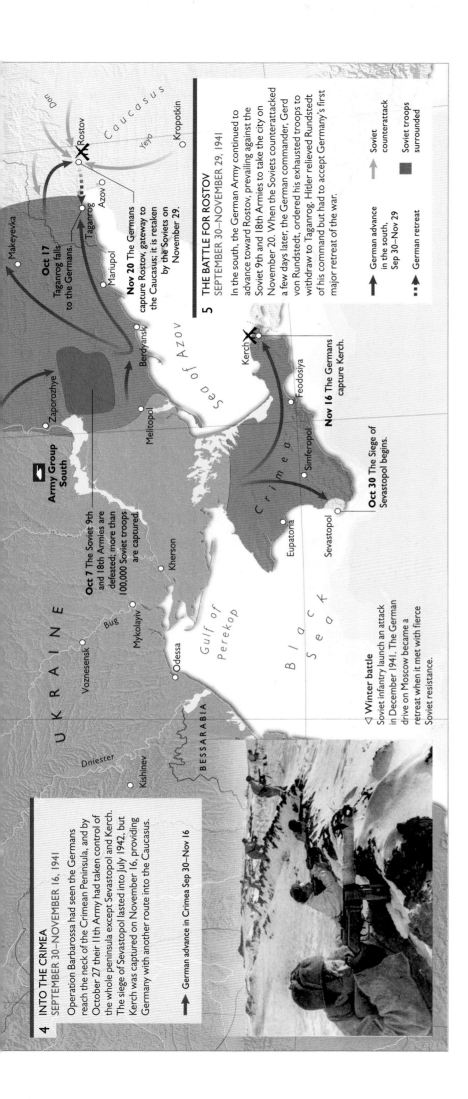

4 INTO THE CRIMEA
SEPTEMBER 30–NOVEMBER 16, 1941

Operation Barbarossa had seen the Germans reach the neck of the Crimean Peninsula, and by October 27 their 11th Army had taken control of the whole peninsula except Sevastopol and Kerch. The siege of Sevastopol lasted into July 1942, but Kerch was captured on November 16, providing Germany with another route into the Caucasus.

→ German advance in Crimea Sep 30–Nov 16

5 THE BATTLE FOR ROSTOV
SEPTEMBER 30–NOVEMBER 29, 1941

In the south, the German Army continued to advance toward Rostov, prevailing against the Soviet 9th and 18th Armies to take the city on November 20. When the Soviets counterattacked a few days later, the German commander, Gerd von Rundstedt, ordered his exhausted troops to withdraw to Taganrog. Hitler relieved Rundstedt of his command but had to accept Germany's first major retreat of the war.

→ German advance in the south, Sep 30–Nov 29
⤏ German retreat
⇧ Soviet counterattack
▮ Soviet troops surrounded

Oct 17 Taganrog falls to the Germans.

Nov 20 The Germans capture Rostov, gateway to the Caucasus; it is retaken by the Soviets on November 29.

Oct 7 The Soviet 9th and 18th Armies are defeated; more than 100,000 Soviet troops are captured.

Nov 16 The Germans capture Kerch.

Oct 30 The Siege of Sevastopol begins.

Army Group South

Map labels: Don, Caucasus, Rostov, Azov, Kropotkin, Yeya, Taganrog, Makeyevka, Mariupol, Berdyansk, Sea of Azov, Kerch, Feodosiya, Crimea, Simferopol, Eupatoria, Sevastopol, Melitopol, Zaporozhye, Kherson, Mykolaiv, Bug, Voznesensk, Odessa, Gulf of Perekop, Black Sea, Kishinev, Dniester, BESSARABIA, UKRAINE

△ Winter battle
Soviet infantry launch an attack in December 1941. The German drive on Moscow became a retreat when it met with fierce Soviet resistance.

MASSACRES IN THE EAST

The German invasion of the Soviet Union in June 1941 brought millions more Jews under Hitler's control. Within weeks, special German units had begun to massacre the Russian Jews, killing up to one million in only five months.

△ **Head of the SS**
Heinrich Himmler was in charge of the *Einsatzgruppen*, and in 1941 he was tasked with implementing Hitler's "Final Solution" to exterminate all European Jews.

The German forces that invaded the USSR as part of Operation Barbarossa (see pp.90–91) were accompanied by *Einsatzgruppen*—special units of the SS tasked with exterminating the Jews who now lived in German-occupied territory. Four groups consisting of around 4,000 men fanned out across the Baltic States, Belorussia, and Ukraine. The killings began at Minsk on July 13, 1941, when over 1,000 Jews were shot, and accelerated as summer progressed. The death squads often used ravines on the edge of large towns, where Jews were shot and the bodies pushed over the edge and buried.

On September 26, the German military command in Kiev ordered the liquidation of the Jewish population. Over 33,000 Jews, believing they were being relocated out of the Kiev ghetto, were taken to the nearby Babi Yar ravine. There, an *Einsatzgruppe*, aided by Ukrainian collaborators, machine-gunned them down. It was the worst single massacre of a campaign that killed between 800,000 and one million Jews by the end of the year, when shootings were replaced by mobile gas vans and extermination camps using either carbon monoxide or hydrogen cyanide (Zyklon B).

△ **Operation Barbarossa**
A German armored unit moves forward during the early stages of Operation Barbarossa—the military invasion of the Soviet Union. The rapid advance of the German army trapped hundreds of thousands of Jews in Nazi-controlled territory.

Post-massacre search
Relatives of massacre victims search for the corpses of their loved ones at Kerch, in Crimea. In fall and winter 1941, the *Einsatzgruppen* brutally murdered an estimated 7,000 Jews from Kerch and its surroundings.

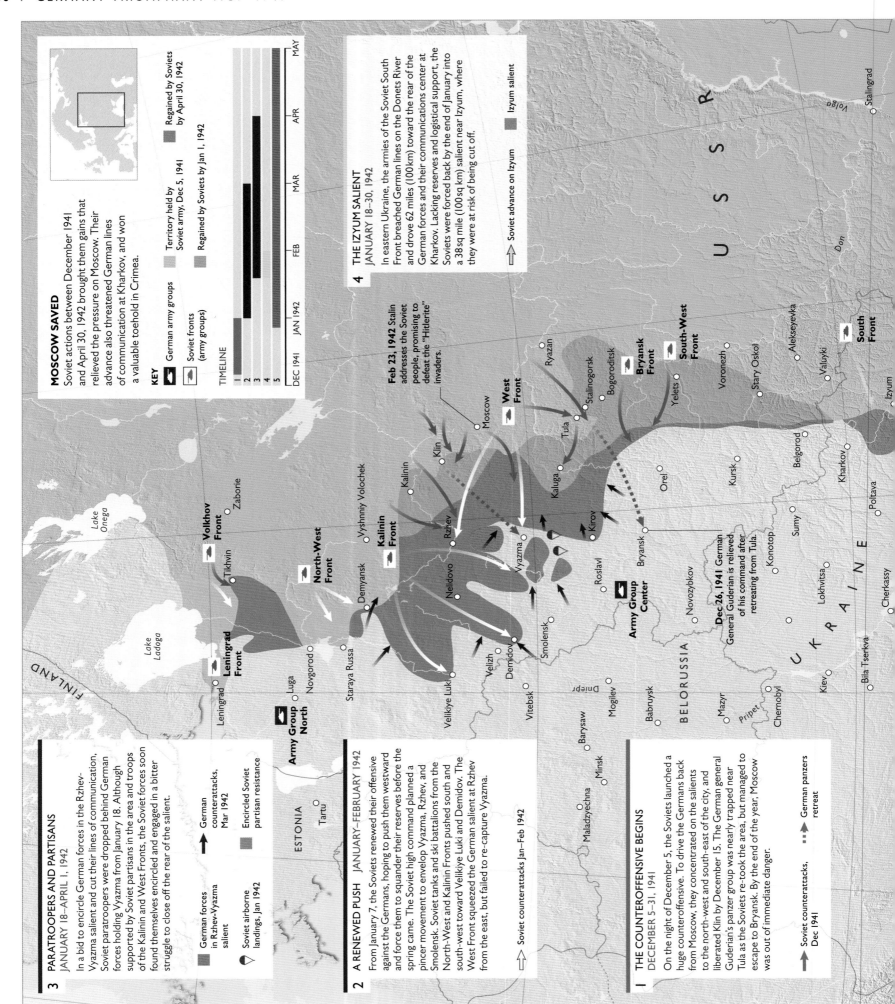

MOSCOW SAVED

Soviet actions between December 1941 and April 30, 1942 brought them gains that relieved the pressure on Moscow. Their advance also threatened German lines of communication at Kharkov, and won a valuable toehold in Crimea.

KEY

- German army groups
- Soviet fronts (army groups)
- Territory held by Soviet army, Dec 5, 1941
- Regained by Soviets by Jan 1, 1942
- Regained by Soviets by April 30, 1942

TIMELINE

DEC 1941 | JAN 1942 | FEB | MAR | APR | MAY

1
2
3
4
5

4 THE IZYUM SALIENT
JANUARY 18–30, 1942

In eastern Ukraine, the armies of the Soviet South Front breached German lines on the Donets River and drove 62 miles (100km) toward the rear of the German forces and their communications center at Kharkov. Lacking reserves and logistical support, the Soviets were forced back by the end of January into a 38sq mile (100sq km) salient near Izyum, where they were at risk of being cut off.

⇨ Soviet advance on Izyum

■ Izyum salient

3 PARATROOPERS AND PARTISANS
JANUARY 18–APRIL 1, 1942

In a bid to encircle German forces in the Rzhev-Vyazma salient and cut their lines of communication, Soviet paratroopers were dropped behind German forces holding Vyazma from January 18. Although supported by Soviet partisans in the area and troops of the Kalinin and West Fronts, the Soviet forces soon found themselves encircled and engaged in a bitter struggle to close off the rear of the salient.

- German forces in Rzhev-Vyazma salient
- Soviet airborne landings, Jan 1942
- German counterattacks, Mar 1942
- Encircled Soviet partisan resistance

2 A RENEWED PUSH JANUARY–FEBRUARY 1942

From January 7, the Soviets renewed their offensive against the Germans, hoping to push them westward and force them to squander their reserves before the spring came. The Soviet high command planned a pincer movement to envelop Vyazma, Rzhev, and Smolensk. Soviet tanks and ski battalions from the North-West and Kalinin Fronts pushed south and south-west toward Velikiye Luki and Demidov. The West Front squeezed the German salient at Rzhev from the east, but failed to re-capture Vyazma.

⇨ Soviet counterattacks Jan–Feb 1942

1 THE COUNTEROFFENSIVE BEGINS
DECEMBER 5–31, 1941

On the night of December 5, the Soviets launched a huge counteroffensive. To drive the Germans back from Moscow, they concentrated on the salients to the north-west and south-east of the city, and liberated Klin by December 15. The German general General Guderian's panzer group was nearly trapped near Tula as the Soviets re-took the area, but managed to escape to Bryansk. By the end of the year, Moscow was out of immediate danger.

➤ Soviet counterattacks, Dec 1941

⇢ German panzers retreat

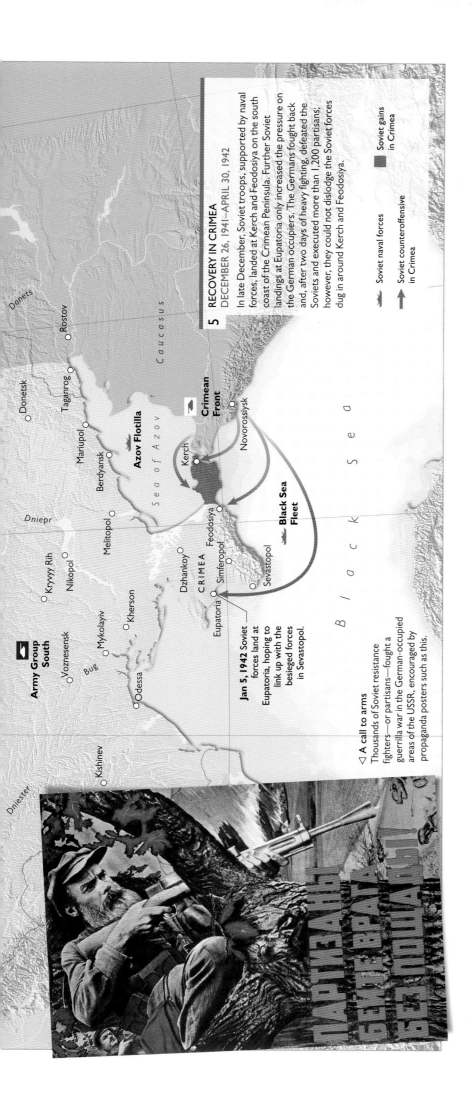

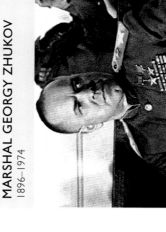

MARSHAL GEORGY ZHUKOV
1896–1974

One of Stalin's most capable commanders, Zhukov organized the defense of Leningrad and Moscow, and led the counterattack at Moscow in December 1941. At Stalingrad, his counteroffensive destroyed the German 6th Army in the city. It was Zhukov who accepted the German surrender in Berlin in 1945. He was made a Marshal of the Soviet Union in 1943, but was sidelined after the war because Stalin saw him as a threat.

5 RECOVERY IN CRIMEA
DECEMBER 26, 1941–APRIL 30, 1942

In late December, Soviet troops, supported by naval forces, landed at Kerch and Feodosiya on the south coast of the Crimean Peninsula. Further Soviet landings at Eupatoria only increased the pressure on the German occupiers. The Germans fought back and, after two days of heavy fighting, defeated the Soviets and executed more than 1,200 partisans; however, they could not dislodge the Soviet forces dug in around Kerch and Feodosiya.

➤ Soviet naval forces

⬆ Soviet counteroffensive in Crimea

■ Soviet gains in Crimea

Jan 5, 1942 Soviet forces land at Eupatoria, hoping to link up with the besieged forces in Sevastopol.

▽ **A call to arms**
Thousands of Soviet resistance fighters—or partisans—fought a guerrilla war in the German-occupied areas of the USSR, encouraged by propaganda posters such as this.

THE RELIEF OF MOSCOW

The Soviets launched a counteroffensive against the German invaders in December 1941, making early gains at several points along the vast Eastern Front and freeing Moscow from immediate danger. However, they could not force a full retreat, and the front remained largely static from February 1942 until a new German offensive began in June.

In late September 1941, Hitler had aimed to take Moscow before the start of the bitter Russian winter (see pp.96–97). Despite German successes at Vyazma and Bryansk on the way to the capital, Soviet opposition forced the German armies to stall and dig in for the winter around Moscow. The German commanders assumed that the Red Army was as depleted as their own. Stalin, however, had armies in reserve in Siberia, most of which he brought forward to bolster the Soviet forces on the Eastern Front.

From December 5, the Soviet commanders launched a huge counteroffensive against the Germans, with operations running along the whole front. To the north, the Volkhov Front managed to regain the strategically important town of Tikhvin, which eased the supply routes to besieged Leningrad (see pp.94–95). Near Moscow,

the German salients around Klin and Tula were quickly pushed back, but it took longer to shift the Germans away from the center of the front. To the south, the Red Army re-took Kerch in Crimea and created a substantial salient at Izyum. The Germans, under orders to defend their positions, continued to fight and made several assaults in March; by April the Soviet counteroffensive had all but ground to a halt. Both sides had suffered huge casualties. The Soviet forces had advanced more than 62 miles (100km) in some places, but they had not been able to force the Germans into a general retreat or re-take the German communications centers at Vyazma and Kharkov. The Soviet failure to follow through their counteroffensive ultimately led to a successful German offensive in the south, and to the Battle of Stalingrad (see pp.148–153).

THE WIDENING WAR 1942

THE US ENTERED THE WAR IN EUROPE AND THE PACIFIC, WHILE IN THE EAST THE SOVIETS STEMMED THE GERMAN ADVANCE. MEANWHILE, THE NAZIS REDOUBLED THEIR PERSECUTION OF THE JEWS.

AMERICA AND JAPAN GO TO WAR

In December 1941, Japan embarked on war with the US, which was blocking its imperial ambitions in Asia. Initial military victories left the Japanese in control of a wide area of Asia and the Pacific, but it faced a fierce US fight back.

△ **Man of influence**
Admiral Isoroku Yamamoto masterminded the surprise Japanese aircraft carrier attack on Pearl Harbor. However, he personally doubted that Japan could win a war against the US.

Throughout the 1930s, the US did not openly confront Japan about its increasing militarism in Asia, such as its invasion of China in 1937. However, following the rapid victory of Hitler's forces in Europe in 1940, Japan stepped up its aggression, recognizing the opportunity to seize Southeast Asia from the European colonial powers—the defeated French and Dutch, and the weakened British.

Hostilities on the rise

Increasingly committed to backing Britain against Nazi Germany, US President Roosevelt accepted responsibility for resisting Japan's expansion in Southeast Asia—a task the British could no longer perform. Japanese encroachment on French Indochina in 1940–1941 met an aggressive response from the US, which placed Japan under economic blockade and demanded that it abandon its ambitions to establish an empire in Asia.

Japan's response was to push ahead with a plan for the conquest of Southeast Asia. They believed a surprise attack on the US fleet at Pearl Harbor, Hawaii, would remove the US temporarily from the equation, allowing

Japan sufficient time to establish a far-flung defensive perimeter in the Pacific. The Japanese hoped their position would then be strong enough to deter the US from retaliation, leaving Japan securely in control of an Asian empire. However, this was a disastrous miscalculation. In reality, their surprise attack on Pearl Harbor on December 7, 1941, so outraged American popular opinion that the US was implacably committed to go to war against Japan and fight to the bitter end, regardless of cost or casualties. The following day, the US declared war against Japan.

Racial hatred of the Japanese was a feature of American attitudes to the Pacific War from the outset, and the mistreatment of Allied prisoners of war by the Japanese provided further fuel for anti-Japanese sentiment.

Germany declares war

Four days after the attack on Pearl Harbor, Hitler declared war on the US, bringing the US into the European conflict. Since Roosevelt saw US interests as more vitally threatened by the power of Nazi Germany than

◁ **Promoting war production**
A US propaganda poster links the Nazi swastika to the Japanese national flag, showing Germany and Japan as a common enemy.

JAPAN'S WAVE OF CONQUEST

For six months after the attack on Pearl Harbor, Japanese forces advanced victoriously through Southeast Asia and across the Pacific. Malaysia and Singapore, the Philippines, the Dutch East Indies, and Burma all fell to Japan, while landings in New Guinea threatened Australia. However, by the end of 1942 the battle of Midway and the extensive fighting at Guadalcanal, both in the Pacific, showed that the Americans were capable of defeating the Japanese both on land and at sea.

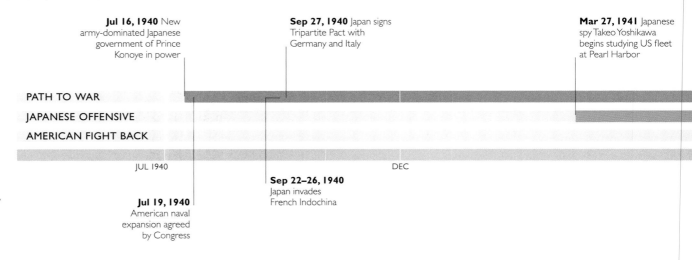

Jul 16, 1940 New army-dominated Japanese government of Prince Konoye in power

Sep 27, 1940 Japan signs Tripartite Pact with Germany and Italy

Mar 27, 1941 Japanese spy Takeo Yoshikawa begins studying US fleet at Pearl Harbor

PATH TO WAR

JAPANESE OFFENSIVE

AMERICAN FIGHT BACK

JUL 1940

DEC

Sep 22–26, 1940 Japan invades French Indochina

Jul 19, 1940 American naval expansion agreed by Congress

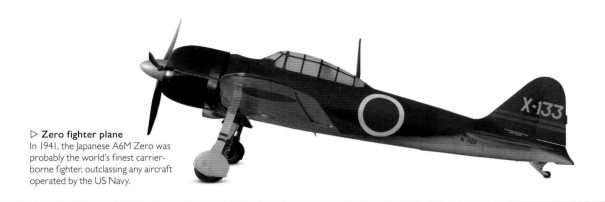

▷ **Zero fighter plane**
In 1941, the Japanese A6M Zero was probably the world's finest carrier-borne fighter, outclassing any aircraft operated by the US Navy.

▽ **Disaster at Pearl Harbor**
Fire spreads through the battleship USS *West Virginia* during the Japanese air strike at Pearl Harbor. Four American battleships were sunk in the attack.

> *"We will gain the inevitable triumph—so help us God."*
>
> PRESIDENT ROOSEVELT, DECEMBER 8, 1941

by Japanese aggression, he decided to prioritize the struggle against Germany in Europe, which slowed the American fight in the Pacific.

In contrast to the Western Allies, who established joint commands and strategies, Japan and Germany fought two totally separate wars. Japan remained at peace with the Soviet Union, Germany's bitterest enemy, until August 1945, when the Soviet Union declared war on Japan after Japan refused to capitulate.

Successes and failures

The initial Japanese offensives in Southeast Asia were very successful against the colonial empires, which lacked both morale and military strength. The spectacle of the British surrender at Singapore, in particular, delivered a fatal blow to European racial prestige. However, in British India only a minority of activists in the nationalist independence movement sided with Nazi Germany and Japan. Overall, the Japanese failed to capitalize on potential support from their fellow Asians, proving at least as exploitative and oppressive as the European colonialists they supplanted.

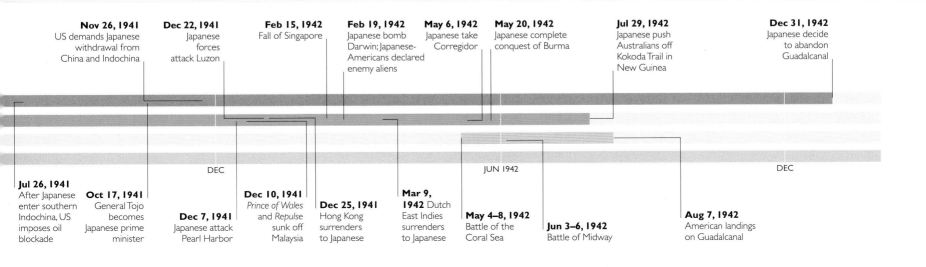

Nov 26, 1941
US demands Japanese withdrawal from China and Indochina

Dec 22, 1941
Japanese forces attack Luzon

Feb 15, 1942
Fall of Singapore

Feb 19, 1942
Japanese bomb Darwin; Japanese-Americans declared enemy aliens

May 6, 1942
Japanese take Corregidor

May 20, 1942
Japanese complete conquest of Burma

Jul 29, 1942
Japanese push Australians off Kokoda Trail in New Guinea

Dec 31, 1942
Japanese decide to abandon Guadalcanal

DEC

JUN 1942

DEC

Jul 26, 1941
After Japanese enter southern Indochina, US imposes oil blockade

Oct 17, 1941
General Tojo becomes Japanese prime minister

Dec 7, 1941
Japanese attack Pearl Harbor

Dec 10, 1941
Prince of Wales and *Repulse* sunk off Malaysia

Dec 25, 1941
Hong Kong surrenders to Japanese

Mar 9, 1942 Dutch East Indies surrenders to Japanese

May 4–8, 1942
Battle of the Coral Sea

Jun 3–6, 1942
Battle of Midway

Aug 7, 1942
American landings on Guadalcanal

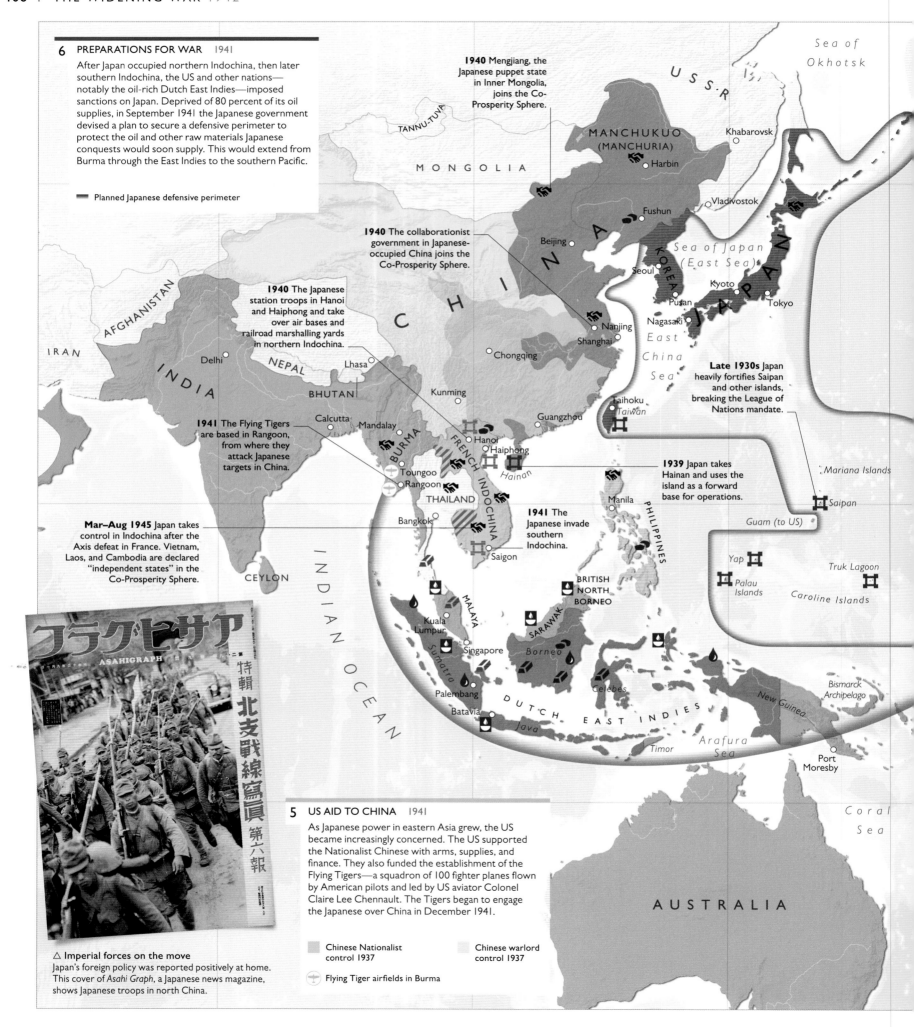

6 PREPARATIONS FOR WAR 1941

After Japan occupied northern Indochina, then later southern Indochina, the US and other nations—notably the oil-rich Dutch East Indies—imposed sanctions on Japan. Deprived of 80 percent of its oil supplies, in September 1941 the Japanese government devised a plan to secure a defensive perimeter to protect the oil and other raw materials Japanese conquests would soon supply. This would extend from Burma through the East Indies to the southern Pacific.

▬▬ Planned Japanese defensive perimeter

1940 Mengjiang, the Japanese puppet state in Inner Mongolia, joins the Co-Prosperity Sphere.

1940 The collaborationist government in Japanese-occupied China joins the Co-Prosperity Sphere.

1940 The Japanese station troops in Hanoi and Haiphong and take over air bases and railroad marshalling yards in northern Indochina.

1941 The Flying Tigers are based in Rangoon, from where they attack Japanese targets in China.

Mar–Aug 1945 Japan takes control in Indochina after the Axis defeat in France. Vietnam, Laos, and Cambodia are declared "independent states" in the Co-Prosperity Sphere.

Late 1930s Japan heavily fortifies Saipan and other islands, breaking the League of Nations mandate.

1939 Japan takes Hainan and uses the island as a forward base for operations.

1941 The Japanese invade southern Indochina.

△ **Imperial forces on the move**
Japan's foreign policy was reported positively at home. This cover of *Asahi Graph*, a Japanese news magazine, shows Japanese troops in north China.

5 US AID TO CHINA 1941

As Japanese power in eastern Asia grew, the US became increasingly concerned. The US supported the Nationalist Chinese with arms, supplies, and finance. They also funded the establishment of the Flying Tigers—a squadron of 100 fighter planes flown by American pilots and led by US aviator Colonel Claire Lee Chennault. The Tigers began to engage the Japanese over China in December 1941.

▢ Chinese Nationalist control 1937

▢ Chinese warlord control 1937

✈ Flying Tiger airfields in Burma

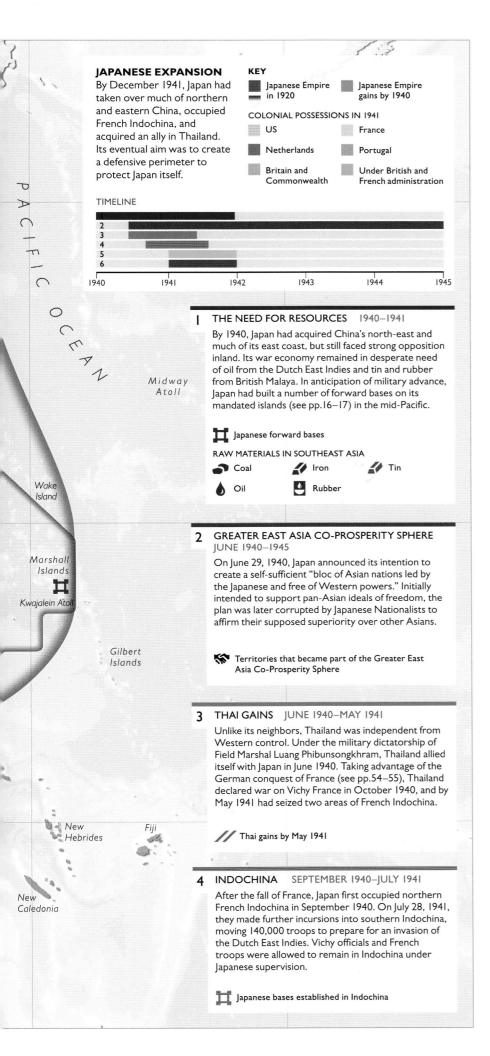

JAPANESE EXPANSION

By December 1941, Japan had taken over much of northern and eastern China, occupied French Indochina, and acquired an ally in Thailand. Its eventual aim was to create a defensive perimeter to protect Japan itself.

KEY

- ■ Japanese Empire in 1920
- ■ Japanese Empire gains by 1940

COLONIAL POSSESSIONS IN 1941

- US
- Netherlands
- Britain and Commonwealth
- France
- Portugal
- Under British and French administration

TIMELINE

	1940	1941	1942	1943	1944	1945
2						
3						
4						
5						
6						

1 THE NEED FOR RESOURCES 1940–1941

By 1940, Japan had acquired China's north-east and much of its east coast, but still faced strong opposition inland. Its war economy remained in desperate need of oil from the Dutch East Indies and tin and rubber from British Malaya. In anticipation of military advance, Japan had built a number of forward bases on its mandated islands (see pp.16–17) in the mid-Pacific.

- Japanese forward bases

RAW MATERIALS IN SOUTHEAST ASIA

- Coal
- Iron
- Tin
- Oil
- Rubber

2 GREATER EAST ASIA CO-PROSPERITY SPHERE
JUNE 1940–1945

On June 29, 1940, Japan announced its intention to create a self-sufficient "bloc of Asian nations led by the Japanese and free of Western powers." Initially intended to support pan-Asian ideals of freedom, the plan was later corrupted by Japanese Nationalists to affirm their supposed superiority over other Asians.

- Territories that became part of the Greater East Asia Co-Prosperity Sphere

3 THAI GAINS JUNE 1940–MAY 1941

Unlike its neighbors, Thailand was independent from Western control. Under the military dictatorship of Field Marshal Luang Phibunsongkhram, Thailand allied itself with Japan in June 1940. Taking advantage of the German conquest of France (see pp.54–55), Thailand declared war on Vichy France in October 1940, and by May 1941 had seized two areas of French Indochina.

- Thai gains by May 1941

4 INDOCHINA SEPTEMBER 1940–JULY 1941

After the fall of France, Japan first occupied northern French Indochina in September 1940. On July 28, 1941, they made further incursions into southern Indochina, moving 140,000 troops to prepare for an invasion of the Dutch East Indies. Vichy officials and French troops were allowed to remain in Indochina under Japanese supervision.

- Japanese bases established in Indochina

JAPANESE AMBITIONS

After the invasion of China, Japan looked elsewhere to expand its empire. By 1941, it became clear that Japan had substantial imperial and economic ambitions in Southeast Asia, particularly regarding the American and European colonies in the region.

Despite its size and its extensive empire, Japan had only limited access to vital raw materials. The oil, coal, steel, iron, and minerals it needed to drive its economy all had to be imported. Japan's conquest of Manchuria in 1931 (see pp.22–23) provided much-needed coal, but demand for oil, tin, and rubber had yet to be met. Japan's incursions into eastern Siberia in the 1930s were defeated by the USSR. The Japanese government thereafter looked toward the resource-rich European colonial territories in Southeast Asia.

Japan used discontent against the colonial powers to propose the Greater East Asia Co-Prosperity Sphere in 1940, promising "Asia for the Asiatics" and independence from oppression (see pp.222–223). Japan also allied with independent Thailand in June 1940, and began to plan for war in April–May 1941. It prepared for an invasion of Southeast Asia by occupying French Indochina in July 1941—an act that prompted an economic embargo of Japan by the Western powers. Faced with impending oil shortages and potential economic collapse, Japan prepared for a larger war, planning its conquests and its defense of a greatly enlarged empire.

> *"I fear we would become a third-class nation after two or three years if we just sat tight."*
>
> PRIME MINISTER HIDEKI TOJO, NOVEMBER 5, 1941

THE ECONOMIC EMBARGO AGAINST JAPAN

In order to deter Japanese military expansion in China and Southeast Asia, the US, Britain, and the Dutch East Indies restricted and then ended sales of oil, iron ore, and steel to Japan. Without oil, the Japanese military would have quickly ground to a halt. The Japanese referred to these embargoes as the ABCD (American-British-Chinese-Dutch) encirclement. In April 1941 they began to draw up plans to seize resource-rich Malaya and the Dutch East Indies.

Dutch soldiers destroy oil reserves in Java

Ready for battle
Cadets from the Imperial Naval Academy, Etajima, near Hiroshima, undergo training in September 1941. They were probably prospective members of the *Kaigun Tokubetsu Rikusentai*—the Japanese equivalent of the Marines.

JAPAN GOES TO WAR

In July 1941, the US imposed sanctions on Japan in retaliation for their occupation of French Indochina, and Britain and the Dutch East Indies followed suit. For Japan, making concessions was not an option.

Faced with a trade embargo that threatened to strangle their economy, Japan's leaders came to the conclusion that war was the only option remaining open to them. As Admiral Osami Nagano, Chief of Staff of the Imperial Japanese Navy, declared in September 1941, "Since Japan is unavoidably facing national ruin whether it decides to fight the United States or submit to its demands, it must by all means choose to fight." The Japanese leadership also believed that time was against them, and that the longer they delayed in mobilizing for war, the smaller their prospects of success would be.

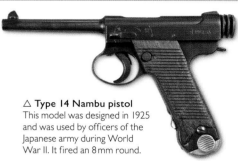

△ **Type 14 Nambu pistol**
This model was designed in 1925 and was used by officers of the Japanese army during World War II. It fired an 8mm round.

The Japanese war plan

Japan's leaders planned to strike in Southeast Asia in order to win control of the US-held Philippines, the oil-rich Dutch East Indies, and the British colonies of Malaya and Singapore. The Japanese recognized that such a move would almost certainly provoke an armed response by American forces, and so decided to take preventative action by planning a surprise attack on the US Pacific Fleet at Pearl Harbor, Hawaii, on December 7, 1941 (see pp.110–111). The Japanese intention was that, by turning the central and southwestern Pacific into an impregnable military bastion, they would force the US into fighting an island-by-island war of attrition, the cost of which would break the Americans' will to fight. However, the reality of the situation proved to be very different.

HIDEKI TOJO
1884–1948

Born in Tokyo to a family of the former samurai caste, Hideki Tojo enlisted as a cadet in the Imperial Japanese Army in 1899 and rose to the rank of general. He went on to serve as prime minister of Japan from 1941 to 1944, and during this time he ordered the infamous attack on US forces at Pearl Harbor. At the end of the war he was arrested shortly after a botched suicide attempt and was tried for war crimes. He was executed in 1948.

PEARL HARBOR

US president Franklin D. Roosevelt called December 7, 1941, the day Japan attacked Pearl Harbor, "a date which will live in infamy." At the time, US negotiations with Japan were still in progress and no declaration of war had been made. The attack transformed the war from a European battle into a worldwide conflict.

Tensions between the US and Japan had been rising since the invasion of Manchuria in 1931 (see pp.22–23). The subsequent expansion of Japanese influence in the region put the US on alert and prompted it to move its Pacific Fleet to Pearl Harbor, Hawaii, in 1940, as a deterrent. When Japan took control of Indochina in mid-1941, the US ceased all exports to the country, so Japan set its sights on the oil-rich Dutch East Indies. The US opened negotiations with Japan that summer in an attempt to improve relations, but no agreement was reached. The Japanese Prime Minister Fumimaro Konoe resigned on October 16, to be replaced by a more hawkish military government under General Hideki Tojo. Final exchanges between the two sides

proved fruitless, and on December 1, Japanese Emperor Hirohito approved a "war against United States, Great Britain, and Holland."

Japanese strategists knew that the US base in Pearl Harbor was vulnerable and had made plans earlier in the year for a strike. Success would prevent the Pacific Fleet from interfering in the Japanese conquest of the Dutch East Indies and Malaya and buy time for Japan to increase its strength in the region. Japan hoped an attack would undermine American morale, forcing the US to seek a compromise peace. When the attack came, the Americans were unprepared, but the effect was the opposite of Japan's hopes. The US public became united behind a total war to the finish.

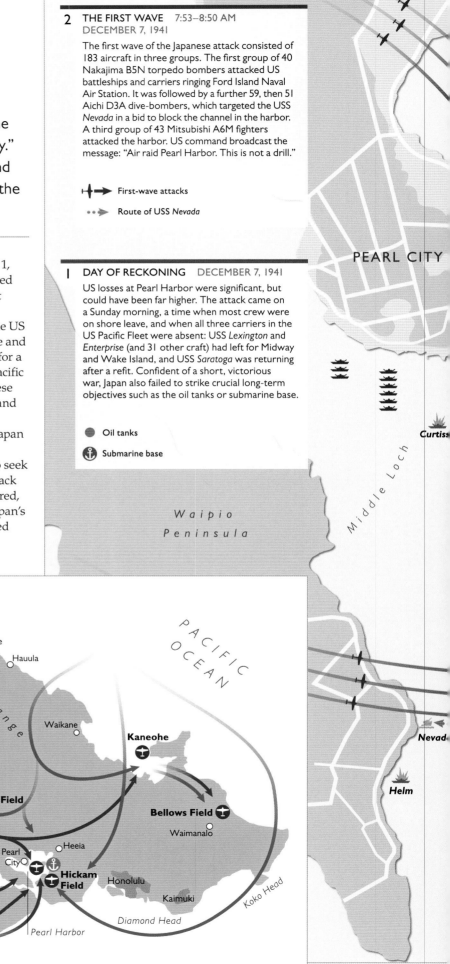

2 THE FIRST WAVE 7:53–8:50 AM
DECEMBER 7, 1941

The first wave of the Japanese attack consisted of 183 aircraft in three groups. The first group of 40 Nakajima B5N torpedo bombers attacked US battleships and carriers ringing Ford Island Naval Air Station. It was followed by a further 59, then 51 Aichi D3A dive-bombers, which targeted the USS *Nevada* in a bid to block the channel in the harbor. A third group of 43 Mitsubishi A6M fighters attacked the harbor. US command broadcast the message: "Air raid Pearl Harbor. This is not a drill."

↦➡ First-wave attacks

•••➤ Route of USS *Nevada*

1 DAY OF RECKONING DECEMBER 7, 1941

US losses at Pearl Harbor were significant, but could have been far higher. The attack came on a Sunday morning, a time when most crew were on shore leave, and when all three carriers in the US Pacific Fleet were absent: USS *Lexington* and *Enterprise* (and 31 other craft) had left for Midway and Wake Island, and USS *Saratoga* was returning after a refit. Confident of a short, victorious war, Japan also failed to strike crucial long-term objectives such as the oil tanks or submarine base.

● Oil tanks

⚓ Submarine base

ROUTE OF THE ATTACK

The Japanese Striking Force, made up of six aircraft carriers carrying more than 400 aircraft, 14 other ships, and eight oil tankers, left the Kurile Islands in northern Japan on November 26 and assembled north of Hawaii. It was supported by 23 submarines from ports in mainland Japan. The plan was to launch two waves of air attacks, targeting not just the vessels in Pearl Harbor but also oil tanks, dockyards, air and naval bases, and military barracks across the island. The first wave of Japanese aircraft was detected by US radar, which mistook it for the scheduled arrival of six B-17 bombers from California.

KEY

➡ First-wave attack 7:53 am

➡ Second-wave attack 8:50 am

🧍 Targeted barracks

✈ Targeted air bases

⚓ Targeted naval base

▪ Key urban areas

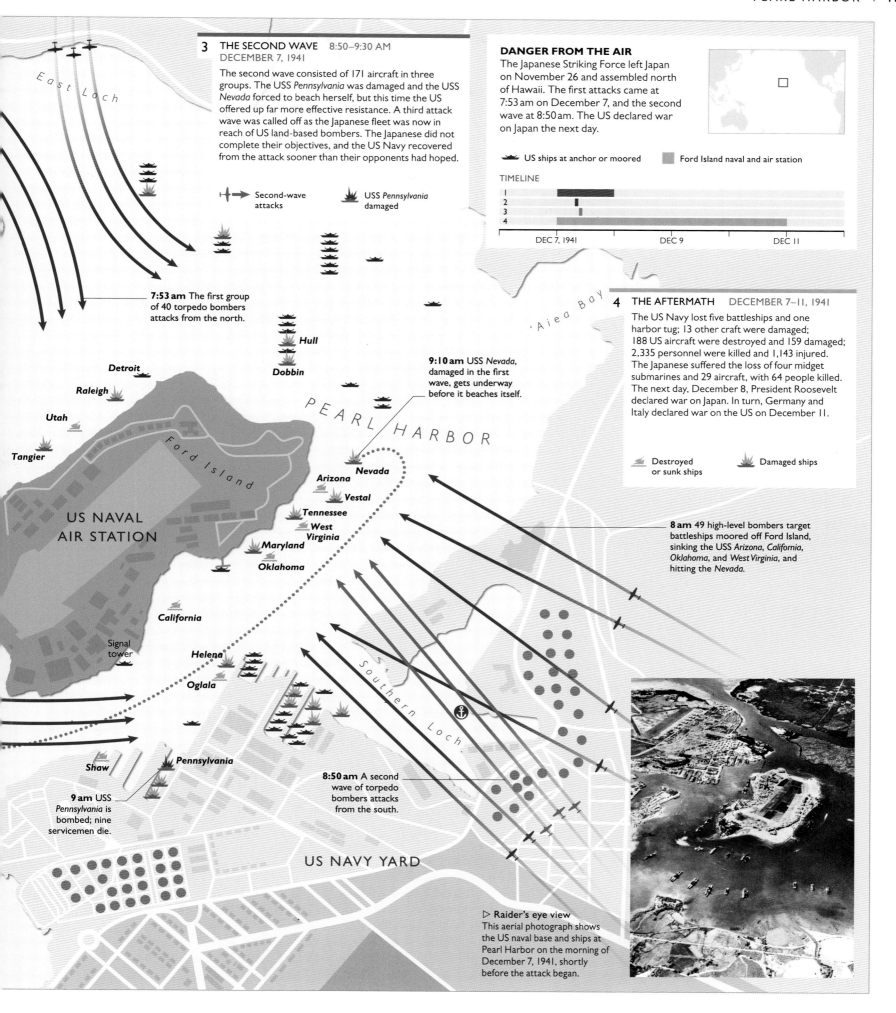

3 THE SECOND WAVE 8:50–9:30 AM
DECEMBER 7, 1941

The second wave consisted of 171 aircraft in three groups. The USS *Pennsylvania* was damaged and the USS *Nevada* forced to beach herself, but this time the US offered up far more effective resistance. A third attack wave was called off as the Japanese fleet was now in reach of US land-based bombers. The Japanese did not complete their objectives, and the US Navy recovered from the attack sooner than their opponents had hoped.

⊢→ Second-wave attacks

💥 USS *Pennsylvania* damaged

7:53 am The first group of 40 torpedo bombers attacks from the north.

East Loch

Hull

Detroit

Raleigh

Utah

Tangier

Dobbin

9:10 am USS *Nevada*, damaged in the first wave, gets underway before it beaches itself.

PEARL HARBOR

'Aiea Bay

DANGER FROM THE AIR
The Japanese Striking Force left Japan on November 26 and assembled north of Hawaii. The first attacks came at 7:53 am on December 7, and the second wave at 8:50 am. The US declared war on Japan the next day.

🚢 US ships at anchor or moored

▨ Ford Island naval and air station

TIMELINE
1
2
3
4

DEC 7, 1941 · · · · · · · DEC 9 · · · · · · · DEC 11

4 THE AFTERMATH DECEMBER 7–11, 1941

The US Navy lost five battleships and one harbor tug; 13 other craft were damaged; 188 US aircraft were destroyed and 159 damaged; 2,335 personnel were killed and 1,143 injured. The Japanese suffered the loss of four midget submarines and 29 aircraft, with 64 people killed. The next day, December 8, President Roosevelt declared war on Japan. In turn, Germany and Italy declared war on the US on December 11.

🚢 Destroyed or sunk ships

💥 Damaged ships

Ford Island

US NAVAL AIR STATION

Nevada

Arizona

Vestal

Tennessee

West Virginia

Maryland

Oklahoma

California

Signal tower

Helena

Oglala

8 am 49 high-level bombers target battleships moored off Ford Island, sinking the USS *Arizona*, *California*, *Oklahoma*, and *West Virginia*, and hitting the *Nevada*.

Southern Loch

⚓

8:50 am A second wave of torpedo bombers attacks from the south.

Shaw

Pennsylvania

9 am USS *Pennsylvania* is bombed; nine servicemen die.

US NAVY YARD

▷ **Raider's eye view**
This aerial photograph shows the US naval base and ships at Pearl Harbor on the morning of December 7, 1941, shortly before the attack began.

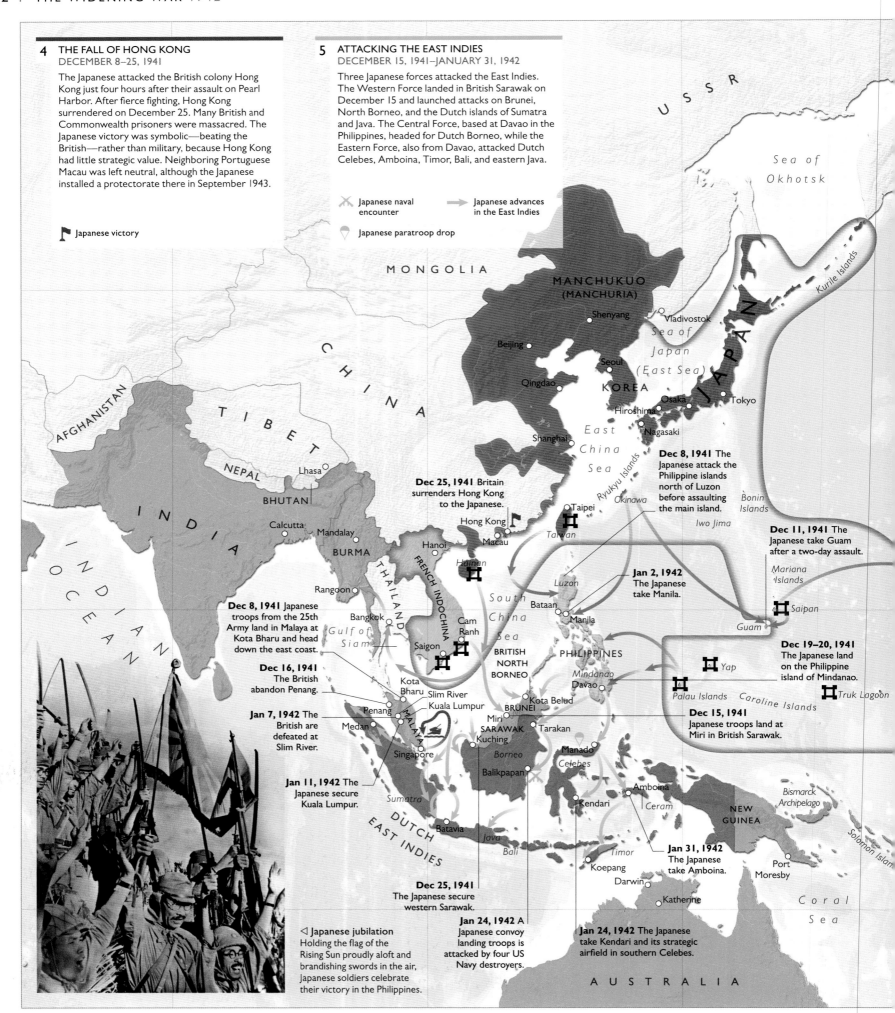

4 THE FALL OF HONG KONG
DECEMBER 8–25, 1941

The Japanese attacked the British colony Hong Kong just four hours after their assault on Pearl Harbor. After fierce fighting, Hong Kong surrendered on December 25. Many British and Commonwealth prisoners were massacred. The Japanese victory was symbolic—beating the British—rather than military, because Hong Kong had little strategic value. Neighboring Portuguese Macau was left neutral, although the Japanese installed a protectorate there in September 1943.

⚑ Japanese victory

5 ATTACKING THE EAST INDIES
DECEMBER 15, 1941–JANUARY 31, 1942

Three Japanese forces attacked the East Indies. The Western Force landed in British Sarawak on December 15 and launched attacks on Brunei, North Borneo, and the Dutch islands of Sumatra and Java. The Central Force, based at Davao in the Philippines, headed for Dutch Borneo, while the Eastern Force, also from Davao, attacked Dutch Celebes, Amboina, Timor, Bali, and eastern Java.

✈ Japanese naval encounter
➔ Japanese advances in the East Indies
⛱ Japanese paratroop drop

Dec 25, 1941 Britain surrenders Hong Kong to the Japanese.

Dec 8, 1941 The Japanese attack the Philippine islands north of Luzon before assaulting the main island.

Dec 11, 1941 The Japanese take Guam after a two-day assault.

Jan 2, 1942 The Japanese take Manila.

Dec 8, 1941 Japanese troops from the 25th Army land in Malaya at Kota Bharu and head down the east coast.

Dec 16, 1941 The British abandon Penang.

Jan 7, 1942 The British are defeated at Slim River.

Dec 19–20, 1941 The Japanese land on the Philippine island of Mindanao.

Dec 15, 1941 Japanese troops land at Miri in British Sarawak.

Jan 11, 1942 The Japanese secure Kuala Lumpur.

Dec 25, 1941 The Japanese secure western Sarawak.

Jan 24, 1942 A Japanese convoy landing troops is attacked by four US Navy destroyers.

Jan 31, 1942 The Japanese take Amboina.

Jan 24, 1942 The Japanese take Kendari and its strategic airfield in southern Celebes.

◁ **Japanese jubilation**
Holding the flag of the Rising Sun proudly aloft and brandishing swords in the air, Japanese soldiers celebrate their victory in the Philippines.

Map labels: USSR, Sea of Okhotsk, Kurile Islands, MONGOLIA, MANCHUKUO (MANCHURIA), Shenyang, Vladivostok, Sea of Japan (East Sea), JAPAN, Beijing, Seoul, KOREA, Osaka, Tokyo, Qingdao, Hiroshima, Nagasaki, AFGHANISTAN, TIBET, Shanghai, East China Sea, NEPAL, Lhasa, BHUTAN, Bonin Islands, Calcutta, Mandalay, INDIA, Hong Kong, Macau, Taipei, Taiwan, Ryukyu Islands, Okinawa, Iwo Jima, BURMA, Hanoi, Hainan, Luzon, Mariana Islands, Rangoon, INDIAN OCEAN, THAILAND, FRENCH INDOCHINA, South China Sea, Bataan, Manila, Saipan, Guam, Bangkok, Cam Ranh, Saigon, Gulf of Siam, Kota Bharu, Slim River, BRITISH NORTH BORNEO, PHILIPPINES, Mindanao, Davao, Yap, Palau Islands, Caroline Islands, Truk Lagoon, Kuala Lumpur, Kota Belud, Penang, Medan, MALAYA, Miri, SARAWAK, Kuching, BRUNEI, Tarakan, Manado, Celebes, Singapore, Borneo, Balikpapan, Amboina, Ceram, Bismarck Archipelago, Kendari, NEW GUINEA, Sumatra, DUTCH EAST INDIES, Batavia, Java, Bali, Timor, Koepang, Darwin, Port Moresby, Solomon Islands, Katherine, Coral Sea, AUSTRALIA

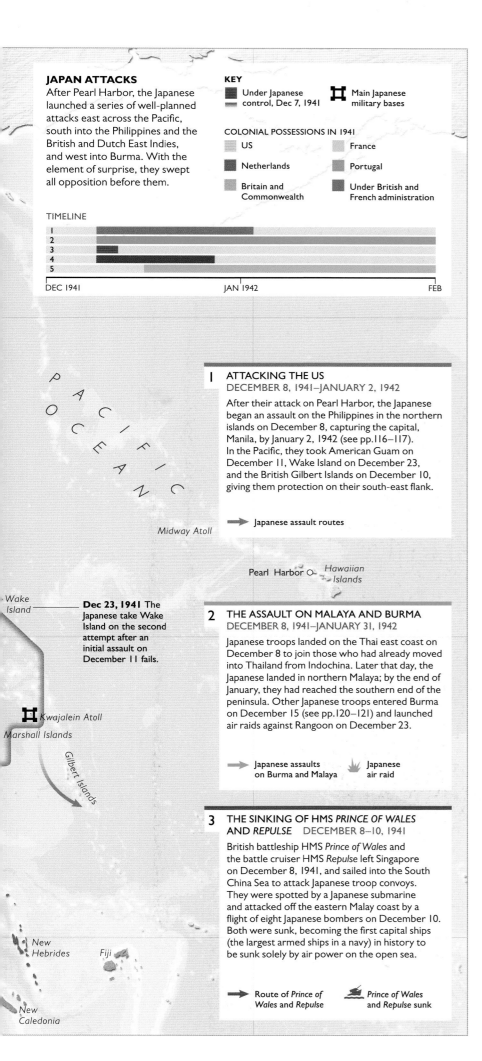

JAPAN ATTACKS

After Pearl Harbor, the Japanese launched a series of well-planned attacks east across the Pacific, south into the Philippines and the British and Dutch East Indies, and west into Burma. With the element of surprise, they swept all opposition before them.

KEY

■ Under Japanese control, Dec 7, 1941

⊞ Main Japanese military bases

COLONIAL POSSESSIONS IN 1941

US
France
Netherlands
Portugal
Britain and Commonwealth
Under British and French administration

TIMELINE

1
2
3
4
5

DEC 1941   JAN 1942   FEB

1 ATTACKING THE US
DECEMBER 8, 1941–JANUARY 2, 1942

After their attack on Pearl Harbor, the Japanese began an assault on the Philippines in the northern islands on December 8, capturing the capital, Manila, by January 2, 1942 (see pp.116–117). In the Pacific, they took American Guam on December 11, Wake Island on December 23, and the British Gilbert Islands on December 10, giving them protection on their south-east flank.

→ Japanese assault routes

Midway Atoll

Pearl Harbor ○ *Hawaiian Islands*

Wake Island — **Dec 23, 1941** The Japanese take Wake Island on the second attempt after an initial assault on December 11 fails.

⊞ *Kwajalein Atoll*
Marshall Islands

Gilbert Islands

2 THE ASSAULT ON MALAYA AND BURMA
DECEMBER 8, 1941–JANUARY 31, 1942

Japanese troops landed on the Thai east coast on December 8 to join those who had already moved into Thailand from Indochina. Later that day, the Japanese landed in northern Malaya; by the end of January, they had reached the southern end of the peninsula. Other Japanese troops entered Burma on December 15 (see pp.120–121) and launched air raids against Rangoon on December 23.

→ Japanese assaults on Burma and Malaya
Japanese air raid

3 THE SINKING OF HMS *PRINCE OF WALES* AND *REPULSE* DECEMBER 8–10, 1941

British battleship HMS *Prince of Wales* and the battle cruiser HMS *Repulse* left Singapore on December 8, 1941, and sailed into the South China Sea to attack Japanese troop convoys. They were spotted by a Japanese submarine and attacked off the eastern Malay coast by a flight of eight Japanese bombers on December 10. Both were sunk, becoming the first capital ships (the largest armed ships in a navy) in history to be sunk solely by air power on the open sea.

→ Route of *Prince of Wales* and *Repulse*
Prince of Wales and *Repulse* sunk

New Hebrides   *Fiji*

New Caledonia

JAPANESE ADVANCES

The attack on Pearl Harbor on December 7, 1941, marked the start of a campaign by the Japanese to extend their control throughout Southeast Asia and the western Pacific. Within days, they had launched a series of daring amphibious and airborne assaults.

A few days before the events of Pearl Harbor (see pp.110–111), Japanese troops had moved through Thailand, positioning themselves for planned actions. On December 7, troop transports gathered in the Gulf of Siam ready for an assault on Malaya, which took place the next morning. The first attack on the Philippines occurred on the same day, with the British East Indies coming under attack a week later. By then, two British capital ships had been sunk in the South China Sea and Hong Kong was under assault. US-controlled Guam and Wake Island were quickly lost, the Dutch East Indies came under sustained attack in early January 1942, and by the end of January mainland Malaya was in Japanese hands.

American, British, and Dutch forces suffered heavy defeats, with many men taken prisoner or massacred by the Japanese. The Japanese attack was geographically wide, with air raids on Rangoon in Burma to the west and the capture of the Gilbert Islands in the Pacific to the east. It was also impeccably planned, with surprise and military experience giving the Japanese some easy victories.

> *"Japan was supreme, and we everywhere were weak and naked."*
>
> WINSTON CHURCHILL, *THE SECOND WORLD WAR*, 1950

THAILAND IN THE WAR

Thailand became increasingly authoritarian with the accession in 1938 of the pro-Fascist Luang Phibunsongkhram (right) as prime minister. A former field marshal who was pro-Japanese, Phibunsongkhram was pressured into allowing Japanese troops to pass through Thailand in late November 1941; however, on December 8 Japan issued an ultimatum and invaded anyway. Phibunsongkhram ordered an armistice and signed an alliance with Japan, undertaking to assist its war; he gained two states in Burma as a reward.

AMERICA AT WAR

With the onset of war, life in the US changed dramatically. Millions of men were conscripted, while at home industry geared up to provide necessities for the war effort, turning the country into what President Franklin D. Roosevelt christened "the arsenal of democracy."

△ **Patriotic duty**
A recruiting poster urges women to enroll as volunteer nurses. Around 74,000 served in the US Army and Navy in World War II.

Following the US's entry into the war in December 1941 (see pp.110–111), Roosevelt used a series of War Power Acts to reorganize the economy and industry for total war. Everyday life across the US changed. Meat, sugar, butter, canned goods, gasoline, fuel oil, clothes, and other commodities were all rationed, and civilians planted "victory gardens" to grow their own food. Americans were encouraged to save scrap metal for the war industries, and armament production soared. To fund the expense of waging a global war, US propaganda urged the public to buy war bonds and victory stamps. Meanwhile, anti-Japanese feeling led to the confinement of nearly 120,000 Japanese Americans in west-coast internment camps.

Changes in the workplace

To replace the men drafted into the armed forces, women joined the workplace in ever-increasing numbers. Many were enthusiastic about their new opportunities, some inspired by an advertisement that told them working in a war plant was "a lot more exciting than polishing the family furniture." The war also offered better jobs to thousands of African Americans, who moved from the south to work in the industrial cities of the north, midwest, and west. It was the start of the largest internal migration in US history. However, racial segregation was still in place, and race riots broke out in some urban centers.

HOLLYWOOD AT WAR

Hollywood played an important role in boosting national morale during the war. Film star and singer Marlene Dietrich (right), who in 1939 renounced her German citizenship and became a US citizen, often entertained the Allied troops. At home, Hollywood star power was used in the drive to raise funds for the war.

Replacing the men
A woman assembles the cowling for an engine of a B-25 bomber. By 1943, around 65 percent of workers in the aircraft industry were women. Their efforts helped the US produce more than 300,000 planes in the course of the war.

JAPAN INVADES THE PHILIPPINES

Following their attack on the US naval base at Pearl Harbor, Hawaii, Japanese troops began to land in the north of the US-held Philippine Islands on December 8, 1941. The US was now under attack across the Pacific Ocean and faced the most serious military challenge that it had known in a generation.

The Japanese began their campaign for the Philippines with heavy air attacks that neutralized US air power in the archipelago. Their first landings were met with little effective resistance, forcing the Commander of US Forces in the East, General Douglas MacArthur, to abandon the capital, Manila, and retreat west to fortify the Bataan Peninsula. Here the American and Filipino troops held out for four more months until forced to surrender on April 9, 1942. The final US redoubt on Corregidor Island fell the next month. The defeat was a blow to American morale, and the Philippine Islands would remain in Japanese hands until their gradual but bloody recovery after October 1944 (see pp.248–249).

The Japanese set up a Council of State to rule the islands until they declared them an independent republic, led by José Laurel, in October 1943. Most of the Filipino elite served the Japanese, but a successful resistance quickly arose, notably on Mindanao, the island furthest from Manila. By the end of the war, some 277 guerrilla units and about 260,000 people were in action. They were so effective that by the end of the war, the Japanese controlled only 12 of the 48 Philippine provinces.

5 THE BATTLE OF CORREGIDOR
MAY 5–6, 1942

Corregidor Island to the south of Bataan guarded access to Manila Harbor—the finest natural harbor in East Asia. After the fall of Bataan, this tiny island was the last US base in the region. The Japanese bombed Corregidor for four weeks before landing their troops on the north-east coast on the night of May 5. US defenses collapsed, and the island surrendered on May 6, 1942.

▢ Last US base in the Philippines

■ Japanese beachhead

✕ Battle

4 THE BATAAN DEATH MARCH
APRIL 10–11, 1942

The Japanese force-marched 80,000 American and Filipino prisoners of war from Bataan to Camp O'Donnell in Capas in the north—a total distance of around 69 miles (112 km). Between 5,500 and 18,650 died in the march, which was later judged to be a war crime. About 12,000 marchers eventually escaped to form guerrilla units in the mountains.

∎∎▶ Route of the Bataan Death March

Port Binanga

Mabayo ○

○ Morong

Mauban ○

Jan 23–26, 1942 Japanese troops attempt to land by sea behind US lines but are contained on their beachheads.

▽ Medal of Honor
This medal was awarded to US General Jonathan Mayhew Wainwright IV, the Commander of the Allied forces in the Philippines, who led his men in the final stand on Corregidor.

THE JAPANESE INVASION BEGINS

The Japanese landed in the northern Philippine Islands on December 8, 1941. After bombing US air bases, they invaded Luzon, the main island in the north, on December 10 and in the south two days later, attacking from Palau, a Pacific island some 620 miles (1,000 km) to the south-east. Further assaults were launched against the southern Mindanao Island on December 19, again from Palau. The main attacks on Luzon came on December 22, when Japanese troops landed in Lingayen Gulf on the west coast, and on December 24, when they landed in Lamon Bay on the east coast. Attacks on the smaller central islands continued until May 1942.

KEY

✸ Japanese air attacks on US bases

➡ Japanese landings

Luzon
Laoag · 10 DEC
10 DEC · Aparri
Vigan
22 DEC · *Luzon*
Lingayen Gulf · Lingayen · *Philippine Sea* · 24 DEC · *PACIFIC OCEAN*
Cabanatuan
Bataan Peninsula · San Fernando
Manila · *Lamon Bay*
See main map
South China Sea
Corregidor Island · Batangas · 12 DEC
Calapan · Legazpi
Mindoro
Calamian Group · *Masbate* · *Samar*
Capiz · Tacloban
Panay
Iloilo · *Leyte*
Puerto Princesa · *Cebu*
Bohol · Surigao
Palawan · *Los Negros*
Bukidnon
Sulu Sea · Pagadian · *Mindanao*
Cotabato · Davao
Zamboanga · *Moro Gulf* · Dulawan · Mati
Basilan
Jolo · 24 DEC · 19 DEC
Borneo

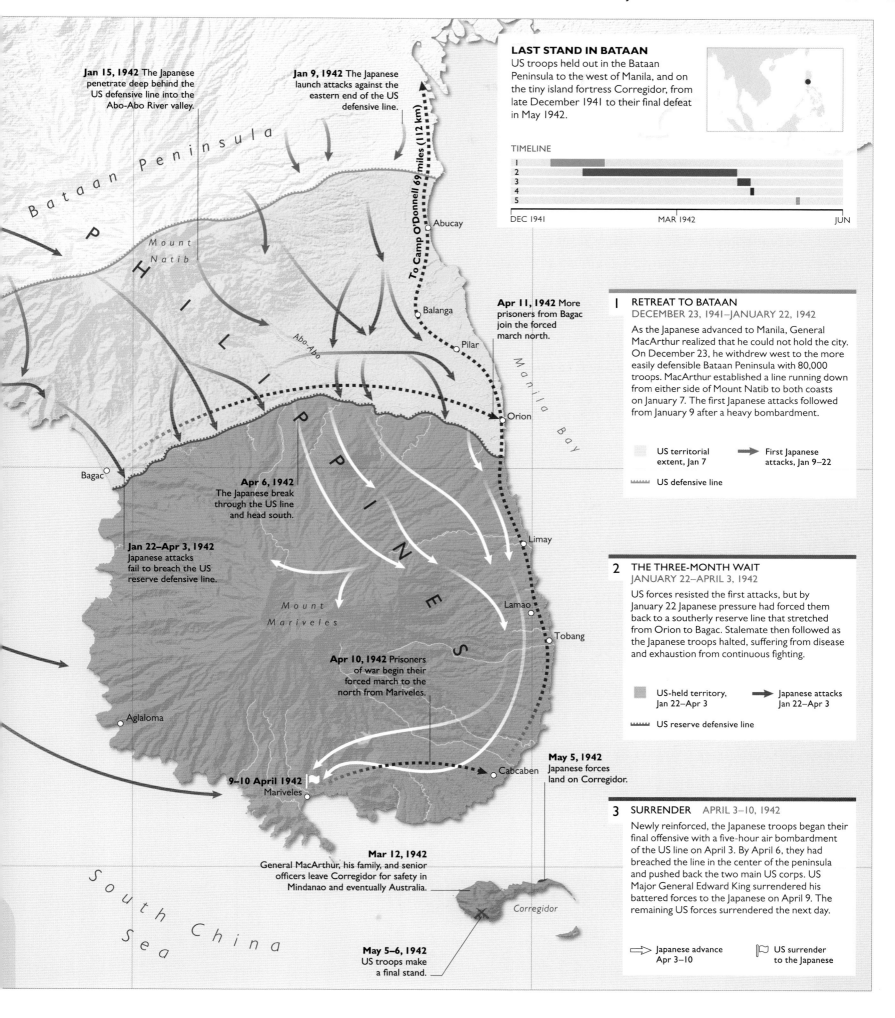

Jan 15, 1942 The Japanese penetrate deep behind the US defensive line into the Abo-Abo River valley.

Jan 9, 1942 The Japanese launch attacks against the eastern end of the US defensive line.

Bataan Peninsula

Mount Natib

Abucay

To Camp O'Donnell 69 miles (112 km)

Balanga

Abo-Abo

Pilar

Apr 11, 1942 More prisoners from Bagac join the forced march north.

Manila Bay

Orion

Bagac

Apr 6, 1942 The Japanese break through the US line and head south.

Jan 22–Apr 3, 1942 Japanese attacks fail to breach the US reserve defensive line.

Limay

Mount Mariveles

Lamao

Tobang

Apr 10, 1942 Prisoners of war begin their forced march to the north from Mariveles.

Aglaloma

9–10 April 1942
Mariveles

Cabcaben

May 5, 1942 Japanese forces land on Corregidor.

Mar 12, 1942 General MacArthur, his family, and senior officers leave Corregidor for safety in Mindanao and eventually Australia.

Corregidor

South China Sea

May 5–6, 1942 US troops make a final stand.

LAST STAND IN BATAAN

US troops held out in the Bataan Peninsula to the west of Manila, and on the tiny island fortress Corregidor, from late December 1941 to their final defeat in May 1942.

TIMELINE

1			
2			
3			
4			
5			

DEC 1941 — MAR 1942 — JUN

1 RETREAT TO BATAAN
DECEMBER 23, 1941–JANUARY 22, 1942

As the Japanese advanced to Manila, General MacArthur realized that he could not hold the city. On December 23, he withdrew west to the more easily defensible Bataan Peninsula with 80,000 troops. MacArthur established a line running down from either side of Mount Natib to both coasts on January 7. The first Japanese attacks followed from January 9 after a heavy bombardment.

US territorial extent, Jan 7

First Japanese attacks, Jan 9–22

US defensive line

2 THE THREE-MONTH WAIT
JANUARY 22–APRIL 3, 1942

US forces resisted the first attacks, but by January 22 Japanese pressure had forced them back to a southerly reserve line that stretched from Orion to Bagac. Stalemate then followed as the Japanese troops halted, suffering from disease and exhaustion from continuous fighting.

US-held territory, Jan 22–Apr 3

Japanese attacks Jan 22–Apr 3

US reserve defensive line

3 SURRENDER   APRIL 3–10, 1942

Newly reinforced, the Japanese troops began their final offensive with a five-hour air bombardment of the US line on April 3. By April 6, they had breached the line in the center of the peninsula and pushed back the two main US corps. US Major General Edward King surrendered his battered forces to the Japanese on April 9. The remaining US forces surrendered the next day.

Japanese advance Apr 3–10

US surrender to the Japanese

SURRENDER AT SINGAPORE

The fall of the British colony of Singapore to the Japanese in February 1942 led to the largest surrender of British-led personnel in military history. It was described by prime minister Winston Churchill as the worst disaster ever to befall the British in wartime.

Japanese forces commanded by General Tomoyuki Yamashita had invaded British Malaya on December 8, 1941 (see pp.112–113). Through superior tactics and mobility they defeated the British and Commonwealth forces, and by January 30, 1942, had reached the Johore Strait at the southern tip of the Malay Peninsula. The exhausted Allied troops crossed to Singapore Island via a causeway, which they then partially destroyed in the hope of delaying Japanese progress. By this time though, the Japanese had reliable intelligence on the weak state of "Fortress Singapore," and invaded on February 9.

> *"My attack on Singapore was a bluff—a bluff that worked."*
>
> GENERAL TOMOYUKI YAMASHITA

Outgunned, outmaneuvered, and with inadequate air support—yet with more than twice the number of troops that the Japanese had—the British and Commonwealth forces were soon pushed back into Singapore city itself. They were forced into a humiliating surrender on February 15. It later became clear that while the British were running out of supplies in the last days of the battle, so were the Japanese, who were low on ammunition for their artillery. However, had the British commander Lieutenant-General Arthur Percival decided to fight on, victory would have been unlikely.

THE BRITISH NAVAL BASE IN SINGAPORE

Completed in 1939 at a staggering cost of $500 million, Singapore's naval base boasted what was then the largest dry dock in the world, the third-largest floating dock (below), and enough fuel tanks to support the entire British navy for six months. It was defended by heavy 15-in naval guns and also by airforce squadrons stationed at Tengah Air Base. Winston Churchill touted it as an impregnable fortress, the "Gibraltar of the East."

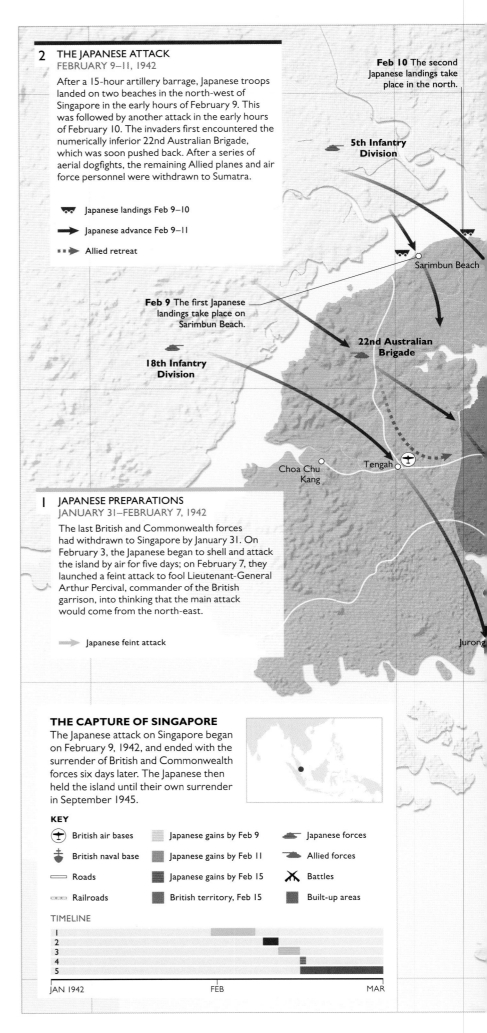

2 THE JAPANESE ATTACK
FEBRUARY 9–11, 1942

After a 15-hour artillery barrage, Japanese troops landed on two beaches in the north-west of Singapore in the early hours of February 9. This was followed by another attack in the early hours of February 10. The invaders first encountered the numerically inferior 22nd Australian Brigade, which was soon pushed back. After a series of aerial dogfights, the remaining Allied planes and air force personnel were withdrawn to Sumatra.

⛟ Japanese landings Feb 9–10

➡ Japanese advance Feb 9–11

▪▪▶ Allied retreat

Feb 10 The second Japanese landings take place in the north.

5th Infantry Division

Sarimbun Beach

Feb 9 The first Japanese landings take place on Sarimbun Beach.

22nd Australian Brigade

18th Infantry Division

Choa Chu Kang

Tengah

1 JAPANESE PREPARATIONS
JANUARY 31–FEBRUARY 7, 1942

The last British and Commonwealth forces had withdrawn to Singapore by January 31. On February 3, the Japanese began to shell and attack the island by air for five days; on February 7, they launched a feint attack to fool Lieutenant-General Arthur Percival, commander of the British garrison, into thinking that the main attack would come from the north-east.

➡ Japanese feint attack

Jurong

THE CAPTURE OF SINGAPORE

The Japanese attack on Singapore began on February 9, 1942, and ended with the surrender of British and Commonwealth forces six days later. The Japanese then held the island until their own surrender in September 1945.

KEY

✈ British air bases	▦ Japanese gains by Feb 9	⛴ Japanese forces
⚓ British naval base	▦ Japanese gains by Feb 11	⛵ Allied forces
═ Roads	▦ Japanese gains by Feb 15	✗ Battles
▭▭ Railroads	▦ British territory, Feb 15	▦ Built-up areas

TIMELINE

1		
2		
3		
4		
5		

JAN 1942 FEB MAR

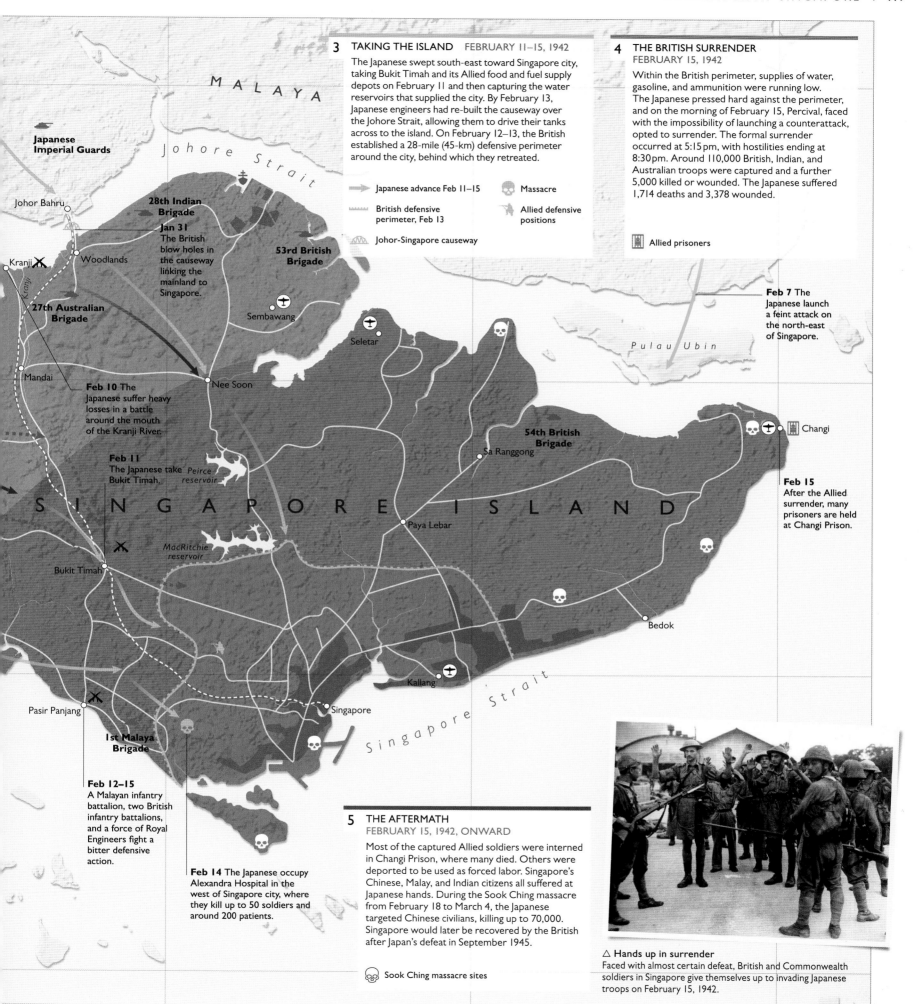

MALAYA

Johore Strait

Japanese Imperial Guards

Johor Bahru

28th Indian Brigade

Jan 31 The British blow holes in the causeway linking the mainland to Singapore.

Kranji

Woodlands

53rd British Brigade

27th Australian Brigade

Mandai

Sembawang

Seletar

Nee Soon

Feb 10 The Japanese suffer heavy losses in a battle around the mouth of the Kranji River.

Feb 11 The Japanese take Bukit Timah.

Peirce reservoir

Pulau Ubin

Feb 7 The Japanese launch a feint attack on the north-east of Singapore.

Sa Ranggong

54th British Brigade

Changi

Feb 15 After the Allied surrender, many prisoners are held at Changi Prison.

SINGAPORE ISLAND

MacRitchie reservoir

Bukit Timah

Paya Lebar

Bedok

Pasir Panjang

1st Malaya Brigade

Kallang

Singapore

Singapore Strait

Feb 12–15 A Malayan infantry battalion, two British infantry battalions, and a force of Royal Engineers fight a bitter defensive action.

Feb 14 The Japanese occupy Alexandra Hospital in the west of Singapore city, where they kill up to 50 soldiers and around 200 patients.

3 TAKING THE ISLAND FEBRUARY 11–15, 1942

The Japanese swept south-east toward Singapore city, taking Bukit Timah and its Allied food and fuel supply depots on February 11 and then capturing the water reservoirs that supplied the city. By February 13, Japanese engineers had re-built the causeway over the Johore Strait, allowing them to drive their tanks across to the island. On February 12–13, the British established a 28-mile (45-km) defensive perimeter around the city, behind which they retreated.

→ Japanese advance Feb 11–15

〜 British defensive perimeter, Feb 13

⌒ Johor–Singapore causeway

☠ Massacre

⚔ Allied defensive positions

▦ Allied prisoners

4 THE BRITISH SURRENDER
FEBRUARY 15, 1942

Within the British perimeter, supplies of water, gasoline, and ammunition were running low. The Japanese pressed hard against the perimeter, and on the morning of February 15, Percival, faced with the impossibility of launching a counterattack, opted to surrender. The formal surrender occurred at 5:15 pm, with hostilities ending at 8:30 pm. Around 110,000 British, Indian, and Australian troops were captured and a further 5,000 killed or wounded. The Japanese suffered 1,714 deaths and 3,378 wounded.

5 THE AFTERMATH
FEBRUARY 15, 1942, ONWARD

Most of the captured Allied soldiers were interned in Changi Prison, where many died. Others were deported to be used as forced labor. Singapore's Chinese, Malay, and Indian citizens all suffered at Japanese hands. During the Sook Ching massacre from February 18 to March 4, the Japanese targeted Chinese civilians, killing up to 70,000. Singapore would later be recovered by the British after Japan's defeat in September 1945.

☠ Sook Ching massacre sites

△ **Hands up in surrender**
Faced with almost certain defeat, British and Commonwealth soldiers in Singapore give themselves up to invading Japanese troops on February 15, 1942.

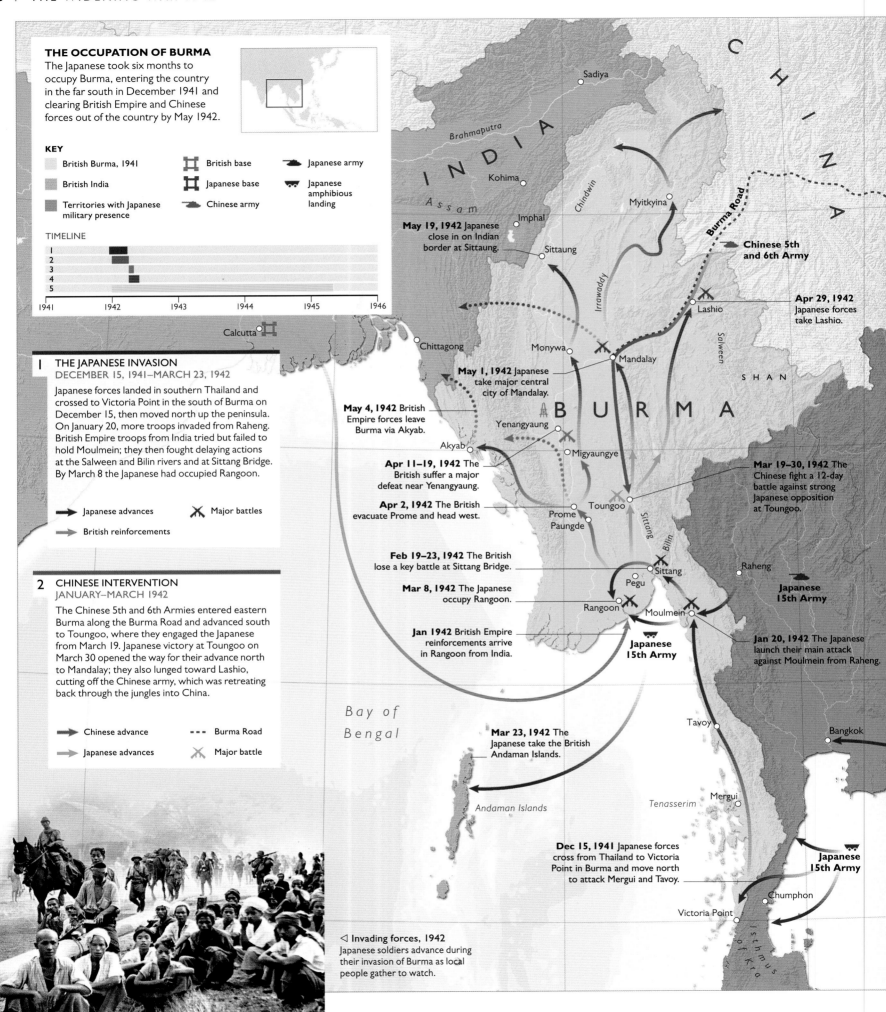

THE OCCUPATION OF BURMA

The Japanese took six months to occupy Burma, entering the country in the far south in December 1941 and clearing British Empire and Chinese forces out of the country by May 1942.

KEY

- British Burma, 1941
- British India
- Territories with Japanese military presence
- British base
- Japanese base
- Chinese army
- Japanese army
- Japanese amphibious landing

TIMELINE

	1941	1942	1943	1944	1945	1946
1						
2						
3						
4						
5						

1 THE JAPANESE INVASION
DECEMBER 15, 1941–MARCH 23, 1942

Japanese forces landed in southern Thailand and crossed to Victoria Point in the south of Burma on December 15, then moved north up the peninsula. On January 20, more troops invaded from Raheng. British Empire troops from India tried but failed to hold Moulmein; they then fought delaying actions at the Salween and Bilin rivers and at Sittang Bridge. By March 8 the Japanese had occupied Rangoon.

- → Japanese advances
- → British reinforcements
- ✕ Major battles

2 CHINESE INTERVENTION
JANUARY–MARCH 1942

The Chinese 5th and 6th Armies entered eastern Burma along the Burma Road and advanced south to Toungoo, where they engaged the Japanese from March 19. Japanese victory at Toungoo on March 30 opened the way for their advance north to Mandalay; they also lunged toward Lashio, cutting off the Chinese army, which was retreating back through the jungles into China.

- → Chinese advance
- → Japanese advances
- - - Burma Road
- ✕ Major battle

May 19, 1942 Japanese close in on Indian border at Sittaung.

Chinese 5th and 6th Army

Apr 29, 1942 Japanese forces take Lashio.

May 1, 1942 Japanese take major central city of Mandalay.

May 4, 1942 British Empire forces leave Burma via Akyab.

Apr 11–19, 1942 The British suffer a major defeat near Yenangyaung.

Mar 19–30, 1942 The Chinese fight a 12-day battle against strong Japanese opposition at Toungoo.

Apr 2, 1942 The British evacuate Prome and head west.

Feb 19–23, 1942 The British lose a key battle at Sittang Bridge.

Mar 8, 1942 The Japanese occupy Rangoon.

Jan 1942 British Empire reinforcements arrive in Rangoon from India.

Jan 20, 1942 The Japanese launch their main attack against Moulmein from Raheng.

Japanese 15th Army

Mar 23, 1942 The Japanese take the British Andaman Islands.

Dec 15, 1941 Japanese forces cross from Thailand to Victoria Point in Burma and move north to attack Mergui and Tavoy.

◁ Invading forces, 1942
Japanese soldiers advance during their invasion of Burma as local people gather to watch.

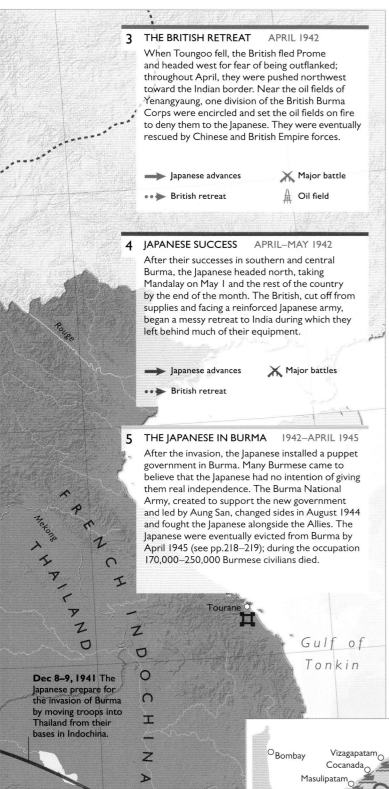

3 THE BRITISH RETREAT APRIL 1942

When Toungoo fell, the British fled Prome and headed west for fear of being outflanked; throughout April, they were pushed northwest toward the Indian border. Near the oil fields of Yenangyaung, one division of the British Burma Corps were encircled and set the oil fields on fire to deny them to the Japanese. They were eventually rescued by Chinese and British Empire forces.

→ Japanese advances

⚔ Major battle

•••► British retreat

⛽ Oil field

4 JAPANESE SUCCESS APRIL–MAY 1942

After their successes in southern and central Burma, the Japanese headed north, taking Mandalay on May 1 and the rest of the country by the end of the month. The British, cut off from supplies and facing a reinforced Japanese army, began a messy retreat to India during which they left behind much of their equipment.

→ Japanese advances

⚔ Major battles

•••► British retreat

5 THE JAPANESE IN BURMA 1942–APRIL 1945

After the invasion, the Japanese installed a puppet government in Burma. Many Burmese came to believe that the Japanese had no intention of giving them real independence. The Burma National Army, created to support the new government and led by Aung San, changed sides in August 1944 and fought the Japanese alongside the Allies. The Japanese were eventually evicted from Burma by April 1945 (see pp.218–219); during the occupation 170,000–250,000 Burmese civilians died.

Dec 8–9, 1941 The Japanese prepare for the invasion of Burma by moving troops into Thailand from their bases in Indochina.

JAPAN TAKES BURMA

The conquest of the British colony of Burma extended the Japanese defensive perimeter to its westernmost point, and cut off Allied supply routes to China. The fighting was fierce and costly, and the result was a decisive Japanese victory in May 1942 that dealt yet another blow to the British after the fall of Singapore.

Japan wished to conquer Burma to gain access to its natural resources of oil, cobalt, and rice, and to gain a buffer zone to protect its planned conquests in Malaya and Singapore. It also wanted to close the Burma Road—a conduit for supplies for the Nationalist forces of Chiang Kai-shek, whom the Japanese had been fighting in China since 1937 (see pp.26–27). Many Burmese, who wished to see the end of British rule in their country, supported the invasion. Among them was Aung San, a Burmese activist, and the Thirty Comrades, who received military training from the Japanese and returned to form the Burma Independence Army.

The Japanese invasion began on December 15, 1941. The British Empire troops were no match for the battle-trained Japanese infantry, who exploited effective tactics and made good use of limited air resources. Delaying actions by the British and a major battle fought at Toungoo by a Chinese Nationalist army in March failed to stop the invaders; the British were forced out of the country by the end of May. Fearful that the Japanese would attack Ceylon, and so take control over the Indian Ocean, the British occupied Vichy-held Madagascar in May 1942 to prevent the Japanese establishing a submarine base there.

> *"Two brigades still east of the river fought to break through the great Sittang railway bridge. Then came tragedy."*
>
> WILLIAM SLIM, COMMANDER OF THE BRITISH BURMA CORPS, 1956

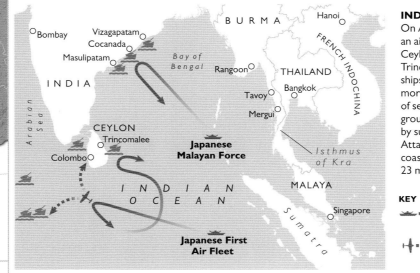

INDIAN OCEAN ATTACKS

On April 5, 1942, the Japanese launched an aircraft carrier attack against Colombo, Ceylon; this was followed by an assault on Trincomalee on April 9. Eight British naval ships and five merchantmen were sunk and more than 40 aircraft were lost; hundreds of servicemen and civilians were killed on the ground. Five more merchantmen were sunk by submarines off the west coast of India. Attacks were also launched against three east coast Indian ports, with the loss of a further 23 merchantmen.

KEY

Japanese fleet movements

Sites of British ship and merchantmen losses

Japanese air attack from aircraft carrier

War in Iraq
Sherman tank crews of the Indian 31st
Armored Division receive instruction on the
use of Browning machine guns in Iraq. They
had been sent to Iraq as part of operations
against the pro-Axis regime of Rashid Ali
in 1941 (see pp.82–83).

INDIA IN WORLD WAR II

Although India fought in the war to defend the British Empire, a Nationalist movement at home gained support, with the aim of shaking off British rule. The nation aided production of arms and raised 2.5 million volunteers, who fought in Europe, North Africa, and Asia.

△ **Recruitment campaign**
The British government ran a highly successful campaign to encourage Indians to join the army, raising the largest volunteer force in history.

As part of the British Empire, India had little choice but to join the war. However, this was opposed by many Indian Nationalists, who withdrew their support from provincial governments that the British had established in 1935. There was also opposition from the "Quit India" movement, which was launched by Mahatma Gandhi in 1942 and called for the British to leave at once. The loss of rice imports from Burma after the Japanese invaded the former British colony, as well as the government's failure to improve food distribution, led in 1943 to a famine in Bengal in which three million died. Some Indians were so opposed to British rule that they fought for the Axis powers—mainly 13,000 troops of Subhash Chandra Bose's Indian National Army raised from prisoners of war.

Fighting for the British

Despite the opposition, the impact of Indians fighting for the Axis was slight compared to the loyalist Indian army, which expanded greatly, reaching 2.6 million members in 1945. Indian units were deployed widely—in Iraq, Ethiopia, North Africa, and Italy—but their main goals were to prevent the Japanese from crossing into India (1942–1944) and to defend Burma against the Japanese—an attempt that failed in spring 1942, but succeeded in 1944–1945, when they drove out the Japanese together with other Allied forces (see pp.218–219).

THE VOICE OF OPPOSITION

Gandhi (center) professed a nonviolence philosophy that led him to oppose India's involvement in the war, while other Nationalist leaders thought helping the British would achieve Indian independence more quickly. In 1942, his "Quit India" movement organized protests to encourage the British to leave. He was jailed for nearly two years.

JAPANESE SETBACKS

In early 1942, Japan sought to extend its defensive perimeter south and east across the Pacific. However, its plans were frustrated in an inconclusive naval battle in the Coral Sea, and its forces went on to suffer defeats in New Guinea.

Japan began its assaults on New Guinea, the Solomon Islands, and Australia from January 1942, and its determination to expand its defensive perimeter was heightened by the Doolittle Raid, a US bombing raid on Tokyo and other Japanese cities on April 18, 1942. While this attack did little damage, it made the Japanese realize the potential threat to their homeland.

To achieve their goals, the Japanese planned to capture Midway Atoll to the east (see pp.126–127) to deny its use to American bombers, to take the Australian base at Port Moresby in New Guinea to the south, and to extend their control over the Solomon Islands. This would isolate Australia from its ally, the US, and leave Allied nations and colonies in the region vulnerable.

The initial invasion of New Guinea and the Solomon Islands began favorably, but the assault against Port Moresby was stalled first by stalemate in the two-day Battle of the Coral Sea in May and then by the Japanese failure to seize the port via the overland Kokoda Trail in July. The Japanese had outrun their supply lines and were forced to retreat. The defeats suffered in and around New Guinea were the first major setbacks to Japanese expansion.

> *"Without a doubt … the Coral Sea was the most confused battle area in world history."*
>
> US VICE ADMIRAL H. S. DUCKWORTH, 1972

ADMIRAL ISOROKU YAMAMOTO 1884–1943

Japanese Admiral Isoroku Yamamoto played a major role in Japan's naval battles in the Pacific Ocean. A student of Harvard University and twice naval attaché in Washington, he opposed war with the US and disagreed with the invasion of China in 1937. Nevertheless, he became an admiral in 1940 and planned the attacks on Pearl Harbor and Midway. He was heavily involved in the Battle of the Coral Sea.

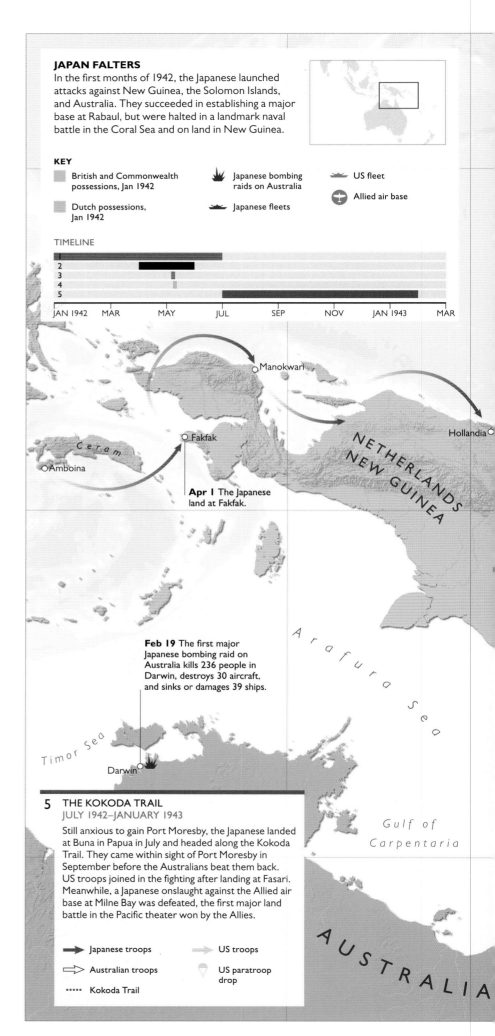

JAPAN FALTERS

In the first months of 1942, the Japanese launched attacks against New Guinea, the Solomon Islands, and Australia. They succeeded in establishing a major base at Rabaul, but were halted in a landmark naval battle in the Coral Sea and on land in New Guinea.

KEY

▨ British and Commonwealth possessions, Jan 1942	🗡 Japanese bombing raids on Australia
▨ Dutch possessions, Jan 1942	⚓ Japanese fleets
	⚓ US fleet
	⊕ Allied air base

TIMELINE

JAN 1942 MAR MAY JUL SEP NOV JAN 1943 MAR

Apr 1 The Japanese land at Fakfak.

Feb 19 The first major Japanese bombing raid on Australia kills 236 people in Darwin, destroys 30 aircraft, and sinks or damages 39 ships.

5 THE KOKODA TRAIL
JULY 1942–JANUARY 1943

Still anxious to gain Port Moresby, the Japanese landed at Buna in Papua in July and headed along the Kokoda Trail. They came within sight of Port Moresby in September before the Australians beat them back. US troops joined in the fighting after landing at Fasari. Meanwhile, a Japanese onslaught against the Allied air base at Milne Bay was defeated, the first major land battle in the Pacific theater won by the Allies.

➡ Japanese troops	➡ US troops
▷ Australian troops	▽ US paratroop drop
····· Kokoda Trail	

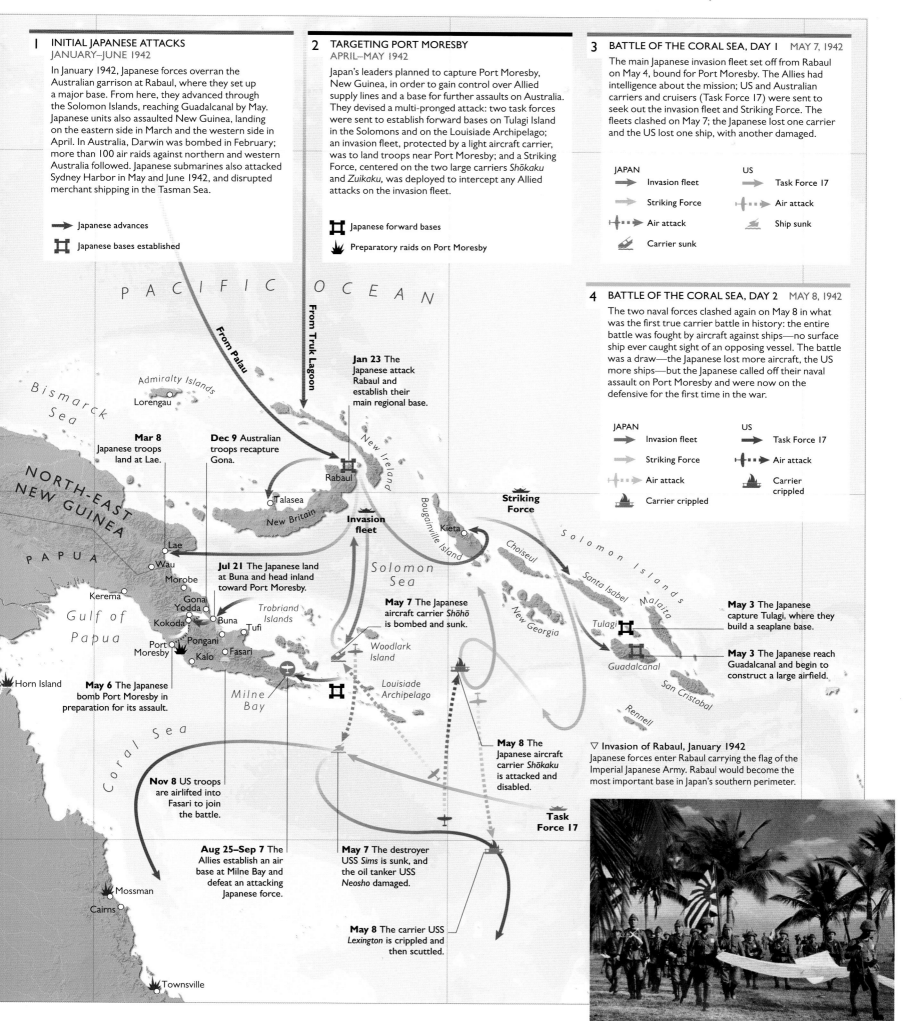

1 INITIAL JAPANESE ATTACKS
JANUARY–JUNE 1942

In January 1942, Japanese forces overran the Australian garrison at Rabaul, where they set up a major base. From here, they advanced through the Solomon Islands, reaching Guadalcanal by May. Japanese units also assaulted New Guinea, landing on the eastern side in March and the western side in April. In Australia, Darwin was bombed in February; more than 100 air raids against northern and western Australia followed. Japanese submarines also attacked Sydney Harbor in May and June 1942, and disrupted merchant shipping in the Tasman Sea.

→ Japanese advances

⊞ Japanese bases established

2 TARGETING PORT MORESBY
APRIL–MAY 1942

Japan's leaders planned to capture Port Moresby, New Guinea, in order to gain control over Allied supply lines and a base for further assaults on Australia. They devised a multi-pronged attack: two task forces were sent to establish forward bases on Tulagi Island in the Solomons and on the Louisiade Archipelago; an invasion fleet, protected by a light aircraft carrier, was to land troops near Port Moresby; and a Striking Force, centered on the two large carriers *Shōkaku* and *Zuikaku,* was deployed to intercept any Allied attacks on the invasion fleet.

⊞ Japanese forward bases

🌿 Preparatory raids on Port Moresby

3 BATTLE OF THE CORAL SEA, DAY I   MAY 7, 1942

The main Japanese invasion fleet set off from Rabaul on May 4, bound for Port Moresby. The Allies had intelligence about the mission; US and Australian carriers and cruisers (Task Force 17) were sent to seek out the invasion fleet and Striking Force. The fleets clashed on May 7; the Japanese lost one carrier and the US lost one ship, with another damaged.

JAPAN
→ Invasion fleet
→ Striking Force
⊢┅► Air attack
⚓ Carrier sunk

US
→ Task Force 17
⊢┅► Air attack
🚢 Ship sunk

4 BATTLE OF THE CORAL SEA, DAY 2   MAY 8, 1942

The two naval forces clashed again on May 8 in what was the first true carrier battle in history: the entire battle was fought by aircraft against ships—no surface ship ever caught sight of an opposing vessel. The battle was a draw—the Japanese lost more aircraft, the US more ships—but the Japanese called off their naval assault on Port Moresby and were now on the defensive for the first time in the war.

JAPAN
→ Invasion fleet
→ Striking Force
⊢┅► Air attack
⚓ Carrier crippled

US
→ Task Force 17
⊢┅► Air attack
🚢 Carrier crippled

▽ Invasion of Rabaul, January 1942
Japanese forces enter Rabaul carrying the flag of the Imperial Japanese Army. Rabaul would become the most important base in Japan's southern perimeter.

PIVOTAL PACIFIC BATTLE

The Battle of Midway was Japan's first naval defeat for centuries. It marked the ascendancy of carriers and their aircraft as the modern weapons with which to dominate the seas.

KEY

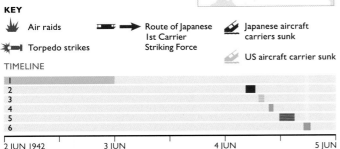

Air raids

Torpedo strikes

Route of Japanese 1st Carrier Striking Force

Japanese aircraft carriers sunk

US aircraft carrier sunk

TIMELINE

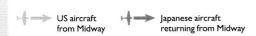

2 JUN 1942   3 JUN   4 JUN   5 JUN

---

1 THE US NAVY LAYS AN AMBUSH
JUNE 2, 1942

By June 2, the US Navy's Task Forces 16 and 17 lay in an area of operations about 350 miles (560 km) north-east of Midway, from where their search planes scoured the ocean for the Japanese. The task forces were formed around three aircraft carriers: USS *Enterprise* and *Hornet*, which Yamamoto thought were in the Solomons; and USS *Yorktown*, which he believed sunk in the Coral Sea.

US Task Force area of operations

US Task Force 16: carriers *Enterprise* and *Hornet*, 152 aircraft, 6 cruisers, 9 destroyers

US Task Force 17: carrier *Yorktown*, 73 aircraft, 2 cruisers, 5 destroyers

---

Jun 5 *Hiryū* is set ablaze; the crew abandons ship while Admiral Yamaguchi and Captain Kaku go down with their vessel.

Hiryū scuttled

5 pm

6:30 pm

---

2 THE JAPANESE STRIKE MIDWAY
4:30–6:40 AM JUNE 4, 1942

The 1st Carrier Striking Force launched an air attack on Midway with 108 aircraft, holding back around half of its planes to deal with possible attacks by US naval forces. At 5:45 am the raiders were spotted and US interceptors scrambled. The Japanese failed to disable Midway's defenses in this attack, and around one-third of the Japanese aircraft were destroyed or damaged by US fighters and antiaircraft fire from the island.

First air attack on Midway

Japanese 1st Carrier Striking Force

Jun 4–5 Route of carriers *Akagi*, *Sōryū*, *Kaga*, and *Hiryū*.

Jun 5 *Akagi* is scuttled at 5 am; Yamamoto calls off the operation against Midway and at midday the Japanese warships withdraw westward.

Sōryū sunk

Akagi scuttled

Kaga sunk

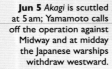

10:25 am

10:15 am

9:45 am

9:28 am

7:10 am

PACIFIC OCEAN

---

3 CONFUSION IN THE JAPANESE FORCE
7:10–8:30 AM JUNE 4, 1942

US bombers from Midway attacked the Japanese 1st Carrier Striking Force with little effect. As the Japanese force changed course following reports of an approaching US naval force, planes began to return from Midway to land and refuel. Deck operations became confused, and planners were unsure whether to rearm aircraft with high-explosive bombs for a second sortie against Midway, or with torpedoes to repel a threat from the US Navy.

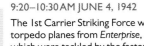

US aircraft from Midway

Japanese aircraft returning from Midway

---

4 A MOMENTOUS MORNING
9:20–10:30 AM JUNE 4, 1942

The 1st Carrier Striking Force was now targeted by torpedo planes from *Enterprise*, *Hornet*, and *Yorktown*, which were tackled by the faster Japanese Zero fighters. However, the Zeros, now out of position and low on ammunition, could not contain a later wave of attacks by dive-bombers. These hit the carriers *Kaga* and *Sōryū* (both sank later that day), the flagship *Akagi* (scuttled the next morning), two battleships, and a destroyer.

Yorktown dive-bomber and torpedo aircraft

Enterprise dive-bomber aircraft

Enterprise torpedo aircraft

Hornet torpedo aircraft

---

5 *YORKTOWN* BECOMES A CASUALTY
11:50 AM–3 PM JUNE 4, 1942

US radar detected planes from the carrier *Hiryū* approaching *Yorktown* from the west. The raiders were intercepted by US fighters, but several broke through and hit *Yorktown* at around noon with three bombs. By 2:30 pm the fires aboard *Yorktown* had been extinguished, but torpedo planes hit her again. By 3 pm *Yorktown* was listing and the order was issued to abandon ship. *Yorktown* finally sank on June 7.

Hiryū dive-bomber aircraft

Hiryū torpedo aircraft

---

6 THE CRIPPLING OF THE *HIRYU*
5 PM–6:30 PM JUNE 4, 1942

Hiryū had been located at 2:30 pm by a scout plane from *Yorktown*. Shortly after 5 pm 40 US dive-bombers attacked the Japanese carrier, which was defended by just a dozen fighters. *Hiryū* was hit many times and set ablaze (she was scuttled the next day). B-17s from Midway followed up the attack on the remains of the Japanese fleet, which was in retreat by June 5.

US dive-bomber aircraft

B-17 aircraft strike from Midway

Jun 6 *Yorktown*, now under tow, is hit by a torpedo from a Japanese submarine and sinks the following day.

US Task Force 16   US Task Force 17

Jun 4 *Yorktown* is hit by bombs.

12 pm

2:40 pm   *Yorktown* torpedoed

6:20 am Jun 4 Japanese carrier aircraft bomb US naval base on Midway Atoll.

△ **Modeling the action**
This diorama by American designer Norman Bel Geddes depicts a scene from the Battle of Midway, with the damaged Japanese ship *Akagi* in the foreground.

THE BATTLE OF MIDWAY

In June 1942, the Japanese sought to neutralize US power in the Pacific by challenging the US in what they hoped would be a decisive naval engagement at Midway Atoll in the westernmost part of the Hawaiian archipelago.

After their attack on Pearl Harbor, the Japanese waged war for months in Southeast Asia and the Pacific. Their advance was only stemmed in May 1942 at the Battle of the Coral Sea (see pp.124–125), when they failed to seize Port Moresby. Alarmed by an American bombing raid on their cities, the Japanese decided to launch an attack on Midway—an island halfway across the Pacific. By mid-1942 the atoll was the most westerly US base in the central Pacific, and Japanese planners recognized its value as a fueling station for US vessels and aircraft.

Admiral Isoroku Yamamoto, commander-in-chief of the Japanese Combined Fleet, argued that Japan's defensive perimeter should be pushed eastward by capturing Midway and US islands in the western Aleutians. His plan involved luring part of the US fleet northward with an attack in the Aleutians, then attacking Midway from the north-west and south-west with three groups. He reasoned that this would draw out the US carrier fleet to be destroyed, but the US fleet knew of this plan, because code breaker Joseph Rochefort had cracked the Japanese cipher, JN-25. As Yamamoto had predicted, the encounter at Midway was decisive, but not in the way he had hoped: the battle marked the end of Japanese dominance in the Pacific.

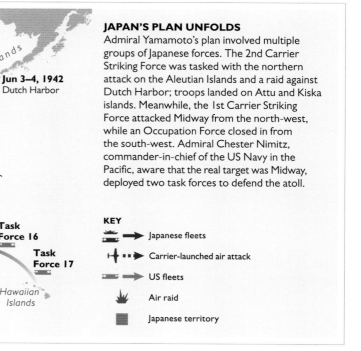

Midway Atoll

JAPAN'S PLAN UNFOLDS
Admiral Yamamoto's plan involved multiple groups of Japanese forces. The 2nd Carrier Striking Force was tasked with the northern attack on the Aleutian Islands and a raid against Dutch Harbor; troops landed on Attu and Kiska islands. Meanwhile, the 1st Carrier Striking Force attacked Midway from the north-west, while an Occupation Force closed in from the south-west. Admiral Chester Nimitz, commander-in-chief of the US Navy in the Pacific, aware that the real target was Midway, deployed two task forces to defend the atoll.

KEY

→ Japanese fleets

→ Carrier-launched air attack

→ US fleets

Air raid

Japanese territory

Logistics map, December 1942
This map, made by the US 1st Marine Amphibious Corps, shows landing sites, anchorages, and tides. Henderson Field can be seen on the north coast, center-left.

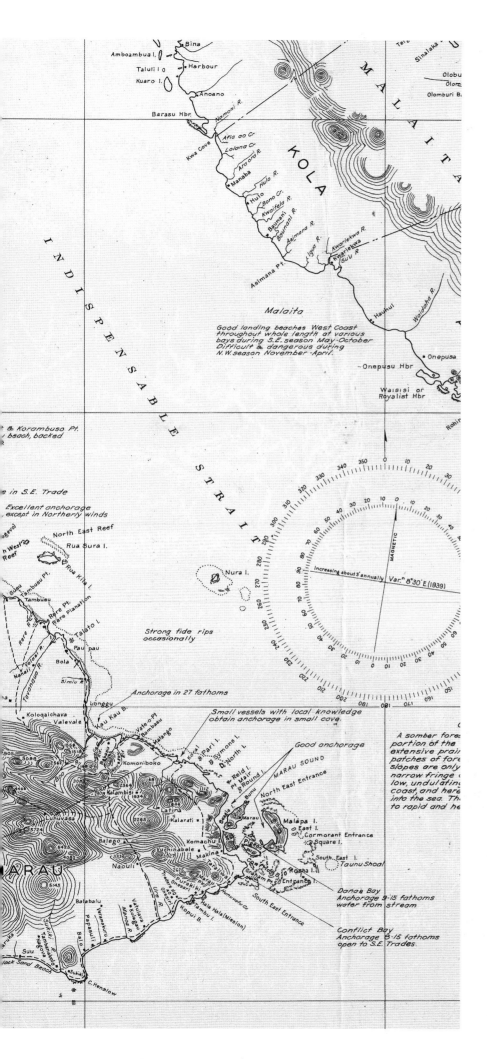

GUADALCANAL

In August 1942 the Allies went on the offensive in the Pacific War, landing on Japanese-held Guadalcanal in the Solomon Islands. Fierce battles raged on land and sea for six months until the Japanese withdrew.

The Japanese established a naval base in the southern Solomon Islands in May 1942 and in July began building an airfield on Guadalcanal. Seeing this as a threat to lines of communication between the US and Australia, the Allies assembled a force of US Marines and US and Australian warships to attack Guadalcanal and the nearby island of Tulagi to the north on August 7. The Japanese were caught by surprise, and 11,000 US Marines were put ashore on Guadalcanal almost unopposed. On the night of August 8–9, however, the Japanese navy counterattacked. Striking at the Allied naval force, they sank four cruisers in the battle of Savo Island, killing more than 1,000 seamen. The rattled Allied fleet withdrew, leaving the Marines ashore to fend for themselves without heavy equipment, which had not yet been landed.

The defense of Henderson Field

While the Japanese strove to organize troop landings to retake Guadalcanal, the US Marines completed construction of the airstrip on the north coast, named Henderson Field. Once US aircraft arrived two weeks after the initial landings, they could stop the Japanese navy operating around the island in daytime. The Japanese resorted to using fast destroyers to ferry troops from their base at Rabaul by night. Through this "Tokyo Express" they built up sufficient forces on Guadalcanal to launch serious attacks on the Marines' defensive perimeter around the airfield from mid-September. The Marines fought off a series of near-suicidal assaults through October, while mounting their own aggressive patrols into the hostile jungle terrain.

The final battles

The climax of the campaign came in mid-November. Japanese warships planned to sail in by night to bombard Henderson Field while transports landed fresh troops. The US Navy responded in force. In two nights of brutal, confused, close-range fighting in darkness, the Japanese lost two battleships and four other warships. The US Navy also suffered substantial losses, but the Japanese troop landings stopped. From here the Americans were able to reinforce their troops on Guadalcanal to 50,000 men. With no prospect of victory, Japan decided their resources would be better employed elsewhere. Troop withdrawals began, and the last Japanese forces left in early February 1943.

▷ **US landings**
Thousands of US Marines landed on the north coast between Koli Point and Lunga Point on August 7, 1942.

WAR IN EUROPE AND AFRICA

Throughout most of 1942, the outcome of the war against Hitler hung in the balance. However, by the year's end, Allied victories on the Eastern front and in the North African desert had decisively turned the tide, and Nazi Germany's era of conquests had ended.

After the US, Soviet Union, and Britain had united against Germany in 1941, the increase in economic resources and population were weighted heavily in favor of the Allies. However, bringing these resources to bear on the battlefield was no easy matter.

German successes

Militarily, the Germans were still capable of inflicting heavy defeats on their enemies. In the Soviet Union, Axis forces repulsed Soviet offensives and resumed their advance eastward, reaching the Volga and the Caucasus. By late summer 1942, Hitler's aim of crippling the Soviets' war effort by capturing their sources of oil supplies and arms production looked within sight.

Meanwhile, in Egypt's Western Desert, the German field marshal Erwin Rommel outfought the British, and by July had advanced to El Alamein, less than 70 miles (100 km) from Britain's major naval base at Alexandria. In the Atlantic, German U-boats attacked American coastal shipping and transoceanic convoys, threatening to block the movement of US arms and troops to the European theater, which depended entirely upon sea transport. Merchant convoys taking military aid to the Soviet Union through its Arctic ports also suffered heavy losses.

▽ **The Americans arrive**
A British policeman gives directions to a newly arrived American soldier. Over 200,000 US personnel were based in Britain by the end of 1942.

◁ **Call for collaboration**
A poster calls for Dutch volunteers to join the Nazis' elite force, the Waffen-SS. Recruits were sought from conquered countries with racially "Aryan" populations, including the Netherlands, Denmark, and Norway. Every nation in occupied Europe produced enthusiastic collaborators, who identified ideologically with the Nazis' racist and anticommunist beliefs.

Domination over cooperation

Throughout this period, the German hold on occupied Europe remained secure. Coastal raids and RAF bombing of cities were too ineffectual to have significant impact. In occupied countries, the Nazis crushed all opposition by force and exploited the resources to the maximum. The scale of resistance activity remained quite limited, despite the efforts of the British Special Operations Executive (SOE) and the growth of Communist-led partisan guerrilla groups after the Soviet Union's entry into the war.

Hitler also had plans for construction of a racially stratified New Order in Europe. In 1942, his policy to massacre all Jews (code named "the Final Solution") became organized into a coherent project to annihilate Europe's Jewish population. Extermination camps industrialized killing, the scale of which was limited only by the need to use Jews as slave labor. The same camps killed off Soviet prisoners of war, political opponents of Nazism, the Romany people, and homosexuals.

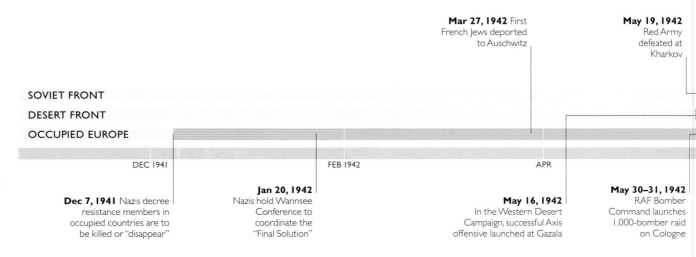

THE TURNING POINT

Throughout the first half of 1942, the Axis powers' victories continued. When German troops reached Stalingrad in August, it appeared another major success was in prospect, but instead the battle was a disaster for Hitler's forces. In North Africa, Field Marshal Rommel's Panzer Army was trapped between the British, who had recently been victorious at the Second Battle of El Alamein, and US troops, which landed in Operation Torch. Meanwhile, the sufferings of the people of Nazi-occupied Europe mounted.

SOVIET FRONT

DESERT FRONT

OCCUPIED EUROPE

DEC 1941   FEB 1942   APR

Mar 27, 1942 First French Jews deported to Auschwitz

May 19, 1942 Red Army defeated at Kharkov

Dec 7, 1941 Nazis decree resistance members in occupied countries are to be killed or "disappear"

Jan 20, 1942 Nazis hold Wannsee Conference to coordinate the "Final Solution"

May 16, 1942 In the Western Desert Campaign, successful Axis offensive launched at Gazala

May 30–31, 1942 RAF Bomber Command launches 1,000-bomber raid on Cologne

◁ **Decisive battle**
Red Army soldiers advance through the ruins of Stalingrad in 1943. The battle for the Soviet city—the largest conflict in World War II—ended in a crushing victory for Stalin's forces, transforming the war on the Eastern front.

Allied successes

Hitler's military strategy was based on the calculation that he could defeat the Soviet Union and so place Germany in an impregnable position in Europe before American strength was brought to bear. However, Soviet forces exhibited formidable resilience, despite suffering great losses of men, equipment, and territory. The encirclement and destruction of a German army at Stalingrad in the winter of 1942–1943 demonstrated that, at the very least, the Soviet Union was not going to be defeated soon.

While battle raged in Stalingrad, the British scored a decisive victory over Axis forces at El Alamein, in the North African desert. Largely responsible for Britain's success was General Bernard Montgomery—a commander who knew how to triumph over a more skillful opponent through patiently deployed material superiority. Meanwhile, landings in French North Africa gave US troops their first experience of fighting the Axis forces. By the end of 1942, US bomber aircraft had begun arriving at bases in Britain, and Allied leaders were discussing a future full-scale invasion of occupied Europe. For Germany, the years of victory were over and a long, tenacious struggle for survival against the odds lay ahead.

▷ **British on the offensive**
At the battle of El Alamein in October 1942, the infantry of Britain's 8th Army advanced to attack well-prepared Axis defensive positions. After lengthy fighting, General Rommel's army was driven into headlong retreat.

Jul 4, 1942
Sevastopol in Crimea falls to Axis forces

Jul 7, 1942
Rommel halted at First Battle of El Alamein

Jul 14, 1942
Beginning of deportation of Dutch Jews to Auschwitz

Aug 10, 1942
Germans reach the outskirts of Stalingrad

Aug 12, 1942
Churchill flies to meet Stalin in Moscow

Aug 19, 1942
Raid by Canadian troops at Dieppe is a costly failure

Nov 19, 1942 Soviets launch operation to surround Axis forces in Stalingrad

Jan 31, 1943
German general Paulus surrenders in Stalingrad

JUL   SEP   NOV   JAN 1943

Jun 10, 1942
Germans massacre civilians at Czech towns of Lidice and Lezaky after assassination of Heydrich in Prague

Jul 16, 1942
Mass arrest of Parisian Jews by French police

Jul 19, 1942
Beginning of dispatch of Polish Jews to extermination camps

Aug 17, 1942
US B-17 Flying Fortresses make first bombing raid in Europe

Oct 23–Nov 4, 1942 Major British offensive— Second Battle of El Alamein

Nov 8, 1942 Operation Torch landings by chiefly US troops in French North Africa

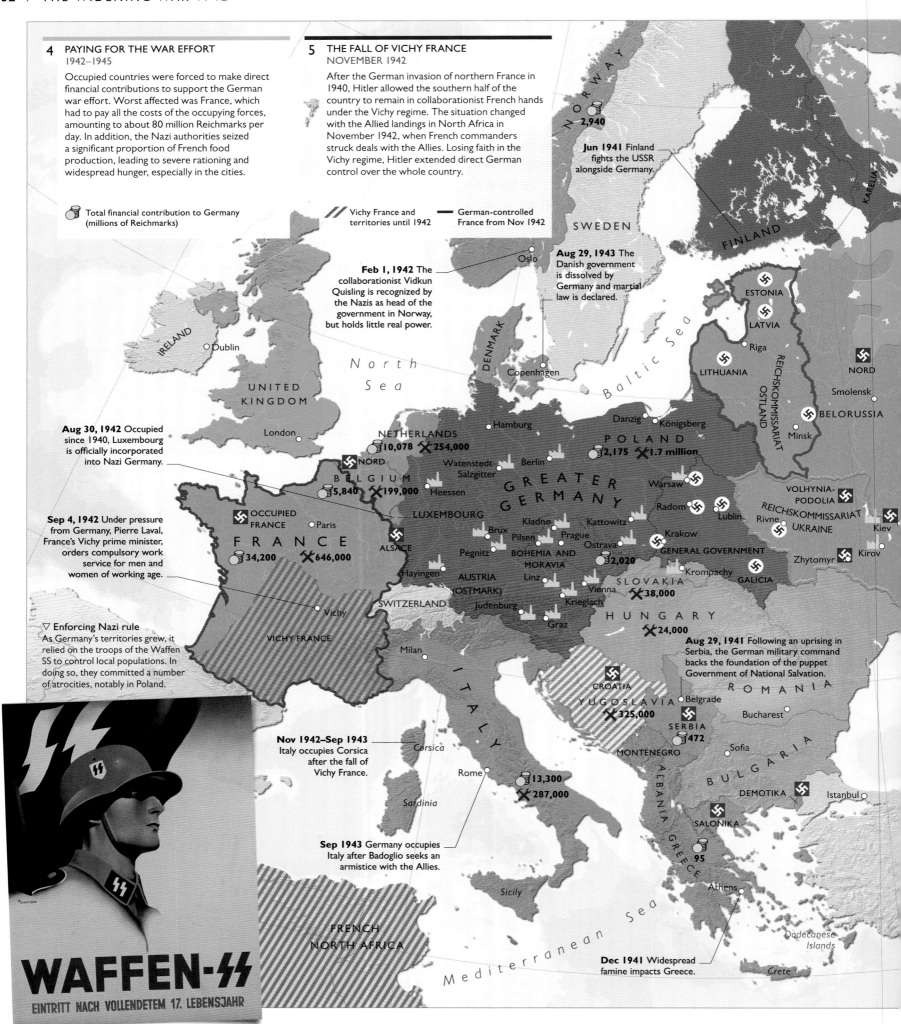

4 PAYING FOR THE WAR EFFORT
1942–1945

Occupied countries were forced to make direct financial contributions to support the German war effort. Worst affected was France, which had to pay all the costs of the occupying forces, amounting to about 80 million Reichmarks per day. In addition, the Nazi authorities seized a significant proportion of French food production, leading to severe rationing and widespread hunger, especially in the cities.

💰 Total financial contribution to Germany (millions of Reichmarks)

5 THE FALL OF VICHY FRANCE
NOVEMBER 1942

After the German invasion of northern France in 1940, Hitler allowed the southern half of the country to remain in collaborationist French hands under the Vichy regime. The situation changed with the Allied landings in North Africa in November 1942, when French commanders struck deals with the Allies. Losing faith in the Vichy regime, Hitler extended direct German control over the whole country.

// Vichy France and territories until 1942

— German-controlled France from Nov 1942

Feb 1, 1942 The collaborationist Vidkun Quisling is recognized by the Nazis as head of the government in Norway, but holds little real power.

Aug 29, 1943 The Danish government is dissolved by Germany and martial law is declared.

Jun 1941 Finland fights the USSR alongside Germany.

Aug 30, 1942 Occupied since 1940, Luxembourg is officially incorporated into Nazi Germany.

Sep 4, 1942 Under pressure from Germany, Pierre Laval, France's Vichy prime minister, orders compulsory work service for men and women of working age.

▽ **Enforcing Nazi rule**
As Germany's territories grew, it relied on the troops of the Waffen SS to control local populations. In doing so, they committed a number of atrocities, notably in Poland.

Nov 1942–Sep 1943 Italy occupies Corsica after the fall of Vichy France.

Sep 1943 Germany occupies Italy after Badoglio seeks an armistice with the Allies.

Aug 29, 1941 Following an uprising in Serbia, the German military command backs the foundation of the puppet Government of National Salvation.

Dec 1941 Widespread famine impacts Greece.

NETHERLANDS 💰10,078 ✗254,000

BELGIUM 💰5,840 ✗199,000

OCCUPIED FRANCE

FRANCE 💰34,200 ✗646,000

💰2,175 ✗1.7 million

💰2,020

SLOVAKIA ✗38,000

HUNGARY ✗24,000

YUGOSLAVIA ✗325,000

SERBIA 💰472

💰13,300 ✗287,000

💰95

💰2,940

WAFFEN-⚡⚡
EINTRITT NACH VOLLENDETEM 17. LEBENSJAHR

NORWAY
SWEDEN
FINLAND
KARELIA
ESTONIA
LATVIA
Riga
NORD
LITHUANIA
REICHSKOMMISSARIAT OSTLAND
Smolensk
BELORUSSIA
Minsk
IRELAND
Dublin
UNITED KINGDOM
London
North Sea
DENMARK
Oslo
Copenhagen
Baltic Sea
Hamburg
Danzig
Königsberg
POLAND
Warsaw
VOLHYNIA-PODOLIA
Watenstedt-Salzgitter
Berlin
GREATER GERMANY
Radom
Lublin
Rivne
REICHSKOMMISSARIAT UKRAINE
Kiev
Heessen
LUXEMBOURG
NORD
Kladno
Brüx
Pilsen
Prague
Kattowitz
Krakow
GENERAL GOVERNMENT
Zhytomyr
Kirov
Pegnitz
BOHEMIA AND MORAVIA
Ostrava
Krompachy
GALICIA
Paris
ALSACE
AUSTRIA (OSTMARK)
Linz
Vienna
Krieglach
SLOVAKIA
Hayingen
Judenburg
Graz
Vichy
SWITZERLAND
VICHY FRANCE
Milan
ITALY
ROMANIA
Belgrade
Bucharest
CROATIA
MONTENEGRO
Sofia
BULGARIA
Corsica
Rome
SERBIA
ALBANIA
DEMOTIKA
Istanbul
Sardinia
SALONIKA
GREECE
Sicily
Athens
FRENCH NORTH AFRICA
Mediterranean Sea
Dodecanese Islands
Crete

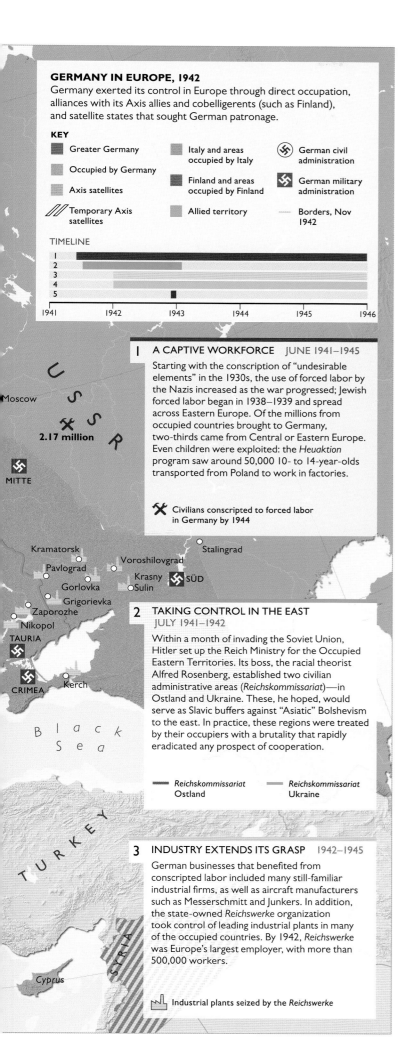

GERMANY IN EUROPE, 1942

Germany exerted its control in Europe through direct occupation, alliances with its Axis allies and cobelligerents (such as Finland), and satellite states that sought German patronage.

KEY

- Greater Germany
- Occupied by Germany
- Axis satellites
- Temporary Axis satellites
- Italy and areas occupied by Italy
- Finland and areas occupied by Finland
- Allied territory
- German civil administration
- German military administration
- Borders, Nov 1942

TIMELINE

1 | 2 | 3 | 4 | 5

1941 | 1942 | 1943 | 1944 | 1945 | 1946

1 A CAPTIVE WORKFORCE JUNE 1941–1945

Starting with the conscription of "undesirable elements" in the 1930s, the use of forced labor by the Nazis increased as the war progressed; Jewish forced labor began in 1938–1939 and spread across Eastern Europe. Of the millions from occupied countries brought to Germany, two-thirds came from Central or Eastern Europe. Even children were exploited: the *Heuaktion* program saw around 50,000 10- to 14-year-olds transported from Poland to work in factories.

Civilians conscripted to forced labor in Germany by 1944

2 TAKING CONTROL IN THE EAST
JULY 1941–1942

Within a month of invading the Soviet Union, Hitler set up the Reich Ministry for the Occupied Eastern Territories. Its boss, the racial theorist Alfred Rosenberg, established two civilian administrative areas (*Reichskommissariat*)—in Ostland and Ukraine. These, he hoped, would serve as Slavic buffers against "Asiatic" Bolshevism to the east. In practice, these regions were treated by their occupiers with a brutality that rapidly eradicated any prospect of cooperation.

Reichskommissariat Ostland

Reichskommissariat Ukraine

3 INDUSTRY EXTENDS ITS GRASP 1942–1945

German businesses that benefited from conscripted labor included many still-familiar industrial firms, as well as aircraft manufacturers such as Messerschmitt and Junkers. In addition, the state-owned *Reichswerke* organization took control of leading industrial plants in many of the occupied countries. By 1942, *Reichswerke* was Europe's largest employer, with more than 500,000 workers.

Industrial plants seized by the *Reichswerke*

NEW ORDER IN EUROPE

At its peak, Greater Germany—Germany and the territories it had annexed—covered much of central Europe, and most other countries on the continent were either occupied by Germany or under its influence. Hitler had begun to fullfil his dream of creating *Lebensraum* ("living space") for the German "master race."

Countries occupied by Germany were treated with degrees of severity that reflected how closely their populations matched the Nazis' Aryan ideal. Norway and Denmark received relatively lenient treatment; Denmark kept its king and its government until mid-1943, when it was placed under military occupation.

The situation in Eastern Europe, however, was very different: the Nazis regarded the people there as inferior, or subject, races and treated them with brutality. The worst regimes were imposed on Poland, occupied USSR, and the Baltic states, where communities were evicted to create living space for ethnic German settlement.

Occupied territories were placed under the control of civilian administrations, headed by Nazi Party officials, or under military administrations. In either case, the countries were exploited financially, economically, and militarily in order to advance the German war effort. Occupied nations were forced to transfer large capital sums to Germany and to provide workers for German factories; when the number of volunteers was considered insufficient, forced labor was introduced on a huge scale. Such measures provoked active resistance movements (see pp.176–177), which the occupation authorities sought to suppress with extreme brutality.

> *"The year 1941 will be, I am convinced, the historical year of a great European New Order."*
>
> ADOLF HITLER, SPEECH AT THE BERLIN *SPORTPALAST*, 1941

ITALY AND *LO SPAZIO VITALE*

Just as *Lebensraum* was a key goal for Germany's Nazis, Italy's Fascists also sought their own living space (*Lo Spazio Vitale*), by expanding their national boundaries across the Mediterranean and into North Africa (see pp.74–75). Fueled by the racist ideologies of figures such as Giuseppe Bottai—who served as Italy's Minister of Education—they argued that Italy was the heir to ancient Rome. Their goal was to create "a new Empire in which Italians would illuminate the world with their art, educate it with their knowledge, and ... their administrative technique and ability."

Giuseppe Bottai, Fascist politician during the early years of the war.

WAVES OF PERSECUTION

The organized and systematic persecution of Jews and other minorities began in Germany, but expanded with the Nazi advances between 1940 and 1942. The most murderous phase took place in 1942 and 1943.

KEY

- Greater Germany, Nov 1942
- Axis-controlled territory
- Allied territory

TIMELINE

1 2 3 4

1930 1935 1940 1945 1950

Sep 12, 1942 The Nazi authorities complete the deportation of 265,000 Jews from the Warsaw ghetto to Treblinka.

Jun 25–29, 1941 An estimated 4,000 Jews are massacred in Kaunas, Lithuania, following the German occupation of the city.

Jan 25, 1945 25,000 prisoners die at the hands of the SS during the evacuation of the Stutthof camp.

Aug 4, 1944 Anne Frank becomes one of 100,000 Dutch Jews sent to the death camps.

Apr 15, 1945 British forces liberate the Bergen-Belsen death camp.

Mar 27, 1942 France's occupation authorities begin deporting 65,000 French Jews through Drancy.

Sep 15, 1935 The Reichstag passes anti-Jewish laws.

Oct 18, 1939 The first Jewish deportees are sent to the Lublin Reservation camp.

Map labels: NORWAY, SWEDEN, North Sea, DENMARK, Copenhagen, Baltic Sea, REICHSKOMMISSARIAT OSTLAND, Kaiserwald, Riga, Jungfernhof, Kaunas, Ponary, Vilnius, Bialystok, FORMER POLAND, Stutthof, Treblinka, Chelmno, Lublin, Warsaw, Sobibor, Lodz, Majdanek, Czestochowa, Sosnowiec, Belzec, Lwow, Gross-Rosen, Plaszow, Krakow, SLOVAKIA, Auschwitz-Birkenau, BOHEMIA AND MORAVIA, Theresienstadt, Prague, Flossenburg, Nuremberg, Mauthausen, Bratislava, Budapest, HUNGARY, Vienna, OSTMARK, Danica, Zagreb, Jasenovac, Stara Gradiska, Djakovo, Belgrade, Tasmajdan, Jadovno, INDEPENDENT STATE OF CROATIA, Sajmiste, SERBIA, Bozen, SWITZERLAND, Natzweiler, Dachau, Fossoli, ITALY, FRANCE, Drancy, UNITED KINGDOM, London, Amsterdam, 'S-Hertogenbosch, NETHERLANDS, Westerbork, Mechelen, Brussels, BELGIUM, Bergen-Belsen, Neuengamme, Ravensbrück, Sachsenhausen, Berlin, GREATER GERMANY, Sachsenburg, Mittelbau-Dora, Buchenwald

1 ANTI-SEMITISM AND THE LAW 1933–1938

Hitler put his anti-Semitism into practice when the Nazi Party came to power in 1933. In April 1933, Jewish shops and businesses were subject to a boycott. Soon, Jews were disbarred from the civil service, practicing law, and owning farms. In 1935, new laws denied Jews citizenship and criminalized sexual relationships between Jews and ethnic Germans. Then, in 1938, the assassination of a Nazi diplomat was used as the excuse for Kristallnacht (see pp.30–31), a pogrom that saw the destruction of Jewish-owned shops and synagogues.

✠ First concentration camp   ✠ Concentration camps

2 GHETTOS AND KILLINGS 1939–1942

The plight of the Jews worsened with the outbreak of war. Many were sent to ghettos in Poland—gathering places for eventual deportation. Jewish populations were rounded up in France, Belgium, the Netherlands, and the former Yugoslavia (where many were massacred). The worst mass killings took place during the invasion of the Soviet Union, when specially-appointed SS *Einsatzgruppen* are thought to have killed almost 500,000 people.

⚡ Locations of *Einsatzgruppen*   ✡ Ghettos
☠ Sites of mass killings

3 THE DEATH CAMPS 1942–1945

Nazi leaders sought a "final solution to the Jewish question in Europe." It was agreed by leading Nazi officials in a meeting in Wannsee, Berlin, in January 1942. By the spring of 1942, freight trains were carrying Jews from the ghettos to camps in the east. The most lethal were the six purpose-built death camps—Chelmno, Auschwitz-Birkenau, Belzec, Majdanek, Sobibor, and Treblinka—in occupied Poland.

✺ Wannsee meeting   ✠ Extermination camps

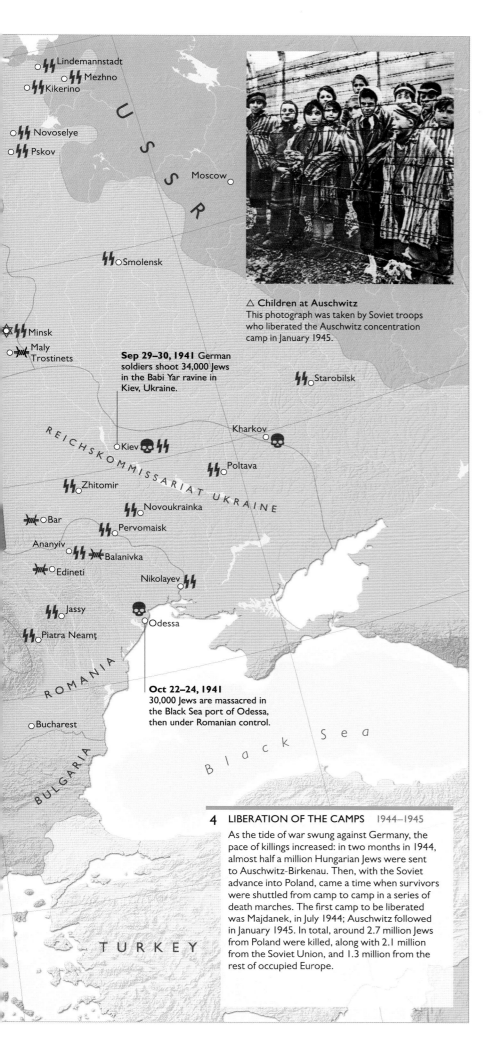

Lindemannstadt
Mezhno
Kikerino

Novoselye
Pskov

Moscow

Smolensk

Sep 29–30, 1941 German
soldiers shoot 34,000 Jews
in the Babi Yar ravine in
Kiev, Ukraine.

Minsk
**Maly
Trostinets**

Starobilsk

Kharkov

Kiev

Poltava

R E I C H S K O M M I S S A R I A T U K R A I N E

Zhitomir

Bar
Novoukrainka

Pervomaisk
Ananyiv
Balanivka
Edineti

Nikolayev

Jassy
Odessa

Piatra Neamț

R O M A N I A

B l a c k   S e a

Bucharest

B U L G A R I A

Oct 22–24, 1941
30,000 Jews are massacred in
the Black Sea port of Odessa,
then under Romanian control.

△ **Children at Auschwitz**
This photograph was taken by Soviet troops
who liberated the Auschwitz concentration
camp in January 1945.

4   LIBERATION OF THE CAMPS   1944–1945

As the tide of war swung against Germany, the
pace of killings increased: in two months in 1944,
almost half a million Hungarian Jews were sent
to Auschwitz-Birkenau. Then, with the Soviet
advance into Poland, came a time when survivors
were shuttled from camp to camp in a series of
death marches. The first camp to be liberated
was Majdanek, in July 1944; Auschwitz followed
in January 1945. In total, around 2.7 million Jews
from Poland were killed, along with 2.1 million
from the Soviet Union, and 1.3 million from the
rest of occupied Europe.

T U R K E Y

THE HOLOCAUST

Hitler and his supporters saw the Jews as a worldwide
enemy conspiring to undermine the German nation.
The Nazi regime embarked on what became known as
the Holocaust—the systematic persecution and murder
of around six million European Jews.

The Nazi rise to power had immediate consequences for Germany's
Jews, who were treated from the start as racial outcasts. From 1935
onward they were denied citizenship and forbidden to marry or
have sexual relations with people of "German blood." The policy
was deliberately aimed at encouraging Jews to flee the country,
and by 1938 about half the Jewish population had done just that.

With the outbreak of war, the situation deteriorated further.
Ghettos were created in the occupied eastern lands where
deportees could be resettled and controlled. During the drive
eastward many Jewish populations were massacred, often in
retaliation for isolated acts of resistance. From late 1941, new
extermination centers were constructed—known as Operation
Reinhard camps—where Jews were sent to the gas chambers or
selected for grueling slave labor, through which thousands more
were worked to death. The results were horrifying: when liberation
finally came, an estimated two-thirds of Europe's pre-war Jewish
population had been wiped out.

*"The Holocaust was not only a Jewish tragedy,
but also a human tragedy."*

SIMON WIESENTHAL, HOLOCAUST SURVIVOR

OTHER PERSECUTED MINORITIES

Jews were not the only minority
group persecuted by the Nazis.
Their victims stretched from
homosexual men and people
with disabilities to Jehovah's
Witnesses, Freemasons, and
Catholic and Protestant
dissidents. In terms of numbers,
ethnic groups suffered the worst
losses. Romani people faced the
same genocidal threat as the
Jews, while the Nazi assault
on the Slavic peoples ended in
the deaths of some 15 million
Soviets and 3 million Poles.

**Roma and Sinti women
at Bergen-Belsen**

THE WARSAW GHETTO

In the 1930s, Warsaw was home to 375,000 Jews—the second largest single Jewish population in the world after New York. Following Germany's invasion of Poland in 1939, the Nazis imposed a multitude of restrictions on Jews, including their enforced relocation to a ghetto.

△ **Identification mark**
Jews in the Warsaw Ghetto were forced to wear a white armband featuring a blue Star of David on their right arm so they could be identified easily.

On October 12, 1940, all Jewish residents of Warsaw and others from outlying districts were forced to move to an area of just 1.3 sq miles (3.4 sq km) in the north of the city. High walls made of stone and barbed wire enclosed the ghetto, and armed guards kept watch; any Jew found outside the walls could be shot. In such a confined space, chronic overcrowding and malnutrition were rife. An estimated 400,000 Jews struggled daily for survival with an average of eight to ten people sharing a single room. The threat of starvation was constant, since the food rations were not sufficient to sustain life. Typhus and other deadly illnesses became endemic.

The Warsaw Ghetto Uprising

Mass deportations of Polish Jews to concentration camps and extermination camps began in July 1942. They resumed in January 1943 and again in early April. This time, the Jews fought back against the Germans, with Jewish resistance fighters giving battle for four weeks. However, they were vastly outnumbered, and the ghetto was incinerated and reduced to rubble. By the time the fighting ended on May 16, 7,000 Jews had been slaughtered on the streets and another 42,000 had been taken captive and deported. The Warsaw concentration camp complex was built on the site of the old ghetto.

THE NAZI CAMPS

Shown here on a contemporary map, concentration and extermination camps were spread throughout the territory of the Third Reich during World War II. Auschwitz-Birkenau in Poland became the most notorious: between 1.1 and 1.3 million Jews were sent there, and at least 960,000 were executed in the gas chambers. An estimated 750,000 perished at Treblinka, also in Poland.

Nazi round-up
Terrified Jewish families are rounded up by Nazi troops in the Warsaw Ghetto prior to their forced deportation to concentration and extermination camps. Attempts by Jewish guerrillas to resist the Nazis ultimately ended in failure.

THE UNDERGROUND WAR

While Hitler's armies rolled across Europe, another, more clandestine war was going on within the occupied lands. Allied operatives carried out surprise raids, while local resistance groups, supported from London, rose up against their oppressors in a variety of ways, such as producing propaganda, sabotage, and direct armed conflict.

KEY

- Allied territory, 1942
- Axis territory, occupations, and cobelligerents, 1942
- Neutral territory, 1942
- Main SOE operations area
- ⊞ SOE main bases
- ⊞ SOE secondary bases
- ✝ Raids and attacks by SOE
- ✹ Sabotage
- ✊ Resistance
- ♟ Partisan support
- ▭ Communications
- ⚲ Supplies delivered by air

TIMELINE

1
2
3
4
5

JAN 1941   JUL   JAN 1942   JUL   JAN 1943   JUL

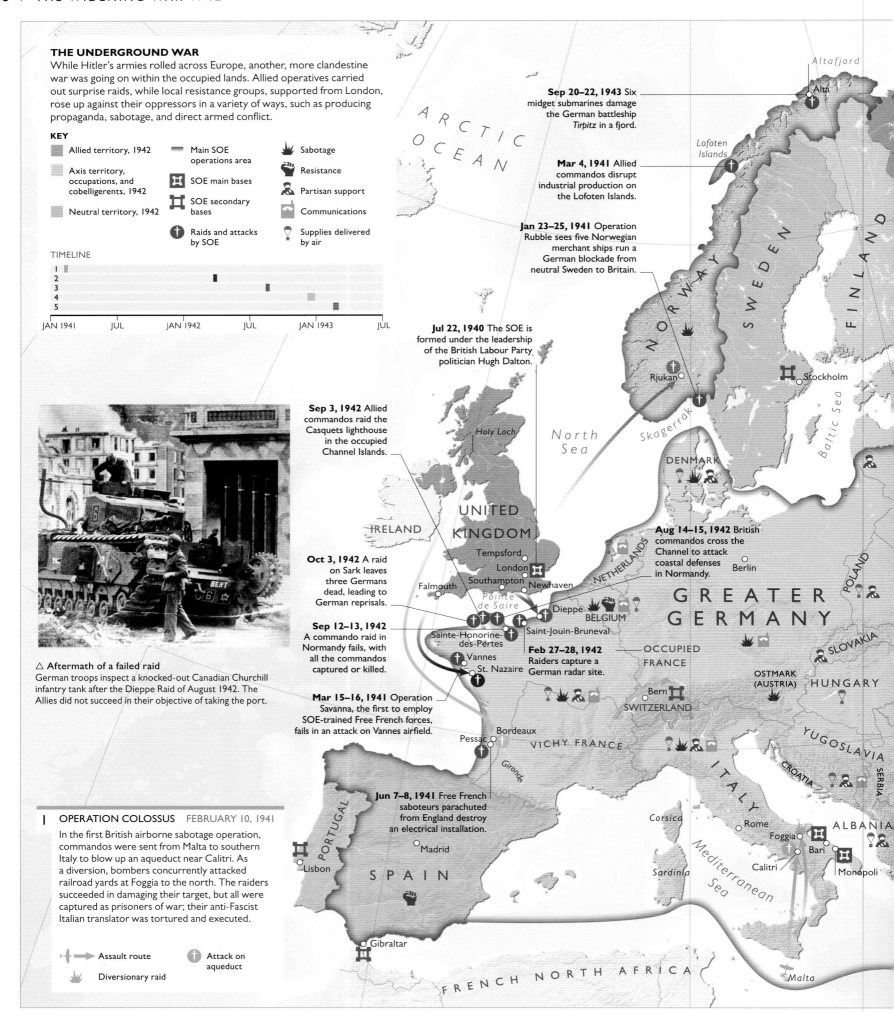

△ **Aftermath of a failed raid**
German troops inspect a knocked-out Canadian Churchill infantry tank after the Dieppe Raid of August 1942. The Allies did not succeed in their objective of taking the port.

OPERATION COLOSSUS FEBRUARY 10, 1941

In the first British airborne sabotage operation, commandos were sent from Malta to southern Italy to blow up an aqueduct near Calitri. As a diversion, bombers concurrently attacked railroad yards at Foggia to the north. The raiders succeeded in damaging their target, but all were captured as prisoners of war; their anti-Fascist Italian translator was tortured and executed.

- ⊢→ Assault route
- ✹ Diversionary raid
- ✝ Attack on aqueduct

Sep 20–22, 1943 Six midget submarines damage the German battleship *Tirpitz* in a fjord.

Mar 4, 1941 Allied commandos disrupt industrial production on the Lofoten Islands.

Jan 23–25, 1941 Operation Rubble sees five Norwegian merchant ships run a German blockade from neutral Sweden to Britain.

Jul 22, 1940 The SOE is formed under the leadership of the British Labour Party politician Hugh Dalton.

Sep 3, 1942 Allied commandos raid the Casquets lighthouse in the occupied Channel Islands.

Oct 3, 1942 A raid on Sark leaves three Germans dead, leading to German reprisals.

Sep 12–13, 1942 A commando raid in Normandy fails, with all the commandos captured or killed.

Aug 14–15, 1942 British commandos cross the Channel to attack coastal defenses in Normandy.

Feb 27–28, 1942 Raiders capture a German radar site.

Mar 15–16, 1941 Operation Savanna, the first to employ SOE-trained Free French forces, fails in an attack on Vannes airfield.

Jun 7–8, 1941 Free French saboteurs parachuted from England destroy an electrical installation.

Map labels

ARCTIC OCEAN
Altafjord
Alta
Lofoten Islands
NORWAY
SWEDEN
FINLAND
Baltic Sea
Skagerrak
North Sea
Rjukan
Stockholm
DENMARK
Holy Loch
IRELAND
UNITED KINGDOM
Tempsford
London
Southampton
Newhaven
Falmouth
Pointe de Saire
Sainte-Honorine-des-Pertes
Vannes
St. Nazaire
Dieppe
Saint-Jouin-Bruneval
NETHERLANDS
BELGIUM
Berlin
POLAND
GREATER GERMANY
OCCUPIED FRANCE
SLOVAKIA
OSTMARK (AUSTRIA)
HUNGARY
Bern
SWITZERLAND
YUGOSLAVIA
CROATIA
SERBIA
Pessac
Bordeaux
Gironde
VICHY FRANCE
ITALY
Corsica
Rome
ALBANIA
Foggia
Bari
Calitri
Monopoli
Sardinia
Mediterranean Sea
Madrid
SPAIN
PORTUGAL
Lisbon
Gibraltar
FRENCH NORTH AFRICA
Malta

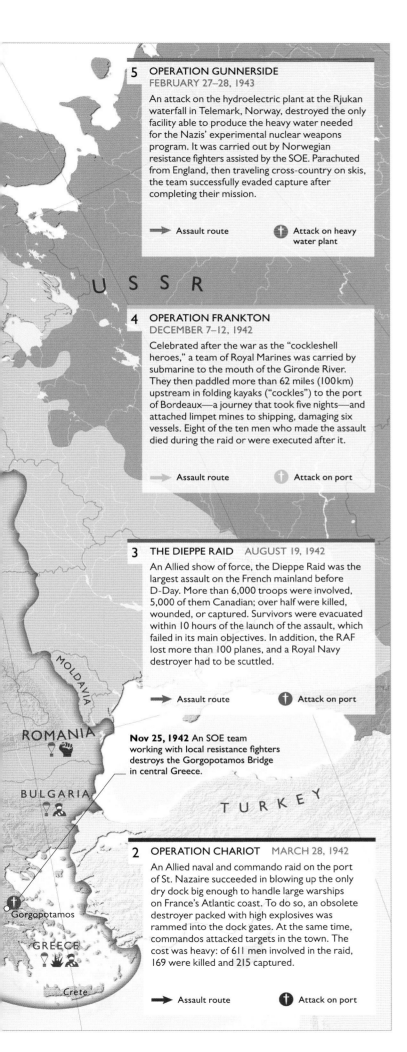

5 OPERATION GUNNERSIDE
FEBRUARY 27–28, 1943

An attack on the hydroelectric plant at the Rjukan waterfall in Telemark, Norway, destroyed the only facility able to produce the heavy water needed for the Nazis' experimental nuclear weapons program. It was carried out by Norwegian resistance fighters assisted by the SOE. Parachuted from England, then traveling cross-country on skis, the team successfully evaded capture after completing their mission.

➡ Assault route   ⊕ Attack on heavy water plant

4 OPERATION FRANKTON
DECEMBER 7–12, 1942

Celebrated after the war as the "cockleshell heroes," a team of Royal Marines was carried by submarine to the mouth of the Gironde River. They then paddled more than 62 miles (100km) upstream in folding kayaks ("cockles") to the port of Bordeaux—a journey that took five nights—and attached limpet mines to shipping, damaging six vessels. Eight of the ten men who made the assault died during the raid or were executed after it.

➡ Assault route   ⊕ Attack on port

3 THE DIEPPE RAID   AUGUST 19, 1942

An Allied show of force, the Dieppe Raid was the largest assault on the French mainland before D-Day. More than 6,000 troops were involved, 5,000 of them Canadian; over half were killed, wounded, or captured. Survivors were evacuated within 10 hours of the launch of the assault, which failed in its main objectives. In addition, the RAF lost more than 100 planes, and a Royal Navy destroyer had to be scuttled.

➡ Assault route   ⊕ Attack on port

Nov 25, 1942 An SOE team working with local resistance fighters destroys the Gorgopotamos Bridge in central Greece.

2 OPERATION CHARIOT   MARCH 28, 1942

An Allied naval and commando raid on the port of St. Nazaire succeeded in blowing up the only dry dock big enough to handle large warships on France's Atlantic coast. To do so, an obsolete destroyer packed with high explosives was rammed into the dock gates. At the same time, commandos attacked targets in the town. The cost was heavy: of 611 men involved in the raid, 169 were killed and 215 captured.

➡ Assault route   ⊕ Attack on port

RAIDS AND SUBVERSIONS

With much of Europe under Nazi control by mid-1940, Britain resorted to unconventional means of attacking the enemy. A secret body—the Special Operations Executive (SOE)—trained commandos in guerrilla tactics and employed special forces to conduct clandestine operations in occupied territory.

At a time when Hitler's plans for Europe seemed close to success, Britain's War Cabinet considered it important to take the offensive by staging surprise attacks on occupied territory. Sometimes these took the form of combined operations, with air, land, and naval forces working together. The first such raid, on the Lofoten Islands in Norway, was conducted successfully in March 1941. Other attacks followed, aimed at spreading fear along the coasts. The most ambitious was the assault on St. Nazaire in March 1942, the success of which encouraged Allied commanders to launch the disastrous Dieppe Raid five months later.

Meanwhile, from early 1941 onward the SOE had been coordinating espionage and sabotage activities in the occupied lands, as well as liaising with resistance movements across the continent (see pp.176–177). Some incursions were conducted by its own operatives, while others employed SOE-trained resistance fighters inserted back into their own homelands to carry out missions. The SOE's activities were sometimes controversial, as they risked triggering Nazi reprisals on local civilians. Yet by striking into the heart of occupied Europe, they kept the spirit of resistance alive and helped prepare the path for D-Day (see pp.186–187).

"In no previous war … have resistance forces been so closely harnessed to the main military effort."

US GENERAL DWIGHT D. EISENHOWER, 1945

MAJOR-GENERAL SIR COLIN GUBBINS
1896–1976

The SOE—also known as "Churchill's secret army"—was officially formed in 1940. The organization was shaped and then led by Colin Gubbins, the son of a British diplomat. Gubbins served with distinction in World War I, winning the Military Cross for rescuing wounded men under fire. He developed an interest in irregular warfare while serving in Russia and then Ireland in the immediate post-war years. In 1940, after service in the brief Norwegian campaign, he was seconded to the newly formed SOE, taking over as its head in 1943. There he coordinated the work of resistance groups in the occupied lands, playing a significant, if little-acknowledged, part in the victorious Allied war effort.

ARCTIC CONVOYS

Allied civilian sailors endured the dangers of extreme Arctic conditions and German air, surface, and U-boat fleets to bring more than 4½ million tons (4 million metric tons) of supplies to Soviet ports between 1941 and 1945. Around 3,000 men died and more than 100 ships were lost in the effort to keep the USSR in the war.

The German invasion of the USSR in June 1941 prompted Stalin to ask Britain and its allies for assistance in supplying the Soviet war effort. From August 1941, convoys undertook what Churchill called the "worst journey in the world," ferrying materiel needed in the war against Germany.

The most direct route took convoys through the Arctic Circle to the Soviet ports of Murmansk and Archangel. Passing close to German-held territory, they were within easy reach of the Luftwaffe and U-boats waiting in ambush, while in the Norwegian fjords, German warships—including the pride of the fleet, the *Tirpitz*—lay in wait.

The convoys faced gales, blizzards, and dense fog in the Arctic Ocean. In summer, they could follow a route that lay further from the Norwegian coast,

but this took them nearer to icebergs drifting into the sea lanes. In winter, the darkness offered cover but the sea ice forced the ships nearer their enemies. Thick ice formed over the vessels and had to be chipped away so that they did not capsize.

The first convoys suffered few losses, but Germany intensified its operations in 1942. The calamitous attack on convoy PQ-17 in July 1942 forced the Allies to improve the security of the convoys. The Allied decision to suspend the convoys while they prepared for Operation Torch (see pp.146–47) in September–December 1942 increased tension with the Soviets, who were desperately fighting for Stalingrad (see pp.150–151). Convoys resumed and ran until the end of the war, but bad feeling between the Eastern and Western Allies remained.

ROUTES TO THE USSR

The Arctic route to the USSR was the shortest, and accounted for almost 25 percent of Allied aid sent to the Soviet Union. However, Soviet ships voyaging from the west coast of the US carried 50 percent. The Soviets also ran a convoy route through the Bering Strait, supplying fuel for Lend-Lease aircraft being transferred from Alaska to Siberia.

KEY
→ Summer Arctic convoy route
→ Winter Arctic convoy route
→ Soviet convoy route
→ US/Soviet convoy route

PERIL ALL AROUND
Squeezed between the ice and the German navy, U-boats, and air bases along the coast of Norway, the Arctic route was the most dangerous supply route to the Soviet Union.

KEY
▮ Axis territories, occupations, and cobelligerents by end of 1942
▮ Allied territories by end of 1942
⁘ Extent of winter sea ice
✈ German air bases
⚓ German naval and U-boat bases
⚓ Allied naval bases

TIMELINE
1 2 3 4 5
1941 — 1942 — 1943 — 1944 — 1945 — 1946

Aug 1941–Jun 1942 Convoys congregate at the Icelandic harbors of Reykjavík and Hvalfjördur before sailing to the USSR.

Aug 1941–May 1945 Convoys set off from numerous naval bases across the British Isles.

Aug 12, 1941 The first convoy "Dervish" sets sail for Archangel via Iceland.

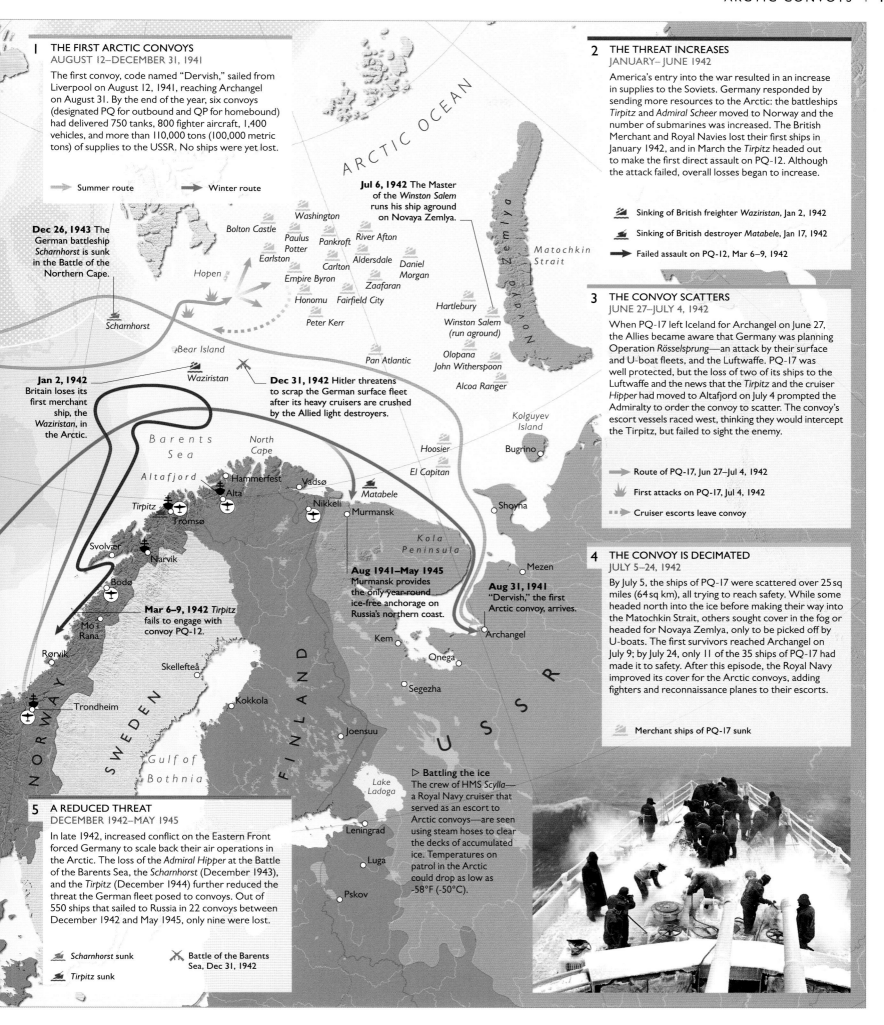

1 THE FIRST ARCTIC CONVOYS
AUGUST 12–DECEMBER 31, 1941

The first convoy, code named "Dervish," sailed from Liverpool on August 12, 1941, reaching Archangel on August 31. By the end of the year, six convoys (designated PQ for outbound and QP for homebound) had delivered 750 tanks, 800 fighter aircraft, 1,400 vehicles, and more than 110,000 tons (100,000 metric tons) of supplies to the USSR. No ships were yet lost.

→ Summer route
→ Winter route

Dec 26, 1943 The German battleship *Scharnhorst* is sunk in the Battle of the Northern Cape.

Jul 6, 1942 The Master of the *Winston Salem* runs his ship aground on Novaya Zemlya.

Jan 2, 1942 Britain loses its first merchant ship, the *Waziristan*, in the Arctic.

Dec 31, 1942 Hitler threatens to scrap the German surface fleet after its heavy cruisers are crushed by the Allied light destroyers.

Mar 6–9, 1942 *Tirpitz* fails to engage with convoy PQ-12.

Aug 1941–May 1945 Murmansk provides the only year-round ice-free anchorage on Russia's northern coast.

Aug 31, 1941 "Dervish," the first Arctic convoy, arrives.

2 THE THREAT INCREASES
JANUARY– JUNE 1942

America's entry into the war resulted in an increase in supplies to the Soviets. Germany responded by sending more resources to the Arctic: the battleships *Tirpitz* and *Admiral Scheer* moved to Norway and the number of submarines was increased. The British Merchant and Royal Navies lost their first ships in January 1942, and in March the *Tirpitz* headed out to make the first direct assault on PQ-12. Although the attack failed, overall losses began to increase.

⚓ Sinking of British freighter *Waziristan*, Jan 2, 1942
⚓ Sinking of British destroyer *Matabele*, Jan 17, 1942
→ Failed assault on PQ-12, Mar 6–9, 1942

3 THE CONVOY SCATTERS
JUNE 27–JULY 4, 1942

When PQ-17 left Iceland for Archangel on June 27, the Allies became aware that Germany was planning Operation *Rösselsprung*—an attack by their surface and U-boat fleets, and the Luftwaffe. PQ-17 was well protected, but the loss of two of its ships to the Luftwaffe and the news that the *Tirpitz* and the cruiser *Hipper* had moved to Altafjord on July 4 prompted the Admiralty to order the convoy to scatter. The convoy's escort vessels raced west, thinking they would intercept the Tirpitz, but failed to sight the enemy.

→ Route of PQ-17, Jun 27–Jul 4, 1942
✹ First attacks on PQ-17, Jul 4, 1942
┅► Cruiser escorts leave convoy

4 THE CONVOY IS DECIMATED
JULY 5–24, 1942

By July 5, the ships of PQ-17 were scattered over 25 sq miles (64 sq km), all trying to reach safety. While some headed north into the ice before making their way into the Matochkin Strait, others sought cover in the fog or headed for Novaya Zemlya, only to be picked off by U-boats. The first survivors reached Archangel on July 9; by July 24, only 11 of the 35 ships of PQ-17 had made it to safety. After this episode, the Royal Navy improved its cover for the Arctic convoys, adding fighters and reconnaissance planes to their escorts.

⚓ Merchant ships of PQ-17 sunk

5 A REDUCED THREAT
DECEMBER 1942–MAY 1945

In late 1942, increased conflict on the Eastern Front forced Germany to scale back their air operations in the Arctic. The loss of the *Admiral Hipper* at the Battle of the Barents Sea, the *Scharnhorst* (December 1943), and the *Tirpitz* (December 1944) further reduced the threat the German fleet posed to convoys. Out of 550 ships that sailed to Russia in 22 convoys between December 1942 and May 1945, only nine were lost.

⚓ *Scharnhorst* sunk
⚓ *Tirpitz* sunk
✕ Battle of the Barents Sea, Dec 31, 1942

▷ **Battling the ice**
The crew of HMS *Scylla*—a Royal Navy cruiser that served as an escort to Arctic convoys—are seen using steam hoses to clear the decks of accumulated ice. Temperatures on patrol in the Arctic could drop as low as -58°F (-50°C).

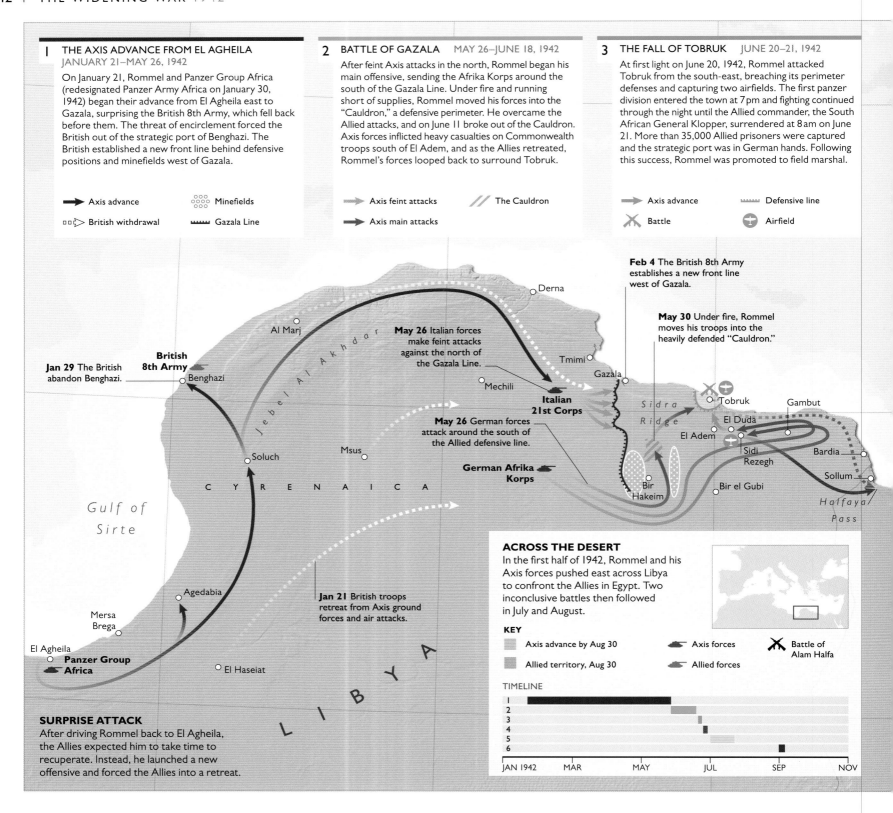

1 THE AXIS ADVANCE FROM EL AGHEILA
JANUARY 21–MAY 26, 1942

On January 21, Rommel and Panzer Group Africa (redesignated Panzer Army Africa on January 30, 1942) began their advance from El Agheila east to Gazala, surprising the British 8th Army, which fell back before them. The threat of encirclement forced the British out of the strategic port of Benghazi. The British established a new front line behind defensive positions and minefields west of Gazala.

→ Axis advance
⊶⊳ British withdrawal
⠿ Minefields
〰 Gazala Line

2 BATTLE OF GAZALA MAY 26–JUNE 18, 1942

After feint Axis attacks in the north, Rommel began his main offensive, sending the Afrika Korps around the south of the Gazala Line. Under fire and running short of supplies, Rommel moved his forces into the "Cauldron," a defensive perimeter. He overcame the Allied attacks, and on June 11 broke out of the Cauldron. Axis forces inflicted heavy casualties on Commonwealth troops south of El Adem, and as the Allies retreated, Rommel's forces looped back to surround Tobruk.

→ Axis feint attacks
→ Axis main attacks
// The Cauldron

3 THE FALL OF TOBRUK JUNE 20–21, 1942

At first light on June 20, 1942, Rommel attacked Tobruk from the south-east, breaching its perimeter defenses and capturing two airfields. The first panzer division entered the town at 7pm and fighting continued through the night until the Allied commander, the South African General Klopper, surrendered at 8am on June 21. More than 35,000 Allied prisoners were captured and the strategic port was in German hands. Following this success, Rommel was promoted to field marshal.

→ Axis advance
〰 Defensive line
✗ Battle
✈ Airfield

SURPRISE ATTACK
After driving Rommel back to El Agheila, the Allies expected him to take time to recuperate. Instead, he launched a new offensive and forced the Allies into a retreat.

ACROSS THE DESERT
In the first half of 1942, Rommel and his Axis forces pushed east across Libya to confront the Allies in Egypt. Two inconclusive battles then followed in July and August.

KEY

▨ Axis advance by Aug 30
▨ Allied territory, Aug 30
🛦 Axis forces
🛦 Allied forces
✗ Battle of Alam Halfa

TIMELINE

ROMMEL'S FINAL ADVANCE

By the start of 1942, the war in North Africa had seemingly turned against Rommel, but the man known as the "desert fox" countered with a new attack. He pushed the Allies into a retreat deep into Egypt, leading to confrontation at El Alamein.

By early January 1942, the Allied Operation Crusader (see pp.76–77) had forced Rommel all the way back from the Egyptian border to El Agheila, on Libya's Gulf of Sirte. This major retreat left the Axis forces (consisting of Italian and German corps) exhausted and their supply lines disrupted. The British assumed that Rommel would be unable to regain the initiative for some time, and so took the opportunity to refit their equipment and allow their troops time to relax. However, Rommel acted swiftly to restore his troops to fighting order and began to advance eastward on January 21, overrunning Benghazi on January 28 and Tmini by early February. The Allies regrouped behind the Gazala Line—a defensive barrier of minefields interspersed with small, fortified keeps—which ran from

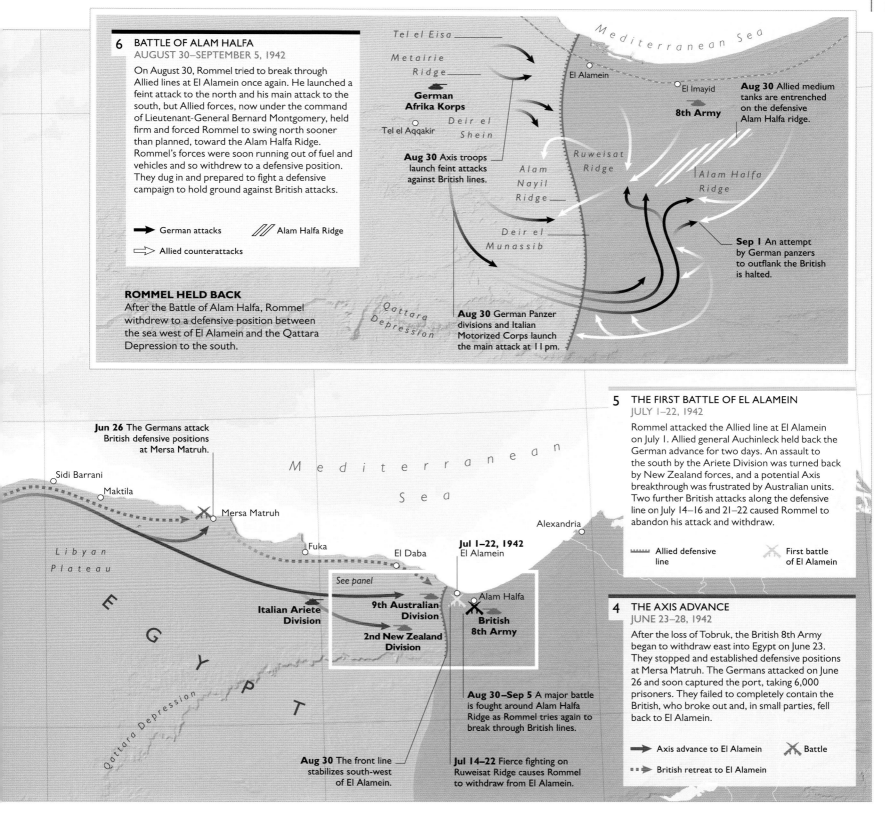

6 BATTLE OF ALAM HALFA
AUGUST 30–SEPTEMBER 5, 1942

On August 30, Rommel tried to break through Allied lines at El Alamein once again. He launched a feint attack to the north and his main attack to the south, but Allied forces, now under the command of Lieutenant-General Bernard Montgomery, held firm and forced Rommel to swing north sooner than planned, toward the Alam Halfa Ridge. Rommel's forces were soon running out of fuel and vehicles and so withdrew to a defensive position. They dug in and prepared to fight a defensive campaign to hold ground against British attacks.

➡ German attacks   ⫽ Alam Halfa Ridge

⇨ Allied counterattacks

ROMMEL HELD BACK
After the Battle of Alam Halfa, Rommel withdrew to a defensive position between the sea west of El Alamein and the Qattara Depression to the south.

Aug 30 Axis troops launch feint attacks against British lines.

Aug 30 German Panzer divisions and Italian Motorized Corps launch the main attack at 11 pm.

Aug 30 Allied medium tanks are entrenched on the defensive Alam Halfa ridge.

Sep 1 An attempt by German panzers to outflank the British is halted.

Mediterranean Sea

Tel el Eisa
Metairie Ridge
German Afrika Korps
Tel el Aqqakir
Deir el Shein
El Alamein
El Imayid
8th Army
Ruweisat Ridge
Alam Nayil Ridge
Alam Halfa Ridge
Deir el Munassib
Qattara Depression

Jun 26 The Germans attack British defensive positions at Mersa Matruh.

Sidi Barrani
Maktila
Mediterranean Sea
Mersa Matruh
Fuka
El Daba
Alexandria
Jul 1–22, 1942 El Alamein
Alam Halfa
Libyan Plateau
Italian Ariete Division
See panel
9th Australian Division
2nd New Zealand Division
British 8th Army
E G Y P T
Qattara Depression

Aug 30 The front line stabilizes south-west of El Alamein.

Aug 30–Sep 5 A major battle is fought around Alam Halfa Ridge as Rommel tries again to break through British lines.

Jul 14–22 Fierce fighting on Ruweisat Ridge causes Rommel to withdraw from El Alamein.

5 THE FIRST BATTLE OF EL ALAMEIN
JULY 1–22, 1942

Rommel attacked the Allied line at El Alamein on July 1. Allied general Auchinleck held back the German advance for two days. An assault to the south by the Ariete Division was turned back by New Zealand forces, and a potential Axis breakthrough was frustrated by Australian units. Two further British attacks along the defensive line on July 14–16 and 21–22 caused Rommel to abandon his attack and withdraw.

▨▨▨ Allied defensive line   ✕ First battle of El Alamein

4 THE AXIS ADVANCE
JUNE 23–28, 1942

After the loss of Tobruk, the British 8th Army began to withdraw east into Egypt on June 23. They stopped and established defensive positions at Mersa Matruh. The Germans attacked on June 26 and soon captured the port, taking 6,000 prisoners. They failed to completely contain the British, who broke out and, in small parties, fell back to El Alamein.

➡ Axis advance to El Alamein   ✕ Battle

▪▪▪➤ British retreat to El Alamein

---

the coast at Gazala to Bir Hakeim about 60 miles (95 km) to the south. Despite fierce resistance—particularly from the Free French forces at Bir Hakeim—and heavy losses on both sides, Rommel prevailed at the Battle of Gazala and forced the Allies to abandon their defensive line and retreat toward the Egyptian border.

By the middle of June, Axis forces had captured Tobruk and the Allies had fallen back to Mersa Matruh, which was itself overcome by the end of the month. The two sides confronted one another in Egypt in two inconclusive battles—El Alamein in July and Alam Halfa in August. Although Rommel had achieved his most impressive victories to date in North Africa, he had ultimately failed to break through Allied lines. His advance had been checked.

◁ **Battle instructions** Erwin Rommel (on the right), the commander of the German and Italian forces in North Africa, gives directions to his officers.

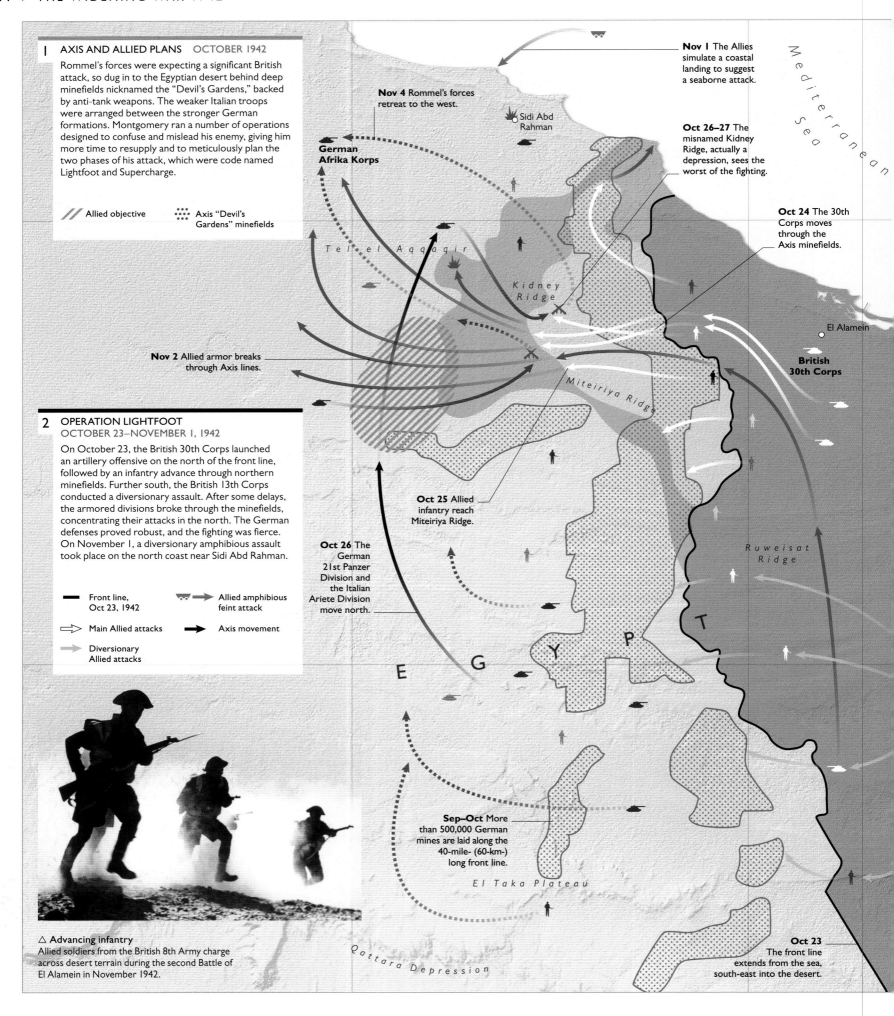

1 AXIS AND ALLIED PLANS OCTOBER 1942

Rommel's forces were expecting a significant British attack, so dug in to the Egyptian desert behind deep minefields nicknamed the "Devil's Gardens," backed by anti-tank weapons. The weaker Italian troops were arranged between the stronger German formations. Montgomery ran a number of operations designed to confuse and mislead his enemy, giving him more time to resupply and to meticulously plan the two phases of his attack, which were code named Lightfoot and Supercharge.

/// Allied objective

⬡ Axis "Devil's Gardens" minefields

2 OPERATION LIGHTFOOT
OCTOBER 23–NOVEMBER 1, 1942

On October 23, the British 30th Corps launched an artillery offensive on the north of the front line, followed by an infantry advance through northern minefields. Further south, the British 13th Corps conducted a diversionary assault. After some delays, the armored divisions broke through the minefields, concentrating their attacks in the north. The German defenses proved robust, and the fighting was fierce. On November 1, a diversionary amphibious assault took place on the north coast near Sidi Abd Rahman.

— Front line, Oct 23, 1942

⬚⇒ Allied amphibious feint attack

⇨ Main Allied attacks

→ Axis movement

⇨ Diversionary Allied attacks

△ **Advancing infantry**
Allied soldiers from the British 8th Army charge across desert terrain during the second Battle of El Alamein in November 1942.

Nov 1 The Allies simulate a coastal landing to suggest a seaborne attack.

Nov 4 Rommel's forces retreat to the west.

Sidi Abd Rahman

German Afrika Korps

Oct 26–27 The misnamed Kidney Ridge, actually a depression, sees the worst of the fighting.

Oct 24 The 30th Corps moves through the Axis minefields.

Tel el Aqqaqir

Kidney Ridge

Nov 2 Allied armor breaks through Axis lines.

El Alamein

British 30th Corps

Miteiriya Ridge

Oct 25 Allied infantry reach Miteiriya Ridge.

Oct 26 The German 21st Panzer Division and the Italian Ariete Division move north.

Ruweisat Ridge

Mediterranean Sea

E G Y P T

Sep–Oct More than 500,000 German mines are laid along the 40-mile- (60-km-) long front line.

El Taka Plateau

Qattara Depression

Oct 23 The front line extends from the sea, south-east into the desert.

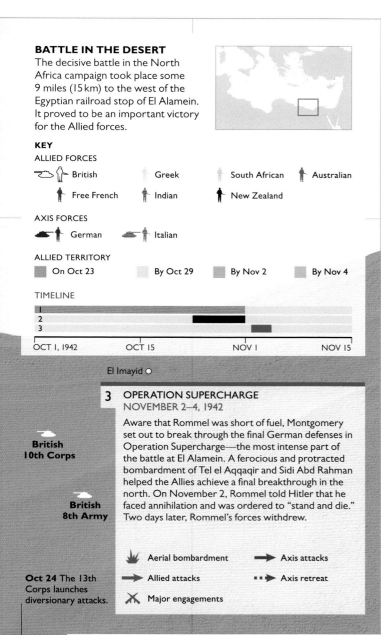

BATTLE IN THE DESERT
The decisive battle in the North Africa campaign took place some 9 miles (15 km) to the west of the Egyptian railroad stop of El Alamein. It proved to be an important victory for the Allied forces.

KEY

ALLIED FORCES

British · Greek · South African · Australian

Free French · Indian · New Zealand

AXIS FORCES

German · Italian

ALLIED TERRITORY

On Oct 23 · By Oct 29 · By Nov 2 · By Nov 4

TIMELINE

1
2
3

OCT 1, 1942 · OCT 15 · NOV 1 · NOV 15

El Imayid

3 OPERATION SUPERCHARGE
NOVEMBER 2–4, 1942

Aware that Rommel was short of fuel, Montgomery set out to break through the final German defenses in Operation Supercharge—the most intense part of the battle at El Alamein. A ferocious and protracted bombardment of Tel el Aqqaqir and Sidi Abd Rahman helped the Allies achieve a final breakthrough in the north. On November 2, Rommel told Hitler that he faced annihilation and was ordered to "stand and die." Two days later, Rommel's forces withdrew.

British 10th Corps

British 8th Army

Oct 24 The 13th Corps launches diversionary attacks.

Aerial bombardment · Axis attacks

Allied attacks · Axis retreat

Major engagements

British 13th Corps

SECOND BATTLE OF EL ALAMEIN

The key battle of the Western Desert Campaign took place around the Egyptian town of El Alamein from October to November 1942. It proved to be a watershed, stopping the Axis advance into Egypt, ending the threat to the Suez Canal, and forcing Rommel's troops, including the formidable Afrika Korps, to retreat into Tunisia.

After their failure to break through British lines at Alam Halfa in August 1942 (see pp.142–143), the Axis forces were on the defensive, and their supply lines were badly overstretched. However, General Montgomery did not immediately counterattack, choosing instead to build up his forces, gather intelligence, and further choke Axis supplies before launching an attack that he hoped would be decisive.

By October, the Axis forces were outnumbered and outgunned. The Allies fielded 195,000 men, 1,029 tanks, 435 armored cars, 900 artillery pieces, 1,451 anti-tank guns, and 750 aircraft. In response, the combined German and Italian forces numbered 116,000 men,

and were equipped with 547 tanks, 192 armored cars, 552 artillery pieces, and up to 1,060 anti-tank guns, as well as around 900 aircraft. The inevitable Allied attack finally came on October 23, 1942, with Rommel away in Germany for medical treatment; he returned to Africa on October 25. The Axis forces put up fierce resistance, but by November 4, Rommel was in retreat toward Tunisia. The Allies had won, and plans were underway to clear the Axis forces from Africa (see pp.146–147).

The second Battle of El Alamein was a turning point for the Western Allies and also a boost to flagging morale, as Britain celebrated a major success, the first for its land forces since 1939.

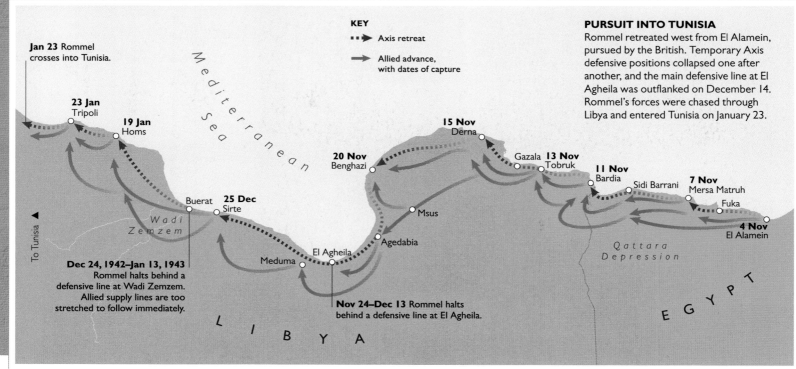

KEY

Axis retreat

Allied advance, with dates of capture

PURSUIT INTO TUNISIA
Rommel retreated west from El Alamein, pursued by the British. Temporary Axis defensive positions collapsed one after another, and the main defensive line at El Agheila was outflanked on December 14. Rommel's forces were chased through Libya and entered Tunisia on January 23.

Jan 23 Rommel crosses into Tunisia.

Mediterranean Sea

23 Jan Tripoli · 19 Jan Homs · 15 Nov Derna · 20 Nov Benghazi · Gazala · 13 Nov Tobruk · 11 Nov Bardia · Sidi Barrani · 7 Nov Mersa Matruh · Fuka

Buerat · 25 Dec Sirte · Wadi Zemzem · Msus · Agedabia · Meduma · El Agheila · Qattara Depression · 4 Nov El Alamein

To Tunisia

Dec 24, 1942–Jan 13, 1943 Rommel halts behind a defensive line at Wadi Zemzem. Allied supply lines are too stretched to follow immediately.

Nov 24–Dec 13 Rommel halts behind a defensive line at El Agheila.

L I B Y A · E G Y P T

OPERATION TORCH

Four days after German field marshal Rommel began his retreat from El Alamein in Egypt, US and British troops began to land in Morocco and Algeria. Known as Operation Torch, this campaign was intended to evict Axis forces from Africa and clear the way for the invasion of Italy.

The Soviet Union wanted its Western allies to open up a second front in Europe to relieve the pressure on the Red Army. The US backed a direct assault on occupied France, but Churchill argued for landings in Africa that would both reduce pressure on British and Commonwealth forces in Egypt and enable the Allies to clear North Africa of Axis troops. The Allies could then use Tunisia as a starting point from which to attack the Axis

through its most vulnerable member—Italy. Such a landing would also help safeguard passage for Allied vessels through the Mediterranean to the Suez Canal. US commanders opposed the British plan, and wanted a three-pronged attack across the English Channel. Roosevelt, however, saw the need for the campaign and ordered that Torch go ahead at the earliest possible date, much to the fury of US planners and the Soviets.

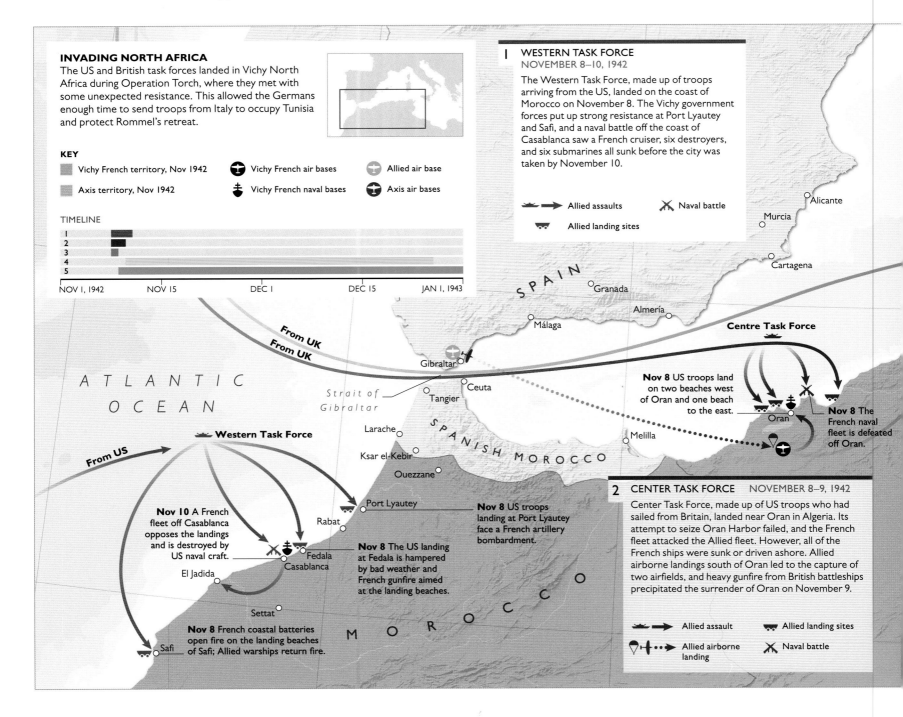

INVADING NORTH AFRICA
The US and British task forces landed in Vichy North Africa during Operation Torch, where they met with some unexpected resistance. This allowed the Germans enough time to send troops from Italy to occupy Tunisia and protect Rommel's retreat.

KEY

Vichy French territory, Nov 1942
Axis territory, Nov 1942
Vichy French air bases
Vichy French naval bases
Allied air base
Axis air bases

TIMELINE
1
2
3
4
5
NOV 1, 1942   NOV 15   DEC 1   DEC 15   JAN 1, 1943

1 WESTERN TASK FORCE
NOVEMBER 8–10, 1942

The Western Task Force, made up of troops arriving from the US, landed on the coast of Morocco on November 8. The Vichy government forces put up strong resistance at Port Lyautey and Safi, and a naval battle off the coast of Casablanca saw a French cruiser, six destroyers, and six submarines all sunk before the city was taken by November 10.

Allied assaults   Naval battle
Allied landing sites

Nov 8 US troops land on two beaches west of Oran and one beach to the east.

Nov 8 The French naval fleet is defeated off Oran.

Centre Task Force

Alicante
Murcia
Cartagena
Granada
Almería
Málaga
SPAIN
Gibraltar
Strait of Gibraltar
Ceuta
Tangier
Melilla
Oran

ATLANTIC OCEAN

Western Task Force

From UK
From UK
From US

Larache
Ksar el-Kebir
Ouezzane
SPANISH MOROCCO
Port Lyautey
Rabat

Nov 10 A French fleet off Casablanca opposes the landings and is destroyed by US naval craft.

Nov 8 US troops landing at Port Lyautey face a French artillery bombardment.

Nov 8 The US landing at Fedala is hampered by bad weather and French gunfire aimed at the landing beaches.

Fedala
Casablanca
El Jadida
Settat
Safi

Nov 8 French coastal batteries open fire on the landing beaches of Safi; Allied warships return fire.

MOROCCO

2 CENTER TASK FORCE   NOVEMBER 8–9, 1942

Center Task Force, made up of US troops who had sailed from Britain, landed near Oran in Algeria. Its attempt to seize Oran Harbor failed, and the French fleet attacked the Allied fleet. However, all of the French ships were sunk or driven ashore. Allied airborne landings south of Oran led to the capture of two airfields, and heavy gunfire from British battleships precipitated the surrender of Oran on November 9.

Allied assault   Allied landing sites
Allied airborne landing   Naval battle

The planned landing areas on the North African coast were under the rule of Vichy France, which controlled tens of thousands of troops. The Allies were uncertain of what the Vichy leaders' response would be to an invasion and sent US Major General Mark Clark on a secret mission to Algiers to gauge their possible reaction. Despite the support of some individual generals, the Vichy governments in Morocco and Algeria opposed the landings, which consequently met with stiff resistance. A further drawback of landing in Morocco was that it was a considerable distance to Tunisia—the ultimate Allied target. As a result, German reinforcements were able to pour into Tunisia from Italy to protect Rommel's rear as he retreated following defeat at El Alamein (see pp.144–145).

"The only tough nut left is in your hands. Crack it open quickly."

EISENHOWER TO PATTON, CASABLANCA, 1943

THE END OF VICHY FRANCE

The failure of Vichy France to resist the Allied landings in North Africa convinced the Germans that it could no longer be trusted. On November 11, German and Italian troops occupied Vichy France and ended its independence. The Germans also launched Operation Lila to capture the units of the French fleet at Toulon and prevent them from sailing to join the Allies. However, the French navy scuttled almost their entire fleet at Toulon on November 27, before the Germans arrived in the port.

The French fleet is scuttled

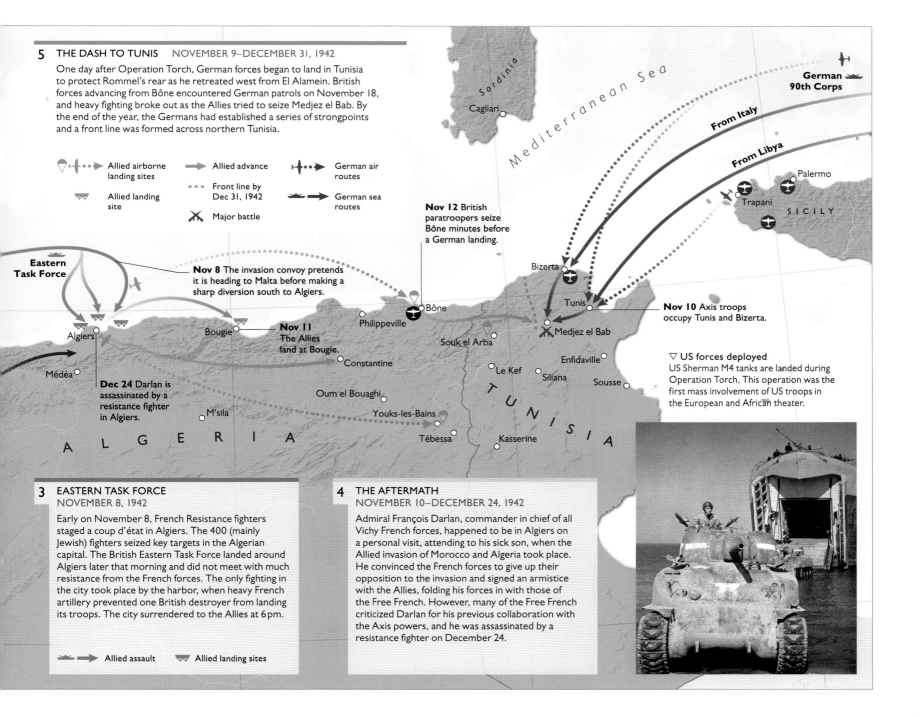

5 THE DASH TO TUNIS   NOVEMBER 9–DECEMBER 31, 1942

One day after Operation Torch, German forces began to land in Tunisia to protect Rommel's rear as he retreated west from El Alamein. British forces advancing from Bône encountered German patrols on November 18, and heavy fighting broke out as the Allies tried to seize Medjez el Bab. By the end of the year, the Germans had established a series of strongpoints and a front line was formed across northern Tunisia.

- Allied airborne landing sites
- Allied landing site
- Allied advance
- Front line by Dec 31, 1942
- Major battle
- German air routes
- German sea routes

Nov 8 The invasion convoy pretends it is heading to Malta before making a sharp diversion south to Algiers.

Nov 12 British paratroopers seize Bône minutes before a German landing.

Eastern Task Force

Nov 11 The Allies land at Bougie.

Nov 10 Axis troops occupy Tunis and Bizerta.

Dec 24 Darlan is assassinated by a resistance fighter in Algiers.

German 90th Corps

From Italy

From Libya

Mediterranean Sea

Sardinia

Cagliari

Palermo

Trapani

SICILY

Bizerta

Tunis

Medjez el Bab

Bône

Philippeville

Souk el Arba

Enfidaville

Le Kef

Siliana

Sousse

Constantine

Bougie

Algiers

Médéa

M'sila

Oum el Bouaghi

Youks-les-Bains

Tébessa

Kasserine

ALGERIA

TUNISIA

△ **US forces deployed**
US Sherman M4 tanks are landed during Operation Torch. This operation was the first mass involvement of US troops in the European and African theater.

3 EASTERN TASK FORCE
NOVEMBER 8, 1942

Early on November 8, French Resistance fighters staged a coup d'état in Algiers. The 400 (mainly Jewish) fighters seized key targets in the Algerian capital. The British Eastern Task Force landed around Algiers later that morning and did not meet with much resistance from the French forces. The only fighting in the city took place by the harbor, when heavy French artillery prevented one British destroyer from landing its troops. The city surrendered to the Allies at 6 pm.

- Allied assault
- Allied landing sites

4 THE AFTERMATH
NOVEMBER 10–DECEMBER 24, 1942

Admiral François Darlan, commander in chief of all Vichy French forces, happened to be in Algiers on a personal visit, attending to his sick son, when the Allied invasion of Morocco and Algeria took place. He convinced the French forces to give up their opposition to the invasion and signed an armistice with the Allies, folding his forces in with those of the Free French. However, many of the Free French criticized Darlan for his previous collaboration with the Axis powers, and he was assassinated by a resistance fighter on December 24.

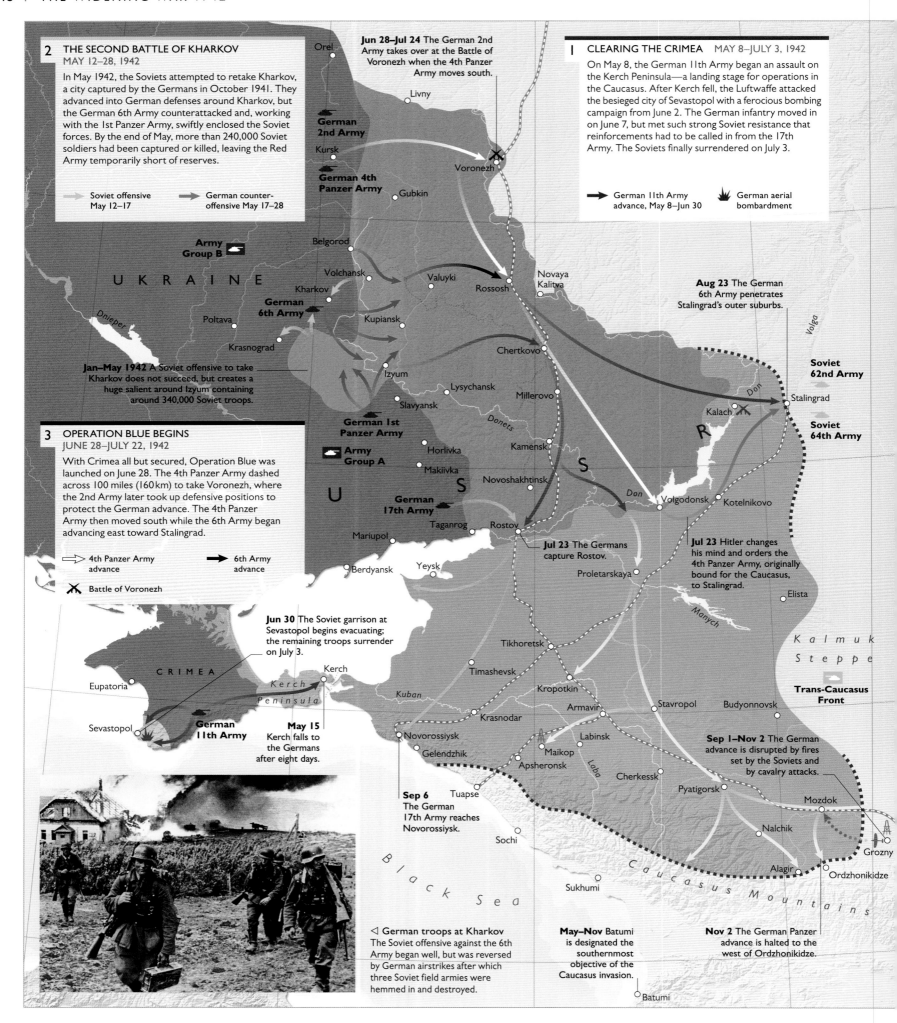

2 THE SECOND BATTLE OF KHARKOV
MAY 12–28, 1942

In May 1942, the Soviets attempted to retake Kharkov, a city captured by the Germans in October 1941. They advanced into German defenses around Kharkov, but the German 6th Army counterattacked and, working with the 1st Panzer Army, swiftly enclosed the Soviet forces. By the end of May, more than 240,000 Soviet soldiers had been captured or killed, leaving the Red Army temporarily short of reserves.

→ Soviet offensive May 12–17
→ German counter-offensive May 17–28

Jan–May 1942 A Soviet offensive to take Kharkov does not succeed, but creates a huge salient around Izyum containing around 340,000 Soviet troops.

3 OPERATION BLUE BEGINS
JUNE 28–JULY 22, 1942

With Crimea all but secured, Operation Blue was launched on June 28. The 4th Panzer Army dashed across 100 miles (160 km) to take Voronezh, where the 2nd Army later took up defensive positions to protect the German advance. The 4th Panzer Army then moved south while the 6th Army began advancing east toward Stalingrad.

⇨ 4th Panzer Army advance
➡ 6th Army advance
✕ Battle of Voronezh

Jun 30 The Soviet garrison at Sevastopol begins evacuating; the remaining troops surrender on July 3.

May 15 Kerch falls to the Germans after eight days.

Sep 6 The German 17th Army reaches Novorossiysk.

◁ **German troops at Kharkov**
The Soviet offensive against the 6th Army began well, but was reversed by German airstrikes after which three Soviet field armies were hemmed in and destroyed.

Jun 28–Jul 24 The German 2nd Army takes over at the Battle of Voronezh when the 4th Panzer Army moves south.

German 2nd Army

German 4th Panzer Army

Army Group B

German 6th Army

German 1st Panzer Army

Army Group A

German 17th Army

Jul 23 The Germans capture Rostov.

1 CLEARING THE CRIMEA   MAY 8–JULY 3, 1942

On May 8, the German 11th Army began an assault on the Kerch Peninsula—a landing stage for operations in the Caucasus. After Kerch fell, the Luftwaffe attacked the besieged city of Sevastopol with a ferocious bombing campaign from June 2. The German infantry moved in on June 7, but met such strong Soviet resistance that reinforcements had to be called in from the 17th Army. The Soviets finally surrendered on July 3.

➡ German 11th Army advance, May 8–Jun 30
✺ German aerial bombardment

German 11th Army

Aug 23 The German 6th Army penetrates Stalingrad's outer suburbs.

Soviet 62nd Army

Soviet 64th Army

Jul 23 Hitler changes his mind and orders the 4th Panzer Army, originally bound for the Caucasus, to Stalingrad.

Kalmuk Steppe

Trans-Caucasus Front

Sep 1–Nov 2 The German advance is disrupted by fires set by the Soviets and by cavalry attacks.

May–Nov Batumi is designated the southernmost objective of the Caucasus invasion.

Nov 2 The German Panzer advance is halted to the west of Ordzhonikidze.

UKRAINE
USSR
CRIMEA
Kerch Peninsula
Black Sea
Caucasus Mountains

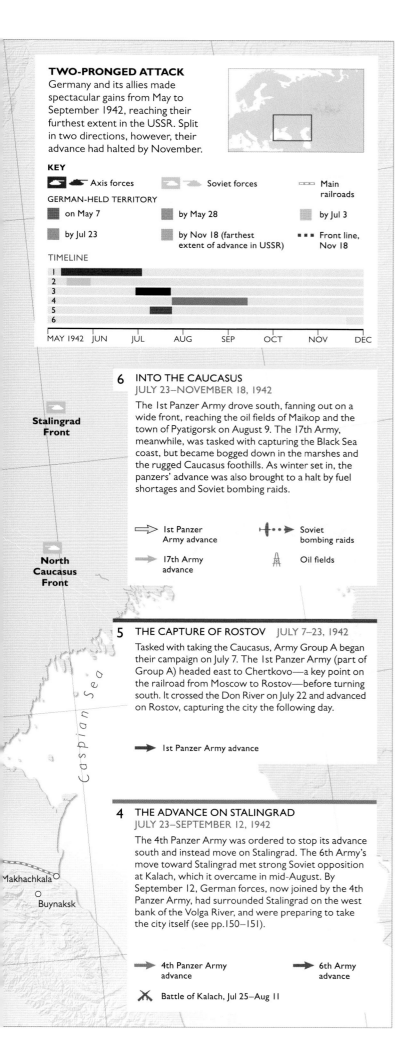

TWO-PRONGED ATTACK
Germany and its allies made spectacular gains from May to September 1942, reaching their furthest extent in the USSR. Split in two directions, however, their advance had halted by November.

KEY

Axis forces   Soviet forces   Main railroads

GERMAN-HELD TERRITORY

on May 7   by May 28   by Jul 3

by Jul 23   by Nov 18 (farthest extent of advance in USSR)   Front line, Nov 18

TIMELINE

1
2
3
4
5
6

MAY 1942   JUN   JUL   AUG   SEP   OCT   NOV   DEC

Stalingrad Front

North Caucasus Front

6 INTO THE CAUCASUS
JULY 23–NOVEMBER 18, 1942

The 1st Panzer Army drove south, fanning out on a wide front, reaching the oil fields of Maikop and the town of Pyatigorsk on August 9. The 17th Army, meanwhile, was tasked with capturing the Black Sea coast, but became bogged down in the marshes and the rugged Caucasus foothills. As winter set in, the panzers' advance was also brought to a halt by fuel shortages and Soviet bombing raids.

1st Panzer Army advance   Soviet bombing raids

17th Army advance   Oil fields

5 THE CAPTURE OF ROSTOV   JULY 7–23, 1942

Tasked with taking the Caucasus, Army Group A began their campaign on July 7. The 1st Panzer Army (part of Group A) headed east to Chertkovo—a key point on the railroad from Moscow to Rostov—before turning south. It crossed the Don River on July 22 and advanced on Rostov, capturing the city the following day.

1st Panzer Army advance

Makhachkala

Buynaksk

4 THE ADVANCE ON STALINGRAD
JULY 23–SEPTEMBER 12, 1942

The 4th Panzer Army was ordered to stop its advance south and instead move on Stalingrad. The 6th Army's move toward Stalingrad met strong Soviet opposition at Kalach, which it overcame in mid-August. By September 12, German forces, now joined by the 4th Panzer Army, had surrounded Stalingrad on the west bank of the Volga River, and were preparing to take the city itself (see pp.150–151).

4th Panzer Army advance   6th Army advance

Battle of Kalach, Jul 25–Aug 11

GERMAN ADVANCE TO STALINGRAD

The Germans launched a huge offensive in the southern USSR in the summer of 1942. Their target was the oil-rich Caucasus region, which they planned to seize after taking the cities in the Don River basin, the USSR's industrial heartland. They advanced rapidly, and by September had closed in on the city of Stalingrad.

Having failed to take Moscow (see pp.100–101), the Germans planned a new offensive that would bypass the capital. Operation Blue (*Fall Blau*) aimed to strike south-east to take the oil fields of the Caucasus, seizing the Red Army's vital fuel supplies for Germany, and also to capture Stalingrad, which would secure transport links into the Caucasus and protect the Germans' flank. Hitler also believed that the Soviets were near breaking point, and that one more major offensive would drive them to defeat.

First, the Germans needed to clear Crimea and the Kharkov area of Soviet forces, a task they achieved by early July. Once *Fall Blau* began, however, Hitler ordered simultaneous attacks on Stalingrad and the Caucasus. To achieve this, Army Group South (including Italian, Hungarian, and Romanian divisions) was split in two on July 7, 1942. Army Group A was to advance through the Caucasus and secure the Black Sea coast as far south as Batumi, while Army Group B was to move on Stalingrad.

Over the next months, resources were switched between the two offensives; by mid-September the Germans were spread across a vast area and neither army group had achieved its objective. Meanwhile, Stalin ordered the Red Army to defend Stalingrad at all costs (see pp.150–151).

> *"If we don't take Maikop and Grozny [oil fields in the Caucasus] then I must put an end to the war."*
>
> ADOLF HITLER, TO HIS GENERALS, JULY 23, 1942

OIL IN THE CAUCASUS

The Caucasus had been an important oil-producing region since the start of the 20th century, and by 1940 the region was producing the majority of the Soviet Union's oil. In 1939–1940, the Soviets supplied oil to Nazi Germany, but the supply was cut off when the two countries went to war. In Operation Blue, Hitler was determined to capture the oil fields to fuel his war machine.

Oil derricks in the Caucasus

STALINGRAD UNDER SIEGE

One of the most colossal conflicts of the war, the Battle of Stalingrad became a symbol of Soviet patriotism as civilians fought alongside soldiers to defend the city street by street. The battle halted Germany's advance in the east, marking a turning point in the war.

In late August 1942, German Army Group B approached the industrial city of Stalingrad. The Luftwaffe rained bombs on the city before German ground forces entered in September. They met a fight that raged from street to street and house to house, and even descended into the sewers; the Germans dubbed it *Rattenkrieg* (Rat War). General Vasily Chuikov, commander of the Soviet 62nd Army, had his men "hug the enemy," fighting in such close proximity that the Germans could not exploit their superior air power and artillery.

The Soviet forces were steadily pressed back to the banks of the Volga River, but Stalin was willing to sacrifice huge numbers of people to serve his purposes and kept up reinforcements. The average life expectancy of a Soviet soldier in the battle was 24 hours; overall, there were around 1.1 million dead, wounded, and missing. Both sides were exhausted by mid-November, but the battle—which would continue until February 1943—had reached a turning point. The Red Army was about to launch a counteroffensive that would begin to turn the tide of the war (see pp.152–153).

> *"It is time to finish retreating. Not one step back!"*
>
> JOSEPH STALIN, ORDER NO. 227, JULY 28, 1942

"PAVLOV'S HOUSE"—A SYMBOL OF RESISTANCE

The Soviets turned ordinary buildings into "fortresses" in their defense of Stalingrad. A platoon of Soviet soldiers, led by Sergeant Yakov Pavlov, held this apartment building for two months against daily German assaults. They fortified it with minefields and barbed wire, dug trenches for supply lines, and placed machine guns at windows and an anti-tank gun on the roof to pick off approaching German forces.

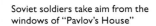
Soviet soldiers take aim from the windows of "Pavlov's House"

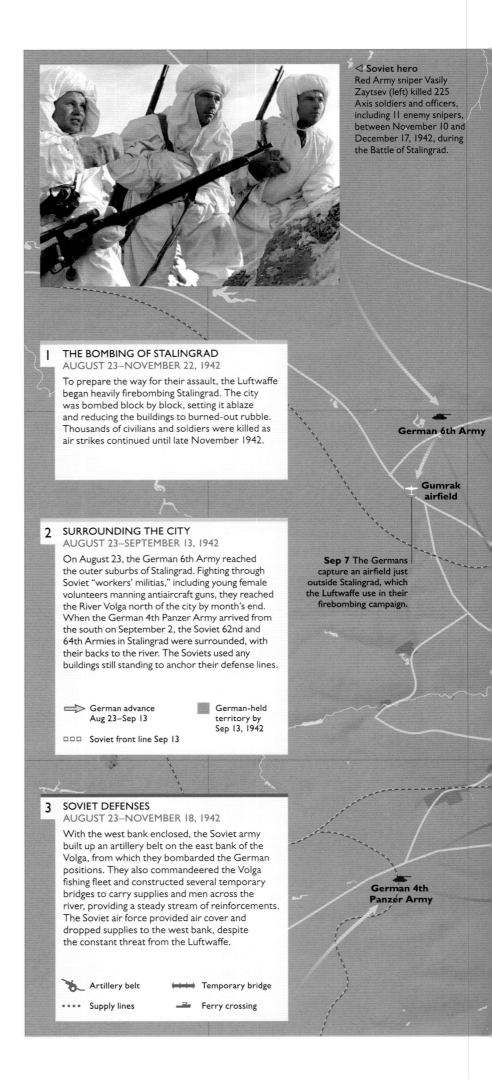

◁ **Soviet hero**
Red Army sniper Vasily Zaytsev (left) killed 225 Axis soldiers and officers, including 11 enemy snipers, between November 10 and December 17, 1942, during the Battle of Stalingrad.

1 THE BOMBING OF STALINGRAD
AUGUST 23–NOVEMBER 22, 1942

To prepare the way for their assault, the Luftwaffe began heavily firebombing Stalingrad. The city was bombed block by block, setting it ablaze and reducing the buildings to burned-out rubble. Thousands of civilians and soldiers were killed as air strikes continued until late November 1942.

German 6th Army

Gumrak airfield

2 SURROUNDING THE CITY
AUGUST 23–SEPTEMBER 13, 1942

On August 23, the German 6th Army reached the outer suburbs of Stalingrad. Fighting through Soviet "workers' militias," including young female volunteers manning antiaircraft guns, they reached the River Volga north of the city by month's end. When the German 4th Panzer Army arrived from the south on September 2, the Soviet 62nd and 64th Armies in Stalingrad were surrounded, with their backs to the river. The Soviets used any buildings still standing to anchor their defense lines.

Sep 7 The Germans capture an airfield just outside Stalingrad, which the Luftwaffe use in their firebombing campaign.

⇒ German advance Aug 23–Sep 13	▨ German-held territory by Sep 13, 1942
□□□ Soviet front line Sep 13	

3 SOVIET DEFENSES
AUGUST 23–NOVEMBER 18, 1942

With the west bank enclosed, the Soviet army built up an artillery belt on the east bank of the Volga, from which they bombarded the German positions. They also commandeered the Volga fishing fleet and constructed several temporary bridges to carry supplies and men across the river, providing a steady stream of reinforcements. The Soviet air force provided air cover and dropped supplies to the west bank, despite the constant threat from the Luftwaffe.

German 4th Panzer Army

⚒ Artillery belt	⊨ Temporary bridge
•••• Supply lines	⛴ Ferry crossing

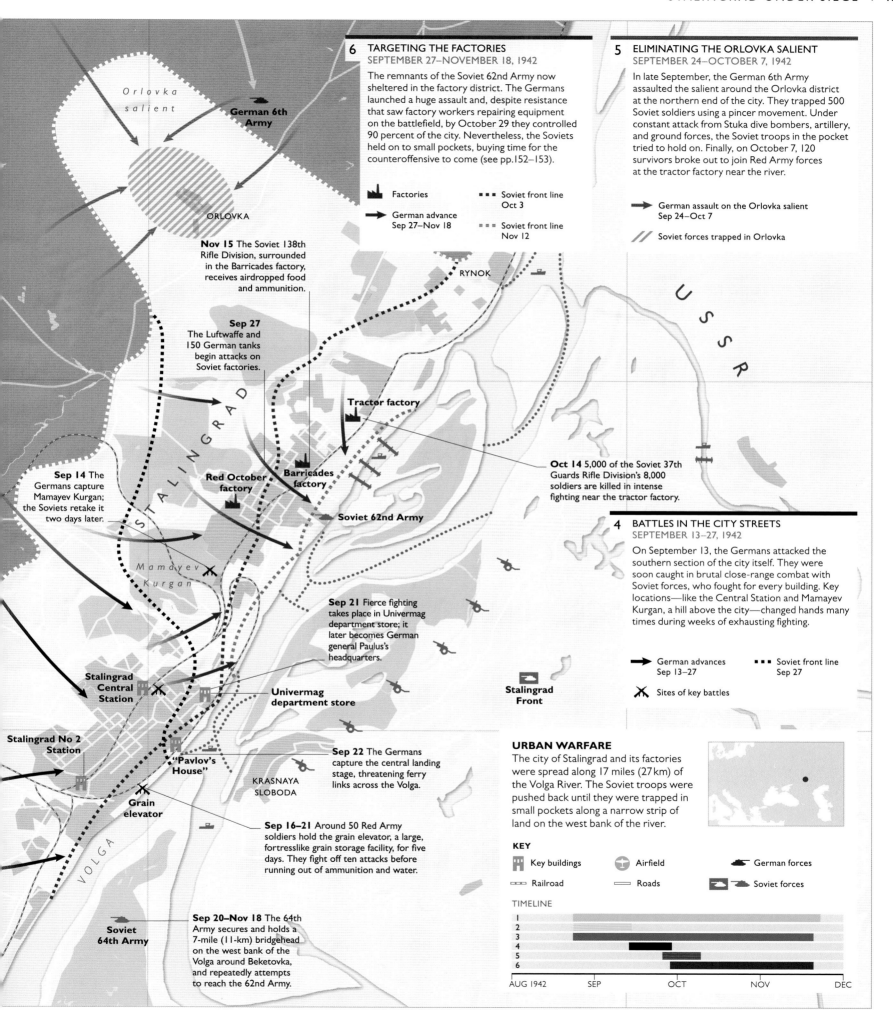

6 TARGETING THE FACTORIES
SEPTEMBER 27–NOVEMBER 18, 1942

The remnants of the Soviet 62nd Army now sheltered in the factory district. The Germans launched a huge assault and, despite resistance that saw factory workers repairing equipment on the battlefield, by October 29 they controlled 90 percent of the city. Nevertheless, the Soviets held on to small pockets, buying time for the counteroffensive to come (see pp.152–153).

- 🏭 Factories
- ➡ German advance Sep 27–Nov 18
- ▪▪▪ Soviet front line Oct 3
- ▪▪▪ Soviet front line Nov 12

5 ELIMINATING THE ORLOVKA SALIENT
SEPTEMBER 24–OCTOBER 7, 1942

In late September, the German 6th Army assaulted the salient around the Orlovka district at the northern end of the city. They trapped 500 Soviet soldiers using a pincer movement. Under constant attack from Stuka dive bombers, artillery, and ground forces, the Soviet troops in the pocket tried to hold on. Finally, on October 7, 120 survivors broke out to join Red Army forces at the tractor factory near the river.

- ➡ German assault on the Orlovka salient Sep 24–Oct 7
- /// Soviet forces trapped in Orlovka

Nov 15 The Soviet 138th Rifle Division, surrounded in the Barricades factory, receives airdropped food and ammunition.

Sep 27 The Luftwaffe and 150 German tanks begin attacks on Soviet factories.

Sep 14 The Germans capture Mamayev Kurgan; the Soviets retake it two days later.

Oct 14 5,000 of the Soviet 37th Guards Rifle Division's 8,000 soldiers are killed in intense fighting near the tractor factory.

Orlovka salient

German 6th Army

ORLOVKA

RYNOK

U S S R

Tractor factory

Red October factory

Barricades factory

Soviet 62nd Army

S T A L I N G R A D

Mamayev Kurgan

4 BATTLES IN THE CITY STREETS
SEPTEMBER 13–27, 1942

On September 13, the Germans attacked the southern section of the city itself. They were soon caught in brutal close-range combat with Soviet forces, who fought for every building. Key locations—like the Central Station and Mamayev Kurgan, a hill above the city—changed hands many times during weeks of exhausting fighting.

- ➡ German advances Sep 13–27
- ▪▪▪ Soviet front line Sep 27
- ✗ Sites of key battles

Sep 21 Fierce fighting takes place in Univermag department store; it later becomes German general Paulus's headquarters.

Stalingrad Front

Stalingrad Central Station

Stalingrad No 2 Station

"Pavlov's House"

KRASNAYA SLOBODA

Grain elevator

Univermag department store

Sep 22 The Germans capture the central landing stage, threatening ferry links across the Volga.

Sep 16–21 Around 50 Red Army soldiers hold the grain elevator, a large, fortresslike grain storage facility, for five days. They fight off ten attacks before running out of ammunition and water.

V O L G A

Soviet 64th Army

Sep 20–Nov 18 The 64th Army secures and holds a 7-mile (11-km) bridgehead on the west bank of the Volga around Beketovka, and repeatedly attempts to reach the 62nd Army.

URBAN WARFARE

The city of Stalingrad and its factories were spread along 17 miles (27 km) of the Volga River. The Soviet troops were pushed back until they were trapped in small pockets along a narrow strip of land on the west bank of the river.

KEY

- 🏛 Key buildings
- 🛬 Airfield
- German forces
- ▭▭▭ Railroad
- ▭ Roads
- Soviet forces

TIMELINE

	AUG 1942	SEP	OCT	NOV	DEC
1					
2					
3					
4					
5					
6					

SOVIET VICTORY AT STALINGRAD

In November 1942, the Soviets launched an unexpected counteroffensive at Stalingrad—not pushing through the front line in the city itself, but encircling the city to cut off, then annihilate, the German army within. Following this victory, the Soviets went on to push the Germans out of the Caucasus and the Don River basin.

The Germans disregarded what limited intelligence they had about a major Soviet counteroffensive, believing that the Soviets could not have the men or equipment to mount such an attack. As a result, the speed and success of the Red Army assault in November 1942 came as a shock to them. The Soviets' plan was ingenious: they targeted Germany's allies, the weaker Romanian, Italian, and Hungarian armies that flanked the German 6th Army in Stalingrad and held the front line along the Don River. By November 23, the 6th Army was isolated from the stronger German forces to the west and south.

The Soviets then launched a series of operations to clear the Don basin and Caucasus. By the time the Red Army launched its final assault on Stalingrad in mid-January 1943, it had decimated the Germans' allies and retaken much of the territory lost to the German advance of 1942 (see pp.148–149). Hitler only averted further disaster by allowing Army Group A to retreat from the Caucasus. It had seemed as if the German retreat might turn into a rout, but by February the Soviet army was overstretched. A successful counterattack at Kharkov boosted German morale as they planned their next offensive (see pp.178–179).

> "18,000 wounded without any supplies or dressings or drugs. Further defense senseless. Collapse inevitable."
>
> GENERAL PAULUS, MESSAGE TO ADOLF HITLER, JANUARY 24, 1943

GERMAN ALLIES AT STALINGRAD

The Italian, Hungarian, and Romanian armies at Stalingrad were expected to protect the Germans' flanks and stabilize the front, but they were fatally overstretched and—as the Soviet marshal Zhukov noted—less well armed, less experienced, and less efficient at defense than the Germans. Having neglected to reinforce their positions along the Don River, Germany's allies provided an easy target for the Soviet counterattack.

Romanian POWs at Stalingrad

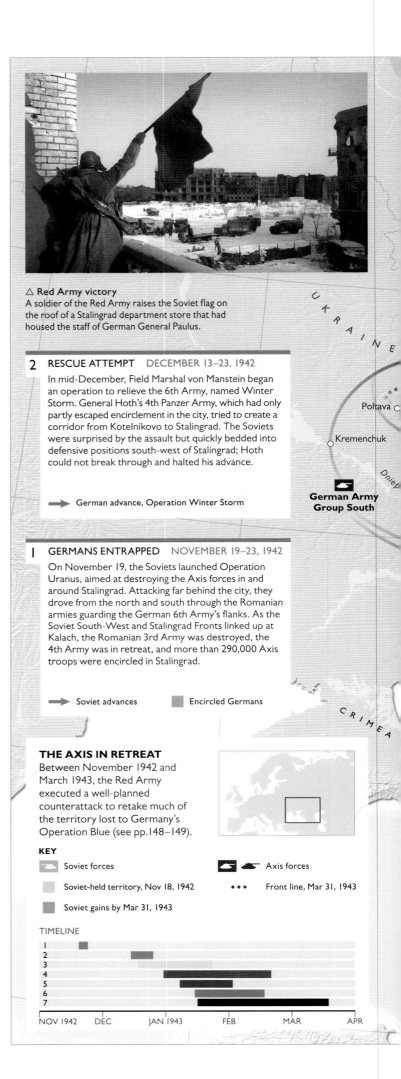

△ Red Army victory
A soldier of the Red Army raises the Soviet flag on the roof of a Stalingrad department store that had housed the staff of German General Paulus.

2 RESCUE ATTEMPT DECEMBER 13–23, 1942
In mid-December, Field Marshal von Manstein began an operation to relieve the 6th Army, named Winter Storm. General Hoth's 4th Panzer Army, which had only partly escaped encirclement in the city, tried to create a corridor from Kotelnikovo to Stalingrad. The Soviets were surprised by the assault but quickly bedded into defensive positions south-west of Stalingrad; Hoth could not break through and halted his advance.

→ German advance, Operation Winter Storm

German Army Group South

1 GERMANS ENTRAPPED NOVEMBER 19–23, 1942
On November 19, the Soviets launched Operation Uranus, aimed at destroying the Axis forces in and around Stalingrad. Attacking far behind the city, they drove from the north and south through the Romanian armies guarding the German 6th Army's flanks. As the Soviet South-West and Stalingrad Fronts linked up at Kalach, the Romanian 3rd Army was destroyed, the 4th Army was in retreat, and more than 290,000 Axis troops were encircled in Stalingrad.

→ Soviet advances   ■ Encircled Germans

Poltava
Kremenchuk

UKRAINE
Dnieper
CRIMEA

THE AXIS IN RETREAT
Between November 1942 and March 1943, the Red Army executed a well-planned counterattack to retake much of the territory lost to Germany's Operation Blue (see pp.148–149).

KEY

◣ Soviet forces		◥ Axis forces	
■ Soviet-held territory, Nov 18, 1942		••• Front line, Mar 31, 1943	
■ Soviet gains by Mar 31, 1943			

TIMELINE

1					
2					
3					
4					
5					
6					
7					
NOV 1942	DEC	JAN 1943	FEB	MAR	APR

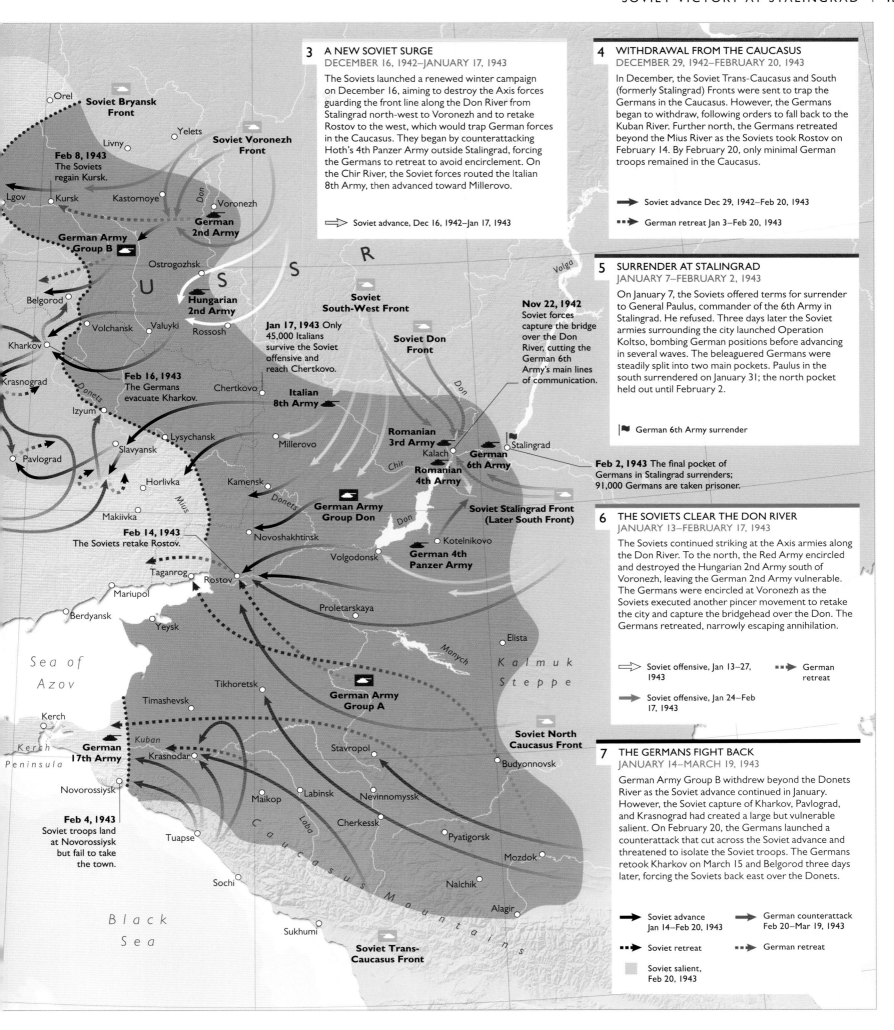

3 A NEW SOVIET SURGE
DECEMBER 16, 1942–JANUARY 17, 1943

The Soviets launched a renewed winter campaign on December 16, aiming to destroy the Axis forces guarding the front line along the Don River from Stalingrad north-west to Voronezh and to retake Rostov to the west, which would trap German forces in the Caucasus. They began by counterattacking Hoth's 4th Panzer Army outside Stalingrad, forcing the Germans to retreat to avoid encirclement. On the Chir River, the Soviet forces routed the Italian 8th Army, then advanced toward Millerovo.

⟹ Soviet advance, Dec 16, 1942–Jan 17, 1943

4 WITHDRAWAL FROM THE CAUCASUS
DECEMBER 29, 1942–FEBRUARY 20, 1943

In December, the Soviet Trans-Caucasus and South (formerly Stalingrad) Fronts were sent to trap the Germans in the Caucasus. However, the Germans began to withdraw, following orders to fall back to the Kuban River. Further north, the Germans retreated beyond the Mius River as the Soviets took Rostov on February 14. By February 20, only minimal German troops remained in the Caucasus.

➡ Soviet advance Dec 29, 1942–Feb 20, 1943

---➤ German retreat Jan 3–Feb 20, 1943

5 SURRENDER AT STALINGRAD
JANUARY 7–FEBRUARY 2, 1943

On January 7, the Soviets offered terms for surrender to General Paulus, commander of the 6th Army in Stalingrad. He refused. Three days later the Soviet armies surrounding the city launched Operation Koltso, bombing German positions before advancing in several waves. The beleaguered Germans were steadily split into two main pockets. Paulus in the south surrendered on January 31; the north pocket held out until February 2.

⚑ German 6th Army surrender

6 THE SOVIETS CLEAR THE DON RIVER
JANUARY 13–FEBRUARY 17, 1943

The Soviets continued striking at the Axis armies along the Don River. To the north, the Red Army encircled and destroyed the Hungarian 2nd Army south of Voronezh, leaving the German 2nd Army vulnerable. The Germans were encircled at Voronezh as the Soviets executed another pincer movement to retake the city and capture the bridgehead over the Don. The Germans retreated, narrowly escaping annihilation.

⟹ Soviet offensive, Jan 13–27, 1943   ➡ German retreat

➡ Soviet offensive, Jan 24–Feb 17, 1943

7 THE GERMANS FIGHT BACK
JANUARY 14–MARCH 19, 1943

German Army Group B withdrew beyond the Donets River as the Soviet advance continued in January. However, the Soviet capture of Kharkov, Pavlograd, and Krasnograd had created a large but vulnerable salient. On February 20, the Germans launched a counterattack that cut across the Soviet advance and threatened to isolate the Soviet troops. The Germans retook Kharkov on March 15 and Belgorod three days later, forcing the Soviets back east over the Donets.

➡ Soviet advance Jan 14–Feb 20, 1943   ➡ German counterattack Feb 20–Mar 19, 1943

---➤ Soviet retreat   ---➤ German retreat

▢ Soviet salient, Feb 20, 1943

Map labels:

Orel
Soviet Bryansk Front
Livny
Yelets
Soviet Voronezh Front
Feb 8, 1943 The Soviets regain Kursk.
Lgov
Kursk
Kastornoye
Voronezh
Don
German 2nd Army
German Army Group B
Ostrogozhsk
Belgorod
Hungarian 2nd Army
Soviet South-West Front
Volchansk
Valuyki
Rossosh
Kharkov
Jan 17, 1943 Only 45,000 Italians survive the Soviet offensive and reach Chertkovo.
Krasnograd
Donets
Feb 16, 1943 The Germans evacuate Kharkov.
Chertkovo
Soviet Don Front
Nov 22, 1942 Soviet forces capture the bridge over the Don River, cutting the German 6th Army's main lines of communication.
Izyum
Slavyansk
Lysychansk
Millerovo
Italian 8th Army
Don
Pavlograd
Horlivka
Kamensk
Romanian 3rd Army
Kalach
German 6th Army
Stalingrad
Volga
Feb 2, 1943 The final pocket of Germans in Stalingrad surrenders; 91,000 Germans are taken prisoner.
Makiivka
Chir
Romanian 4th Army
Mius
Donets
German Army Group Don
Soviet Stalingrad Front (Later South Front)
Feb 14, 1943 The Soviets retake Rostov.
Novoshakhtinsk
Don
Taganrog
Rostov
Volgodonsk
Kotelnikovo
German 4th Panzer Army
Mariupol
Proletarskaya
Berdyansk
Yeysk
Elista
Manych
Kalmuk Steppe
Sea of Azov
Tikhoretsk
German Army Group A
Kerch
Timashevsk
Soviet North Caucasus Front
Kerch Peninsula
German 17th Army
Kuban
Krasnodar
Stavropol
Budyonnovsk
Novorossiysk
Feb 4, 1943 Soviet troops land at Novorossiysk but fail to take the town.
Maikop
Labinsk
Nevinnomyssk
Laba
Cherkessk
Pyatigorsk
Mozdok
Tuapse
Caucasus Mountains
Sochi
Nalchik
Alagir
Black Sea
Sukhumi
Soviet Trans-Caucasus Front

U S S R

PRISONERS OF WAR

Millions of Allied and Axis solders were captured during World War II and sent to prisoner-of-war (POW) camps. Despite international agreements that were supposed to protect such prisoners, conditions in the camps could be dire.

Rapid advances made by the German army in the opening stages of the war meant that the Germans soon held several million French and Polish prisoners, and opened a network of camps to hold them. The invading Germans also encircled vast numbers of Soviet soldiers, and by December 1941 they had captured 3.2 million of them. However, the tables turned in Stalingrad in 1942, when the Germans experienced their first major defeat, and ultimately around 1.5 million German troops fell into Soviet hands.

△ **Bare necessities**
Prisoners had few possessions and so were forced to improvise, creating their own utensils such as this hand-carved spoon in a box with the prisoner's inmate number.

Variable conditions

The Geneva Convention of 1929 had laid down standards for captured POWs, but the Soviet Union had not signed it and Japan had not ratified it, so conditions in Soviet and Japanese camps during World War II were often appalling. The Germans generally treated prisoners from Britain, France, the US, and other western Allies according to the Geneva Convention, but not so the Soviets. As a result, almost 60 percent of Soviet POWs held by the Germans died, many of typhus, dysentery, exposure, or starvation.

Prisoners taken on the Western Front usually fared better: officers did not have to work, while rank-and-file soldiers were supposed to do work without military value, and the Red Cross dispatched 36 million food parcels to supplement their diet. Most were released soon after the war, although the last German POW held by the Soviet Union was not repatriated until 1956.

COLDITZ CASTLE

The Renaissance castle at Colditz in Saxony, Germany, was used by the German army from 1940 to detain POWs who had tried to escape from other camps. Security was tight, but escape attempts were rife, and a total of 30 prisoners managed to break out to freedom. One notable attempt involved a homemade glider.

Caught out in the cold
Prisoners were often at their most vulnerable immediately after capture, when they were transported to camps. Here, German soldiers taken in Alsace in January 1945 endure freezing conditions as they are moved from the frontline.

TURNING THE TIDE 1943–1944

WITH THE ALLIED INVASION OF NORMANDY, THE SOVIETS PRESSING
FROM THE EAST, AND THE US CAMPAIGNING ACROSS THE PACIFIC,
THE AXIS POWERS FACED THEIR HARDEST FIGHT YET.

GERMAN DEFIANCE

As 1943 progressed, it became increasingly evident that Nazi Germany would eventually be defeated. However, Hitler remained defiant, and the war continued in 1944 with unabated ferocity as the Allies pressed on toward the German homeland.

△ **Sicily landings**
British troops wade ashore during Operation Husky, the Allied invasion of Sicily, in July 1943. The invasion led to the overthrow of the Italian fascist dictator Benito Mussolini.

By 1943, superior manpower and industrial strength gave the Allies a huge advantage over Germany. Yet at crucial points in the war, the Germans came very close to major successes. In the battle of the Atlantic, the German submarine campaign inflicted almost unsustainable losses on Allied shipping before the Allies finally defeated the U-boat menace. On the Eastern front, Soviet forces won the battle of Kursk, but at huge cost. Germany suffered under the impact of British and US bombing, but losses on the Allied side were heavy as well. Even when Italy was invaded and sued for peace, the Germans were able to block the Allied advance northward.

Yet the most determined efforts of German fighting forces were eventually in vain. The Allies made sensible decisions to produce relatively simple equipment on a vast scale, and they had the manpower and organizational skills to put the arms into action effectively. The Germans had the best tanks and a great deal

of other superior technology, but despite this and their extensive use of slave labor, Germany could not match Allied industrial output.

Germany struggles to keep control

As conditions in Nazi-occupied Europe worsened, with food shortages and the mass conscription of men to work in German factories, armed resistance spread. This meant large numbers of German troops were needed to suppress subversive activities. Also, the Allied bombings forced Germany to devote substantial resources to home defense, as well as hampering arms production and fuel supplies.

As shown by their bombing of German cities, the Western Allies had learned the ruthlessness of total war. Their undertaking to pursue "unconditional surrender" committed them to the complete military defeat of Germany without negotiation or compromise. Hitler hoped the Allied countries would have a major disagreement, but despite ideological differences, the Soviet Union, Britain, and the US held together. Hitler also dreamed of a technological miracle—wonder weapons that would

◁ **King Tiger**
Introduced in 1944, the German Tiger II was the heaviest tank used in the war. Its thick armor gave good protection, giving it a considerable advantage over Allied tanks in head-on confrontations.

NAZI GERMANY'S CHANGING FORTUNES

In early 1943, the Germans remained in control of continental Europe, despite their surrender at Stalingrad. However, that summer the Allied invasion of Italy and the Soviet victory at Kursk placed German forces under mounting pressure. After Allied troops landed at Normandy in June 1944, while Soviet forces were advancing rapidly from the east, it appeared that Nazi resistance might collapse, even though Allied military progress faltered at the German frontiers.

Jan 14–24, 1943 Allies decide on "unconditional surrender" of Germany at Casablanca Conference

May 16–17, 1943 Dambuster raid on Ruhr dams

Jul 10, 1943 Allied troops stage landings in Sicily

Jul 27–28, 1943 Bombing of Hamburg causes firestorm, killing c.37,000

Sep 9, 1943 Allies launch invasion of Italian mainland, resisted by Germans

WESTERN EUROPE

EASTERN FRONT

RESISTANCE

JAN 1943

MAY

SEP

May 12, 1943 Axis forces in Tunisia surrender, ending war in North Africa

Jul 5, 1943 Beginning of Battle of Kursk; ends in major Soviet victory (August 23)

Jul 25, 1943 Mussolini is deposed and Italy seeks an armistice

Aug 17, 1943 US Air Force loses 60 bombers in daylight raids on Schweinfurt and Regensburg

◁ **Ruins of Warsaw**
After suppressing an uprising by Polish resistance fighters in the summer of 1944, German troops systematically destroyed Warsaw, leaving four-fifths of the city in ruins.

> *"The free men of the world are marching together to Victory!"*
>
> GENERAL DWIGHT D. EISENHOWER, "ORDER OF THE DAY" STATEMENT, JUNE 5, 1944

▽ **Liberation of Paris**
US soldiers and Parisian women celebrate in front of the Eiffel Tower after the liberation of Paris in August 1944. The city had been under German occupation for four years.

transform the war. But although the Germans introduced flying bombs, rockets, and jet aircraft, the weapons were too little, too late to have any decisive impact.

The final stages

By summer 1944, the Soviets were advancing toward Germany from the east, while the Western Allies had invaded Normandy. However, the euphoria of liberation as Allied forces raced across France and Belgium that August was followed by frustration when they ground to a halt in the fall. The failure of a coup against Hitler left him securely in control and determined to fight to the end. Political conflicts came to the fore, with Communist-led partisan movements clashing with Nationalists and Fascists in Yugoslavia, Greece, and Italy.

The suffering across Europe in the latter stages of the war was tremendous. The extermination of Jews continued, and the Allied aerial bombing campaign took a heavy toll on civilians in German cities and elsewhere. Liberation from Nazi rule brought joy to many, but death or humiliation to those judged as traitors—from collaborators in France to Crimean Tatars subject to mass deportation in the USSR. Millions of ethnic German civilians from the Baltic and central Europe fled west in the face of the advancing Soviet armies. A post-war Europe scarred by ideological division, ruins, and refugees was already taking shape while the fighting approached its climax.

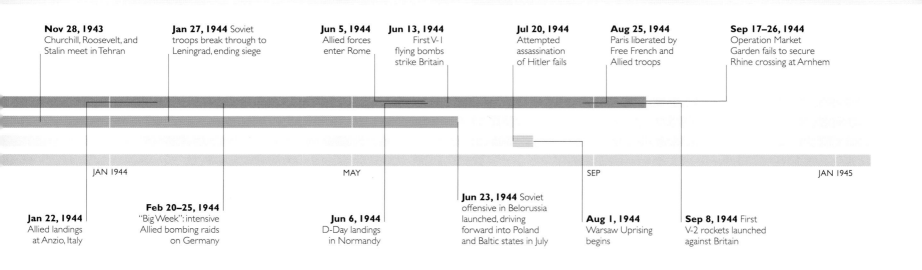

Nov 28, 1943
Churchill, Roosevelt, and Stalin meet in Tehran

Jan 27, 1944 Soviet troops break through to Leningrad, ending siege

Jun 5, 1944
Allied forces enter Rome

Jun 13, 1944
First V-1 flying bombs strike Britain

Jul 20, 1944
Attempted assassination of Hitler fails

Aug 25, 1944
Paris liberated by Free French and Allied troops

Sep 17–26, 1944
Operation Market Garden fails to secure Rhine crossing at Arnhem

JAN 1944　　　　　MAY　　　　　SEP　　　　　JAN 1945

Jan 22, 1944
Allied landings at Anzio, Italy

Feb 20–25, 1944
"Big Week": intensive Allied bombing raids on Germany

Jun 6, 1944
D-Day landings in Normandy

Jun 23, 1944 Soviet offensive in Belorussia launched, driving forward into Poland and Baltic states in July

Aug 1, 1944
Warsaw Uprising begins

Sep 8, 1944 First V-2 rockets launched against Britain

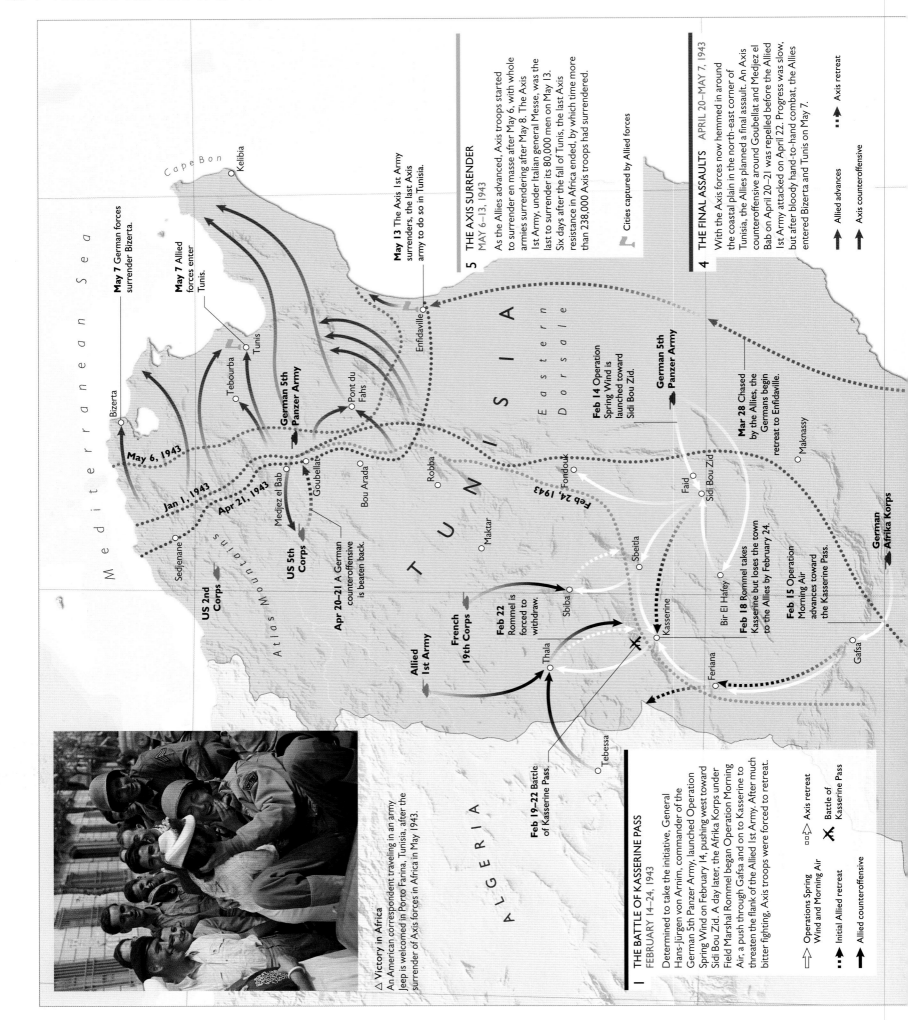

Mediterranean Sea

Cape Bon

○ Kelibia

May 7 German forces surrender Bizerta.

May 7 Allied forces enter Tunis.

May 13 The Axis 1st Army surrenders, the last Axis army to do so in Tunisia.

○ Bizerta

May 6, 1943

○ Tunis

○ Tebourba

German 5th Panzer Army

○ Pont du Fahs

○ Enfidaville

Jan 1, 1943

Apr 21, 1943

○ Sedjenane

○ Medjez el Bab

○ Goubellat

US 5th Corps

○ Bou Arada

○ Robba

○ Fondouk

Feb 24, 1943

○ Faid

○ Sidi Bou Zid

German 5th Panzer Army

Feb 14 Operation Spring Wind is launched toward Sidi Bou Zid.

Mar 28 Chased by the Allies, the Germans begin retreat to Enfidaville.

○ Makmassy

Apr 20–21 A German counteroffensive is beaten back.

US 2nd Corps

Atlas Mountains

○ Maktar

○ Sbeitla

US 5th Corps

French 19th Corps

Feb 22 Rommel is forced to withdraw.

○ Sbiba

○ Thala

○ Kasserine

Feb 18 Rommel takes Kasserine but loses the town to the Allies by February 24.

○ Bir El Hafey

Feb 15 Operation Morning Air advances toward the Kasserine Pass.

German Afrika Korps

Allied 1st Army

○ Feriana

○ Gafsa

T U N I S I A

Eastern Dorsale

Feb 19–22 Battle of Kasserine Pass.

○ Tebessa

A L G E R I A

5 THE AXIS SURRENDER MAY 6–13, 1943

As the Allies advanced, Axis troops started to surrender en masse after May 6, with whole armies surrendering after May 8. The Axis 1st Army, under Italian general Messe, was the last to surrender its 80,000 men on May 13. Six days after the fall of Tunis, the last Axis resistance in Africa ended, by which time more than 238,000 Axis troops had surrendered.

⌐ Cities captured by Allied forces

4 THE FINAL ASSAULTS APRIL 20–MAY 7, 1943

With the Axis forces now hemmed in around the coastal plain in the north-east corner of Tunisia, the Allies planned a final assault. An Axis counteroffensive around Goubellat and Medjez el Bab on April 20–21 was repelled before the Allied 1st Army attacked on April 22. Progress was slow, but after bloody hand-to-hand combat, the Allies entered Bizerta and Tunis on May 7.

↑ Allied advances   ↑ Axis retreat

↑ Allied counteroffensive   ↑ Axis counteroffensive

△ Victory in Africa

An American correspondent traveling in an army Jeep is welcomed in Porto Farina, Tunisia, after the surrender of Axis forces in Africa in May 1943.

I THE BATTLE OF KASSERINE PASS FEBRUARY 14–24, 1943

Determined to take the initiative, General Hans-Jürgen von Arnim, commander of the German 5th Panzer Army, launched Operation Spring Wind on February 14, pushing west toward Sidi Bou Zid. A day later, the Afrika Korps under Field Marshal Rommel began Operation Morning Air, a push through Gafsa and on to Kasserine to threaten the flank of the Allied 1st Army. After much bitter fighting, Axis troops were forced to retreat.

⇨ Operations Spring Wind and Morning Air

▪▪▷ Axis retreat

✕ Battle of Kasserine Pass

▪▪▪ Initial Allied retreat

↑ Allied counteroffensive

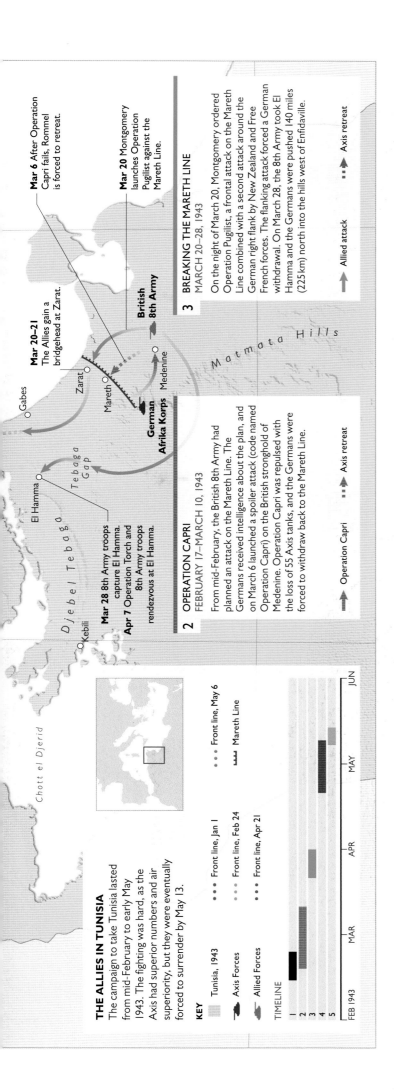

Mar 6 After Operation Capri fails, Rommel is forced to retreat.

Mar 20 Montgomery launches Operation Pugilist against the Mareth Line.

Mar 20–21 The Allies gain a bridgehead at Zarat.

British 8th Army

German Afrika Korps

Matmata Hills

Gabes
Zarat
Mareth
Medenine
El Hamma
Tebaga Gap
Djebel Tebaga
Kebili

Chott el Djerid

3 BREAKING THE MARETH LINE
MARCH 20–28, 1943

On the night of March 20, Montgomery ordered Operation Pugilist, a frontal attack on the Mareth Line combined with a second attack around the German right flank by New Zealand and Free French forces. The flanking attack forced a German withdrawal. On March 28, the 8th Army took El Hamma and the Germans were pushed 140 miles (225 km) north into the hills west of Enfidaville.

Allied attack ⟶   Axis retreat ⟶

2 OPERATION CAPRI
FEBRUARY 17–MARCH 10, 1943

From mid-February, the British 8th Army had planned an attack on the Mareth Line. The Germans received intelligence about the plan, and on March 6 launched a spoiler attack (code named Operation Capri) on the British stronghold of Medenine. Operation Capri was repulsed with the loss of 55 Axis tanks, and the Germans were forced to withdraw back to the Mareth Line.

Mar 28 8th Army troops capture El Hamma.
Apr 7 Operation Torch and 8th Army troops rendezvous at El Hamma.

Operation Capri ⟶   Axis retreat ⟶

THE ALLIES IN TUNISIA
The campaign to take Tunisia lasted from mid-February to early May 1943. The fighting was hard, as the Axis had superior numbers and air superiority, but they were eventually forced to surrender by May 13.

KEY
- Tunisia, 1943
- Axis Forces
- Allied Forces
- Front line, Jan 1
- Front line, Feb 24
- Front line, Apr 21
- Front line, May 6
- Mareth Line

TIMELINE
1 / 2 / 3 / 4 / 5
FEB 1943 — MAR — APR — MAY — JUN

VICTORY IN THE DESERT

Following the British victory at El Alamein to their east and the successful Allied landings of Operation Torch in Algeria and Morocco to their west, the Axis armies were forced to fight a defensive campaign in Tunisia. Resupplied and reinforced by air and by convoys arriving in Tunis, they dug in and prepared for a long battle.

A key goal of Operation Torch (see pp.146–147) had been to provide a route through Tunisia by which the Allies could attack Italy—the "soft underbelly" of the Axis, according to Churchill. In order to avoid Axis air attacks, Operation Torch had landed its forces some 500 miles (800 km) west of Tunis, and although they raced east across Algeria as soon as they landed, the Germans acted swiftly to reinforce their positions in Tunisia. The Vichy French governor of Tunisia, Admiral Jean-Pierre Esteva, allowed German aircraft to fly in additional troops, tanks (including the new Tiger tanks), artillery pieces, and other supplies. By the beginning of 1943, around 250,000

Axis troops had arrived in Tunisia, forming a substantial force. The Germans also benefited from the close proximity of their airfields in Sicily. Rommel's army, consisting of German and Italian corps, in retreat after the second Battle of El Alamein (see pp.144–145), was also in Tunisia, having taken up positions on the defensive Mareth Line—a former French colonial defensive line running 22 miles (35 km) from the coast to the mountains. The advances that Allied forces had made from Algeria since the Torch landings came to an end as they reached the Eastern Dorsale (the eastern extension of the Atlas Mountains), which effectively became the front line of the conflict in Tunisia.

January 1943 saw sporadic fighting on the long front as both sides struggled to resupply their forces. The Allies repulsed a significant Axis advance toward Kasserine in February 1943, and their attacks on the Mareth Line in March overwhelmed the Axis defenders. The Axis armies retreated toward north-east Tunisia, finally surrendering by May 13. The war in Africa was over.

"I want to impose on everyone that the bad times are over, they are finished!"

GENERAL BERNARD MONTGOMERY, 1942

THE 8TH ARMY

The British 8th Army was a multinational force. In addition to the UK, units came from Australia, New Zealand, India, South Africa, Rhodesia, Canada, Greece, and Poland, as well as a sizeable Free French contingent—a total of more than 220,000 men. For much of its operational life in North Africa and Italy, it was led by General Bernard Montgomery.

SUMMIT CONFERENCES

The global alliance that emerged in 1941 to oppose the Axis powers needed to make difficult strategic decisions. As a result, a series of summit meetings were arranged in 1943 to coordinate a joint Allied approach.

The Allies faced conflicting priorities. At a summit in Moscow in September 1941, they discussed the distribution of Lend-Lease Aid, the US scheme to help their allies by giving military supplies and raw materials on credit (see pp.70–71). This was followed in January 1943 by a conference in Morocco, attended by British prime minister Winston Churchill and US president Franklin D. Roosevelt. The two leaders decided on a combined bomber offensive against Germany, and on the policy of Germany's unconditional surrender. They also agreed a "Mediterranean First" strategy, prioritizing the defeat of Axis forces in North Africa and Italy over opening a new front in France.

△ **Soviet anti-German poster**
The shared goal of beating Germany encouraged Soviet collaboration with other powers.

Cairo and Tehran

In November 1943, the Allies met in Cairo and Tehran. In Cairo, Roosevelt, Churchill, and Chinese leader Chiang Kai-shek discussed strategies for the defeat of Japan, agreeing that an offensive against the Japanese in China took priority over recapturing Malaysia. In Tehran, Stalin joined the Allied leaders to discuss Poland, Japan, and more.

△ **Tehran conference**
Allied leaders Stalin, Roosevelt, and Churchill were all present at a conference in November 1943, held in the USSR's legation in Tehran. The leaders reached agreement over the invasion of occupied France and discussed the division of Germany.

Moroccan conference
President Roosevelt and Prime Minister Churchill speak to the press during the Casablanca Conference (code named "Symbol") in 1943. Germany's attack on Stalingrad prevented Joseph Stalin from attending the meeting.

SICILY AND ITALY INVADED

After the defeat of Axis forces in Tunisia, Axis-controlled southern Europe appeared vulnerable. Germany was led to believe that Allied interests lay in Sardinia or Corsica, but in January 1943 the Allies decided to invade Sicily. Six months later the invasion (Operation Husky) began.

In 1943, Axis forces on Sicily were under the command of General Alfredo Guzzoni. However, the only reliable troops in his 6th Army were two German divisions in Hans Hube's 14th Panzer Corps; Italy's own soldiers were poorly motivated.

The Allied forces for the invasion were Patton's US 7th Army and Montgomery's British and Commonwealth 8th Army, both under the overall command of Britain's General Harold Alexander. The initial

plan was for the British to attack up the east coast, taking Catania and then Messina, with their flank and rear protected by the Americans. On August 5, the British took Catania, and by August 17 the Allies controlled Sicily. In late July, Mussolini was deposed and replaced as prime minister by Marshal Pietro Badoglio. When news broke on September 8 that Badoglio had agreed an armistice, the Germans seized Rome and effectively occupied Italy.

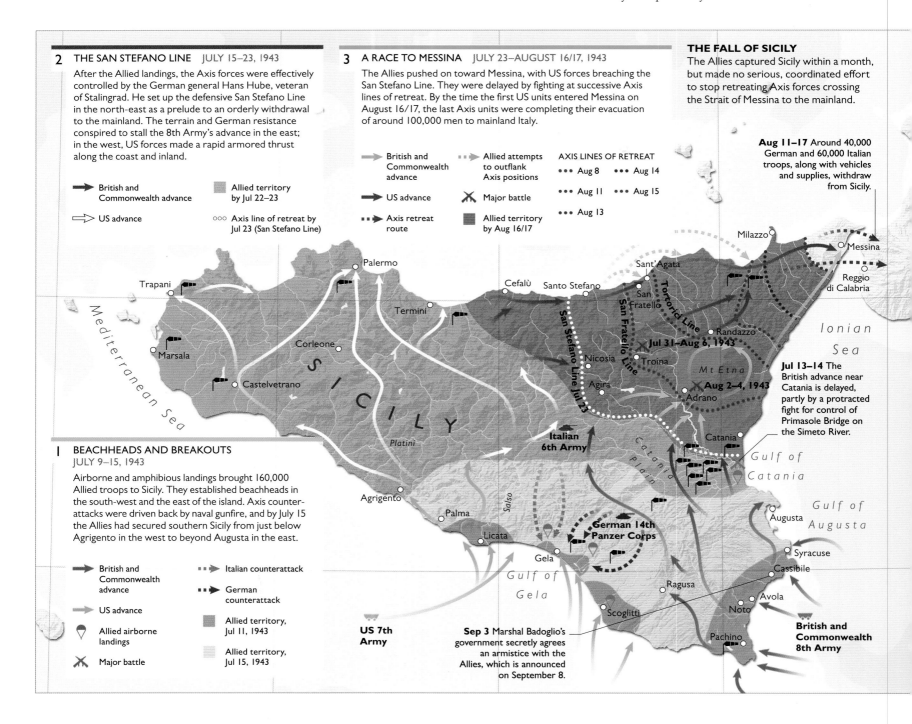

2 THE SAN STEFANO LINE JULY 15–23, 1943

After the Allied landings, the Axis forces were effectively controlled by the German general Hans Hube, veteran of Stalingrad. He set up the defensive San Stefano Line in the north-east as a prelude to an orderly withdrawal to the mainland. The terrain and German resistance conspired to stall the 8th Army's advance in the east; in the west, US forces made a rapid armored thrust along the coast and inland.

- → British and Commonwealth advance
- ⇨ US advance
- ▨ Allied territory by Jul 22–23
- ooo Axis line of retreat by Jul 23 (San Stefano Line)

3 A RACE TO MESSINA JULY 23–AUGUST 16/17, 1943

The Allies pushed on toward Messina, with US forces breaching the San Stefano Line. They were delayed by fighting at successive Axis lines of retreat. By the time the first US units entered Messina on August 16/17, the last Axis units were completing their evacuation of around 100,000 men to mainland Italy.

- → British and Commonwealth advance
- → US advance
- ⇢ Axis retreat route
- ⇢ Allied attempts to outflank Axis positions
- ✕ Major battle
- ▨ Allied territory by Aug 16/17

AXIS LINES OF RETREAT
- ••• Aug 8
- ••• Aug 11
- ••• Aug 13
- ••• Aug 14
- ••• Aug 15

THE FALL OF SICILY

The Allies captured Sicily within a month, but made no serious, coordinated effort to stop retreating Axis forces crossing the Strait of Messina to the mainland.

Aug 11–17 Around 40,000 German and 60,000 Italian troops, along with vehicles and supplies, withdraw from Sicily.

Jul 13–14 The British advance near Catania is delayed, partly by a protracted fight for control of Primasole Bridge on the Simeto River.

1 BEACHHEADS AND BREAKOUTS JULY 9–15, 1943

Airborne and amphibious landings brought 160,000 Allied troops to Sicily. They established beachheads in the south-west and the east of the island. Axis counter-attacks were driven back by naval gunfire, and by July 15 the Allies had secured southern Sicily from just below Agrigento in the west to beyond Augusta in the east.

- → British and Commonwealth advance
- → US advance
- ⬤ Allied airborne landings
- ✕ Major battle
- ⇢ Italian counterattack
- ⇢ German counterattack
- ▨ Allied territory, Jul 11, 1943
- ▨ Allied territory, Jul 15, 1943

Sep 3 Marshal Badoglio's government secretly agrees an armistice with the Allies, which is announced on September 8.

Map labels: Trapani, Palermo, Cefalù, Santo Stefano, Sant'Agata, Milazzo, Messina, Reggio di Calabria, Termini, San Fratello, Randazzo, Marsala, Corleone, Nicosia, Troina, Mt Etna, Castelvetrano, Agira, Adrano, Catania, Agrigento, Palma, Licata, Gela, Scoglitti, Syracuse, Cassibile, Ragusa, Avola, Noto, Pachino, Augusta, San Stefano Line Jul 23, San Fratello Line, Tortorici Line, Italian 6th Army, German 14th Panzer Corps, US 7th Army, British and Commonwealth 8th Army, Mediterranean Sea, Ionian Sea, Gulf of Catania, Gulf of Augusta, Gulf of Gela, Platini, Salso, Catania Plain, SICILY

Jul 31–Aug 6, 1943
Aug 2–4, 1943

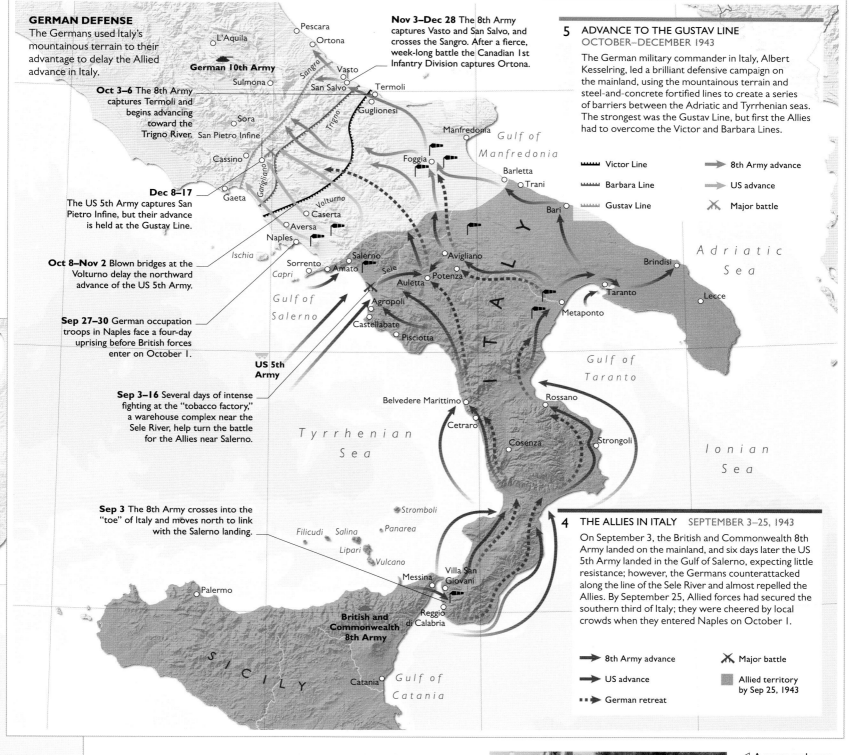

GERMAN DEFENSE

The Germans used Italy's mountainous terrain to their advantage to delay the Allied advance in Italy.

German 10th Army

Oct 3–6 The 8th Army captures Termoli and begins advancing toward the Trigno River.

Dec 8–17 The US 5th Army captures San Pietro Infine, but their advance is held at the Gustav Line.

Oct 8–Nov 2 Blown bridges at the Volturno delay the northward advance of the US 5th Army.

Sep 27–30 German occupation troops in Naples face a four-day uprising before British forces enter on October 1.

US 5th Army

Sep 3–16 Several days of intense fighting at the "tobacco factory," a warehouse complex near the Sele River, help turn the battle for the Allies near Salerno.

Sep 3 The 8th Army crosses into the "toe" of Italy and moves north to link with the Salerno landing.

British and Commonwealth 8th Army

Nov 3–Dec 28 The 8th Army captures Vasto and San Salvo, and crosses the Sangro. After a fierce, week-long battle the Canadian 1st Infantry Division captures Ortona.

5 ADVANCE TO THE GUSTAV LINE
OCTOBER–DECEMBER 1943

The German military commander in Italy, Albert Kesselring, led a brilliant defensive campaign on the mainland, using the mountainous terrain and steel-and-concrete fortified lines to create a series of barriers between the Adriatic and Tyrrhenian seas. The strongest was the Gustav Line, but first the Allies had to overcome the Victor and Barbara Lines.

﹀﹀﹀ Victor Line	→	8th Army advance
﹀﹀﹀ Barbara Line	→	US advance
﹀﹀﹀ Gustav Line	✗	Major battle

4 THE ALLIES IN ITALY SEPTEMBER 3–25, 1943

On September 3, the British and Commonwealth 8th Army landed on the mainland, and six days later the US 5th Army landed in the Gulf of Salerno, expecting little resistance; however, the Germans counterattacked along the line of the Sele River and almost repelled the Allies. By September 25, Allied forces had secured the southern third of Italy; they were cheered by local crowds when they entered Naples on October 1.

→ 8th Army advance	✗	Major battle
→ US advance		Allied territory by Sep 25, 1943
▶▶▶ German retreat		

BREAKING THE AXIS

By transferring the campaign in the Mediterranean from North Africa to Italy, the Allies believed that General Harold Alexander's 15th Army Group could end the war by 1944.

KEY

British and Commonwealth forces	US forces	Italian forces
	German forces	Airfields constructed by the Allies

TIMELINE

1
2
3
4
5

JUL 1943   AUG   SEP   OCT   NOV   DEC   JAN 1944

◁ **A warm welcome**
Sicilian children join British soldiers on an M4 Sherman tank as the Allied forces are welcomed into Milo, in north-eastern Sicily, on August 15, 1943.

FROM ANZIO TO THE GOTHIC LINE

The Allies' campaign in Italy resumed in January 1944 with a long-held objective: to liberate Rome. They landed at Anzio, south of Rome, but their advance north was slowed by a series of defensive lines masterminded by German field marshal Albert Kesselring. The battles in Italy's mountainous terrain produced some of the toughest fighting of the war.

By the end of 1943, German forces in Italy had retreated to the fortified Gustav Line, also called the Winter Line. On this line lay Monte Cassino, a strategic location at the base of the Liri and Rapido river valleys that guarded Route 6—the road north to Rome.

Days before their first attack on Cassino, the Allies landed at Anzio, well behind the Gustav Line, in an attempt to outflank the Germans and cut their lines of communication. The US 6th Corps made an amphibious landing north of the Pontine Marshes, 35 miles (56 km) from Rome. However, hesitation by the US commander at Anzio led to his units being hemmed in at the beachhead. At Cassino, a series of bloody and very costly Allied

assaults began on January 24. Despite air support from Allied bombers flying from bases in North Africa, and later southern Italy, it took until May for the Allies to break through at Cassino.

The US 5th Army then pushed up the coast toward Anzio while the British 8th Army advanced up the Liri River—a combined attack that the Germans could not withstand. After five months of attrition, progress toward—and then beyond—Rome was achieved swiftly. However, the Germans withdrew skillfully, falling back behind the Trasimene and Arno Lines, which gave them time to create another well-fortified line, the Gothic Line, to the north. It was here, in August 1944, that the Allies paused again.

LIBERATION AND DIVISION

Rome was the first capital city to be liberated when the US 5th Army entered on June 4, 1944 (pictured). However, just two days later the Allies made the D-Day landings in Normandy (see pp.186–187), and within two months Allied troops in Italy had been redeployed. The US 6th Corps and the French Expeditionary Corps were transferred from the US 5th Army to the French Riviera for Operation Dragoon (see pp.194–195). These changes allowed German forces more time to make their retreat.

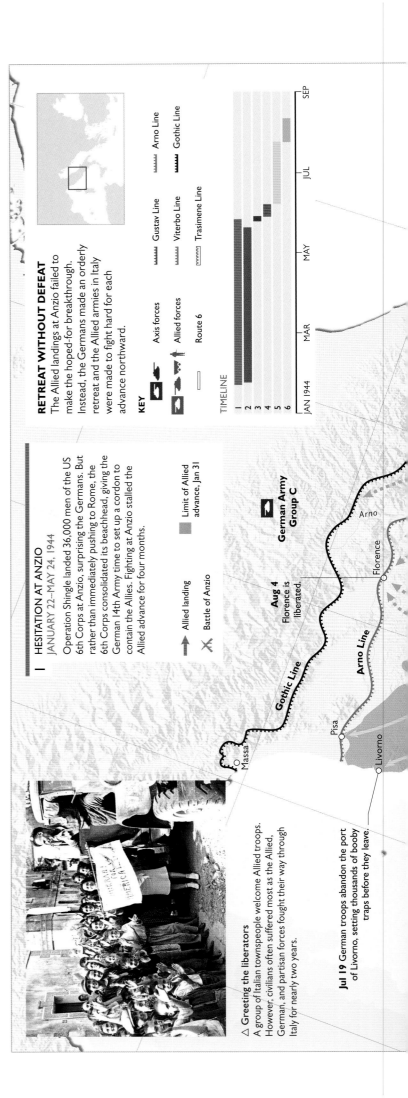

△ Greeting the liberators
A group of Italian townspeople welcome Allied troops. However, civilians often suffered most as the Allied, German, and partisan forces fought their way through Italy for nearly two years.

Jul 19 German troops abandon the port of Livorno, setting thousands of booby traps before they leave.

HESITATION AT ANZIO
JANUARY 22–MAY 24, 1944

Operation Shingle landed 36,000 men of the US 6th Corps at Anzio, surprising the Germans. But rather than immediately pushing to Rome, the 6th Corps consolidated its beachhead, giving the German 14th Army time to set up a cordon to contain the Allies. Fighting at Anzio stalled the Allied advance for four months.

↑ Allied landing

✕ Battle of Anzio

▨ Limit of Allied advance, Jan 31

RETREAT WITHOUT DEFEAT

The Allied landings at Anzio failed to make the hoped-for breakthrough. Instead, the Germans made an orderly retreat and the Allied armies in Italy were made to fight hard for each advance northward.

KEY

Axis forces	
Allied forces	
Route 6	

‒‒‒‒ Gustav Line   ‒‒‒‒ Arno Line

‒‒‒‒ Viterbo Line   ━━━ Gothic Line

▨▨▨ Trasimene Line

TIMELINE

JAN 1944   MAR   MAY   JUL   SEP

1
2
3
4
5
6

Aug 4 Florence is liberated.

German Army Group C

Arno

Florence

Gothic Line

Arno Line

Massa

Pisa

Livorno

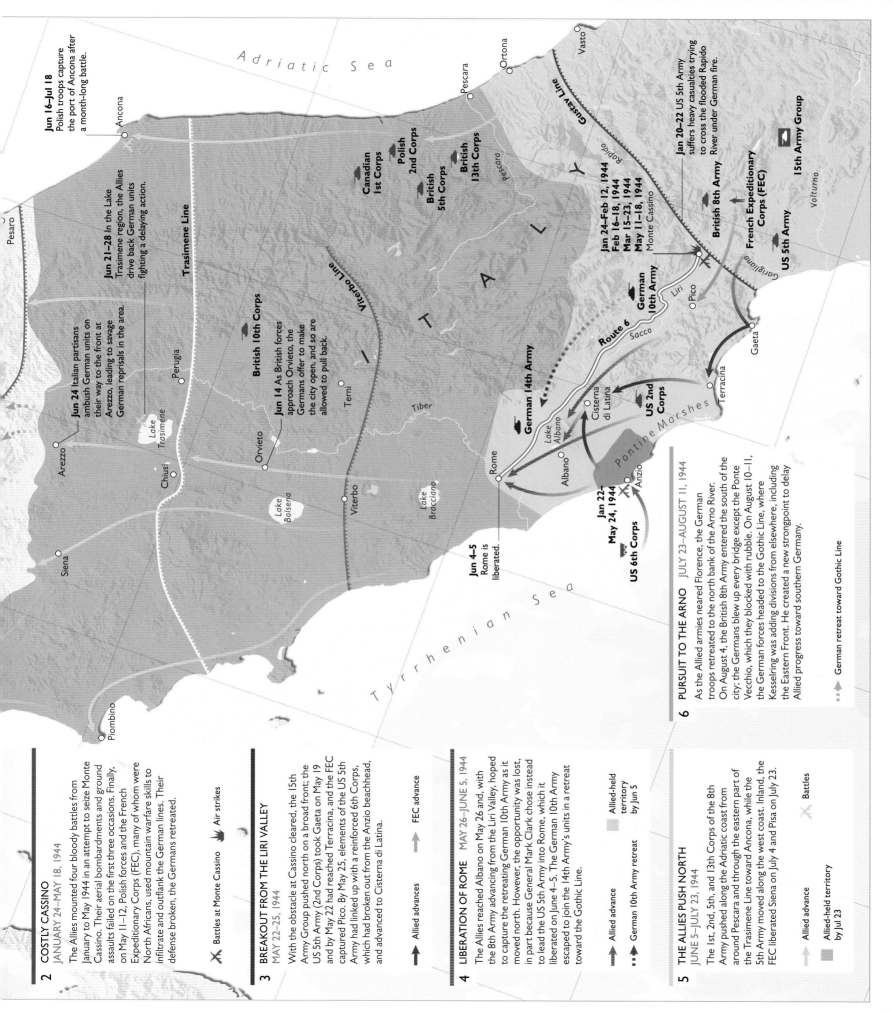

Adriatic Sea

Jun 16–Jul 18 Polish troops capture the port of Ancona after a month-long battle.

Jun 21–28 In the Lake Trasimene region, the Allies drive back German units fighting a delaying action.

Trasimene Line

Jun 24 Italian partisans ambush German units on their way to the front at Arezzo, leading to savage German reprisals in the area.

Viterbo Line

British 10th Corps

Jun 14 As British forces approach Orvieto, the Germans offer to make the city open, and so are allowed to pull back.

Gustav Line

Canadian 1st Corps

Polish 2nd Corps

British 5th Corps

British 13th Corps

Jan 24–Feb 12, 1944
Feb 16–18, 1944
Mar 15–23, 1944
May 11–18, 1944
Monte Cassino

Jan 20–22 US 5th Army suffers heavy casualties trying to cross the flooded Rapido River under German fire.

British 8th Army

French Expeditionary Corps (FEC)

US 5th Army

15th Army Group

German 10th Army

Route 6

German 14th Army

Cisterna di Latina

US 2nd Corps

Pontine Marshes

Jun 4–5 Rome is liberated.

May 24, 1944
Jan 22, 1944
US 6th Corps

Rome

Albano

Anzio

Gaeta

Terracina

Italy

Pesaro

Ancona

Perugia

Arezzo

Lake Trasimene

Siena

Chiusi

Orvieto

Terni

Tiber

Viterbo

Lake Bolsena

Lake Bracciano

Piombino

Ortona

Pescara

Vasto

Pescara

Rapido

Garigliano

Volturno

Liri

Pico

Sacco

Lake Albano

Tyrrhenian Sea

---

2   COSTLY CASSINO
JANUARY 24–MAY 18, 1944

The Allies mounted four bloody battles from January to May 1944 in an attempt to seize Monte Cassino. Their aerial bombardments and ground assaults failed on the first three occasions. Finally, on May 11–12, Polish forces and the French Expeditionary Corps (FEC), many of whom were North Africans, used mountain warfare skills to infiltrate and outflank the German lines. Their defense broken, the Germans retreated.

✕ Battles at Monte Cassino   ⤵ Air strikes

3   BREAKOUT FROM THE LIRI VALLEY
MAY 22–25, 1944

With the obstacle at Cassino cleared, the 15th Army Group pushed north on a broad front; the US 5th Army (2nd Corps) took Gaeta on May 19 and by May 22 had reached Terracina, and the FEC captured Pico. By May 25, elements of the US 5th Army had linked up with a reinforced 6th Corps, which had broken out from the Anzio beachhead, and advanced to Cisterna di Latina.

⬆ Allied advances   ⬆ FEC advance

4   LIBERATION OF ROME   MAY 26–JUNE 5, 1944

The Allies reached Albano on May 26 and, with the 8th Army advancing from the Liri Valley, hoped to capture the retreating German 10th Army as it moved north. However, the opportunity was lost, in part because General Mark Clark chose instead to lead the US 5th Army into Rome, which it liberated on June 4–5. The German 10th Army escaped to join the 14th Army's units in a retreat toward the Gothic Line.

⬆ Allied advance   ⬆ German 10th Army retreat   ▨ Allied-held territory by Jun 5

5   THE ALLIES PUSH NORTH
JUNE 5–JULY 23, 1944

The 1st, 2nd, 5th, and 13th Corps of the 8th Army pushed along the Adriatic coast from around Pescara and through the eastern part of the Trasimene Line toward Ancona, while the 5th Army moved along the west coast. Inland, the FEC liberated Siena on July 4 and Pisa on July 23.

⬆ Allied advance   ✕ Battles   ▨ Allied-held territory by Jul 23

6   PURSUIT TO THE ARNO   JULY 23–AUGUST 11, 1944

As the Allied armies neared Florence, the German troops retreated to the north bank of the Arno River. On August 4, the British 8th Army entered the south of the city; the Germans blew up every bridge except the Ponte Vecchio, which they blocked with rubble. On August 10–11, the German forces headed to the Gothic Line, where Kesselring was adding divisions from elsewhere, including the Eastern Front. He created a new strongpoint to delay Allied progress toward southern Germany.

⤴ German retreat toward Gothic Line

DEFEAT OF THE U-BOATS

America's entry into the war began a new wave of U-boat activity in 1942 as the submarines hunted ships off the US east coast. Improved defenses soon drove the U-boats out into the mid-Atlantic, where they faced increasingly effective countermeasures by 1943.

After Germany declared war on the US in December 1941, the Atlantic Ocean became the theater for the early conflict between the nations. Admiral Karl Dönitz, commander of the German U-boat fleet, launched Operation Drumbeat to harass merchant ships moving along the US east coast. The first casualty was a British tanker, sunk on January 14, 1942, and by June of that year a total of 492 Allied ships had been lost, even though there were never more than a dozen German submarines operating in the area.

As the US improved its coastal defenses, the focus of the sea battle shifted to the mid-Atlantic, with additional attacks continuing in the Caribbean Sea. Germany poured ever-increasing resources into its submarine fleet and by November 1942, more than 80 U-boats were active in the Atlantic theater. That month was to prove the deadliest of all for the Allies, who lost over 88,000 tons (80,000 metric tons) of merchant shipping; the tally for the year 1942 amounted to over 6 million tons (5.4 million metric tons).

The tide of the war in the Atlantic turned in favor of the Allies in the spring of 1943. Faced by a real threat to Britain's oil supplies, the Allies deployed long-range aircraft equipped with improved radar, as well as hunting packs of anti-submarine vessels, typically escorted by small escort aircraft carriers. The tactic worked. In May 1943, when 41 U-boats were sunk, Admiral Dönitz unwillingly recalled all his vessels from the North Atlantic. Although they would return later, the U-boats never again presented the grave threat that they had in the early years of the war.

ADMIRAL KARL DÖNITZ 1891–1980

Karl Dönitz served as a submarine officer in World War I. In the mid 1930s he took charge of the clandestine program to rebuild Germany's U-boat fleet, which had been banned in 1919. Promoted to Rear-Admiral in 1939, he proved a skillful strategist—so much so that he was made Commander-in-Chief of the German navy in January 1943. For his loyalty, Hitler chose him as his successor, and he briefly served as Germany's head of state following the Führer's suicide in 1945.

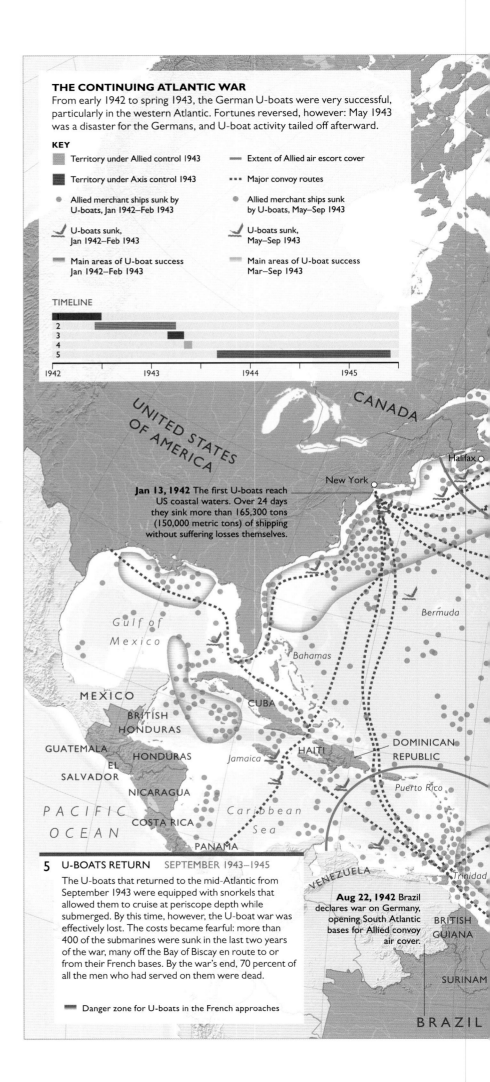

THE CONTINUING ATLANTIC WAR

From early 1942 to spring 1943, the German U-boats were very successful, particularly in the western Atlantic. Fortunes reversed, however: May 1943 was a disaster for the Germans, and U-boat activity tailed off afterward.

KEY

- Territory under Allied control 1943
- Territory under Axis control 1943
- Allied merchant ships sunk by U-boats, Jan 1942–Feb 1943
- U-boats sunk, Jan 1942–Feb 1943
- Main areas of U-boat success Jan 1942–Feb 1943
- Extent of Allied air escort cover
- Major convoy routes
- Allied merchant ships sunk by U-boats, May–Sep 1943
- U-boats sunk, May–Sep 1943
- Main areas of U-boat success Mar–Sep 1943

TIMELINE

1942 1943 1944 1945

Jan 13, 1942 The first U-boats reach US coastal waters. Over 24 days they sink more than 165,300 tons (150,000 metric tons) of shipping without suffering losses themselves.

5 U-BOATS RETURN SEPTEMBER 1943–1945

The U-boats that returned to the mid-Atlantic from September 1943 were equipped with snorkels that allowed them to cruise at periscope depth while submerged. By this time, however, the U-boat war was effectively lost. The costs became fearful: more than 400 of the submarines were sunk in the last two years of the war, many off the Bay of Biscay en route to or from their French bases. By the war's end, 70 percent of all the men who had served on them were dead.

- Danger zone for U-boats in the French approaches

Aug 22, 1942 Brazil declares war on Germany, opening South Atlantic bases for Allied convoy air cover.

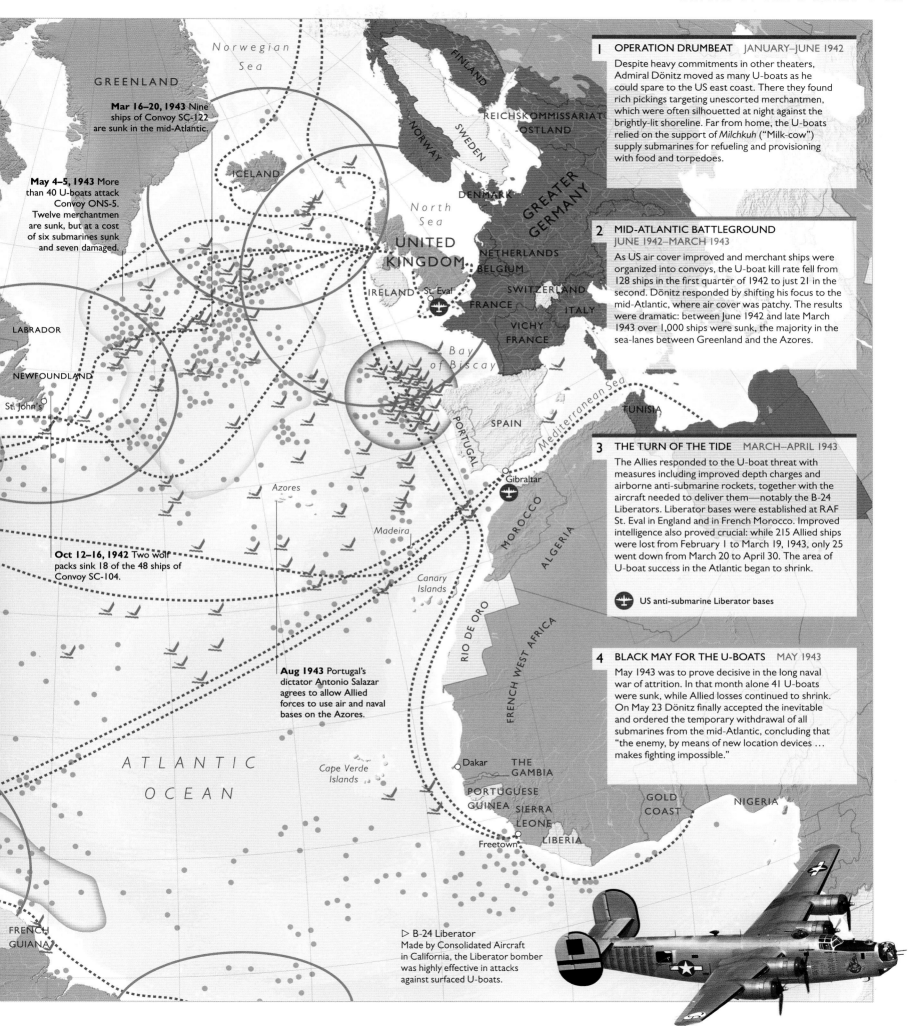

1 OPERATION DRUMBEAT JANUARY–JUNE 1942

Despite heavy commitments in other theaters, Admiral Dönitz moved as many U-boats as he could spare to the US east coast. There they found rich pickings targeting unescorted merchantmen, which were often silhouetted at night against the brightly-lit shoreline. Far from home, the U-boats relied on the support of *Milchkuh* ("Milk-cow") supply submarines for refueling and provisioning with food and torpedoes.

2 MID-ATLANTIC BATTLEGROUND JUNE 1942–MARCH 1943

As US air cover improved and merchant ships were organized into convoys, the U-boat kill rate fell from 128 ships in the first quarter of 1942 to just 21 in the second. Dönitz responded by shifting his focus to the mid-Atlantic, where air cover was patchy. The results were dramatic: between June 1942 and late March 1943 over 1,000 ships were sunk, the majority in the sea-lanes between Greenland and the Azores.

3 THE TURN OF THE TIDE MARCH–APRIL 1943

The Allies responded to the U-boat threat with measures including improved depth charges and airborne anti-submarine rockets, together with the aircraft needed to deliver them—notably the B-24 Liberators. Liberator bases were established at RAF St. Eval in England and in French Morocco. Improved intelligence also proved crucial: while 215 Allied ships were lost from February 1 to March 19, 1943, only 25 went down from March 20 to April 30. The area of U-boat success in the Atlantic began to shrink.

✈ US anti-submarine Liberator bases

4 BLACK MAY FOR THE U-BOATS MAY 1943

May 1943 was to prove decisive in the long naval war of attrition. In that month alone 41 U-boats were sunk, while Allied losses continued to shrink. On May 23 Dönitz finally accepted the inevitable and ordered the temporary withdrawal of all submarines from the mid-Atlantic, concluding that "the enemy, by means of new location devices … makes fighting impossible."

Mar 16–20, 1943 Nine ships of Convoy SC-122 are sunk in the mid-Atlantic.

May 4–5, 1943 More than 40 U-boats attack Convoy ONS-5. Twelve merchantmen are sunk, but at a cost of six submarines sunk and seven damaged.

Oct 12–16, 1942 Two wolf packs sink 18 of the 48 ships of Convoy SC-104.

Aug 1943 Portugal's dictator Antonio Salazar agrees to allow Allied forces to use air and naval bases on the Azores.

▷ B-24 Liberator
Made by Consolidated Aircraft in California, the Liberator bomber was highly effective in attacks against surfaced U-boats.

CODE-BREAKING

Both the Axis powers and the Allies devoted significant resources to breaking the ciphers used by governments and armed forces to conceal their communications. The Allies, in particular, achieved great success in this field.

Both sides stood to gain a huge advantage if they could intercept and decrypt enemy radio transmissions. However, gathering signals intelligence (SIGINT) was a complex and laborious process, made harder by machine-encoding devices such as Enigma (Germany), Typex (Britain), and Purple (Japan).

△ **Converting into code**
German soldiers encipher a message using an Enigma machine. Errors and shortcuts made by operators in a hurry often provided a way into the code.

The code war
In fall 1939, the British set up a specialist cryptography department, Ultra, at Bletchley Park, Buckinghamshire, staffed by civilian and military experts. By April 1941, these cryptographers, using electro-mechanic decoding devices called "bombes," could read transmissions from the German Luftwaffe, followed by variants of the code used by other German services.

This information was strategically vital, and included Rommel's intentions before El Alamein (see pp.76–77), German U-boat locations in the North Atlantic (see pp.64–65), and German deployments in Normandy before D-Day (see pp.186–189). However, the intelligence had to be used sparingly to prevent the Axis powers realizing the Enigma code had been broken. Elsewhere, the work of US code-breakers (MAGIC) on Japanese diplomatic codes and the JN-25 naval code yielded valuable intelligence in the Pacific theater, while German SIGINT on the Soviets was poor due to effective Soviet coding.

ENIGMA MACHINE

The German Enigma machine used a typewriter key attached to a series of rotating wheels (rotors), internal wiring, and a plugboard, which produced billions of variants for each letter depressed. In 1938, the Polish intelligence service provided information on the Enigma's construction, which proved key to cracking the code.

Code-breaking at Bletchley Park
Electronic devices, such as the Colossus (seen here in operation), allowed cryptographers to run multiple attempts to crack an Enigma message in a very short time. The Colossus could process 5,000 characters a second.

BOMBING BY DAY AND NIGHT

From 1942 onward, the RAF sought to stage a Blitz in reverse by pursuing the Strategic Bombing Offensive— an aerial campaign designed to shatter enemy morale. The arrival of the US 8th Air Force in England later that year further increased the pressure on Germany.

"The bomber will always get through," British politician Stanley Baldwin had opined in 1932, and this view was still widely held at the start of the war. Even though the Blitz's failure to destroy British morale contradicted this theory, the RAF looked to Bomber Command to take the fight to German soil. The British initially targeted military and industrial installations in nighttime raids, but these suffered from a lack of accuracy, so in 1942 they turned to the less discriminate "area bombing" that targeted industrial cities and their populations.

The US 8th Air Force units, which arrived in England in late 1942, favored a different strategy—precision bombing in daylight. However, this approach proved costly, with many aircraft lost to German fighters. In January 1943, the Allies agreed a joint policy in Casablanca (see pp.162–163), which prioritized attacks on enemy infrastructure. In the months that followed, the effectiveness of their raids improved with the introduction of new aircraft (notably the Avro Lancaster), better navigational aids, and the use of Pathfinder units to help locate targets. By the turn of the year, the Allies had the upper hand and the Luftwaffe had been forced onto the defensive.

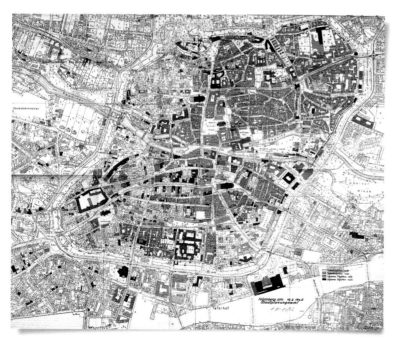

△ **Bomb damage in Nuremberg**
This German map from 1945 shows the new damage (dark red and black) to Nuremberg's old town after a huge Allied air raid on January 2, 1945. Bright red and blue areas show older damage from previous raids.

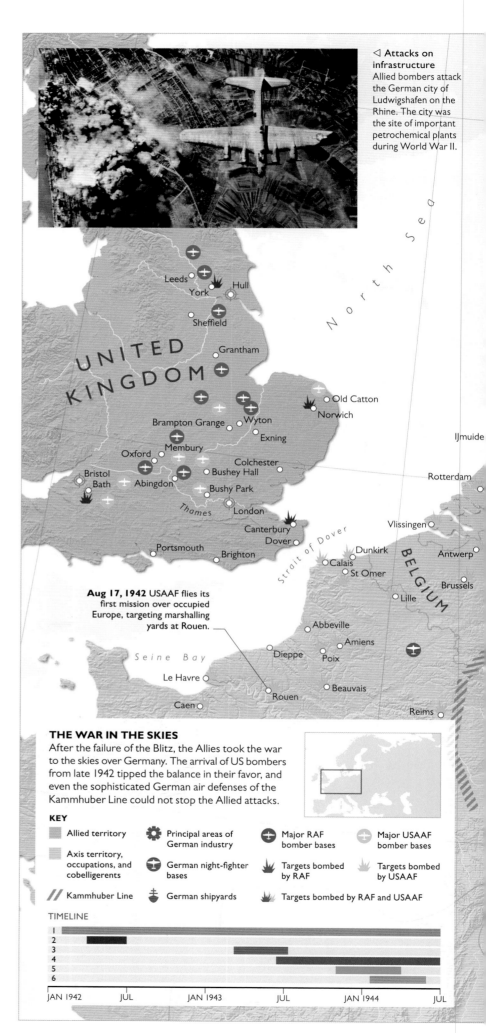

◁ **Attacks on infrastructure**
Allied bombers attack the German city of Ludwigshafen on the Rhine. The city was the site of important petrochemical plants during World War II.

Aug 17, 1942 USAAF flies its first mission over occupied Europe, targeting marshalling yards at Rouen.

THE WAR IN THE SKIES
After the failure of the Blitz, the Allies took the war to the skies over Germany. The arrival of US bombers from late 1942 tipped the balance in their favor, and even the sophisticated German air defenses of the Kammhuber Line could not stop the Allied attacks.

KEY

▬ Allied territory	⚙ Principal areas of German industry	⬤ Major RAF bomber bases
▬ Axis territory, occupations, and cobelligerents	⬤ German night-fighter bases	⬤ Major USAAF bomber bases
⫻ Kammhuber Line	⚓ German shipyards	Targets bombed by RAF
		Targets bombed by USAAF
		Targets bombed by RAF and USAAF

TIMELINE

JAN 1942   JUL   JAN 1943   JUL   JAN 1944   JUL

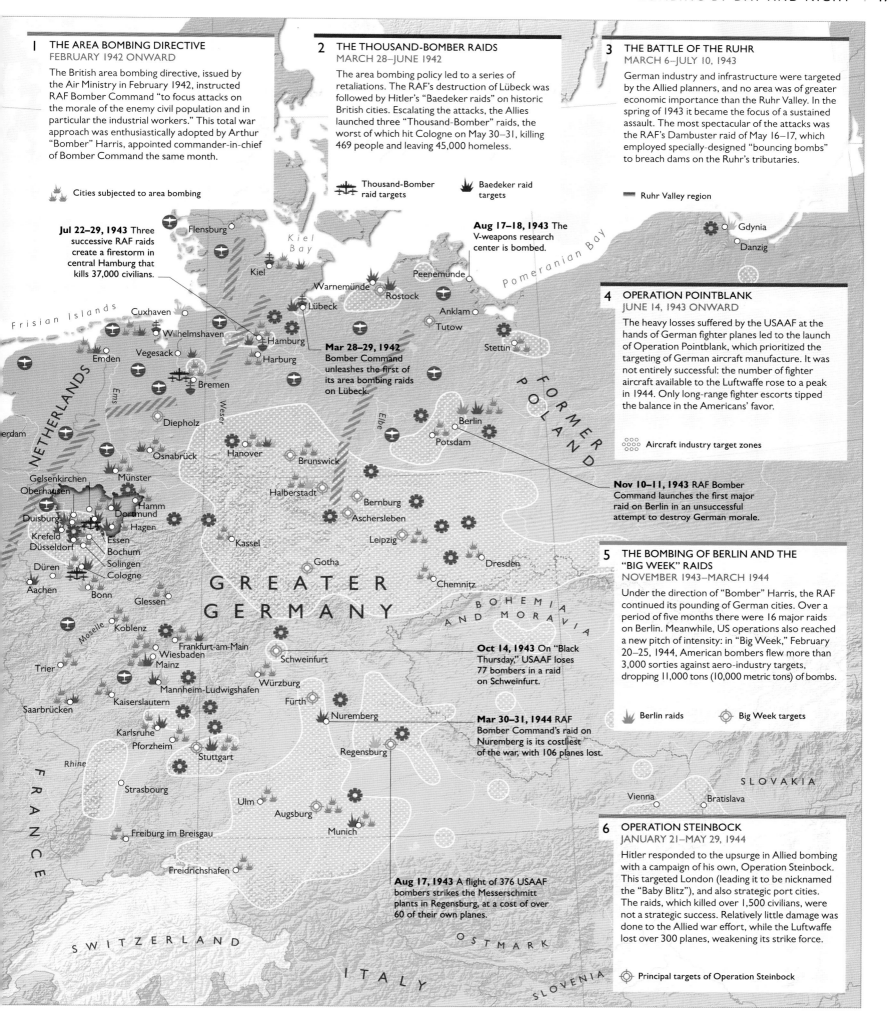

1 THE AREA BOMBING DIRECTIVE
FEBRUARY 1942 ONWARD

The British area bombing directive, issued by the Air Ministry in February 1942, instructed RAF Bomber Command "to focus attacks on the morale of the enemy civil population and in particular the industrial workers." This total war approach was enthusiastically adopted by Arthur "Bomber" Harris, appointed commander-in-chief of Bomber Command the same month.

🌿 Cities subjected to area bombing

2 THE THOUSAND-BOMBER RAIDS
MARCH 28–JUNE 1942

The area bombing policy led to a series of retaliations. The RAF's destruction of Lübeck was followed by Hitler's "Baedeker raids" on historic British cities. Escalating the attacks, the Allies launched three "Thousand-Bomber" raids, the worst of which hit Cologne on May 30–31, killing 469 people and leaving 45,000 homeless.

✈ Thousand-Bomber raid targets   🌿 Baedeker raid targets

3 THE BATTLE OF THE RUHR
MARCH 6–JULY 10, 1943

German industry and infrastructure were targeted by the Allied planners, and no area was of greater economic importance than the Ruhr Valley. In the spring of 1943 it became the focus of a sustained assault. The most spectacular of the attacks was the RAF's Dambuster raid of May 16–17, which employed specially-designed "bouncing bombs" to breach dams on the Ruhr's tributaries.

▬ Ruhr Valley region

Jul 22–29, 1943 Three successive RAF raids create a firestorm in central Hamburg that kills 37,000 civilians.

Aug 17–18, 1943 The V-weapons research center is bombed.

Mar 28–29, 1942 Bomber Command unleashes the first of its area bombing raids on Lübeck.

4 OPERATION POINTBLANK
JUNE 14, 1943 ONWARD

The heavy losses suffered by the USAAF at the hands of German fighter planes led to the launch of Operation Pointblank, which prioritized the targeting of German aircraft manufacture. It was not entirely successful: the number of fighter aircraft available to the Luftwaffe rose to a peak in 1944. Only long-range fighter escorts tipped the balance in the Americans' favor.

⊙ Aircraft industry target zones

Nov 10–11, 1943 RAF Bomber Command launches the first major raid on Berlin in an unsuccessful attempt to destroy German morale.

5 THE BOMBING OF BERLIN AND THE "BIG WEEK" RAIDS
NOVEMBER 1943–MARCH 1944

Under the direction of "Bomber" Harris, the RAF continued its pounding of German cities. Over a period of five months there were 16 major raids on Berlin. Meanwhile, US operations also reached a new pitch of intensity: in "Big Week," February 20–25, 1944, American bombers flew more than 3,000 sorties against aero-industry targets, dropping 11,000 tons (10,000 metric tons) of bombs.

🌿 Berlin raids   ◎ Big Week targets

Oct 14, 1943 On "Black Thursday," USAAF loses 77 bombers in a raid on Schweinfurt.

Mar 30–31, 1944 RAF Bomber Command's raid on Nuremberg is its costliest of the war, with 106 planes lost.

Aug 17, 1943 A flight of 376 USAAF bombers strikes the Messerschmitt plants in Regensburg, at a cost of over 60 of their own planes.

6 OPERATION STEINBOCK
JANUARY 21–MAY 29, 1944

Hitler responded to the upsurge in Allied bombing with a campaign of his own, Operation Steinbock. This targeted London (leading it to be nicknamed the "Baby Blitz"), and also strategic port cities. The raids, which killed over 1,500 civilians, were not a strategic success. Relatively little damage was done to the Allied war effort, while the Luftwaffe lost over 300 planes, weakening its strike force.

◎ Principal targets of Operation Steinbock

SPEER AND THE WAR INDUSTRY

From 1942, Germany's war production effort became much more efficient under the direction of Albert Speer. As Minister of Armaments and Munitions, he increased output at a challenging time in the final years of the war.

△ **New plan for Berlin**
Speer surveys his plans for a redevelopment of Berlin, which Hitler commissioned in 1937. Most plans were abandoned due to the war.

In the early stages of the war, the German economy was not well mobilized for the needs of the armed forces; resources were not allocated efficiently, and the military interfered in production. Fritz Todt, a civil engineer who had supervised the construction of the Westwall fortifications along the Franco–German border, became Minister of Armaments and Munitions in 1940. He set in motion the reforms that would improve German industry, before dying in a plane crash in 1942.

Streamlining operations

Todt's replacement was architect and urban planner Albert Speer, who had designed the parade grounds for the Nuremberg rallies. Speer amalgamated military agencies to establish a central planning board, set up production committees for major weapons types, and excluded the armed forces from decisions about war production. He also used forced labor to boost production. As a result, despite Allied bombing offensives from 1943 onward, Speer tripled Germany's armaments production, enabling it to sustain the war into 1945. He was the only Nazi at the Nuremberg trials to admit guilt.

△ **Close associates**
Speer (far left) developed a close working relationship with Hitler, enabling Speer to secure necessary resources and overcome military objections to his industrial reorganizations. Here, he inspects a new weapons system with the Führer.

Heinkel aircraft factory
Speer took control of aircraft production in 1944. Prior to this, his close cooperation with Luftwaffe technical director Erhard Milch meant that German annual production of aircraft nearly quadrupled to 39,000 by 1944.

6 THE ITALIAN PARTISAN WAR
SEPTEMBER 1943–MAY 1945

The Italian resistance had its roots in anti-Fascist groups opposed to Mussolini before the war, but its activities expanded hugely after the Allied invasion in 1943 and the German occupation of the country. Nationalist, Communist, and Catholic groups combined to resist the invaders, often under the leadership of Italian former officers. In September 1943, the National Liberation Committee was founded to coordinate opposition to the Nazi forces.

🗲 Clashes between Germans and Partisan forces

7 THE DUTCH HUNGER WINTER
SEPTEMBER 1944–MAY 1945

In the Netherlands, underground fighters helped the Allies with intelligence and acts of sabotage. In 1944, with the southern half of the country already liberated, railroad workers went on strike, leading the Nazi authorities to retaliate by cutting off supply lines. The result was the Hunger Winter of 1944–1945, during which up to 20,000 people starved to death.

— Pre-war Netherlands   → Main escape routes

🚶 Major reprisal

△ **Fighting in the streets**
In August 1944, resistance members on the streets of Paris take aim from their makeshift barracks. At this time there were an estimated 100,000 members of the resistance across France.

5 POLISH RESISTANCE
NOVEMBER 1939–MAY 1945

Poland suffered more under Nazi occupation than any other country (see pp.38–39). Resistance centered on the Polish Home Army, loyal to the government in exile in London, and the pro-Communist People's Army. In August 1944 the Home Army launched an uprising in Warsaw (see pp.184–185) that was brutally crushed by Waffen-SS units, while the approaching Red Army was unable to assist. When it was over, the city was in ruins, and over 150,000 people were dead.

▭ Pre-war Poland

▨ Principal Polish Partisan areas

✊ Armed uprisings in Jewish ghettos

🗲 Clashes between Partisans and German forces 1941–1942

Jun 10, 1944 In retaliation for resistance activity in central France, Waffen-SS troops wipe out the entire population of the village of Oradour-sur-Glane.

4 NATIONAL LIBERATION FOR GREECE
MAY 1941–OCTOBER 1944

The Greek resistance movement was fractured between many different groups, who often fought among themselves and resisted attempts by the Allies to bring them together (see pp.202–203). The most successful was the Communist-inspired National Liberation Front (EAM), whose guerrilla forces won control of much of the mountainous interior of Greece. In March 1944, EAM set up the Political Committee of National Liberation, which became the de facto government of the liberated areas.

— Pre-war Greece   ✊ Initial centers of resistance

May 9, 1944 Norwegian saboteurs blow up a train carrying mineral supplies for export to Germany.

Jul 20, 1944 An attempt by Claus von Stauffenberg and other German officers to assassinate Hitler fails.

May 27, 1942 SOE-trained Czech resistance fighters assassinate Nazi *Reichsprotektor* Reinhard Heydrich, triggering reprisals.

Mar 26, 1943 Polish resistance fighters free 25 captives from a Nazi prison van.

Feb 18, 1943 Nazi authorities break up the White Rose group.

Aug 29, 1944 Slovak resistance forces launch an armed uprising against Nazi troops occupying the country.

Jul 3, 1944 The Resistance declares a Free Republic of Vercors; the insurrection is viciously suppressed by the Germans.

Sep 27–30, 1943 Townspeople and resistance fighters join to drive out the occupying forces.

Mar 6, 1943 Yugoslav Partisans under Marshal Tito evade Axis forces by a strategic retreat in the Battle of the Neretva River.

FINLAND

NORWAY   Orkdal   Bergen   Oslo   Stavanger

SWEDEN

DENMARK   Silkeborg   Herning   Arhus   Copenhagen

REICHSKOMMISSARIAT OSTLAND

Rastenburg   Nowogródek   Nieswiez   Krynks   Bialystok   Treblinka   Kleck   Warsaw   Radom   Sobibor   Częstochowa   POLAND   Będzin   Tarnów

UNITED KINGDOM   London

NETHERLANDS   The Hague   Amsterdam   Berlin

Brussels   Lille   Brest   Le Havre   Rouen   Paris   BELGIUM   LUXEMBOURG   Luxembourg   Metz   Strasbourg

OCCUPIED FRANCE

GREATER GERMANY   Prague   Kladno   Stefanau   Munich   SLOVAKIA

SPAIN   PORTUGAL   Madrid   Lisbon   Barcelona

VICHY FRANCE   Oradour-sur-Glane   Beyssenac   SWITZERLAND   Grenoble   Toulouse   Vercors   Marseille

Marburg   HUNGARY   Bolzano   Milan   Turin   Fossoli   Padua   Trieste   Stari   Genoa   La Spezia   Bologna   Florence   Monte Battaglia   Piombino

Coka   Petrila   Báctopolya   Timişoara   Aninoasa   Petrovgrad   Zasayi   Belgrade   Lupeni   Šabac   Čačak   Zaječar   ROMANIA   Kruševac   Niš   BULGARIA   Sofia   Plovadiv   Topollica   Tirane   ALBANIA   Salonika

YUGOSLAVIA   Neretva

ITALY   Rome   Naples   Corsica   Sardinia   Sicily

GREECE   Athens   Patras

FRENCH NORTH AFRICA   TUNISIA

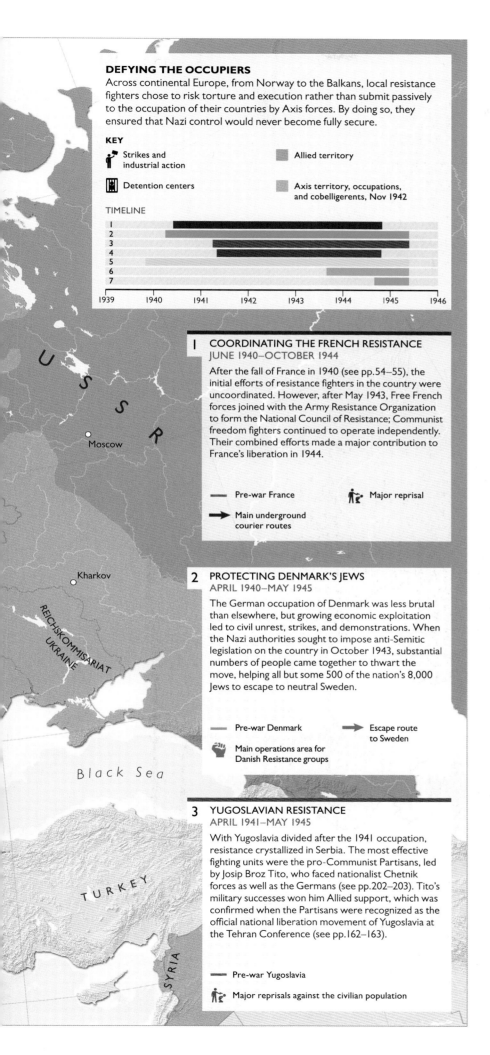

DEFYING THE OCCUPIERS

Across continental Europe, from Norway to the Balkans, local resistance fighters chose to risk torture and execution rather than submit passively to the occupation of their countries by Axis forces. By doing so, they ensured that Nazi control would never become fully secure.

KEY

Strikes and industrial action

Allied territory

Detention centers

Axis territory, occupations, and cobelligerents, Nov 1942

TIMELINE

1
2
3
4
5
6
7

1939   1940   1941   1942   1943   1944   1945   1946

1 COORDINATING THE FRENCH RESISTANCE
JUNE 1940–OCTOBER 1944

After the fall of France in 1940 (see pp.54–55), the initial efforts of resistance fighters in the country were uncoordinated. However, after May 1943, Free French forces joined with the Army Resistance Organization to form the National Council of Resistance; Communist freedom fighters continued to operate independently. Their combined efforts made a major contribution to France's liberation in 1944.

— Pre-war France

Major reprisal

➔ Main underground courier routes

2 PROTECTING DENMARK'S JEWS
APRIL 1940–MAY 1945

The German occupation of Denmark was less brutal than elsewhere, but growing economic exploitation led to civil unrest, strikes, and demonstrations. When the Nazi authorities sought to impose anti-Semitic legislation on the country in October 1943, substantial numbers of people came together to thwart the move, helping all but some 500 of the nation's 8,000 Jews to escape to neutral Sweden.

— Pre-war Denmark

➔ Escape route to Sweden

Main operations area for Danish Resistance groups

3 YUGOSLAVIAN RESISTANCE
APRIL 1941–MAY 1945

With Yugoslavia divided after the 1941 occupation, resistance crystallized in Serbia. The most effective fighting units were the pro-Communist Partisans, led by Josip Broz Tito, who faced nationalist Chetnik forces as well as the Germans (see pp.202–203). Tito's military successes won him Allied support, which was confirmed when the Partisans were recognized as the official national liberation movement of Yugoslavia at the Tehran Conference (see pp.162–163).

— Pre-war Yugoslavia

Major reprisals against the civilian population

RESISTANCE IN EUROPE

The brutality of Nazi rule led to the rise of resistance movements in every occupied country. These local groups received assistance, wherever possible, from Britain's Special Operations Executive (SOE), while the Soviet Union helped pro-Communist guerrillas in Eastern Europe.

Resistance groups often emerged spontaneously. Their operations took various forms, from passive opposition, such as that practiced in Germany by White Rose activists who distributed anti-Nazi pamphlets, to large-scale military activity. The mountainous terrain of the Balkans lent itself particularly well to the latter, and Yugoslavia and Greece experienced years of guerrilla warfare.

Elsewhere, opposition activities ranged from sabotage missions against military and industrial facilities to espionage and intelligence gathering. Sometimes local operatives carried out the actions, but the SOE (see pp.138–139) also inserted agents secretly by boat or parachute. Capture by the German authorities or collaborators usually meant torture and death, and successful ventures risked violent reprisals against the local population. However, such acts of resistance helped to divert valuable Axis resources from the two war fronts, as well as depleting the occupiers' morale. Equally important, resistance to the Nazi regime asserted human dignity in the face of oppression.

"France has lost a battle, but she has not lost the war."

GENERAL CHARLES DE GAULLE, 1940

RESISTANCE WRITING

Swaying public opinion was a vital part of the war effort: Vichy French authorities used propaganda to mobilize hostility to the resistance and the reprisals that they provoked. In response, resistance fighters set up underground newspapers that helped keep protest alive. In France there was *Libération* and *Combat* (edited by philosopher Albert Camus) and in Belgium *La Libre Belgique*, while in the Netherlands there were more than 1,000 publications.

Combat, May 29, 1944

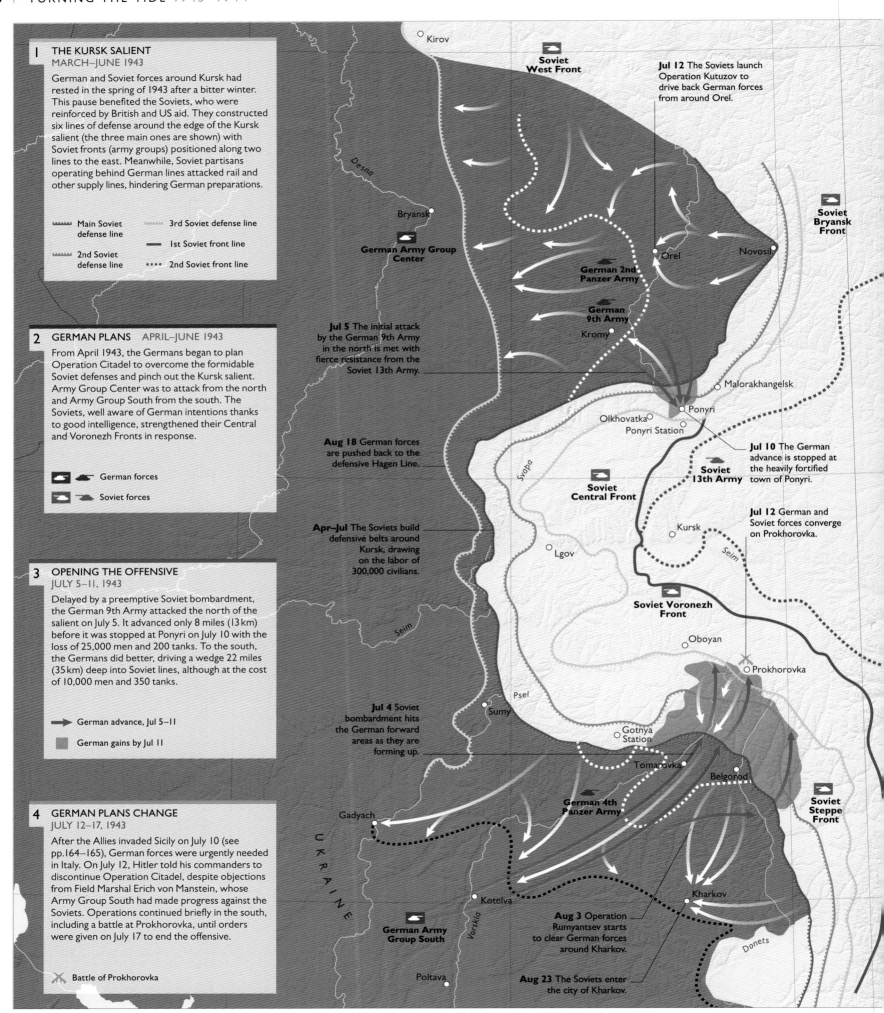

1 THE KURSK SALIENT
MARCH–JUNE 1943

German and Soviet forces around Kursk had rested in the spring of 1943 after a bitter winter. This pause benefited the Soviets, who were reinforced by British and US aid. They constructed six lines of defense around the edge of the Kursk salient (the three main ones are shown) with Soviet fronts (army groups) positioned along two lines to the east. Meanwhile, Soviet partisans operating behind German lines attacked rail and other supply lines, hindering German preparations.

〰️	Main Soviet defense line	〰️	3rd Soviet defense line
〰️	2nd Soviet defense line	▬	1st Soviet front line
		┄	2nd Soviet front line

2 GERMAN PLANS   APRIL–JUNE 1943

From April 1943, the Germans began to plan Operation Citadel to overcome the formidable Soviet defenses and pinch out the Kursk salient. Army Group Center was to attack from the north and Army Group South from the south. The Soviets, well aware of German intentions thanks to good intelligence, strengthened their Central and Voronezh Fronts in response.

- 🛡️ German forces
- 🛡️ Soviet forces

3 OPENING THE OFFENSIVE
JULY 5–11, 1943

Delayed by a preemptive Soviet bombardment, the German 9th Army attacked the north of the salient on July 5. It advanced only 8 miles (13 km) before it was stopped at Ponyri on July 10 with the loss of 25,000 men and 200 tanks. To the south, the Germans did better, driving a wedge 22 miles (35 km) deep into Soviet lines, although at the cost of 10,000 men and 350 tanks.

- ➡️ German advance, Jul 5–11
- ⬛ German gains by Jul 11

4 GERMAN PLANS CHANGE
JULY 12–17, 1943

After the Allies invaded Sicily on July 10 (see pp.164–165), German forces were urgently needed in Italy. On July 12, Hitler told his commanders to discontinue Operation Citadel, despite objections from Field Marshal Erich von Manstein, whose Army Group South had made progress against the Soviets. Operations continued briefly in the south, including a battle at Prokhorovka, until orders were given on July 17 to end the offensive.

- ✕ Battle of Prokhorovka

Soviet West Front

Jul 12 The Soviets launch Operation Kutuzov to drive back German forces from around Orel.

Soviet Bryansk Front

Kirov

Bryansk

German Army Group Center

Orel

Novosil

German 2nd Panzer Army

German 9th Army

Kromy

Jul 5 The initial attack by the German 9th Army in the north is met with fierce resistance from the Soviet 13th Army.

Malorakhangelsk

Olkhovatka Ponyri
Ponyri Station

Jul 10 The German advance is stopped at the heavily fortified town of Ponyri.

Aug 18 German forces are pushed back to the defensive Hagen Line.

Soviet 13th Army

Soviet Central Front

Jul 12 German and Soviet forces converge on Prokhorovka.

Kursk

Svapa

Apr–Jul The Soviets build defensive belts around Kursk, drawing on the labor of 300,000 civilians.

Lgov

Seim

Seim

Soviet Voronezh Front

Oboyan

Prokhorovka

Psel

Sumy

Jul 4 Soviet bombardment hits the German forward areas as they are forming up.

Gotnya Station

Tomarovka

Belgorod

Soviet Steppe Front

Gadyach

German 4th Panzer Army

U K R A I N E

Kotelva

Vorskla

German Army Group South

Aug 3 Operation Rumyantsev starts to clear German forces around Kharkov.

Kharkov

Donets

Poltava

Aug 23 The Soviets enter the city of Kharkov.

A FORTIFIED SALIENT

The battle for control of the Kursk salient began on July 5, 1943, with a massive German onslaught that was at first held off by dense fortifications, then forced back by superior Soviet numbers.

KEY

▨ German-held territory, Jul 4

TIMELINE

1	
2	
3	
4	
5	

MAR 1943   MAY   JUL   SEP

△ **Soviet counterattack**
Soviet troops follow their T-34 tanks during a counterattack near Kursk. The Soviets defended the salient with great bravery, often running close to German tanks to throw grenades under their tracks.

U   S   S   R

Apr–Jul Heavily defended front lines are drawn up, manned by the Soviet Central and Voronezh Fronts.

5   THE SOVIETS ADVANCE
JULY 12–AUGUST 23, 1943

As the Germans faltered, the Soviets attacked Army Group Center around Orel, north of Kursk, on July 12. The Germans were forced back across their defensive Hagen Line by August 18, and suffered huge losses. To the south, the Voronezh and Steppe Fronts advanced on August 3 and converged on Kharkov, forcing the Germans out by August 23.

Soviet South-west Front

⇨ Soviet advances   ▫▫▫ Front line, Aug 5

▦▦▦ German Hagen Line   ▪▪▪ Front line, Aug 23

THE BATTLE OF KURSK

In the summer of 1943, German forces in the USSR found themselves facing a huge, well-fortified Soviet salient around the city of Kursk, some 280 miles (450 km) south of Moscow. The resulting battle to remove the salient became a monumental clash of armor and was one of the largest tank battles of the war.

In early 1943, Soviet advances, combined with German retreats and counterattacks (see pp.152–153), resulted in a huge salient around Kursk. A vast, pivotal battle for the salient—an area of land 112 miles (180 km) wide and 62 miles (100 km) deep—followed in the summer, involving more than 8,000 tanks and 1.7 million men on both sides. Some 4,000 aircraft also played a vital role, both sides having recognized the effectiveness of air power—such as the lethal German Stuka dive-bomber—against tank armor.

The eventual Soviet victory at Kursk was a turning point in the war: it was the first time that a German strategic offensive had been halted before it could break through enemy lines; and it was Germany's final strategic offensive on the Eastern Front, where until now it had been dominant. From this point onward, Germany was on the defensive: the Wehrmacht had lost its armored supremacy, and the Luftwaffe had surrendered its dominance in the sky.

The Soviets' victory cost them three times more casualties than the Germans, but the losses were huge on both sides. Overall, more than 230,000 men were killed, missing, or wounded in battle, and more than 2,000 tanks and 600 aircraft were destroyed.

"The battle of Kursk ... and the liberation of Kiev, left Hitlerite Germany facing catastrophe."

VASILY IVANOVICH CHUIKOV, SOVIET GENERAL, 1968

RIVAL GERMAN AND SOVIET TANKS

The main Soviet tank at Kursk was the T-34 medium tank, supported by T-70 light tanks and Lend-Lease tanks supplied by the US and Britain. The Germans deployed mainly Panzer IV tanks, along with limited numbers of powerful Tiger heavy tanks and the new Panther medium tanks. The Panther suffered numerous technical problems during the battle and did not have enough firepower against enemy infantry; by contrast, the Soviets' highly mobile and rugged T-34 could be repaired quickly on the front line.

The powerful Tiger tank was heavily featured in propaganda as a symbol of German might

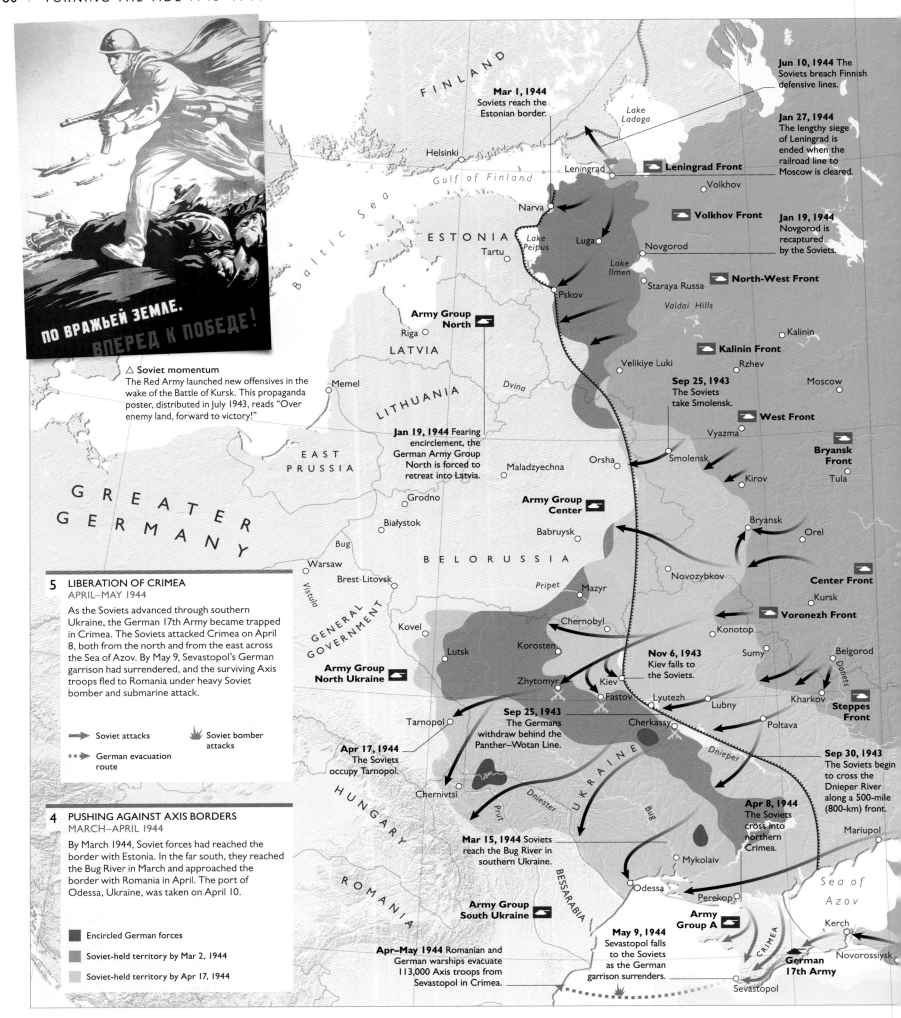

Jun 10, 1944 The Soviets breach Finnish defensive lines.

Mar 1, 1944 Soviets reach the Estonian border.

Jan 27, 1944 The lengthy siege of Leningrad is ended when the railroad line to Moscow is cleared.

Jan 19, 1944 Novgorod is recaptured by the Soviets.

Leningrad Front

Volkhov Front

North-West Front

Army Group North

Kalinin Front

Sep 25, 1943 The Soviets take Smolensk.

West Front

Bryansk Front

Jan 19, 1944 Fearing encirclement, the German Army Group North is forced to retreat into Latvia.

Army Group Center

Center Front

Voronezh Front

Nov 6, 1943 Kiev falls to the Soviets.

△ **Soviet momentum**
The Red Army launched new offensives in the wake of the Battle of Kursk. This propaganda poster, distributed in July 1943, reads "Over enemy land, forward to victory!"

Sep 25, 1943 The Germans withdraw behind the Panther–Wotan Line.

Apr 17, 1944 The Soviets occupy Tarnopol.

Steppes Front

Army Group North Ukraine

Sep 30, 1943 The Soviets begin to cross the Dnieper River along a 500-mile (800-km) front.

5 LIBERATION OF CRIMEA
APRIL–MAY 1944

As the Soviets advanced through southern Ukraine, the German 17th Army became trapped in Crimea. The Soviets attacked Crimea on April 8, both from the north and from the east across the Sea of Azov. By May 9, Sevastopol's German garrison had surrendered, and the surviving Axis troops fled to Romania under heavy Soviet bomber and submarine attack.

Apr 8, 1944 The Soviets cross into northern Crimea.

→ Soviet attacks

🗡 Soviet bomber attacks

‑ ‑ ‑► German evacuation route

Mar 15, 1944 Soviets reach the Bug River in southern Ukraine.

4 PUSHING AGAINST AXIS BORDERS
MARCH–APRIL 1944

By March 1944, Soviet forces had reached the border with Estonia. In the far south, they reached the Bug River in March and approached the border with Romania in April. The port of Odessa, Ukraine, was taken on April 10.

Army Group South Ukraine

Army Group A

German 17th Army

■ Encircled German forces

■ Soviet-held territory by Mar 2, 1944

□ Soviet-held territory by Apr 17, 1944

Apr–May 1944 Romanian and German warships evacuate 113,000 Axis troops from Sevastopol in Crimea.

May 9, 1944 Sevastopol falls to the Soviets as the German garrison surrenders.

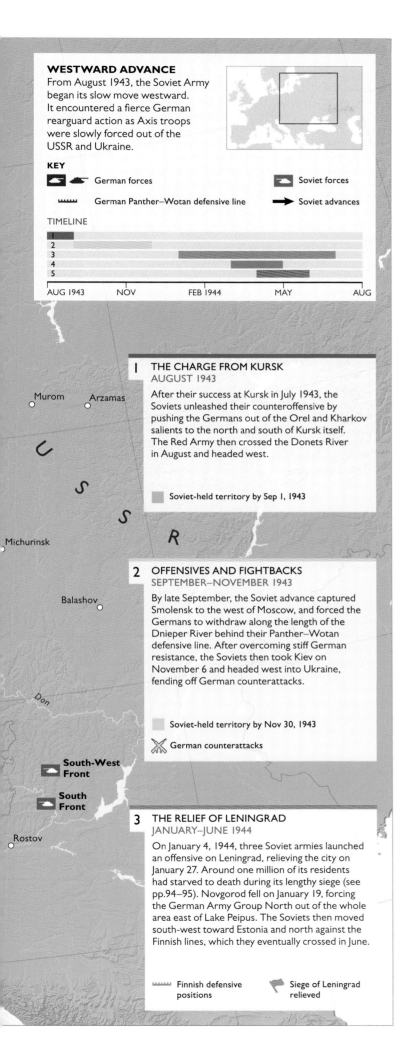

WESTWARD ADVANCE
From August 1943, the Soviet Army began its slow move westward. It encountered a fierce German rearguard action as Axis troops were slowly forced out of the USSR and Ukraine.

KEY

⬛ 🔺 German forces

⬛ Soviet forces

〰〰 German Panther–Wotan defensive line

➡ Soviet advances

TIMELINE

1
2
3
4
5

AUG 1943   NOV   FEB 1944   MAY   AUG

1 THE CHARGE FROM KURSK
AUGUST 1943

After their success at Kursk in July 1943, the Soviets unleashed their counteroffensive by pushing the Germans out of the Orel and Kharkov salients to the north and south of Kursk itself. The Red Army then crossed the Donets River in August and headed west.

⬛ Soviet-held territory by Sep 1, 1943

2 OFFENSIVES AND FIGHTBACKS
SEPTEMBER–NOVEMBER 1943

By late September, the Soviet advance captured Smolensk to the west of Moscow, and forced the Germans to withdraw along the length of the Dnieper River behind their Panther–Wotan defensive line. After overcoming stiff German resistance, the Soviets then took Kiev on November 6 and headed west into Ukraine, fending off German counterattacks.

⬛ Soviet-held territory by Nov 30, 1943

✕ German counterattacks

South-West Front

South Front

3 THE RELIEF OF LENINGRAD
JANUARY–JUNE 1944

On January 4, 1944, three Soviet armies launched an offensive on Leningrad, relieving the city on January 27. Around one million of its residents had starved to death during its lengthy siege (see pp.94–95). Novgorod fell on January 19, forcing the German Army Group North out of the whole area east of Lake Peipus. The Soviets then moved south-west toward Estonia and north against the Finnish lines, which they eventually crossed in June.

〰〰 Finnish defensive positions

🚩 Siege of Leningrad relieved

THE SOVIETS SWEEP FORWARD

The Soviet victory at the Battle of Kursk handed the initiative to the Red Army. It was now ready to attack the Germans on a wider front in order to push them out of the western USSR and Ukraine. The Germans never regained momentum in the east, and Hitler's ambitions for the USSR were crushed.

Following the huge Battle of Kursk (see pp.178–179), the Germans believed, despite their losses, that they had crippled the USSR, rendering it incapable of launching a counterattack. However, the Soviets regrouped quickly, and from summer 1943 German troops found themselves facing Soviet offensives on a front that stretched from Leningrad in the north to Crimea in the south.

In a series of major battles, with only a few setbacks, the Soviets fought their way to the western frontiers of the USSR by May 1944. The German forces on the Eastern Front were depleted due to the diversion of troops to Italy following the Allied landings there (see pp.164–165),

but they nevertheless fought fiercely, giving ground grudgingly and at great cost to the enemy. They made tactical retreats behind new defensive lines built after the defeat at Kursk, particularly the Panther–Wotan Line.

Both sides suffered huge casualties, but the Soviets gained the upper hand: they lifted the 872-day siege of Leningrad; liberated Kiev, Smolensk, and Odessa; and cleared Crimea and its naval port Sevastopol of German forces. The way was now open for the Red Army to launch Operation Bagration (see pp.182–183) to clear the rest of the USSR of German troops and allow the Soviets to head into Eastern Europe.

"An extraordinary day. The entire city is waiting ... any moment now!"

VERA INBER, LENINGRAD CITIZEN, JANUARY 16, 1944

KONSTANTIN ROKOSSOVSKY, 1896–1968

After serving in World War I, Soviet and Polish officer Rokossovsky fought for the Bolsheviks in the Russian Civil War and soon climbed the ranks of the Red Army. He was imprisoned during Stalin's purges in the late 1930s, but was released in 1941 so the USSR could make use of his military skills. He gained fame for his defense of Moscow in 1941–1942 and his success at Stalingrad, where he led the Don Front in trapping the German 6th Army (see pp.152–153). He also played central roles at the Battle of Kursk and in Operation Bagration. It was Rokossovsky's army group that ended the war in north Germany (see pp.242–243). After the war, he became a member of the Communist Polish government.

OPERATION BAGRATION

Operation Bagration was the code name of the massive Soviet assault against German-occupied Belorussia that took place from June 22 to August 14, 1944. The assault, launched exactly three years after Germany invaded the USSR, involved millions of Soviet troops and was instrumental in bringing the war in Europe to an end.

Operation Bagration was named after Pyotr Ivanovich, Prince Bagration (1765–1812), a Russian general who had distinguished himself in the Napoleonic Wars by his use of innovative military tactics. The new campaign in his name was to be equally daring: it was intended to wipe out the German Army Group Center and clear German troops out of the western USSR.

In a series of brilliant but brutal assaults, striking where the Germans least expected, the Red Army swept all before it and advanced hundreds of miles in a couple of months. Soviet troops poured into the German-occupied areas of Belorussia, heading

"The German troops now resemble a wounded beast which is compelled to crawl back to the frontiers of its lair ..."

JOSEPH STALIN, MAY 1, 1944

north into Latvia and Lithuania, and west into Poland. A later operation in the south overran Romania and took Bulgaria out of the war. By the end of Bagration, Soviet troops were on the Vistula River in central Poland, facing Warsaw on the opposite bank; they were close to the shores of the Baltic Sea in the north; and they stood on the borders with Slovakia and Hungary in the south-west. Most threateningly for Germany, the Red Army was close to the eastern border of German East Prussia and the Third Reich itself.

The Soviet campaign was one of the largest Allied operations of the entire war, engaging more than 2.3 million Soviet troops and resulting in the destruction of the German Army Group Center. Losses on both sides were immense, with 180,000 Soviets killed or missing, and the Germans losing around 400,000 men, including nine generals killed and 22 captured. Up to 260,000 German troops were taken prisoner. Coming after German losses at Stalingrad (see pp.148–153) and then Kursk (see pp.178–179), Operation Bagration was another huge defeat for the German forces.

SOVIET MASKIROVKA

Maskirovka, meaning "camouflage" or "deception" in Russian, was a technique that the Soviets used with great success in Operation Bagration. They consistently misled the Germans about where they would attack along the broad front, positioning dummy armies, camouflaging trenches (see above), and sending false communications to suggest that the attack would come in Ukraine; in reality, Soviet troops were moving secretly and gradually by night to Belorussia. The Germans were deceived into moving their troops to the wrong locations on the Eastern Front.

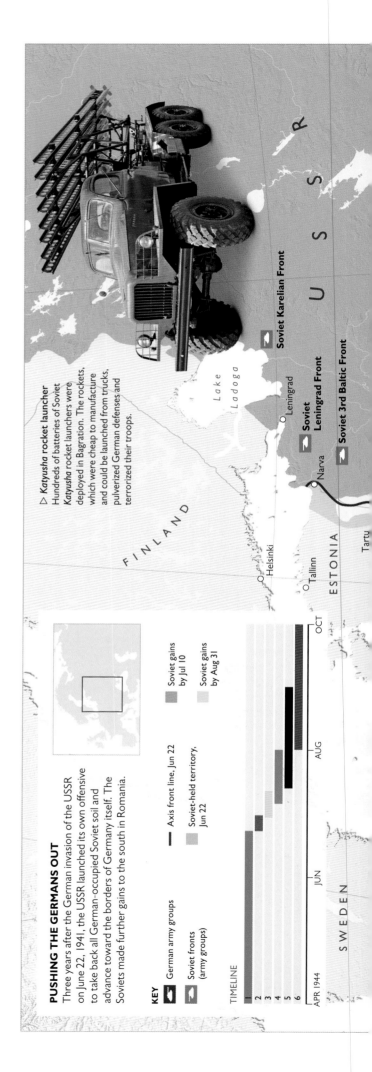

△ **Katyusha rocket launcher**
Hundreds of batteries of Soviet *Katyusha* rocket launchers were deployed in Bagration. The rockets, which were cheap to manufacture and could be launched from trucks, pulverized German defenses and terrorized their troops.

PUSHING THE GERMANS OUT
Three years after the German invasion of the USSR on June 22, 1941, the USSR launched its own offensive to take back all German-occupied Soviet soil and advance toward the borders of Germany itself. The Soviets made further gains to the south in Romania.

KEY

- German army groups
- Soviet fronts (army groups)
- Axis front line, Jun 22
- Soviet-held territory, Jun 22
- Soviet gains by Jul 10
- Soviet gains by Aug 31

TIMELINE

APR 1944 | JUN | AUG | OCT

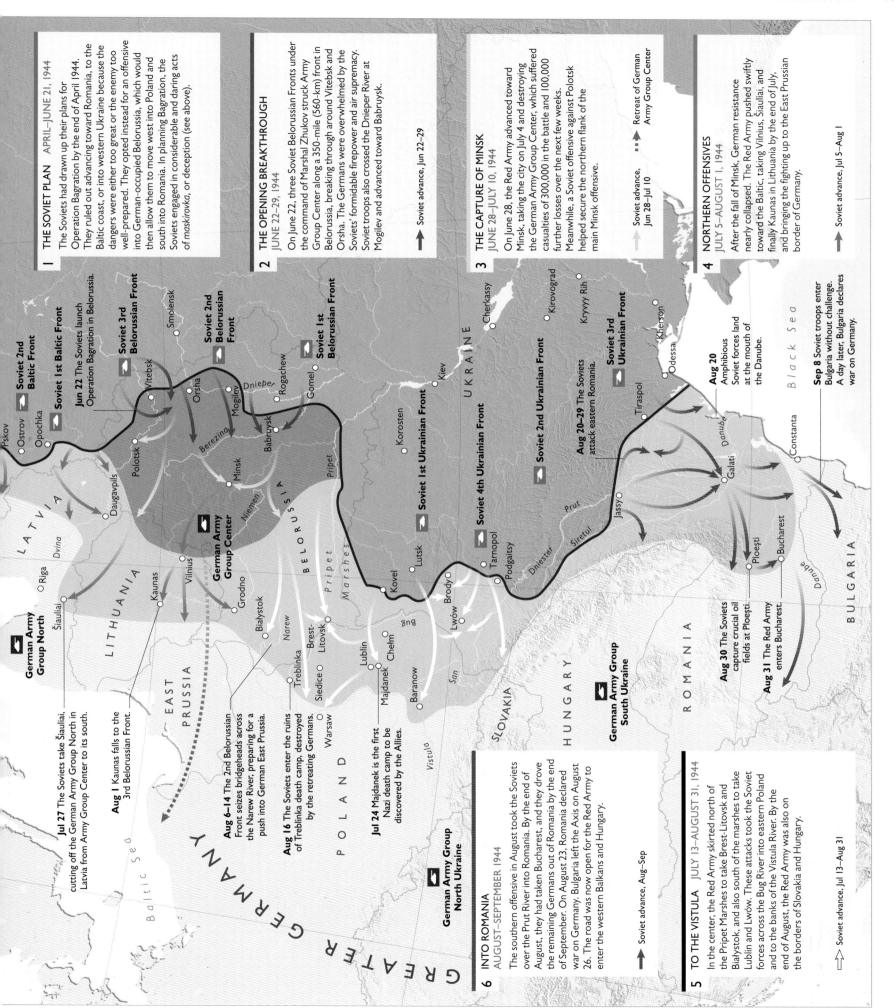

1 THE SOVIET PLAN APRIL–JUNE 21, 1944

The Soviets had drawn up their plans for Operation Bagration by the end of April 1944. They ruled out advancing toward Romania, to the Baltic coast, or into western Ukraine because the dangers were either too great or the enemy too well-prepared. They opted instead for an offensive into German-occupied Belorussia, which would then allow them to move west into Poland and south into Romania. In planning Bagration, the Soviets engaged in considerable and daring acts of *maskirovka*, or deception (see above).

2 THE OPENING BREAKTHROUGH JUNE 22–29, 1944

On June 22, three Soviet Belorussian Fronts under the command of Marshal Zhukov struck Army Group Center along a 350-mile (560-km) front in Belorussia, breaking through around Vitebsk and Orsha. The Germans were overwhelmed by the Soviets' formidable firepower and air supremacy. Soviet troops also crossed the Dnieper River at Mogilev and advanced toward Babruysk.

→ Soviet advance, Jun 22–29

3 THE CAPTURE OF MINSK JUNE 28–JULY 10, 1944

On June 28, the Red Army advanced toward Minsk, taking the city on July 4 and destroying the German Army Group Center, which suffered casualties of 300,000 in the battle and 100,000 further losses over the next few weeks. Meanwhile, a Soviet offensive against Polotsk helped secure the northern flank of the main Minsk offensive.

→ Soviet advance, Jun 28–Jul 10   ⇢ Retreat of German Army Group Center

4 NORTHERN OFFENSIVES JULY 5–AUGUST 1, 1944

After the fall of Minsk, German resistance nearly collapsed. The Red Army pushed swiftly toward the Baltic, taking Vilnius, Šiauliai, and finally Kaunas in Lithuania by the end of July, and bringing the fighting up to the East Prussian border of Germany.

→ Soviet advance, Jul 5–Aug 1

6 INTO ROMANIA AUGUST–SEPTEMBER 1944

The southern offensive in August took the Soviets over the Prut River into Romania. By the end of August, they had taken Bucharest, and they drove the remaining Germans out of Romania by the end of September. On August 23, Romania declared war on Germany. Bulgaria left the Axis on August 26. The road was now open for the Red Army to enter the western Balkans and Hungary.

→ Soviet advance, Aug–Sep

5 TO THE VISTULA JULY 13–AUGUST 31, 1944

In the center, the Red Army skirted north of the Pripet Marshes to take Brest-Litovsk and Bialystok, and also south of the marshes to take Lublin and Lwów. These attacks took the Soviet forces across the Bug River into eastern Poland and to the banks of the Vistula River. By the end of August, the Red Army was also on the borders of Slovakia and Hungary.

⇨ Soviet advance, Jul 13–Aug 31

Jul 27 The Soviets take Šiauliai, cutting off the German Army Group North in Latvia from Army Group Center to its south.

Aug 1 Kaunas falls to the 3rd Belorussian Front.

Aug 6–14 The 2nd Belorussian Front seizes bridgeheads across the Narew River, preparing for a push into German East Prussia.

Aug 16 The Soviets enter the ruins of Treblinka death camp, destroyed by the retreating Germans.

Jul 24 Majdanek is the first Nazi death camp to be discovered by the Allies.

Jun 22 The Soviets launch Operation Bagration in Belorussia.

Aug 20 Amphibious Soviet forces land at the mouth of the Danube.

Aug 20–29 The Soviets attack eastern Romania.

Aug 30 The Soviets capture crucial oil fields at Ploești.

Aug 31 The Red Army enters Bucharest.

Sep 8 Soviet troops enter Bulgaria without challenge. A day later, Bulgaria declares war on Germany.

Soviet 2nd Baltic Front

Soviet 1st Baltic Front

Soviet 3rd Belorussian Front

Soviet 2nd Belorussian Front

Soviet 1st Belorussian Front

Soviet 1st Ukrainian Front

Soviet 4th Ukrainian Front

Soviet 2nd Ukrainian Front

Soviet 3rd Ukrainian Front

German Army Group North

German Army Group Center

German Army Group North Ukraine

German Army Group South Ukraine

LATVIA

LITHUANIA

EAST PRUSSIA

BELORUSSIA

Pripet Marshes

POLAND

SLOVAKIA

HUNGARY

ROMANIA

BULGARIA

UKRAINE

GREATER GERMANY

Black Sea

Baltic Sea

Pskov · Ostrov · Opochka · Riga · Šiauliai · Daugavpils · Polotsk · Vitebsk · Smolensk · Orsha · Mogilev · Rogachew · Gomel · Minsk · Babruysk · Vilnius · Kaunas · Grodno · Bialystok · Narew · Treblinka · Brest-Litovsk · Siedlce · Warsaw · Lublin · Chełm · Majdanek · Baranow · Kovel · Lutsk · Korosten · Kiev · Cherkassy · Kirovograd · Kryvyy Rih · Kherson · Odessa · Brody · Lwów · Tarnopol · Podgaitsy · Tiraspol · Jassy · Galati · Constanța · Ploești · Bucharest

Dnieper · Berezina · Niemen · Dvina · Dnieper · Bug · San · Vistula · Prut · Dniester · Siretul · Danube

THE WARSAW UPRISING

In 1944, the main Polish resistance movement, the Home Army, embarked on an uprising to liberate their cities before the Soviets arrived. For nine weeks, resistance fighters battled the superior German forces.

△ **Insurgent's weapon**
Polish insurgents made thousands of weapons in secret factories, including copies of the British Sten Mark II submachine gun.

When the Soviets pushed the Germans back into Poland in July 1944, General Bor-Koromowski, commander of the Polish Home Army, decided to launch an operation to liberate Warsaw. With the Red Army approaching the Vistula river on August 1, 1944, about 37,000 Polish insurgents fell on the German garrison, which was caught off balance. Although lacking armaments—only one in seven had weapons—the resistance fighters rapidly took key parts of the city.

The Germans held key strategic positions such as railway stations, and on August 25 launched a counteroffensive. Some 20,000 heavily armed German troops, supported by aircraft, fought street battles with the Home Army. In the rubble of destroyed houses, and moving through makeshift tunnels, the Poles resisted for five weeks before surrendering on October 1. All this time, the Soviet army paused its offensive and offered no help, even denying the Western Allies access to airfields to resupply the insurgents. The Home Army lost 17,000 fighters and effectively disbanded, and Warsaw was destroyed on Hitler's orders. When the Soviets finally captured the city in January 1945, former resistance members were arrested, deported, or killed.

△ **Prisoners of war**
The suppression of the Warsaw Uprising was brutal; in the first few days, 40,000 civilians were massacred. The Home Army fought back fiercely, despite being outnumbered; here, German prisoners captured by the Polish resistance are forced to wear swastika-emblazoned shirts.

Fighting for liberty
Home Army fighters take shelter behind a makeshift barricade. Around 50 percent of Warsaw's buildings were destroyed during the German recapture of the city, and around 300,000 inhabitants became refugees.

THE D-DAY LANDINGS

On June 6, 1944, the largest seaborne invasion in history took place on the beaches of Normandy. Code named Operation Neptune, and usually referred to as D-Day, it began the liberation of France and the opening of another front in Europe.

At the Washington Conference of May 1943, the Allied leaders met to discuss their future strategy in Europe, and set a date of May 1944 for the invasion of France. Numerous sites for the offensive were considered. The obvious choice, an invasion across the narrowest part of the Channel to France's northernmost point, the Pas-de-Calais, was ruled out because it was the most heavily defended. Normandy was favored for the broad front it offered into central France.

The naval operations, led by British admiral Sir Bertram Ramsay, were described by historian Corelli Barnett as a "never surpassed masterpiece of planning" and involved a 6,939-strong invasion fleet. This consisted of 1,213 warships, 4,126 landing craft, 736 ancillary craft (including minesweepers), and 864 merchant vessels from eight different Allied navies, carrying 176,000 troops in all. German defenses consisted of around 50,000 troops and 170 artillery guns.

Allied planners identified the ideal conditions for the landings— low tide, clear skies, and a full moon—and suggested a window of June 5–7. Poor weather on June 5 delayed the landings by a day, but even so the seas remained rough when the invasion began in the early hours of June 6, 1944. A naval and aerial bombardment was followed by an airborne and amphibious assault by troops from the US, Britain, and Canada under the supreme command of US general Dwight D. Eisenhower.

THE DECEPTION PLAN

The Allies convinced Hitler that their attack would be centered on the Pas-de-Calais using a variety of methods. A bogus US 1st Army Group with fake tanks was created in south-east England. As the real invasion fleet headed for Normandy, naval launches headed to Calais and Boulogne towing barrage balloons to create radar echoes similar to those of troop ships. Dummy parachutists were also dropped in the area.

Allied troops lift an inflatable decoy tank

OPERATION NEPTUNE

All five landing beaches were given code names— from west to east: Utah, Omaha, Gold, Juno, and Sword. The Allied goal was to link up the four easterly beaches and establish a front line 10 miles (16km) inland from the coast no later than midnight on June 6.

KEY

- Allied territory, Jun 6
- Axis territory, Jun 6
- Normandy beaches
- Allied gains, Jun 6
- Allied objective at 12:00 midnight Jun 6
- German mine barrier
- German gun batteries
- German infantry divisions
- German panzer division

TIMELINE

1
2
3
4
5
6
7

JUN 5, 1944   JUN 6   JUN 7

▽ **After the fighting**
US soldiers at Omaha Beach cover their dead and dying. Their landing craft sunk by German artillery, these troops could only reach Omaha by using a life raft.

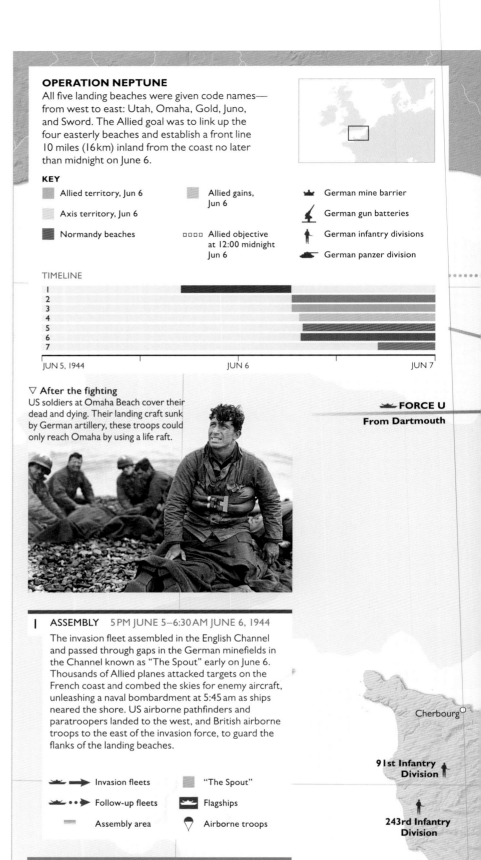

FORCE U
From Dartmouth

| ASSEMBLY   5PM JUNE 5–6:30AM JUNE 6, 1944

The invasion fleet assembled in the English Channel and passed through gaps in the German minefields in the Channel known as "The Spout" early on June 6. Thousands of Allied planes attacked targets on the French coast and combed the skies for enemy aircraft, unleashing a naval bombardment at 5:45 am as ships neared the shore. US airborne pathfinders and paratroopers landed to the west, and British airborne troops to the east of the invasion force, to guard the flanks of the landing beaches.

- Invasion fleets
- Follow-up fleets
- Assembly area
- "The Spout"
- Flagships
- Airborne troops

Cherbourg

91st Infantry Division

243rd Infantry Division

2   US LANDINGS ON UTAH BEACH
6:30AM–END OF DAY JUNE 6, 1944

The first US troops landed on Utah beach at 6:30am. Strong currents pushed their landing craft 1 mile (1.8km) to the south, but their new landing site turned out to be more favorable than the intended one. There, US troops set up a beachhead and made contact with airborne troops. By the end of the day, 21,000 troops had landed with just 197 casualties.

- US landing craft
- US troop movements

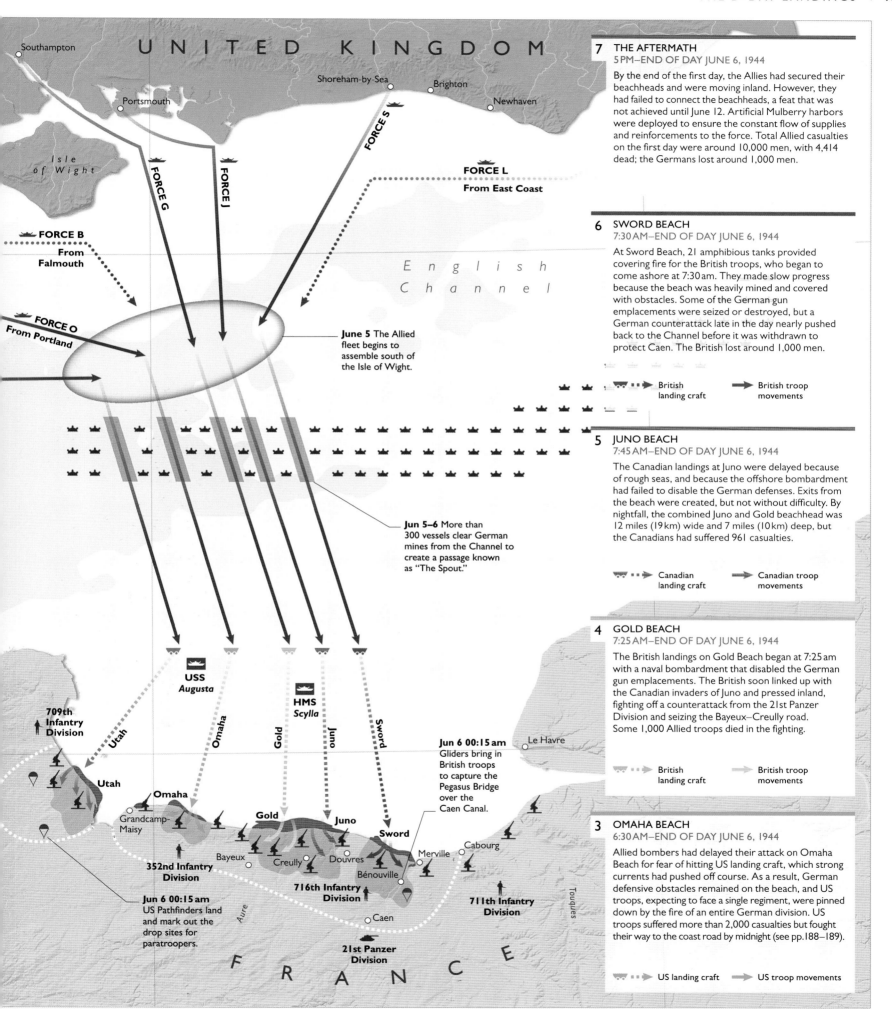

UNITED KINGDOM

Southampton

Portsmouth

Shoreham-by-Sea

Brighton

Newhaven

Isle of Wight

FORCE S

FORCE G

FORCE J

FORCE L
From East Coast

E n g l i s h

FORCE B
From Falmouth

C h a n n e l

FORCE O
From Portland

June 5 The Allied fleet begins to assemble south of the Isle of Wight.

Jun 5–6 More than 300 vessels clear German mines from the Channel to create a passage known as "The Spout."

USS *Augusta*

HMS *Scylla*

709th Infantry Division

Utah

Jun 6 00:15 am Gliders bring in British troops to capture the Pegasus Bridge over the Caen Canal.

Le Havre

Omaha

Gold

Juno

Sword

Utah

Omaha

Grandcamp-Maisy

Gold

Juno

Sword

Merville

Cabourg

352nd Infantry Division

Bayeux

Creully

Douvres

Bénouville

711th Infantry Division

Touques

716th Infantry Division

Jun 6 00:15 am US Pathfinders land and mark out the drop sites for paratroopers.

Aure

Caen

21st Panzer Division

F R A N C E

---

7 THE AFTERMATH
5 PM–END OF DAY JUNE 6, 1944

By the end of the first day, the Allies had secured their beachheads and were moving inland. However, they had failed to connect the beachheads, a feat that was not achieved until June 12. Artificial Mulberry harbors were deployed to ensure the constant flow of supplies and reinforcements to the force. Total Allied casualties on the first day were around 10,000 men, with 4,414 dead; the Germans lost around 1,000 men.

---

6 SWORD BEACH
7:30 AM–END OF DAY JUNE 6, 1944

At Sword Beach, 21 amphibious tanks provided covering fire for the British troops, who began to come ashore at 7:30am. They made slow progress because the beach was heavily mined and covered with obstacles. Some of the German gun emplacements were seized or destroyed, but a German counterattack late in the day nearly pushed back to the Channel before it was withdrawn to protect Caen. The British lost around 1,000 men.

➤ British landing craft ➡ British troop movements

---

5 JUNO BEACH
7:45 AM–END OF DAY JUNE 6, 1944

The Canadian landings at Juno were delayed because of rough seas, and because the offshore bombardment had failed to disable the German defenses. Exits from the beach were created, but not without difficulty. By nightfall, the combined Juno and Gold beachhead was 12 miles (19km) wide and 7 miles (10km) deep, but the Canadians had suffered 961 casualties.

➤ Canadian landing craft ➡ Canadian troop movements

---

4 GOLD BEACH
7:25 AM–END OF DAY JUNE 6, 1944

The British landings on Gold Beach began at 7:25am with a naval bombardment that disabled the German gun emplacements. The British soon linked up with the Canadian invaders of Juno and pressed inland, fighting off a counterattack from the 21st Panzer Division and seizing the Bayeux–Creully road. Some 1,000 Allied troops died in the fighting.

➤ British landing craft ➡ British troop movements

---

3 OMAHA BEACH
6:30 AM–END OF DAY JUNE 6, 1944

Allied bombers had delayed their attack on Omaha Beach for fear of hitting US landing craft, which strong currents had pushed off course. As a result, German defensive obstacles remained on the beach, and US troops, expecting to face a single regiment, were pinned down by the fire of an entire German division. US troops suffered more than 2,000 casualties but fought their way to the coast road by midnight (see pp.188–189).

➤ US landing craft ➡ US troop movements

OMAHA BEACH

Of the five D-Day landings in Normandy on June 6, 1944, Omaha was the costliest for the Allies. Hampered by deep, rising water, and assaulted by heavy German fire from well-defended cliffs, around 2,400 US soldiers were killed or injured in the landing.

△ **Anti-tank mine**
The Normandy beaches were defended by mines such as this German T-42, devised to explode when a tank drove over it.

The US 1st and 29th Infantry Divisions were tasked with securing a beachhead 6 miles (10 km) long at Omaha beach, then linking up with other Allies landing at Utah beach to the west and Gold beach to the east.

The assault started at 6:35 am with a first wave of troops from the US 1st Infantry Division, but the operation did not go according to plan. The Allied bombers providing air cover missed their targets, and the naval gunfire was poorly directed. As soon as the landing craft hit the beach, the Germans defending the cliffs rained shell, mortar, and machine-gun fire on the US troops as they tried to disembark. Most of the amphibious tanks were swamped and sank in the heavy swell, as did the supporting artillery. Within minutes of the initial landing, one-third of the assault troops had become casualties. Lieutenant-General Omar N. Bradley had to make a snap decision on whether to continue the landings, or pull out and switch reinforcements to Utah beach. He chose to continue.

Gaining a foothold

The landing started to improve as the Americans, reinforced by a second wave from the 29th Infantry Division, slowly managed to move up the beach and toward the surrounding bluffs. A flotilla of Allied destroyers steamed close inshore to provide much-needed artillery support. By late afternoon, tanks and other vehicles were moving off the beach. Despite determined resistance by the German defenders, by the end of the day some 34,000 US troops had landed at Omaha beach and secured a beachhead.

COMMAND DIFFERENCES

The German response to the invasion was slowed by power struggles. Rommel (center) argued for a fight on the beaches, whereas Gerd von Rundstedt, his superior, planned for a counterattack when the Allies were ashore. However, the need for Hitler's permission delayed von Rundstedt's plan until the afternoon of D-Day.

Wading ashore
E Company, 16th Infantry Regiment, land on Omaha beach at around 6:40am on D-Day. Two German regiments defended the beach from the cliffs at the rear, and defensive obstacles were placed in the water to wreck landing craft.

Normandy bridgehead

This German situation map from August 1, 1944, shows the progress made by Allied forces (represented by red flags along the coast) by July 31, 1944. They have broken out of the bridgehead, but the advance is slowed by German defenses (shown as blue flags). Areas shaded in red show French resistance activities.

THE BATTLE OF NORMANDY

Some of the hardest fighting of the war took place in the two months after the D-Day landings. The Allies suffered around 100,000 casualties in a grueling struggle to break out of their bridgehead in Normandy.

The D-Day landings (see pp.186–187) put Allied troops ashore on the Normandy coast, but their progress inland stalled as elite panzer divisions rushed to Normandy, blocking their movement out of the bridgehead. The terrain favored the defenders, and bad weather reduced the effectiveness of Allied air power. According to Allied plans, the city of Caen, which is about 9 miles (14 km) from the coast, should have been swiftly captured by British and Canadian troops of the 2nd Army while the US 1st Army advanced west up the Cotentin Peninsula to seize the port of Cherbourg. In reality, the Americans did not take Cherbourg until three weeks after the landings and Caen was still firmly in German hands at the end of June. British general Bernard Montgomery, in command of Allied ground forces, was criticized by some US generals for the failure to make progress. A sense of crisis was also mounting on the German side; Hitler fired Field Marshal Gerd von Rundstedt as Commander-in-Chief West (headquartered with Army Group D in Paris) on July 1 after he called for a withdrawal from Normandy and an end to the war.

The Allied breakout

On July 18, after carpet-bombing by Allied air forces destroyed Caen and flattened much of its surrounding area, Montgomery launched Operation Goodwood, an offensive by three armored divisions east of the city. The British lost 300 tanks in the fighting and failed to break through the German lines. However, it drew the best German divisions away from the sector facing the US 1st Army. On July 25, the Americans launched Operation Cobra, overcoming much-weakened German resistance to break out toward Avranches. The US 3rd Army under General George Patton joined in the offensive, pouring through the gap opened in the enemy line. German tanks counterattacking on August 7 were destroyed by Allied ground-attack aircraft and US artillery. Much of the German army fleeing from Normandy escaped encirclement in the Falaise Pocket (see p.194–95), but the Allied path into France was now open.

▷ **Heavy artillery**
US soldiers fire howitzer shells at German soldiers near the town of Carentan, on the Cotentin Peninsula.

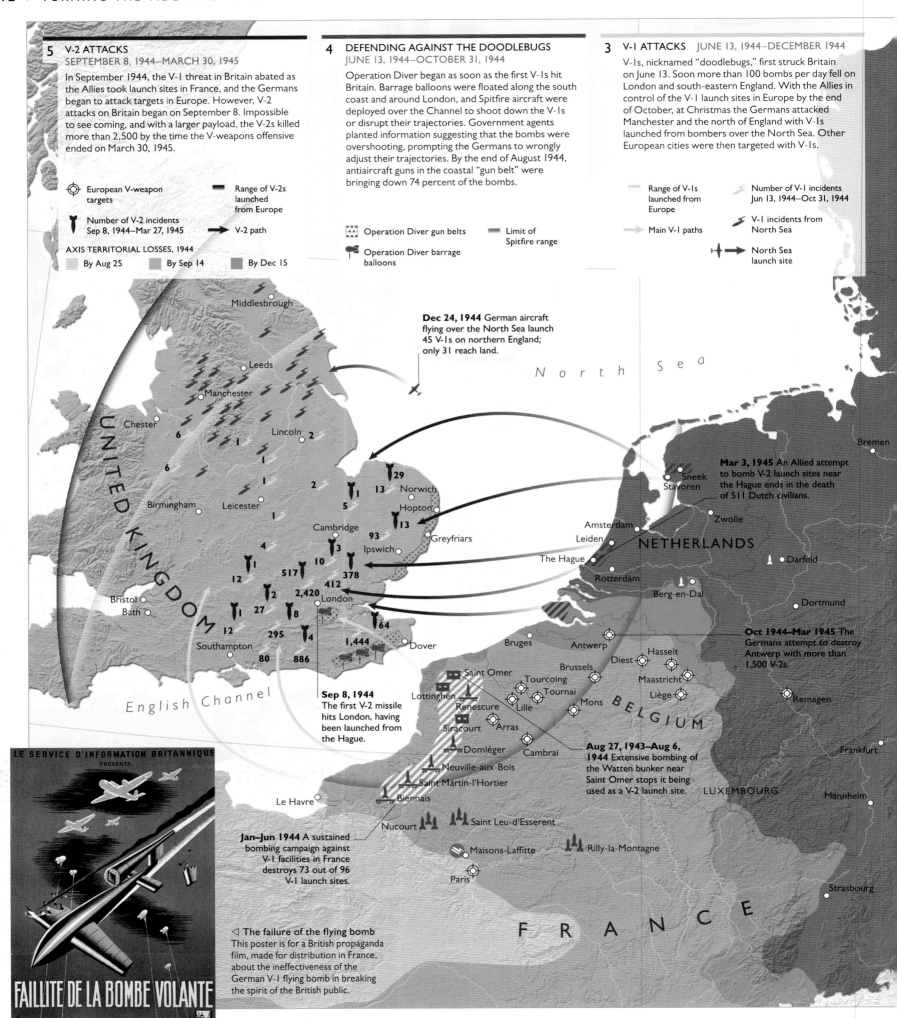

5 V-2 ATTACKS
SEPTEMBER 8, 1944–MARCH 30, 1945

In September 1944, the V-1 threat in Britain abated as the Allies took launch sites in France, and the Germans began to attack targets in Europe. However, V-2 attacks on Britain began on September 8. Impossible to see coming, and with a larger payload, the V-2s killed more than 2,500 by the time the V-weapons offensive ended on March 30, 1945.

- European V-weapon targets
- Number of V-2 incidents Sep 8, 1944–Mar 27, 1945
- Range of V-2s launched from Europe
- V-2 path

AXIS TERRITORIAL LOSSES, 1944
- By Aug 25
- By Sep 14
- By Dec 15

4 DEFENDING AGAINST THE DOODLEBUGS
JUNE 13, 1944–OCTOBER 31, 1944

Operation Diver began as soon as the first V-1s hit Britain. Barrage balloons were floated along the south coast and around London, and Spitfire aircraft were deployed over the Channel to shoot down the V-1s or disrupt their trajectories. Government agents planted information suggesting that the bombs were overshooting, prompting the Germans to wrongly adjust their trajectories. By the end of August 1944, antiaircraft guns in the coastal "gun belt" were bringing down 74 percent of the bombs.

- Operation Diver gun belts
- Operation Diver barrage balloons
- Limit of Spitfire range

3 V-1 ATTACKS   JUNE 13, 1944–DECEMBER 1944

V-1s, nicknamed "doodlebugs," first struck Britain on June 13. Soon more than 100 bombs per day fell on London and south-eastern England. With the Allies in control of the V-1 launch sites in Europe by the end of October, at Christmas the Germans attacked Manchester and the north of England with V-1s launched from bombers over the North Sea. Other European cities were then targeted with V-1s.

- Range of V-1s launched from Europe
- Main V-1 paths
- Number of V-1 incidents Jun 13, 1944–Oct 31, 1944
- V-1 incidents from North Sea
- North Sea launch site

Dec 24, 1944 German aircraft flying over the North Sea launch 45 V-1s on northern England; only 31 reach land.

Mar 3, 1945 An Allied attempt to bomb V-2 launch sites near the Hague ends in the death of 511 Dutch civilians.

Oct 1944–Mar 1945 The Germans attempt to destroy Antwerp with more than 1,500 V-2s.

Sep 8, 1944 The first V-2 missile hits London, having been launched from the Hague.

Aug 27, 1943–Aug 6, 1944 Extensive bombing of the Watten bunker near Saint Omer stops it being used as a V-2 launch site.

Jan–Jun 1944 A sustained bombing campaign against V-1 facilities in France destroys 73 out of 96 V-1 launch sites.

◁ **The failure of the flying bomb**
This poster is for a British propaganda film, made for distribution in France, about the ineffectiveness of the German V-1 flying bomb in breaking the spirit of the British public.

LE SERVICE D'INFORMATION BRITANNIQUE PRÉSENTE

FAILLITE DE LA BOMBE VOLANTE

V-WEAPONS

In June 1944, the Germans began targeting Britain with new V-weapons (from *Vergeltungswaffen*, meaning "reprisal weapons" in response to Allied bombing). They succeeded—at first—in their goal of inflicting terror on the population and destroying infrastructure.

Rumors that Germany was developing long-range missiles were confirmed in 1943 when Polish intelligence agents smuggled details of the *Vergeltungswaffen* to the British. As well as terrorizing Allied civilians, these "wonder weapons" were intended to boost morale in Germany. The Allies responded with Operation Crossbow, intended to disrupt the production, transport, and launch of the weapons. Nevertheless, the first V-1 flying bombs fell on London in June 1944 and continued to affect a swathe of England throughout the summer. These simple steel and plywood missiles were powered by a pulse-jet that made a buzzing sound, which cut out when the bomb was about to fall. Thousands of Londoners fled the city, but they began to return when defensive countermeasures introduced in Operation Diver took effect, disabling or destroying nearly half of the 12,000 missiles fired. Those that did reach Britain caused 45,000 casualties.

The unleashing of the V-2—a large, fast, rocket-powered missile—in September 1944 added to the toll, both in Britain and in the cities targeted in Europe. As the Allies advanced through France to the Netherlands in March 1945, they knocked out German launch sites, and Europe was finally freed from the terror of the V-weapons.

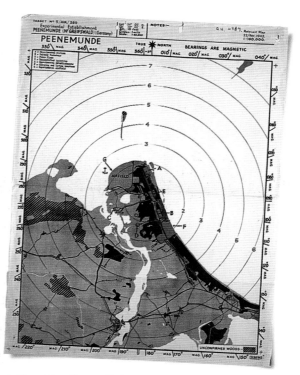

△ **The raid on Peenemünde**
This British map from 1943 shows the targets of Operation Hydra— the bombing raid on Peenemünde on the night of August 17–18, 1943. It forced the Germans to move V-2 production to the *Mittelwerk* factory.

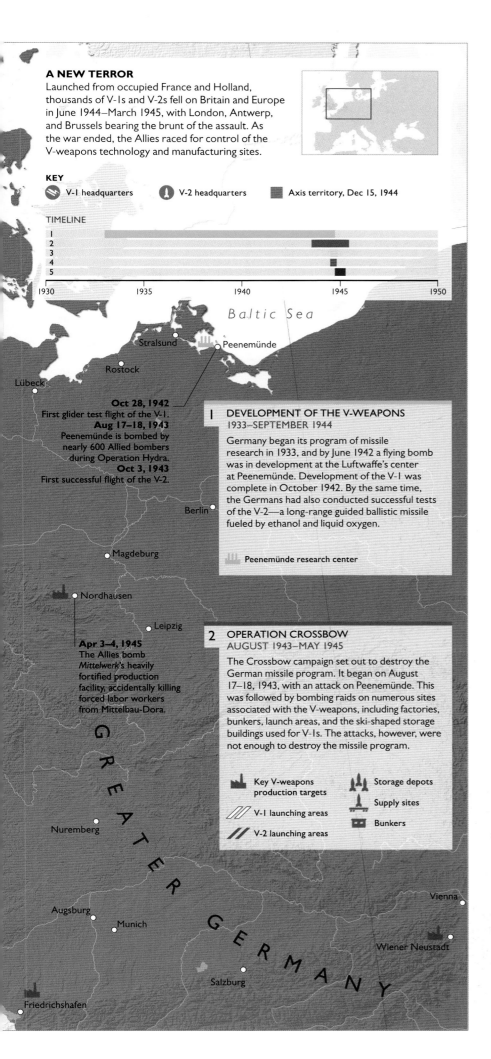

A NEW TERROR

Launched from occupied France and Holland, thousands of V-1s and V-2s fell on Britain and Europe in June 1944–March 1945, with London, Antwerp, and Brussels bearing the brunt of the assault. As the war ended, the Allies raced for control of the V-weapons technology and manufacturing sites.

KEY

- ⊗ V-1 headquarters
- ⬧ V-2 headquarters
- ▪ Axis territory, Dec 15, 1944

TIMELINE

1
2
3
4
5

1930　1935　1940　1945　1950

Baltic Sea

Stralsund
Peenemünde
Rostock
Lübeck

Oct 28, 1942
First glider test flight of the V-1.
Aug 17–18, 1943
Peenemünde is bombed by nearly 600 Allied bombers during Operation Hydra.
Oct 3, 1943
First successful flight of the V-2.

Berlin

Magdeburg

Nordhausen

Leipzig

Apr 3–4, 1945
The Allies bomb *Mittelwerk*'s heavily fortified production facility, accidentally killing forced labor workers from Mittelbau-Dora.

Nuremberg

Augsburg
Munich

Salzburg

Friedrichshafen

Vienna

Wiener Neustadt

GREATER GERMANY

1 DEVELOPMENT OF THE V-WEAPONS
1933–SEPTEMBER 1944

Germany began its program of missile research in 1933, and by June 1942 a flying bomb was in development at the Luftwaffe's center at Peenemünde. Development of the V-1 was complete in October 1942. By the same time, the Germans had also conducted successful tests of the V-2—a long-range guided ballistic missile fueled by ethanol and liquid oxygen.

🏭 Peenemünde research center

2 OPERATION CROSSBOW
AUGUST 1943–MAY 1945

The Crossbow campaign set out to destroy the German missile program. It began on August 17–18, 1943, with an attack on Peenemünde. This was followed by bombing raids on numerous sites associated with the V-weapons, including factories, bunkers, launch areas, and the ski-shaped storage buildings used for V-1s. The attacks, however, were not enough to destroy the missile program.

🏭 Key V-weapons production targets
▨ V-1 launching areas
▧ V-2 launching areas
🚀 Storage depots
🚀 Supply sites
▭ Bunkers

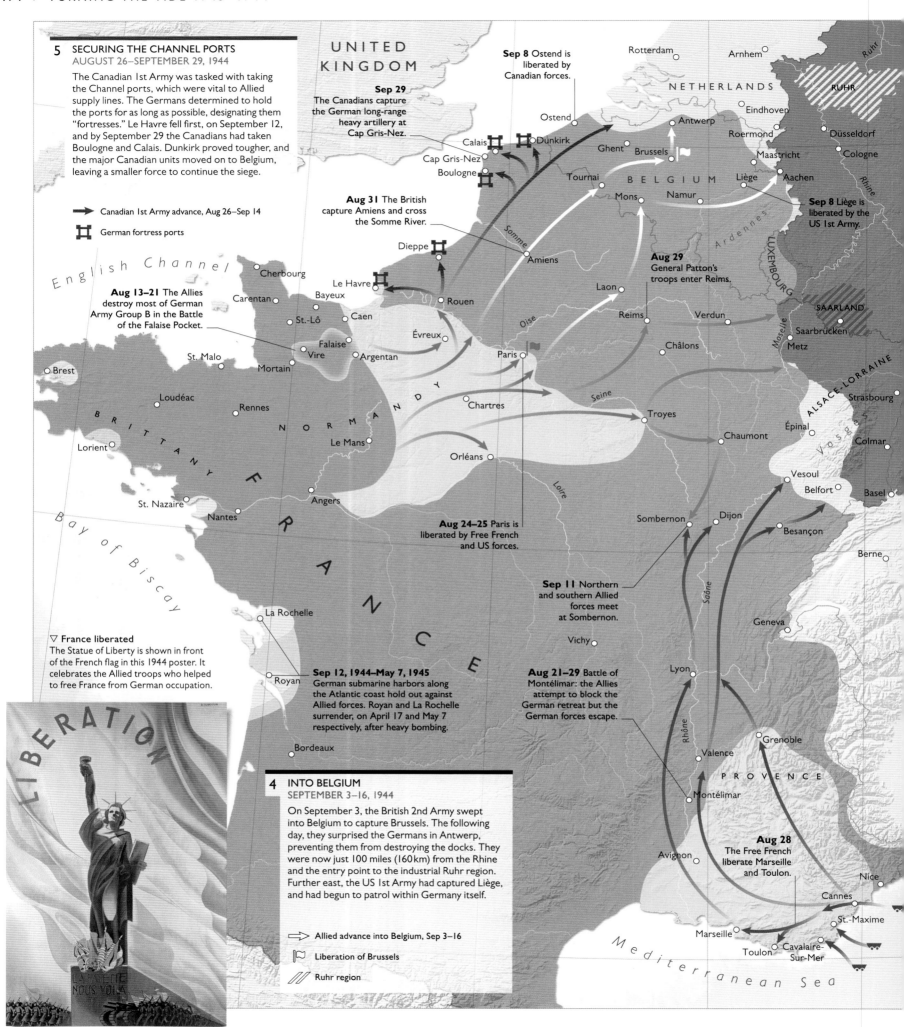

5 SECURING THE CHANNEL PORTS
AUGUST 26–SEPTEMBER 29, 1944

The Canadian 1st Army was tasked with taking the Channel ports, which were vital to Allied supply lines. The Germans determined to hold the ports for as long as possible, designating them "fortresses." Le Havre fell first, on September 12, and by September 29 the Canadians had taken Boulogne and Calais. Dunkirk proved tougher, and the major Canadian units moved on to Belgium, leaving a smaller force to continue the siege.

→ Canadian 1st Army advance, Aug 26–Sep 14

⊞ German fortress ports

Sep 29 The Canadians capture the German long-range heavy artillery at Cap Gris-Nez.

Sep 8 Ostend is liberated by Canadian forces.

Sep 8 Liège is liberated by the US 1st Army.

Aug 31 The British capture Amiens and cross the Somme River.

Aug 29 General Patton's troops enter Reims.

Aug 13–21 The Allies destroy most of German Army Group B in the Battle of the Falaise Pocket.

Aug 24–25 Paris is liberated by Free French and US forces.

Sep 11 Northern and southern Allied forces meet at Sombernon.

▽ **France liberated**
The Statue of Liberty is shown in front of the French flag in this 1944 poster. It celebrates the Allied troops who helped to free France from German occupation.

Sep 12, 1944–May 7, 1945 German submarine harbors along the Atlantic coast hold out against Allied forces. Royan and La Rochelle surrender, on April 17 and May 7 respectively, after heavy bombing.

Aug 21–29 Battle of Montélimar: the Allies attempt to block the German retreat but the German forces escape.

Aug 28 The Free French liberate Marseille and Toulon.

4 INTO BELGIUM
SEPTEMBER 3–16, 1944

On September 3, the British 2nd Army swept into Belgium to capture Brussels. The following day, they surprised the Germans in Antwerp, preventing them from destroying the docks. They were now just 100 miles (160km) from the Rhine and the entry point to the industrial Ruhr region. Further east, the US 1st Army had captured Liège, and had begun to patrol within Germany itself.

⇨ Allied advance into Belgium, Sep 3–16

⚑ Liberation of Brussels

⫽ Ruhr region

LIBERATION

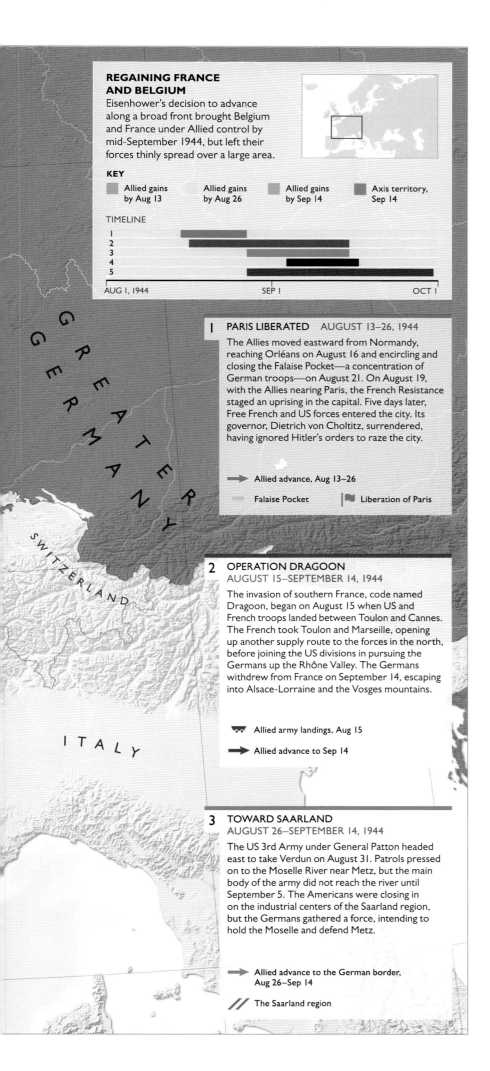

REGAINING FRANCE AND BELGIUM

Eisenhower's decision to advance along a broad front brought Belgium and France under Allied control by mid-September 1944, but left their forces thinly spread over a large area.

KEY

Allied gains by Aug 13	Allied gains by Aug 26	Allied gains by Sep 14	Axis territory, Sep 14

TIMELINE

1
2
3
4
5

AUG 1, 1944   SEP 1   OCT 1

GREATER GERMANY

SWITZERLAND

ITALY

1   PARIS LIBERATED   AUGUST 13–26, 1944

The Allies moved eastward from Normandy, reaching Orléans on August 16 and encircling and closing the Falaise Pocket—a concentration of German troops—on August 21. On August 19, with the Allies nearing Paris, the French Resistance staged an uprising in the capital. Five days later, Free French and US forces entered the city. Its governor, Dietrich von Choltitz, surrendered, having ignored Hitler's orders to raze the city.

→ Allied advance, Aug 13–26

▨ Falaise Pocket   ⚑ Liberation of Paris

2   OPERATION DRAGOON
AUGUST 15–SEPTEMBER 14, 1944

The invasion of southern France, code named Dragoon, began on August 15 when US and French troops landed between Toulon and Cannes. The French took Toulon and Marseille, opening up another supply route to the forces in the north, before joining the US divisions in pursuing the Germans up the Rhône Valley. The Germans withdrew from France on September 14, escaping into Alsace-Lorraine and the Vosges mountains.

⋁ Allied army landings, Aug 15

→ Allied advance to Sep 14

3   TOWARD SAARLAND
AUGUST 26–SEPTEMBER 14, 1944

The US 3rd Army under General Patton headed east to take Verdun on August 31. Patrols pressed on to the Moselle River near Metz, but the main body of the army did not reach the river until September 5. The Americans were closing in on the industrial centers of the Saarland region, but the Germans gathered a force, intending to hold the Moselle and defend Metz.

→ Allied advance to the German border, Aug 26–Sep 14

// The Saarland region

THE BREAKOUT

Within three months of the D-Day landings, the Allies had broken out of Normandy, liberating France and most of Belgium. They swept eastward to reach the German border by the middle of September. However, a hard fight lay ahead.

In August, the Allied breakout from Normandy developed into a rout as their forces spread east, chasing the Germans from northern France. By the end of the month, they had cleared Brittany, reached the Loire, and moved as far as Troyes to the east. Paris was liberated, having been under Nazi control since June 1940, and General de Gaulle was installed in the city. Meanwhile, a French and US force had landed in Provence and begun to drive the Germans from the south.

The Allies disagreed on how best to proceed. British Field Marshal Bernard Montgomery wished to advance on a narrow front and push north-east through Belgium to reach the Ruhr Valley. However, US General Dwight Eisenhower—Supreme Commander of the Allied forces in Europe—rejected Montgomery's plan, favoring a "broad front" strategy in which troops would be deployed along the entire Western Front before driving into Germany. By mid-September, the Allies were stretched across a front from Antwerp in the north to the Swiss border near Belfort in the south. The British were poised to make a dramatic attempt to invade Germany through the Netherlands (see pp.198–199), while the US forces were within touching distance of the economically vital Saarland and Ruhr regions. However, both faced increasing German resistance.

> *"Steady, Monty. You can't speak to me like that. I'm your boss."*

EISENHOWER TO MONTGOMERY, SEPTEMBER 10, 1944

THE RED BALL EXPRESS

For 83 days, from August 25 to November 16, 1944, convoys of trucks emblazoned with red balls and driven predominantly by African Americans carried food, fuel, and munitions along the road from Cherbourg to the Allied logistics base at Chartres. At its peak, the Red Ball Express operated nearly 6,000 vehicles, carrying 12,500 tons (11,300 metric tons) of supplies each day. The convoy system was abandoned once the port of Antwerp and the French railroad lines were re-opened and fuel pipes installed.

A US soldier on the Red Ball Highway

After the blast
Leading Nazi officials Martin Bormann (second from left) and Hermann Göring (fourth from left) inspect the wrecked conference room where the bomb was detonated. A stout table leg had helped shield Hitler from the explosion.

THE PLOT TO KILL HITLER

As the Allies drew closer on two fronts, within Germany a hostile faction plotted to overthrow Hitler and make peace. On July 20, 1944, there was an assassination attempt that came close to success.

Planned by a group of senior German military officers, the July Plot was set in motion when Colonel Claus von Stauffenberg planted a briefcase-bomb in a meeting at the "Wolf's Lair," Hitler's field headquarters in East Prussia. After the bomb went off, Stauffenberg flew to Berlin to claim that the SS had assassinated Hitler and order the German Replacement Army to overthrow the Nazi regime. However, Hitler was not dead. Although three other Nazis were killed, Hitler suffered only minor injuries.

△ **Key plotter**
After being severely injured in Tunisia in 1943, Stauffenberg joined other conspirators to save Germany from destruction.

The conspiracy fails

Not realizing that Hitler was still alive, the conspirators instructed the Replacement Army to arrest various officials; meanwhile, counter-orders were given by Hitler. When Major Otto Remer, acting on the conspirators' orders, arrived to arrest the Propaganda Minister Joseph Goebbels, he was informed by Goebbels that the Führer was still alive. To prove his point, Goebbels phoned Hitler, who spoke to Remer and ordered that he crush the rebellion immediately. Remer's troops moved on the War Ministry, where, after a brief gun battle, the conspirators surrendered. The leading figures were sentenced to death, with Stauffenberg shot that same evening.

▷ **Living to tell the tale**
Hitler greets Joseph Goebbels only hours after surviving the bomb blast that was intended to assassinate him. Following the attempted coup, more than 7,000 alleged conspirators were arrested; up to 5,000 ended up dead, either executed or forced to commit suicide.

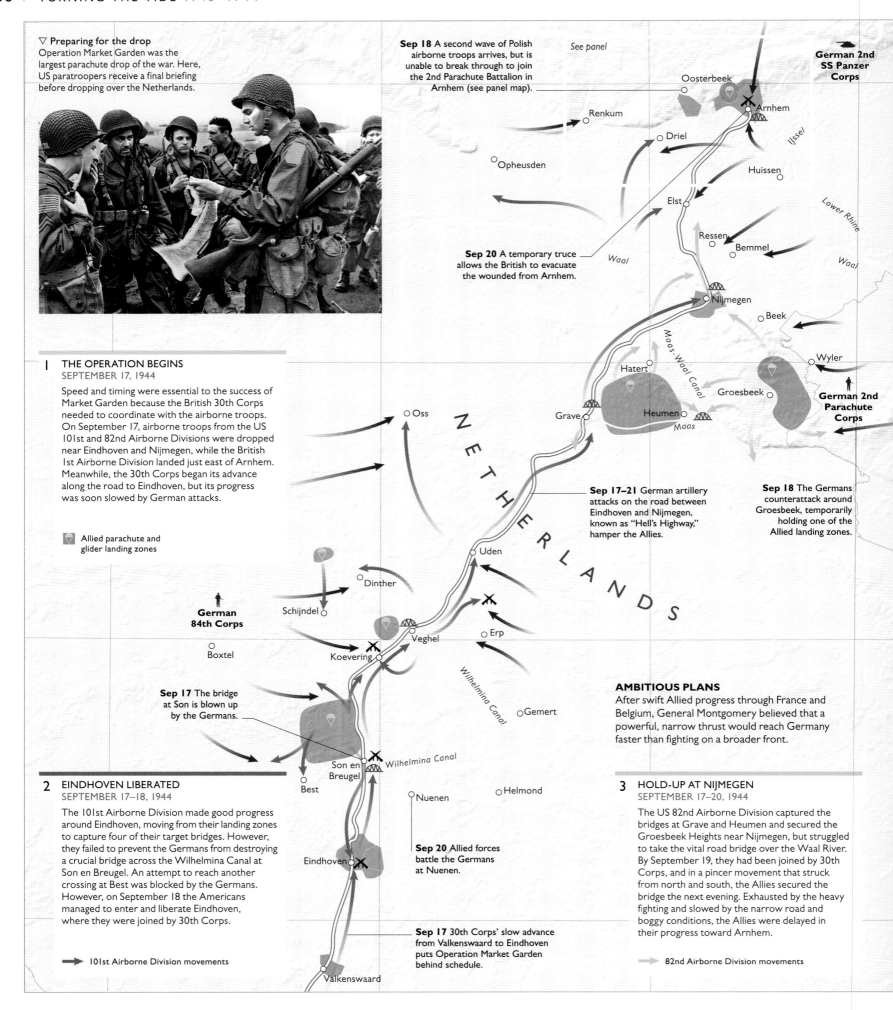

▽ **Preparing for the drop**
Operation Market Garden was the largest parachute drop of the war. Here, US paratroopers receive a final briefing before dropping over the Netherlands.

Sep 18 A second wave of Polish airborne troops arrives, but is unable to break through to join the 2nd Parachute Battalion in Arnhem (see panel map).

See panel

German 2nd SS Panzer Corps

Sep 20 A temporary truce allows the British to evacuate the wounded from Arnhem.

German 2nd Parachute Corps

1 THE OPERATION BEGINS
SEPTEMBER 17, 1944

Speed and timing were essential to the success of Market Garden because the British 30th Corps needed to coordinate with the airborne troops. On September 17, airborne troops from the US 101st and 82nd Airborne Divisions were dropped near Eindhoven and Nijmegen, while the British 1st Airborne Division landed just east of Arnhem. Meanwhile, the 30th Corps began its advance along the road to Eindhoven, but its progress was soon slowed by German attacks.

▨ Allied parachute and glider landing zones

Sep 17–21 German artillery attacks on the road between Eindhoven and Nijmegen, known as "Hell's Highway," hamper the Allies.

Sep 18 The Germans counterattack around Groesbeek, temporarily holding one of the Allied landing zones.

German 84th Corps

AMBITIOUS PLANS

After swift Allied progress through France and Belgium, General Montgomery believed that a powerful, narrow thrust would reach Germany faster than fighting on a broader front.

Sep 17 The bridge at Son is blown up by the Germans.

2 EINDHOVEN LIBERATED
SEPTEMBER 17–18, 1944

The 101st Airborne Division made good progress around Eindhoven, moving from their landing zones to capture four of their target bridges. However, they failed to prevent the Germans from destroying a crucial bridge across the Wilhelmina Canal at Son en Breugel. An attempt to reach another crossing at Best was blocked by the Germans. However, on September 18 the Americans managed to enter and liberate Eindhoven, where they were joined by 30th Corps.

➡ 101st Airborne Division movements

Sep 20 Allied forces battle the Germans at Nuenen.

Sep 17 30th Corps' slow advance from Valkenswaard to Eindhoven puts Operation Market Garden behind schedule.

3 HOLD-UP AT NIJMEGEN
SEPTEMBER 17–20, 1944

The US 82nd Airborne Division captured the bridges at Grave and Heumen and secured the Groesbeek Heights near Nijmegen, but struggled to take the vital road bridge over the Waal River. By September 19, they had been joined by 30th Corps, and in a pincer movement that struck from north and south, the Allies secured the bridge the next evening. Exhausted by the heavy fighting and slowed by the narrow road and boggy conditions, the Allies were delayed in their progress toward Arnhem.

➡ 82nd Airborne Division movements

Map labels: Oosterbeek, Renkum, Driel, Opheusden, Arnhem, IJssel, Huissen, Elst, Ressen, Bemmel, Lower Rhine, Waal, Nijmegen, Beek, Wyler, Hatert, Maas-Waal Canal, Groesbeek, Grave, Heumen, Maas, Oss, N E T H E R L A N D S, Uden, Dinther, Schijndel, Erp, Veghel, Boxtel, Koevering, Gemert, Wilhelmina Canal, Son en Breugel, Best, Nuenen, Helmond, Eindhoven, Valkenswaard

OPERATION MARKET GARDEN

In one of the boldest plans of the war, the Allies dropped thousands of troops behind enemy lines in the Netherlands, near the German border. This operation—designated Market Garden—aimed to clear a path for the Allies into Germany, but it turned out to be a costly failure.

By mid-September 1944, the Allies—sensing stiffening resistance—were desperate to break through into Germany. In a hastily conceived plan, Field Marshal Montgomery believed that he could push through the Netherlands and into Germany, bypassing the heavily defended Westwall, or Siegfried Line (see pp.200–201). On September 17–18, 35,000 airborne troops were delivered by glider and parachute to around Nijmegen, Eindhoven, and Arnhem. Their task was to secure bridges along the road between these cities; the British 30th Corps would then advance over this route and cross the Lower Rhine at Arnhem, after which the Allies would have easy access into Germany's industrial heartland in the Ruhr.

However, the Allies never managed to take the bridge over the Rhine at Arnhem, and after a week of bitter fighting, in which over 1,000 Allied troops died, they were forced to evacuate. Market Garden failed, wasting resources that would have been invaluable over the coming months, when the Allies tackled German defenses over a broader front.

A FLAWED PLAN
Montgomery planned to secure the bridges along the road from Eindhoven to Arnhem with airborne troops, creating a safe corridor for his ground forces. He anticipated little resistance.

KEY

→ Main German attacks

➡ Advance of 30th Corps ground forces

⋀⋀ Key bridges

✖ Major battles

German forces

▭ Road from Eindhoven to Arnhem

Key urban areas

TIMELINE

1
2
3
4
5

SEP 15, 1944 — SEP 20 — SEP 25 — SEP 30

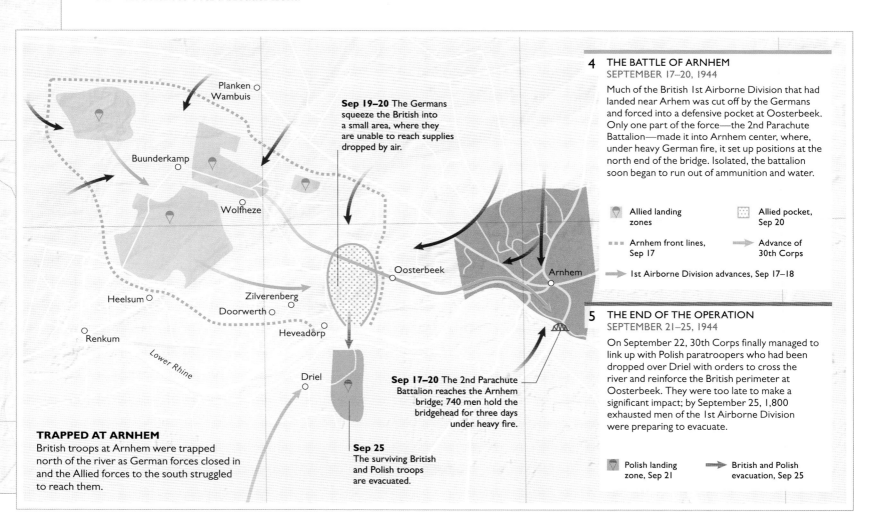

4 THE BATTLE OF ARNHEM
SEPTEMBER 17–20, 1944

Much of the British 1st Airborne Division that had landed near Arhem was cut off by the Germans and forced into a defensive pocket at Oosterbeek. Only one part of the force—the 2nd Parachute Battalion—made it into Arnhem center, where, under heavy German fire, it set up positions at the north end of the bridge. Isolated, the battalion soon began to run out of ammunition and water.

Allied landing zones

Allied pocket, Sep 20

Arnhem front lines, Sep 17

Advance of 30th Corps

1st Airborne Division advances, Sep 17–18

5 THE END OF THE OPERATION
SEPTEMBER 21–25, 1944

On September 22, 30th Corps finally managed to link up with Polish paratroopers who had been dropped over Driel with orders to cross the river and reinforce the British perimeter at Oosterbeek. They were too late to make a significant impact; by September 25, 1,800 exhausted men of the 1st Airborne Division were preparing to evacuate.

Polish landing zone, Sep 21

British and Polish evacuation, Sep 25

Planken Wambuis

Sep 19–20 The Germans squeeze the British into a small area, where they are unable to reach supplies dropped by air.

Buunderkamp

Wolfheze

Heelsum

Zilverenberg

Doorwerth

Renkum

Heveadorp

Lower Rhine

Oosterbeek

Arnhem

Driel

Sep 17–20 The 2nd Parachute Battalion reaches the Arnhem bridge; 740 men hold the bridgehead for three days under heavy fire.

TRAPPED AT ARNHEM
British troops at Arnhem were trapped north of the river as German forces closed in and the Allied forces to the south struggled to reach them.

Sep 25
The surviving British and Polish troops are evacuated.

GREATER GERMANY

BATTLES AT GERMANY'S GATE

Weary from the Battle of Normandy and their advance across France, the Allies faced organized German resistance as they tried to cross the German border in late 1944. Although they made gains in Alsace–Lorraine and in Germany itself, exhausting campaigns in the Scheldt and Hürtgen Forest depleted their forces.

In Operation Market Garden (see pp.198–199) the Allies had failed to cross the Rhine and to establish an invasion route into Germany. This, together with their severely overstretched supply lines, lost the Allies the initiative they had won after their breakout from Normandy (see pp.194–195) and so their chances of bringing the war to an end in 1944. Instead, they spent the fall and early winter trying to breach German defenses along the borders in Belgium, the Netherlands, and France.

After a grueling battle, the Allies cleared the German defenses on the Scheldt Estuary in the Netherlands, opening up the port of Antwerp in Belgium as a supply route for their forces. However, to reach the Rhine River, the Allies now had to contend

with two formidable deterrents: the Westwall (or Siegfried Line), a 373-mile (600-km) German defensive line of bunkers, tank traps, and tunnels; and the increasingly cold, wet weather.

The US 7th Army and French 1st Army met with success on the southern end of the front, advancing toward the German industrial region of the Saarland and reducing the Germans in eastern France to a small pocket around Colmar; and the Canadians and British succeeded in bringing Antwerp back into operation. However, the Allies' aim to reach the Ruhr Valley, Germany's most economically important region, was hampered when the US 1st Army was defeated and suffered more than 33,000 casualties in a long battle in the Hürtgen Forest.

> *"In Hürtgen they just froze up hard; and it was so cold they froze up with ruddy faces."*
>
> ERNEST HEMINGWAY, *ACROSS THE RIVER AND INTO THE TREES*, 1950

▷ **Fallen bunker**
This bunker on Germany's Westwall defensive line has been destroyed by Allied armor-piercing weapons. In 1944, Hitler ordered a large-scale reinforcement of the line, but the bunkers became vulnerable to newly-developed Allied weaponry.

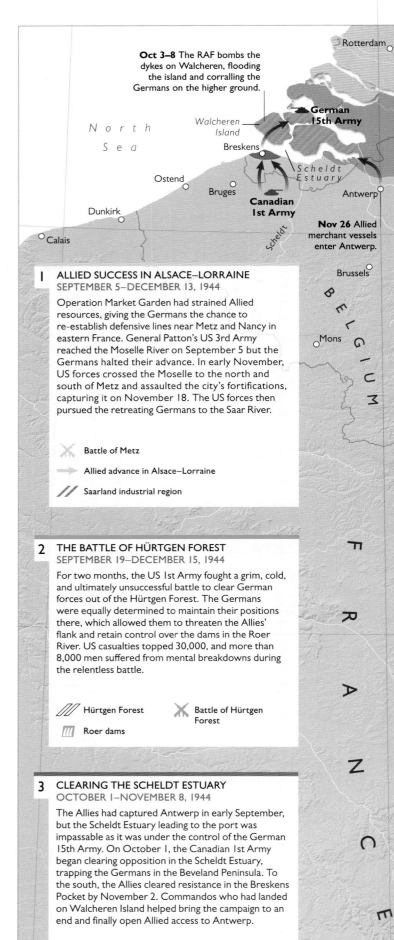

Oct 3–8 The RAF bombs the dykes on Walcheren, flooding the island and corralling the Germans on the higher ground.

Nov 26 Allied merchant vessels enter Antwerp.

1 ALLIED SUCCESS IN ALSACE–LORRAINE
SEPTEMBER 5–DECEMBER 13, 1944

Operation Market Garden had strained Allied resources, giving the Germans the chance to re-establish defensive lines near Metz and Nancy in eastern France. General Patton's US 3rd Army reached the Moselle River on September 5 but the Germans halted their advance. In early November, US forces crossed the Moselle to the north and south of Metz and assaulted the city's fortifications, capturing it on November 18. The US forces then pursued the retreating Germans to the Saar River.

✕ Battle of Metz

→ Allied advance in Alsace–Lorraine

// Saarland industrial region

2 THE BATTLE OF HÜRTGEN FOREST
SEPTEMBER 19–DECEMBER 15, 1944

For two months, the US 1st Army fought a grim, cold, and ultimately unsuccessful battle to clear German forces out of the Hürtgen Forest. The Germans were equally determined to maintain their positions there, which allowed them to threaten the Allies' flank and retain control over the dams in the Roer River. US casualties topped 30,000, and more than 8,000 men suffered from mental breakdowns during the relentless battle.

/// Hürtgen Forest

▥ Roer dams

✕ Battle of Hürtgen Forest

3 CLEARING THE SCHELDT ESTUARY
OCTOBER 1–NOVEMBER 8, 1944

The Allies had captured Antwerp in early September, but the Scheldt Estuary leading to the port was impassable as it was under the control of the German 15th Army. On October 1, the Canadian 1st Army began clearing opposition in the Scheldt Estuary, trapping the Germans in the Beveland Peninsula. To the south, the Allies cleared resistance in the Breskens Pocket by November 2. Commandos who had landed on Walcheren Island helped bring the campaign to an end and finally open Allied access to Antwerp.

// Beveland Peninsula

■ Breskens Pocket

→ Canadian 1st Army advance

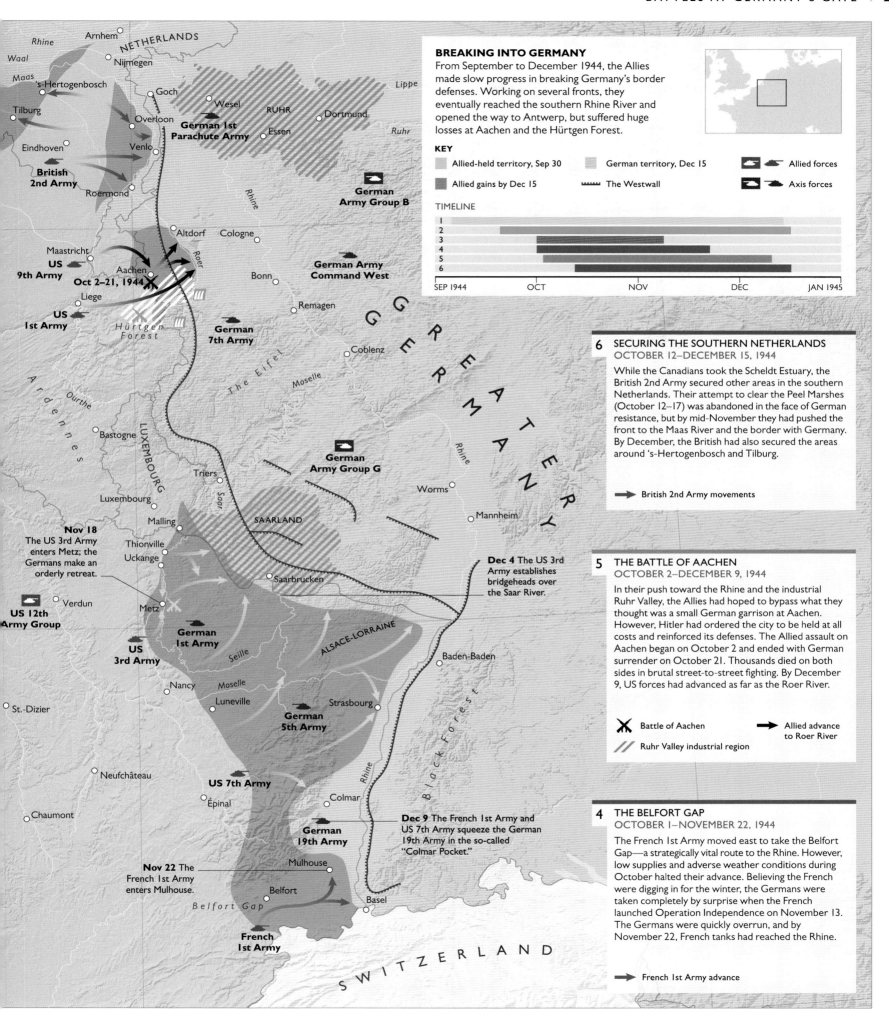

BREAKING INTO GERMANY

From September to December 1944, the Allies made slow progress in breaking Germany's border defenses. Working on several fronts, they eventually reached the southern Rhine River and opened the way to Antwerp, but suffered huge losses at Aachen and the Hürtgen Forest.

KEY

Allied-held territory, Sep 30	German territory, Dec 15
Allied gains by Dec 15	The Westwall

Allied forces
Axis forces

TIMELINE

SEP 1944 — OCT — NOV — DEC — JAN 1945

---

6 SECURING THE SOUTHERN NETHERLANDS
OCTOBER 12–DECEMBER 15, 1944

While the Canadians took the Scheldt Estuary, the British 2nd Army secured other areas in the southern Netherlands. Their attempt to clear the Peel Marshes (October 12–17) was abandoned in the face of German resistance, but by mid-November they had pushed the front to the Maas River and the border with Germany. By December, the British had also secured the areas around 's-Hertogenbosch and Tilburg.

→ British 2nd Army movements

---

5 THE BATTLE OF AACHEN
OCTOBER 2–DECEMBER 9, 1944

In their push toward the Rhine and the industrial Ruhr Valley, the Allies had hoped to bypass what they thought was a small German garrison at Aachen. However, Hitler had ordered the city to be held at all costs and reinforced its defenses. The Allied assault on Aachen began on October 2 and ended with German surrender on October 21. Thousands died on both sides in brutal street-to-street fighting. By December 9, US forces had advanced as far as the Roer River.

✕ Battle of Aachen
→ Allied advance to Roer River
/// Ruhr Valley industrial region

---

4 THE BELFORT GAP
OCTOBER 1–NOVEMBER 22, 1944

The French 1st Army moved east to take the Belfort Gap—a strategically vital route to the Rhine. However, low supplies and adverse weather conditions during October halted their advance. Believing the French were digging in for the winter, the Germans were taken completely by surprise when the French launched Operation Independence on November 13. The Germans were quickly overrun, and by November 22, French tanks had reached the Rhine.

→ French 1st Army advance

Map labels:

Rhine, Waal, Maas, Arnhem, NETHERLANDS, Nijmegen, 's-Hertogenbosch, Tilburg, Goch, Wesel, Lippe, RUHR, Dortmund, Essen, Ruhr, Eindhoven, Overloon, Venlo, **German 1st Parachute Army**, Roermond, **British 2nd Army**, Altdorf, Cologne, Rhine, **German Army Group B**, Maastricht, Roer, US 9th Army, Aachen, **Oct 2–21, 1944**, Liege, Bonn, **German Army Command West**, US 1st Army, Hürtgen Forest, Remagen, **German 7th Army**, The Eifel, Coblenz, Moselle, GREATER GERMANY, Ardennes, Ourthe, LUXEMBOURG, Bastogne, Triers, **German Army Group G**, Luxembourg, Rhine, Worms, Malling, SAARLAND, Thionville, Uckange, Saarbrucken, Mannheim, **Nov 18** The US 3rd Army enters Metz; the Germans make an orderly retreat., Verdun, **US 12th Army Group**, Metz, **German 1st Army**, **Dec 4** The US 3rd Army establishes bridgeheads over the Saar River., **US 3rd Army**, Seille, ALSACE-LORRAINE, Baden-Baden, Nancy, Moselle, St.-Dizier, Luneville, Strasbourg, **German 5th Army**, Black Forest, Neufchâteau, **US 7th Army**, Colmar, Rhine, Épinal, Chaumont, **Dec 9** The French 1st Army and US 7th Army squeeze the German 19th Army in the so-called "Colmar Pocket.", **German 19th Army**, **Nov 22** The French 1st Army enters Mulhouse., Mulhouse, Belfort, Basel, Belfort Gap, **French 1st Army**, SWITZERLAND

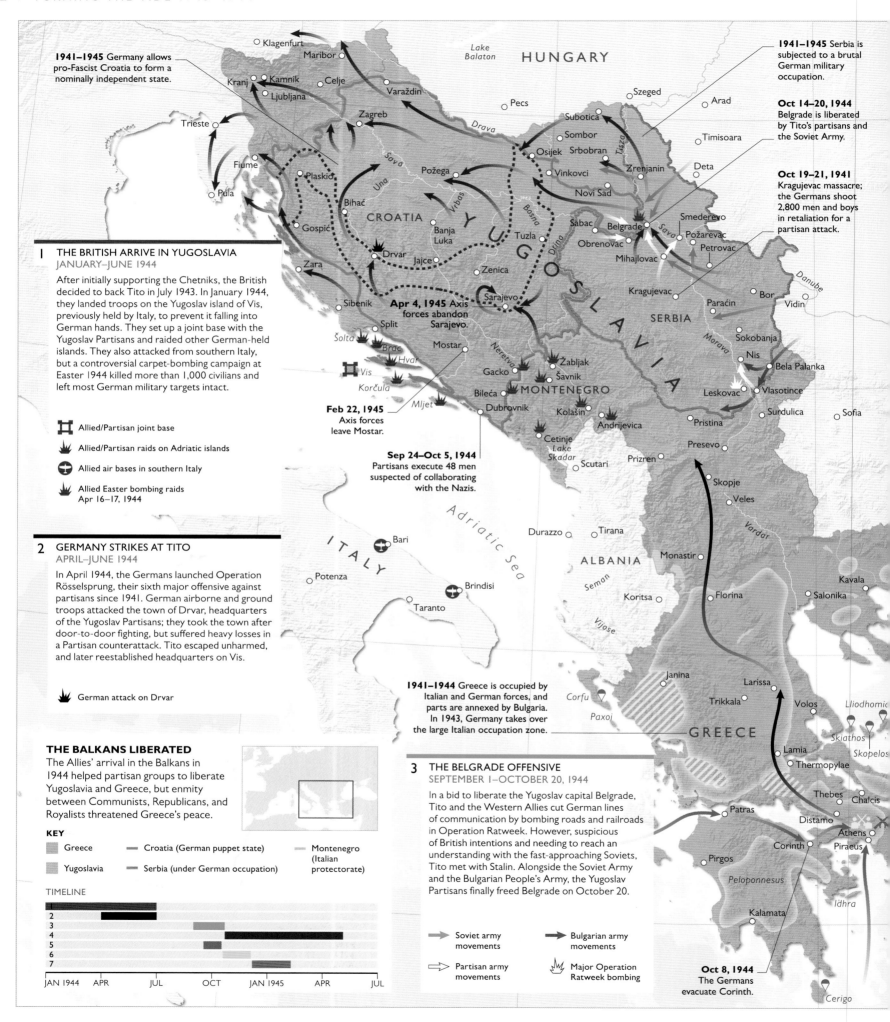

1941–1945 Germany allows pro-Fascist Croatia to form a nominally independent state.

1941–1945 Serbia is subjected to a brutal German military occupation.

Oct 14–20, 1944 Belgrade is liberated by Tito's partisans and the Soviet Army.

Oct 19–21, 1941 Kragujevac massacre; the Germans shoot 2,800 men and boys in retaliation for a partisan attack.

Apr 4, 1945 Axis forces abandon Sarajevo.

Feb 22, 1945 Axis forces leave Mostar.

Sep 24–Oct 5, 1944 Partisans execute 48 men suspected of collaborating with the Nazis.

1 THE BRITISH ARRIVE IN YUGOSLAVIA
JANUARY–JUNE 1944

After initially supporting the Chetniks, the British decided to back Tito in July 1943. In January 1944, they landed troops on the Yugoslav island of Vis, previously held by Italy, to prevent it falling into German hands. They set up a joint base with the Yugoslav Partisans and raided other German-held islands. They also attacked from southern Italy, but a controversial carpet-bombing campaign at Easter 1944 killed more than 1,000 civilians and left most German military targets intact.

⌖ Allied/Partisan joint base

☸ Allied/Partisan raids on Adriatic islands

⊕ Allied air bases in southern Italy

☸ Allied Easter bombing raids Apr 16–17, 1944

2 GERMANY STRIKES AT TITO
APRIL–JUNE 1944

In April 1944, the Germans launched Operation Rösselsprung, their sixth major offensive against partisans since 1941. German airborne and ground troops attacked the town of Drvar, headquarters of the Yugoslav Partisans; they took the town after door-to-door fighting, but suffered heavy losses in a Partisan counterattack. Tito escaped unharmed, and later reestablished headquarters on Vis.

☸ German attack on Drvar

THE BALKANS LIBERATED

The Allies' arrival in the Balkans in 1944 helped partisan groups to liberate Yugoslavia and Greece, but enmity between Communists, Republicans, and Royalists threatened Greece's peace.

KEY

▦ Greece	▬ Croatia (German puppet state)	▬ Montenegro (Italian protectorate)
▦ Yugoslavia	▬ Serbia (under German occupation)	

TIMELINE

JAN 1944	APR	JUL	OCT	JAN 1945	APR	JUL

1941–1944 Greece is occupied by Italian and German forces, and parts are annexed by Bulgaria. In 1943, Germany takes over the large Italian occupation zone.

3 THE BELGRADE OFFENSIVE
SEPTEMBER 1–OCTOBER 20, 1944

In a bid to liberate the Yugoslav capital Belgrade, Tito and the Western Allies cut German lines of communication by bombing roads and railroads in Operation Ratweek. However, suspicious of British intentions and needing to reach an understanding with the fast-approaching Soviets, Tito met with Stalin. Alongside the Soviet Army and the Bulgarian People's Army, the Yugoslav Partisans finally freed Belgrade on October 20.

→ Soviet army movements

➡ Bulgarian army movements

⇨ Partisan army movements

☸ Major Operation Ratweek bombing

Oct 8, 1944 The Germans evacuate Corinth.

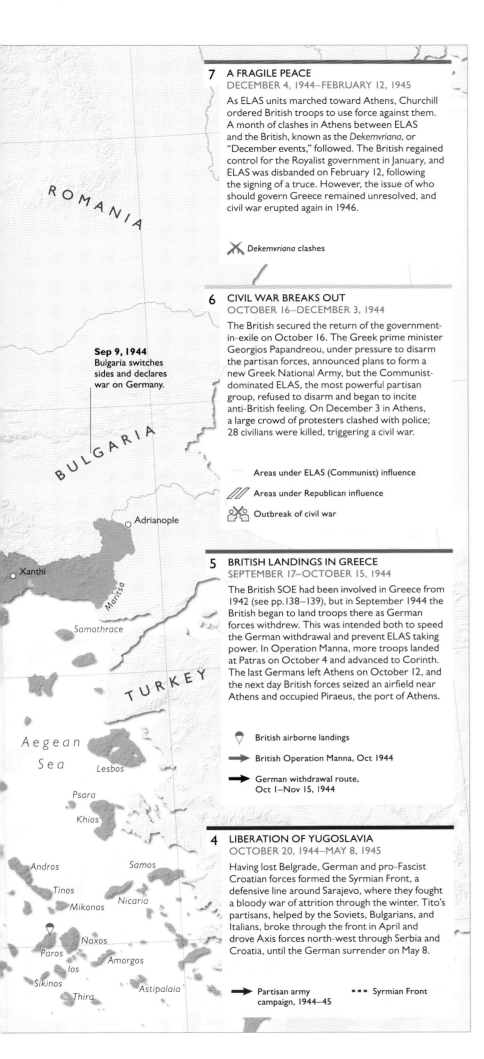

7 A FRAGILE PEACE
DECEMBER 4, 1944–FEBRUARY 12, 1945

As ELAS units marched toward Athens, Churchill ordered British troops to use force against them. A month of clashes in Athens between ELAS and the British, known as the *Dekemvriana*, or "December events," followed. The British regained control for the Royalist government in January, and ELAS was disbanded on February 12, following the signing of a truce. However, the issue of who should govern Greece remained unresolved, and civil war erupted again in 1946.

✕ *Dekemvriana* clashes

6 CIVIL WAR BREAKS OUT
OCTOBER 16–DECEMBER 3, 1944

The British secured the return of the government-in-exile on October 16. The Greek prime minister Georgios Papandreou, under pressure to disarm the partisan forces, announced plans to form a new Greek National Army, but the Communist-dominated ELAS, the most powerful partisan group, refused to disarm and began to incite anti-British feeling. On December 3 in Athens, a large crowd of protesters clashed with police; 28 civilians were killed, triggering a civil war.

Sep 9, 1944
Bulgaria switches sides and declares war on Germany.

Areas under ELAS (Communist) influence

/// Areas under Republican influence

⚔ Outbreak of civil war

5 BRITISH LANDINGS IN GREECE
SEPTEMBER 17–OCTOBER 15, 1944

The British SOE had been involved in Greece from 1942 (see pp.138–139), but in September 1944 the British began to land troops there as German forces withdrew. This was intended both to speed the German withdrawal and prevent ELAS taking power. In Operation Manna, more troops landed at Patras on October 4 and advanced to Corinth. The last Germans left Athens on October 12, and the next day British forces seized an airfield near Athens and occupied Piraeus, the port of Athens.

⊙ British airborne landings

➡ British Operation Manna, Oct 1944

➡ German withdrawal route, Oct 1–Nov 15, 1944

4 LIBERATION OF YUGOSLAVIA
OCTOBER 20, 1944–MAY 8, 1945

Having lost Belgrade, German and pro-Fascist Croatian forces formed the Syrmian Front, a defensive line around Sarajevo, where they fought a bloody war of attrition through the winter. Tito's partisans, helped by the Soviets, Bulgarians, and Italians, broke through the front in April and drove Axis forces north-west through Serbia and Croatia, until the German surrender on May 8.

➡ Partisan army campaign, 1944–45   ▪▪▪ Syrmian Front

GREECE AND YUGOSLAVIA

After Axis armies occupied Greece and Yugoslavia in 1941, partisan factions fought fiercely against them, but also against each other. As Axis control over the Balkans crumbled from 1943 onward, the Allies became embroiled in the complex politics of the region.

Following the invasion of the Balkans (see pp.80–81), Italy occupied most of Greece, while Yugoslavia—now divided into three states and with its remaining land annexed by its neighbors—was dominated by Germany. After Italy surrendered in September 1943 (see pp.164–165), the Germans occupied the whole region, but the approach of the Soviet Army in September 1944 (see pp.182–183) threatened to encircle them and they withdrew. At the same time, Churchill and Stalin agreed that Britain would have a free hand in Greece, while the USSR would have influence over the other Balkan nations.

In both countries, resistance to the occupying forces formed under competing groups. In Yugoslavia, Colonel Draža Mihailović led the Royalist Chetniks, and Josip Broz, known as Tito, led the Communist Yugoslav Partisans. By 1943, it was clear that Tito was more effective against the Germans, and when the Chetniks began collaborating with the Nazis against the Communists, Tito won Allied support. In Greece, Communist and Republican partisan groups shared mutual dislike of the British-supported Royalist government-in-exile. As liberation drew nearer, the British were alarmed by the increasing power of the Communist-dominated partisan group EAM and its armed wing, ELAS. Their attempts to broker a Greek government that would bring all factions together tipped into a civil war.

△ **Greek partisans on the move**
A line of partisans marches to join Allied forces in Greece in October 1944. Partisan forces in Greece and Yugoslavia offered a serious challenge to German troops, keeping them from joining Axis campaigns elsewhere.

WAR AGAINST JAPAN

In 1943–1944, the Japanese ground forces suffered a succession of defeats against the US, which had the advantages of a larger population and greater industrial capacity. The once-proud Imperial Japanese Navy was almost totally destroyed.

△ **Rosie the Riveter**
The name "Rosie the Riveter" was coined for American women working in heavy industry during World War II. This US propaganda poster exploits the stereotype to encourage the national effort for victory.

The feat of organization involved in the US's massive expansion in the production of arms, ships, and aircraft from 1942 onward was extraordinary. Business, the armed forces, and federal bureaucracy cooperated effectively to develop and manufacture the hardware needed to win the war. With US government spending quadrupling between 1941 and 1944, the unemployment of the Depression years was replaced by labor shortages. This had notable effects on American society. Women took jobs in heavy industry, and African Americans from the rural Deep South migrated to work in California and in northern cities—a population shift that provoked race riots in Detroit in summer 1943. The Roosevelt administration made tentative progress with desegregation of employment, but the US armed forces remained racially segregated.

Japan could not match the US's industrial output, nor the quality of its weapons. Despite the forced labor of Javanese, Korean, Chinese, and Allied prisoners of war, Japan was unable to fulfill its military and civilian manpower needs.

▷ **Amphibious landing**
US Marines go ashore on New Britain island, New Guinea, in December 1943. The use of landing craft and amphibious vehicles was a Marine speciality.

THE FIGHT FOR SUPREMACY

American "island-hopping" across the Pacific began in November 1943 at the Gilbert Islands and reached the Marianas in July 1944. The US offensive in the south-west Pacific led up to landings in the Philippines in October 1944, while the defeat of Japan's naval force left the Japanese exposed to potential invasion of their mainland. Meanwhile, fighting between Japan and China reached a new intensity, and the British advanced into Japanese-occupied Burma after repelling an attack on India.

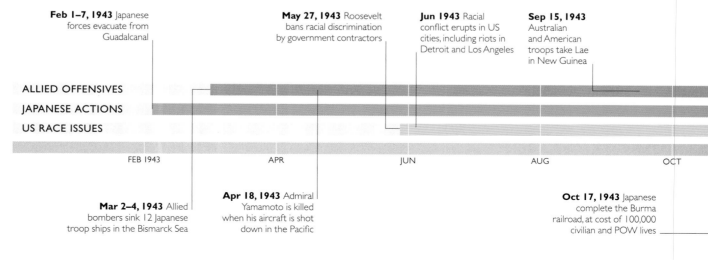

Feb 1–7, 1943 Japanese forces evacuate from Guadalcanal

May 27, 1943 Roosevelt bans racial discrimination by government contractors

Jun 1943 Racial conflict erupts in US cities, including riots in Detroit and Los Angeles

Sep 15, 1943 Australian and American troops take Lae in New Guinea

ALLIED OFFENSIVES

JAPANESE ACTIONS

US RACE ISSUES

FEB 1943   APR   JUN   AUG   OCT

Mar 2–4, 1943 Allied bombers sink 12 Japanese troop ships in the Bismarck Sea

Apr 18, 1943 Admiral Yamamoto is killed when his aircraft is shot down in the Pacific

Oct 17, 1943 Japanese complete the Burma railroad, at cost of 100,000 civilian and POW lives

◁ **Operations in China**
Japanese soldiers pose on their Type 97 medium tank during the 1944 Ichigo offensive in China. The operation showed the unbroken fighting strength of the Japanese army.

US strategy

US command in the Pacific War was divided between General Douglas MacArthur in the south-west Pacific sector, where the US Army predominated, and Admiral Chester Nimitz in the central and South Pacific, where the US Marines and the US Navy led the charge. Nimitz's island-hopping strategy across the central Pacific toward Japan proved most decisive. The Marines employed a range of new amphibious equipment in a series of landings on Japanese-held islands, which fell one by one, despite a defense-to-the-death mounted by their outnumbered garrisons. When the Japanese navy tried to intervene against the US landings on the Pacific island of Saipan in June 1944, it found that its carrier aircraft and pilots had ceased to be any match for their American opponents.

The Philippines campaign

Meanwhile, MacArthur's forces sidestepped Japanese strongpoints, such as Rabaul in New Guinea, to begin the reconquest of the Philippines. The naval battle of Leyte Gulf, fought during the Philippine landings in October 1944, destroyed the Japanese Imperial Navy as an effective fighting force.

Fighting spirit

Despite Japan's inferior military resources, there was no decline in its martial spirit. In spring 1944, Japanese troops from Burma invaded British India, and they mustered half a million men for one of the largest offensives of its long war in China. On the Pacific islands, US casualties mounted, and on Saipan, the Americans were shocked by the mass suicide of Japanese civilians and soldiers, who chose death over surrender. By autumn 1944, the US conquest of the Mariana Islands provided a Pacific base for America's new B-29 bombers to attack the Japanese mainland, and the balance of forces in favor of the US and its allies had become overwhelming.

▽ **Battle of Leyte Gulf**
Ships of the US Navy's Fast Carrier Task Force 38 sail in line astern at the battle of Leyte Gulf in October 1944. Deploying 36 carriers of all types, the US managed to regain the Philippines.

"I have returned. By the grace of Almighty God our forces stand again on Philippine soil …"

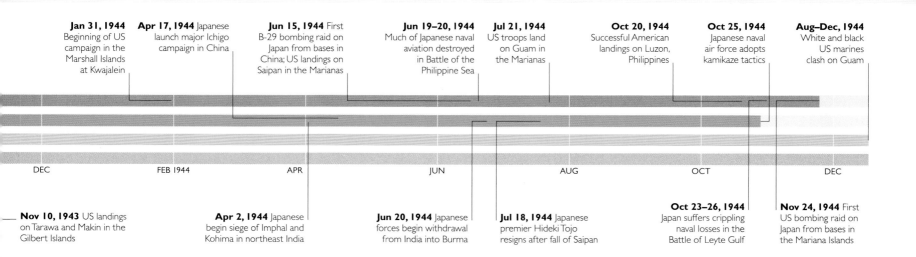

Jan 31, 1944 Beginning of US campaign in the Marshall Islands at Kwajalein

Apr 17, 1944 Japanese launch major Ichigo campaign in China

Jun 15, 1944 First B-29 bombing raid on Japan from bases in China; US landings on Saipan in the Marianas

Jun 19–20, 1944 Much of Japanese naval aviation destroyed in Battle of the Philippine Sea

Jul 21, 1944 US troops land on Guam in the Marianas

Oct 20, 1944 Successful American landings on Luzon, Philippines

Oct 25, 1944 Japanese naval air force adopts kamikaze tactics

Aug–Dec, 1944 White and black US marines clash on Guam

DEC   FEB 1944   APR   JUN   AUG   OCT   DEC

Nov 10, 1943 US landings on Tarawa and Makin in the Gilbert Islands

Apr 2, 1944 Japanese begin siege of Imphal and Kohima in northeast India

Jun 20, 1944 Japanese forces begin withdrawal from India into Burma

Jul 18, 1944 Japanese premier Hideki Tojo resigns after fall of Saipan

Oct 23–26, 1944 Japan suffers crippling naval losses in the Battle of Leyte Gulf

Nov 24, 1944 First US bombing raid on Japan from bases in the Mariana Islands

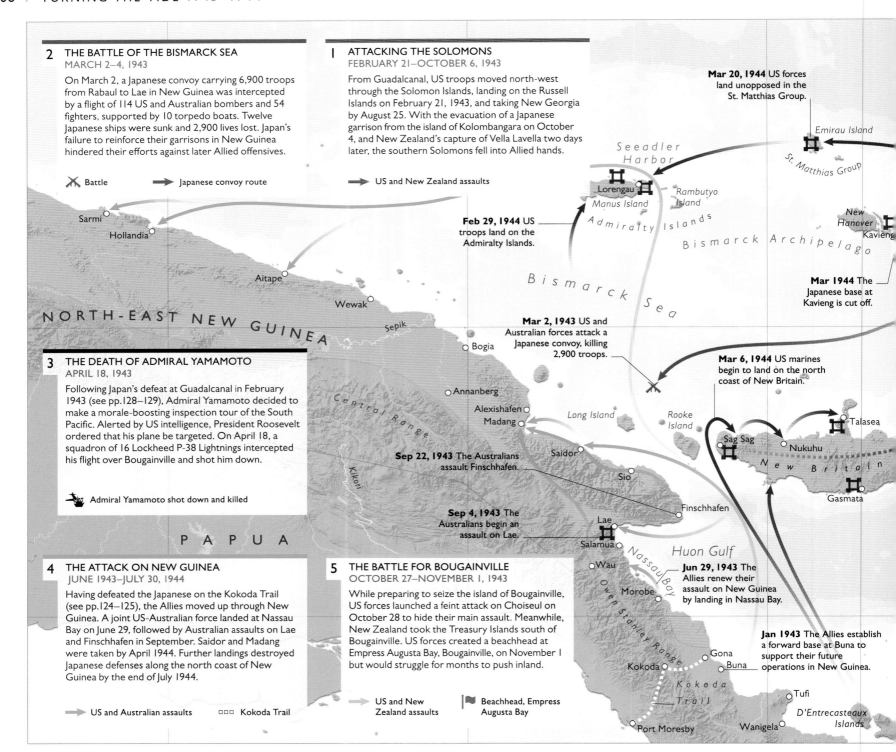

2 THE BATTLE OF THE BISMARCK SEA
MARCH 2–4, 1943

On March 2, a Japanese convoy carrying 6,900 troops from Rabaul to Lae in New Guinea was intercepted by a flight of 114 US and Australian bombers and 54 fighters, supported by 10 torpedo boats. Twelve Japanese ships were sunk and 2,900 lives lost. Japan's failure to reinforce their garrisons in New Guinea hindered their efforts against later Allied offensives.

✕ Battle   → Japanese convoy route

1 ATTACKING THE SOLOMONS
FEBRUARY 21–OCTOBER 6, 1943

From Guadalcanal, US troops moved north-west through the Solomon Islands, landing on the Russell Islands on February 21, 1943, and taking New Georgia by August 25. With the evacuation of a Japanese garrison from the island of Kolombangara on October 4, and New Zealand's capture of Vella Lavella two days later, the southern Solomons fell into Allied hands.

→ US and New Zealand assaults

3 THE DEATH OF ADMIRAL YAMAMOTO
APRIL 18, 1943

Following Japan's defeat at Guadalcanal in February 1943 (see pp.128–129), Admiral Yamamoto decided to make a morale-boosting inspection tour of the South Pacific. Alerted by US intelligence, President Roosevelt ordered that his plane be targeted. On April 18, a squadron of 16 Lockheed P-38 Lightnings intercepted his flight over Bougainville and shot him down.

🛩 Admiral Yamamoto shot down and killed

4 THE ATTACK ON NEW GUINEA
JUNE 1943–JULY 30, 1944

Having defeated the Japanese on the Kokoda Trail (see pp.124–125), the Allies moved up through New Guinea. A joint US-Australian force landed at Nassau Bay on June 29, followed by Australian assaults on Lae and Finschhafen in September. Saidor and Madang were taken by April 1944. Further landings destroyed Japanese defenses along the north coast of New Guinea by the end of July 1944.

→ US and Australian assaults   ▫▫▫ Kokoda Trail

5 THE BATTLE FOR BOUGAINVILLE
OCTOBER 27–NOVEMBER 1, 1943

While preparing to seize the island of Bougainville, US forces launched a feint attack on Choiseul on October 28 to hide their main assault. Meanwhile, New Zealand took the Treasury Islands south of Bougainville. US forces created a beachhead at Empress Augusta Bay, Bougainville, on November 1 but would struggle for months to push inland.

→ US and New Zealand assaults   ⚑ Beachhead, Empress Augusta Bay

Map labels:
Mar 20, 1944 US forces land unopposed in the St. Matthias Group.
Feb 29, 1944 US troops land on the Admiralty Islands.
Mar 1944 The Japanese base at Kavieng is cut off.
Mar 2, 1943 US and Australian forces attack a Japanese convoy, killing 2,900 troops.
Mar 6, 1944 US marines begin to land on the north coast of New Britain.
Sep 22, 1943 The Australians assault Finschhafen.
Sep 4, 1943 The Australians begin an assault on Lae.
Jun 29, 1943 The Allies renew their assault on New Guinea by landing in Nassau Bay.
Jan 1943 The Allies establish a forward base at Buna to support their future operations in New Guinea.

OPERATION CARTWHEEL

In early 1943, the Americans drew up a series of plans to challenge the Japanese in the south-west Pacific, known collectively as Operation Cartwheel. The objective was audacious: to advance through the Solomon Islands in the east and along New Guinea in the west in order to encircle and neutralize the major Japanese base at Rabaul in New Britain.

Operation Cartwheel was approved by US president Franklin D. Roosevelt and British prime minister Winston Churchill at the Casablanca Conference in January 1943 (see pp.162–163). Under the overall command of US general Douglas MacArthur, it consisted of 13 separate planned operations, of which 10 were undertaken and three were dropped because they were considered too costly. Cartwheel saw the movement of Allied forces in two large wings—one up the coast of New Guinea, the other up along the Solomon chain. The aim of this pincer action was to encircle Rabaul, a base that supported a large fleet of aircraft and gave the Japanese control of shipping in the south-west Pacific—a major obstacle to the eventual Allied goal of capturing the Philippines.

The Allied campaign aimed to avoid major concentrations of Japanese forces and focused instead on severing their lines of supply and communication, and on establishing airfields and bases to

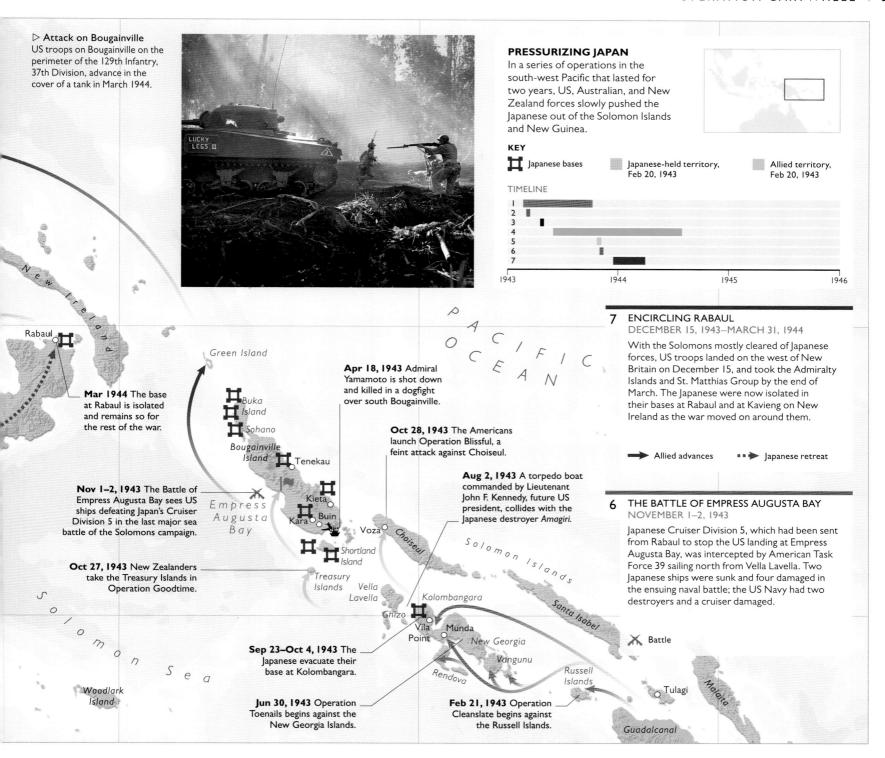

▷ **Attack on Bougainville**
US troops on Bougainville on the perimeter of the 129th Infantry, 37th Division, advance in the cover of a tank in March 1944.

PRESSURIZING JAPAN

In a series of operations in the south-west Pacific that lasted for two years, US, Australian, and New Zealand forces slowly pushed the Japanese out of the Solomon Islands and New Guinea.

KEY

⌗ Japanese bases ▪ Japanese-held territory, Feb 20, 1943 ▪ Allied territory, Feb 20, 1943

TIMELINE

1
2
3
4
5
6
7

1943   1944   1945   1946

---

7 ENCIRCLING RABAUL
DECEMBER 15, 1943–MARCH 31, 1944

With the Solomons mostly cleared of Japanese forces, US troops landed on the west of New Britain on December 15, and took the Admiralty Islands and St. Matthias Group by the end of March. The Japanese were now isolated in their bases at Rabaul and at Kavieng on New Ireland as the war moved on around them.

→ Allied advances ▪▪▶ Japanese retreat

---

6 THE BATTLE OF EMPRESS AUGUSTA BAY
NOVEMBER 1–2, 1943

Japanese Cruiser Division 5, which had been sent from Rabaul to stop the US landing at Empress Augusta Bay, was intercepted by American Task Force 39 sailing north from Vella Lavella. Two Japanese ships were sunk and four damaged in the ensuing naval battle; the US Navy had two destroyers and a cruiser damaged.

Map labels

New Ireland

Rabaul ⌗

Mar 1944 The base at Rabaul is isolated and remains so for the rest of the war.

Green Island

PACIFIC OCEAN

Buka Island ⌗
Sohano ⌗
Bougainville Island

Apr 18, 1943 Admiral Yamamoto is shot down and killed in a dogfight over south Bougainville.

Tenekau ⌗

Oct 28, 1943 The Americans launch Operation Blissful, a feint attack against Choiseul.

Nov 1–2, 1943 The Battle of Empress Augusta Bay sees US ships defeating Japan's Cruiser Division 5 in the last major sea battle of the Solomons campaign.

Empress Augusta Bay

Kieta ⌗
Kara ⌗ Buin
Voza
Choiseul

Aug 2, 1943 A torpedo boat commanded by Lieutenant John F. Kennedy, future US president, collides with the Japanese destroyer *Amagiri*.

Solomon Islands

Oct 27, 1943 New Zealanders take the Treasury Islands in Operation Goodtime.

Shortland Island ⌗

Treasury Islands
Vella Lavella
Ghizo ⌗

Kolombangara

Santa Isabel

Vila Point
Munda
New Georgia
Vangunu

X Battle

Solomon Sea

Sep 23–Oct 4, 1943 The Japanese evacuate their base at Kolombangara.

Rendova
Russell Islands

Tulagi
Malaita

Woodlark Island

Jun 30, 1943 Operation Toenails begins against the New Georgia Islands.

Feb 21, 1943 Operation Cleanslate begins against the Russell Islands.

Guadalcanal

---

support Allied logistics. Nevertheless, fighting throughout the campaign was intense, with the Japanese resisting all naval landings and fighting rearguard actions on many of the islands.

The Allies disrupted Japanese troop movements during the Battle of the Bismarck Sea in March 1943, and the shooting down of Admiral Yamamoto (see p.124), commander-in-chief of the Japanese Combined Fleet, severely dented Japanese morale. On reaching Rabaul, the Allies—much to General MacArthur's disapproval—opted not to attack in order to avoid unnecessary casualties, and instead surrounded and isolated the base, which remained in Japanese hands until the end of the war.

Cartwheel took more than a year to achieve, but its eventual success removed the Japanese from the south-west Pacific and allowed the Allies to start new campaigns against them in the Pacific islands to the north (see pp.210–211).

LOCKHEED P-38 LIGHTNING

The Lockheed P-38 Lightning— the aircraft that shot down Japan's Admiral Yamamoto—was a key American fighter aircraft produced in large numbers throughout the war. Used for bombing raids, night fighting, interception, escort, and reconnaissance work, it shot down more Japanese planes than any other aircraft during World War II. Its twin engines mounted on pods allowed it to carry heavier armaments than its competitors.

US AMPHIBIOUS WARFARE

In the Pacific, the campaigns were often fought over far-flung archipelagos. As a result, the US Marine Corps developed particular expertise in amphibious landings, which drove the Japanese from their island strongholds.

△ **War tales**
The Marine campaigns in the Pacific sparked a lively industry in books relating their exploits, such as this 1961 publication.

Following the Japanese attack on the US naval base at Pearl Harbor, Hawaii, in December 1941, the US joined World War II. It was clear from the start that the US Marine Corps—established during the American Revolution as the navy's land-fighting force—would be necessary to defend and recapture a series of island groups in the Pacific from the Japanese.

Marines on board

Although the Marines were involved in defensive campaigns early in the war, they came into their own in August 1942, when their special forces Raider battalions mounted highly effective raids during the invasion of Guadalcanal (see pp.128–129). In the island-hopping campaigns through the Marshall and Gilbert islands in 1943 (see pp.210–211), the Marines developed true amphibious assault capability, landing tanks and other assault vehicles. By 1945, the Marine Corps had expanded to six divisions, including parachute battalions and defense garrison battalions. They took part in most major operations, including the hard-fought battles for the Japanese islands of Iwo Jima (see pp.250–251) and Okinawa (see pp.254–255); at the latter, fierce resistance cost the Marines 3,440 dead and 15,487 wounded.

SPECIALIZED LANDING CRAFT

From mid-1943, the Marines used tank landing ships, with lowerable bow doors, to deliver tanks and other vehicles directly to beaches. Among the vehicles they carried was the Weasel—an armored troop carrier, which sometimes carried weapons and had tracks to prevent it becoming bogged down in wet sand.

An M29C
Weasel

Beach landing
Marines wade ashore, their rifles held high above the water, at Cape Gloucester, on the island of New Britain, Papua New Guinea, in December 1943. The aim of the operation was to capture a Japanese airfield that dominated the island.

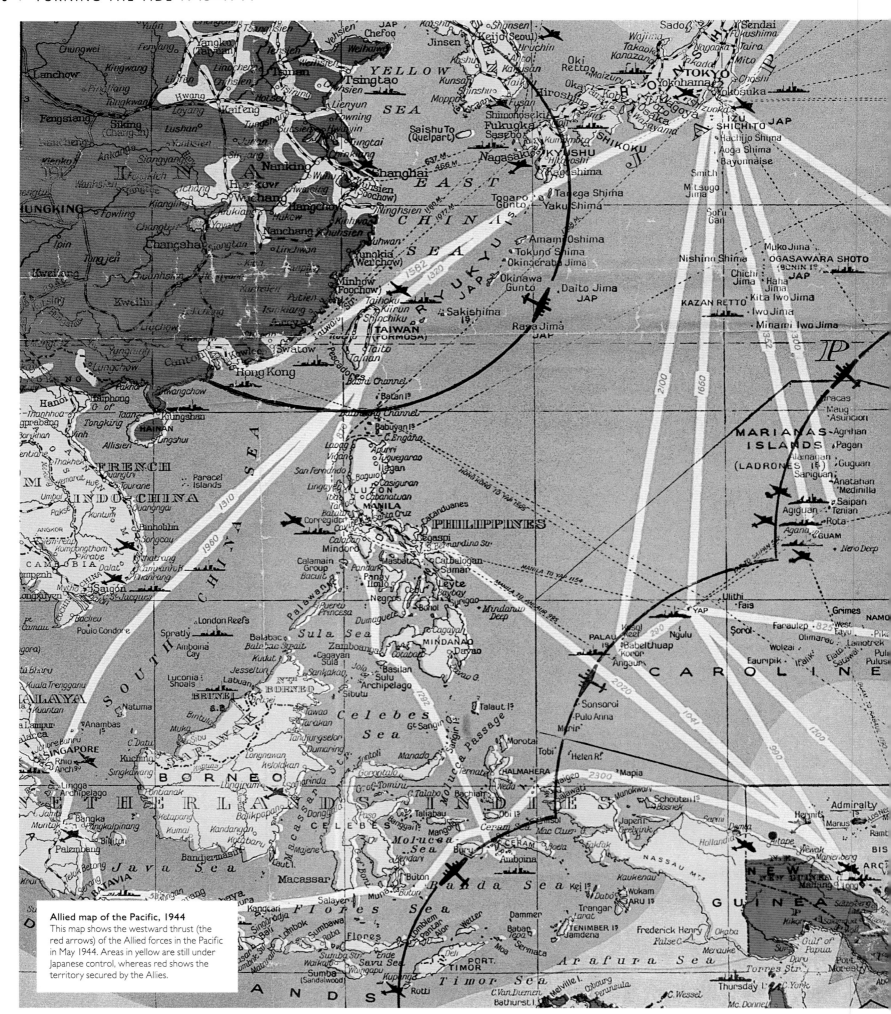

Allied map of the Pacific, 1944
This map shows the westward thrust (the red arrows) of the Allied forces in the Pacific in May 1944. Areas in yellow are still under Japanese control, whereas red shows the territory secured by the Allies.

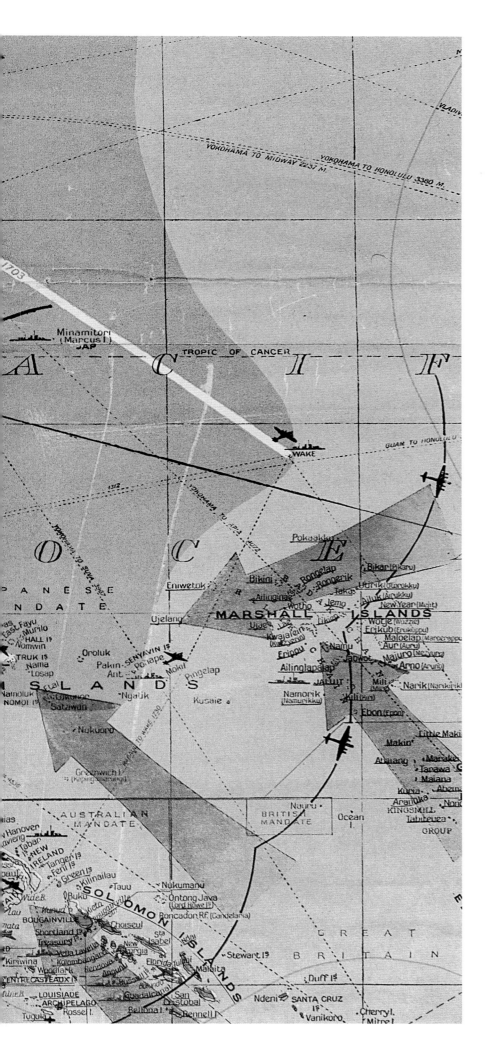

ISLAND-HOPPING IN THE PACIFIC

In autumn 1943, the US Navy and Marines initiated a drive across the central Pacific toward the Marianas. Advancing island by island, they took the war ever closer to the Japanese home islands, but at a heavy cost in lives.

Nearly two years after entering the war, the Japanese still held most of the far-flung defensive perimeter they had established in the Pacific (see pp.106–107), which stretched as far as the remote Gilbert and Marshall Islands (right-hand edge of the map). An American fightback in these islands was initially delayed by a lack of naval resources, but by November 1943, US Admiral Chester Nimitz was ready to take the offensive. Operation Cartwheel (see pp.206–207) was already under way in the Solomon Islands and New Guinea (bottom right on the map). Nimitz's first targets were Tarawa and Makin, tiny coral atolls in the Gilbert Islands. He was able to deploy a fleet of 17 aircraft carriers and 12 battleships—enough to prevent any major intervention by the Imperial Japanese Navy. The assault force possessed an array of landing craft and amphibious vehicles developed for Pacific operations.

Fierce defense

Tarawa was defended by fewer than 3,000 Japanese soldiers, but their commander, Rear Admiral Keiji Shibazaki, had strengthened the atoll's defenses. It took 18,000 US Marines four days to seize Tarawa, at a cost of over 1,000 dead and 2,000 wounded. The Japanese fought suicidally to the end; only 17 of the island's defenders survived. Another 66 US Army soldiers were killed in the simultaneous assault on Makin Atoll (Butaritari), while the navy lost 644 men when an escort carrier was sunk by a Japanese submarine. The scale of the casualties in taking such relatively minor objectives was a shock to the Americans.

The next targets were the Marshall Islands, which had been a Japanese mandate since 1920. The main fighting occurred at Eniwetok Atoll and Kwajalein Atoll. The Americans had learned lessons from Tarawa, but still suffered over 1,000 casualties. Further west, the major Japanese naval base at Truk (Chuuk) Lagoon in the Caroline Islands was devastated by US aircraft. Japan's defensive perimeter was disintegrating, and the path to the Mariana Islands (see pp.212–213) was opening up—with the eventual US aim of closing in on Japan itself.

▷ **Japanese prayer flag**
Japanese soldiers in World War II sometimes wore or carried flags inscribed with prayers from their loved ones to bring them luck.

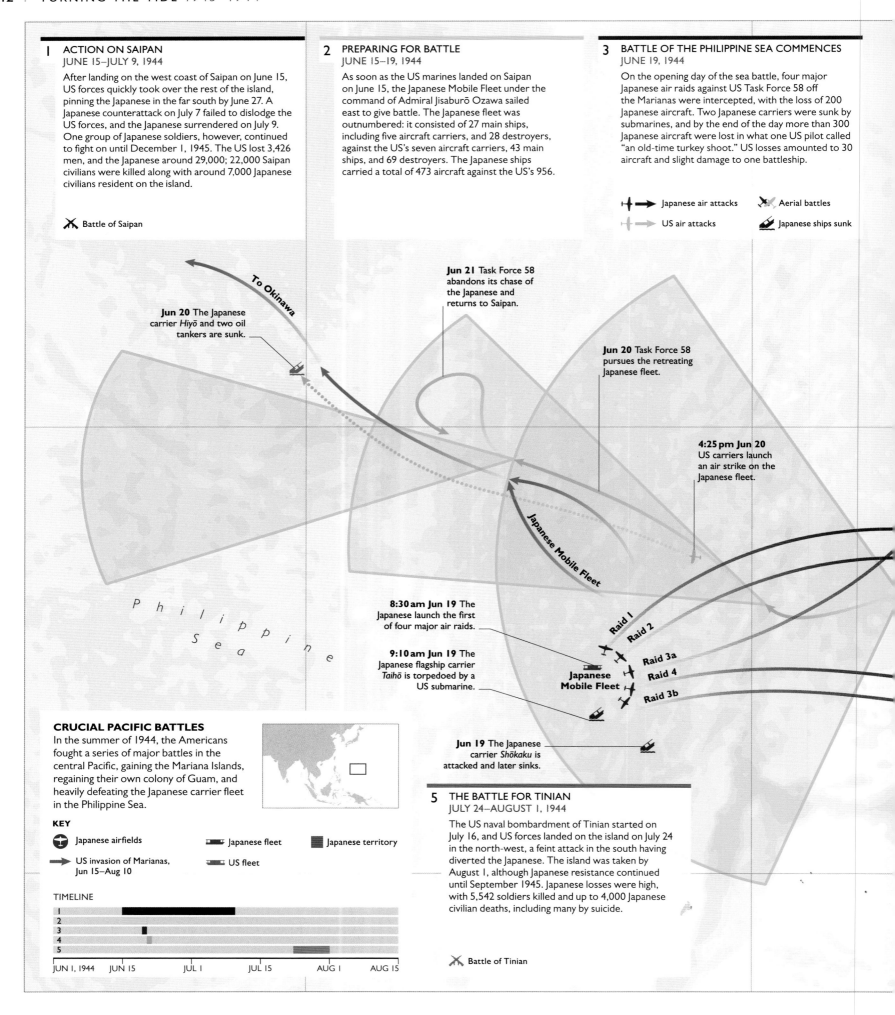

1 ACTION ON SAIPAN
JUNE 15–JULY 9, 1944

After landing on the west coast of Saipan on June 15, US forces quickly took over the rest of the island, pinning the Japanese in the far south by June 27. A Japanese counterattack on July 7 failed to dislodge the US forces, and the Japanese surrendered on July 9. One group of Japanese soldiers, however, continued to fight on until December 1, 1945. The US lost 3,426 men, and the Japanese around 29,000; 22,000 Saipan civilians were killed along with around 7,000 Japanese civilians resident on the island.

✕ Battle of Saipan

2 PREPARING FOR BATTLE
JUNE 15–19, 1944

As soon as the US marines landed on Saipan on June 15, the Japanese Mobile Fleet under the command of Admiral Jisaburō Ozawa sailed east to give battle. The Japanese fleet was outnumbered: it consisted of 27 main ships, including five aircraft carriers, and 28 destroyers, against the US's seven aircraft carriers, 43 main ships, and 69 destroyers. The Japanese ships carried a total of 473 aircraft against the US's 956.

3 BATTLE OF THE PHILIPPINE SEA COMMENCES
JUNE 19, 1944

On the opening day of the sea battle, four major Japanese air raids against US Task Force 58 off the Marianas were intercepted, with the loss of 200 Japanese aircraft. Two Japanese carriers were sunk by submarines, and by the end of the day more than 300 Japanese aircraft were lost in what one US pilot called "an old-time turkey shoot." US losses amounted to 30 aircraft and slight damage to one battleship.

⊢➤ Japanese air attacks ✕ Aerial battles

⊢⟶ US air attacks 🚢 Japanese ships sunk

Jun 21 Task Force 58 abandons its chase of the Japanese and returns to Saipan.

Jun 20 The Japanese carrier *Hiyō* and two oil tankers are sunk.

To Okinawa

Jun 20 Task Force 58 pursues the retreating Japanese fleet.

4:25 pm Jun 20 US carriers launch an air strike on the Japanese fleet.

Japanese Mobile Fleet

8:30 am Jun 19 The Japanese launch the first of four major air raids.

9:10 am Jun 19 The Japanese flagship carrier *Taihō* is torpedoed by a US submarine.

Raid 1
Raid 2
Raid 3a
Raid 4
Raid 3b

Japanese Mobile Fleet

Philippine Sea

Jun 19 The Japanese carrier *Shōkaku* is attacked and later sinks.

CRUCIAL PACIFIC BATTLES

In the summer of 1944, the Americans fought a series of major battles in the central Pacific, gaining the Mariana Islands, regaining their own colony of Guam, and heavily defeating the Japanese carrier fleet in the Philippine Sea.

KEY

🛪 Japanese airfields

➤ US invasion of Marianas, Jun 15–Aug 10

▭ Japanese fleet

▭ US fleet

▮ Japanese territory

5 THE BATTLE FOR TINIAN
JULY 24–AUGUST 1, 1944

The US naval bombardment of Tinian started on July 16, and US forces landed on the island on July 24 in the north-west, a feint attack in the south having diverted the Japanese. The island was taken by August 1, although Japanese resistance continued until September 1945. Japanese losses were high, with 5,542 soldiers killed and up to 4,000 Japanese civilian deaths, including many by suicide.

✕ Battle of Tinian

TIMELINE

1
2
3
4
5

JUN 1, 1944   JUN 15   JUL 1   JUL 15   AUG 1   AUG 15

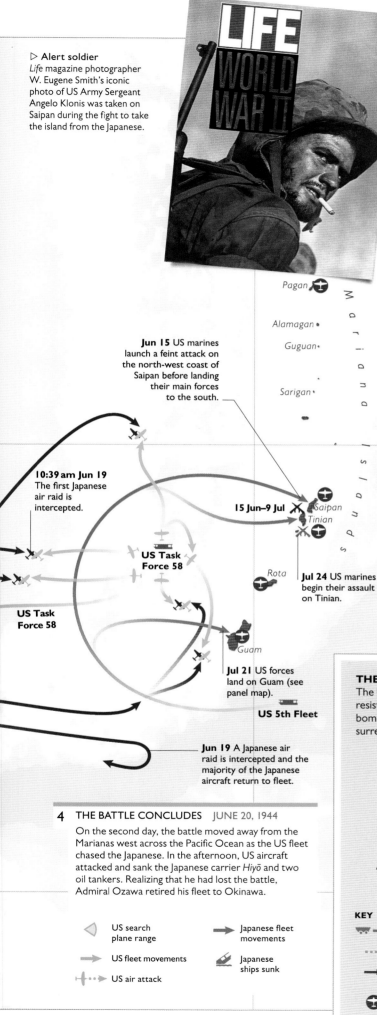

▷ **Alert soldier**
Life magazine photographer W. Eugene Smith's iconic photo of US Army Sergeant Angelo Klonis was taken on Saipan during the fight to take the island from the Japanese.

BATTLE FOR THE MARIANAS

In June 1944, the greatest carrier battle of the war took place in the central Pacific in the Battle of the Philippine Sea. The Japanese were roundly defeated by the US Navy, losing the bulk of their carrier fleet and control of the strategically important Marianas. The US moved within striking distance of the Japanese home islands.

By February 1944, the Americans had secured the Gilbert and the Marshall Islands (see pp.210–211), and destroyed the Japanese base on Truk Lagoon in the Caroline Islands. The next US objective was to capture the Mariana Islands, notably the main Japanese bases on Saipan, Tinian, and Guam. Possession of these islands would provide the US with bases for a bombing campaign against the Japanese mainland and enable them to cut Japan off from the Philippines and its other gains in Southeast Asia— a loss that the Japanese could not allow to go unchallenged.

The US began its offensive in June 1944, with the landing of Marines on Saipan, supported by the 5th Fleet. The Japanese Mobile Fleet under Admiral Jisaburō Ozawa responded by attacking the US Navy, but was defeated by superior US tactics, intelligence, and technology in the two-day Battle of the Philippine Sea.

The Japanese suffered a crippling blow, losing three of their carriers along with 445 carrier-based aircraft and over 200 aircraft from the Marianas. They were left with a vastly reduced number of planes and aircrew with which to equip their remaining carriers.

The two-day naval battle that took place in the Philippine Sea was the last of the five major carrier-versus-carrier battles of the Pacific War, and the largest carrier battle in history.

Jun 15 US marines launch a feint attack on the north-west coast of Saipan before landing their main forces to the south.

10:39 am Jun 19 The first Japanese air raid is intercepted.

15 Jun–9 Jul

US Task Force 58

US Task Force 58

Pagan

Alamagan

Guguan

Sarigan

Saipan
Tinian

Rota

Guam

Jul 24 US marines begin their assault on Tinian.

Jul 21 US forces land on Guam (see panel map).

US 5th Fleet

Jun 19 A Japanese air raid is intercepted and the majority of the Japanese aircraft return to fleet.

4 THE BATTLE CONCLUDES JUNE 20, 1944

On the second day, the battle moved away from the Marianas west across the Pacific Ocean as the US fleet chased the Japanese. In the afternoon, US aircraft attacked and sank the Japanese carrier *Hiyō* and two oil tankers. Realizing that he had lost the battle, Admiral Ozawa retired his fleet to Okinawa.

KEY			
◁	US search plane range	⟶	Japanese fleet movements
⟶	US fleet movements	🚢	Japanese ships sunk
✈···⟶	US air attack		

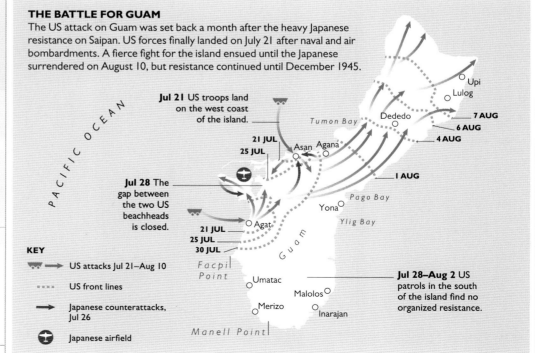

THE BATTLE FOR GUAM
The US attack on Guam was set back a month after the heavy Japanese resistance on Saipan. US forces finally landed on July 21 after naval and air bombardments. A fierce fight for the island ensued until the Japanese surrendered on August 10, but resistance continued until December 1945.

Jul 21 US troops land on the west coast of the island.

Jul 28 The gap between the two US beachheads is closed.

Upi
Lulog
Dededo
Tumon Bay
Asan Agana
Pago Bay
Yona
Ylig Bay
Agat
Umatac
Merizo
Malolos
Inarajan
Facpil Point
Manell Point
Guam

21 JUL / 25 JUL
21 JUL / 25 JUL / 30 JUL

7 AUG
6 AUG
4 AUG
1 AUG

Jul 28–Aug 2 US patrols in the south of the island find no organized resistance.

KEY	
🛥⟶	US attacks Jul 21–Aug 10
·····	US front lines
⟶	Japanese counterattacks, Jul 26
✈	Japanese airfield

PACIFIC OCEAN

THE BATTLE OF LEYTE GULF

On March 11, 1942, US General Douglas MacArthur and his family left the Philippines after his forces were surrounded by Japanese troops. He famously stated that: "I came through and I shall return." On October 20, 1944, he fulfilled that vow when US troops landed on Leyte Island in the eastern Philippines.

After capturing most of the Mariana Islands (see pp.212–213), the US Joint Chiefs of Staff debated what move to make next. Some favored an attack on Taiwan—part of the Japanese Empire—or putting additional resources into the war in China, but General MacArthur successfully championed an attack on the Philippines. His personal affront was to be avenged.

US forces landed at Leyte Gulf in the Philippines on October 20, a move that caused the Japanese to summon much of their remaining navy to fend off the invasion. Allied fleets met the Japanese fleet in a series of engagements around the Philippines over the next three days.

Cumulatively, these engagements constituted the largest naval battle of the war. They involved 70 Japanese warships and 210 American and Australian vessels, and resulted in the shattering of Japanese sea power. The Japanese lost 28 ships and more than 300 aircraft; moreover, their ability to move oil and other key resources from Southeast Asia to their home islands was destroyed. In comparison, the US suffered far lighter losses of six ships and around 200 aircraft.

The US secured beachheads on Leyte and opened the road for their forces to recover the entire Philippine archipelago (see pp.248–249).

> "Leyte was tantamount to the loss of the Philippines ... I felt that it was the end."
>
> ADMIRAL MITSUMASA YONAI, JAPANESE NAVY MINISTER, 1946

GENERAL DOUGLAS MACARTHUR

Douglas MacArthur (1880–1964) was Chief of Staff of the US Army from 1930 to 1935, before retiring from active service in 1937 to become military advisor to the Philippine government. Recalled to active duty in 1941 as commander of the US Army Forces in the Far East, he was forced out of the Philippines by the Japanese in 1942, returning in 1944 and officially accepting Japan's surrender in September 1945. His successes in World War II made him a hugely popular public figure in the US.

General Douglas MacArthur with his famous corn cob pipe

Japanese 2nd Striking Force

△ **Leyte liberated**
US soldiers and members of the US Coast Guard pose with a Japanese battle flag, which they captured while taking a beach on Leyte Island.

South China Sea

5 BATTLE OF CAPE ENGAÑO
OCTOBER 24–25, 1944

The Japanese sent a decoy carrier force to the north-east of the Philippines to lure the US fleet away from Leyte Gulf. Three US task groups sailed north to engage the carrier fleet. Though they lost the light carrier USS *Princeton*, sunk by land-based aircraft on October 24, the US groups sank four Japanese carriers and five other ships.

→ Japanese decoy carrier force movements

✕ Battle of Cape Engaño, Oct 25, 1944

→ US task force movements

⊦■■▶ US air attacks from carrier task force

⊻ US aircraft carrier sunk

⊻ Japanese aircraft carrier sunk

Oct 23 US submarines sink Japanese cruisers *Atago* and *Maya* to the west of Palawan Island.

4 THE BATTLE OF SURIGAO STRAIT
OCTOBER 24–25, 1944

Japanese Task Force C sailed east from Borneo into the Surigao Strait; it was soon followed there by the 2nd Striking Force, which had sailed from Taiwan to the north. The Japanese vessels encountered US and Australian cruisers, destroyers, and torpedo boats in the early hours of October 25. All but one of the seven vessels of Task Force C were destroyed before the Japanese withdrew, and most of the remaining fleet was sunk in later engagements around Leyte.

→ Japanese Task Force C

✕ Battle of Surigao Strait, Oct 25, 1944

→ Japanese 2nd Striking Force

Palawan Passage

Palawan

Japanese Task force A

Japanese Task force C

North Borneo

Brunei Bay

Brunei

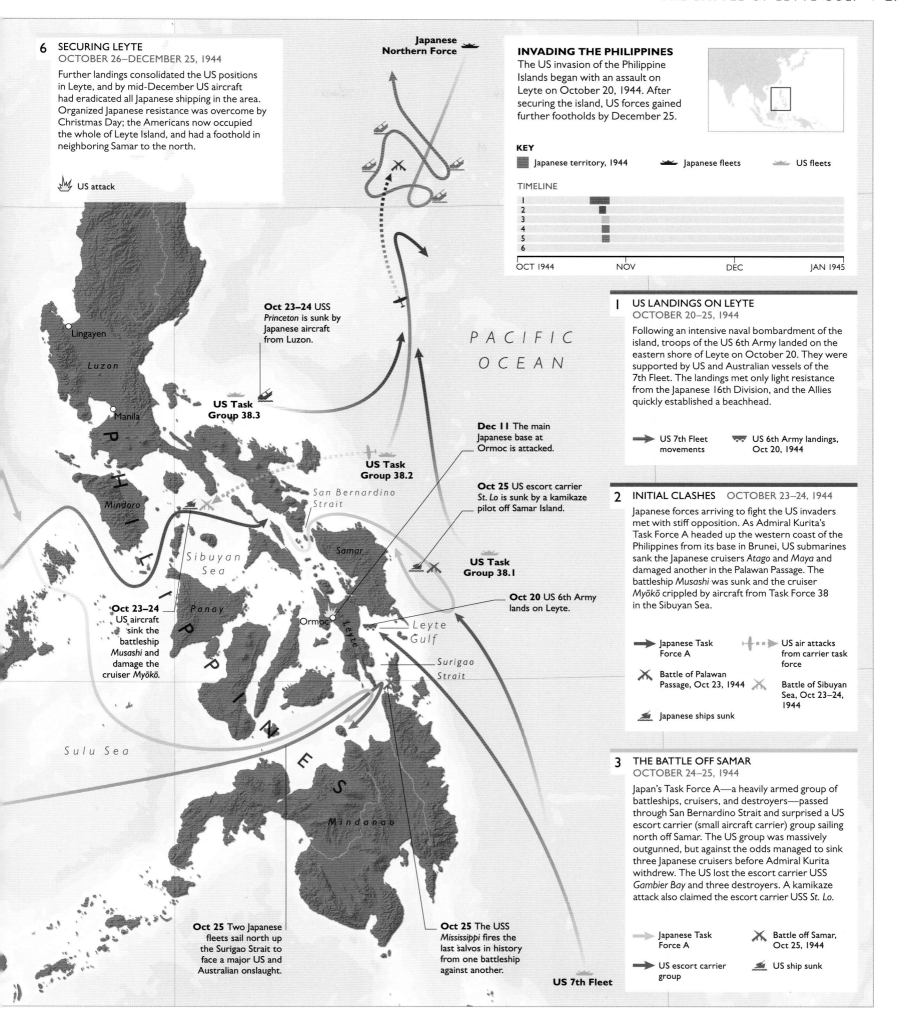

Japanese Northern Force

6 SECURING LEYTE
OCTOBER 26–DECEMBER 25, 1944

Further landings consolidated the US positions in Leyte, and by mid-December US aircraft had eradicated all Japanese shipping in the area. Organized Japanese resistance was overcome by Christmas Day; the Americans now occupied the whole of Leyte Island, and had a foothold in neighboring Samar to the north.

★ US attack

INVADING THE PHILIPPINES

The US invasion of the Philippine Islands began with an assault on Leyte on October 20, 1944. After securing the island, US forces gained further footholds by December 25.

KEY

▰ Japanese territory, 1944   ⬟ Japanese fleets   ⬟ US fleets

TIMELINE

1	
2	
3	
4	
5	
6	

OCT 1944   NOV   DEC   JAN 1945

Oct 23–24 USS *Princeton* is sunk by Japanese aircraft from Luzon.

US Task Group 38.3

US Task Group 38.2

Dec 11 The main Japanese base at Ormoc is attacked.

Oct 25 US escort carrier *St. Lo* is sunk by a kamikaze pilot off Samar Island.

US Task Group 38.1

Oct 23–24 US aircraft sink the battleship *Musashi* and damage the cruiser *Myōkō*.

Oct 20 US 6th Army lands on Leyte.

Oct 25 Two Japanese fleets sail north up the Surigao Strait to face a major US and Australian onslaught.

Oct 25 The USS *Mississippi* fires the last salvos in history from one battleship against another.

US 7th Fleet

Lingayen
Luzon
Manila
Mindoro
Sibuyan Sea
Panay
Ormoc
Samar
Leyte Gulf
Surigao Strait
Sulu Sea
Mindanao
San Bernardino Strait

PACIFIC OCEAN

PHILIPPINES

---

1 US LANDINGS ON LEYTE
OCTOBER 20–25, 1944

Following an intensive naval bombardment of the island, troops of the US 6th Army landed on the eastern shore of Leyte on October 20. They were supported by US and Australian vessels of the 7th Fleet. The landings met only light resistance from the Japanese 16th Division, and the Allies quickly established a beachhead.

➡ US 7th Fleet movements   ⬇ US 6th Army landings, Oct 20, 1944

---

2 INITIAL CLASHES   OCTOBER 23–24, 1944

Japanese forces arriving to fight the US invaders met with stiff opposition. As Admiral Kurita's Task Force A headed up the western coast of the Philippines from its base in Brunei, US submarines sank the Japanese cruisers *Atago* and *Maya* and damaged another in the Palawan Passage. The battleship *Musashi* was sunk and the cruiser *Myōkō* crippled by aircraft from Task Force 38 in the Sibuyan Sea.

➡ Japanese Task Force A   ⊢⊣→ US air attacks from carrier task force

✗ Battle of Palawan Passage, Oct 23, 1944   ✗ Battle of Sibuyan Sea, Oct 23–24, 1944

⬟ Japanese ships sunk

---

3 THE BATTLE OFF SAMAR
OCTOBER 24–25, 1944

Japan's Task Force A—a heavily armed group of battleships, cruisers, and destroyers—passed through San Bernardino Strait and surprised a US escort carrier (small aircraft carrier) group sailing north off Samar. The US group was massively outgunned, but against the odds managed to sink three Japanese cruisers before Admiral Kurita withdrew. The US lost the escort carrier USS *Gambier Bay* and three destroyers. A kamikaze attack also claimed the escort carrier USS *St. Lo*.

➡ Japanese Task Force A   ✗ Battle off Samar, Oct 25, 1944

➡ US escort carrier group   ⬟ US ship sunk

KAMIKAZE TACTICS

In 1944, the Japanese military ordered suicide pilots—known as kamikaze—into action, in a desperate attempt to stem the tide of defeat. Thousands of volunteers enlisted to undertake crash-dive attacks with their planes, prepared to sacrifice their lives for Japan.

△ **Propaganda poster**
Japanese posters such as this one glorified kamikaze missions. Many young Japanese, often students, came forward to volunteer.

Toward the end of 1944, Japan was in a critical situation. The country had suffered catastrophic military defeats, both the navy and air force had lost their offensive capability, and a diminished economy meant resources were limited. The civilian population of Japan was mobilized for defense, but due to lack of funds some were armed only with bamboo spears.

Realizing that conventional bombing methods would not halt the advancing American forces, the Japanese high command attempted to decimate the US fleet by initiating mass suicide attacks. Named after the "divine wind" that, according to Japanese legend, had scattered an invading Mongol fleet in 1274, the kamikaze suicide bombers were the brainchild of Vice-Admiral Onishi Takijuro. Volunteer pilots were instructed to crash-dive planes laden with explosives, torpedoes, and full fuel tanks into Allied warships. The operation, code named Floating Chrysanthemum, drew upon the Japanese military tradition of death being more honorable and less shameful than defeat, capture, and surrender.

The first kamikaze attacks were launched against the American fleet on October 25, 1944, at the Battle of Leyte Gulf (see pp.214–215), and the attacks continued until the end of the war. In total, the use of kamikaze strikes resulted in the loss of 34 US ships, and a further 368 US vessels were badly damaged.

THE PILOTS

The average age of kamikazes was between 17 and 20 years old, and some of them had as few as 40 hours of flying experience before they were sent on their final mission. More than 2,500 kamikazes had sacrificed their lives by the end of World War II, and their success rate is estimated at around 19 percent.

Attack on USS *Bunker Hill*
US aircraft carrier *Bunker Hill* blazes after being attacked by two kamikazes off Okinawa on May 11, 1945. The two planes plunged into the carrier's flight deck, heavily damaging the ship and forcing it to retire for repair.

THE FIGHTBACK IN BURMA

Occupied by Japan in spring 1942, Burma was recaptured by British Empire troops toward the end of the war. The campaign was characterized by tactical innovation and fierce jungle fighting.

When the Japanese invaded Burma in 1942, they stopped at the border with British India, having achieved their goal to cut the Allied supply route from the port of Rangoon (shown here, right) to Nationalist China. Any attempt to recapture Burma by an advance from north-east India would involve fighting across formidable terrain of mountain and jungle. The difficulty of conducting such an offensive led the Allies to develop Long Range Penetration groups—specially trained infantry dropped into the jungle by parachute or glider. These groups—the British Chindits led by General Orde Wingate, and their American equivalents, Merrill's Marauders, under General Frank Merrill— operated for months behind Japanese lines in 1943–1944, carrying out guerrilla attacks on troops and communications.

In response, the Japanese mounted an offensive across the Indian border into Assam. Their 15th Army under General Renya Mutaguchi advanced swiftly northward in March 1944, surrounding more than 100,000 troops of the British Indian Army at Imphal. They also attacked Kohima on the road north of Imphal, where a garrison of 1,500 men came under siege on April 4. By the time the undernourished and disease-ridden Japanese troops were forced to withdraw into Burma in July, they had suffered more than 50,000 casualties.

The drive to Rangoon

The failed Assam invasion left the Japanese vulnerable to an Allied counteroffensive. British and Indian forces under General William Slim pressed southward from Imphal, crossing the Irrawaddy River south of Mandalay in February 1945. Meanwhile, Chinese Nationalist troops cleared the Japanese from north-eastern Burma. After Slim's forces captured Mandalay and the important road junction at Meiktila, they met determined counterattacks, but the balance of forces had swung against the Japanese. Burmese anti-colonialists, who had welcomed the Japanese in 1942, switched sides, and the Burma National Army joined in the British advance to Rangoon. The British secured the port city in May after amphibious landings.

◁ **Burma patrol**
Allied soldiers search for Japanese soldiers. After May 1945, Japanese troops remained in Burma but their operations were of little significance.

Intelligence gathering, Rangoon
A map created by British Intelligence in April 1945 shows features of strategic importance in the Burmese port city of Rangoon. After capturing Mandalay in March 1945, the Allies sought to take Rangoon before the onset of the monsoon season in May.

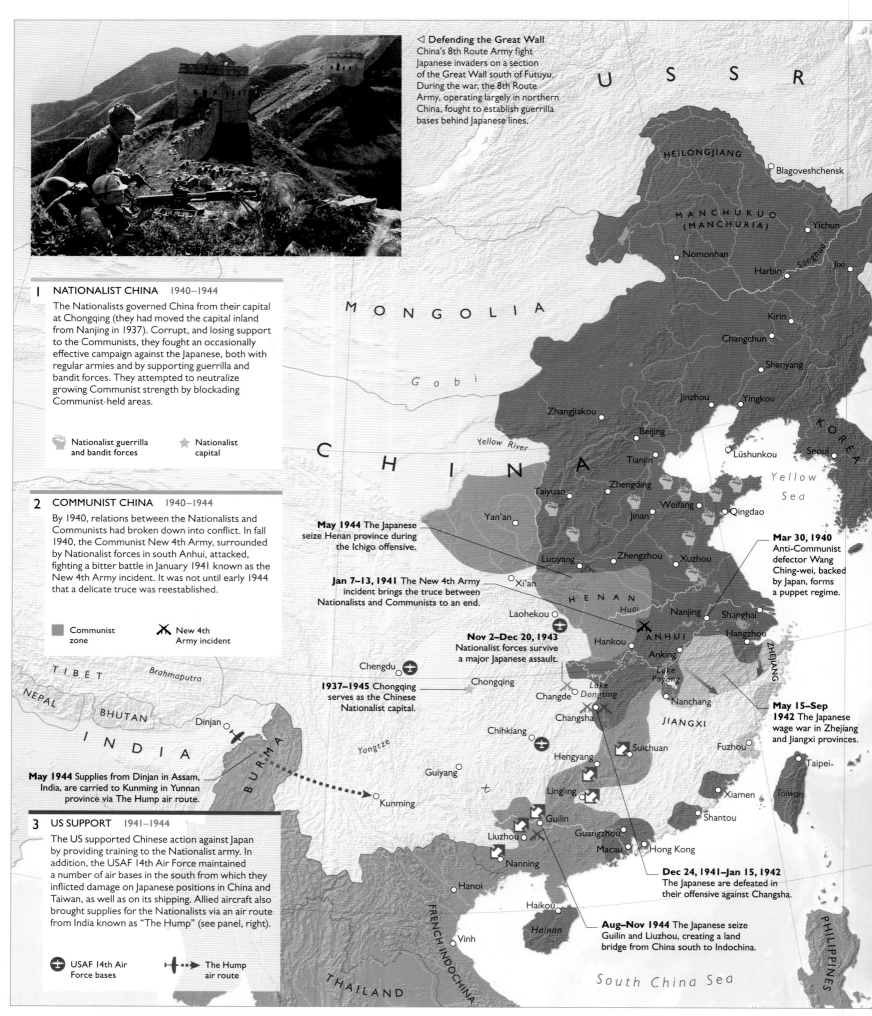

◁ **Defending the Great Wall**
China's 8th Route Army fight Japanese invaders on a section of the Great Wall south of Futuyu. During the war, the 8th Route Army, operating largely in northern China, fought to establish guerrilla bases behind Japanese lines.

1 NATIONALIST CHINA 1940–1944

The Nationalists governed China from their capital at Chongqing (they had moved the capital inland from Nanjing in 1937). Corrupt, and losing support to the Communists, they fought an occasionally effective campaign against the Japanese, both with regular armies and by supporting guerrilla and bandit forces. They attempted to neutralize growing Communist strength by blockading Communist-held areas.

🖐 Nationalist guerrilla and bandit forces

★ Nationalist capital

2 COMMUNIST CHINA 1940–1944

By 1940, relations between the Nationalists and Communists had broken down into conflict. In fall 1940, the Communist New 4th Army, surrounded by Nationalist forces in south Anhui, attacked, fighting a bitter battle in January 1941 known as the New 4th Army incident. It was not until early 1944 that a delicate truce was reestablished.

⬛ Communist zone

✕ New 4th Army incident

3 US SUPPORT 1941–1944

The US supported Chinese action against Japan by providing training to the Nationalist army. In addition, the USAF 14th Air Force maintained a number of air bases in the south from which they inflicted damage on Japanese positions in China and Taiwan, as well as on its shipping. Allied aircraft also brought supplies for the Nationalists via an air route from India known as "The Hump" (see panel, right).

✈ USAF 14th Air Force bases

✈--▶ The Hump air route

May 1944 The Japanese seize Henan province during the Ichigo offensive.

Jan 7–13, 1941 The New 4th Army incident brings the truce between Nationalists and Communists to an end.

Nov 2–Dec 20, 1943 Nationalist forces survive a major Japanese assault.

1937–1945 Chongqing serves as the Chinese Nationalist capital.

May 1944 Supplies from Dinjan in Assam, India, are carried to Kunming in Yunnan province via The Hump air route.

Mar 30, 1940 Anti-Communist defector Wang Ching-wei, backed by Japan, forms a puppet regime.

May 15–Sep 1942 The Japanese wage war in Zhejiang and Jiangxi provinces.

Dec 24, 1941–Jan 15, 1942 The Japanese are defeated in their offensive against Changsha.

Aug–Nov 1944 The Japanese seize Guilin and Liuzhou, creating a land bridge from China south to Indochina.

4 EARLY JAPANESE OFFENSIVES
DECEMBER 1941–SEPTEMBER 1942

The first major Japanese attack in China after Pearl Harbor began in late December 1941 and resulted in defeat at the hands of the Nationalists at Changsha. In May 1942, the Japanese launched an offensive in the provinces of Zhejiang and Jiangxi aimed at destroying US air bases and punishing the Chinese who supported US activity. More than 250,000 Chinese civilians were killed by Japanese biological weapons.

- Japan and its territories by 1941
- Japanese gains in China 1941–1942
- Other regions under Japanese control 1941–1942
- Battle site
- Japanese advances in Zhejiang–Jiangxi

5 STALEMATE   JUNE 1942–DECEMBER 1943

Little action took place in China after mid-1942 as the Japanese focused on other goals in the Pacific. In 1943 they launched a series of "rice offensives"— attacks designed to battle-harden their new troops and to seize food supplies from the starving Chinese. However, with US help the Chinese managed to fight the Japanese to a stalemate at Changde, a battle in which the Japanese continued to use chemical weapons, including mustard gas.

- Battle site

6 OPERATION ICHIGO
APRIL 19–DECEMBER 31, 1944

In 1944 Japan launched its largest campaign in China to create a land bridge between its conquests in the east of the country and its gains in Indochina, and to eradicate the US air bases supporting B-29 Superfortress bombers. The Japanese fought three major battles with the Chinese. Losses were huge, with the Chinese suffering up to 700,000 casualties.

- Battle sites
- Captured US air bases
- Territory held by the Japanese after Operation Ichigo

JAPANESE CHINA

By 1941, Japan controlled much of northern and eastern China. After sporadic fighting between Japanese and Nationalist Chinese, the Japanese made advances in the south and center during Operation Ichigo in 1944, with both sides suffering major casualties.

TIMELINE

1940 · 1941 · 1942 · 1943 · 1944 · 1945

CHINA AND JAPAN AT WAR

Despite a truce between China's Nationalist and Communist factions following the Japanese invasion in 1937, wartime China remained bitterly divided. Japan sought to capitalize on this, stretching its resources across China to wage an eight-year expansionist war.

While bitter fighting had raged between Chinese and Japanese forces since 1937, after the Japanese attack on Pearl Harbor in December 1941 the conflict became incorporated into the larger war that erupted in the Pacific. The US provided air and military support from India for the Nationalists, who managed to inflict several defeats on the Japanese, but the aid was never enough to turn the tide of the war in favor of the Chinese. Japan's offensives in the months following Pearl Harbor were sporadic, with attacks on US air bases in the south of China as well as the massacre of 250,000 civilians using biological agents such as cholera and typhoid. Further offensives in 1943 were also accompanied by chemical weapons. It was not until 1944 that Japan launched a huge offensive, Operation Ichigo, in which 500,000 troops attempted to carve out a path to Japanese-occupied Indochina and remove the threat from the US air bases used to bomb Japanese cities. The campaign was a success, and the Japanese largely kept the gains from Operation Ichigo until the end of the war.

> *"The Greater East Asian War was justified and righteous."*
>
> HIDEKI TOJO, FORMER JAPANESE PRIME MINISTER, 1946

FLYING THE HUMP

In 1942, the US set up an air route from Assam in India to supply Nationalist Chinese forces across the country. Nicknamed "The Hump" by pilots, it passed over the eastern end of the Himalayas, and was extremely dangerous due to consistently poor weather and a lack of charts and radio navigation aids. By August 1945, more than 728,000 tons (660,000 metric tons) of materiel had been flown in to China, with a great loss of Allied aircraft.

A US Army transport flies over the Himalayas

The bridge to Saigon
Japanese troops head into Saigon, in French
Indochina, in 1940 as part of an invasion that
secured the French colonies by 1941. The
French administered Indochina until March
1945, when the Japanese took control until
the war's end.

JAPANESE RULE IN EAST ASIA

Japan acquired an extensive colonial empire before and during World War II, in part to secure raw material supplies for its economy. Little political freedom was permitted in its colonies, and conditions were harsh.

Before World War I, Japan had annexed Taiwan and Korea, and it acquired former German Pacific islands as mandates after the war. In the 1930s it invaded Manchuria, large parts of eastern China, and Southeast Asia from 1940 (see pp.106–107). Where possible, the economies of these territories were shaped to supply Japan's war effort; steel production in Manchuria increased, agricultural output rose in Taiwan, and electricity production soared in Korea.

Little consideration was given to local needs, and there were widespread food shortages. Many thousands of women were forced into sexual slavery as "comfort women" for the army. Japan also clamped down harshly on dissent. Allied prisoners of war (POWs) suffered greatly, including the 80,000 taken when Singapore fell in February 1942. The Japanese military code looked down on surrender, and Allied POWs routinely received minimal rations, were beaten, and were put to hard labor, including constructing the Burma railway, through 260 miles (420km) of mountainous jungle. The death toll was high—of the 36,000 US troops taken prisoner by the Japanese, almost 40 percent died.

△ **Pan-Asian solidarity**
Japanese propaganda extolled the virtues of pan-Asian solidarity, such as on this poster, which promotes cooperation between Manchuria, Japan, and China.

GREATER EAST ASIA CONFERENCE

In 1940, the Japanese government announced a Greater East Asia Co-Prosperity Sphere. Ostensibly a bloc of Asian powers to promote prosperity and political freedom, it was in reality completely directed by Japan. At its 1943 Conference in Tokyo, pro-Japanese leaders attended, such as Ba Maw of Burma (far left) and José P. Laurel of the Philippines (second from right).

ENDGAME AND AFTERMATH 1944–1955

AS THE WAR REACHED ITS FINALE IN EUROPE, THE US AND JAPAN INTENSIFIED THEIR BITTER STRUGGLE IN THE PACIFIC. THE DROPPING OF THE ATOMIC BOMB USHERED IN A NEW AND UNCERTAIN ERA.

ALLIED VICTORY IN EUROPE

Hitler's determination to fight to the finish condemned Germany to massive destruction in the final phase of the war in Europe. However, victory for the Allies was not achieved until Soviet troops raised the hammer and sickle flag over the ruins of Berlin.

△ **The face of war**
A soldier from an SS panzer division shows signs of combat exhaustion during the Battle of the Bulge in the winter of 1944–1945.

In December 1944, with the Allies closing in on Germany, Hitler made a last attempt to turn the tide of the war, launching a surprise offensive in the Ardennes, in Belgium, Luxembourg, and northeastern France. The initial success of this operation—named the Battle of the Bulge because of the bulging shape created when the Germans pushed through the Allied front line—was testimony to the remarkable tenacity of the German army, but Hitler's plan for a decisive breakthrough failed. The US troops held key positions and once poor weather had cleared, the Allies could resume their air attacks, which were having a decisive effect. Meanwhile, the Germans were running out of fuel.

▷ **Meeting at Torgau**
US and Soviet troops meet in friendly fashion at Torgau, on the Elbe, as the Allies overrun Germany from east and west in April 1945.

False hopes

By January 1945, with the Ardennes offensive failing and Soviet troops ready to invade Germany from the east, the German position seemed hopeless. However, the Nazi regime retained the will to fight and many of its people remained loyal. While the Führer dreamed of miracles, young and old were marshalled for a final, desperate homeland defense. Hitler's remaining hope was for the Western Allies and the Soviet Union to have a major disagreement, but this did not happen. The Yalta conference of Allied leaders in February confirmed broad agreement on the immediate practical concerns of the wartime alliance, such as the military occupation of Germany, while skirting around more intractable future political issues. There was no "race for Berlin"; instead, the Western Allies were content to let the Soviets enjoy the honor—and suffer the casualties—involved in taking the city.

Carnage on an epic scale

The scale of the destruction and disruption in the last months of the war was staggering. The resumption of the Soviet advance in January 1945 triggered the mass evacuation of German civilians from East Prussia and the Baltic. Having won control of the air over Germany at great cost, the Allied air forces proceeded to destroy German towns and cities in attacks that no longer served any clear military purpose.

As Soviet forces fought their way into Berlin in late April, US and Soviet troops met at the Elbe River. The discovery of the Nazi death

THE THIRD REICH'S LAST STAND

The Ardennes operation, launched on December 16, 1944, was the German army's last offensive. The Soviet advance on Germany, which began in January 1945, carried the fighting deep into the country, and the Western Allies crossed the Rhine in March. The death of Roosevelt on April 12 gave Hitler a glimmer of hope, but it made no difference to the conduct of the war. Hostilities continued for a week after Hitler's suicide as surrenders were arranged on different fronts.

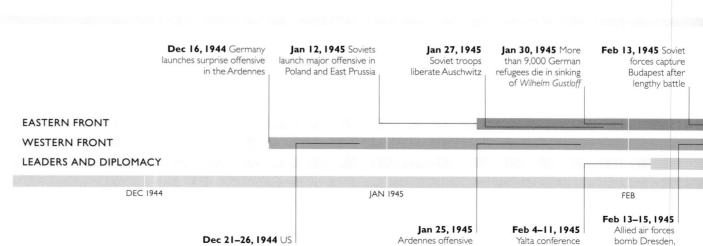

	Dec 16, 1944 Germany launches surprise offensive in the Ardennes	**Jan 12, 1945** Soviets launch major offensive in Poland and East Prussia	**Jan 27, 1945** Soviet troops liberate Auschwitz	**Jan 30, 1945** More than 9,000 German refugees die in sinking of *Wilhelm Gustloff*	**Feb 13, 1945** Soviet forces capture Budapest after lengthy battle

EASTERN FRONT
WESTERN FRONT
LEADERS AND DIPLOMACY

DEC 1944   JAN 1945   FEB

Dec 21–26, 1944 US troops hold out under siege at Bastogne

Jan 25, 1945 Ardennes offensive ends in costly German defeat

Feb 4–11, 1945 Yalta conference attended by Churchill, Roosevelt, and Stalin

Feb 13–15, 1945 Allied air forces bomb Dresden, killing some 35,000 people

◁ **Mustang fighter**
The North American Mustang P-51 was a key aircraft in the war's final stages, acting as a long-range fighter escort for bombers and as a ground-attack aircraft armed with rockets and bombs.

▽ **Raising the flag**
As a symbol of Soviet victory, soldiers raise a flag over the Reichstag building amid the ruins of Berlin on May 2, 1945.

camps shocked the advancing Allied forces. A series of German surrenders began in Italy, where Mussolini met a grim end at the hands of Italian partisans on April 28. Two days later, Hitler died by suicide at his Berlin bunker, denouncing the German army and people as unworthy of his leadership. On May 8, the war in Europe was declared over.

Allied-occupied Germany

The victors of World War II reigned over a continent in ruins. Political conflicts between Communists and their enemies were already surfacing before the war ended: for example in Greece, where British intervention prevented Communist-led partisans from taking power. But in Germany itself, where prolonged Nazi resistance had been expected and feared, there was instead only the struggle to survive or, in the case of prominent Nazis, to escape retribution. The Allies carried out their plan for the four-way division of Germany, including Berlin, into military occupation zones, France having won the right to be included in the share-out. Occupation by the Soviet Union was, to say the least, an ambiguous "liberation" for many of the peoples of Central and Eastern Europe. However, despite the suffering that followed, Europe could at least now hope to move toward a brighter future.

"This is your victory! It is the victory of freedom in every land."

WINSTON CHURCHILL, SPEECH, MAY 8, 1945

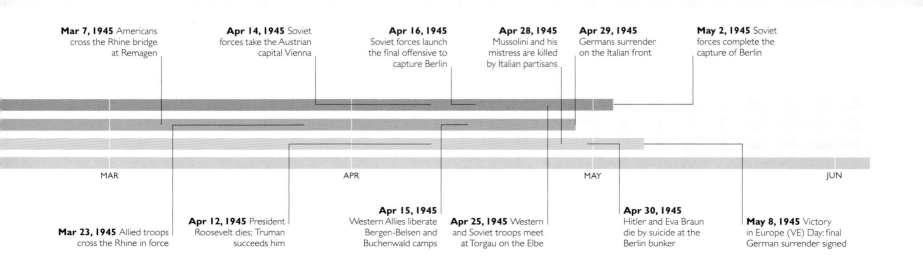

Mar 7, 1945 Americans cross the Rhine bridge at Remagen

Apr 14, 1945 Soviet forces take the Austrian capital Vienna

Apr 16, 1945 Soviet forces launch the final offensive to capture Berlin

Apr 28, 1945 Mussolini and his mistress are killed by Italian partisans

Apr 29, 1945 Germans surrender on the Italian front

May 2, 1945 Soviet forces complete the capture of Berlin

MAR   APR   MAY   JUN

Mar 23, 1945 Allied troops cross the Rhine in force

Apr 12, 1945 President Roosevelt dies; Truman succeeds him

Apr 15, 1945 Western Allies liberate Bergen-Belsen and Buchenwald camps

Apr 25, 1945 Western and Soviet troops meet at Torgau on the Elbe

Apr 30, 1945 Hitler and Eva Braun die by suicide at the Berlin bunker

May 8, 1945 Victory in Europe (VE) Day: final German surrender signed

2 GERMAN ADVANCE DECEMBER 17–20, 1944

The Germans pushed west for the next four days, and attempted to deploy paratroopers behind American lines. They had planned to take control of Antwerp by December 20, but were held up by American resistance, notably at St. Vith in the central sector and Bastogne in the south, both key road junctions.

→ German advance Dec 17–20, 1944

⚫ German paratroop drop zone

▪▪▪▪ Front lines Dec 20, 1944

3 THE FURTHEST POINT DECEMBER 21–24, 1944

The Germans reached the peak of their advance when they took Celles on December 24. Still 62 miles (100 km) short of Antwerp, the attacking units had failed to cross the Meuse River, held back by the Allied defensive force. The German vanguard was left occupying a narrow neck of land increasingly under threat from Allied pressure to the north and south.

→ German advance Dec 21–24, 1944

→ US counterattacks from Dec 24, 1944

EARLY ADVANCES

The most rapid German advance was in the central sector of the bulge, where Clervaux fell in three days.

Dec 17, 1944 German plans to land 1,300 paratroopers behind Allied lines fail.

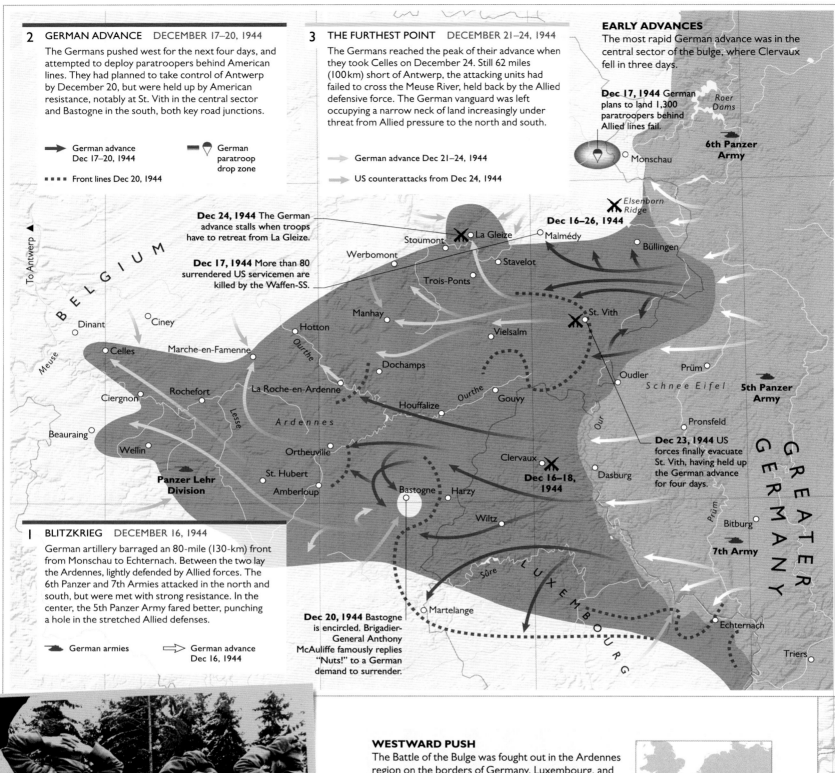

Dec 24, 1944 The German advance stalls when troops have to retreat from La Gleize.

Dec 17, 1944 More than 80 surrendered US servicemen are killed by the Waffen-SS.

Dec 23, 1944 US forces finally evacuate St. Vith, having held up the German advance for four days.

1 BLITZKRIEG DECEMBER 16, 1944

German artillery barraged an 80-mile (130-km) front from Monschau to Echternach. Between the two lay the Ardennes, lightly defended by Allied forces. The 6th Panzer and 7th Armies attacked in the north and south, but were met with strong resistance. In the center, the 5th Panzer Army fared better, punching a hole in the stretched Allied defenses.

▅ German armies

⇨ German advance Dec 16, 1944

Dec 20, 1944 Bastogne is encircled. Brigadier-General Anthony McAuliffe famously replies "Nuts!" to a German demand to surrender.

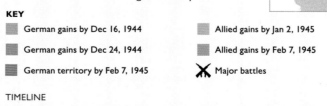

△ **German advance halted**
Captured German soldiers put their hands above their heads as they surrender to a US soldier, January 1945. Poor weather conditions coupled with Allied resistance at key junctions prevented the Germans reaching their goal.

WESTWARD PUSH

The Battle of the Bulge was fought out in the Ardennes region on the borders of Germany, Luxembourg, and Belgium. The German attack began on December 16, 1944, but their push westward was halted by the Allies, who eliminated the German gains in early 1945.

KEY

▨ German gains by Dec 16, 1944

▨ German gains by Dec 24, 1944

▨ German territory by Feb 7, 1945

▨ Allied gains by Jan 2, 1945

▨ Allied gains by Feb 7, 1945

✕ Major battles

TIMELINE

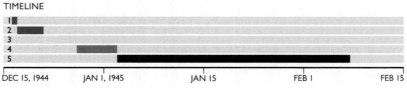

DEC 15, 1944   JAN 1, 1945   JAN 15   FEB 1   FEB 15

BATTLE OF THE BULGE

Shaken by the Allies' advance on Germany, Hitler decided on a final gamble in winter 1944. His counter-offensive punched a deep wedge in Allied lines, leading Western newspapers to call it the Battle of the Bulge. It was the last major German offensive of the war, and the largest fought on the Western Front.

Desperate to regain the initiative in Europe, Hitler chose a move that startled even his own generals: an attack through the hilly, wooded Ardennes region bordering Germany to the port of Antwerp in Belgium, covering 112 miles (180 km). This action was intended to cut the Allied forces in two and disrupt their supplies. Allied commanders had discounted the possibility of such an attack, so the assault achieved almost total surprise. However, the German forces soon encountered exactly those problems the military planners had foreseen. Poor roads led to transportation

bottlenecks and the winter weather made conditions difficult. Hitler's plan depended on an almost impossibly tight schedule, but his forces soon found themselves bogged down by the difficult terrain and held back by determined US resistance.

After three weeks, when it had become apparent that the planned breakthrough had not happened, Hitler ordered his troops back to Germany. The operation had been a huge failure. The killed and wounded on both sides numbered close to 100,000, and crucially Germany had also lost over 500 tanks and 1,000 aircraft.

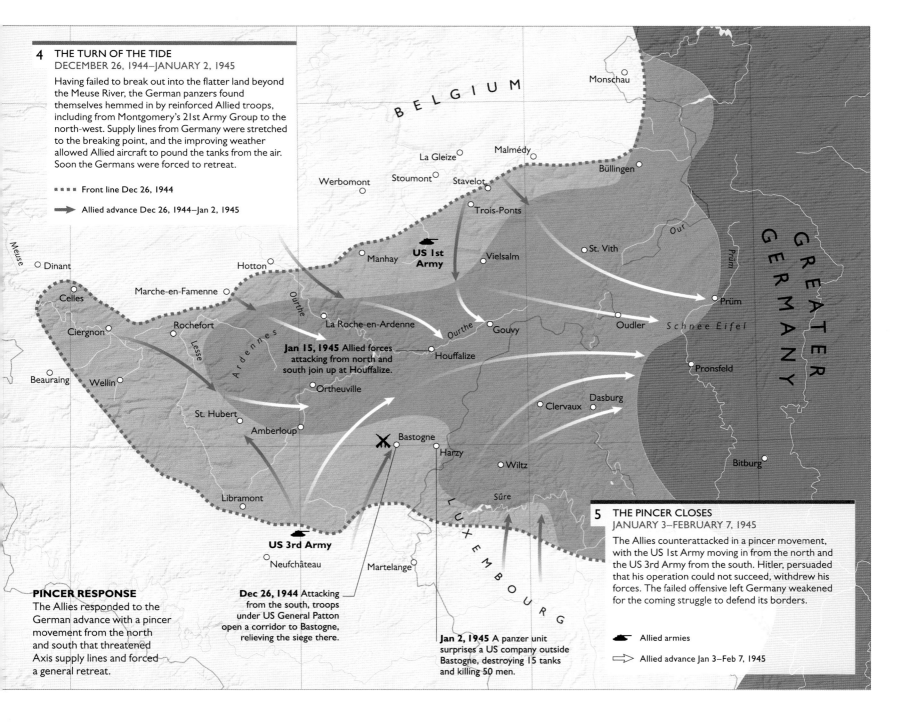

4 THE TURN OF THE TIDE
DECEMBER 26, 1944–JANUARY 2, 1945

Having failed to break out into the flatter land beyond the Meuse River, the German panzers found themselves hemmed in by reinforced Allied troops, including from Montgomery's 21st Army Group to the north-west. Supply lines from Germany were stretched to the breaking point, and the improving weather allowed Allied aircraft to pound the tanks from the air. Soon the Germans were forced to retreat.

▪▪▪▪ Front line Dec 26, 1944

➡ Allied advance Dec 26, 1944–Jan 2, 1945

Jan 15, 1945 Allied forces attacking from north and south join up at Houffalize.

US 1st Army

US 3rd Army

PINCER RESPONSE
The Allies responded to the German advance with a pincer movement from the north and south that threatened Axis supply lines and forced a general retreat.

Dec 26, 1944 Attacking from the south, troops under US General Patton open a corridor to Bastogne, relieving the siege there.

Jan 2, 1945 A panzer unit surprises a US company outside Bastogne, destroying 15 tanks and killing 50 men.

5 THE PINCER CLOSES
JANUARY 3–FEBRUARY 7, 1945

The Allies counterattacked in a pincer movement, with the US 1st Army moving in from the north and the US 3rd Army from the south. Hitler, persuaded that his operation could not succeed, withdrew his forces. The failed offensive left Germany weakened for the coming struggle to defend its borders.

◆ Allied armies

⇨ Allied advance Jan 3–Feb 7, 1945

YALTA AND POTSDAM

In February 1945, the three Allied leaders—Roosevelt, Churchill, and Stalin—met at Yalta in Crimea to decide the fate of the post-war world. Five months later, the nations' leaders met again at Potsdam, near Berlin.

△ **Memorial for a leader**
The 1945 Yalta conference was a historical landmark, as this postage stamp from the former French colony of Togo, issued to mark Churchill's death in 1965, confirms.

One of the main aims of Yalta was to decide what should happen to Germany after the war. The Big Three—as Roosevelt, Churchill, and Stalin were known—agreed to divide the country into four occupation zones administered by the US, Britain, the USSR, and France, with control of Berlin split between the four powers. They agreed to establish a provisional government in Poland as a preliminary to holding elections. Similarly, the other freed peoples of Eastern Europe would be helped in setting up democratic regimes. Stalin agreed to join the war against Japan once Germany surrendered, and to join the UN.

Broken pledges

The Yalta agreements were initially heralded as a success, but the mood did not last. By the time they met again at Potsdam between July 7 and August 2, with Harry S Truman and Clement Attlee replacing Roosevelt and Churchill respectively, the tensions between the West and the USSR were obvious. Although the divided and disarmed state of Germany was confirmed, there was disagreement about the amount of reparations the Germans should pay. Refugees from the east were flooding westward, displaced by the adjustment of the Polish–German frontier in Poland's favor. Additionally, it was clear that Stalin, despite his promises, would not allow free elections to take place in the territories his armies had liberated.

THE POTSDAM DECLARATION

Following Potsdam, the US, UK, and China called for Japan's unconditional surrender, threatening "prompt and utter destruction" if it did not comply. Although Stalin was also present at the conference, the USSR and Japan had a treaty of nonaggression at the time, so he did not sign the declaration.

The Big Three
Winston Churchill, Franklin D. Roosevelt, and Joseph Stalin at the Yalta conference in February 1945. Roosevelt was suffering health problems at the time of the conference, and he died that year on April 12 in the US state of Georgia.

CROSSING THE RHINE

After driving back the German counteroffensive in the Ardennes, Allied forces met their next major challenge—fighting their way over the Rhine. They then spent a month advancing across Germany toward the Elbe to meet Soviet troops advancing from the east.

More than 1,310 ft (400 m) wide in places and fiercely defended on its eastern bank, the Rhine was a formidable barrier to Allied progress into Germany. The Supreme Commander of the Allied forces, General Eisenhower, made careful plans for a coordinated assault to storm across the river. In the end, the initial crossing took place almost by chance over a bridge at Remagen that German defenders had failed to blow up. The campaign then proceeded according to Eisenhower's plan, and by March 24 the Allies had established three substantial bridgeheads on the waterway's far bank.

"One of those rare and fleeting opportunities which occasionally arise in war."

GENERAL EISENHOWER ON THE CAPTURE OF REMAGEN

Germany now lay open before the Allies, but political considerations imposed a degree of caution. It had been agreed at Yalta (see pp.230–231) that the eastern approaches to Berlin were to remain in the Soviet zone, so instead of hastening toward the German capital, the Western Allied advance proceeded more haltingly. British troops uncovered horrors when they liberated the Bergen-Belsen concentration camp in mid-April, and US forces reached the Dachau camp two weeks later.

GENERAL GEORGE PATTON 1885–1945

Born into a prosperous family in California, George Patton graduated from the US Military Academy at West Point in 1909. He represented his country in the modern pentathlon at the Stockholm Olympics in 1912 and pioneered the use of tanks by the US in World War I. He had already established a formidable fighting reputation in North Africa and Sicily before taking charge of the US 3rd Army early in 1944. Under his command the forces won a reputation for highly aggressive action.

PATHS THROUGH GERMANY
After crossing the Rhine, the way lay open for Allied armies to advance across central Germany and meet up with Soviet forces at the Elbe River.

KEY

German army groups	Allied gains by Dec 15, 1944	Supplies delivered by air	
German armies	Allied gains by Mar 21, 1945		
Allied army groups	Allied gains by Apr 18, 1945		
Allied armies	Concentration camp		

TIMELINE

JAN 1945 — FEB — MAR — APRIL — MAY — JUN

Apr 29–May 8 Food drops from Allied bombers help alleviate the suffering of Dutch civilians facing famine after the Hunger Winter of 1944–1945.

1 TO THE RHINE'S BANK
JANUARY–MARCH 5, 1945

Before crossing the Rhine, Allied forces first had to clear the approaches to the river. The Canadian 1st Army advanced through the southern Netherlands; US 9th Army troops moved through München-Gladbach, their progress delayed as German troops flooded the Roer valley; and US 1st Army troops entered Cologne on the river's west bank on March 5, 1945.

Allied operations ⟶ Allied advances

2 THE BRIDGE AT REMAGEN
MARCH 7–21, 1945

On March 7, troops of the US 1st Army unexpectedly found the Ludendorff railroad bridge at Remagen still intact. They crossed the bridge under heavy enemy fire and established the first Allied bridgehead on the east bank of the Rhine. US engineers put additional pontoon bridges in place, and by March 21 more than 25,000 troops had crossed. Infuriated, Hitler had four officers executed for failing to prevent the breach.

Battle of Remagen — Bridgehead at Remagen

3 ACROSS THE RHINE
MARCH 22–25, 1945

The Remagen crossing preempted an Allied assault across the river planned for the night of March 23. The British 21st Army Group under Field Marshal Montgomery made a series of crossings in northern Germany, by which time General Patton had crossed at Oppenheim to the south. By March 25, two more substantial bridgeheads had been established.

Bridgeheads established March 23–25

Amsterdam
Rotterdam
Rhi

UNITED KINGDOM

British 21st Army Group
Brussels
BELGIUM
Lille

Seine
Reims
Loire

FRANCE

Troyes

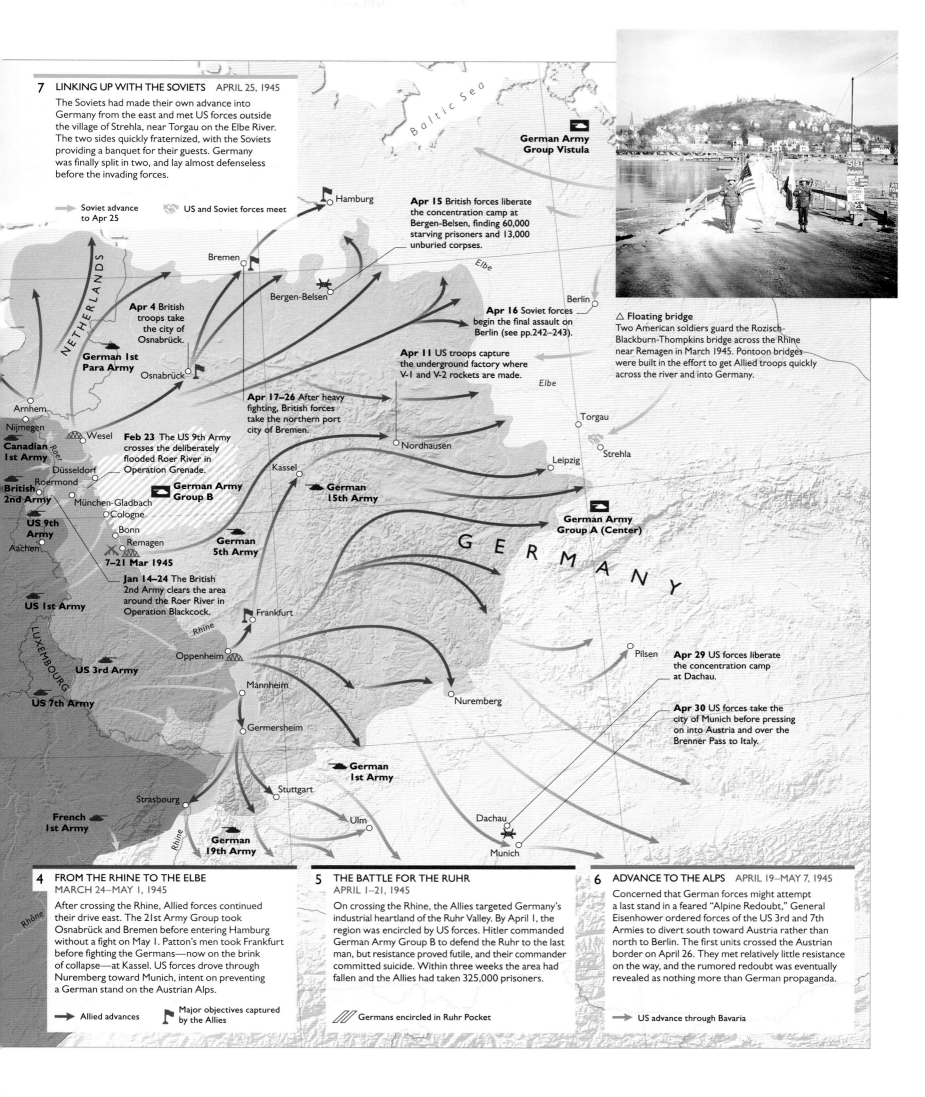

7 LINKING UP WITH THE SOVIETS APRIL 25, 1945

The Soviets had made their own advance into Germany from the east and met US forces outside the village of Strehla, near Torgau on the Elbe River. The two sides quickly fraternized, with the Soviets providing a banquet for their guests. Germany was finally split in two, and lay almost defenseless before the invading forces.

→ Soviet advance to Apr 25

🤝 US and Soviet forces meet

Baltic Sea

German Army Group Vistula

Apr 15 British forces liberate the concentration camp at Bergen-Belsen, finding 60,000 starving prisoners and 13,000 unburied corpses.

Apr 16 Soviet forces begin the final assault on Berlin (see pp.242–243).

Apr 11 US troops capture the underground factory where V-1 and V-2 rockets are made.

Apr 17–26 After heavy fighting, British forces take the northern port city of Bremen.

Feb 23 The US 9th Army crosses the deliberately flooded Roer River in Operation Grenade.

German Army Group B

Apr 4 British troops take the city of Osnabrück.

German 1st Para Army

Jan 14–24 The British 2nd Army clears the area around the Roer River in Operation Blackcock.

7–21 Mar 1945

△ Floating bridge
Two American soldiers guard the Rozisch-Blackburn-Thompkins bridge across the Rhine near Remagen in March 1945. Pontoon bridges were built in the effort to get Allied troops quickly across the river and into Germany.

Hamburg

Bremen

Bergen-Belsen

Berlin

Elbe

Elbe

Torgau

Strehla

Leipzig

Nordhausen

Kassel

German 15th Army

German Army Group A (Center)

G E R M A N Y

NETHERLANDS

Arnhem

Nijmegen

Canadian 1st Army

Wesel

Roer

Düsseldorf

British 2nd Army

Roermond

München-Gladbach

Cologne

US 9th Army

Bonn

Aachen

Remagen

Osnabrück

German 5th Army

LUXEMBOURG

US 1st Army

US 3rd Army

US 7th Army

Rhine

Frankfurt

Oppenheim

Mannheim

Germersheim

Pilsen

Apr 29 US forces liberate the concentration camp at Dachau.

Apr 30 US forces take the city of Munich before pressing on into Austria and over the Brenner Pass to Italy.

Nuremberg

German 1st Army

French 1st Army

Strasbourg

Stuttgart

Ulm

Dachau

Rhine

German 19th Army

Munich

Rhône

Rhône

---

4 FROM THE RHINE TO THE ELBE
MARCH 24–MAY 1, 1945

After crossing the Rhine, Allied forces continued their drive east. The 21st Army Group took Osnabrück and Bremen before entering Hamburg without a fight on May 1. Patton's men took Frankfurt before fighting the Germans—now on the brink of collapse—at Kassel. US forces drove through Nuremberg toward Munich, intent on preventing a German stand on the Austrian Alps.

→ Allied advances

⚑ Major objectives captured by the Allies

5 THE BATTLE FOR THE RUHR
APRIL 1–21, 1945

On crossing the Rhine, the Allies targeted Germany's industrial heartland of the Ruhr Valley. By April 1, the region was encircled by US forces. Hitler commanded German Army Group B to defend the Ruhr to the last man, but resistance proved futile, and their commander committed suicide. Within three weeks the area had fallen and the Allies had taken 325,000 prisoners.

/// Germans encircled in Ruhr Pocket

6 ADVANCE TO THE ALPS APRIL 19–MAY 7, 1945

Concerned that German forces might attempt a last stand in a feared "Alpine Redoubt," General Eisenhower ordered forces of the US 3rd and 7th Armies to divert south toward Austria rather than north to Berlin. The first units crossed the Austrian border on April 26. They met relatively little resistance on the way, and the rumored redoubt was eventually revealed as nothing more than German propaganda.

→ US advance through Bavaria

GERMANY LOSES THE AIR WAR

The nature of the air war over Europe changed with the Allied landings in Normandy. The Luftwaffe was forced increasingly onto the defensive, and by late 1944, fuel shortages and loss of men and materiel had made it largely a spent force.

From mid-1944, the balance in the air war over Europe tipped decisively in the Allies' favor. This was in no small part due to the arrival in Europe of the P-51B Mustang—a fast fighter with enough range to provide effective cover for B-17 and B-24 bombers. Among the best fighters of the war, the P-51B could outperform the heavy fighters used by the Luftwaffe against the USAAF raiders, so Allied bombing raids became increasingly effective in disrupting German aircraft production and interrupting the development of new designs.

The Luftwaffe's activities were also curtailed by a chronic shortage of fuel caused by the Allied bombers' selective targeting of Germany's oil resources. By September 1944, the Luftwaffe had access to only 11,000 tons (10,000 metric tons) of octane each month instead of the 176,400 tons (160,000 metric tons) that it needed to fuel its operations. The USAAF mainly undertook the precision bombing of oil facilities, while the RAF under "Bomber" Harris turned their attention to the area bombing of cities.

Running out of legitimate strategic and industrial targets, the Allies dropped their bombs wherever they would cause maximum confusion to their enemy. In total, more than 350,000 German civilians were killed in Allied attacks; the rate of fatalities grew to 13,000 people a month from July 1944 to January 1945. The mass casualties of civilians that resulted in Hamburg, Dresden, Leipzig, Chemnitz, and other centers were controversial at the time, and have attracted growing criticism ever since.

THE P-51 MUSTANG

Originally designed by North American Aviation in 1940, the single-seater, long-range Mustang fighter took a major step forward in performance with the introduction of the B model, powered by a Rolls-Royce engine. From late 1943 onward, P-51Bs, along with the later C and D (shown here) models, were used as escorts on long-distance bombing raids, targeting German fighters and helping secure Allied victory in the skies.

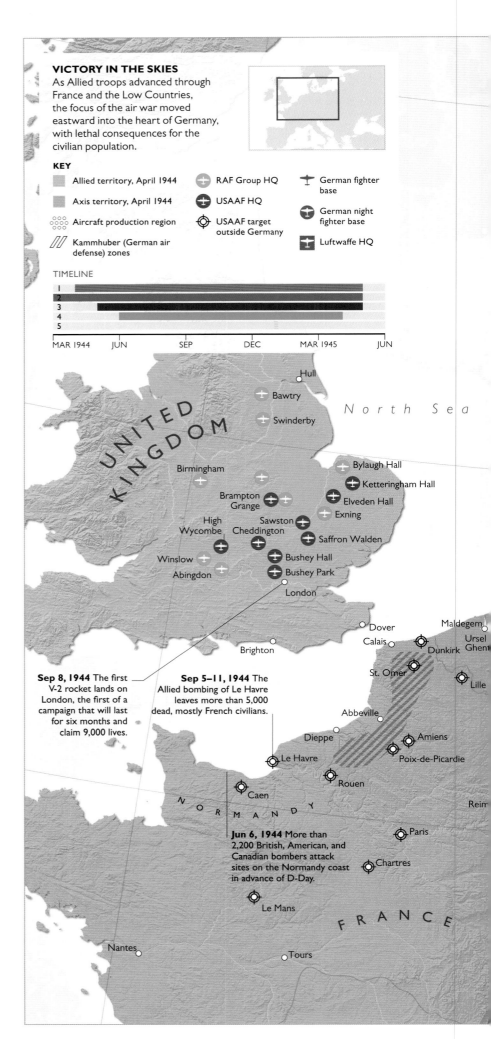

VICTORY IN THE SKIES
As Allied troops advanced through France and the Low Countries, the focus of the air war moved eastward into the heart of Germany, with lethal consequences for the civilian population.

KEY

- Allied territory, April 1944
- Axis territory, April 1944
- Aircraft production region
- Kammhuber (German air defense) zones
- RAF Group HQ
- USAAF HQ
- USAAF target outside Germany
- German fighter base
- German night fighter base
- Luftwaffe HQ

TIMELINE

MAR 1944   JUN   SEP   DEC   MAR 1945   JUN

Sep 8, 1944 The first V-2 rocket lands on London, the first of a campaign that will last for six months and claim 9,000 lives.

Sep 5–11, 1944 The Allied bombing of Le Havre leaves more than 5,000 dead, mostly French civilians.

Jun 6, 1944 More than 2,200 British, American, and Canadian bombers attack sites on the Normandy coast in advance of D-Day.

North Sea

UNITED KINGDOM

Hull
Bawtry
Swinderby
Birmingham
Bylaugh Hall
Ketteringham Hall
Brampton Grange
Elveden Hall
Exning
High Wycombe
Sawston
Cheddington
Saffron Walden
Winslow
Bushey Hall
Abingdon
Bushey Park
London
Dover
Calais
Maldegem
Ursel
Dunkirk
Ghent
Brighton
St. Omer
Lille
Abbeville
Dieppe
Amiens
Le Havre
Poix-de-Picardie
Rouen
Caen
NORMANDY
Reim
Paris
Le Mans
Chartres
FRANCE
Nantes
Tours

1 CROSSBOW OPERATIONS
APRIL 1944–APRIL 1945

Allied surveillance provided evidence of V-1 launch sites (see pp.192–193) as early as May 1943. The first raids against the German long-range V-1 and V-2 weapons—part of an operation code named Crossbow—took place later that year and intensified in April 1944. Of 6,380 V-1s launched against Britain, 4,380 were brought down by fighter planes or antiaircraft fire.

/// V-1 launch site areas   /// V-2 launch site areas

2 AERIAL BOMBARDMENT
UP TO APRIL 1945

Throughout the air war, the RAF's "Bomber" Harris pursued his goal of destroying German morale through aerial attacks on cities. One of the most devastating was the assault on the historic center of Dresden (see pp.236–237), previously unscathed. Four raids over two nights created a firestorm that killed an estimated 25,000 people on the night of February 13/14, 1945.

German cities suffering 50–100 percent destruction in raids in 1944–1945

3 TARGETING OIL AND TRANSPORTATION
MAY 1944–APRIL 1945

As well as targeting the German aircraft industry, the Allies turned their attention to cutting off oil supplies to the Luftwaffe. Allied planes flying from liberated southern Italy attacked refineries at Ploeşti in Romania, while raids on fuel sites and transportation infrastructure in Germany and the occupied lands reduced production by 95 percent.

Oil targets   Transportation target zones

4 EXTENDING THE STRIKE RANGE
JUNE 1944–APRIL 4, 1945

As the war neared its end, the targets of Allied bombing moved farther east. The improved design of bombers, such as the US B-24 Liberator, gave the Allies longer reach, as did the availability of airfields in continental Europe (after D-Day) and in southern Italy. In 1944, Stalin allowed the US to establish bases in Ukraine, but US–Soviet suspicions quickly limited their effectiveness.

Operational ranges of Allied bombers

5 THE LUFTWAFFE'S LAST OFFENSIVE
JANUARY 1, 1945

By 1945 the Luftwaffe was almost spent, but managed to stage a last surprise attack, Operation *Bodenplatte* (Baseplate), which sought to neutralize Allied air power in the Low Countries as part of the Battle of the Bulge offensive (see pp.228–229). The assault destroyed more than 300 Allied planes, but German losses were equally heavy, and the operation brought no lasting gains.

Allied air bases attacked on Jan 1, 1945

Apr 9, 1945 British bombers sink the cruiser *Admiral Scheer* in Kiel harbor, one of several missions against the last remnants of German naval power.

Mar 3, 1945 RAF bombers targeting a V-2 missile site mistakenly hit the Bezuidenhout suburb of The Hague, killing 500 Dutch civilians.

Mar 12, 1945 Dortmund is largely destroyed by a force of more than 1,100 aircraft.

1944–1945 German air defenses—the most sophisticated in the world—cannot stop Allied bombing.

Sep 11, 1944 A dogfight over the Ore Mountains costs 29 German and 50 American lives.

Feb 14, 1945 Prague, still under German occupation, is accidentally bombed by American aircraft.

Feb 23–24, 1945 An RAF assault on the medieval city of Pforzheim leaves a third of the population dead and over 80 percent of its buildings destroyed.

Map labels

DENMARK
Baltic Sea
NETHERLANDS
BELGIUM
GREATER GERMANY
SWITZERLAND
SLOVAKIA
HUNGARY
Ore Mountains
From Italy
From USSR
From United Kingdom

Kiel
Rostock
Schwerin
Stettin
Bremerhaven
Wilhelmshaven
Hamburg
Emden
Bremen
Sneek
Leiden
The Hague
Rotterdam
Heesch
Gilze en Rijen
Volkel
Woensdrecht
Eindhoven
Antwerp
Ophoven
Asch
Sint-Truiden
Brussels
Le Culot
Osnabrück
Hanover
Hildesheim
Berlin
Dessau
Leipzig
Dresden
Chemnitz
Brüx
Dec
Prague
Dortmund
Essen
Hagen
München-Gladbach
Cologne
Bonn
Giessen
Koblenz
Kassel
Schweinfurt
Wiesbaden
Hanau
Mainz
Frankfurt
Trier
Würzburg
Nuremberg
Darmstadt
Mannheim
Saarbrücken
Heilbronn
St.-Dizier
Metz
Karlsruhe
Pforzheim
Stuttgart
Nancy
Regensburg
Ulm
Augsburg
Lagerlechfeld
Munich
Friedrichshafen
Dijon
Vienna
Graz

THE BOMBING OF DRESDEN

From around 10 pm on February 13, 1945, until noon the following day, the historic city of Dresden in eastern Germany was subjected to one of the most intensive bombing raids of the war. The savage attack was sudden and unexpected, and the results were devastating.

Known as Operation Thunderclap, the attack began with 244 RAF Lancasters dropping more than 890 tons (810 tonnes) of high explosive and incendiary bombs on the center and inner suburbs of the city. After a 25-minute pause, a further 529 bombers arrived, dropping over 2,000 tons (1,800 tonnes) of bombs to fuel the firestorm the initial attack had kindled. The second attack lasted 40 minutes. By the time it ended, Dresden had been utterly devastated. The following morning, as the surviving residents stumbled into the streets to survey the damage, the air-raid sirens wailed again. Some 311 USAAF Flying Fortresses dropped a further 860 tons (770 tonnes) of bombs on the stricken city. Around 25,000 Dresdeners were killed.

△ **Air-raid warning**
A handheld air-raid siren of the type used in Dresden. The city's citizens had little warning of the initial attack.

A display of might

Whether such a destructive attack on Dresden was justified has provoked debate ever since. The Allies bombed eastern German cities in order to aid the Soviet advance and prevent a German retreat to an Alpine redoubt (or fortress). However, RAF Bomber Command's Arthur Harris briefed his aircrews to bomb densely packed residential zones, causing huge numbers of civilian deaths.

△ **The second attack**
Two months after the initial attack on Dresden by the RAF Lancasters, B-17 Flying Fortresses of the US 8th Air Force bombed Dresden by daylight on April 17, 1945. The aim of the mission was to sever the city's southeastern rail links. It was the final attack on Dresden, an ancient cathedral city that Germans referred to as "Florence on the Elbe."

Dresden in ruins
This view from the tower of Dresden's *Rathaus* (city hall) southward over the city reveals the extent of the destruction caused by Allied area bombing. Much of the city center remained rubble into the 1950s.

THE FINAL SOVIET ATTACK

In the final stage of the war in Europe, a series of hard-fought victories brought Soviet armies into the heart of central Europe and the Balkans, with major consequences for both the war and the continent itself.

The Red Army's advance of summer 1944 had cleared the Germans from Soviet soil and penetrated Poland, Romania, and the Baltic states. However, it stalled outside Warsaw while the Germans crushed an uprising by the Polish Home Army (see pp.184–185). To the south, Soviet forces invaded Bulgaria before taking the Yugoslav capital, Belgrade, with Josip Broz Tito's partisans. In Hungary, the Red Army beat a path to Budapest in December, but took almost two months to capture the city, which was defended by German and Hungarian forces.

Overwhelming forces

The final push into Germany began on January 12, 1945, with an offensive by Marshal Zhukov's 1st Ukrainian Front, joined two days later by Marshal Konev's 1st Belorussian Front (see right). With more than two million men and 4,000 tanks, the armies advanced almost 300 miles (500 km) by early February, with Zhukov penetrating the industrial area of Silesia, and Konev reaching the River Oder, less than 45 miles (70 km) east of Berlin. The Soviet advance liberated Auschwitz on January 27, and droves of German civilian refugees fled west, panicked by reports of Soviet atrocities. Zhukov halted at the Oder to resupply his army, while in the north the Soviets took control of East Prussia and the Baltic states. The Soviets began their final assault on April 16 (see pp.242–243). After four days Zhukov broke the defenses; by April 20 Berlin was encircled. On April 25, US and Soviet troops met triumphantly at Torgau on the Elbe.

△ **The Allies meet**
A lieutenant from the US 69th Infantry Division (in helmet) poses with soldiers from the Soviet 58th Guards Division in Torgau, Germany, in April 1945. The site would become the border of their future military occupation zones.

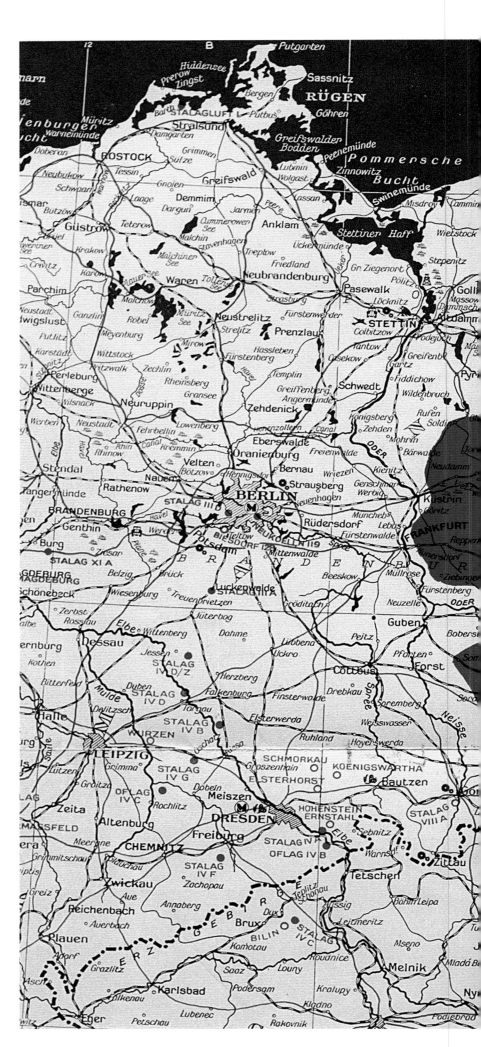

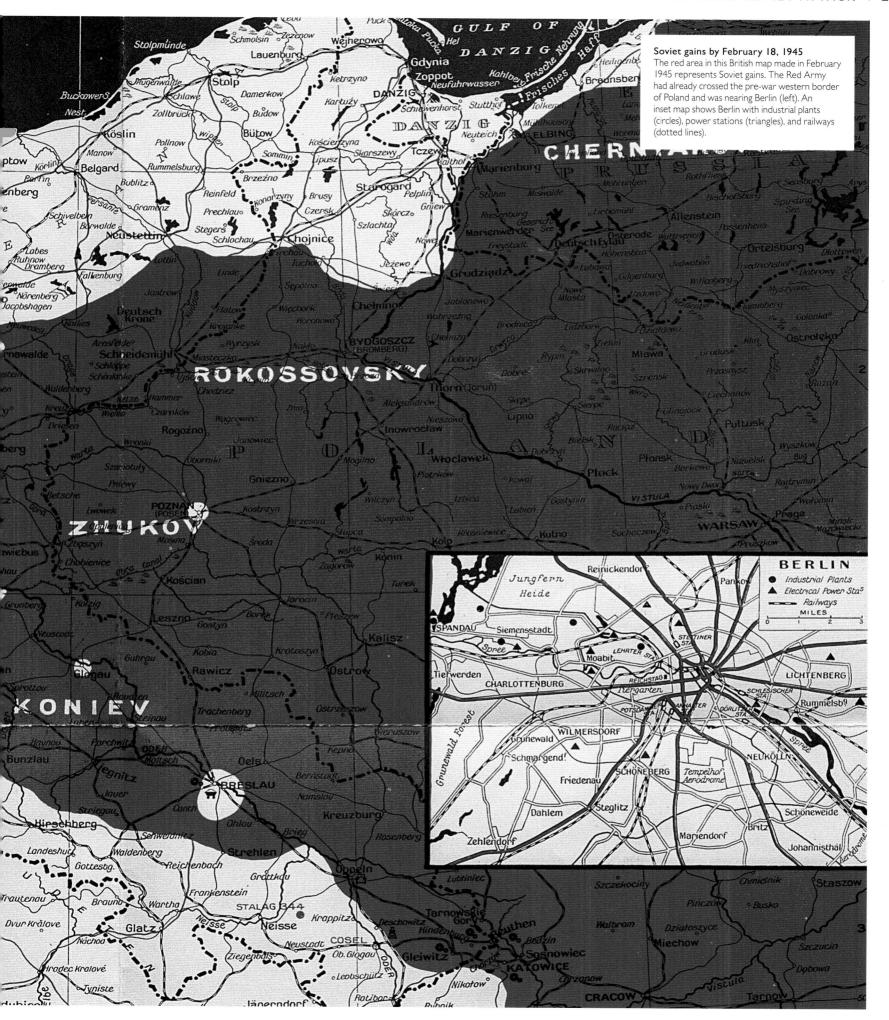

Soviet gains by February 18, 1945
The red area in this British map made in February 1945 represents Soviet gains. The Red Army had already crossed the pre-war western border of Poland and was nearing Berlin (left). An inset map shows Berlin with industrial plants (circles), power stations (triangles), and railways (dotted lines).

FINAL STRUGGLES IN ITALY

In 1944, the Allies pushed northward through Italy, eventually forcing the Germans behind the Gothic Line—a formidable defensive line that ran the width of the country. Following a winter of military stalemate, the Allies achieved a decisive breakthrough in spring 1945 that finally brought the war in Italy to an end.

German field marshal Albert Kesselring continued to frustrate the pursuing Allies by conducting a skillful defensive retreat. Under his orders, 15,000 slave laborers built the Gothic Line (also known as the Green Line)—a series of bunkers, anti-tank ditches, machine-gun posts, minefields, and other defenses. The location of the Gothic Line in the Apennine Mountains meant that the most viable places for the Allies to attack were along both coasts and at a few mountain passes—points that the Germans heavily defended. In September 1944, some Allied divisions broke through at the eastern end of the line, but otherwise the barrier held out

until the following spring, when the Allies launched a decisive offensive. The battle for the Gothic Line was one of the largest fought in the war, involving more than 1.2 million men.

As the Allies turned their focus to the Western Front after D-Day (see pp.186–187), the Italian campaign came to be seen as something of a sideshow. But for those involved, it was a long, punishing struggle that claimed the lives of around 250,000 soldiers and 150,000 noncombatants. Under Kesselring's orders, German troops responded brutally to any opposition, killing thousands of civilians in reprisal for partisan attacks or disobedience.

> *"A soldier's first duty is to obey, otherwise you might as well do away with soldiering."*
>
> FIELD MARSHAL ALBERT KESSELRING, 1946

ITALIAN PARTISANS

After the fall of Rome in June 1944 (see pp.166–167), some pro-Fascist Italian forces continued to fight alongside German troops. However, they were matched by the number of partisans fighting against the occupiers and against Mussolini's Italian Social Republic (the Republic of Salò: see Box 5). Italian partisans liberated many cities before the arrival of the Allies, including Milan, Genoa, and Turin. After the German forces were expelled, partisan groups executed thousands of collaborators.

Partisans enter the freed city of Milan on April 25, 1945

LAST STAND IN ITALY

The Germans pinned their last hopes of halting the Allied advance in Italy on their fortified Gothic Line. However, they could not contain the sustained attacks and were forced to capitulate in May 1945.

KEY

Allied forces	Massacres	Areas of Italian partisan activity

TIMELINE

	JUL 1944	SEP	NOV	JAN 1945	MAR	MAY	JUL
1							
2							
3							
4							
5							

Geneva

1 RETREAT TO THE GOTHIC LINE
AUGUST 1944

By early August, Allied forces had pushed the Germans as far north as the Arno River and had taken the city of Florence. The Germans withdrew behind the Gothic Line, a defensive line that stretched 200 miles (320 km) between Italy's east and west coasts. The fortifications, which were 10 miles (16 km) deep in some places, would be the last major line of defense for the Germans in Italy.

Gothic Line	Allied advance
Battle	Allied territory by Aug 25, 1944

Novar

Vercelli

Turin

Alessandri

2 ALLIES BREACH THE GOTHIC LINE
AUGUST–DECEMBER 1944

The Allies gave the Germans every indication that they would assault the Gothic Line on the west coast, but the move was a feint to allow the British 8th Army to break through in the east, taking the port of Rimini. US forces made progress in the Apennine Mountains. The last Allied victory of 1944 came on December 5 with the capture of the east-coast city of Ravenna.

Mondovì

Allied advance	Allied territory by Dec 31, 1944
Battles	

San Remo

Ligurian Sea

3 WINTER STALEMATE
DECEMBER 1944–APRIL 9, 1945

The winter of 1944–1945 was harsh, and neither side made much progress. The inactivity enabled both sides to move forces to areas where they were needed more urgently. In March, the Allies bombed Axis-held Venice; the same month, Hitler promoted Kesselring to Commander-in-Chief on the Western Front. Morale dropped on both sides, as troops realized that the conflict in western Europe was taking priority over Italy.

Allied territory by Apr 9, 1945	Allied air attack

Zürich

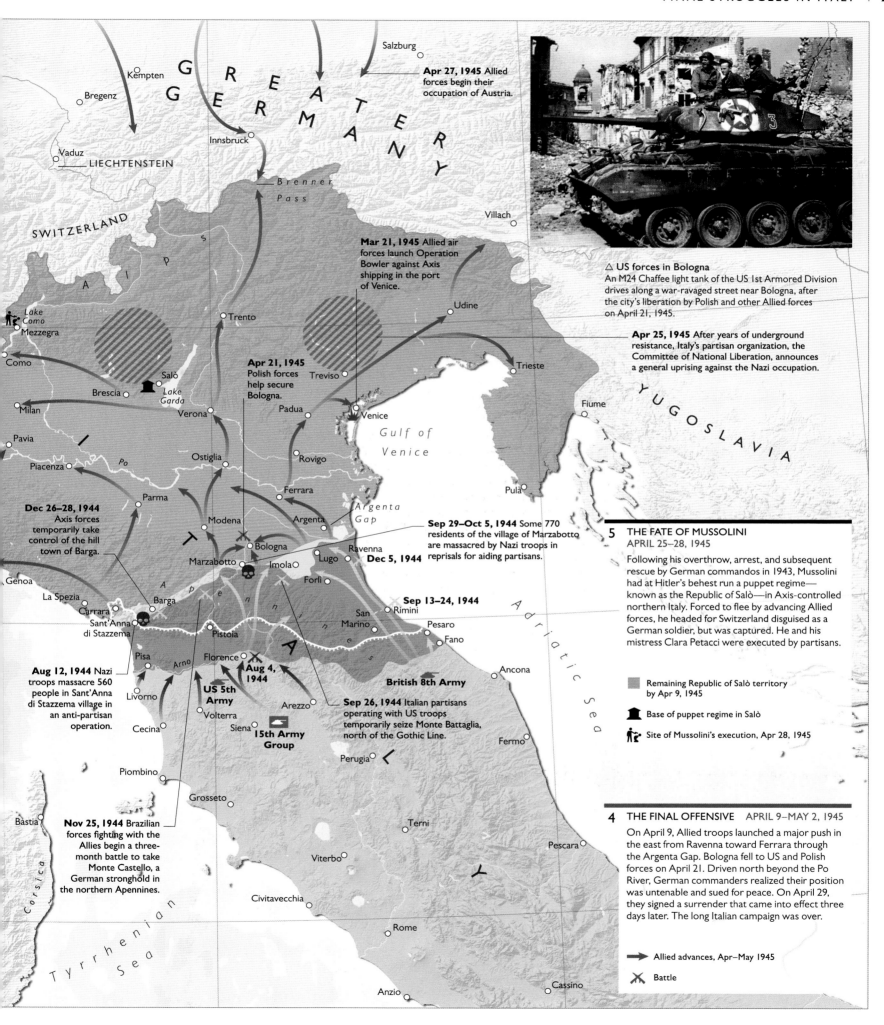

Apr 27, 1945 Allied forces begin their occupation of Austria.

Mar 21, 1945 Allied air forces launch Operation Bowler against Axis shipping in the port of Venice.

Apr 21, 1945 Polish forces help secure Bologna.

Dec 26–28, 1944 Axis forces temporarily take control of the hill town of Barga.

Sep 29–Oct 5, 1944 Some 770 residents of the village of Marzabotto are massacred by Nazi troops in reprisals for aiding partisans.

Dec 5, 1944

Sep 13–24, 1944

Aug 12, 1944 Nazi troops massacre 560 people in Sant'Anna di Stazzema village in an anti-partisan operation.

Aug 4, 1944

US 5th Army

15th Army Group

Sep 26, 1944 Italian partisans operating with US troops temporarily seize Monte Battaglia, north of the Gothic Line.

British 8th Army

Nov 25, 1944 Brazilian forces fighting with the Allies begin a three-month battle to take Monte Castello, a German stronghold in the northern Apennines.

△ **US forces in Bologna**
An M24 Chaffee light tank of the US 1st Armored Division drives along a war-ravaged street near Bologna, after the city's liberation by Polish and other Allied forces on April 21, 1945.

Apr 25, 1945 After years of underground resistance, Italy's partisan organization, the Committee of National Liberation, announces a general uprising against the Nazi occupation.

---

5 THE FATE OF MUSSOLINI
APRIL 25–28, 1945

Following his overthrow, arrest, and subsequent rescue by German commandos in 1943, Mussolini had at Hitler's behest run a puppet regime—known as the Republic of Salò—in Axis-controlled northern Italy. Forced to flee by advancing Allied forces, he headed for Switzerland disguised as a German soldier, but was captured. He and his mistress Clara Petacci were executed by partisans.

▨ Remaining Republic of Salò territory by Apr 9, 1945

♟ Base of puppet regime in Salò

🏃 Site of Mussolini's execution, Apr 28, 1945

---

4 THE FINAL OFFENSIVE APRIL 9–MAY 2, 1945

On April 9, Allied troops launched a major push in the east from Ravenna toward Ferrara through the Argenta Gap. Bologna fell to US and Polish forces on April 21. Driven north beyond the Po River, German commanders realized their position was untenable and sued for peace. On April 29, they signed a surrender that came into effect three days later. The long Italian campaign was over.

➡ Allied advances, Apr–May 1945

✕ Battle

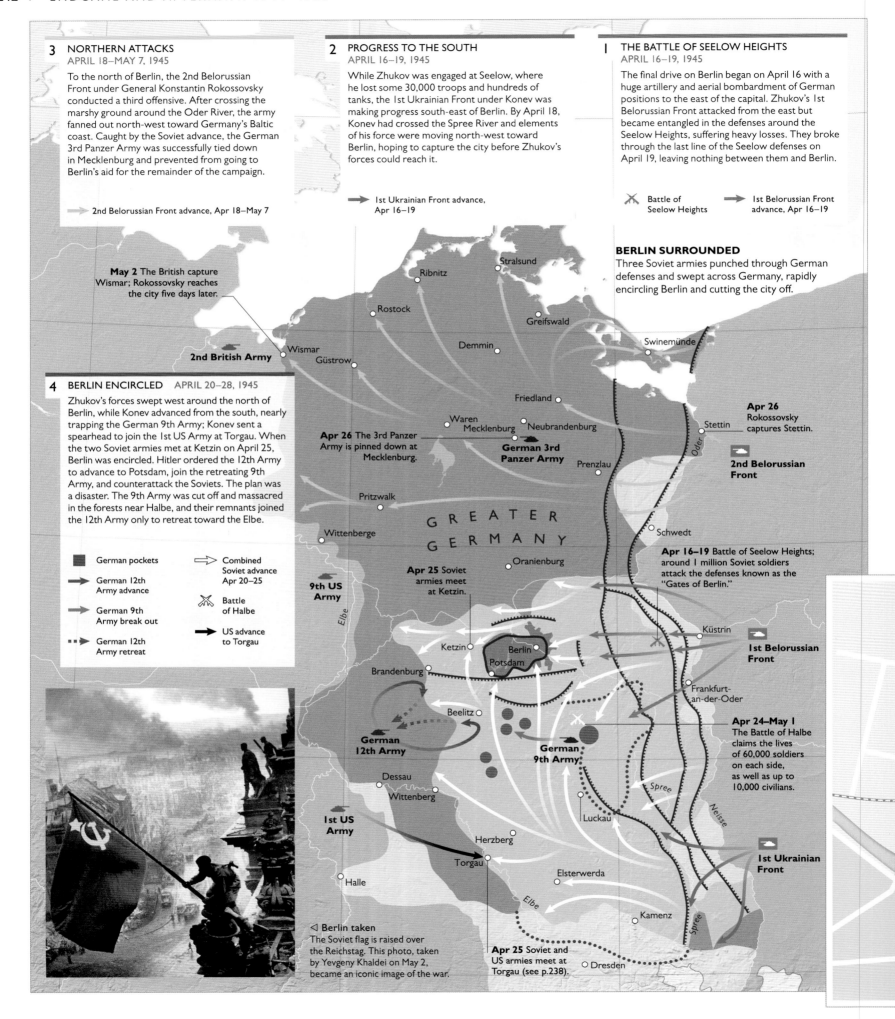

3 NORTHERN ATTACKS
APRIL 18–MAY 7, 1945

To the north of Berlin, the 2nd Belorussian Front under General Konstantin Rokossovsky conducted a third offensive. After crossing the marshy ground around the Oder River, the army fanned out north-west toward Germany's Baltic coast. Caught by the Soviet advance, the German 3rd Panzer Army was successfully tied down in Mecklenburg and prevented from going to Berlin's aid for the remainder of the campaign.

→ 2nd Belorussian Front advance, Apr 18–May 7

2 PROGRESS TO THE SOUTH
APRIL 16–19, 1945

While Zhukov was engaged at Seelow, where he lost some 30,000 troops and hundreds of tanks, the 1st Ukrainian Front under Konev was making progress south-east of Berlin. By April 18, Konev had crossed the Spree River and elements of his force were moving north-west toward Berlin, hoping to capture the city before Zhukov's forces could reach it.

→ 1st Ukrainian Front advance, Apr 16–19

1 THE BATTLE OF SEELOW HEIGHTS
APRIL 16–19, 1945

The final drive on Berlin began on April 16 with a huge artillery and aerial bombardment of German positions to the east of the capital. Zhukov's 1st Belorussian Front attacked from the east but became entangled in the defenses around the Seelow Heights, suffering heavy losses. They broke through the last line of the Seelow defenses on April 19, leaving nothing between them and Berlin.

⚔ Battle of Seelow Heights   → 1st Belorussian Front advance, Apr 16–19

BERLIN SURROUNDED

Three Soviet armies punched through German defenses and swept across Germany, rapidly encircling Berlin and cutting the city off.

May 2 The British capture Wismar; Rokossovsky reaches the city five days later.

2nd British Army

4 BERLIN ENCIRCLED   APRIL 20–28, 1945

Zhukov's forces swept west around the north of Berlin, while Konev advanced from the south, nearly trapping the German 9th Army; Konev sent a spearhead to join the 1st US Army at Torgau. When the two Soviet armies met at Ketzin on April 25, Berlin was encircled. Hitler ordered the 12th Army to advance to Potsdam, join the retreating 9th Army, and counterattack the Soviets. The plan was a disaster. The 9th Army was cut off and massacred in the forests near Halbe, and their remnants joined the 12th Army only to retreat toward the Elbe.

- ▪ German pockets
- → German 12th Army advance
- → German 9th Army break out
- ▪▪→ German 12th Army retreat
- ⇨ Combined Soviet advance Apr 20–25
- ⚔ Battle of Halbe
- → US advance to Torgau

Apr 26 The 3rd Panzer Army is pinned down at Mecklenburg.

Apr 26 Rokossovsky captures Stettin.

2nd Belorussian Front

German 3rd Panzer Army

Apr 16–19 Battle of Seelow Heights; around 1 million Soviet soldiers attack the defenses known as the "Gates of Berlin."

Apr 25 Soviet armies meet at Ketzin.

9th US Army

1st US Army

1st Belorussian Front

German 12th Army

German 9th Army

Apr 24–May 1 The Battle of Halbe claims the lives of 60,000 soldiers on each side, as well as up to 10,000 civilians.

1st Ukrainian Front

◁ **Berlin taken**
The Soviet flag is raised over the Reichstag. This photo, taken by Yevgeny Khaldei on May 2, became an iconic image of the war.

Apr 25 Soviet and US armies meet at Torgau (see p.238).

Labels on map: Stralsund, Ribnitz, Rostock, Greifswald, Demmin, Swinemünde, Wismar, Güstrow, Friedland, Waren, Mecklenburg, Neubrandenburg, Stettin, Prenzlau, Pritzwalk, Schwedt, GREATER GERMANY, Wittenberge, Oranienburg, Küstrin, Ketzin, Berlin, Potsdam, Brandenburg, Frankfurt-an-der-Oder, Beelitz, Dessau, Wittenberg, Luckau, Spree, Neisse, Herzberg, Torgau, Halle, Elsterwerda, Elbe, Kamenz, Spree, Dresden, Oder, Elbe

THE FALL OF BERLIN

In April 1945, the city of Berlin—already devastated by two years of Allied bombing—faced an overwhelming Red Army advance that drove the war in Europe to its bloody finale. The human cost was vast on both sides as vengeful Soviet troops attacked the German capital.

By mid-April 1945, the Red Army had amassed 2.5 million troops, 6,000 tanks, and more than 40,000 artillery pieces along the Oder and Neisse Rivers in preparation for their final assault on Berlin. Caught between the advancing British and American armies to the west and the Red Army's 200 divisions to the east were around 1 million German soldiers and 1,500 tanks. Many of the German soldiers were sick, wounded, or starving, but found themselves motivated to fight by their fear of what the Red Army might do in retribution for the millions of Soviet soldiers killed in the war.

Wishing to avoid a clash between the US and the Soviets, Eisenhower told Stalin that the US would not advance on Berlin. Stalin did not believe this and sped up his plans, pitting two generals—Konev and Zhukov—against each other in a race for the capital. Following a massive artillery bombardment of the city, the Red Army surrounded Berlin by April 25. Hitler, hiding in his bunker, pinned his hopes on a planned counterattack by his 9th and 12th Armies. It never came. Instead, the Red Army closed in and, as it tightened its grip on the city center, Hitler and Goebbels committed suicide. Berlin surrendered to the Soviets on May 2, and five days later the war in Europe was over.

GERMANY OVERRUN

Prevented from escaping westwards due to the advancing British and American armies, Germany's remaining armies were overwhelmed by the Red Army in just a few weeks from April to May 1945. By the time Berlin surrendered on May 2, Hitler had already been dead for two days.

KEY

British and US forces		German defensive lines		
Soviet forces		Front lines of German counterattacks		
German forces		German territory, 28 Apr		

ALLIED TERRITORIAL GAINS

Apr 15	Apr 28
Apr 18	Urban areas
Apr 25	

TIMELINE

APR 15 ,1945   APR 20   APR 25   APR 30   MAY 5   MAY 10

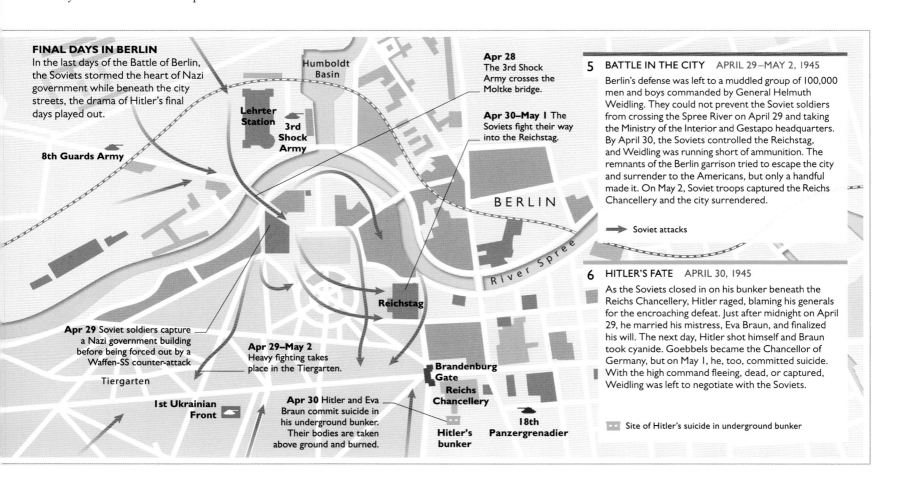

FINAL DAYS IN BERLIN
In the last days of the Battle of Berlin, the Soviets stormed the heart of Nazi government while beneath the city streets, the drama of Hitler's final days played out.

Humboldt Basin

Lehrter Station

3rd Shock Army

8th Guards Army

Apr 28 The 3rd Shock Army crosses the Moltke bridge.

Apr 30–May 1 The Soviets fight their way into the Reichstag.

BERLIN

Reichstag

River Spree

Apr 29 Soviet soldiers capture a Nazi government building before being forced out by a Waffen-SS counter-attack

Tiergarten

Apr 29–May 2 Heavy fighting takes place in the Tiergarten.

1st Ukrainian Front

Apr 30 Hitler and Eva Braun commit suicide in his underground bunker. Their bodies are taken above ground and burned.

Hitler's bunker

Brandenburg Gate
Reichs Chancellery

18th Panzergrenadier

5   BATTLE IN THE CITY   APRIL 29–MAY 2, 1945

Berlin's defense was left to a muddled group of 100,000 men and boys commanded by General Helmuth Weidling. They could not prevent the Soviet soldiers from crossing the Spree River on April 29 and taking the Ministry of the Interior and Gestapo headquarters. By April 30, the Soviets controlled the Reichstag, and Weidling was running short of ammunition. The remnants of the Berlin garrison tried to escape the city and surrender to the Americans, but only a handful made it. On May 2, Soviet troops captured the Reichs Chancellery and the city surrendered.

→ Soviet attacks

6   HITLER'S FATE   APRIL 30, 1945

As the Soviets closed in on his bunker beneath the Reichs Chancellery, Hitler raged, blaming his generals for the encroaching defeat. Just after midnight on April 29, he married his mistress, Eva Braun, and finalized his will. The next day, Hitler shot himself and Braun took cyanide. Goebbels became the Chancellor of Germany, but on May 1, he, too, committed suicide. With the high command fleeing, dead, or captured, Weidling was left to negotiate with the Soviets.

Site of Hitler's suicide in underground bunker

VE DAY

Germany's surrender on May 7, 1945, was celebrated across the Western world the following day. Hitler had killed himself in his bunker eight days previously, and war in Europe had finally ended.

△ **Special edition**
A commemorative edition of the UK magazine *Picture Post* celebrates VE Day. The magazine had previously campaigned against the Nazi regime.

On May 7, 1945, the Supreme Allied Commander, General Dwight D. Eisenhower, accepted the unconditional surrender of all German land, sea, and air forces at his headquarters in Reims, in northeastern France. In Britain, the news that the surrender document had been signed was broadcast that evening on the BBC. The following day, which was named Victory in Europe Day (usually abbreviated to VE Day), was declared a national holiday.

Celebrating victory

Even before the start of the official celebrations, the festivities began. In London, more than a million people took to the streets, while celebratory bonfires blazed the length and breadth of the country. Effigies of Hitler were burned on many of them. In America, the celebrations were slightly more subdued, primarily because the US was still mourning the death of President Franklin D. Roosevelt, who had died less than a month earlier. However, 15,000 policemen were still mobilized to control the huge crowds that had massed in Times Square, New York. There were also huge celebrations in Paris, with parades on the Champs-Élysées, and in France May 8 (*La fête de la Victoire*) continues to be a public holiday. In the USSR, however, because Stalin refused to recognize the signature at Reims and insisted on a formal surrender ceremony in Berlin on May 8, celebrations did not take place until May 9.

△ **Nazi downfall**
Soldiers from the US 7th Army fly the Stars and Stripes flag to celebrate victory, perched on what had been Hitler's viewing podium in the Luitpold Arena, Nuremberg, where the Nazi Party's infamous rallies had been held.

Dancing for joy
British girls dance with US GIs in London during the celebrations to mark the end of war in Europe. Thousands headed to Buckingham Palace, where Prime Minister Winston Churchill and the Royal Family greeted the ecstatic crowd.

DEFEAT OF JAPAN

By 1945, the eventual outcome of the war with Japan seemed inevitable. However, it was unclear how Japan's leaders could be brought to acknowledge defeat. In the end, the planned invasion of the Japanese mainland proved unnecessary, since the Allies' nuclear destruction of Hiroshima and Nagasaki was followed by Japan's surrender a few days later.

▽ **Targeting cities**
A US Army Air Forces map designates a key industrial target in Osaka, Japan. Over 200,000 Japanese were killed in non-nuclear strategic bombing.

By any objective measure, Japan had already lost the war by spring 1945. US aircraft based on Pacific islands were carrying out mass raids against Japanese cities, and a naval blockade both starved the civilian population and crippled the nation's war machine through a lack of fuel and other supplies. Japan's overseas armies were giving up territory that they had conquered in Burma, the Philippines, and New Guinea.

△ **Display of might**
A propaganda poster boasts of Japanese air power. In reality, by 1945 Japan's aircraft were outnumbered and outclassed by those of their opponents.

When Germany surrendered in May 1945, it meant that the military resources of the Allies could now be transferred to the Pacific theater. However, the Japanese continued to show every sign of determination to fight to the last man, as exhibited in the fierce battles for Iwo Jima and Okinawa; indeed, America believed that the war against Japan could continue well into 1946. In June 1945, the US Army planned to land in Japan the following November, with follow-up landings in March 1946. The expectation was of heavy losses in prolonged campaigns.

Japan faces up to defeat

The Japanese leadership finally faced up to the certainty of defeat after the fall of Okinawa in June. Knowing the war was lost, the Japanese war council split into two factions known as the "peace" and "war" parties. The peace party sought some way to end the conflict that would leave Japan independent and unoccupied—a prospect that the Allies would probably never have accepted. The war party favored a fight to the death, devising a plan for

ENDGAME IN THE PACIFIC WAR

In the first half of 1945, the US suffered mounting casualties in fighting against resolute Japanese troops. Some 26,000 Americans were killed or wounded in the battle for the small island of Iwo Jima, and the subsequent capture of Okinawa cost the US over 50,000 casualties. In August, however, the dropping of atomic bombs on two Japanese cities, and a Soviet invasion of Manchuria, propelled the Japanese government into surrendering at last.

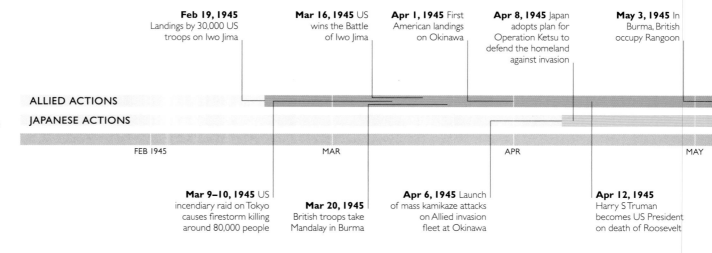

◁ **Soviet offensive**
Motorized Soviet infantry advance into Japanese-occupied Manchuria in August 1945. The invasion of Manchuria by the Soviet Union was a major factor in persuading Japan to recognize the need for surrender.

the defense of the homeland involving the entire population in suicidal resistance, under the slogan "The Glorious Death of One Hundred Million." Emperor Hirohito leaned toward support of the peace party, but at this point no decisions were made. The peace party's hopes for a compromise deal with the Allies was unrealistic, and the war party remained adamant.

The dropping of the bomb

Unknown to all but a few, even in the Allied political and military leadership, the Manhattan Project had been pursuing development of the atomic bomb, initially intended for use against Germany. The new weapon was successfully tested the day before the opening of an Allied conference at Potsdam, Germany, one of the aims of which was to encourage the Soviet Union to join the war against Japan. Although some doubts were raised behind the scenes, vetoing the dropping of atomic bombs on Japanese cities was never seriously considered. The Potsdam Declaration, calling on Japan to surrender or face destruction, was issued before the bombing, but its threats were too vague to influence Japanese policy. In early August 1945, atomic bombs were dropped on Hiroshima and Nagasaki, and the Soviet Union declared war on Japan. Emperor Hirohito and the peace party finally surrendered, although even then Japanese officers tried to prevent the announcement from being broadcast.

▽ **Raising the flag**
A famous photograph shows US Marines planting the Stars and Stripes flag on Mount Suribachi on Iwo Jima in March 1945. The capture of the Pacific island took five weeks of intensive fighting, and was one of the bloodiest battles against Japan in World War II.

> *"Despite the best that has been done by everyone… the war situation has developed not necessarily to Japan's advantage."*
>
> EMPEROR HIROHITO, SURRENDER BROADCAST, AUGUST 15, 1945

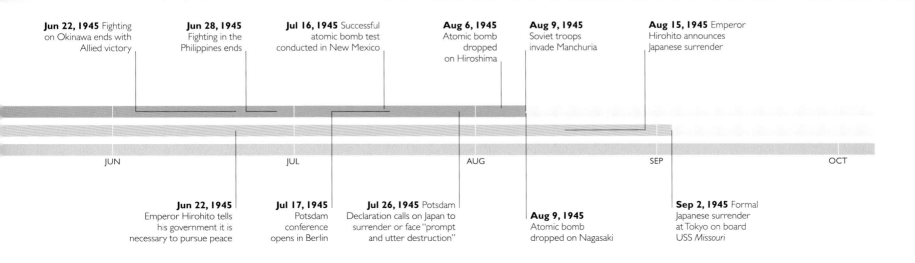

Jun 22, 1945 Fighting on Okinawa ends with Allied victory

Jun 28, 1945 Fighting in the Philippines ends

Jul 16, 1945 Successful atomic bomb test conducted in New Mexico

Aug 6, 1945 Atomic bomb dropped on Hiroshima

Aug 9, 1945 Soviet troops invade Manchuria

Aug 15, 1945 Emperor Hirohito announces Japanese surrender

JUN   JUL   AUG   SEP   OCT

Jun 22, 1945 Emperor Hirohito tells his government it is necessary to pursue peace

Jul 17, 1945 Potsdam conference opens in Berlin

Jul 26, 1945 Potsdam Declaration calls on Japan to surrender or face "prompt and utter destruction"

Aug 9, 1945 Atomic bomb dropped on Nagasaki

Sep 2, 1945 Formal Japanese surrender at Tokyo on board USS *Missouri*

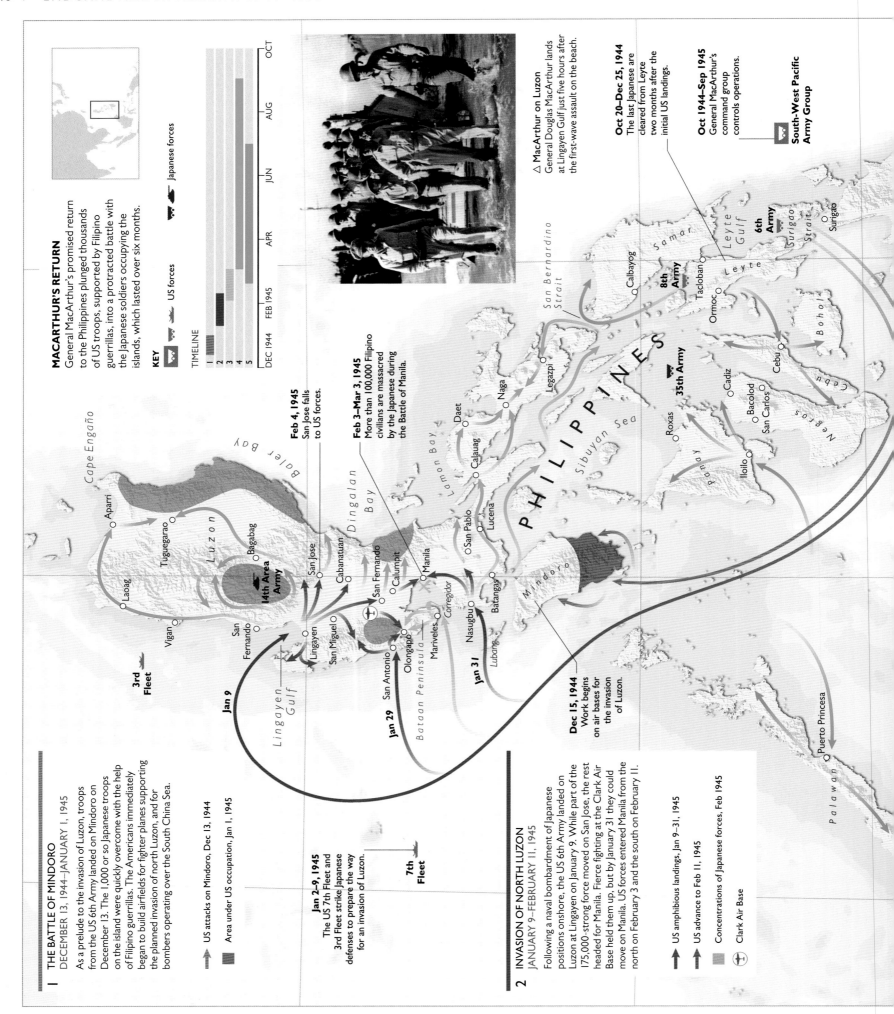

MACARTHUR'S RETURN

General MacArthur's promised return to the Philippines plunged thousands of US troops, supported by Filipino guerrillas, into a protracted battle with the Japanese soldiers occupying the islands, which lasted over six months.

KEY

US forces

Japanese forces

TIMELINE

1
2
3
4
5

DEC 1944   FEB 1945   APR   JUN   AUG   OCT

△ MacArthur on Luzon
General Douglas MacArthur lands at Lingayen Gulf just five hours after the first-wave assault on the beach.

Oct 20–Dec 25, 1944
The last Japanese are cleared from Leyte two months after the initial US landings.

Oct 1944–Sep 1945
General MacArthur's command group controls operations.

South-West Pacific
Army Group

1 THE BATTLE OF MINDORO
DECEMBER 13, 1944–JANUARY 1, 1945

As a prelude to the invasion of Luzon, troops from the US 6th Army landed on Mindoro on December 13. The 1,000 or so Japanese troops on the island were quickly overcome with the help of Filipino guerrillas. The Americans immediately began to build airfields for fighter planes supporting the planned invasion of north Luzon, and for bombers operating over the South China Sea.

US attacks on Mindoro, Dec 13, 1944

Area under US occupation, Jan 1, 1945

Jan 2–9, 1945
The US 7th Fleet and 3rd Fleet strike Japanese defenses to prepare the way for an invasion of Luzon.

7th Fleet

2 INVASION OF NORTH LUZON
JANUARY 9–FEBRUARY 11, 1945

Following a naval bombardment of Japanese positions onshore, the US 6th Army landed on Luzon at Lingayen on January 9. While part of the 175,000-strong force moved on San Jose, the rest headed for Manila. Fierce fighting at the Clark Air Base held them up, but by January 31 they could move on Manila. US forces entered Manila from the north on February 3 and the south on February 11.

US amphibious landings, Jan 9–31, 1945

US advance to Feb 11, 1945

Concentrations of Japanese forces, Feb 1945

Clark Air Base

Feb 4, 1945
San Jose falls to US forces.

Feb 3–Mar 3, 1945
More than 100,000 Filipino civilians are massacred by the Japanese during the Battle of Manila.

Dec 15, 1944
Work begins on air bases for the invasion of Luzon.

Jan 9

Jan 29

Jan 31

3rd Fleet

14th Area Army

35th Army

6th Army

8th Army

Cape Engaño

Baler Bay

Dingalan Bay

Lamon Bay

Lingayen Gulf

Bataan Peninsula

Sibuyan Sea

San Bernardino Strait

Surigao Strait

Leyte Gulf

PHILIPPINES

Luzon

Mindoro

Samar

Leyte

Bohol

Cebu

Negros

Panay

Palawan

Aparri
Laoag
Tuguegarao
Vigan
Bagabag
San Fernando
San Jose
Cabanatuan
San Fernando
Calumpit
Lingayen
San Miguel
San Antonio
Olongapo
Mariveles
Corregidor
Nasugbu
Batangas
Lubang
Manila
San Pablo
Lucena
Calauag
Daet
Naga
Legazpi
Roxas
Iloilo
Bacolod
San Carlos
Cadiz
Cebu
Calbayog
Ormoc
Tacloban
Surigato
Puerto Princesa

RETAKING THE PHILIPPINES

The US Navy's success in the Battle of Leyte Gulf in October 1944 was followed by a painful advance through the Philippine islands from January 1945 that cost the lives of more than 10,000 US soldiers, 200,000 Japanese soldiers, and 120,000 civilians. The campaign tied up US troops for longer than US General Douglas MacArthur expected, and with little strategic need.

Having broken the Imperial Japanese Navy's power in the Battle of Leyte Gulf (see pp.214–215), the US Navy saw little to gain in clearing the Japanese from the Philippine islands, with some strategists favoring a direct assault on Japan. General MacArthur, however, having promised to return after defeat in 1942, was set on retaking the Philippines. In January 1945, he began an invasion of

the main island, Luzon, where around 250,000 soldiers of the Japanese 14th Area Army under the command of General Tomoyuki Yamashita were concentrated in the north around Manila, and on the high ground leading into the Bataan Peninsula.

The main invasion of Luzon began with landings by forces from the US 6th Army at Lingayen Gulf. The Filipino guerrillas were eager to take back control after the brutality of the Japanese regime and supported the Americans by striking the Japanese forces and carrying out reconnaissance activities. Still, progress was slow and brutal in the face of the Japanese refusal to surrender. Manila finally fell on March 3, 1945, by which time the US 8th Army had begun to move through the southern islands. In both north and south, the Americans were kept occupied until the end of the war.

"Have your troops hoist the colors to its peak, and let no enemy ever haul them down."

GENERAL DOUGLAS MACARTHUR, PHILIPPINES, 1945

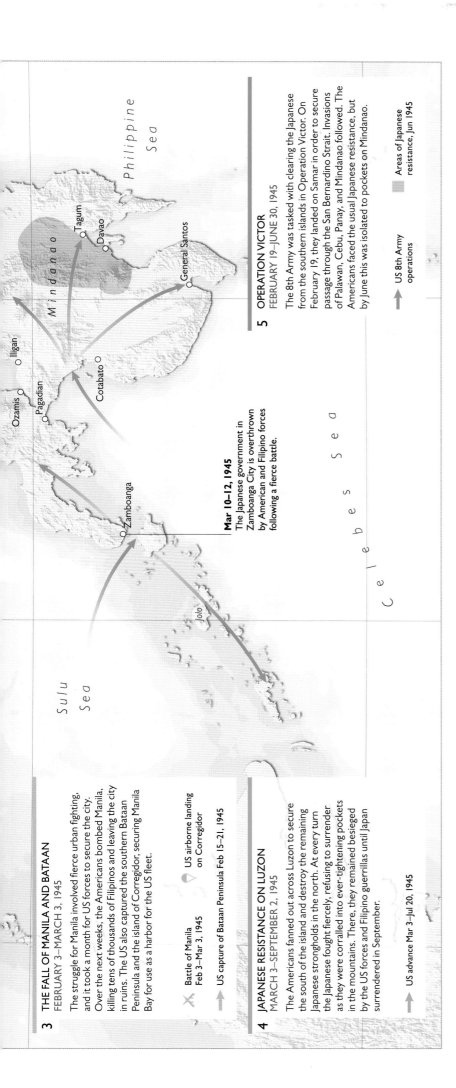

3 THE FALL OF MANILA AND BATAAN
FEBRUARY 3–MARCH 3, 1945

The struggle for Manila involved fierce urban fighting, and it took a month for US forces to secure the city. Over the next weeks, the Americans bombed Manila, killing tens of thousands of Filipinos and leaving the city in ruins. The US also captured the southern Bataan Peninsula and the island of Corregidor, securing Manila Bay for use as a harbor for the US fleet.

✕ Battle of Manila
Feb 3–Mar 3, 1945

◢ US airborne landing on Corregidor

⬆ US capture of Bataan Peninsula Feb 15–21, 1945

4 JAPANESE RESISTANCE ON LUZON
MARCH 3–SEPTEMBER 2, 1945

The Americans fanned out across Luzon to secure the south of the island and destroy the remaining Japanese strongholds in the north. At every turn the Japanese fought fiercely, refusing to surrender as they were corralled into ever-tightening pockets in the mountains. There, they remained besieged by the US forces and Filipino guerrillas until Japan surrendered in September.

⬆ US advance Mar 3–Jul 20, 1945

Mar 10–12, 1945
The Japanese government in Zamboanga City is overthrown by American and Filipino forces following a fierce battle.

5 OPERATION VICTOR
FEBRUARY 19–JUNE 30, 1945

The 8th Army was tasked with clearing the Japanese from the southern islands in Operation Victor. On February 19, they landed on Samar in order to secure passage through the San Bernardino Strait. Invasions of Palawan, Cebu, Panay, and Mindanao followed. The Americans faced the usual Japanese resistance, but by June this was isolated to pockets on Mindanao.

⬆ US 8th Army operations

▨ Areas of Japanese resistance, Jun 1945

Philippine Sea

Mindanao

Tagum
Davao
General Santos
Cotabato
Iligan
Ozamis
Pagadian
Zamboanga
Jolo

Sulu Sea

Celebes Sea

NO SURRENDER

Hiroo Onoda (1922–2014) was one of several Japanese soldiers who remained hidden in the Philippines' jungles, unaware or not believing that the war had ended. Cut off from his unit on Lubang Island in 1945, Onoda refused to surrender until his former commanding officer traveled to the Philippines in 1974 and relieved him of duty (below).

IWO JIMA OVERRUN

Over five bloody weeks in February and March 1945, US Marines spread across Iwo Jima, moving out from their beachheads to capture the island in four stages.

KEY

	US TERRITORIAL GAINS, 1945	
☐ Airstrip	Beachhead on Feb 19	by Feb 24
	by Mar 9	by Mar 1
		by Mar 14

TIMELINE

1
2
3
4

JAN 1944   JUL   JAN 1945   JUL

2 THE INITIAL LANDINGS   FEBRUARY 19, 1945

On February 19, 30,000 men from the 3rd, 4th, and 5th US Marine Divisions landed on the beaches of southeast Iwo Jima. The Japanese opened fire on the Americans, who were exposed because they could not dig foxholes in the soft volcanic ash of the beach. By the time the Marines reached the west coast of the island, almost 2,000 of their men had been killed or wounded.

🛖 US Marine divisions   ➡ US landings

3 CAPTURE OF MOUNT SURIBACHI AND THE AIRFIELDS   FEBRUARY 20–24, 1945

The Marines edged forward, capturing the first of Iwo Jima's two functioning airfields on February 20 and the second three days later. That same day a small group of Marines reached the summit of Mount Suribachi, the 554-ft (169-m) peak in the south of the island—an event recorded in what was one of the most iconic photographs to emerge from World War II (see p.247).

✈ Airfield   ➡ US advance Feb 20–24, 1945

🛣 Airfield (under construction)

◁ **Density of defenses**
A US map from early 1945 plots all the observed Japanese gun emplacements and defensive installations (red) on Iwo Jima.

1 OPENING MOVES

MARCH 1944–FEBRUARY 18, 1945

In 1944, General Tadamichi Kuribayashi, in charge of the 21,000 Japanese soldiers on Iwo Jima, began transforming the island into a fortress. He created a massive network of bunkers and hidden gun emplacements, digging 1,500 rooms in the island's rock and linking them with 11 miles (18km) of tunnels. Sheltering underground, the Japanese garrison was largely unaffected by the intense bombing of the island by US naval and air forces that had been launched to soften up the defenses.

〰 Main lines of defense
〰 Secondary line of defense
▬ Artillery positions

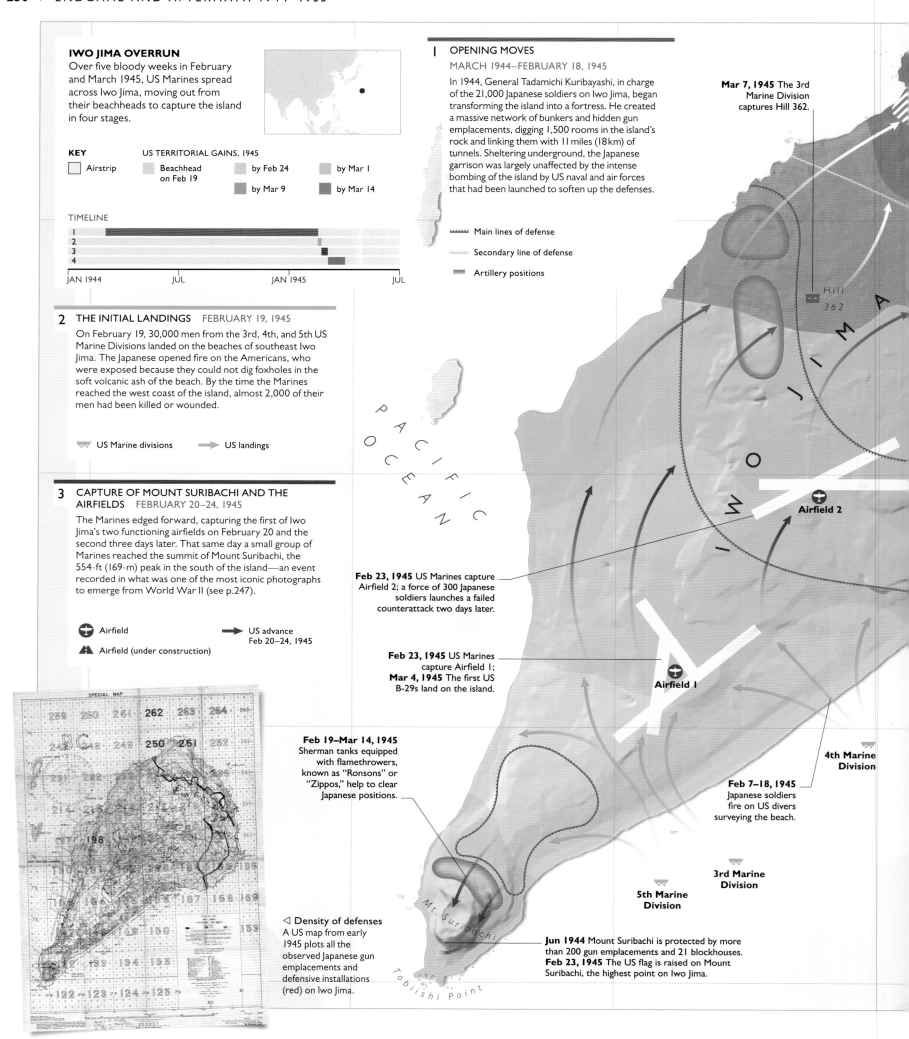

Mar 7, 1945 The 3rd Marine Division captures Hill 362.

Hill 362

Feb 23, 1945 US Marines capture Airfield 2; a force of 300 Japanese soldiers launches a failed counterattack two days later.

Airfield 2

Feb 23, 1945 US Marines capture Airfield 1;
Mar 4, 1945 The first US B-29s land on the island.

Airfield 1

Feb 19–Mar 14, 1945 Sherman tanks equipped with flamethrowers, known as "Ronsons" or "Zippos," help to clear Japanese positions.

4th Marine Division

Feb 7–18, 1945 Japanese soldiers fire on US divers surveying the beach.

3rd Marine Division

5th Marine Division

Mt. Suribachi

Jun 1944 Mount Suribachi is protected by more than 200 gun emplacements and 21 blockhouses.
Feb 23, 1945 The US flag is raised on Mount Suribachi, the highest point on Iwo Jima.

Tobiishi Point

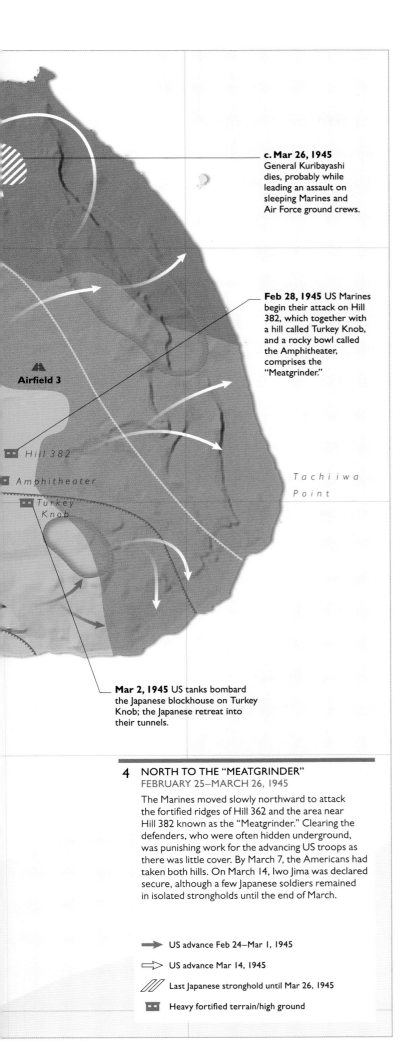

c. Mar 26, 1945
General Kuribayashi dies, probably while leading an assault on sleeping Marines and Air Force ground crews.

Feb 28, 1945 US Marines begin their attack on Hill 382, which together with a hill called Turkey Knob, and a rocky bowl called the Amphitheater, comprises the "Meatgrinder."

Airfield 3

Hill 382

Amphitheater

Turkey Knob

Tachiiwa Point

Mar 2, 1945 US tanks bombard the Japanese blockhouse on Turkey Knob; the Japanese retreat into their tunnels.

4   **NORTH TO THE "MEATGRINDER"**
FEBRUARY 25–MARCH 26, 1945

The Marines moved slowly northward to attack the fortified ridges of Hill 362 and the area near Hill 382 known as the "Meatgrinder." Clearing the defenders, who were often hidden underground, was punishing work for the advancing US troops as there was little cover. By March 7, the Americans had taken both hills. On March 14, Iwo Jima was declared secure, although a few Japanese soldiers remained in isolated strongholds until the end of March.

→ US advance Feb 24–Mar 1, 1945

⇨ US advance Mar 14, 1945

▨ Last Japanese stronghold until Mar 26, 1945

▨ Heavy fortified terrain/high ground

IWO JIMA

The Japanese island of Iwo Jima, which lies some 800 miles (1,300 km) from mainland Japan, was a strategic target for the US. The Marines who took the island from the small number of Japanese forces based there in early 1945 encountered some of the bloodiest fighting of the Pacific War.

By the start of 1945, US forces had moved far west across the Pacific, reaching Leyte and Luzon in the Philippines and inflicting terrible damage on the Imperial Japanese Navy and its air force in the process. In February 1945, US Marines invaded the tiny Pacific island of Iwo Jima, a Japanese military base. Their aim was strategic: they wanted to secure the island's airfields, which would provide a base for Allied fighter planes needed to escort the bombers raiding Japan from the Marianas (see pp.252–53)—and for the B-29 bombers themselves.

The Japanese were aware of the impending threat and as a result had made their preparations: sending reinforcements to Iwo Jima, ordering the evacuation of its civilian population, and placing the island's defense into the hands of one of their most brilliant and experienced generals, Tadamichi Kuribayashi.

Lacking naval or air support and commanding a relatively small force, Kuribayashi knew that an American victory was near inevitable, but he was determined to make it as costly as possible, and to delay his enemy's advance. Instead of defending the island's landing beaches, he ordered the construction of a huge network of caves, tunnels, and pillboxes inland. The invading US troops on the surface— often without cover—were at the mercy of the defenders, who would suddenly emerge from their underground bunkers to launch attacks. Casualties were huge on both sides.

"Japan has started a war with a formidable enemy and we must brace ourselves accordingly."

GENERAL TADAMICHI KURIBAYASHI, 1944

FIGHT TO THE DEATH

Over 20,000 of the 21,000 Japanese soldiers on Iwo Jima died in the fighting while following the instructions set out in General Kuribayashi's six "Courageous Battle Vows." The vows pledged soldiers to defend the island with all their strength, to attack the enemy with suicidal bravery, to not die until they had killed at least ten enemy soldiers, and to continue fighting to the last man.

US Marines destroy a Japanese bunker on Iwo Jima

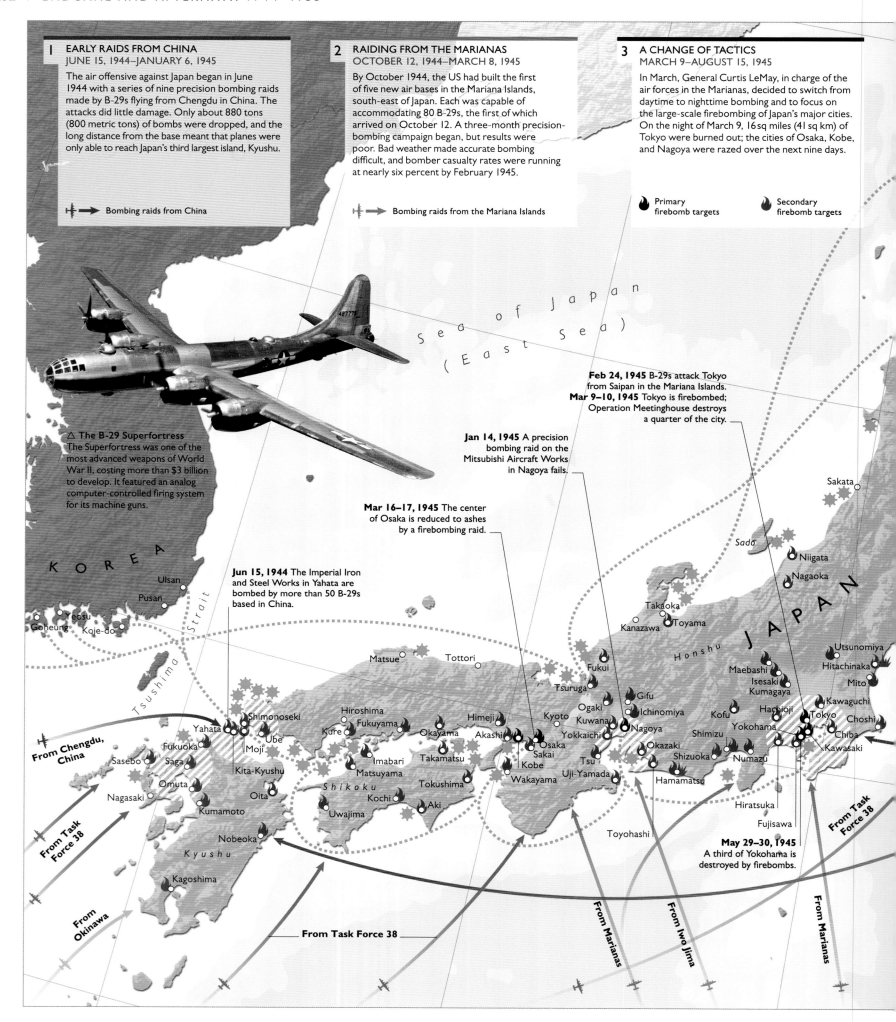

1 EARLY RAIDS FROM CHINA
JUNE 15, 1944–JANUARY 6, 1945

The air offensive against Japan began in June 1944 with a series of nine precision bombing raids made by B-29s flying from Chengdu in China. The attacks did little damage. Only about 880 tons (800 metric tons) of bombs were dropped, and the long distance from the base meant that planes were only able to reach Japan's third largest island, Kyushu.

⊬→ Bombing raids from China

2 RAIDING FROM THE MARIANAS
OCTOBER 12, 1944–MARCH 8, 1945

By October 1944, the US had built the first of five new air bases in the Mariana Islands, south-east of Japan. Each was capable of accommodating 80 B-29s, the first of which arrived on October 12. A three-month precision-bombing campaign began, but results were poor. Bad weather made accurate bombing difficult, and bomber casualty rates were running at nearly six percent by February 1945.

⊬→ Bombing raids from the Mariana Islands

3 A CHANGE OF TACTICS
MARCH 9–AUGUST 15, 1945

In March, General Curtis LeMay, in charge of the air forces in the Marianas, decided to switch from daytime to nighttime bombing and to focus on the large-scale firebombing of Japan's major cities. On the night of March 9, 16 sq miles (41 sq km) of Tokyo were burned out; the cities of Osaka, Kobe, and Nagoya were razed over the next nine days.

🔥 Primary firebomb targets   🔥 Secondary firebomb targets

△ The B-29 Superfortress
The Superfortress was one of the most advanced weapons of World War II, costing more than $3 billion to develop. It featured an analog computer-controlled firing system for its machine guns.

Feb 24, 1945 B-29s attack Tokyo from Saipan in the Mariana Islands.
Mar 9–10, 1945 Tokyo is firebombed; Operation Meetinghouse destroys a quarter of the city.

Jan 14, 1945 A precision bombing raid on the Mitsubishi Aircraft Works in Nagoya fails.

Mar 16–17, 1945 The center of Osaka is reduced to ashes by a firebombing raid.

Jun 15, 1944 The Imperial Iron and Steel Works in Yahata are bombed by more than 50 B-29s based in China.

May 29–30, 1945 A third of Yokohama is destroyed by firebombs.

Sea of Japan (East Sea)

KOREA

Tsushima Strait

JAPAN

Honshu

Shikoku

Kyushu

From Chengdu, China

From Task Force 38

From Okinawa

From Task Force 38

From Marianas

From Iwo Jima

From Marianas

Ulsan
Pusan
Yeosu
Goheung
Koje-do

Matsue
Tottori
Hiroshima
Fukuyama
Kure
Okayama
Imabari
Matsuyama
Takamatsu
Kochi
Uwajima
Aki
Tokushima

Yahata
Shimonoseki
Ube
Moji
Fukuoka
Saga
Kita-Kyushu
Sasebo
Omuta
Kumamoto
Oita
Nagasaki
Nobeoka
Kagoshima

Himeji
Akashi
Osaka
Sakai
Kobe
Wakayama
Kyoto
Kuwana
Yokkaichi
Tsu
Uji-Yamada

Fukui
Tsuruga
Ogaki
Gifu
Ichinomiya
Nagoya
Okazaki
Shizuoka
Hamamatsu
Toyohashi

Takaoka
Kanazawa
Toyama

Maebashi
Isesaki
Kumagaya
Kofu
Shimizu
Numazu
Hiratsuka
Fujisawa

Hachioji
Yokohama
Tokyo
Kawaguchi
Choshi
Chiba
Kawasaki

Utsunomiya
Hitachinaka
Mito

Sakata
Niigata
Nagaoka

Sado

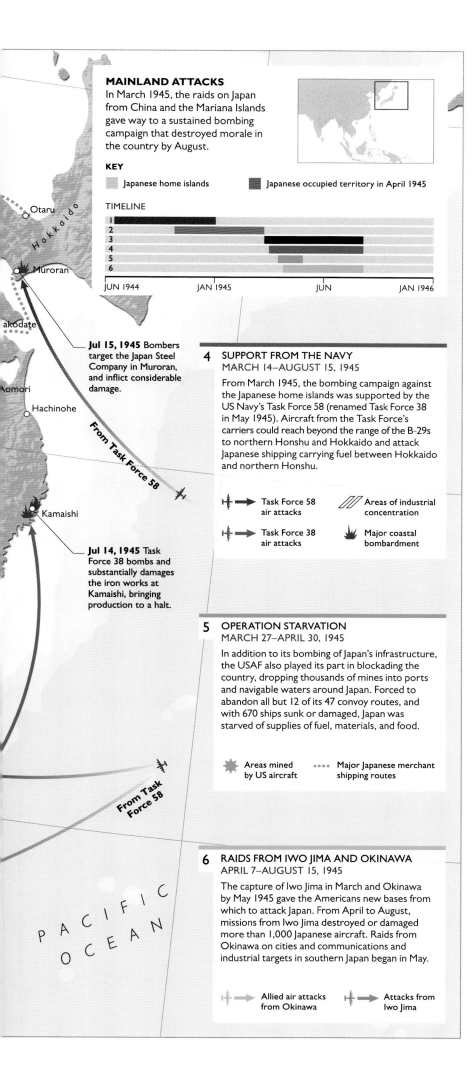

MAINLAND ATTACKS

In March 1945, the raids on Japan from China and the Mariana Islands gave way to a sustained bombing campaign that destroyed morale in the country by August.

KEY

▪ Japanese home islands ▪ Japanese occupied territory in April 1945

TIMELINE

1	
2	
3	
4	
5	
6	

JUN 1944   JAN 1945   JUN   JAN 1946

Jul 15, 1945 Bombers target the Japan Steel Company in Muroran, and inflict considerable damage.

Jul 14, 1945 Task Force 38 bombs and substantially damages the iron works at Kamaishi, bringing production to a halt.

From Task Force 58

From Task Force 58

Otaru
Muroran
Hakodate
Aomori
Hachinohe
Kamaishi

Hokkaido

PACIFIC OCEAN

4 SUPPORT FROM THE NAVY
MARCH 14–AUGUST 15, 1945

From March 1945, the bombing campaign against the Japanese home islands was supported by the US Navy's Task Force 58 (renamed Task Force 38 in May 1945). Aircraft from the Task Force's carriers could reach beyond the range of the B-29s to northern Honshu and Hokkaido and attack Japanese shipping carrying fuel between Hokkaido and northern Honshu.

⊢⊢→ Task Force 58 air attacks
⊢⊢→ Task Force 38 air attacks
/// Areas of industrial concentration
✹ Major coastal bombardment

5 OPERATION STARVATION
MARCH 27–APRIL 30, 1945

In addition to its bombing of Japan's infrastructure, the USAF also played its part in blockading the country, dropping thousands of mines into ports and navigable waters around Japan. Forced to abandon all but 12 of its 47 convoy routes, and with 670 ships sunk or damaged, Japan was starved of supplies of fuel, materials, and food.

✹ Areas mined by US aircraft
···· Major Japanese merchant shipping routes

6 RAIDS FROM IWO JIMA AND OKINAWA
APRIL 7–AUGUST 15, 1945

The capture of Iwo Jima in March and Okinawa by May 1945 gave the Americans new bases from which to attack Japan. From April to August, missions from Iwo Jima destroyed or damaged more than 1,000 Japanese aircraft. Raids from Okinawa on cities and communications and industrial targets in southern Japan began in May.

→ Allied air attacks from Okinawa
⊢⊢→ Attacks from Iwo Jima

THE BOMBING OF JAPAN

In June 1944, the Allies began the aerial bombardment of Japan. Aimed initially at shutting down Japanese industrial production for its war machine and cutting off the country's supplies, the campaign turned into a devastating assault on Japan's cities.

The Allies had long realized that the aerial bombardment of Japan would be an essential element in bringing the Japanese Empire to its knees. Early in the Pacific War, the US had launched a mostly unsuccessful air raid on Japan from an aircraft carrier—the Doolittle Raid of April 18, 1942—but had not targeted the country since.

In early 1944, the US deployed the advanced B-29 Superfortress in the Pacific theater. The aircraft was capable of carrying 10 tons (9 metric tons) of bombs over long distances and was used from June 1944 until the end of the war in the sustained bombing of the Japanese home islands. The campaign began poorly; raids from China proved problematic, and precision bombing did little to disrupt Japanese industry. However, as the campaign progressed and the USAF changed tactics, carpet-bombing Japan's cities with napalm and incendiary bombs, the results were dramatic. By August, a third of Japan's buildings and more than 600 factories had been destroyed, tens of thousands of its citizens had been killed, millions were homeless, and Japanese morale was decimated.

"This fire left nothing but twisted, tumbled-down rubble in its path."

GENERAL CURTIS LEMAY ON THE BOMBING OF TOKYO

THE TOKYO FIRESTORM

On the night of March 9–10, 1945, the USAF unleashed Operation Meetinghouse on Tokyo. In a devastating raid, 279 B-29s dropped 1,665 tons (1,510 metric tons) of bombs on the capital city. These napalm or gasoline and white phosphorus incendiary bombs ignited on impact, setting fire to huge swathes of the city, including the densely populated dock districts. A quarter of Tokyo's buildings were destroyed, leaving one million people homeless, and at least 80,000 people were killed.

Tokyo ablaze

THE BATTLE OF OKINAWA

As the conflict in Europe was nearing its end, the US was still fighting a brutal war in the Pacific. Its planned conquest of the isolated island of Okinawa resulted in one of the bloodiest battles of the entire conflict, which earned the nickname "Typhoon of Steel."

With their assault on Iwo Jima still underway (see pp.250–251), US commanders began preparing for Operation Iceberg—the invasion of Okinawa, the largest island in the Ryukyu Archipelago. Just 60 miles (96 km) long and 20 miles (32 km) wide at its widest, Okinawa is equidistant from Taiwan, Japan, and China, and US strategists saw it as the ideal base for the final assaults on the main Japanese islands. Like Iwo Jima, Okinawa was heavily fortified, with artillery hidden in caves, and garrisoned by 100,000 men under Lieutenant General Ushijima Mitsuru.

Familiar with the fierce determination of the Japanese army and aware that losses in the battle would probably overtake those on Iwo Jima, the US began the campaign with a massive bombardment to soften up the island's defenses. This was followed by the US military's biggest amphibious landing of the Pacific War. Nonetheless, it took the US forces more than two months to capture the entire island. In the end 12,000 US soldiers, 100,000 Japanese soldiers, and 100,000 civilians died in a campaign that was made obsolete by the events at Hiroshima and Nagasaki (see pp.258–259).

"The Japanese bayonets were fixed; ours weren't. We used the knives …"

FORMER US MARINE WILLIAM MANCHESTER, 1987

CAUGHT IN THE CROSSFIRE

Both Japanese and American soldiers committed atrocities against civilians during the battle. The Japanese also confiscated the Okinawans' food, causing mass starvation. When an American victory seemed certain, thousands of Okinawans committed suicide under pressure from the government. Among the civilians killed on Okinawa were also many who had been forced to serve in the Japanese army.

A US Marine shares his rations with children on Okinawa

OKINAWA CAPTURED

In four broad phases extending from April 1 to June 21, the Americans gradually gained control of Okinawa. The battle for the island played out on land and at sea.

KEY

Allied forces   Japanese airfields

UNDER US CONTROL 1945

Mar 31   Apr 4   Apr 21

May 12   Jun 21

TIMELINE

1
2
3
4
5
6

MAR 1945   APR   MAY   JUN   JUL

1 ALLIED PREPARATION
MARCH 18–31, 1945

Ahead of the invasion, Allied aircraft from carriers in Task Force 58 launched raids on Kyushu—the most south-westerly of Japan's main islands. They destroyed hundreds of Japanese aircraft, reducing the threat to the invasion of Okinawa. On March 26, US forces landed on the Kerama Islands west of Okinawa, which could be used as fleet anchorage, and on Keise Shima, from which artillery could provide fire support across most of southern Okinawa.

Aguni Shima

Preliminary US landings

Mar–Apr The US 10th Army consists of more than 180,000 personnel at the start of the invasion.

US 10th Army

2 THE INVASION OF OKINAWA
APRIL 1–4, 1945

Troops of the US 10th Army landed at Hagushi on April 1. By the end of the day, 50,000 US soldiers were on Okinawa and had taken key targets, including airfields. Ultimately, 170,000 troops landed on the island. At first they faced little resistance as they moved inland; by April 4 they had divided the island in two.

US landings and advance across Okinawa

Japanese forces on Apr 1

East China Sea

3 THE CONQUEST OF NORTH OKINAWA
APRIL 4–21, 1945

After taking south central Okinawa, General Buckner, commander of the US 10th Army, sent troops north. They encountered strong resistance from Japanese forces cornered in ridged, wooded terrain around Mount Yae in the Motobu Peninsula. By April 20, the US held the north, and had secured the islet of Ie Shima.

Kerama Islands

US advance north

Resistance around Mount Yae

Task Force 51

6 COLLAPSE OF THE SOUTHERN DEFENSE
MAY 12–JUNE 21, 1945

US troops continued their grueling advance through monsoon rains and took Shuri Castle on May 29—a major breakthrough. The Japanese retreated south to the Kiyan Peninsula, where the remnants held out until June 21. Fewer than 10,000 of over 100,000 Japanese and Okinawan soldiers surrendered were finally captured.

→ US advance   ☐ Last pocket of Japanese resistance

⌗ Shuri Castle

5 COUNTERATTACK AT SEA
APRIL 6–JUNE 22, 1945

On April 6, Japan targeted Task Force 58, off the coast of Okinawa, with a campaign of kamikaze attacks launched from the Japanese island of Kyushu to the north. Many smaller ships were sunk and larger warships were damaged. A Japanese naval task force led by the *Yamato*—the world's largest battleship—was intercepted by US torpedo bombers and destroyed long before it reached Okinawa.

➤ Kamikaze attacks on Allied Fleet

Apr 13 US Marines reach Hedo, the northernmost point of the island.

Cape Hedo

Hedo

Aha

Tako

Taira

Apr 6 Kamikaze aircraft from Kyushu attack US Task Force 58.

Task Force 58

Ie Shima

Bise

Motobu Peninsula

Mount Yae

Apr 16–21 US forces capture Ie Shima and its air base; Pulitzer Prize–winning US journalist Ernie Pyle is killed while covering the invasion.

Nago

Apr 13–20 Japanese troops fight to defend the hills of Mount Yae, before being overrun.

Kin

Mar 26–30 US frogmen and minesweepers clear the invasion beaches of obstacles.

Kurawa

Hagushi Bay

Hagushi

4 THE PUSH SOUTH   APRIL 4–MAY 12, 1945

US forces pushing south faced intensive fighting but by April 9 reached the heavily fortified Shuri Line. As in Iwo Jima, the Japanese hid in and fought from caves; the US Marines and soldiers resorted to flamethrowers as they fought hill by hill to advance. They were repelled numerous times, with mounting casualties, before breaking through to Naha on May 12.

→ US advance   〰 Shuri Line

Mar 31 US artillery is positioned on Keise Shima islets.

Kuba

Apr 10 US troops land and clear the island.

Tsugen Shima

Keise Shima

Naha Shuri

Japanese 32nd Army

Yonabaru

Oruku Peninsula

Jun 4 US Marines land; 4,000 Japanese troops hidden in the underground naval headquarters commit suicide on June 13.

Itoman

Kiyan Peninsula

▷ **Beachhead on Okinawa**
The invasion was a logistical challenge for the US forces, who needed to land thousands of men and large amounts of supplies onto a remote island. Here, stores are loaded onto the beach during the operation.

OKINAWA

PACIFIC OCEAN

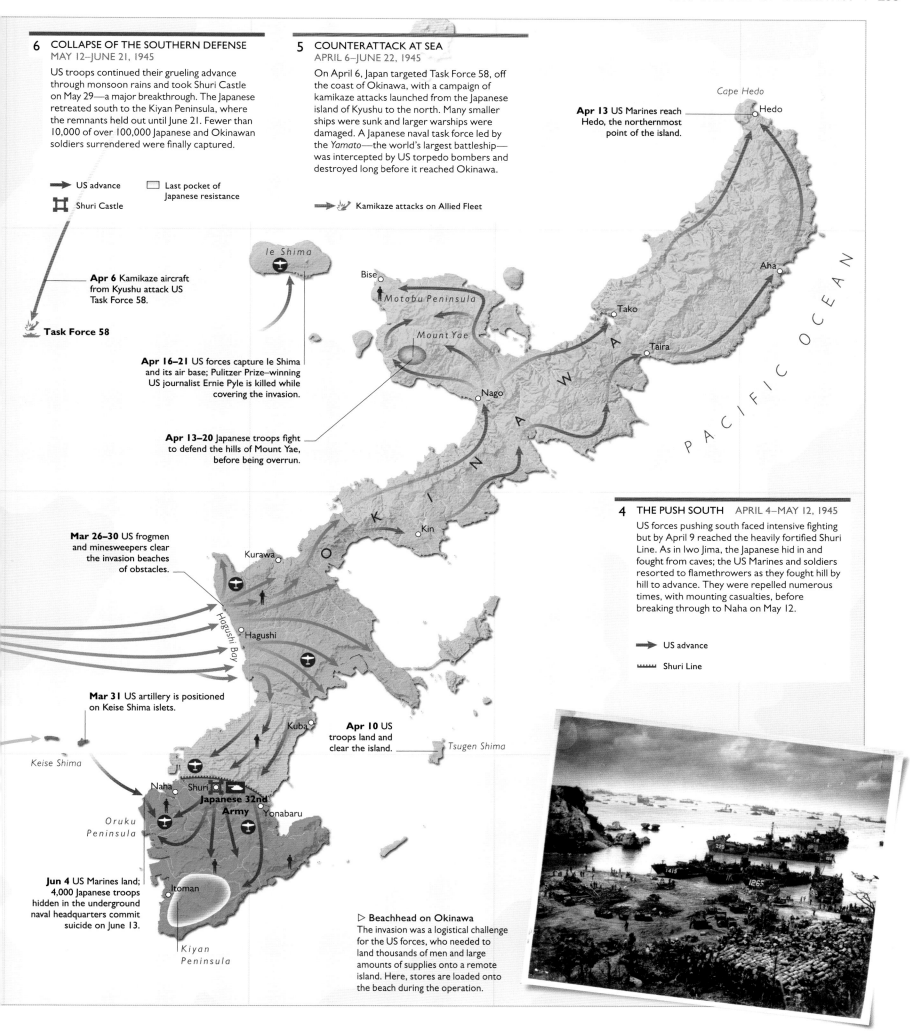

MANHATTAN PROJECT

The Manhattan Project was one of several programs working on developing nuclear weapons in the 1940s, and it was the most successful. In July 1945, the project team detonated the world's first atomic bomb.

Knowledge about atomic physics developed very quickly. In 1896, French physicist Henri Becquerel discovered radioactivity, and by 1920, New Zealand-born physicist Ernest Rutherford had split the atom, and Danish physicist Niels Bohr had completed his atomic theory. With the discovery of nuclear fission by German

△ **"Fat Man" replica**
Code named "Fat Man," the atomic bomb that was dropped on the Japanese city of Nagasaki in August 1945 was even more powerful than the one used at Hiroshima.

scientists Otto Hahn and Fritz Strassman in 1938, the race to develop an atomic weapon had begun. The US-based Manhattan Project, set up in 1941, quickly outpaced the British program. In 1943, Britain's Tube Alloys program and the Manhattan Project merged, while the Allies successfully sabotaged Germany's atomic program with an attack on the Vemork heavy water plant (see pp.138–139).

The bomb as a reality
On July 16, 1945, the US army successfully detonated an atomic bomb at Almagordo, New Mexico. Churchill heard of the test through a note handed to him at the Potsdam Conference that said, "Babies satisfactorily born." The atomic bomb was now a reality, and was dropped to devastating effect on Japan in August of the same year, at Hiroshima and Nagasaki (see pp.258–259).

△ **The beginning of the end**
The world's first atomic bomb exploded at 5:29 am on July 16, 1945, in New Mexico, in an operation code named "Trinity."

▷ **Team photo display**
The Manhattan Project's team consisted of many scientists who had left Britain or fled Europe before or during the war.

Harold M. Agnew

Luis Alvarez

Athena V. Berry

Richard P. Feynman

Al Clark

R. Oppenheimer

Katherine Oppenheimer

Elinor Hempelmann

Marion L. Arnold

Leandro S. Ortiz

Viola M. Vigil

Elmer L. Hilton

John R. Von Neumann

Gladys Grinsel

Seth H. Neddermeyer

zel R. Greenbacker

Amadon Garcia

Sara Lea Peddicord

Gilbert J. Gutierrez

HIROSHIMA AND NAGASAKI

On August 6, 1945, a B-29 bomber dropped a nuclear weapon on Hiroshima that killed around 80,000 people instantly and left 70 percent of the city's buildings in ruins. A second bomb was dropped on Nagasaki three days later, claiming another 40,000 lives. The bombs helped to bring the Pacific war to an end, but at an appalling cost.

As the war in the west came to an end in May 1945, the Allied forces began drawing up plans to invade Japan. However, the Japanese had a large number of troops, along with a vast civilian militia, and US military planners feared that an invasion could result in a long-running conflict with extensive casualties on both sides. They considered using chemical and biological weapons, but, despite some opposition, President Truman made the decision to use nuclear weapons (see pp.256–257) against Japan.

Three nuclear bombs were built. The first prototype was tested over the New Mexico desert on July 16, 1945. The other two bombs were to be dropped on the cities of Hiroshima and Kokura, chosen for their industrial and military significance; however, poor weather conditions on the day of the attack resulted in one of the bombers diverting from Kokura to Nagasaki. The two explosions caused casualties on a vast scale, and their impact started a debate about the morality of nuclear weapons that still rages today.

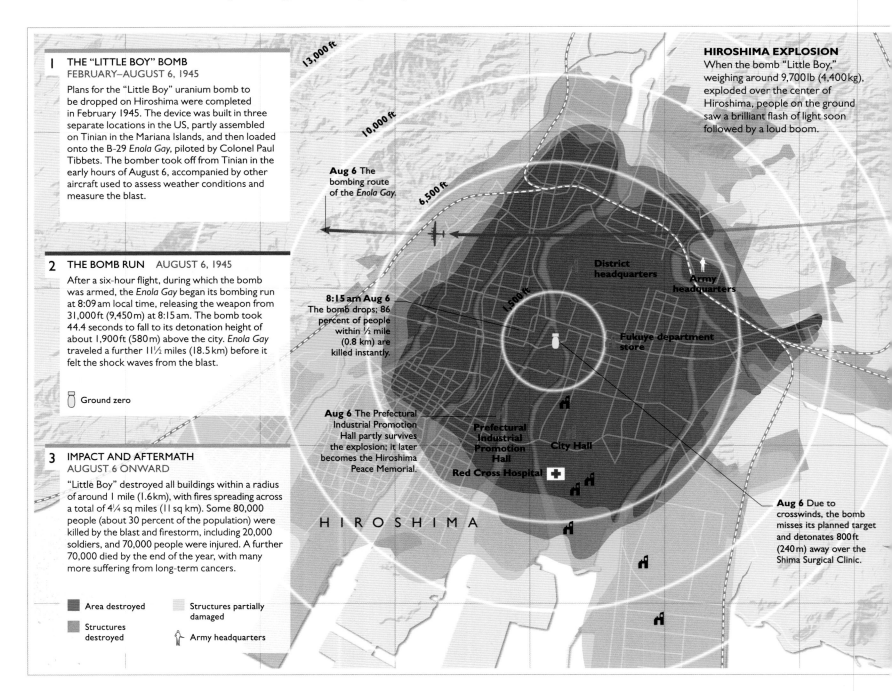

1 THE "LITTLE BOY" BOMB
FEBRUARY–AUGUST 6, 1945

Plans for the "Little Boy" uranium bomb to be dropped on Hiroshima were completed in February 1945. The device was built in three separate locations in the US, partly assembled on Tinian in the Mariana Islands, and then loaded onto the B-29 *Enola Gay*, piloted by Colonel Paul Tibbets. The bomber took off from Tinian in the early hours of August 6, accompanied by other aircraft used to assess weather conditions and measure the blast.

2 THE BOMB RUN   AUGUST 6, 1945

After a six-hour flight, during which the bomb was armed, the *Enola Gay* began its bombing run at 8:09 am local time, releasing the weapon from 31,000 ft (9,450 m) at 8:15 am. The bomb took 44.4 seconds to fall to its detonation height of about 1,900 ft (580 m) above the city. *Enola Gay* traveled a further 11½ miles (18.5 km) before it felt the shock waves from the blast.

🍶 Ground zero

3 IMPACT AND AFTERMATH
AUGUST 6 ONWARD

"Little Boy" destroyed all buildings within a radius of around 1 mile (1.6 km), with fires spreading across a total of 4¼ sq miles (11 sq km). Some 80,000 people (about 30 percent of the population) were killed by the blast and firestorm, including 20,000 soldiers, and 70,000 people were injured. A further 70,000 died by the end of the year, with many more suffering from long-term cancers.

■ Area destroyed
■ Structures destroyed
■ Structures partially damaged
🍶 Army headquarters

13,000 ft

10,000 ft

6,500 ft

Aug 6 The bombing route of the *Enola Gay*.

HIROSHIMA EXPLOSION
When the bomb "Little Boy," weighing around 9,700 lb (4,400 kg), exploded over the center of Hiroshima, people on the ground saw a brilliant flash of light soon followed by a loud boom.

8:15 am Aug 6 The bomb drops; 86 percent of people within ½ mile (0.8 km) are killed instantly.

1,500 ft

District headquarters

Army headquarters

Fukuye department store

Aug 6 The Prefectural Industrial Promotion Hall partly survives the explosion; it later becomes the Hiroshima Peace Memorial.

Prefectural Industrial Promotion Hall

City Hall

Red Cross Hospital ✚

Aug 6 Due to crosswinds, the bomb misses its planned target and detonates 800 ft (240 m) away over the Shima Surgical Clinic.

H I R O S H I M A

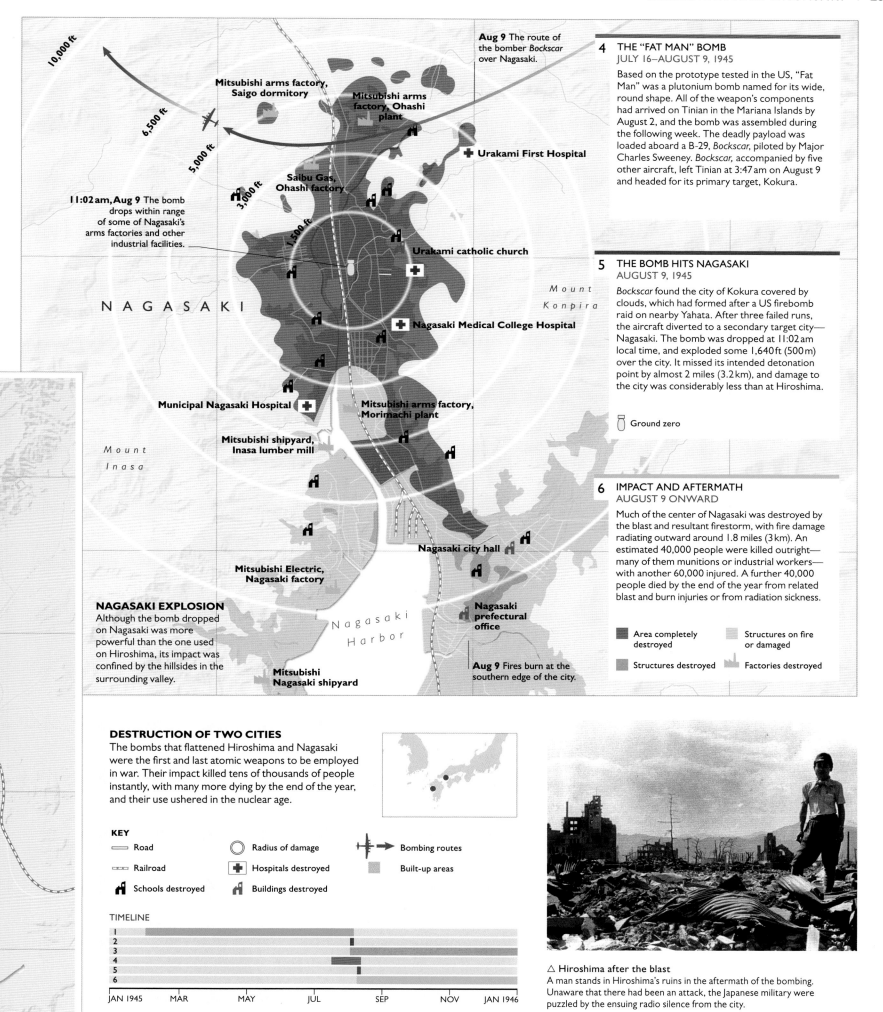

Aug 9 The route of the bomber *Bockscar* over Nagasaki.

Mitsubishi arms factory, Saigo dormitory

Mitsubishi arms factory, Ohashi plant

✚ Urakami First Hospital

Saibu Gas, Ohashi factory

11:02 am, Aug 9 The bomb drops within range of some of Nagasaki's arms factories and other industrial facilities.

Urakami catholic church

N A G A S A K I

Mount Konpira

Nagasaki Medical College Hospital

Municipal Nagasaki Hospital ✚

Mount Inasa

Mitsubishi arms factory, Morimachi plant

Mitsubishi shipyard, Inasa lumber mill

Nagasaki city hall

Mitsubishi Electric, Nagasaki factory

Nagasaki prefectural office

Nagasaki Harbor

NAGASAKI EXPLOSION
Although the bomb dropped on Nagasaki was more powerful than the one used on Hiroshima, its impact was confined by the hillsides in the surrounding valley.

Aug 9 Fires burn at the southern edge of the city.

Mitsubishi Nagasaki shipyard

4 THE "FAT MAN" BOMB
JULY 16–AUGUST 9, 1945
Based on the prototype tested in the US, "Fat Man" was a plutonium bomb named for its wide, round shape. All of the weapon's components had arrived on Tinian in the Mariana Islands by August 2, and the bomb was assembled during the following week. The deadly payload was loaded aboard a B-29, *Bockscar*, piloted by Major Charles Sweeney. *Bockscar*, accompanied by five other aircraft, left Tinian at 3:47 am on August 9 and headed for its primary target, Kokura.

5 THE BOMB HITS NAGASAKI
AUGUST 9, 1945
Bockscar found the city of Kokura covered by clouds, which had formed after a US firebomb raid on nearby Yahata. After three failed runs, the aircraft diverted to a secondary target city—Nagasaki. The bomb was dropped at 11:02 am local time, and exploded some 1,640 ft (500 m) over the city. It missed its intended detonation point by almost 2 miles (3.2 km), and damage to the city was considerably less than at Hiroshima.

⬚ Ground zero

6 IMPACT AND AFTERMATH
AUGUST 9 ONWARD
Much of the center of Nagasaki was destroyed by the blast and resultant firestorm, with fire damage radiating outward around 1.8 miles (3 km). An estimated 40,000 people were killed outright—many of them munitions or industrial workers—with another 60,000 injured. A further 40,000 people died by the end of the year from related blast and burn injuries or from radiation sickness.

■ Area completely destroyed

■ Structures on fire or damaged

■ Structures destroyed

⚒ Factories destroyed

DESTRUCTION OF TWO CITIES
The bombs that flattened Hiroshima and Nagasaki were the first and last atomic weapons to be employed in war. Their impact killed tens of thousands of people instantly, with many more dying by the end of the year, and their use ushered in the nuclear age.

KEY
▭ Road

◯ Radius of damage

✈ Bombing routes

▱ Railroad

✚ Hospitals destroyed

▨ Built-up areas

⚑ Schools destroyed

⚒ Buildings destroyed

TIMELINE
1
2
3
4
5
6

JAN 1945   MAR   MAY   JUL   SEP   NOV   JAN 1946

△ **Hiroshima after the blast**
A man stands in Hiroshima's ruins in the aftermath of the bombing. Unaware that there had been an attack, the Japanese military were puzzled by the ensuing radio silence from the city.

PEACE IN THE PACIFIC

Japan surrendered to the Allies on August 15, 1945, around three months after the capitulation of Axis forces in Europe. It brought World War II to an end, and prevented a US invasion of Japan's home islands that would almost certainly have cost many more lives.

△ **Hot news**
The Stars and Stripes, the US military newspaper, splashes news of Japan's unconditional surrender and the end of the war.

While Japan's surrender is often attributed to the bombing of Hiroshima and Nagasaki (see pp.258–259), there were other elements involved. The Potsdam Declaration (see pp.230–231) had demanded unconditional Japanese surrender, and Japan's Supreme Council for the Direction of the War, or "Big Six," appealed to the USSR—secretly and unsuccessfully—to negotiate a surrender on more favorable terms. On August 6, the US dropped an atom bomb on Hiroshima, and a few days later they dropped another on Nagasaki. On August 8, the USSR declared war on Japan; the following day, Soviet forces began their invasion of Manchuria.

As the odds stacked up against Japan, Emperor Hirohito ordered the "Big Six" to accept the Allies' terms of surrender. A failed coup d'etat by pro-war factions ensued, and on August 15 Hirohito issued a radio broadcast declaring surrender. It was a crushing blow to the nation, and a few military personnel refused to accept it, fighting on for months and even years. US forces began occupying Japan on August 28, and the surrender ceremony took place on September 2.

△ **Laying down of arms**
Japanese officers surrender their ceremonial samurai swords to soldiers of the 25th Indian Division at Kuala Lumpur, Malaya. In his capitulation speech, Emperor Hirohito had declared that if the Japanese continued to fight "it would not only result in an ultimate collapse and obliteration of the Japanese nation, but would lead to the total extinction of human civilization."

Ceremony in Tokyo Bay
Sailors and soldiers crowd the decks of the USS *Missouri* to witness the Japanese Foreign Minister Mamoru Shigemitsu and Army Chief of Staff General Umezu Yoshijiro sign the Instrument of Surrender. General Douglas MacArthur accepted the surrender on behalf of the Allies.

THE AFTERMATH OF WAR

The most destructive war in history, World War II was followed by a nuclear arms race between the US and the Soviet Union that created the potential for mass destruction on an unprecedented and almost unimaginable scale. Recovery from the material damage of the war was relatively swift, but achieving genuine peace proved an elusive goal.

△ **People on the move**
In the wake of World War II, there were at least 11 million civilian refugees throughout Europe who needed to find new homes.

Across most of Europe and Asia, World War II left a legacy of ruined cities and displaced lives. In contrast, the US was strengthened by the war, both economically and militarily, and became globally dominant. The Soviet Union had greatly extended its territory and possessed a formidable army, but it had suffered some of the worst damage of any country in the war, and could not compete with the US in economic strength. For Britain and France, although they had been on the winning side, the war had been humbling, and their imperial prestige would never be restored. By 1955, most countries in South and Southeast Asia had gained independence from colonial rule.

The Cold War sets in

The high ideals professed by the victors during World War II found embodiment in the United Nations and provided the basis for war crime trials of Nazi and Japanese leaders. However, the alliance between the Soviet Union and the Western powers soon fell apart, and Europe became divided by the "Iron Curtain," which separated the Soviet-dominated Communist East from the US-dominated capitalist West. By 1950, after the triumph of Mao Zedong in the Chinese Civil War, Communist societies stretched from Central Europe to the Pacific, while the US adopted the role of leader of the "Free World." As the US

◁ **Nuclear arms race**
The 1952 explosion of the first hydrogen bomb at Eniwetok Atoll, in the Pacific, further expanded the destructive power of nuclear arsenals.

EUROPE AND ASIA

Unable to agree on Germany's future, the Allies turned their temporary military occupation zones into separate states. The Soviet Union's zone became East Germany, and the Western powers' zones formed West Germany. Berlin remained divided between the four powers, but within East German territory. Later, West Germany integrated into NATO, and East Germany into the Warsaw Pact. Japan was only occupied by the Americans, and was reconstructed as a constitutional monarchy.

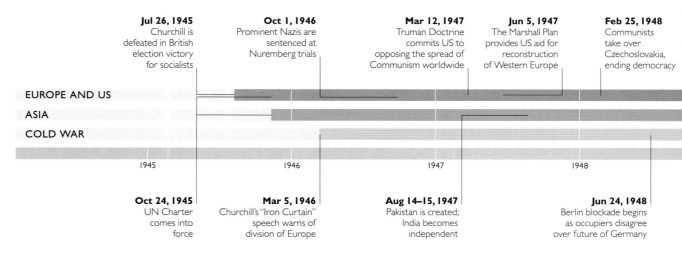

Jul 26, 1945
Churchill is defeated in British election victory for socialists

Oct 1, 1946
Prominent Nazis are sentenced at Nuremberg trials

Mar 12, 1947
Truman Doctrine commits US to opposing the spread of Communism worldwide

Jun 5, 1947
The Marshall Plan provides US aid for reconstruction of Western Europe

Feb 25, 1948
Communists take over Czechoslovakia, ending democracy

EUROPE AND US
ASIA
COLD WAR

1945   1946   1947   1948

Oct 24, 1945
UN Charter comes into force

Mar 5, 1946
Churchill's "Iron Curtain" speech warns of division of Europe

Aug 14–15, 1947
Pakistan is created; India becomes independent

Jun 24, 1948
Berlin blockade begins as occupiers disagree over future of Germany

◁ **Back on track**
The mass production of the Volkswagen (meaning "people's car") became a symbol of West Germany's economic and political recovery in the 1950s.

> *"Shall we put an end to the human race; or shall mankind renounce war?"*
>
> BERTRAND RUSSELL, THE RUSSELL–EINSTEIN MANIFESTO, 1955

and USSR (the "superpowers") engaged in a nuclear arms race, and the US fought the Chinese Communist troops in Korea, fears of an even more destructive World War III were only too real.

Economic recovery

Across the world, political recovery and economic reconstruction were surprisingly successful. As a global economy was restored (excluding the Communist states), there was no return to the mass unemployment of the Depression years, and in many countries, consumer demand was soon driving high growth rates. Japan and Germany had seen enough of the horrors of war and, unlike after World War I, there were no calls to avenge defeat. Japan was reestablished as a constitutional monarchy, and Hiroshima and Nagasaki were restored as flourishing cities. In West Germany, democracy took root, and industrial growth was rapid. Across much of Western Europe, forms of social democracy with mixed economies became standard. Progressive innovations included votes for women in France and the National Health Service in Britain.

The post-war world

The victorious powers fell far short of fulfilling the ideals they had expressed during the conflict. In the Soviet-controlled sphere—which included Albania, Bulgaria, Czechoslovakia, Hungary, East Germany, Poland, Romania, and Yugoslavia—prison camps and the denial of individual freedom negated the promise of liberation. Meanwhile, the US was prepared to support right-wing dictators serving the anticommunist cause, as in Francoist Spain and much of Latin America. For decades, the colonial powers still fought local wars against subject populations, while in the Middle East, the founding of Israel confirmed a chronic instability in the region. Instead of disarmament, there was a headlong race to expand both nuclear and conventional military arsenals. However, amid these conflicts and uncertainties, many individuals found a chance to build new lives in rapidly changing societies. The post-war world did not necessarily offer justice, peace, or security, but it did offer hope.

△ **Mao's China**
A poster celebrates the anniversary of the founding of Communist China, led by Chairman Mao Zedong. In the 1960s, about one third of the world's population lived under Communist rule.

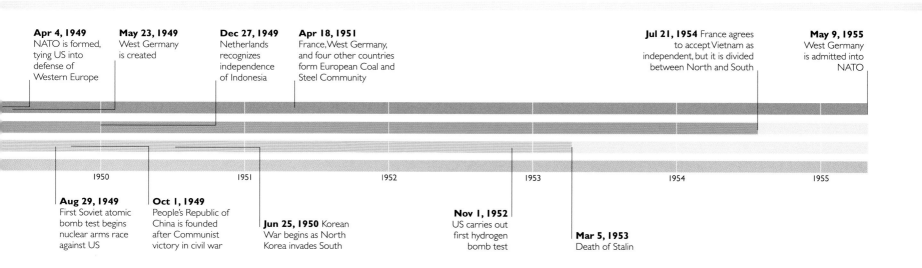

Apr 4, 1949 NATO is formed, tying US into defense of Western Europe

May 23, 1949 West Germany is created

Dec 27, 1949 Netherlands recognizes independence of Indonesia

Apr 18, 1951 France, West Germany, and four other countries form European Coal and Steel Community

Jul 21, 1954 France agrees to accept Vietnam as independent, but it is divided between North and South

May 9, 1955 West Germany is admitted into NATO

1950   1951   1952   1953   1954   1955

Aug 29, 1949 First Soviet atomic bomb test begins nuclear arms race against US

Oct 1, 1949 People's Republic of China is founded after Communist victory in civil war

Jun 25, 1950 Korean War begins as North Korea invades South

Nov 1, 1952 US carries out first hydrogen bomb test

Mar 5, 1953 Death of Stalin

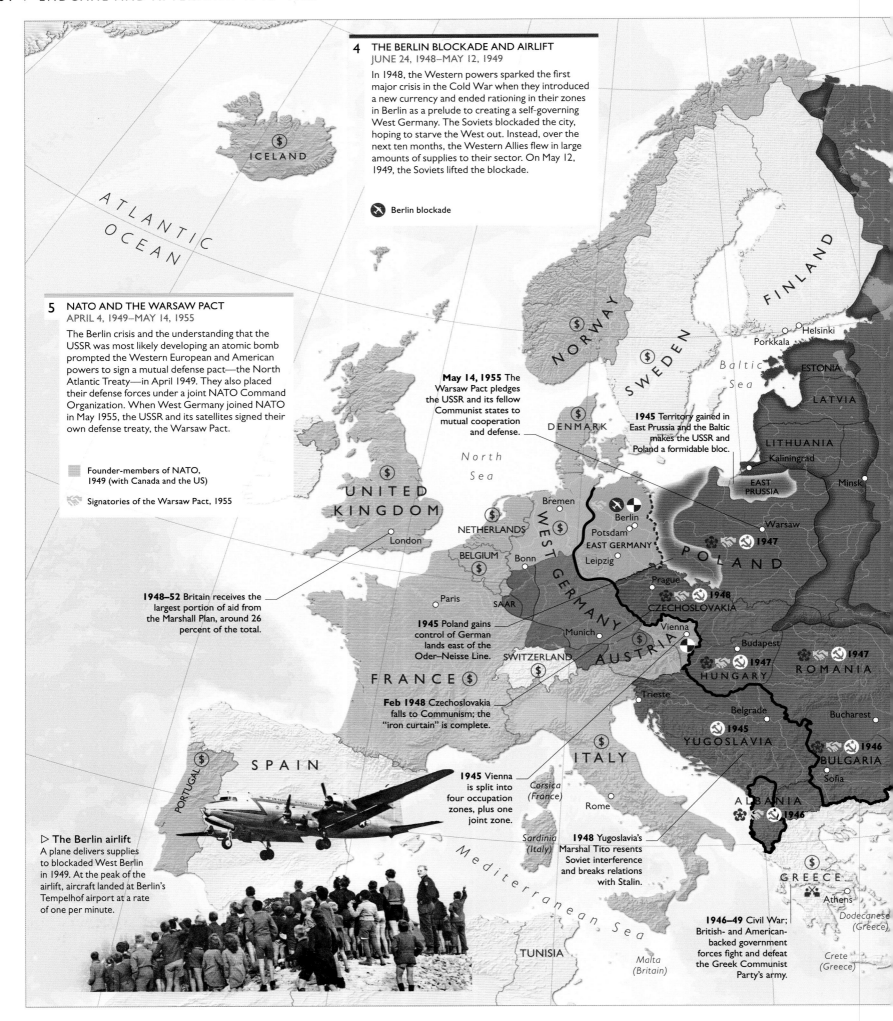

4 THE BERLIN BLOCKADE AND AIRLIFT
JUNE 24, 1948–MAY 12, 1949

In 1948, the Western powers sparked the first major crisis in the Cold War when they introduced a new currency and ended rationing in their zones in Berlin as a prelude to creating a self-governing West Germany. The Soviets blockaded the city, hoping to starve the West out. Instead, over the next ten months, the Western Allies flew in large amounts of supplies to their sector. On May 12, 1949, the Soviets lifted the blockade.

✈ Berlin blockade

5 NATO AND THE WARSAW PACT
APRIL 4, 1949–MAY 14, 1955

The Berlin crisis and the understanding that the USSR was most likely developing an atomic bomb prompted the Western European and American powers to sign a mutual defense pact—the North Atlantic Treaty—in April 1949. They also placed their defense forces under a joint NATO Command Organization. When West Germany joined NATO in May 1955, the USSR and its satellites signed their own defense treaty, the Warsaw Pact.

Founder-members of NATO, 1949 (with Canada and the US)

Signatories of the Warsaw Pact, 1955

May 14, 1955 The Warsaw Pact pledges the USSR and its fellow Communist states to mutual cooperation and defense.

1945 Territory gained in East Prussia and the Baltic makes the USSR and Poland a formidable bloc.

1948–52 Britain receives the largest portion of aid from the Marshall Plan, around 26 percent of the total.

1945 Poland gains control of German lands east of the Oder–Neisse Line.

Feb 1948 Czechoslovakia falls to Communism; the "iron curtain" is complete.

1945 Vienna is split into four occupation zones, plus one joint zone.

▷ **The Berlin airlift**
A plane delivers supplies to blockaded West Berlin in 1949. At the peak of the airlift, aircraft landed at Berlin's Tempelhof airport at a rate of one per minute.

1948 Yugoslavia's Marshal Tito resents Soviet interference and breaks relations with Stalin.

1946–49 Civil War; British- and American-backed government forces fight and defeat the Greek Communist Party's army.

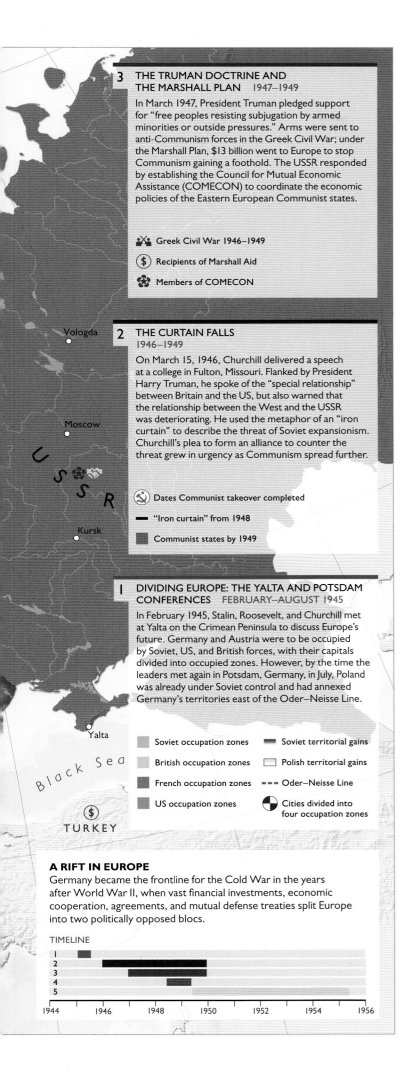

3 THE TRUMAN DOCTRINE AND THE MARSHALL PLAN 1947–1949

In March 1947, President Truman pledged support for "free peoples resisting subjugation by armed minorities or outside pressures." Arms were sent to anti-Communism forces in the Greek Civil War; under the Marshall Plan, $13 billion went to Europe to stop Communism gaining a foothold. The USSR responded by establishing the Council for Mutual Economic Assistance (COMECON) to coordinate the economic policies of the Eastern European Communist states.

- Greek Civil War 1946–1949
- $ Recipients of Marshall Aid
- Members of COMECON

2 THE CURTAIN FALLS 1946–1949

On March 15, 1946, Churchill delivered a speech at a college in Fulton, Missouri. Flanked by President Harry Truman, he spoke of the "special relationship" between Britain and the US, but also warned that the relationship between the West and the USSR was deteriorating. He used the metaphor of an "iron curtain" to describe the threat of Soviet expansionism. Churchill's plea to form an alliance to counter the threat grew in urgency as Communism spread further.

- Dates Communist takeover completed
- "Iron curtain" from 1948
- Communist states by 1949

1 DIVIDING EUROPE: THE YALTA AND POTSDAM CONFERENCES FEBRUARY–AUGUST 1945

In February 1945, Stalin, Roosevelt, and Churchill met at Yalta on the Crimean Peninsula to discuss Europe's future. Germany and Austria were to be occupied by Soviet, US, and British forces, with their capitals divided into occupied zones. However, by the time the leaders met again in Potsdam, Germany, in July, Poland was already under Soviet control and had annexed Germany's territories east of the Oder–Neisse Line.

- Soviet occupation zones
- British occupation zones
- French occupation zones
- US occupation zones
- Soviet territorial gains
- Polish territorial gains
- - - Oder–Neisse Line
- Cities divided into four occupation zones

A RIFT IN EUROPE

Germany became the frontline for the Cold War in the years after World War II, when vast financial investments, economic cooperation, agreements, and mutual defense treaties split Europe into two politically opposed blocs.

TIMELINE

	1944	1946	1948	1950	1952	1954	1956
1							
2							
3							
4							
5							

THE IRON CURTAIN

After the end of World War II, Europe was divided by an ideological "iron curtain" that separated the Communist states of the East from the democracies of the West. The division deepened to create two economic and military blocs that existed at a tense stand-off for the next 40 years.

The goodwill between the USSR and its Western allies drained away toward the end of the war, and historic tensions between the powers began to resurface by the time the Allied leaders met to discuss the reorganization of Europe at Yalta in February 1945 (see pp.230–231).

As much of Eastern Europe fell into Communist hands over the next few years, the US gradually came to heed Churchill's warning—originally dismissed as warmongering—that an "iron curtain" was descending on Europe and that the West needed protection from the spread of Communism. Rivalry and antagonism between the former allies grew rapidly into the Cold War, a term originally coined by the English writer George Orwell. This war was expressed not through direct military conflict, but rather through general non-cooperation, propaganda, and economic measures, which created two opposed economic blocs—Western Europe and North America on one side, and the USSR and her satellite Communist states on the other.

The Cold War nearly tipped into armed conflict during the Berlin blockade in 1948. After this, both sides created mutual defense treaties—the North Atlantic Treaty and the Warsaw Pact—that successfully prevented war, despite later moments of crisis, such as the Cuban Missile Crisis in 1962. Relations between the two blocs would eventually thaw in the 1980s with the liberalization of the USSR under Mikhail Gorbachev.

△ **Germany divided**
This map, produced in Frankfurt, Germany, in 1945, shows the division of the country into Occupation Zones. The symbol over Berlin shows the split of the city into four sectors.

THE CHINESE CIVIL WAR

After Japan's defeat in 1945, the uneasy wartime alliance between Chiang Kai-shek's Chinese Nationalist Party and Mao Zedong's Chinese Communist Party fell apart. The long battle for control of a unified China entered its final phase.

On September 9, 1945, a week after Japan's surrender ended World War II, Japanese forces in China (excluding those in Manchuria) surrendered to the Chinese Nationalist Party, or Guomindang (GMD), ending a merciless conflict that had lasted eight years (see pp.220–221). However, lingering political rivalries left China divided and would soon plunge the country into a bitter civil war.

The GMD government returned to power at its pre-war capital, Nanjing, but its perceived weakness and corruption caused its popularity to drop. Meanwhile, promises of land reform made by Mao's Chinese Communist Party (CCP) greatly appealed to the Chinese peasantry. Mao and Chiang Kai-shek met in Chongqing in an attempt to negotiate a peaceful way toward a united China, but despite the intervention of the US, war broke out. The GMD forces were numerically superior but had been weakened by years of war; they faced the Communists, who, during the wartime occupation, had supplemented their conventional army, which was renamed the People's Liberation Army (PLA).

Three campaigns were crucial to the PLA's victory: Liaoning-Shenyang, which drove the GMD from Manchuria; Huaihai, which destroyed the GMD stronghold of Xuzhou; and Pingjin, which led to Mao entering Beijing (then Beiping) on January 21, 1949. The GMD's then-capital Nanjing fell in April, and in December the GMD fled to Taiwan. One of the far-reaching effects of the war was the emergence of Communist China as a great power in the modern world.

MAO ZEDONG

Mao Zedong (1893–1976) was born into a well-off peasant family in Hunan, south-west China. He fought in the 1911 revolution, worked at the university in Beijing as a librarian, and became a founder member of the Chinese Communist Party in 1921. Later he returned to Hunan as a trade union organizer. He believed that the revolutionary movement could win mass support in China by radicalizing the peasantry rather than the urban industrial working class.

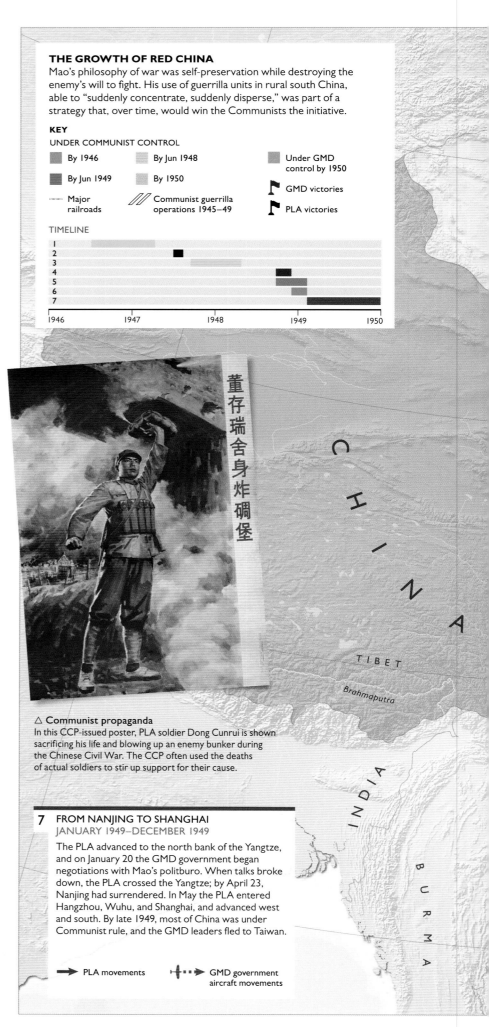

THE GROWTH OF RED CHINA

Mao's philosophy of war was self-preservation while destroying the enemy's will to fight. His use of guerrilla units in rural south China, able to "suddenly concentrate, suddenly disperse," was part of a strategy that, over time, would win the Communists the initiative.

KEY

UNDER COMMUNIST CONTROL

■ By 1946	▨ By Jun 1948	▨ Under GMD control by 1950
■ By Jun 1949	▨ By 1950	
----- Major railroads	/// Communist guerrilla operations 1945–49	⚑ GMD victories
		⚑ PLA victories

TIMELINE

1946 — 1947 — 1948 — 1949 — 1950

△ **Communist propaganda**
In this CCP-issued poster, PLA soldier Dong Cunrui is shown sacrificing his life and blowing up an enemy bunker during the Chinese Civil War. The CCP often used the deaths of actual soldiers to stir up support for their cause.

7 FROM NANJING TO SHANGHAI
JANUARY 1949–DECEMBER 1949

The PLA advanced to the north bank of the Yangtze, and on January 20 the GMD government began negotiations with Mao's politburo. When talks broke down, the PLA crossed the Yangtze; by April 23, Nanjing had surrendered. In May the PLA entered Hangzhou, Wuhu, and Shanghai, and advanced west and south. By late 1949, most of China was under Communist rule, and the GMD leaders fled to Taiwan.

→ PLA movements ⊹⊹⊱ GMD government aircraft movements

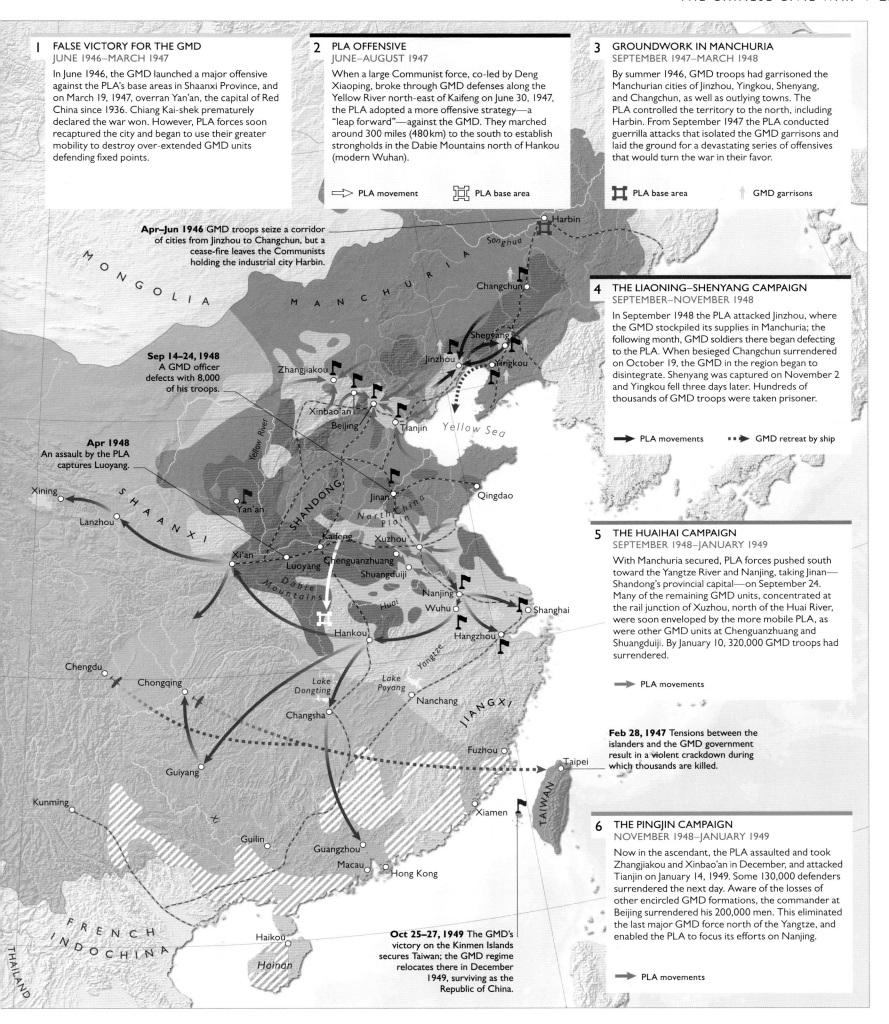

1 FALSE VICTORY FOR THE GMD
JUNE 1946–MARCH 1947

In June 1946, the GMD launched a major offensive against the PLA's base areas in Shaanxi Province, and on March 19, 1947, overran Yan'an, the capital of Red China since 1936. Chiang Kai-shek prematurely declared the war won. However, PLA forces soon recaptured the city and began to use their greater mobility to destroy over-extended GMD units defending fixed points.

2 PLA OFFENSIVE
JUNE–AUGUST 1947

When a large Communist force, co-led by Deng Xiaoping, broke through GMD defenses along the Yellow River north-east of Kaifeng on June 30, 1947, the PLA adopted a more offensive strategy—a "leap forward"—against the GMD. They marched around 300 miles (480km) to the south to establish strongholds in the Dabie Mountains north of Hankou (modern Wuhan).

⇨ PLA movement   ⊞ PLA base area

3 GROUNDWORK IN MANCHURIA
SEPTEMBER 1947–MARCH 1948

By summer 1946, GMD troops had garrisoned the Manchurian cities of Jinzhou, Yingkou, Shenyang, and Changchun, as well as outlying towns. The PLA controlled the territory to the north, including Harbin. From September 1947 the PLA conducted guerrilla attacks that isolated the GMD garrisons and laid the ground for a devastating series of offensives that would turn the war in their favor.

⊞ PLA base area   ⚑ GMD garrisons

4 THE LIAONING–SHENYANG CAMPAIGN
SEPTEMBER–NOVEMBER 1948

In September 1948 the PLA attacked Jinzhou, where the GMD stockpiled its supplies in Manchuria; the following month, GMD soldiers there began defecting to the PLA. When besieged Changchun surrendered on October 19, the GMD in the region began to disintegrate. Shenyang was captured on November 2 and Yingkou fell three days later. Hundreds of thousands of GMD troops were taken prisoner.

➡ PLA movements   ⇢ GMD retreat by ship

5 THE HUAIHAI CAMPAIGN
SEPTEMBER 1948–JANUARY 1949

With Manchuria secured, PLA forces pushed south toward the Yangtze River and Nanjing, taking Jinan—Shandong's provincial capital—on September 24. Many of the remaining GMD units, concentrated at the rail junction of Xuzhou, north of the Huai River, were soon enveloped by the more mobile PLA, as were other GMD units at Chenguanzhuang and Shuangduiji. By January 10, 320,000 GMD troops had surrendered.

➡ PLA movements

6 THE PINGJIN CAMPAIGN
NOVEMBER 1948–JANUARY 1949

Now in the ascendant, the PLA assaulted and took Zhangjiakou and Xinbao'an in December, and attacked Tianjin on January 14, 1949. Some 130,000 defenders surrendered the next day. Aware of the losses of other encircled GMD formations, the commander at Beijing surrendered his 200,000 men. This eliminated the last major GMD force north of the Yangtze, and enabled the PLA to focus its efforts on Nanjing.

➡ PLA movements

Apr–Jun 1946 GMD troops seize a corridor of cities from Jinzhou to Changchun, but a cease-fire leaves the Communists holding the industrial city Harbin.

Sep 14–24, 1948 A GMD officer defects with 8,000 of his troops.

Apr 1948 An assault by the PLA captures Luoyang.

Feb 28, 1947 Tensions between the islanders and the GMD government result in a violent crackdown during which thousands are killed.

Oct 25–27, 1949 The GMD's victory on the Kinmen Islands secures Taiwan; the GMD regime relocates there in December 1949, surviving as the Republic of China.

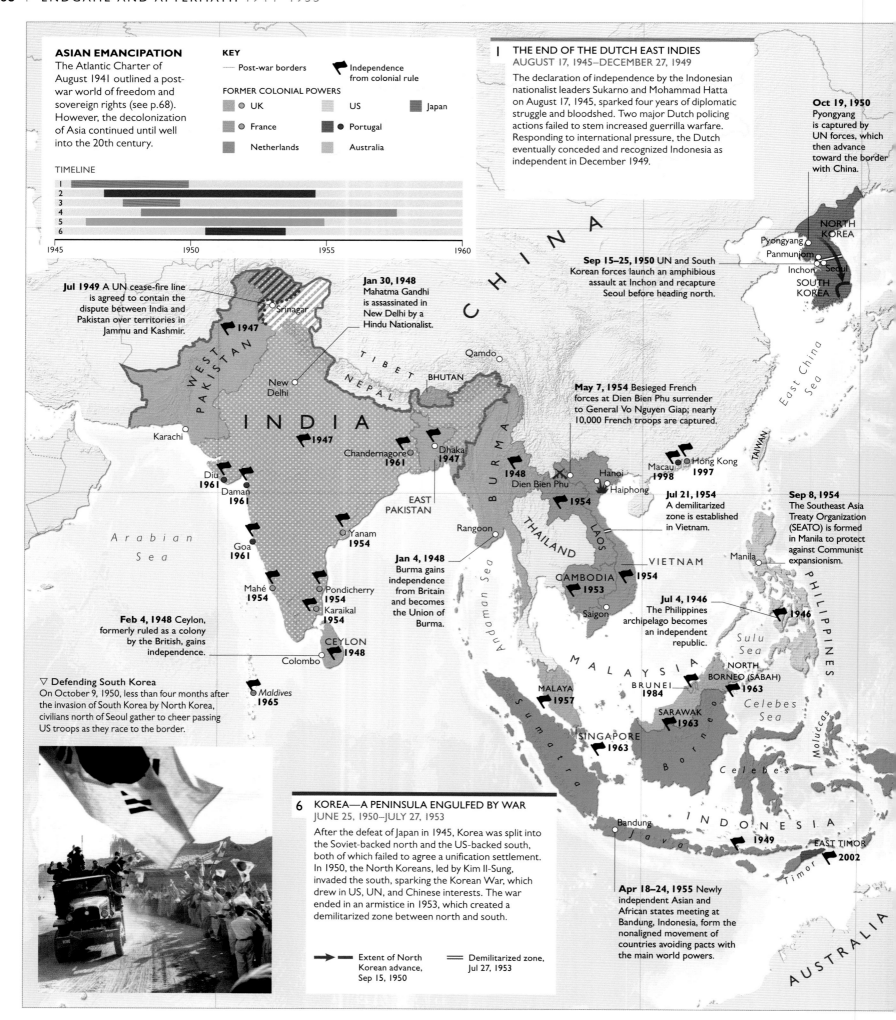

ASIAN EMANCIPATION
The Atlantic Charter of August 1941 outlined a post-war world of freedom and sovereign rights (see p.68). However, the decolonization of Asia continued until well into the 20th century.

KEY

— Post-war borders

🏴 Independence from colonial rule

FORMER COLONIAL POWERS

- UK
- US
- Japan
- France
- Portugal
- Netherlands
- Australia

TIMELINE

1
2
3
4
5
6

1945   1950   1955   1960

I THE END OF THE DUTCH EAST INDIES
AUGUST 17, 1945–DECEMBER 27, 1949

The declaration of independence by the Indonesian nationalist leaders Sukarno and Mohammad Hatta on August 17, 1945, sparked four years of diplomatic struggle and bloodshed. Two major Dutch policing actions failed to stem increased guerrilla warfare. Responding to international pressure, the Dutch eventually conceded and recognized Indonesia as independent in December 1949.

Oct 19, 1950 Pyongyang is captured by UN forces, which then advance toward the border with China.

Sep 15–25, 1950 UN and South Korean forces launch an amphibious assault at Inchon and recapture Seoul before heading north.

Jul 1949 A UN cease-fire line is agreed to contain the dispute between India and Pakistan over territories in Jammu and Kashmir.

Jan 30, 1948 Mahatma Gandhi is assassinated in New Delhi by a Hindu Nationalist.

May 7, 1954 Besieged French forces at Dien Bien Phu surrender to General Vo Nguyen Giap; nearly 10,000 French troops are captured.

Jul 21, 1954 A demilitarized zone is established in Vietnam.

Sep 8, 1954 The Southeast Asia Treaty Organization (SEATO) is formed in Manila to protect against Communist expansionism.

Jan 4, 1948 Burma gains independence from Britain and becomes the Union of Burma.

Feb 4, 1948 Ceylon, formerly ruled as a colony by the British, gains independence.

Jul 4, 1946 The Philippines archipelago becomes an independent republic.

▽ **Defending South Korea**
On October 9, 1950, less than four months after the invasion of South Korea by North Korea, civilians north of Seoul gather to cheer passing US troops as they race to the border.

6 KOREA—A PENINSULA ENGULFED BY WAR
JUNE 25, 1950–JULY 27, 1953

After the defeat of Japan in 1945, Korea was split into the Soviet-backed north and the US-backed south, both of which failed to agree a unification settlement. In 1950, the North Koreans, led by Kim Il-Sung, invaded the south, sparking the Korean War, which drew in US, UN, and Chinese interests. The war ended in an armistice in 1953, which created a demilitarized zone between north and south.

Apr 18–24, 1955 Newly independent Asian and African states meeting at Bandung, Indonesia, form the nonaligned movement of countries avoiding pacts with the main world powers.

➤ ▬ Extent of North Korean advance, Sep 15, 1950

═ Demilitarized zone, Jul 27, 1953

Map labels:

NORTH KOREA
Pyongyang
Panmunjom
Inchon Seoul
SOUTH KOREA

CHINA
East China Sea
TAIWAN

WEST PAKISTAN
Srinagar 1947
New Delhi
Karachi
TIBET
NEPAL
BHUTAN
Qamdo

INDIA 1947
Chandernagore 1961
Dhaka 1947
EAST PAKISTAN

Diu 1961
Daman 1961
Goa 1961
Mahé 1954
Yanam 1954
Pondicherry 1954
Karaikal 1954

Arabian Sea

CEYLON 1948
Colombo

Maldives 1965

BURMA 1948
Rangoon

Dien Bien Phu 1954
Hanoi
Haiphong
Macau 1998
Hong Kong 1997

THAILAND
LAOS
VIETNAM
CAMBODIA 1953
Saigon 1954

Andaman Sea

Manila
PHILIPPINES 1946

MALAYSIA
MALAYA 1957
SINGAPORE 1963
SARAWAK 1963
BRUNEI 1984
NORTH BORNEO (SABAH) 1963

Sulu Sea
Celebes Sea
Borneo
Celebes
Moluccas

Sumatra
Java
Bandung 1949
INDONESIA
Timor
EAST TIMOR 2002

AUSTRALIA

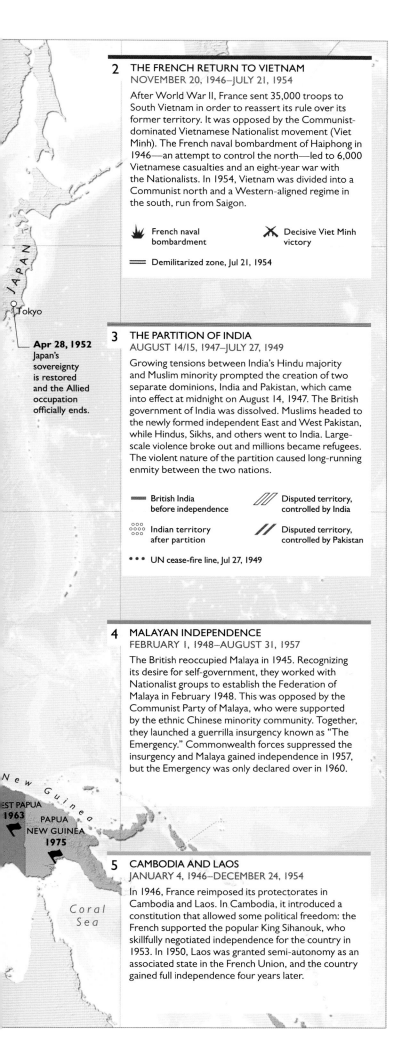

2 THE FRENCH RETURN TO VIETNAM
NOVEMBER 20, 1946–JULY 21, 1954

After World War II, France sent 35,000 troops to South Vietnam in order to reassert its rule over its former territory. It was opposed by the Communist-dominated Vietnamese Nationalist movement (Viet Minh). The French naval bombardment of Haiphong in 1946—an attempt to control the north—led to 6,000 Vietnamese casualties and an eight-year war with the Nationalists. In 1954, Vietnam was divided into a Communist north and a Western-aligned regime in the south, run from Saigon.

- ⚜ French naval bombardment
- ✕ Decisive Viet Minh victory
- ═══ Demilitarized zone, Jul 21, 1954

Apr 28, 1952 Japan's sovereignty is restored and the Allied occupation officially ends.

3 THE PARTITION OF INDIA
AUGUST 14/15, 1947–JULY 27, 1949

Growing tensions between India's Hindu majority and Muslim minority prompted the creation of two separate dominions, India and Pakistan, which came into effect at midnight on August 14, 1947. The British government of India was dissolved. Muslims headed to the newly formed independent East and West Pakistan, while Hindus, Sikhs, and others went to India. Large-scale violence broke out and millions became refugees. The violent nature of the partition caused long-running enmity between the two nations.

- ─── British India before independence
- ▨ Disputed territory, controlled by India
- ▨ Indian territory after partition
- ▨ Disputed territory, controlled by Pakistan
- ••• UN cease-fire line, Jul 27, 1949

4 MALAYAN INDEPENDENCE
FEBRUARY 1, 1948–AUGUST 31, 1957

The British reoccupied Malaya in 1945. Recognizing its desire for self-government, they worked with Nationalist groups to establish the Federation of Malaya in February 1948. This was opposed by the Communist Party of Malaya, who were supported by the ethnic Chinese minority community. Together, they launched a guerrilla insurgency known as "The Emergency." Commonwealth forces suppressed the insurgency and Malaya gained independence in 1957, but the Emergency was only declared over in 1960.

5 CAMBODIA AND LAOS
JANUARY 4, 1946–DECEMBER 24, 1954

In 1946, France reimposed its protectorates in Cambodia and Laos. In Cambodia, it introduced a constitution that allowed some political freedom: the French supported the popular King Sihanouk, who skillfully negotiated independence for the country in 1953. In 1950, Laos was granted semi-autonomy as an associated state in the French Union, and the country gained full independence four years later.

DECOLONIZATION OF ASIA

After the liberation of Japan's Asian colonies, many more Asian nations fought for independence. Anti-imperialist movements began to gain widespread popular legitimacy, and as a result many of the occupying powers were forced to reassess their old colonial outposts.

Japan's advance through Southeast Asia during World War II exposed the fragile hold that the Western powers had on their colonies. Even though the Allied powers emerged as victors in 1945, most were unwilling or unable to restore their colonial regimes.

A greatly weakened Britain was disinclined to defend its empire. Indian pressure for self-governance had grown since the foundation of the Indian National Congress in 1885, and for many it seemed inevitable that Britain would leave the subcontinent. Britain aimed to avert conflict by granting self-government, whereas the Netherlands and France tried to revive their empires in the East Indies and Indochina. This approach plunged both countries into wars that would prove to be unwinnable, and served as a warning to any outside power tempted to try to impose its will on the region.

The pattern of decolonization in Asia was affected not only by the countries involved, but also by shifting ideologies. Competing capitalist and Communist visions of society in a post-war world fueled the Cold War, which lasted for most of the 20th century (see pp.264–265). Fears surrounding Communist expansionism ignited war in the Korean peninsula in 1950, and would become a defining feature of Asia in this era.

"At the stroke of the midnight hour, while the world sleeps, India will awake to life and freedom."

JAWAHARLAL NEHRU, 1947

INDIAN INDEPENDENCE

The Indian National Congress (INC), the most influential group in the campaign for independence in India, was led by Mahatma Gandhi and Jawaharlal Nehru, both of whom had studied law in London. Under the leadership of Gandhi from 1921 to the mid-1930s the INC changed from an elite project to a mass movement of nonviolent civil disobedience. Nehru, who succeeded Gandhi as head of the party in 1929, rejected Dominion status, instead demanding full independence. He became India's first prime minister in 1947.

Nehru (left) and Gandhi meet in Bombay, India

New arrivals
Refugees from Eastern Europe, Turkey, and Tunisia prepare to go ashore at Haifa in early summer of 1949. In 1950 the Israeli Law of Return was passed, giving any Jew the legal right to settle in Israel.

THE CREATION OF ISRAEL

In 1917, Britain had pledged its support for "a national home for the Jewish people" in Palestine, in a statement now known as the Balfour Declaration. However, it was not until after World War II that Israel became a state.

After World War I, Britain controlled Palestine under the terms of the League of Nations mandate and aimed to create a home there for Jews. Since Arabs formed 90 percent of the population, many were opposed to the idea. Tensions escalated in the 1930s and 1940s when many Jews fleeing from the Nazis traveled to Palestine to seek a safe refuge.

Caught in the dispute between the Arabs and the Jews, Britain imposed strict quotas on Jewish immigration. Thousands of Jewish immigrants were imprisoned in British camps, and violence escalated. In 1947, the British government handed over control to the United Nations, which planned to partition Palestine and create one state for Arabs and another for Jews. However, the Arabs rejected the idea.

△ **Commemorative stamp**
A 1949 stamp depicts the foundation of modern Tel Aviv. The city was established in 1909 by 60 Jewish families, 15 miles (24 km) northwest of Jerusalem.

The first Arab–Israeli war

On May 14, 1948, the British mandate terminated and a Zionist organization proclaimed the establishment of the independent State of Israel. A military coalition of Arab states fought to gain control, but by the time a cease-fire was agreed in 1949, the Israelis had taken control of all the territories the UN had allocated to them, and made further gains at the expense of their Arab neighbors. Hundreds of thousands of Palestinian Arabs fled their homelands to become stateless refugees, while Israel held its first elections later that year.

VOYAGE OF THE EXODUS

Hundreds of would-be Jewish immigrants crowded the decks of the refugee ship SS *Exodus* in the port of Haifa, then part of Palestine, in July 1947. The British intercepted the ship as it tried to make an illicit landfall. The passengers were forcibly disembarked and then shipped back across the Mediterranean to France.

THE PRICE OF WAR

World War II affected most of the globe, and cost more than 50 million lives. The Eastern Front accounted for many of the military deaths, while the Holocaust, bombings, and land war left millions of civilians dead. In Europe, many survivors faced a desperate scramble to find homes in new places.

The human cost of World War II exceeded anything that came before it. Military casualty rates in north-west Europe in 1944–1945 matched—and sometimes exceeded—those of World War I, while the bitter war of attrition at the Eastern Front claimed further millions of lives. An unprecedented proportion of those who died in the war were civilians. Six million Jews, 130,000–200,000 Roma, and 250,000 disabled people died in the Nazi Holocaust, while the brutality of the Soviet, Nazi, and Japanese regimes added to the vast toll, as did the Allied bombing of cities in Germany and, most

destructively, in Japan. By the end of the war, Poland had lost 16 percent of its 1939 population, and the Soviet Union around 15 percent.

The human suffering did not end as the war came to a close. Millions of Germans who were living in Eastern Europe were forced to flee the advancing Red Army in 1944 and hundreds of thousands of them died from violence, malnutrition, or disease. And as Europe's boundaries were redrawn, the war's survivors faced the task of rebuilding their countries, their cities, and their lives in the midst of terrible devastation.

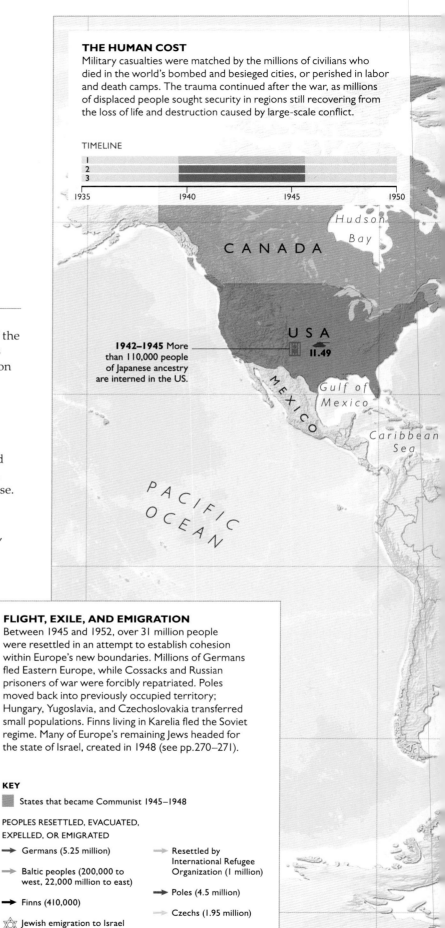

THE HUMAN COST
Military casualties were matched by the millions of civilians who died in the world's bombed and besieged cities, or perished in labor and death camps. The trauma continued after the war, as millions of displaced people sought security in regions still recovering from the loss of life and destruction caused by large-scale conflict.

TIMELINE

1942–1945 More than 110,000 people of Japanese ancestry are interned in the US.

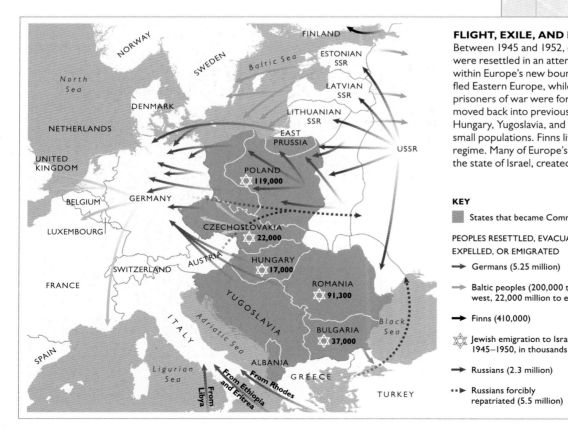

FLIGHT, EXILE, AND EMIGRATION
Between 1945 and 1952, over 31 million people were resettled in an attempt to establish cohesion within Europe's new boundaries. Millions of Germans fled Eastern Europe, while Cossacks and Russian prisoners of war were forcibly repatriated. Poles moved back into previously occupied territory; Hungary, Yugoslavia, and Czechoslovakia transferred small populations. Finns living in Karelia fled the Soviet regime. Many of Europe's remaining Jews headed for the state of Israel, created in 1948 (see pp.270–271).

KEY

■ States that became Communist 1945–1948

PEOPLES RESETTLED, EVACUATED, EXPELLED, OR EMIGRATED

→ Germans (5.25 million)

→ Baltic peoples (200,000 to west, 22,000 million to east)

→ Finns (410,000)

✡ Jewish emigration to Israel 1945–1950, in thousands

→ Russians (2.3 million)

▪▪▶ Russians forcibly repatriated (5.5 million)

→ Resettled by International Refugee Organization (1 million)

→ Poles (4.5 million)

→ Czechs (1.95 million)

→ Turks (130,000)

→ Italians (230,000)

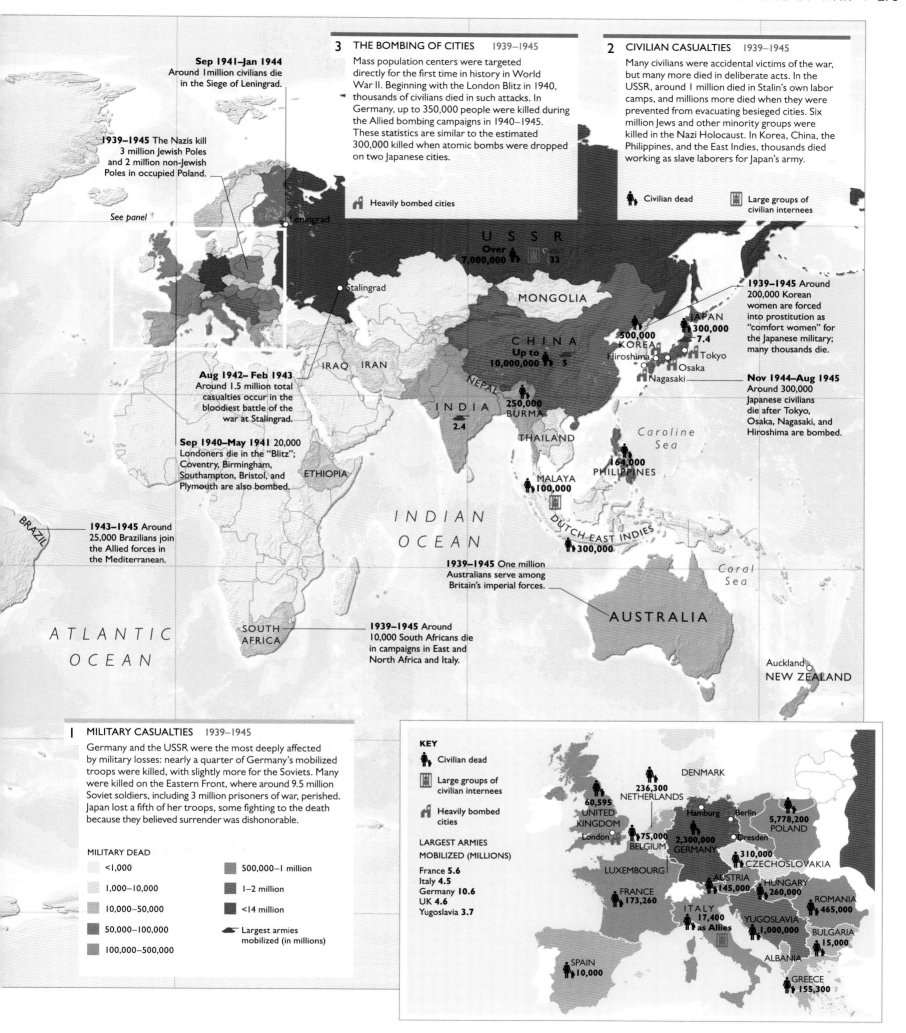

Sep 1941–Jan 1944 Around 1 million civilians die in the Siege of Leningrad.

1939–1945 The Nazis kill 3 million Jewish Poles and 2 million non-Jewish Poles in occupied Poland.

See panel

3 THE BOMBING OF CITIES 1939–1945

Mass population centers were targeted directly for the first time in history in World War II. Beginning with the London Blitz in 1940, thousands of civilians died in such attacks. In Germany, up to 350,000 people were killed during the Allied bombing campaigns in 1940–1945. These statistics are similar to the estimated 300,000 killed when atomic bombs were dropped on two Japanese cities.

🏛 Heavily bombed cities

2 CIVILIAN CASUALTIES 1939–1945

Many civilians were accidental victims of the war, but many more died in deliberate acts. In the USSR, around 1 million died in Stalin's own labor camps, and millions more died when they were prevented from evacuating besieged cities. Six million Jews and other minority groups were killed in the Nazi Holocaust. In Korea, China, the Philippines, and the East Indies, thousands died working as slave laborers for Japan's army.

👥 Civilian dead   ▨ Large groups of civilian internees

USSR Over 7,000,000 — 33

1939–1945 Around 200,000 Korean women are forced into prostitution as "comfort women" for the Japanese military; many thousands die.

JAPAN 300,000 — 7.4

KOREA 500,000

Hiroshima, Tokyo, Osaka, Nagasaki

CHINA Up to 10,000,000 — 5

Aug 1942– Feb 1943 Around 1.5 million total casualties occur in the bloodiest battle of the war at Stalingrad.

Nov 1944–Aug 1945 Around 300,000 Japanese civilians die after Tokyo, Osaka, Nagasaki, and Hiroshima are bombed.

INDIA 2.4

BURMA 250,000

Sep 1940–May 1941 20,000 Londoners die in the "Blitz"; Coventry, Birmingham, Southampton, Bristol, and Plymouth are also bombed.

PHILIPPINES 164,000

MALAYA 100,000

DUTCH EAST INDIES 300,000

1943–1945 Around 25,000 Brazilians join the Allied forces in the Mediterranean.

1939–1945 One million Australians serve among Britain's imperial forces.

1939–1945 Around 10,000 South Africans die in campaigns in East and North Africa and Italy.

Caroline Sea

Coral Sea

AUSTRALIA

Auckland
NEW ZEALAND

INDIAN OCEAN

ATLANTIC OCEAN

1 MILITARY CASUALTIES 1939–1945

Germany and the USSR were the most deeply affected by military losses: nearly a quarter of Germany's mobilized troops were killed, with slightly more for the Soviets. Many were killed on the Eastern Front, where around 9.5 million Soviet soldiers, including 3 million prisoners of war, perished. Japan lost a fifth of her troops, some fighting to the death because they believed surrender was dishonorable.

MILITARY DEAD

☐ <1,000	☐ 500,000–1 million
☐ 1,000–10,000	☐ 1–2 million
☐ 10,000–50,000	☐ <14 million
☐ 50,000–100,000	◄ Largest armies mobilized (in millions)
☐ 100,000–500,000	

KEY

👥 Civilian dead

▨ Large groups of civilian internees

🏛 Heavily bombed cities

LARGEST ARMIES MOBILIZED (MILLIONS)

France **5.6**
Italy **4.5**
Germany **10.6**
UK **4.6**
Yugoslavia **3.7**

UNITED KINGDOM 60,595
London

DENMARK

NETHERLANDS 236,300

BELGIUM 75,000

Hamburg, Berlin, Dresden

GERMANY 2,300,000

POLAND 5,778,200

LUXEMBOURG

CZECHOSLOVAKIA 310,000

FRANCE 173,260

AUSTRIA 145,000

HUNGARY 260,000

ITALY 17,400 as Allies

YUGOSLAVIA 1,000,000

ROMANIA 465,000

BULGARIA 15,000

SPAIN 10,000

ALBANIA

GREECE 155,300

REMEMBRANCE

The memory of World War II is kept alive by most of the participating countries, not only in ceremonies and monuments but also in each nation's particular view of the war and of the sacrifices made by both combatants and civilians.

△ **Makeshift memorial**
A hastily erected marker on a Normandy beach marks the grave of a US soldier killed during the D-Day landings in 1944.

Most Allied nations have an annual day of remembrance, including Veterans Day in the US, Anzac day in Australia and New Zealand, Victory Day in France and the Czech Republic, and Liberation Day in the Netherlands and Norway.

Russia commemorates victory on May 9 with parades and ceremonies. The war, specifically the period 1941–1945, is known as the Great Patriotic War, and its remembrance acknowledges the nation's huge sacrifice in lives. Among the events is the March of the Immortal Regiment, in which millions of citizens assemble carrying portraits and photographs of World War II veterans, victims, and survivors. Many countries also commemorate individual events. In the US, Pearl Harbor Remembrance Day takes place annually on the anniversary of the attack (see pp.110–111), while in Britain, Battle of Britain Day commemorates Fighter Command's victory over the Luftwaffe in 1940 (see pp.58–59).

Axis nations remember
In Japan, the war remains a controversial subject; nevertheless, the site of the Hiroshima bombing (see pp.258–259) is now the Hiroshima Peace Memorial Park. In Germany, remembrance of the war is characterized by somber reflection. Some former concentration camps are preserved as museums, and the Berlin monument to the Holocaust (right) serves as a stark reminder. In recent years, more open discussion of the war has been encouraged.

MUSIC FOR LENINGRAD

A native of Leningrad, the composer Dmitri Shostakovich wrote the first two movements of his monumental Symphony No. 7 in 1941, while the city was under siege by the Germans. Eventually safely evacuated, he christened the work the Leningrad Symphony to honor the city's heroic resistance. It premiered in 1942.

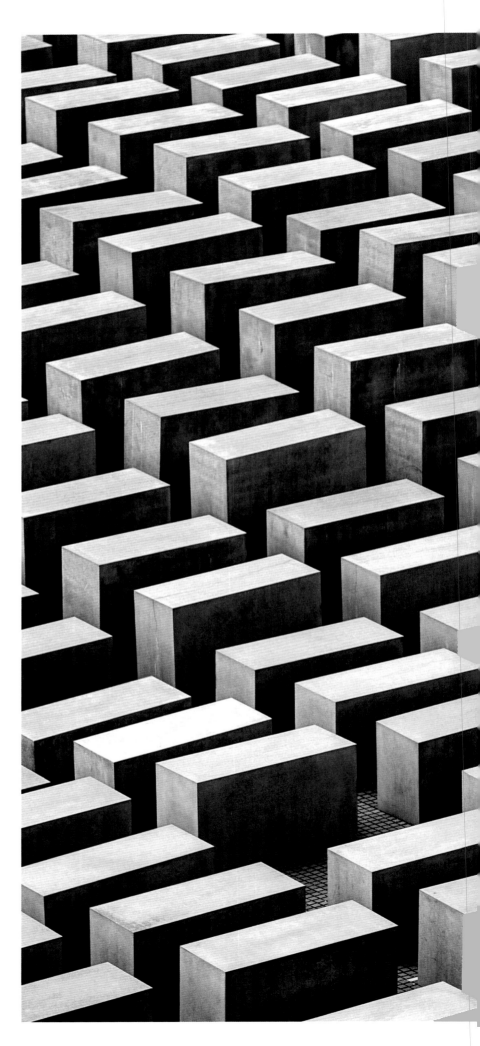

Holocaust memorial in Berlin
Designed by US architect Peter Eisenman
and consisting of 2,711 concrete blocks,
Berlin's "Memorial to the Murdered Jews of
Europe" is often interpreted as representing
an ordered system that has lost touch
with reason.

GLOSSARY

Afrika Korps German expeditionary force, commanded by Erwin Rommel and sent to North Africa in spring 1941 to support the Italians following a string of defeats by the British. Later it was substantially reinforced to become Panzerarmee Afrika (Panzer Army Africa).

aircraft carrier Large naval vessel capable of launching and recovering aircraft, such as torpedo bombers, dive-bombers, and protective fighters.

Anschluss The absorption of Austria into Germany on March 13, 1938, the day after Hitler's troops marched into the country on the pretext of restoring order.

area bombing Blanket aerial bombardment of large urban areas.

armistice The temporary suspension of hostilities between warring countries so that negotiations for a formal peace agreement can take place.

army group The largest military land formation used in World War II, consisting of two or more armies serving under a single commander.

Atlantic Wall The massive coastal defenses the Germans built to repulse an Allied invasion of Western Europe.

Axis, Rome–Berlin The friendship pact agreed between Germany and Italy in November 1936, followed by the Pact of Steel, a formal military alliance in May 1939, and the Tripartite Pact, signed by Germany, Italy, and Japan in September 1940. Other Axis powers included Hungary, Romania, Slovakia, Bulgaria, and Croatia.

battalion Military unit typically consisting of between 300 and 800 soldiers, subdivided into companies and platoons. Battalions are commanded by lieutenant-colonels with a major as second-in-command. Generally, three or more battalions grouped together make up a regiment.

battleship An extremely large, heavily-armored warship, principally armed with large-caliber guns mounted in rotating turrets. Although vitally important to both the Allied and Axis powers, battleships proved highly vulnerable to air attack by carrier-borne aircraft.

beachhead An area close to the sea or a river that, when captured by attacking troops, is the foundation for a subsequent advance deeper into enemy-held territory.

"Big Six" The six members of the Japanese Imperial General Headquarters-Government Liaison Conference (later the Supreme Council for the Direction of the War): the Prime Minister, Minister for Foreign Affairs, Minister of War, Minister of the Navy, the Chief of the Army General Staff, and the Chief of the Naval General Staff.

Bletchley Park Headquarters of Britain's Government Code & Cypher School, tasked with decoding enemy military communications.

Blitz The Luftwaffe's mass bombing campaign against British cities, ports, and towns from September 1940 to May 1941.

Blitzkrieg As employed by the Germans, blitzkrieg ("lightning war") involved mass tank formations, supported by dive-bombers and motorized artillery, making a thrust forward on a narrow front.

Bomber Command The branch of the RAF specializing in bomber operations from 1936 to 1968.

bouncing bomb A spinning cylindrical bomb, invented by British engineer Barnes Wallis to destroy the Ruhr hydroelectric dams.

bridgehead *see* beachhead

brigade Military formation, typically consisting of three to six battalions plus supporting reconnaissance, artillery, engineers, supply, and transport elements.

BEF British Expeditionary Force. British troops sent to France in 1939.

capital ship One of a navy's most important warships. Traditionally a battleship or battle cruiser and, from 1942 onward, an aircraft carrier.

carpet bombing *see* area bombing

corps A military formation, consisting of two or more divisions and typically commanded by a lieutenant-general.

Desert Rats The nickname of the soldiers of the British 7th Armored Division during the fighting in the 1940–1943 North African campaign. It later was applied to the entire 8th Army.

division Military formation consisting of a team of all arms and services required to sustain independent operations. An army can have anything from four to ten divisions.

Eastern Front In World War II, the theater of war between the Axis powers and Finland—a co-belligerent—against the USSR. It took place in central and Eastern Europe, the Baltics, and the Balkans. In the former USSR this part of the war is known as the Great Patriotic War.

Einsatzgruppen Four battalion-sized mobile killing squads that targeted Jews and political enemies in territories occupied by Germany.

enfiladed Gunfire directed from a flanking point along the length of an enemy battle line.

escort carrier Smaller and slower than aircraft carriers, escort carriers were largely converted merchant ships carrying aircraft. They were principally tasked with escorting convoys carrying materiel and supplies.

Fighter Command Branch of the RAF specializing in fighter operations, founded in 1936. Integral in defeating the Luftwaffe during the Battle of Britain in 1940.

Free French French citizens who rallied to General Charles de Gaulle following his call for a continuation of the war after France's capitulation in June 1940.

front (Soviet) The Soviet equivalent of a Western army group. A front was generally made up of three to five armies, plus an army-size air wing to provide ground forces with aerial support.

Führer German word meaning leader. Hitler took it as a title in 1921 to signify his position as leader of the Nazi party.

Geneva Conventions Four political conventions, plus additional protocols, regulating the laws of war and allowing for the protection of POWs and civilians during war. First ratified in 1864, the Geneva Conventions were amended and extended in 1906, 1929, and 1949.

German high command Germany's military leadership, the *Oberkommando der Wehrmacht* ,was set up by Hitler in 1938 to help him establish undisputed control of the armed forces.

gulag Network of forced labor camps that operated in the USSR from the 1920s onward. Although the government agency administrating the gulags closed in 1960, forced labor in the USSR persisted for decades.

Habforce A British military force raised in Palestine in April 1941 and sent to relieve the RAF base at Habbaniyah in Iraq, before being besieged by rebel Iraqi forces.

howitzer A large artillery piece, generally with a comparatively short barrel, capable of firing shells at a high angle of elevation with a steep descent. Depending on the type of howitzer, range varied from around 5 miles (8 km) to 20 miles (30 km).

Imperial Japanese Navy Navy of the Empire of Japan from 1868 until 1945.

kamikaze Japanese pilots of World War II who, from October 1944, launched mass suicide attacks against Allied shipping.

Karelian Isthmus The stretch of land between the Gulf of Finland and Lake Lagoda where the Finns built the fortified Mannerheim Line.

Kriegsmarine The name by which the German navy was known from 1935 until the end of the war.

League of Nations Organization created after World War I to provide a forum for the resolution of international disputes.

Lebensraum A German word meaning "living space," the demand for which formed the basis for Nazi Germany's commitment to territorial expansion.

Lend-Lease US aid program initiated in March 1941 to guarantee the free supply of arms, ammunition, food, and other essential material, notably fuel, to Britain and subsequently to other allies.

legation Group of diplomats and other officials representing their government in a foreign country, but with less status than that of an embassy. A legation is headed by a minister as opposed to an ambassador.

Liberty ships Cargo ships, mass-produced in the US during World War II. Such ships were cheap and easy to build. In all, 2,711 were built, 200 being sunk by enemy action.

Lo Spazio Vitale The Italian equivalent of *Lebensraum*. Fascist Italy's aim was to establish dominance over North Africa and in the Mediterranean area.

Low Countries A collective term for Belgium, the Netherlands, and Luxembourg. Also known as the Benelux countries after the initial letters of their names.

Luftwaffe Officially created in 1935, Germany's Luftwaffe was the most modern air force in the world when war broke out in 1939.

materiel Collective word describing arms, ammunition, and military equipment and supplies in general.

Molotov–Ribbentrop Pact Nonaggression pact concluded by Soviet and German foreign ministers before the start of World War II that partitioned Poland between the two powers.

nautical mile Unit of measurement slightly greater than a land mile and equal to one minute of a degree of latitude.

Nazi party Abbreviated title of the *Nationalsozialistische Deutsche Arbeiterpartei* (National Socialist German Workers' Party).

partisans Members of the armed resistance groups that sprung up in Nazi-occupied territory during the war.

plebiscite A vote by which the people of a country expresses approval or disapproval of a specific proposal. After World War I and in the run-up to World War II, plebiscites were used in Europe to address the issues created by displaced populations.

pocket battleship A type of powerful heavy cruiser built by Germany in the 1930s. The Nazis built three in total: *Deutschland* (later renamed *Lutzow*), *Admiral Scheer*, and *Admiral Graf Spee*. Their main armament consisted of six 11-in guns.

POW Prisoner of war. A person, usually a combatant, held prisoner during an armed conflict.

putsch An illegal attempt to overthrow a government by force of arms. Hitler's so-called Beer Hall Putsch, which he launched against the Bavarian government in Munich in November 1923, though a failure, was a notable step along his road to power.

RAF Royal Air Force. Britain's air force, established in April 1918, and the world's oldest independent air force.

Red Army The Soviet government's army following the 1917 Bolshevik Revolution. The name was dropped in 1946.

Regia Aeronautica The Italian Royal Air Force, founded in 1923. Though on the surface numerically impressive, many of its aircraft were obsolete, and the ill-organized Italian aircraft industry failed to keep pace with its military losses.

regiment *see* battalion.

Reichskommissariat Administrative unit led by a Reichskommissar and tasked with governing regions of German-occupied Europe including the Netherlands, Norway, Belgium, and northern France. Five others were established in the east in a bid to break up the Soviet Union.

Reichstag The parliament of the Third Reich. Its role was largely ceremonial, unanimously approving Hitler's decisions.

Rhineland Area of western Germany along the River Rhine. Following World War I it was demilitarized by the terms of the 1925 Locarno Treaty.

Royal Navy The British navy, the strongest in the world at the start of World War II, fielding 15 battleships and battle cruisers, seven aircraft carriers, 66 cruisers, 184 destroyers, and 60 submarines.

ROC Royal Observer Corps. Civil defense organization tasked with plotting enemy aircraft movements over Britain during World War II.

Saarland Province of south-western Germany, administered by the League of Nations from 1920 to 1935.

salient A battlefield projection, also known as a bulge, surrounded by the enemy on multiple sides, making the troops holding it vulnerable to attack.

SOE Special Operations Executive. British secret intelligence organization tasked with aiding resistance movements in enemy-occupied territories and carrying out spying and sabotage activities.

SS *Schutzstaffel*. The elite paramilitary corps of the Nazi party. Led by Heinrich Himmler from 1929 onward.

SA *Sturmabteilung*. Otherwise known as the Brownshirts, the SA was the original paramilitary force of the Nazis that became gradually overshadowed by the SS.

sue for peace The initiation of negotiations for peace, usually a step taken by the losing party in an attempt to avoid an unconditional surrender.

task force A term coined by the US Navy in 1941 to describe naval units combined to undertake a specific military mission.

Third Reich The official name the Nazis gave Germany after coming to power in 1933. In their version of history the Holy Roman Empire, which lasted from 800 to 1806, constituted the First Reich, and the German Empire (1871–1918) constituted the Second Reich.

Treaty of Versailles The peace treaty that formally concluded World War I following the 1918 armistice between the Allies and Germany. Its contentious clauses on war guilt and its demand

for the payment of reparations caused lasting German resentment that helped fuel the rise of the Nazi party.

U-boats German submarines. While used to attack enemy warships, U-boats were primarily used to create a naval blockade of Allied shipping routes and to allow for commerce raiding.

United Nations International organization established in October 1945 with the aim of preventing future wars.

USAAF United States Army Air Forces. Formed in 1941 as the successor to the Army Air Corps. After the US entered World War II, its strength rose dramatically from just 4,000 aircraft to 75,000 by the end of the war.

Vichy France The name of the state set up under the leadership of Marshal Philippe Pétain to rule unoccupied France following the French surrender in June 1940. Its capital was the spa town of Vichy.

V-weapons The name coined by the Germans for the so-called "vengeance weapons" they deployed in 1944. They consisted of the V-1 pilotless flying bomb and the V-2 long-range rocket.

Waffen-SS The armed branch of the SS and the Wehrmacht's elite fighting formations. It was judged at the post-war Nuremberg trials to be a criminal organization due to its involvement in war crimes and crimes against humanity.

Wehrmacht The generic name for Germany's armed forces from 1935 to the end of the war. It consisted of the Herr (army), the Kriegsmarine (navy), and Luftwaffe (air force) with Hitler as the supreme commander.

Western Front In World War II, the theater of conflict taking place in Belgium, Denmark, Norway, France, Germany, Italy, Luxembourg, and the Netherlands.

INDEX

ACKNOWLEDGMENTS

Dorling Kindersley would like to thank the following people for their help in the preparation of this book: Phil Gamble for additional map design; Steve Crozier for image retouching; Garima Agarwal, Simar Dhamija, and Bianca Zambrea for design assistance; Jaypal Singh Chauhan for DTP assistance; Martyn Page and Kate Taylor for editorial assistance; Katie John for proofreading; and Helen Peters for indexing. Additional map references: maps courtesy of the USMA, Department of History; contains map data © OpenStreetMap contributors.

Editors' note: place names are mostly given in their contemporary forms, except China, where Pinyin Romanization is used. Tonnage is given in metric tonnes and US tons.

The publisher would like to thank the following for their kind permission to reproduce their photographs:

(Key: a-above; b-below/bottom; c-centre; f-far; l-left; r-right; t-top)

2 Dorling Kindersley: Wardrobe Museum, Salisbury. **4 Getty Images:** Bettmann (tl); Henry Guttmann Collection / Hulton Archive (tr). **4-5 Getty Images:** Ullstein bild Dtl.. **5 Getty Images:** Henry Guttmann Collection / Hulton Archive (tl); J. R. Eyerman / The LIFE Picture Collection (tr). **6 Getty Images:** Sgt Robert Howard / Hulton Archive (tl, tr). **6-7 Getty Images:** Ullstein bild Dtl.. **7 The US National Archives and Records Administration:** Photographer: Joe Rosenthal (tl). **8-9 John Calvin / www.wwii-photos-maps.com. 10-11 Getty Images:** Bettmann. **12 Getty Images:** Photo 12 / UIG (tl). **13 Getty Images:** De Agostini / Biblioteca Ambrosiana (cr); Popperfoto (tl). **14 Getty Images:** Swim ink 2 llc / Corbis Historical (tl). **15 Getty Images:** Universal History Archive / Universal Images Group (br). **16 Alamy Stock Photo:** Photo 12 (tl). **18 Getty Images:** Stefano Bianchetti / Corbis Historical (bl). **19 Alamy Stock Photo:** IanDagnall Computing (br). **20-21 Getty Images:** Bettmann. **20 Getty Images:** Bettmann (bc); Adoc-photos / Corbis Historical (cl). **22 Alamy Stock Photo:** Granger Historical Picture Archive (bc). **Getty Images:** Universal History Archive / Universal Images Group (tr). **24 Alamy Stock Photo:** Pictorial Press Ltd (bl). **Getty Images:** Ullstein bild Dtl. (br). **26 akg-images:** Pictures From History (bl). **26-27 Imperial War Museum. 28 akg-images:** (tr). **Getty Images:** Keystone / Hulton Archive (bc). **30-31 Bridgeman Images:** Pictures from History. **31 Bridgeman Images:** Pictures from History (br). **Dorling Kindersley:** By kind permission of The Trustees of the Imperial War Museum, London (cr). **32 Getty Images:** Print Collector / Hulton Archive (bc). **33 Getty Images:** Michael Nicholson / Corbis Historical (tr). **34-35 Getty Images:** Henry Guttmann Collection / Hulton Archive. **36 Alamy Stock Photo:** Chronicle (tl); Heritage Image Partnership Ltd (c). **37 Getty Images:** Hugo Jaeger / Timepix / The Life Picture Collection (cr); IWM / Imperial War Museums (tl). **38 Wikipedia:** Julien Bryan (bl). **40-41 Getty Images:** Gaston Paris / Roger Viollet. **41 Alamy Stock Photo:** Hi-Story (c). **Getty Images:** Lt. L A Puttnam / IWM (br). **43 Alamy Stock Photo:** World History Archive (br). **44 Getty Images:** Bettmann (tr). **46 Getty Images:** Ullstein bild Dtl. (tl). **47 akg-images:** TT News Agency / SVT (tr). **48-49 Advanced Archival Associates Research**. **49 Getty Images:** Ullstein bild Dtl. (br). **50-51 Alamy Stock Photo:** Everett Collection Historica. **51 Bridgeman Images:** Tallandier (br). **Dorling Kindersley:** Wardrobe Museum, Salisbury (cr). **52 Getty Images:** Culture Club / Hulton Archive (bl). **53 Getty Images:** Hulton-Deutsch / Corbis Historical (br). **54 Getty Images:** Adoc-photos / Corbis Historical (bc, tr). **56 Getty Images:** Photo Josse / Leemage / Corbis Historical (clb). **58 Rex by Shutterstock:** Associated Newspapers / Associated Newspapers (bc). **59 Getty Images:** IWM / Imperial War Museums (br). **60-61 London Metropolitan Archives**. **61 Alamy Stock Photo:** Shawshots (br). **62 Alamy Stock Photo:** Pictorial Press Ltd (cla); Trinity Mirror / Mirrorpix (bc). **62-63 Getty Images:** Hulton-Deutsch Collection / Corbis. **64 Alamy Stock Photo:** Interfoto (bc); John Frost Newspapers (cr). **66 Getty Images:** Ullstein bild Dtl. (bc). **67 Alamy Stock Photo:** Trinity Mirror / Mirrorpix (crb). **68-69 Getty Images:** Bettmann. **68 Getty Images:** Capt. Horton / IWM (bl); Photo 12 / UIG (cl). **70 Alamy Stock Photo:** Everett Collection Inc (bc). **71 Getty Images:** Museum of Science and Industry, Chicago / Archive Photos (tr). **72 Getty Images:** Keystone-France / Gamma-Rapho (tl). **73 akg-images:** (r). **Getty Images:** Universal History Archive / UIG (tl). **75 Getty Images:** Haynes Archive / Popperfoto (br). **77 Getty Images:** Galerie Bilderwelt / Hulton Archive (tr); Michael Nicholson / Corbis Historical (br). **79 Getty Images:** Photo 12 / Universal Images Group (clb); Fototeca Storica Nazionale. / Hulton Archive (br). **81 akg-images:** (cr). **82 Bridgeman Images:** © SZ Photo / Scherl (br). **84 Getty Images:** Haynes Archive / Popperfoto (br); Bettmann (bl). **86-87 Getty Images:** Hulton Archive. **86 Alamy Stock Photo:** The Picture Art Collection (bl). **Getty Images:** Dan Burn-Forti / The Image Bank (cl). **88 Dorling Kindersley:** Musée des blindés, Saumur, France (tr). **Getty Images:** Galerie Bilderwelt (cl). **89 Getty Images:** Mondadori Portfolio (cr); Print Collector (t). **90 Alamy Stock Photo:** Pictorial Press Ltd (bl). **91 Getty Images:** Heritage Images / Hulton Archive (br). **92 Dorling Kindersley:** Wardrobe Museum, Salisbury (cl). **Getty Images:** Horace Abrahams / Hulton Archive (bc). **92-93 Getty Images:** TASS. **94 Getty Images:** Ullstein bild Dtl. (bl). **94-95 John Calvin / www.wwii-photos-maps.com**. **97 Getty Images:** Ullstein bild Dtl. (bc); Alexander Ustinov / Hulton Archive (tc). **98-99 Getty Images:** TASS. **98 akg-images:** Ullstein bild (cla). **Getty Images:** ullstein bild Dtl. (bl). **101 akg-images:** Pictures From History (tc). **Getty Images:** Time & Life Pictures / The LIFE Picture Collection (bl). **102-103 Getty Images:** J. R. Eyerman / The LIFE Picture Collection. **104 akg-images:** (cb). **Alamy Stock Photo:** World History Archive (tl). **105 Dorling Kindersley:** Planes of Fame Air Museum, Chino, California (ca). **Getty Images:** Universal History Archive / UIG (cr). **106 Alamy Stock Photo:** Shawshots (bl). **107 Alamy Stock Photo:** Everett Collection Inc (br). **108-109 Getty Images:** The Asahi Shimbun. **109 Bridgeman Images:** Universal History Archive / UIG (br). **Dorling Kindersley:** Imperial War Museum, Duxford (cr). **111 Alamy Stock Photo:** Granger Historical Picture Archive (br). **112 Getty Images:** Keystone / Hulton Archive (bl). **113 Getty Images:** Dmitri Kessel / The LIFE Picture Collection (br). **114-115 Getty Images:** Alfred T. Palmer / Buyenlarge. **114 akg-images:** akg / John Parrot / Stocktrek Images (cl). **Getty Images:** PhotoQuest / Archive Photos (bc). **116 Bridgeman Images:** West Point Museum, New York, USA / Photo © Don Troiani (br). **118 Getty Images:** Carl Mydans / The LIFE Picture Collection (bl). **119 Getty Images:** Mondadori Portfolio (br). **120 Getty Images:** Bettmann (bl). **122-123 Getty Images:** IWM. **123 akg-images:** GandhiServe India (br). **Getty Images:** Bettmann (c). **124 Alamy Stock Photo:** The Picture Art Collection (bc). **125 Alamy Stock Photo:** Historic Images (br). **127 Alamy Stock Photo:** Archivah (cl). **128-129 Alamy Stock Photo:** Hum Historical. **129 Getty Images:** Keystone / Hulton Archive (br). **130 Getty Images:** Photo 12 / UIG (ca); David E. Scherman / Time Life Pictures (clb). **131 akg-images:** (t). **Getty Images:** Sgt. Chetwyn / IWM (cr). **132 Bridgeman Images:** Deutsches Historisches Museum, Berlin, Germany / © DHM (bl). **133 Getty Images:** Ullstein bild Dtl. (br). **135 Alamy Stock Photo:** Pictorial Press Ltd (tc). **Bridgeman Images:** © Galerie Bilderwelt (br). **136-137 Alamy Stock Photo:** Pictorial Press Ltd. **136 akg-images:** Fototeca Gilardi (bc). **United States Holocaust Memorial Museum:** (cla). **138 Getty Images:** Keystone / Hulton Archive (cl). **139 Getty Images:** Evening Standard / Hulton Archive (br). **141 Alamy Stock Photo:** Pictorial Press Ltd (br). **143 Getty Images:** Jean Desmarteau / Gamma-Rapho (br). **144 Getty Images:** Universal History Archive / Universal Images Group (bl). **147 Bridgeman Images:** American Photographer, (20th century) / Private Collection / Peter Newark American Pictures (br). **Getty Images:** British Official Photo / The LIFE Picture Collection (tr). **148 akg-images:** (bl). **149 Getty Images:** Windmill Books / Universal Images Group (br). **150 Getty Images:** TASS (bc). **www.mediadrumworld.com:** (tc). **152 Getty Images:** Serge Plantureux / Corbis Historical (bc). **www.mediadrumworld.com:** (tr). **154-155 Getty Images:** AFP Contributor. **154 Alamy Stock Photo:** Trinity Mirror / Mirrorpix (bc). **Dorling Kindersley:** Imperial War Museum, Duxford (c). **156-157 Getty Images:** Sgt Robert Howard / Hulton Archive. **158 Dorling Kindersley:** Musée des blindés, Saumur, France (cb). **Getty Images:** Popperfoto (tl). **159 Bridgeman Images:** Photo © AGIP (cr). **Getty Images:** Sovfoto / UIG (tl). **160 akg-images:** Stocktrek Images (bl). **161 akg-images:** Heritage-Images / The Print Collector (tr). **162-163 Alamy Stock Photo:** Granger Historical Picture Archive. **162 Alamy Stock Photo:** Peter Horree (ca). **Getty Images:** Lt. D C Oulds / IWM (bl). **165 Getty Images:** Lt. L Chetwyn / Imperial War Museums (bc). **166 akg-images:** (bc). **Bridgeman Images:** © Galerie Bilderwelt (tc). **168 akg-images:** (bl). **169 Getty Images:** aviation-images.com / Universal Images Group (br). **170-171 Getty Images:** Bletchley Park Trust / Sspl. **170 Alamy Stock Photo:** James King-Holmes (bc). **Getty Images:** Time Life Pictures / National Archives / The Life Picture Collection (ca). **172 Getty Images:** Hulton Deutsch / Corbis Historical (tr). **Wikipedia:** Stadt Nürnberg (bl). **174 Bridgeman Images:** SZ Photo / Sammlung Megele (cla). **Getty Images:** Ullstein bild Dtl. (bl). **174-175 Getty Images:** Roger Viollet. **176 Getty Images:** Robert Doisneau / Masters (tl). **177 Alamy Stock Photo:** John Frost Newspapers (br). **179 akg-images:** (br); Sputnik (cl). **180 Bridgeman Images:** Peter Newark Military Pictures (tl). **181 Alamy Stock Photo:** ITAR-TASS News Agency (br). **182 akg-images:** Sputnik (tl). **Dreamstime.com:** Yuri4u80 (tr). **184 Dorling Kindersley:** The Combined Military Services Museum (CMSM) (cla). **Getty Images:** Keystone Features / Hulton Archive (bl). **184-185 Getty Images:** Universal History Archive. **186 Bridgeman Images:** Colorized reproduction of original photograph by Walter Rosenblum, Omaha Beach Rescue, D-Day +1 / © Galerie Bilderwelt (cr). **Getty Images:** Roger Viollet (bl). **188-189 Getty Images:** Smith Collection / Gado. **188 akg-images:** (bc). **Dorling Kindersley:** By kind permission of The Trustees of the Imperial War Museum, London (cla). **190-191 John Calvin / www.wwii-photos-maps.com**. **191 Getty Images:** Franklin / Hulton Archive (br). **192 Bridgeman Images:** French School, (20th century) / Private Collection / Archives Charmet (bl). **193 The National Archives:** (br). **194 akg-images:** Interfoto (bl). **196-197 TopFoto.co.uk:** Ullstein Bild. **196 Getty Images:** Interim Archives / Archive Photos (br). **197 Alamy Stock Photo:** History and Art Collection (cra). **Getty Images:** Heinrich Hoffmann / The Life Picture Collection (br). **198 Alamy Stock Photo:** Granger Historical Picture Archive (tl). **200 Getty Images:** Galerie Bilderwelt / Hulton Archive (bc). **203 Getty Images:** Mondadori Portfolio (br). **204 Bridgeman Images:** Private Collection / Peter Newark Pictures (cr).

Getty Images: Historical / Corbis Historical (tl). **205 Alamy Stock Photo:** American Photo Archive (crb). **Bridgeman Images:** Pictures from History (t). **207 Alamy Stock Photo:** Aviation history now (br). **Getty Images:** Time Life Pictures / The LIFE Picture Collection (tl). **208-209 Getty Images:** Sgt Robert Howard / Hulton Archive. **208 Bridgeman Images:** Private Collection / Peter Newark Pictures (cla). **Dorling Kindersley:** Musée des blindés, Saumur, France (bl). **210-211 Imperial War Museum. 213 Getty Images:** W. Eugene Smith / The LIFE Picture Collection (tc). **214 Getty Images:** Bettmann (bc); Keystone / Hulton Archive (tr). **216 Alamy Stock Photo:** Hi-Story (cl). **Getty Images:** Hulton-Deutsch Collection / Corbis (bc). **216-217 Naval History and Heritage Command. 218-219 Imperial War Museum. 218 Getty Images:** Keystone / Hulton Archive (bl). **220 Getty Images:** Sovfoto / Universal Images Group (tl). **221 Getty Images:** PhotoQuest / Archive Photos (br). **222-223 Getty Images:** Roger Viollet. **223 Getty Images:** Universal History Archive (br). **Wikipedia:** Manchukuo State Council of Emperor Kang-de Puyi (cra). **224-225 The US National Archives and Records Administration:** Photographer: Joe Rosenthal. **226 Getty Images:** Bettmann (c); Time Life Pictures (tl). **227 Bridgeman Images:** Pictures from History (cr). **Dorling Kindersley:** Royal Airforce Museum, London (tl). **228 Getty Images:** Time Life Pictures / The LIFE Picture Collection (bl). **230-231 akg-images:** Heritage-Images / Keystone Archives. **230 Alamy Stock Photo:** DBI Studio (cla). **Getty Images:** Hulton-Deutsch Collection / Corbis (bc). **232 Getty Images:** PhotoQuest / Archive Photos (bc). **233 Getty Images:** Galerie Bilderwelt / Hulton Archive (tr). **234 Getty Images:** PhotoQuest / Archive Photos (bl). **236-237 akg-images:** Picture-Alliance / ZB / Richard Peter sen.. **236 Alamy Stock Photo:** Everett Collection Inc (bl). **Imperial War Museum:** (ca). **238-239 Imperial War Museum. 238 Getty Images:** PhotoQuest / Archive Photos (bl). **240 akg-images:** Fototeca Gilardi (bc). **241 Getty Images:** Galerie Bilderwelt / Hulton Archive (tr). **242 akg-images:** (c) Khaldei / Voller Ernst (bl). **244-245 Getty Images:** Photo12 / UIG. **244 Getty Images:** Hulton-Deutsch Collection / Corbis (bl); Picture Post / Hulton Archive (cla). **246 Getty Images:** De Agostini

Picture Library (tr). **Stanford Libraries:** (c). **247 Getty Images:** Sovfoto / UIG (tl). **The US National Archives and Records Administration:** Photographer: Joe Rosenthal (c). **248 Getty Images:** Carl Mydans / The LIFE Picture Collection (tc). **249 Getty Images:** Jiji Press / AFP (tr). **250 Bridgeman Images:** Museum of Fine Arts, Houston, Texas, USA / gift of Will Michels in honor of Jim and Erika Liu (bl). **251 Getty Images:** W. Eugene Smith / The LIFE Picture Collection (br). **252 akg-images:** (cla). **253 Getty Images:** Time Life Pictures / The LIFE Picture Collection (br). **254 Getty Images:** US Signal Corps / The LIFE Picture Collection (bc). **255 Getty Images:** Time Life Pictures / The LIFE Picture Collection (br). **256-257 Alamy Stock Photo:** Everett Collection Inc. **256 Alamy Stock Photo:** DOD Photo (bl). **Dorling Kindersley:** Bradbury Science Museum, Los Alamos (ca). **259 Getty Images:** The Asahi Shimbun (br). **260-261 Getty Images:** MPI / Archive Photos. **260 Alamy Stock Photo:** John Frost Newspapers (cl); Military Images (bl). **262 akg-images:** (tl). **Getty Images:** Roger Viollet (cl). **263 Bridgeman Images:** Universal History Archive / UIG (cr). **Getty Images:** Keystone-France / Gamma-Keystone (tl). **264 Alamy Stock Photo:** Everett Collection Historical (bc). **265 David Rumsey Map Collection www.davidrumsey.com:** (br). **266 Bridgeman Images:** Pictures from History (bc). **Getty Images:** David Pollack / Corbis Historical (cr). **268 Alamy Stock Photo:** Everett Collection Historical (bl). **269 Getty Images:** Universal History Archive / Universal Images Group (br). **270-271 Magnum Photos:** Robert Capa. **271 Alamy Stock Photo:** Eddie Gerald (cr). **Getty Images:** Frank Shershel / GPO (br). **274-275 Alamy Stock Photo:** DPA Picture Alliance. **274 akg-images:** (bl). **Getty Images:** Popperfoto (cla)

Endpaper images: Front: **akg-images:** Back: **akg-images:** Ullstein bild.

All other images © Dorling Kindersley
For further information see: www.dkimages.com